DATE DUE

Workers in America

Workers in America

A Historical Encyclopedia

VOLUME 2: M–Y

ROBERT E. WEIR

ABC-CLIO

Santa Barbara, California • Denver, Colorado • Oxford, England

Copyright 2013 by ABC-CLIO, LLC

Library of Congress Cataloging-in-Publication Data

Workers in America : a historical encyclopedia / Robert E. Weir.
v. cm.
Rev. ed. of: Historical encyclopedia of American labor / edited by Robert Weir and James P. Hanlan. c2004.
Includes bibliographical references and index.
ISBN 978–1–59884–718–5 (hbk. : alk. paper) — ISBN 978–1–59884–719–2 (ebook)
1. Labor—United States—History—Encyclopedias. 2. Working class—United States—History—Encyclopedias. 3. Labor movement—United States—History—Encyclopedias. 4. Industrial relations—United States—History—Encyclopedias. 5. Labor laws and legislation—United States—History—Encyclopedias. I. Weir, Robert E., 1952–
II. Historical encyclopedia of American labor.
HD8066.H57   2013
331.0973'03—dc23   2012014153

ISBN: 978–1–59884–718–5
EISBN: 978–1–59884–719–2

17 16 15 14 13   1 2 3 4 5

This book is also available on the World Wide Web as an eBook.
Visit www.abc-clio.com for details.

ABC-CLIO, LLC
130 Cremona Drive, P.O. Box 1911
Santa Barbara, California 93116-1911

This book is printed on acid-free paper ∞

Manufactured in the United States of America

Entries appearing in these volumes are revised and expanded from Robert E. Weir and James P. Hanlan, eds., *Historical Encyclopedia of American Labor*. Westport: Greenwood Publishing Group, 2004.

Contents

M

MACHINE POLITICS AND LABOR

The term "political machine" carries many negative connotations and is often associated with corruption, graft, and misuse of public funds. Although such abuses have undoubtedly existed, a political machine is also an organized political body devoted to securing electoral victory and political influence for a given party. Strong-willed individuals—dubbed political "bosses"—who are adept at organizing and skilled at commanding political underlings head many political machines. Political machines generally control some patronage jobs, which they dole out as rewards to loyal supporters and their friends. As such, machine politics have long been (and remain) an important source for employment within American society.

President Andrew Jackson is often wrongly credited for the remark, "To the victor go the spoils." Jackson uttered this phrase, as would many others, but it had been in currency since at least the days of the ancient Roman Republic. Jackson merely voiced a view that was understood to be standard political operating procedure. The federal civil service was created in 1792, but despite the Civil Service Act of 1832, it was not until the passage of the Pendleton Civil Service Act of 1883 that objective standards came into wide use in appointing individuals to government-funded positions. The latter law set up an examination system to test the merit of perspective candidates. Prior to 1883, whatever political party was in power also controlled a patronage system that gave supporters access to jobs. Even after the passage of the Pendleton Act, certain jobs remained exempt, especially those in federal law enforcement, military, and diplomatic agencies. Even today the president of the United States has the right to dole out limited patronage in federal agencies under the executive branch that he commands.

Individual states and municipalities have their own codes that regulate civil service, public works, and contract work. In many cases those codes are far less restrictive than federal laws, even when modeled on federal standards. Historically, state and local government handed out a large number of patronage jobs. In large cities, political machines emerged to contest political power. Those that won and consolidated their power base frequently operated as de facto employers in all matters related to public spending. City politics were organized by wards, each headed by a "boss" or "captain" who represented the local party leader. Electoral loyalty was guaranteed by handing out favors such as jobs, awarding building projects to friendly contractors, assisting troubled ward residents, and acting as emergency social agencies. In many cities, the ward boss was known as the person who could get things done. In the 19th century, he was also likely to be a member of the dominant ethnic group within the ward and to shower favors on that group. Labor unions and central labor councils learned to cultivate friendly relations with ward bosses. As cities grew as a result of the **Industrial Revolution**, unionized construction workers often sought to curry favor with ward bosses so that they could secure contracts to build the expanding city infrastructure.

Political machines had (and have) great potential for abuse. New York City's infamous Tweed Ring bilked the municipality for tens of millions of dollars in the 1860s before it was brought down in 1871, but the Tweed Ring was notable only by the extent of its corruption. Much of the rest of New York State was controlled by a powerful Republican machine for much of the last part of the 19th century that was frequently just as corrupt, and Republican Party machines were instrumental in bypassing the will of the electorate in the disputed presidential election of 1876. Attacks on political machines took place throughout the 19th century and reforming municipal government was a major goal during the **Progressive Era**, but the very nature of American competitive politics dictates the survival of get-out-the-vote political machines. There is scarcely a major American city whose political life has not, at some time or other, been under the sway of a political machine. Kansas City, Missouri, for instance, was under the control of the Pendergast family for much of the 19th and 20th centuries, and some New Deal figures were said to be political bosses. The Byrd family controlled Virginia politics for most of the 20th century, as did the Daley family in Chicago. Boston politics was long dominated by Irish Catholic machine politicians such as James Michael Curley and the Kennedy family.

It is important to distinguish machines that exercised political savvy from those rooted in corruption. The political right often attacks labor unions as political machines, taking their cue from past labor leaders such as **George Meany**, who openly called the **American Federation of Labor-Congress of Industrial Organizations** (AFL-CIO), which he headed, a "political machine." At heart, a political machine is an organization dedicated to winning elections. Organized labor has often built alliances with the machines, especially those of the more union-friendly **Democratic Party**, because such liaisons give unions access to power, lobbying clout, and job opportunities for members. In return, unions often use fundraising mechanisms such as political action committees to drum up support and financial contributions for labor-friendly politicians. It is probably naïve to think that machine politics will disappear as long as political campaigns can be privately funded and victors can hand out spoils.

Myth holds that modern American society is a meritocracy that rewards talent and hard work. In fact, by the early 21st century, between 75 and 80 percent of all job openings were never advertised. This figure highlights the importance of access, however one obtains it. Defenders of machine politics point out that there is little substantive difference between securing a job through political channels and finding one through "networking" with business and professional contacts. Both systems have a built-in potential for abuse, but both persist because they succeed in delivering favors. Modern labor unions worry that their declining numbers limit their ability to pressure politicians to pass laws favorable to job creation and worker protection. Publicly funded workers in unions such as the

American Federation of State, County and Municipal Employees, the **National Education Association**, and various **white-collar** organizations are keenly aware of the links between jobs, **wages**, **collective bargaining** rights, and politics. They are also aware that the **Republican Party** is often hostile toward unions and toward public-sector employment in general. Unions often defend old-style Democratic Party machine-style politics on the grounds that such organizations are more worker friendly.

Suggested Reading

Christopher K. Ansel and Arthur L. Burris, "Bosses of the City Unite! Labor Politics and Political Machine Consolidation, 1870–1910," *Studies in American Political Development* 11 (1997): 1–4; Thomas P. Clifford, *The Political Machine: An American Institution*, 1975; Harry Holloway, "Interest Groups in the Postpartisan Era: The Political Machine of the AFL-CIO," *Political Science Quarterly* 94, no. 1 (Spring 1979): 117–133; Mary Ryan, *Civic Wars, Democracy and Public Life in the American City during the 19th Century*, 1998.

MAINTENANCE OF MEMBERSHIP

Maintenance of membership is a provision in some union **contracts** that requires those who join a union to retain their membership through the life of that contract. Rudimentary maintenance of membership clauses were negotiated during World War I, but most such clauses date from the World War II era. As the United States was drawn into the gathering world conflict, President Franklin Roosevelt wanted to ensure that wartime production would not be interrupted. Key to this assurance was avoiding capital/labor conflict. Unions pressured the Roosevelt administration to set up **closed shops** that hired only union workers, but this plan met with vigorous opposition from the business community. Unions, however, remembered the assault on organized labor after World War I and were determined not to be left vulnerable a second time. In April 1941, the National Defense Mediation Board proposed maintenance of membership clauses as a compromise between unions and employers.

In 1942, President Roosevelt authorized the formation of the **National War Labor Board** (NWLB). The NWLB set up an **arbitration** system in which disputes would be resolved by representatives of labor, business, and the public. Most unions were willing to sign **no-strike pledges** for the duration of the war if they could be assured that wartime conditions would not weaken the labor movement. Both the **American Federation of Labor** (AFL) and the **Congress of Industrial Organizations** (CIO) viewed the **strike** as labor's best weapon in forcing employers to improve **wages** and working conditions. They sought guarantees that the labor movement would not be eviscerated when that weapon was withdrawn and worried that it would be more difficult to retain members and recruit new ones if militancy was curtailed. Continuation of maintenance of membership clauses was given as enticement to secure agreement among unions that did not enjoy closed shops. Such agreements stabilized membership during the life of contracts, thereby protecting union treasuries. They stipulated that an individual worker could not quit his or her union if the person had joined when a contract was in effect.

Some observers hailed this compromise for freeing labor leaders to concentrate on **collective bargaining** and assuring wartime production. Critics argued that it hastened the rise **business unionism** practices that ignored rank-and-file concerns. Still others, including **John L. Lewis**, were suspicious of most wartime agreements and viewed them as ways of securing labor peace by forcing unions to make compromises the business community was not required to make. The postwar period did, indeed, see the business community seek to impose its will much as it had done after World War I—a seeming vindication of Lewis's skepticism, although the actions of his own **United Mine Workers** union during the war is cited by some as having provided some of the justification for a business counter-assault.

Suggested Reading

James Atleson, *Labor and the Wartime State*, 1998; Nelson Lichtenstein, *Labor's War at Home*, 1982; Joel Seidman, *American Labour from Defense to Reconversion*, 1978.

MAJOR LEAGUE BASEBALL PLAYERS ASSOCIATION

The Major League Baseball Players Association (MLBPA) is perhaps the United States' most powerful labor union. Since 1968, when the MLBPA won its first contract, the union has reversed more than a century of management dominance over the economics of Major League Baseball (MLB). In 2006, the MLBPA reached a five-year agreement with owners that raised the average player **salary** to $3.34 million per year by 2010, and set a salary floor of $400,000 per annum. These numbers represent a spectacular reversal of fortunes; as recently as the mid-1960s, the minimum salary was only $6,000—roughly $40,370 in 2009 dollars—and most players took other jobs in the off-season. Only a handful of superstars commanded salaries in excess of $50,000 ($366,440 in 2009 terms). Today, players, coaches, managers, and trainers enjoy full **collective bargaining** rights, binding **arbitration** clauses, and the ability to become free agents after six years of service.

The power today enjoyed by the MLBPA is an outgrowth of a century-long struggle against parsimonious and sometimes abusive MLB owners. The first attempt at a players' union came in 1885, when John Montgomery Ward of the New York Giants formed the Brotherhood of Base Ball Players in response to salary caps imposed by owners, the chattel-like manner in which some owners sold players, and the conditions under which players often had to perform. Management resisted with such force that, in 1890, numerous players bolted and formed a rival league, the Players' Association. It collapsed after a single season and the Brotherhood was crushed.

The Players' Protective Association (PPA) was formed in 1900, but any hope it had of attaining significant power vanished in 1903. Two years earlier, National League (NL) star Napoleon Lajoie had tried to invalidate his contract with Philadelphia Phillies to play for the Philadelphia Athletics in the newly formed American League (AL). The Phillies obtained an **injunction** against Lajoie in 1902, with NL lawyers arguing that a "reserve clause" bound Lajoie to his NL club until such time as it chose to release him. Lajoie managed to dodge the injunction through a technicality—it applied only in Pennsylvania and Lajoie simply signed with a team in Cleveland—but in 1903, the NL and AL signed baseball's National Agreement, which set up a two-league MLB structure. Both the NL and the AL agreed to uphold the reserve clause, thus dooming the efforts of any future Napoleon Lajoie and rendering the PPA and its successors powerless.

In 1914, the newly proposed Federal League challenged the reserve clause as a violation of federal antitrust laws, but the Supreme Court upheld it and the upstart league managed only two seasons (1914, 1915) before folding. The case was revisited in 1951, and the court agreed it erred in 1914, but left the matter in the hands of Congress to change antitrust laws. Congress declined to do so. In 1966, players hired former **United Steelworkers of America** official Marvin Miller to represent them; from this new beginning, the current MLBPA was formed. In 1968, Miller helped players negotiate the first-ever professional sports union contract. He directed an effort in which St. Louis Cardinals star Curt Flood challenged MLB's exemption from antitrust laws. In 1972, the Supreme Court again passed the matter to Congress. Although Flood lost his bid to become a free agent, three years later a federal arbitrator ruled in favor of two players (pitchers Andy Messersmith and Dave McNally, thereby opening the door to future free-agency bids. From 1975 onward, MLB salaries began to soar as owners were forced to bid for player services in a competitive market in which players frequently changed teams when their contracts expired.

Large free-agency contracts and rising salaries have led to contentious labor/management relations, with player **strikes** occurring in 1972, 1980, 1981, 1985, and 1994–1995. Most of these strikes occurred in the off-season, though 86 games were cancelled in 1972 and more than 700 in 1981. The 1994 strike was particularly acrimonious; 920 games were cancelled, and the World Series was aborted for the first time since it was instituted in 1904. In addition, owners **locked out** players in 1973, 1976, and 1990. In 1990, MLB owners were forced to pay the MLBPA more than $280 million for colluding to hold down salaries by refusing to sign free agents.

Owners in small-market cities lacking lucrative media broadcast contracts complain that they can no longer field competitive teams, and many claim they are losing money. At the end of 2001, the Arizona Diamondbacks purportedly lost in excess of $40 million, although they won the World Series. During the winter of 2002, MLB Commissioner Allan H. "Bud" Selig announced plans to eliminate two teams before the start of the season. The MLBPA, plus groups in several cities rumored to be targets of contraction, sued MLB, which was forced to back down. Owners continued to insist that the MLBPA needed to make **concessions**, or that only a handful of teams could make a profit or be competitive on the field. Foremost among the owner demands was that the MLBPA accept a salary cap, the likes of which were already in place in professional basketball and hockey. Instead, MLB instituted a revenue-sharing plan in 2002, which allowed teams in large markets to spend what they wished on payroll, but placed a "luxury" tax on payroll above the league average; the results of this tax were then shared with teams below it.

Revenue sharing has divided owners, especially when figures leaked to the media revealed that MLB finances were in much better shape than some owners claimed. The Florida (now Miami) Marlins, Texas Rangers, Tampa Bay Rays, Los Angeles Angels, Seattle Mariners, and Pittsburgh Pirates each claimed to have lost money between 2007 and 2009, but careful analysis of data revealed they had not. The case of the Pirates was particularly egregious; although Pittsburgh had endured 18 consecutive losing seasons by 2010, it routinely returned profits in excess of $20 million per year to team partners. By contrast, baseball's richest franchise, the New York Yankees, claimed to have lost money in the 2006 season due to revenue sharing. Exacerbating the owners' already weak case against high salaries won by the MLBPA are the record sums that new owners pay for franchises as well as data revealing that MLB has actually been *more* competitive than professional sports leagues that have salary caps. The wealth of the New York Yankees notwithstanding, 13 different teams won the World Series between 1990 and 2010, and 8 of those Series winners played in small markets.

The 2006 contract between owners and the MLBPA did not include a salary cap or league contraction discussion, though it did grant a higher salary scale and raise luxury taxes on high-revenue teams. Many analysts foresee future showdowns between the MLBPA and MLB; several, however, think that the coming battle will be between team owners paying high luxury taxes and those pocketing those revenues. There is gathering sentiment for a payroll *floor* rather than a ceiling. The current MLBPA president is Michael Weiner, who replaced Donald Fehr, who retired in 2009.

Suggested Reading

CBS News, "Multimillion-Dollar Scores for Losing MLB Team," August 23, 2010, http://www.cbsnews.com/stories/2010/08/23/business/main6797677.shtml, accessed February 25, 2011; John Feinstein, *Play Ball: The Life and Hard Times of Major League Baseball*, 1993; Charles P. Korr, *The End of Baseball as We Knew It: The Players Union, 1960–81*, 2002; Major League Baseball Players Association, http://mlbplayers.mlb.com/pa/info/, accessed February 25, 2011; Andrew Zimbalist, *May the Best Team Win: Baseball Economics and Public Policy*, 2003.

MANIFEST DESTINY AND WORK

Manifest Destiny—a term coined by journalist John O'Sullivan in 1845—describes the ideology that Caucasians were destined to expand the borders of the United States from the Atlantic to the Pacific Ocean. Those sentiments were put into practice during the period between 1846 and 1890. During this span, the United States annexed lands formerly held by Mexico, secured additional land by treaty, and fought a series of wars against **Native Americans** that placed most Indians on reservations and opened millions of acres for white settlers. Historians have long understood the racial, geopolitical, and imperialist dimensions of Manifest Destiny, including the desires of antebellum Southern planters to open new lands suitable for agricultural production supported by **slavery**. In popular mythology,

Manifest Destiny also provided new opportunities for farmers, ranchers, homesteaders, and fortune-seekers.

Like all myths, a kernel of truth is embedded within a problematic narrative with regard to the Manifest Destiny philosophy. Between 1849 and 1855, for instance, approximately 300,000 fortune-seekers made their way to California after the discovery of gold in 1848. Some did well, but the vast majority of prospectors found little or only moderate amounts of gold. The greatest profits were made, in fact, by furnishing agents who outfitted prospectors—including Levi Strauss—rather than by miners. By 1850, most of the easily retrievable gold had been claimed and the ore that was left was located deep underground. Getting this gold required expensive machinery and extensive manpower. Thousands who went to California, Nevada, Colorado, and other Western locales arrived dreaming of becoming independently wealthy, but ended up as wage-earners for large corporations. This pattern was repeated in gold rushes such as those at Pike's Peak (1858–1859) and the Black Hills of South Dakota (1874), in silver strikes such as Nevada's Comstock Lode (1859), and in the extraction of other hard-rock ores such as copper and coal. In each case, individual fortunes were relatively few in number and confined to the earliest prospectors to arrive. Long-term fortunes went to big companies such as Hearst, Haggis, Tevin and Company, and Guggenheim. As individual opportunities declined, native-born Caucasians often fell prey to Sinophobia, anti-Irish nativism, and calls for Indian removal.

As in the case of mining, only a handful of farmers and homesteaders rushing to newly opened lands in the Great Plains ever became wealthy. The Homestead Act of 1862—and various revisions to the bill—opened some 270 million acres of land to settlers between 1862 and 1934, but six of ten individuals claiming 160-acre allotments failed to reside on the land for the requisite six months to gain title of the land. Allotment sizes increased with revisions to the 1862 bill, but millions of acres of land that were eventually exploited for timber, water, oil, and minerals extraction passed into the hands of corporations rather than individuals. Railroads, for instance, became the largest owners of trans-Mississippi lands. Corporate interests held powerful sway. Railroads dictated monopolistic freight and grain elevator rates, while ranchers often found themselves at the mercy of companies that controlled water rights in arid regions. Some farmers and ranchers did well, but it should be understood that the **cowboys** of American legend were wage-earners, not independent entrepreneurs. The same was true for tens of thousands of laborers who built railroads across the Great Plains and Great Basin.

The term "Manifest Destiny" passed from popularity before 1890, when the U.S. Census Bureau declared the frontier closed, by which it meant there were no more vast unclaimed tracts of land available for settlement. (Individual homestead allotments continued until 1976.) Frederick Jackson Turner's famed 1893 "frontier thesis" speech helped cement the myth of independence and rugged individualism, but most scholars now caution that it be approached critically rather than literally. Manifest Destiny undoubtedly led to economic expansion that made the United States a powerful nation, but it also exacted a toll from America's neighbors, from non-whites and Native Americans, and even from Caucasian supporters. Far from being an ideal that eliminated class struggle, Manifest Destiny often widened the gap between rich and non-rich.

Suggested Reading

Paul W. Gates, *The Jeffersonian Dream: Studies in the History of American Land Policy and Development*, 1996; J. S. Holliday, *The World Rushed in: The California Gold Rush Experience*, 1981; Henry Nash Smith, *Virgin Land: The American West as Symbol and Myth*, 1959.

MAQUILADORA

Maquiladora is a Spanish term deriving from the verb *maquilar*, meaning "to do a task for another." It once referred to the in-kind payment made to millers grinding peasants' grain, but it now infers foreign-owned companies operating in Mexico, especially those whose corporate headquarters are located in Canada or the United States. The bulk of *maquiladoras* are owned by U.S. corporations and are located in cities close to the U.S. border such as Ciudad Juarez, Mexicali, Nogales, Nuevo Laredo, Rio Bravo, and Tijuana. The products made or assembled in Mexico are then reimported to the country operating the factory. Although still associated with Mexico in the popular mind, *maquiladoras* have become global.

American firms have long moved parts of their operations to Mexico to take advantage of lower labor costs, lax environmental standards, and favorable tax policies. The 1965 Mexico Border Industrialization Program led to an upsurge of foreign investment in Mexico, and in the 1980s business **deregulation** and changes in the tax code made it easier for U.S. companies to move across the border. The 1994 **North American Free Trade Agreement** (NAFTA)—passed over the strenuous objections of organized labor in the United States and in Canada—has sped the process even more.

The benefits for U.S. or Canadian firms desiring to relocate to Mexico are potentially enormous. Under NAFTA, a company can set up either a direct subsidiary or a "shelter agreement," in which it supplies raw materials and manufacturing equipment while a Mexican company provides everything else from labor to legal permits. These operate as de facto **subcontracting** arrangements. Under NAFTA, most *maquiladora* products are taxed only if they are imported outside of North America. Devaluations of the Mexican peso in 1982, and several more times in the 1990s, made Mexican labor so cheap that even Asian firms located some production there. By the mid-1990s, Mexican workers averaged the equivalent of about $19 per week, a figure eclipsed by the hourly rate of many U.S. and Canadian workers. Although many companies relocating in Mexico claimed to be helping Mexicans rise from poverty, in 2002 it was estimated that the average *maquiladora* worker in Tijuana had to work for 90 minutes to earn enough to buy a kilogram of rice.

The business community argues that *maquiladoras* are good for American consumers because they ensure that products can be sold for lower prices, though most companies make little attempt to hide the fact that they are also drawn to low-wage, non-union, weak regulatory environments. Several consulting firms—such as

North American Production Sharing, Inc.—specialize in aiding businesses in shifting part or all of their production to Mexico. Labor unions complain that NAFTA and similar programs are little more than taxpayer-subsidized **slave**-labor bills used by unscrupulous companies to avoid corporate taxes, eliminate jobs, and drive down **wages** in the United States and Canada by blackmailing workers into accepting lower wages lest their jobs be moved elsewhere. Of concern to the global community is Mexico's lack of strong environmental laws. Weak oversight allows companies to pollute in ways that jeopardize regional, if not worldwide, ecosystems. Many U.S.-based unions—including the **United Auto Workers of America**, the **United Electrical Workers**, and the International Longshoremen's and Warehouse Workers—have attempted to organize Mexican workers, though Mexico also lacks many of the labor laws that protect workers from retaliation by employers.

There is little doubt that American jobs have been lost to *maquila* production. According to the **National Association of Manufacturers**, more than 3,450 foreign firms operated in Mexico as of 2002; by 2010, that figure had risen to more than 18,000. In the first six years that NAFTA was in effect (1994–2000), more than 800,000 of the 1.2 million jobs involved in *maquiladora* production came at the expense of lost jobs in the United States. Some economists claimed that most of the lost jobs occurred in **assembly-line** and labor-intensive industries that were already in severe decline, or involved undesirable work incompatible with American preferences and lifestyles. Those claims were countered by data revealing that 78 percent of the lost jobs came from the high-wage manufacturing sector of the economy. Although critics of NAFTA concede there was an overall increase of nearly 27 million jobs in the United States during the period between 1993 and 2007, they also note that most of the growth took place in **service industry** jobs. There have been numerous documented cases of highly profitable plants closing in the United States simply because even greater profits could be made in Mexico.

The recession of the early 21st century took its toll on *maquiladoras*, with Mexican plants shedding nearly 250,000 jobs in 2001 and 2002 alone. By 2005, *maquila* production still accounted for more than half of Mexico's exports, but the lingering recession and competition from **globalism**—especially the rising economic might of China, India, Malaysia, and Vietnam—has cooled the *maquiladora* boom. Deteriorating conditions inside Mexico, such as narcotics-related violence, the kidnapping of foreign nationals, and political instability, have made the country increasingly less attractive to foreign investors.

American labor unions often call for the repeal of NAFTA, though such an action on its own would by no means lead to more jobs in the United States. The current logic of global **capitalism** often involves a "race to the bottom" on wages, and the *maquiladora* phenomenon must now be viewed as global, rather than just a trend involving production in Mexico. Some textile firms, for instance, have bypassed Mexico in favor of moving their manufacturing operations to Honduras or Nicaragua. In recent years, some investors have come agree with organized labor's view that the race to the bottom will not serve the long-term health of the American economy. With nearly one-fourth of all full-time workers in the United

States earning wages that would not raise a family of four above the poverty line, they have come to embrace the idea that robust profits require consumers with means.

Suggested Reading

Eileen Applebaum, Annette Bernhardt, and Richard Murnane, eds., *Low-Wage America: How Employers Are Reshaping Opportunity in the Workplace*, 2003; Jennifer Bickham Mendez, Gilbert Joseph, and Emily Rosenberg, eds., *From the Revolution to the Maquiladoras: Gender, Labor, and Globalization in Nicaragua*, 2005; Alejandro Ruelas-Gossi, "Mexico's Maquiladora Syndrome," *Harvard Business Review*, October 15, 2010; U.S. Government Accountability, *International Trade: Mexico's Maquiladora Decline Affects U.S.-Mexico Border Communities and Trade*, 2011.

MARCH ON WASHINGTON (1963)

The March on Washington took place on August 28, 1963, and was one of the most dramatic moments in the history of the civil rights movement. It was on this day that the Reverend Martin Luther King, Jr., delivered the "I Have a Dream" speech destined to become one of the most famous addresses in American history. The speech, in fact, became so famous that it now overshadows the social and labor dimensions of the event. The event was officially known as the "March on Washington for Jobs and Freedom" and drew its inspiration from **A. Philip Randolph**, president of the **Brotherhood of Sleeping Car Porters** (BSCP). In 1941, Randolph planned a march similar to the 1963 event. It did not take place, but the very threat of such an event led President Franklin Roosevelt to create the **Fair Employment Practices Commission** to investigate complaints of racist hiring practices in the defense industry.

Randolph was also one of the major organizers of the 1963 march, along with King and Bayard Rustin of the Southern Christian Leadership Conference, John Lewis of the Student Nonviolent Coordinating Committee, Whitney Young of the National Urban League, James Farmer of the Congress of Racial Equality, and Roy Wilkins of the National Association for the Advancement of Colored People. In keeping with the theme of jobs and freedom, the organizers stressed the need for strong civil rights legislation and enforcement of the U.S. Supreme Court's 1954 *Brown v. the Board of Education of Topeka, Kansas* ruling ordering the desegregation of public schools. But organizers also called for raising the **minimum wage** to $2 per hour, ending discriminatory practices in the workplace, and creating a federal public works project to hire the unemployed. All of these messages were conveyed before a rally attended by as many as 300,000 people.

The March on Washington proved a challenge for organized labor. **George Meany**, the president of the **American Federation of Labor-Congress of Industrial Organizations** (AFL-CIO), was uncomfortable with the street demonstrations, marches, and acts of civil disobedience associated with the civil rights movement. In addition, many AFL-CIO affiliates had long practiced some of the discriminatory workplace practices denounced by civil rights leaders. As a result, the AFL-CIO refused to endorse the 1963 march. Because of the AFL-CIO's practice of **voluntarism**, however, individual unions within the **labor federation** were free to formulate their own responses to the march. Randolph participated simultaneously as a civil rights leader, the president of the BSCP, and the head of the AFL-CIO's Negro American Labor Council. In addition, **Walter Reuther** of the **United Auto Workers of America** (UAW) spoke at the rally and stood beside King as he gave his famed address. Numerous other labor leaders—including the UAW's Cleveland Robinson and Lewis Carliner, who headed the AFL-CIO's Industrial Union Department—took active roles in the march and rally. The **United Packinghouse Workers of America** also sent a large contingent to Washington, as did various **longshoremen's** unions. In between speeches, the crowd sang civil rights anthems, but also labor standards such "Which Side Are You On?" and a reworked version of the **Joe Hill** classic "Hallelujah, I'm a Bum." In his speech, James Farmer made direct parallels between the civil rights and labor movements.

The March on Washington helped create pressure for the passage of the 1964 Civil Rights Act and the 1965 Voting Rights Act. For organized labor, though, it highlighted the tensions between conservatives and liberals within its ranks. Civil rights and the rise of the **counterculture** placed a strain on the **Cold War** unionism that had become commonplace inside the AFL-CIO. Meany frequently clashed with both Randolph and Reuther, with the latter coming to view Meany as out-of-touch and reactionary. Reuther would eventually lead the UAW to quit the AFL-CIO and join a rival federation he headed, the Alliance for Labor Action. Reuther and King remained friends and allies, and each fought for agendas that combined civil and labor rights for the rest of their lives. The 1963 March on Washington should be remembered for its emphasis on both of those issues as well as King's speech.

Suggested Reading

Eric Arnesen and James Randall, eds., *The Black Worker: Race, Labor, and Civil Rights Since Emancipation*, 2007; Peter B. Levy, *The New Left and Labor*, 1994; Paul Moreno, *Black Americans and Organized Labor: A New History*, 2007; Kate Tuttle, "March on Washington, 1963," *Africana: The Encyclopedia of the African and African American Experience*, 1999.

MARXISM AND LABOR

Karl Marx (1818–1883) was undoubtedly one of the most influential thinkers and social theorists in Western history. It is important, however, to recognize that assessing his impact on the American labor movement differs depends on whether one is speaking of Marxism's influence on social criticism or Marxism's strength as an organized movement. The influence of each has waxed and waned at various moments in American history, but generally speaking Marxist **socialism** has had enormous impact on how workers, intellectuals, and reformers have viewed the world, whereas it has had only periodic and fleeting impact as an organized political movement.

The Communist Manifesto (1848), which Marx coauthored with Friedrich Engels, was widely read worldwide and could be found in labor union reading rooms in the

United States. It was even more widely discussed. Marx and Engels defined class in terms of power relationships determined by ownership of the means of production. They described a propertied bourgeoisie that owned the means of production and, therefore, dominated the proletariat (**working class**) from which it exacted toil and robbed of most of the fruits of its labor. Marx and Engels believed that the dominance of exploitative bourgeois capitalists would create **class consciousness**, which would ultimately yield class struggle. It was no stretch for many American workers to see capitalists as parasitical or society as dualistic. Many clung to views positing that the value of all goods and services ought to depend solely on the amount of labor that went into it. From that perspective, the employing class was often viewed as one of nonproducers, and worker rhetoric that predated the **Workingmen's movement** or Marx routinely divided the world into categories such "millionaires" and "tramps." If anything, the maturation of the **Industrial Revolution** made such distinctions sharper by introducing investment capitalists, absentee ownership, and harsh production systems that prompted some activists to equate **wage**-earning with **slavery**. Increasing numbers of workers were without property as well, making it easier to accept Marx's critique of private property. In addition, Marx and Engels viewed trade unions as both revolutionary bodies and the building blocks upon which society would be rebuilt once **capitalism** was overthrown. Marx predicted that, after a brief period of state-directed socialism, the state would wither and a **communist** society would emerge in which neither social classes nor private property would exist.

From its inception, Marxism was more appealing as social thought than as a social organization. Marx's views led to the founding of the International Workingmen's Association (IWA) in 1864. The IWA, often called the First International, sought to become a worldwide revolutionary socialist movement. Several Americans were in attendance at the IWA's founding, but there was no significant presence of the IWA in America until 1872, when the First International relocated to New York City. By then, Marxist organizations were already splintered, with **anarchists** having argued with Marx over tactics and goals. The IWA made inroads in cities with large immigrant populations—a development that was both a blessing and a curse, as the IWA was widely viewed as a foreign import by native-born workers. The great **railway strike of 1877** saw the IWA coordinate strategy in Chicago and St. Louis, but it was largely absent elsewhere, and it suffered a decline when trade unions faltered after the strike was crushed.

Marx's work was widely discussed in 19th-century America, albeit mostly in digest form—most of the writings that followed *The Communist Manifesto* were too theoretical and obtuse for most readers. Marxists made some headway among New York City **Knights of Labor** (KOL) in the late 1870s, but increasingly gave way to **Lassalleans** whose electoral socialism and skepticism over trade unions was a better fit inside the KOL. Nor would Marxists be successful in capturing control of the **American Federation of Labor** (AFL) when it formed in 1886; its founder, **Samuel Gompers**, had admired Marx as a younger man but subsequently rejected Marxist ideals and came to accept the permanence of capitalism. As organized labor flexed its muscles during the **Great Upheaval**, Marxists competed with anarchists and alternative forms of socialism. Nevertheless, the bulk of the American working class—though prone to evoking fiery rhetoric in their struggles for social justice—belonged to none of the various radical left groups. Marxists reorganized in 1889 and announced the formation of the Second International, and they briefly captured control of the KOL in 1893, when **Daniel DeLeon** of the Socialist Labor Party fashioned a coalition that ousted **Terence Powderly** as KOL head. By then, however, the KOL was in severe decline and DeLeon's mannerisms and doctrinarism served only to fracture it further; in 1895, he bolted from the KOL and formed the Socialist Trade and Labor Alliance. Marxists claimed some credit for unseating Gompers as AFL head in 1894 as well, though his one-term successor, John McBride, was more of a **Populist** than a Marxist.

By the early 20th century, doctrinaire Marxist thought had largely been supplanted by electoral socialism to its right and revolutionary **anarcho-syndicalism** to its left. DeLeon was present at the 1905 founding of the **Industrial Workers of the World** (IWW), but he quickly grew disenchanted with **direct action** tactics, the IWW's distaste for the ballot box (which he had come to see as a useful propaganda tool), and a line of thought that DeLeon deemed insufficiently analytical. As he had done with the KOL, DeLeon split the IWW in 1908 and attempted to form a Detroit-based organization eventually called the Workers' International Industrial Union. That effort sputtered after a promising start and officially disbanded in 1925, though it had been barely alive for a decade.

The Socialist Party (SP) of **Eugene V. Debs** largely dominated the political left of the first two decades of the 20th century. Debs received more than 900,000 votes for president of the United States in 1912, and several socialist **labor journals** enjoyed robust circulation. Again, however, the combined political left in the United States continued to be more inspirational than organizational. At a time in which separate **labor parties** were forming in Europe, the German economist Werner Sombart wrote a 1906 work titled *Why Is There No Socialism in the United States?* Sombart overstated the issue, as numerous socialists won elected municipal offices, but the U.S. left did appear pale when compared to its counterparts in Europe and Australasia.

The fate of Marxism in the United States changed dramatically after the 1917 Bolshevik revolution in Russia. The Communist Party of the United States of America (CPUSA) formed in 1919 and claimed 60,000 members by year's end, making it larger than the SP and siphoning members from the IWW, which was hemorrhaging membership from attacks during the post-World War I **Red Scare**. Under the guidance of **William Z. Foster**, the CPUSA set up the Trade Union Educational League (TUEL), whose goal was to "bore within" AFL unions and convert rank-and-file unionists to communism. This tactic met with only limited success. In turn, the CPUSA abandoned the effort in 1929 and set up a separate communist union, the **Trade Union Unity League** (TUUL), which lasted until 1935.

The coming of the Great Depression would push the CPUSA to the height of its influence among American workers, many of whom thought that the Russian model should be imported to America. Even **Walter Reuther** and his brothers would travel to the Soviet Union in 1933, and all of the Reuthers briefly became communists. Communists proved to be devoted grassroots organizers who skillfully managed resistance to evictions, led protests, manned soup lines, and orchestrated rent and hunger strikes during the early days of the crisis. In 1930, the CPUSA set up the International Workers Order (IWO), a fraternal group that offered insurance plans and financial assistance for members. Its camps and clubs were rich repositories of working-class culture as well as training sessions in which activists learned organizational skills. By 1938, the IWO may have had as many as 140,000 members and the CPUSA more than 200,000 members. Communist organizers were instrumental in many of the organizational drives held by the **Congress of Industrial Organizations** (CIO) after 1935 and into the 1940s.

A key sticking point for the CPUSA was its relationship to Moscow. The Third International (Comintern) was created in 1919, and all national parties were expected to take direction from Russia. It was, however, Marxist-Leninist, with the Soviet Union purporting to be a "dictatorship of the proletariate." For the CPUSA, adhering to this policy meant abrupt shifts in tactics, such as disbanding the TUEL in favor of the TUUL. It also placed American communists in an ambiguous position concerning the New Deal and made them beholden to foreign policy decisions fashioned in Moscow.

As fascism rose in Europe, in 1934 the Comintern advised the CPUSA to forge a **Popular Front** with liberalism, socialists, and other antifascist groups. This policy also led to dismantling of the TUUL. The 1939 Hitler-Stalin pact threw the CPUSA into crisis and forced it to end the Popular Front. Thousands of members quit the CPUSA in disgust, and the group lost credibility within the labor movement that it would never recover, not even after Germany invaded the Soviet Union. CPUSA leader **Earl Browder** tried to reverse course and, in 1944, dismantled the CPUSA as a separate party and endorsed Franklin Roosevelt's reelection.

Although the CPUSA—always a pariah among mainstream politicians—would be tolerated during World War II and the Soviet Union praised as a U.S. ally, these were but wartime conveniences. The end of World War II marked the decline of significant Marxist organizational influence in the American labor movement. The 1947 **Taft-Hartley Act** required labor leaders to sign affidavits stating that they were not communists, and the emergence of **Cold War** unionism led labor organizations to purge communists from their ranks. Between 1948 and 1950, the CIO dumped approximately 20 percent of its membership by expelling affiliates thought to be under the sway of Marxist-Leninists. A continued purge of communists was among the conditions of the 1955 AFL-CIO merger. Both **George Meany**, who feared communism, and Walter Reuther, by then a democratic socialist suspicious of communist motives, agreed on this point, even when they clashed on other matters. The post-World War II Red Scare would surpass that of World War I in intensity. Numerous CPUSA officials were jailed, including **Elizabeth Gurley Flynn**. In 1956, revelations of Josef Stalin's crimes against humanity further damaged the reputation of the CPUSA. By the late 1950s, the CPUSA had fewer than 10,000 members, many of them Federal Bureau of Investigation (FBI) informants posing as communists.

The CPUSA had a minor resurgence in the 1960s among some civil rights workers and members of the **counterculture**, but aside from black radicals in groups such as the **Dodge Revolutionary Union Movement** and some **assembly-line** workers influenced by Students for a Democratic Society, Marxism's impact within the labor movement was minimal. Moreover, although some New Left intellectuals and activists were devoted Marxist ideologues, far more New Left figures were willing to compromise on doctrine in the name of tactical efficiency. Moreover, Marxism did not enjoy unrivaled ideological consideration: Many New Left thinkers embraced anarchism, Maoism, Trotskyism, and other leftist political ideals.

From the late 1970s onward, American Marxists kept up a dedicated fight for social and economic justice, but their influence within organized labor steadily eroded. A few older leaders still recalled Marxist contributions, but by the time the Soviet Union collapsed in 1991, Marxism was viewed as a historical artifact more than as an organizational method.

It would be a mistake, however, to dismiss Marxism cavalierly. It has been, and continues to be, a powerful analytical tool. Many scholars of American labor have been deeply influenced by Marx's critique of capitalism, power, and social class. Intellectuals often use Marxist analysis to analyze the condition of American labor in both the past and the present, and many would argue that Marx's sociological instincts were, in fact, far sharper than his political insights. Marxist thought has been so central that critics claim scholars have romanticized labor history, have failed to separate inflammatory rhetoric from actual behavior, and have imposed revolutionary intent upon workers who struck back against oppression. These charges may have merit, though the Marxist understanding of how material wealth, power, politics, and social class intersect remains difficult to refute.

Suggested Reading

Harvey Klehr, *The Heyday of American Communism: The Depression Decade*, 1984; Harvey Klehr and John Earl Haynes, *The American Communist Movement: Storming Heaven Itself*, 1992; Timothy Messer-Krause, *The Yankee International: Marxism and the American Reform Tradition*, 1998; Fraser M. Ottanelli, *The Communist Party of the United States: From the Depression to World War II*, 1991; Erik Olin Wright, ed., *Approaches to Class Analysis*, 2005.

MASCULINITY AND LABOR

Although women have always worked in America, one of the by-products of the factory system was that working for **wages** for an extended period of time became both a male prerogative and an obligation. This ideal became so ingrained in American society that many aspects of work in the United States remain biased toward male workers.

Archaeological evidence suggests that **division of labor** by sex dates at least from Neolithic times. Such divisions were certainly present in the agrarian economy of colonial and preindustrial America, and they lingered into the early republic. Nonetheless, the advent of industrialization changed the way society valued certain

A power house mechanic working on a steam pump, 1920. Photograph by Lewis Hine. (National Archives and Records Administration)

types of labor. This can be expressed as the shift from a "family economy" to a "**family wage**." In an economy dominated by **agrarianism**, there was relatively little distinction between production and consumption. In such a family economy, the labor of each individual was necessary for the collective family to survive and thrive. Women's labor was valued, even when subsumed within a paternalistic ideal that women's work should supplement male occupations. Even children had assigned roles. When the American economy shifted to money-based exchange systems, however, the family-as-producer model began to erode, and earning income became the key to supporting the family-as-consumer.

The early **Industrial Revolution** corresponded with an emergent **middle-class ideology** that placed an emphasis on a family wage—a single income adequate for supporting a family. The middle-class view of family was also rooted in the idea that men and women had fundamentally different biological natures that made them naturally suited to prescribed social roles. From this perspective—variously called "domestic ideology," the "doctrine of the two spheres," and the "cult of true womanhood"—women were viewed as psychologically and physically suited to household duties such as nurturing children, assuming household duties, and making their homes moral fortresses to which men could retreat. Males were deemed better suited to the competitive, cutthroat public world of work and business. Although these ideals developed first among elites and the middle class, by the mid-19th century they had become hegemonic. Put simply, males were expected to provide for their families. A short period of work was acceptable for young, single **working-class** women, but they were expected to retreat to their households when they married. Some professions, including teaching, actually *required* that women resign when they married. The reality of working-class life throughout the 19th century was such that many women (and children) had to work for the family to survive, but family wage ideology became so thoroughly engrained as a norm that many working-class males felt dishonored by the need for wives to work. Likewise, many labor unions used the family wage ideal as leverage in seeking higher wages. By the Gilded Age, masculinity and reputation were so intertwined that the term "manly" was routinely applied to anyone, regardless of sex, whose conduct was honest, forthright, and principled.

The **Knights of Labor** (KOL) organized women and supported issues such as equal pay for equal work, women's suffrage, and the passage of an equal rights act, but the actions of individual Knights infused with prevailing views of male paternalism and privilege did not always correspond to the KOL's official position on gender. Male privilege was even more deeply entrenched among **craft unionists**, and many affiliates of the **American Federation of Labor** restricted or forbade female members of the trade. In some cases, such as mining and the maritime trades, the mere presence of women in the workplace was said to bring bad luck.

The decline of the KOL of and the collapse of **labor Populism** in the 1890s heightened the association between wage-earning and masculinity. Although radical groups such as the **Industrial Workers of the World** welcomed female members and a handful of unions such as the **International Ladies' Garment Workers' Union** organized women, their overall influence within the organized labor movement declined in the early 20th century. Women often complained of chauvinist behavior on the part of male unionists. The coming of the Great Depression did little to help matters. Soaring unemployment levels led workingmen to pressure employers to hire male breadwinners and dismiss female staff, a position largely supported by both management and labor unions. Even New Deal work programs routinely excluded women, with the assumption again being that men were responsible for securing a family wage.

World War II presented a serious challenge to traditional views of masculinity. As they had during World War I, large numbers of women took on war production jobs between 1942 and 1945. When victory was secured in World War II, **blue-collar** males returning to civilian life expected to return to their jobs and resume their roles as breadwinners. Millions of women returned to the domestic sphere but contrary to popular opinion, millions did not, though most high-paying jobs went back into male hands. The postwar economic boom ushered in unprecedented levels of consumer spending and gave working-class families access to material goods, but at a cost. Many families needed more than one wage-earner to support their buying and spending habits. Although the years 1946 to 1964 have been classified as the Baby Boom era, it was also a time period in which rising numbers of women entered the job market. By 1956, more than one-third of all women were in the workforce; more tellingly, one-fourth of all married women worked and the family wage ideal became increasingly antiquated. By the mid-1980s, more than half of all married women worked.

Women's increased entry into the workplace was not accomplished easily. Although greater numbers worked, a sexual division of labor prevailed. Women were heavily concentrated in low-wage jobs, and certain professions—such as elementary school teaching, secretarial work, telephone switchboard operation, and nursing—were so identified with women that some commentators dubbed these jobs a "pink-collar ghetto." By 1963, the year in which the **Equal Pay Act** was passed, the average working woman made just 59 cents for every dollar earned by males. Popular parlance of the day associated women's work with "pin money," meaning extra cash to be spent on luxuries and frivolities. Male wages, in contrast, continued to be viewed as those that supported families. In like fashion, workplace culture was geared toward a view of men as strong, aggressive, and sexually powerful.

Such social arrangements were ripe for challenge, and the birth of second-wave feminism provided it. The women's movement of the 1960s and 1970s called into question views of masculinity that entailed the subordination of women. Female activists did not shy away from challenging men in presumably progressive areas such as the **counterculture** and organized labor. Unions that prided themselves on being liberal, such as the **United Auto Workers of America**, held tumultuous conventions in which male chauvinism was challenged. Moreover, as a result of court challenges and the implementation of **affirmative action** programs, women began to enter professions that were once male bastions, including law enforcement, firefighting, warehouse work, and construction.

The devastating stagflation of the 1970s and 1980s dealt another severe blow to masculinity, as did the wave of **deindustrialization** and **downsizing** that followed. By the mid-1980s, many high-paying factory jobs had disappeared; in those that remained, unions were plagued by demands for **concessions**. In the last quarter of the 20th century, the rise in family income was due almost entirely to a single factor: the entry of more women into the workplace. Many men felt betrayal, anger, and shame over the erosion of the family wage. A backlash against feminism emerged in the 1980s, though it has been quelled to some extent over the past few decades. Women now make up a larger percentage of the workforce than men. Moreover, the family wage ideal has faded amidst the reality that it is now difficult to sustain households and consumer spending on a single income.

It would, however, be a mistake to assume that masculinity no longer shapes work in American society. Women often complain that the workplace remains hostile toward women and that male work patterns are still dominant. Female employees have filed numerous sexual harassment suits since the 1970s. Today's feminists also point to the fact that the vast majority of chief executive officers (CEOs), upper-level management, line supervisors, and high-paid production workers are male. Recent trends toward **equity pay** have arisen in response to data revealing that nearly 50 years after the Equal Pay Act was passed, women still earn just 77 percent of what males earn; this discrepancy persists even when men and women work in the same occupations. Labor unions have made great strides in removing sexism from their ranks, but it would seem that hyper-masculinity remains a problem in many American workplaces.

Suggested Reading

Ava Baron, *Work Engendered: Toward a New History of American Labor*, 1991; Mary Ann Clawson, *Constructing Brotherhood: Class, Gender, and Fraternalism*, 1989; Susan Faludi,

Stiffed: The Betrayal of the American Man, 2000; Carol Groneman and Mary-Beth Norton, eds., *"To Toil the Livelong Day:" America's Women at Work, 1780–1980*, 1987; Michael Kimmel, *Manhood in America*, 1996; Ruth Milkman, ed., *Women, Work and Protest: A Century of U.S. Women's Labor History*, 1991.

MASTER CRAFTSMAN

A master craftsman is an individual who risen to the highest and most prestigious level of a trade or craft. This designation is an old one, dating to the medieval guild system. The term is a holdover from the medieval guild system and was transplanted to preindustrial North America by European settlers, where it became the basis of colonial **artisan** labor. Master craftsmen were independent shop owners and manufacturers who took in **apprentices** and hired **journeymen**. Master status limited the number of workers practicing a trade, regulated the quality of goods produced, and protected **wage** and price bargaining in preindustrial and precapitalist markets that did not operate according to the logic of competition and the laws of supply and demand.

The emergence of the factory system in the early 19th century challenged preindustrial norms, though its full implications were not yet obvious and demand for skilled labor remained high. In many cases—textiles, for instance —machines merely spun thread or wove cloth, which was then given to skilled tailors to be fashioned into garments. By the 1820s, however, the distinction between master craftsmen and journeymen began to blur, though skill remained primary to each. Skilled artisans usually commanded the highest wages, and they were among the first to form associations to protect those wages, retain craft privileges, set their own prices, and pressure businesses and consumers to buy their products based on the quality and limited supply. In the early 19th century, skilled artisans dominated crafts such as furniture-making, brewing, baking, plumbing, carpentry, and masonry. Although journeymen took the lead, master craftsmen were among the earliest **craft unionists**. Nonetheless, industrialization and mechanization eroded the importance of skilled craftsmen in the 1830s, most notably in the shoe and textile industries.

It is easy to exaggerate the pace at which the **Industrial Revolution** transformed American work. Artisanal labor remained important throughout the 19th century, and American factories often more resembled a warren of interconnected craft shops than the integrated **assembly line** of the popular imagination. Many unions resisted technological changes that replaced master craftsmen with machines and reduced their status to that of unskilled or semiskilled workers. In fact, the **American Federation of Labor** (AFL) formed partly to protect craft workers; cofounder **Samuel Gompers** headed the Cigar Makers International Union, an organization whose craft was particularly threatened by deskilling. The enduring importance of skilled labor explains, in part, why the AFL survived while its chief rival, the **Knights of Labor**—which had a far greater representation among unskilled and prototypical **industrial unionists**—declined after 1890.

The path hewn by the Knights would come to dominate, however. By the late 19th century, mass-production industries had replaced many of its artisans. In 1892, for example, Carnegie Steel easily replaced skilled workers with machines and unskilled **scab** labor during the **Homestead Steel lockout**. By the 20th century, assembly-line production perfected by Henry Ford and other auto manufacturers was becoming widespread and many union activists argued that AFL conceptions of craft ideals were outmoded by technological reality. In the 1930s, this critique gave birth to the **Congress of Industrial Organizations**, a **labor federation** based on industrial union ideals. Skilled craftsmen continued to dominate in fields such as precision machine grinding, carpentry, and tailoring, but the pattern of **blue-collar** work in the 20th century was an inexorable march toward deskilling. In the late 20th century, **outsourcing**, **globalism**, and **deindustrialization** hastened the erosion of artisan labor. In addition, American businesses launched aggressive campaigns to cut labor costs, often replacing high-paid artisan workers by shifting their work to offshore low-wage nations.

Craft work has lost much of its association with the everyday work world and has become identified with niche markets, specialty goods, leisure pursuits, and the fine arts. Society retains craft workers such as plumbers, electricians, carpenters, pipe fitters, and painters, but older craft ideals are now most dominant among **white-collar** professions such as doctors and lawyers, and in professional unions such as the **National Education Association**. Union apprenticeship programs keep blue-collar ideals of craft alive, as do vocational technical schools, certification requirements, and licensing boards. Today, the title of master craftsman is generally conferred to workers who have completed an approved apprenticeship program.

Suggested Reading

Alan Dawley, *Class and Community*, 1976; James Green, *The World of the Worker*, 1990; Bruce Laurie, *Artisans into Workers*, 1989.

MATEWAN

Matewan is a small coal-patch town in Mingo County, West Virginia, where striking coal miners were involved in a bloody shootout with the Baldwin-Felts Agency on May 19, 1920. It was part of the larger West Virginia–Kentucky coal **strike** that convulsed the region between 1920 and 1923. The violence in this section of West Virginia was so severe that the region was dubbed "Bloody Mingo County." The events in Matewan later appeared in fictionalized form in a 1987 **film** by John Sayles.

The events in Matewan occurred in the midst of a **United Mine Workers of America** (UMWA) campaign to organize West Virginia coal miners. New UMWA president **John L. Lewis** made this effort the centerpiece of his plan to revitalize the moribund UMWA. Despite firings and blacklists of UMWA members, the union began to make major inroads in the southern Appalachians. One estimate holds that more than 15,000 miners in the Tug Creek region of West Virginia near Matewan signed with the UMWA. Regional coal operators and the out-of-state interests that controlled them kept up steady harassment of the UMWA, including the importa-tion of **goons** and gun thugs. Some activists were shot or beaten, and rumors abounded that coal companies were murdering miners. By the spring of 1920, min-ers were armed for self-protection. Into this tense atmosphere came the Baldwin-Felts Agency. The firm, like the **Pinkerton** Detective Agency and the Burns Agency, specialized in company "security," a term that generally referred to strong-arm union-busting. Residents complained that agents threatened local citizens and harassed women.

Albert and Lee Felts arrived in Matewan on May 15, 1920. Because Matewan was largely a **company town**, their first order of business was to carry out orders from the Red Jacket Coal Company to evict the families of striking miners from company-owned housing. Several UMWA leaders recognized the potential for vio-lence and sought to have the evictions carried out by the Mingo County sheriff instead of Baldwin-Felts agents, but their efforts were rebuffed by U.S. Attorney General A. Mitchell Palmer, a man whose antilabor biases were well known and who had launched the post-World War I **Red Scare** that decimated unions.

The decision to act aggressively led to tragedy. On May 19, 13 new Baldwin-Felts agents arrived in Matewan. They carried out several evictions until confronted by Matewan chief of police Sid Hatfield, who was also a UMWA member. Hatfield and Matewan mayor Cabell Testerman forced them stop on the grounds that the agents lacked the proper paperwork to continue the evictions. A heated discussion ensued, and legend holds that Hatfield attempted to arrest Albert and Lee Felts, brothers of agency president Tom Felts. When the agents attempted to board a train, gunfire broke out. After a brief volley, the Felts brothers, five other detectives, two miners, and Testerman lay dead.

The shootout at Matewan galvanized miners, and they flooded to UMWA ranks. It also turned the mountains into a war zone marked by periodic sniper fire from both sides. Tom Felts vowed revenge on Hatfield, who along with 15 miners was charged with the murder of Albert Felts. All were acquitted in January 1921. Felts, however, charged that jury members were influenced by **communists** and the UMWA, and convinced the West Virginia legislature to pass the Jury Bill, which allowed judges and juries to be imported from outside the county. In a move of dubious constitutionality, the Matewan defendants were retried, this time for the murders of the six remaining Baldwin-Felts agents. (They could not be charged with the murder of Albert Felts, as that would constitute double jeopardy.) Hatfield never made it trial. Baldwin-Felts agents assassinated him and UMWA member Ed Chambers on August 1, 1921, as they were ascending the courthouse steps. No one was charged with their murders, but the mountains erupted in violence that culminated in the **Battle of Blair Mountain**, which cost at least 25 miners their lives and led President Warren G. Harding to place the region under martial law. In the end, the UMWA suffered a brutal setback. By the 1930s, however, the union had organized nearly all the region's miners.

Matewan's notoriety faded quickly, and not many Americans knew of it until the appearance of the labor movie *Matewan* in 1987. Independent director John Sayles thoroughly researched the film, but his account is not a documentary.

Sayles did not alter the basic historical truth of the Matewan massacre, but he took artistic license in several key areas. For instance, the film's central character, ex-**Industrial Worker of the World** (IWW) activist Joe Kenehan, is a composite character based in part on real-life UMWA leaders Frank Keeney and Fred Mooney. Neither man belonged to the IWW, though Keeney once belonged to the Socialist Party, and both men had been involved in the 1912 Paint Creek strike in which the IWW played a minor role. Sayles also plucked protagonist Few Clothes Johnson from a later episode in the strike to give his film a central African American character.

Suggested Reading

David Corbin, *Life, Work, and Rebellion in the Coal Fields: The Southern West Virginia Miners, 1880–1922*, 1981; Lon Savage, *Thunder in the Mountain: The West Virginia Mine War*, 1990; John Sayles, *Thinking in Pictures: The Making of Matewan*, 1987.

MAY DAY

May Day, held on or about May 1, is celebrated in many nations as a day to honor workers. Long associated with the political left, May Day is not celebrated in the United States with the fervor it evokes elsewhere, though, in an ironic twist, the holiday originated there.

The first May Day occurred on May 1, 1886, and was part and parcel of a failed **general strike** in support of the **eight-hour movement**. An alliance of trade unionists, radicals, and **Knights of Labor** (KOL) called for a nationwide walkout on May 1 to force recalcitrant employers to grant laborers an eight-hour workday. At the time, most factories routinely defined a workday as between nine and 12 hours. Despite early enthusiasm for the idea, the idea began to fizzle in advance of May 1, in part due to opposition from KOL leaders, who felt the actions premature and were troubled by the presence of **anarchist** organizers in some cities. In the end, the KOL refused to endorse the action, though some rank-and-file Knights defied their leaders and participated anyway. The KOL's pullout meant that May Day turnouts were low except in a few cities. Instead of the 1 million strikers organizers had hoped for, only some 300,000 left their jobs.

The biggest crowds were in Chicago, where May Day happened to coincide with a strike against the McCormick-Harvester company. Within the city, some 40,000 workers turned out. The International Working Peoples' Association (IWPA), an anarchist federation, was active in organizing the event and held several massive parades in support of the eight-hour day prior to May 1. On the day itself, clashes in front of the McCormick factory led to scuffles in which several strikers were killed. In protest, the IWPA and others called for a massive protest three days later, a fateful call that culminated in the **Haymarket bombing** tragedy. The Haymarket event proved disastrous for the KOL. Despite the group's denunciation of anarchism and criticism directed at the organization when its head, **Terence Powderly**, refused to endorse a clemency movement directed at individuals arrested for the Haymarket bombing, employers launched an aggressive campaign to weaken the KOL.

May Day also became associated with **anarchism** and the political left. May Day rallies were held after 1886, and in 1889 the International Socialist Congress, held in Paris, proclaimed May 1 as International Workers' Day. This, however, served only to distance moderate and liberal workers and unions from the event, all whom preferred to celebrate a separate **Labor Day**, the celebration of which predated May Day. The **American Federation of Labor** did hold some May Day rallies in the 1890s, but May Day dropped further from favor after the 1917 Bolshevik Revolution in Russia. The newly created Soviet Union appropriated May Day as a holiday to extol the glories of **communism** and as a symbol of **working-class** revolutionary fervor and Soviet military might. May Day enjoyed a brief resurgence among U.S. radicals in the 1930s, but even then most workers favored Labor Day as a time to honor workers. The **Red Scares** following World War I and World War II pushed May Day further into the orbit of the radical left. May Day is still commemorated in the United States, but its appeal is limited mostly to ideologues.

Suggested Reading

Paul Avrich, *The Haymarket Tragedy*, 1984; Eric Hobsbawm and Terence Ranger, eds., *The Invention of Tradition*, 1984; Robert E. Weir, *Beyond Labor's Veil: The Culture of the Knights of Labor*, 1996.

McGUIRE, PETER JAMES

Peter James McGuire (July 6, 1852–February 18, 1906) was a cofounder of the **United Brotherhood of Carpenters and Joiners** (UBC) and of the **American Federation of Labor** (AFL). McGuire was such an important figure in the late 19th century that he is often credited with organizing the first **Labor Day**, though he did not. During the 1880s and the 1890s, he competed with **Samuel Gompers** and other conservative figures for the ideological leadership of skilled workers.

McGuire was born in 1852 in New York City, the oldest of five children born to John J. and Catherine Hand (O'Riley) McGuire, both of whom were Irish immigrants. McGuire's father was a porter in a department store. McGuire attended parochial schools as a boy, but left at the age of 11 to help support his family after his father enlisted in the Union army during the **Civil War**. The youthful McGuire held a variety of menial jobs, including bootblack, stable hand, and newsboy until taking up the cabinet-making trade when he turned 17. As an employee at the Haynes Piano Company, he became interested in the union movement and joined the Cabinet Makers Union of New York. He also developed an interest in politics by attending night classes and lectures at Cooper Union, a free institute for the education of **working-class** men and women. Cooper Union first introduced McGuire to the various strains of socialist thought, and he grew enamored of **Lassalleanism**. Throughout his career, McGuire would be attacked from the right by conservatives who rejected **socialism**, and from the left by revolutionary socialists who rejected Lassalleanism's emphasis on electoral politics.

McGuire first attracted public attention during the Panic of 1873. He was deeply involved with the Committee of Public Safety, which demanded relief for the unemployed. On January 13, 1874, he led a parade that was broken up by mounted police. The **Tompkins Square riot** led McGuire to involvement with the Socialist Labor Party, on whose behalf he became known as a capable recruiter, organizer, and orator. In 1878, he moved to St. Louis, Missouri, and, in 1879, assisted in securing a state **Bureau of Labor Statistics** in the United States. He also joined the St. Louis Carpenters' Union at a time in which **artisan labor** was in the throes of transformation. The carpenters were witnessing the erosion of traditional **apprenticeship** programs and mass-produced machine-made goods were replacing many goods completed by the **master craftsman** of yore. In addition, **wages** were declining. In April 1881, McGuire was the secretary of a committee of the St. Louis Carpenters' Union that led the charge for a national federation of carpenters' unions. From this effort, the UBC was formed. McGuire was elected national secretary and held the office for the next 20 years. McGuire's steady leadership and his editorship of *The Carpenter* made the UBC one of the most powerful trade unions in the country.

McGuire was also active in the 1881 convention that formed the Federation of Organized Trades and Labor Unions (FOTLU), a federation of national trade unions. The FOTLU was not very effective, but when it reorganized as the AFL five years later, McGuire became its first secretary. McGuire hoped that the AFL would serve two purposes: protecting the day-to-day interests of workers in the short term and preparing the path for a future socialist commonwealth. He advocated the formation of a **labor party** that would win control of the government and use federal funds to establish worker-owned large-scale industrial **cooperatives**. During the 1880s and 1890s, both the UBC and the AFL prospered, and McGuire became one of the most influential figures in the labor movement.

McGuire's socialism put him on a collision course with AFL President Samuel Gompers and with cautious trade union leaders. Whereas McGuire dreamed of a redeemed society, AFL craft unionists increasingly gravitated toward a form of **pure and simple** unionism that accepted the permanence of **capitalism**. In 1900, McGuire was forced to resign as vice president of the AFL due to poor health and a descent into alcoholism. Two years later he was expelled from the UBC in the wake of trumped-up charges of embezzlement. McGuire died in Camden, New Jersey, on February 18, 1906.

Suggested Reading

Robert Christie, *Empire in Wood: A History of the Carpenters Union*, 1956; Mark Ehrlich, "Peter J. McGuire's Trade Unionism: Socialism of a Trades Union Kind," *Labor History* 24, no. 2 (Spring 1983): 165–197; Walter Galenson, *The United Brotherhood of Carpenters: The First Hundred Years*, 1983.

McKEE'S ROCK

McKee's Rock is a town in western Pennsylvania near Pittsburgh, where the **Industrial Workers of the World** (IWW) led an important **strike** in the steel mills of the Pressed Steel Car Company in the summer of 1909. Although more than a dozen people lost their lives, and several hundred were injured, the strike ended in partial victory for the IWW. For a brief moment, it appeared that **collective bargaining** would emerge in one of the most union-resistant industries in the United States.

The events in McKee's Rock mirrored those of nearby **Homestead**, where an 1892 strike ended in a rout of labor. Like Homestead, McKee's Rock was largely a **company town** in which workers rented homes and purchased utilities from the corporation. Also like Homestead, the town was dominated by immigrant laborers who lived in crushing poverty. Their nations of origin included Russia, Poland, Austria, Germany, France, and Italy. Many immigrant laborers were paid by a pool system in which wages for an entire work gang were paid to a foreman, who then distributed them. Favoritism and graft abounded. The **American Federation of Labor** (AFL) represented a small number of skilled workers, but deemed most of the immigrant workforce to be unorganizable.

Difficulties began in McKee's Rock during the economic recession of 1907, when **wages** were slashed and new work rules were implemented—the two most troublesome of which were new standards for computing the piece-rate pay under which many workers were compensated and changes to the pooling system that penalized all line workers if any one of them failed to meet quotas. In addition, workers were docked for downtime. By 1909, the recession was over, but wages were still below pre-1907 levels. On Saturday, July 10, 1909, some workers grumbled that their pay was unfairly computed, and on Monday about 40 men refused to work; they were promptly fired. The company's refusal to meet with a workers' committee on July 14 led to a spontaneous walkout of approximately 600 workers; by afternoon, more than 5,000 of the plant's employees were out, with only about 500 skilled AFL men staying on the job.

The strike officially began on Thursday, July 15, with demands for a wage increase, the implementation of a formal **grievance** procedure, and an end to the pooling system. The first day of the strike saw a small-scale repeat of the Homestead events of 21 years earlier, when workers fired upon coal and iron police seeking to enter the plant by boat from the Ohio River. Violence also broke out when the State Constabulary sought to evict workers from their homes and house **scabs** there. Women screaming "Kill the Cossacks" greeted those efforts, and more than 100 individuals on both sides were injured. It is not certain exactly when the IWW entered the fray, but by the end of July, William Trautmann was busily organizing immigrant workers. Violence plagued the strike, and on August 22 a clash between immigrant workers and police forces led to at least seven deaths. State troopers subsequently ransacked workers' homes in search of weapons. Trautmann was arrested on minor charges, but the IWW quickly dispatched Joe Ettor to replace him, and the strike continued.

On September 8, 1909, the Pressed Steel Company capitulated to worker demands. Scabs were dismissed, the pooling system was dismantled, and an immediate 5 percent raise was implemented, with another 10 percent raise promised within 60 days. Pressed Steel no doubt decided to end the strike partly in hopes of deterring the increased IWW organizing. Most negotiations were held with AFL machinists and electricians, who were not sympathetic to foreigners. Ettor led 4,000 immigrant workers out on strike again on September 14, but violent clashes that led to more deaths and AFL opposition collapsed the strike within 24 hours.

The IWW briefly threatened to organize steel. Victory at McKee's Rock was followed by successful actions at two plants in East Chicago, Indiana, and another in Hammond, Indiana. In the end, however, Pressed Steel's strategy worked. By dealing with small AFL unions, steel firms avoided **collective bargaining** with the masses and crippled IWW hopes. The IWW's membership at McKee's Rock plummeted from 6,000 in October 1909 to just 20 in August 1912. The events at McKee's Rock sealed the enmity between the IWW and the AFL, which would be routinely called the "American Separation of Labor" by disgusted IWW members. The clash between the two groups did steelworkers little good. Most steelworkers remained unorganized until the emergence of the Steel Workers Organizing Committee in the 1930s and the founding of the **United Steelworkers of America**.

Suggested Reading

Melvyn Dubofsky, *We Shall Be All: A History of the Industrial Workers of the World*, 1969; Sidney Lens, *The Labor Wars: From the Molly Maguires to the Sitdowns*, 1973; Fred Thompson and Patrick Murfin, *The I.W.W.: The First Seventy Years, 1905–1975*, 1976.

McNEILL, GEORGE EDWIN

George McNeill (August 4, 1837–May 19, 1906) was president of the International Labor Union (ILU), a member of the **Knights of Labor** (KOL), and a founding member of the **American Federation of Labor** (AFL). He was so active in the Eight-Hour League that some contemporaries dubbed him the "father of the **eight-hour movement**," though most historians believe that title should go to **Ira Steward**. Very few 19th-century labor leaders enjoyed as much respect across the ideological spectrum as McNeill, one of the few people who could mediate KOL/ AFL disputes.

McNeill was born in Amesbury, Massachusetts, the son of John and Abigail (Hickey) McNeill, Scots-Irish immigrants. He attended school until the age of 15, when he began work, first in woolen mills, then as a shoemaker. When McNeill was 19, he moved to Boston, met Steward, and took up the eight-hour cause. He served as president of Boston's Eight-Hour League from 1869 to 1874. McNeill also lobbied for the creation of a Massachusetts **Bureau of Labor Statistics** (BLS) and in 1869, was appointed as deputy state constable of the Commonwealth's newly created BLS.

In 1872, McNeill helped compile a statistical report of trade unions, but a controversial report—later published as *Factory Children: A Report upon the Schooling and Hours of Labor of Children Employed in the Manufacturing and Mechanical Establishments of Massachusetts*—led to his dismissal from the bureau when business interests charged it was inflammatory and inaccurate. Despite his problems with the BLS, the Massachusetts office became the model from which a national BLS was later fashioned. McNeill championed the creation of such a body when he joined the

KOL in 1883 because he shared the KOL's belief that BLS statistics would ultimately enlighten the public about the problems facing working people and make it receptive to labor unions.

After his firing from the BLS, McNeill renewed his efforts with the Eight-Hour League, studied Steward's economic theories, and came to blame economic instability on the **wage** system and under-consumption. Like Steward, McNeill joined the Boston Christian Labor Union, a faith-based **socialist** organization. McNeill became the senior warden of a Boston parish headed by Episcopal priest W. D. P. Bliss, who was also a KOL member. McNeill would flirt with various forms of socialism during his career, but the teachings of Bliss remained central to his thought.

McNeill appears to have joined the Socialist Labor Party (SLP) at its inception in 1876. The SLP would split over the question of whether it should be primarily a labor organization or a political entity, with McNeill among those labor reformers suspicious of political parties. The SLP's decision to become a de facto **labor party** caused Steward and several other Eight-Hour League members to shy away from the party. McNeill also kept his distance, but the SLP's various campaigns did awaken his interest in **labor journalism**. When the financially strapped *Labor Standard*, a **Marxist** weekly and official SLP organ, was near bankruptcy in May 1877, a group headed by editor J. P. McDonnell took over the paper and moved operations first to Boston, then to Fall River, Massachusetts, where McNeill joined the editorial board and soon matched Steward in becoming a regular contributor. After December 1877, the *Labor Standard* ceased to be an official SLP paper. The paper was the organ of the short-lived International Labor Union, a group with approximately 7,000 members in 17 states in 1878. The ILU participated in several unsuccessful **strikes** and was defunct by 1881, save a single branch in Newark, New Jersey.

With the demise of the ILU, McNeill turned to the KOL, where he quickly became one of the most respected members of the organization and one of the few figures aside from its national leader, **Terence Powderly**, whose reputation extended beyond his local region. McNeill served in several posts with District Assembly 30, which was the KOL's largest district and represented most of Massachusetts. His socialist views ultimately led to clashes with Powderly and others within the KOL who disagreed with McNeill's views that trade unions could become the basis upon which society could be reformed. At the May 25, 1886, Special General Assembly of the KOL in Cleveland, McNeill was a member of a committee seeking to negotiate peace between the KOL and various trade unions that had lodged complaints against the KOL's insistence that trade union ideals should be subsumed within a greater **solidarity** based on social class and the ideals of the KOL. McNeill remained a committed trade unionist, and when rapprochement failed, McNeill participated in the December 8, 1886, founding of the AFL. A month earlier, he had failed in his bid to be elected mayor of Boston.

McNeill was the editor of the Boston *Labor Leader* until late 1887 and an occasional contributor thereafter. Ironically, McNeill's conversion to the **pure and simple unionism** ideals of the AFL led to more criticism of him within the socialist press than inside the KOL, where he retained many friends despite quitting the organization in late 1886. Though outside the KOL and dismissive of Powderly, whom he believed was controlled by an internal faction, McNeill remained hopeful for the KOL's prospects. Editorial jealousy also played a role in McNeill's dislike of Powderly. In 1886, McNeill published *The Labor Movement: The Problem of To-Day*. McNeill advertised that Powderly had endorsed the volume, which he denied. In 1889, Powderly published his own *Thirty Years of Labor*, which covered many of the same themes as McNeill's book. By then, McNeill had also authored *Eight Hour Primer*.

The public spat with Powderly came just as McNeill's most active work with organized labor was winding down. He published *The Philosophy of the Labor Movement* in 1893 and continued to work within the AFL—he represented it at an 1897 British Trade Union Congress—but opted to lower his public profile as a labor activist. Although McNeill was also active in the Anti-Imperialist League from 1898 until his death in 1906, the work for which he is best known after 1890 was with the Massachusetts Mutual Accidental Insurance Company, which he founded in 1883. "Mass Mutual"—as it continues to be called—was originally designed as a mutual aid and benefits scheme for workers. It evolved into a modern insurance company that regularly earns profits in excess of $1 billion per year.

In 1903, McNeill published a volume of mystical Christian socialist poetry, *Unfrequented Paths: Songs of Nature, Love, and Men*. He died in Somerville, Massachusetts.

Suggested Reading

James Green and Hugh C. Donahue, *Boston's Workers: A Labor History*, 1979; Herbert Gutman, *Work, Culture, and Society in Industrializing America*, 1976; Robert E. Weir, *Knights Unhorsed: Internal Conflict in a Gilded Age Labor Movement*, 2000.

MEANY, GEORGE

George Meany (August 16, 1894–January 10, 1980) was a gruff, burly, cigar-smoking labor administrator from the Bronx who was the most powerful figure in the American labor movement in the middle years of the 20th century. He was also among its most controversial participants. Meany served as president of the **American Federation of Labor** (AFL) from 1952 to 1955, fashioned the AFL's merger with the **Congress of Industrial Organizations** (CIO) in 1955, and thereafter served as **American Federation of Labor-Congress of Industrial Organizations** (AFL-CIO) president until his retirement in 1979.

Meany was born into a Roman Catholic, **working-class** family in New York City, the son of Michael, a union plumber, and Anne (Cullen) Meany, a homemaker. He attended New York public schools until age 14, when he left to train in his father's trade. He worked as a plumber from 1916 to 1922, when he took a paid position with the local branch of the plumbers' union. From that time until his death 58 years later, Meany worked as a trade-union official. Later critics would cite his relative lack of work experience and label him a classic **business unionist** out of touch with the rank-and-file, but such criticisms lay in the future. Meany quickly established a reputation as a skilled bureaucrat, effective lobbyist, and ferocious political infighter. These attributes put him on a fast track to promotion and by 1932—just 10 years removed from school—Meany was elected vice president of the New York State Federation of Labor.

Meany lobbied the New York state legislature to implement New Deal programs within the Empire State and to design its own work-relief schemes. Such efforts brought him to the attention of AFL President **William Green** who, in 1939, named him the AFL's secretary-treasurer, the second-ranking position in the federation. Many observers say that Meany was the de facto leader of the AFL well in advance of Green's death in 1952, and that Meany deserves credit for initiatives such as working to give refuge to Jewish trade unionists fleeing Nazi Germany, and for coordinating the AFL's cooperation with the **National War Labor Board** during World War II. Meany also sparked the development of the AFL's first political action committee, which was set up in direct response to the passage of the 1947 **Taft-Hartley Act.**

When Green died in 1952, Meany was named as AFL president and immediately put his stamp on the federation. He was an ardent opponent of **communism** and led the AFL to participate in **Cold War** unionism initiatives such as giving logistical and financial support to the International Confederation of Free Trade Unions, which some observers believe was sometimes a CIA front. That point is debatable, but without question Meany's greatest achievement in the 1950s was engineering the merger of the AFL and the CIO. Meany was sympathetic to the **craft unionism** of older AFL heads, but he also recognized it as outmoded and sought to bring rapprochement between the AFL's craft unions and the CIO's **industrial unions.** After two years of painstaking negotiations, AFL and CIO leaders agreed to merge their organizations in 1955. Keys to forging the alliance were agreements to set up an Industrial Union Department headed by CIO head **Walter Reuther** and to address racial discrimination among AFL affiliates. Because the AFL had almost twice as many members as the CIO, Meany became president of the new federation, which represented approximately 15.5 million working people.

Meany sought to position the AFL-CIO as a powerful voice in national affairs. Both the AFL and the CIO had forged ties with the **Democratic Party** in the 1930s; after the formation of the AFL-CIO, those connections deepened under Meany. He enjoyed easy access to Democratic Presidents John Kennedy and Lyndon Johnson, in particular, whom he advised on labor issues such as raising the **minimum wage** as well as foreign policy decisions. Meany continually prodded Congress to pass social-welfare legislation that he believed would benefit union workers. At critical points in the 1960s, Meany also supported civil rights legislation and was instrumental in lobbying for the Civil Rights Act of 1964. He was nonetheless troubled by protests and public activism and, therefore, kept his distance from many liberal and radical initiatives. As a consummate insider, Meany distrusted social movements that operated outside the realm of Congress and the White House, and he had little but contempt for the **counterculture.** Meany was disgusted by activists who criticized **capitalism** or showed any sympathy whatsoever for communism. Meany considered even the mildest critique of the Cold War as bordering on treason, and he was appalled by opposition to the Vietnam War, which he considered a noble cause.

By the late 1960s, some AFL-CIO officials had come to see Meany as bullheaded, obstructionist, and perhaps as antiquated in his thinking as Green had been in his final years. While he worked hard to preserve labor's gains, Meany had no interest in extending the AFL-CIO's reach through grassroots organizing efforts. His control over the AFL-CIO's bureaucracy gave him the means to marginalize those union officials pushing the federation to be more aggressive in supporting social causes such as the antiwar movement, civil rights, and feminism. His clashes with Reuther and **A. Philip Randolph** were often acrimonious, and Meany essentially forced the **United Auto Workers of America** (UAW)—one of the AFL-CIO's largest affiliates—out of the federation when UAW President Reuther criticized Meany's leadership.

Meany's conservative approach to union affairs left the federation ill prepared to deal with the economic and political changes of the 1970s. In mid-decade, **deindustrialization** had led corporations to slash many of the industrial jobs that had been at the heart of the union movement. Moreover, Presidents Nixon, Ford, or Carter did not prove to be reliable allies to the labor movement. By the mid-1970s, Meany lacked the mental acuity and physical strength to help the AFL-CIO respond to the profound challenges facing it, though he stubbornly refused to relinquish power. Though wracked by ill health, he remained the federation's president until November 1979, when he turned over the reins of power to his handpicked successor, **Lane Kirkland**. Meany died three months later. He left behind his wife of more than 60 years, the former Eugenia McMahon, and three daughters.

In 1974, the National Labor College, which Meany played a key role in establishing, named its archives after him. In like fashion, the **Department of Labor** posthumously inducted Meany into Labor's Hall of Fame in 1989. Nonetheless, Meany's reputation among scholars has declined in recent years. Although many researchers give Meany high marks for bureaucratic finesse and strong leadership traits, he is also viewed as having overstayed his tenure as AFL-CIO head and as having been inflexible and obstinate. Meany misunderstood the social movements of the 1960s and continued to view the world through the bipolar logic of the early Cold War. His brand of business unionism sometimes veered toward autocracy, and his decision to centralize the AFL-CIO bureaucracy at the expense of grassroots organizing has been roundly criticized. It is probably unfair to lay blame at his feet—as some scholars have done—for the subsequent decline of labor union strength. The United States underwent economic transformations from the 1970s onward whose final implications remain uncertain. Although Meany's business unionism precepts did little to help organized labor cope with those changes, it is by no means certain that a different kind of leader would have fared better.

Suggested Reading

Paul Buhle, *Taking Care of Business: Samuel Gompers, George Meany, Lane Kirkland, and the Tragedy of American Labor*, 1999; Joseph Goulden, *Meany: The Unchallenged Strong-Man of American Labor*, 1972; Archie Robinson, *George Meany and His Times: A Biography*, 1981; Robert Zieger, "George Meany: Labor's Organization Man," in *Labor Leaders in America*, Melvyn Dubofsky and Warren Van Tine, eds., 1987.

MEATPACKING. *See* Butchers.

MECHANICS. *See* Artisan Labor.

MECHANIZATION. *See* Automation.

MEDIATION. *See* Arbitration/Conciliation/Mediation.

MERIT RAISE

A merit raise, or "pay-for-performance," is an increase in an individual's **wage**, usually granted by management, to reward outstanding job-related performance. It differs from a bonus in that merit increases are ongoing additions to a worker's pay, whereas bonuses are generally one-time lump-sum awards. Merit raises also are generally determined by measuring a worker's output or performance vis-à-vis established objectives and goals. Merit pay is usually based on criteria predetermined by the employer and is a private arrangement between management and the wage-earner. For that reason, labor unions are often suspicious of this form of pay. They have historical reasons for adopting this stance, as, in the past, merit raises were integral to **Taylorism** and, along with other tools such as bonus pay, **piecework**, and **profit sharing**, were often little more than ways for employers to achieve substantially greater output at a fraction of the cost that would be involved in paying **overtime** or increasing the workforce. In that regard, merit raises are often backdoor versions of **speed-ups** and **stretch-outs**.

Proponents of merit pay argue that it rewards efficiency, loyalty, and hard work, whereas critics charge that it is too often based on management's subjective interpretation of a job exceptionally well done, is divisive in terms of workplace **solidarity**, is used to break employee **stints**, and is prone to cronyism and favoritism. Merit raises are generally absent in union **contracts**, as most unions argue that across-the-board increases are more democratic. Merit raises are more common among white-collar professionals, though their potential to engender resentment and jealousy often leads employers to adopt the fiction that part of a predetermined annual raise is designated as a "merit" increase and is given to all workers within a particular unit. There is also growing evidence that merit pay does not really work in terms of enhancing productivity, as it harms workforce cohesion. Those workers who do not receive merit pay often feel resentment and may lower their output in response, thereby decreasing the aggregate output.

Merit pay has proved exceptionally divisive in **white-collar** professions such as teaching. Although rewarding good teachers sounds good in theory, the criteria upon which teacher performance is based owe more to politics than to sound educational theory. For example, teachers are often rewarded if a high percentage of their students pass standardized tests. Such a criterion is inherently biased, in that it does not take into account the relative intelligence of students, their previous educational experience, or the resources available within a district to educate children. In many cases standardized tests do little but reflect the nature of American class system. Although the **National Education Association** and the **American Federation of Teachers** have softened their adamant stance against all merit increases, both worry that merit raises for teachers are an attempt to weaken teachers' unions. There is no doubt that merit pay has been used as a union-busting tactic by management in the past.

Merit pay is now a common feature in private business. In one 2009 survey, more than three-fourths of all employers said they give merit increases and nearly 50 percent said they withhold them for low performance. The **Department of Labor** takes the view that the **Fair Labor Standards Act** is not applicable to merit increase questions, but a future court challenge to that interpretation would seem likely.

Suggested Reading

Ann Bates, "The End of Merit Increase?," http://compforce.typepad.com/compensation _force/2009/06/death-knell-for-the-merit-increase.html, accessed March 8, 2011; Samuel Briedner, *To Hell with School Vouchers, Charter Schools, and Merit Pay*, 2002; Robert Heneman, *Merit Pay: Linking Pay to Performance in a Changing World*, 2000.

MIDDLE-CLASS IDEOLOGY

The relationship between the **working class** and the middle class has long been a vexing issue for the organized labor movement and, in the post-World War II era, one that cuts to the very core of individual and group identity. In contemporary America, the vast majority of individuals *think* they belong to the middle class, even when the jobs they hold, the **wages** they earn, and the material comforts they enjoy might suggest otherwise. As an analytical category, the term "middle class" often measures identity and aspirations with more accuracy than it describes objective reality or actual social status. The term has been and remains imprecise. The middle class is defined by negation; its members are part of neither an elite upper class nor a precarious lower class, yet they often share ideological and cultural values of those above them and the need to work with those below them. Moreover, there is such profound diversity within the middle class in terms of wealth, status, prestige, and security that most social scientists subdivide the middle class into categories such as upper-middle, middle-middle, and lower-middle class categories.

The middle class was born amidst ambiguity that came into somewhat sharper focus during the **Industrial Revolution**. In American Colonial society and the early republic, some individuals were neither wealthy landowners nor independent yeomen, but much of the activity of merchants, shopkeepers, lawyers, and clerks was ancillary to an **agrarian** economy based on the land and its products. Historians routinely refer to such individuals as "middling sorts," as most of them lacked **class consciousness** and did not perceive themselves, as **Marxists** later put it, as a class apart. Land ownership remained a powerful ideal, and many of the middling sorts aspired to control property. This was true also of wage-earners such as craft workers, domestic servants, **indentured servants**, and casual laborers. Wage earning was viewed as a temporary status to be abandoned once capital was raised and land was acquired, or, in the case of women, after marriage to a land-owning male was secured.

The Industrial Revolution accelerated trends first made manifest in the first two decades of the 19th century. The agrarian economy began to give way to one based on money, material wealth, property ownership, and income in the form of wages, salaries, and rent. In essence, it ushered in **capitalism**—a shift that altered social class composition. The traditional elites of the upper class possessed great prestige and political influence, but many lacked the monetary wealth possessed by the *nouveau riche* in economic sectors such as manufacturing, investment, and professional employment. The demands of the new economy also froze many workers into a permanent wage-earning status that led to creation of a distinct **working class**.

This factor gave rise to one of the primary distinctions between the middle and the working class. Both classes were dependent upon work for sustenance, but those in the middle classes obtained it through mental labor and those in the working class via manual labor. Middle-class work often entailed a need for greater education or mental training than that of the working class, or at least was perceived that way. By mid-century, middle-class individuals had come to view themselves as society's moral guardians and often resented the snobbery, perceived decadence, and special privileges of the upper class. By the same token, they also saw the lower orders as debased, dangerous, and dependent. Middle-class ideology was, therefore, uncertain in several ways. Middle-class individuals often tried to cultivate taste by aping the values, politics, and cultural practices of the elites they distrusted. In turn, the refined upper classes frequently viewed the middle class as ill-bred social climbers seeking to hide their coarseness behind a wall of conspicuous consumption. Because both capitalism and middle-class wealth were relatively new, few middle-class individuals of the lower-middle class could afford to live off investments, and few of the titans of new commercial or industrial enterprises chose to do so. Hard work became a hallmark of middle-class ideology, so much so that future generations would confuse toil itself with middle-class status. The emphasis on work gave a prestige boost to middle class **white collar** labor.

The passage of time further muddied middle-class identity. By the late 19th century, some families, such as the Rockefellers and the Vanderbilts, had been wealthy for several generations. Their commercial pursuits still made them suspect to old-wealth elites, but the patronage of wealthy individuals had come to sustain upper-class cultural institutions such as museums, the opera, posh churches, and symphony orchestras. If it was unclear to which class ultra-rich investors and manufacturers belonged, it nonetheless made little sense to consider them in the same category as lower-level managers, functionaries, and service-providing professions.

Middle-class composition and ideology were ill defined, though the complexities of each were such that the American middle class did not correspond neatly with **Marxist** class analysis. The American middle class was not akin to the European bourgeoisie; in fact, many middle-class Americans embraced **socialism**, albeit usually a non-Marxist variety.

Evolving middle-class values jumped class boundaries. Over time, some middle-class ideals and practices departed from those of the upper class. "Character" became more important than "honor," for example, and conceptions of "respectability" became linked to meaningful and productive work rather than to dilettantism and idle luxury. Education came to be seen as something that should yield pragmatic returns rather than as an end in its own right. Morality, broadly construed but often narrowly defined, became another marker of middle-class identity, as did a tendency toward sentimentality. These values, in turn, filtered down to a working class that was constantly being replenished by **immigrant** labor. Those workers seeking to differentiate themselves from new arrivals often copied middle-class culture, much in the same manner that the middle class once mimicked elites. This was especially true of skilled **artisans**, some of whom earned wages comparable to the salaries of the lower-middle class. Some working-class families also cultivated respectability by appropriating middle-class markers such as fashion, purchasing pianos, mimicking their reading habits, replicating paternalism, and frequenting middle-class cultural venues. Because most workers could only approximate a middle-class standard of living, however, and distinct forms of working-class culture remained, hazy lines between the two classes remained.

Three factors made these distinctions murkier. First, the emergence of popular, mass-culture entertainments such as professional sports, the circus, and amusement parks led many within the middle class to shift their cultural practices toward activities once mostly associated with the working class. In the 20th century, innovations such as dance hall culture, phonographs, radio, and movies served to homogenize culture. More important still were changing perceptions of capitalism.

For most of the 19th century, capitalism was contested, even as it expanded, but by the 20th it was clearly dominant and **labor federations** such the **American Federation of Labor** (AFL) had come to accept its permanence. Instead of contemplating a future society that would eliminate or subjugate nonproducers, labor unions now shifted their focus to securing more of the material goods of society cherished by the middle classes. This involved a profound ideological shift—the second factor blurring distinctions between the various social classes. Earlier members of the working class had dreamed of transforming society and held to a radical critique of existing conditions. Middle-class ideology, by contrast, was more conservative; rather than seeking to replace the status quo, it generally focused on maximizing the ability of the individual to benefit from society's opportunities.

The third great shift involved the changing nature of work. Agricultural production remained important into the early 20th century, but it would not remain so. The relatively small middle class of the 19th century grew enormously in the 20th century as the American economy shifted toward production of goods and services. In 1910, nearly 35 percent of all U.S. workers were involved in agricultural production, a figure that was more than halved by 1950, and is now less than 2 percent. By contrast, the explosion in **service industry** jobs—which first became more numerous than both agriculture and manufacturing jobs in 1920—led to increases in white-collar labor in the form of positions ranging from plant managers and college professors to retail clerks and office workers. As white-collar options expanded, however, the gap between those at the top and those at the bottom widened, with clerks and other service workers often earning less money and living less-lavish lifestyles than some high-waged members of the working class.

In the 20th century, social scientists such as W. Lloyd Warner and Robert and Helen Lynd noted the ways in which class categories seemed to be collapsing. The Lynds, for example, noticed that **Labor Day** celebrations had lost their zeal and that the allure of popular culture, automobiles, and consumer goods often generated more enthusiasm. The Great Depression delayed dreams of material prosperity for millions of Americans and led to a surge of radical challenges to capitalism, albeit not to the degree that might have been anticipated. Even though millions of workers went on **strike** and grassroots activism emerged, New Deal programs proved more popular to most workers than the appeals of **communists** and other radicals. Leftist scholars would later argue that the American working class was seduced by false hopes blandished by middle-class ideologues, but the power of those hopes should not be underestimated. Moreover, much of the radical challenge to capitalism and middle-class ideology evaporated in the waves of nationalism and full employment during World War II.

The end of the war saw the largest economic expansion in American history. In contrast to the deprivation of the Great Depression and wartime rationing, the postwar period made the American Dream more attainable for the masses. Soon even labor leaders such as AFL head **George Meany** began to assert that American workers were becoming members of the middle class. Although the prosperity thesis has been greatly exaggerated, it was true enough to establish itself as a powerful ideal that passed as truth. It also collided with **Cold War** unionism (a time in which organized labor largely acceded to the foreign policy objectives of the United States), the ideological assumptions embedded in the post-World War II **Red Scare**, and the claims of international business interests that global capitalism would ensure domestic prosperity. Many Americans experienced pressure to conform to prevailing norms. Although these norms were often expressed as the "American way of life," their parameters were defined by middle-class ideology, by then a nexus of work, ownership of property, consumerism, family, faith, and mainstream social and political values. Labor unions already reeling from the 1947 **Taft-Hartley Act** purged radicals from their ranks—actions whose long-term effect was to weaken activism, deemphasize working-class culture, dilute critiques of economic inequality, and institutionalize **business unionism**. In many ways, Cold War unionism completed the transformation of the labor movement from an oppositional force to one that sought to leverage capitalism to greater advantage.

By the end of the 1950s, the term "working class" was in decline and many labor leaders preferred to reference the hypothetical "average" American, a term also regularly invoked by political office-seekers. In 1956, the number of professional white-collar jobs surpassed those classified as blue-collar for the first time. Thus, by the time the social challenges of the 1960s and 1970s occurred, the term "working class" was as likely to be invoked by members of the **counterculture** as those inside the organized labor movement. Although the **American Federation of Labor-Congress of Industrial Organizations** (AFL-CIO) contained many older leaders who recalled the class-based struggles of the 1930s, increasing numbers of union campaigns centered on preserving the middle-class lifestyles of American workers occasioned by nearly two decades' worth of rise in real wages. Ominously, however, by 1970 just 35 percent of workers held blue-collar jobs.

In the late 1970s and beyond, **deindustrialization** accelerated due to stagflation, globalization, **runaway capital**, and the anti-union policies of President **Ronald Reagan**. In an ironic twist, Reagan enjoyed wide support among American wage-earners, many of whom had come to believe that they were members of the middle class. Politicians in both parties discovered that presenting the middle class as imperiled yielded political gain. Those appeals had impact; several studies suggest that a "fear of falling" had long been a defining characteristic of the middle class. By the 1980s, a majority of Americans had come to believe that the United States was a middle-class society and that they were members of that endangered group. Accordingly, in some cases a fear of falling made some voters more prone to embrace conservative politics.

The degree to which middle-class ideology and conservative politics are linked is debatable, but an idealized middle class had clearly become the central political metaphor. In the 2000 presidential campaign, for instance, the only candidate to reference the working class with conviction or frequency was ultra-conservative Patrick Buchanan, and both **Democrats** and **Republicans** denounced his call for economic **protectionism** as unsound policy. In 2008, Democrat John Edwards based a presidential primary campaign around the theme of rebuilding the working class, gained very little traction, and was forced to withdraw from the race (though he later became a vice presidential candidate on John Kerry's failed ticket).

Contemporary Americans believe in the idea of a middle-class society, even if they have little idea of what that means. A 2008 Pew Research Center poll showed that more than half of all Americans identified as middle class, and its findings are unique only in the sense of yielding such a low figure. The National Center for Opinion Research shows a rock-steady belief on the part of most Americans that they are members of the middle class, and some surveys return figures as high as 95 percent. Middle-class ideology has so penetrated American perceptions that it is very difficult to measure class objectively. The 2009 median family income was less than $50,000 for the nation as a whole. If an old-fashioned quintile method is used to measure class, and the middle class is collectively considered as those making 80 percent to 120 percent of the median income, no more than 40 percent of Americans could possibly qualify as middle class. Even so, some polling data reveal that more than one-third of families surviving on less than $15,000 per year consider themselves middle class. Such numbers tell us little about what the middle class is, but it speaks volumes about how potent middle-class ideology has become.

Suggested Reading

Martin J. Burke, *The Conundrum of Class: Public Discourse on the Social Order in America*, 1995; Barbara Ehrenreich, *Fear of Falling: The Inner Life of the Middle Class*, 1990; Robert Frank, *Falling Behind: How Rising Inequality Harms the Middle Class*, 2007; Theresa Sullivan, Elizabeth Warren, and Jay Westbrook, *The Fragile Middle Class: Americans in Debt*, 2001.

MIGRANT AND SEASONAL AGRICULTURAL WORKER PROTECTION ACT. *See* Agricultural Labor Relations Act.

MILITARY AND THE WORKING CLASS

The American **working class** has had a long association with the U.S. military in terms of service, support for the armed forces, and work in defense-related industries. Nonetheless, social class as well as patriotism have historically complicated how the military meets its personnel needs. The armed forces fill its ranks through either volunteer or compulsory methods, the latter of which has often met with resistance. In addition, social class has historically shaped how a military recruit is assigned, promoted, and treated.

During the American Revolution, most of the leaders came from the upper class. Local militias, which saw limited action and seldom left their home region, were generally composed of farmers. By contrast, the Continental Army consisted primarily of **artisans** and **journeymen**, many of whom suffered great privation. Most were paid in scrip and greenbacks that proved of little value after the war, an impoverishing factor that led to postwar popular uprisings such as Shays' Rebellion and the Whiskey Rebellion. Nonetheless, farmers, artisans, and journeymen once again served during the War of 1812.

Laboring people proved willing to serve, but conscription was another matter. Forced service was so distasteful that General George Washington rejected the idea during the Revolutionary War, even though he was chronically short of troops. During the **Civil War**, both the Confederacy and the Union used conscription to meet military needs, but those moves met with resistance in both North and South.

The Southern law passed on April 16, 1862, made all whites aged 18 to 35 eligible for three years of military service. Subsequent amendments raised the upper age limit to 45, then 50. The Confederate draft was decidedly class based. Until popular anger caused its revocation, it was possible for wealthy southerners to hire substitutes, and all forms of the draft exempted those who held more than 20 slaves. There were also exemptions for civil servants and other professions that favored the privileged, and the southern draft met resistance in the backcountry, where small farmers were less likely to own slaves or possess the economic means to avoid service.

The North enacted a draft on March 3, 1863, which met with immediate disapproval from many Union residents. Some resented being drafted to fight for the end of **slavery**, while many recent **immigrants** saw the law as forcing the poor to fight a rich man's war. That charge had merit: Numerous upper and **middle-class** occupations were exempt from the draft and it was possible to hire a substitute or buy an exemption for $300, a trifling sum for the rich but more than a half-year's pay for most laborers. In New York City, the draft law sparked several days of rioting that left dozens dead and inflicted millions of dollars of property damage. The draft was so unpopular that more substitutes than draftees served; in some places, such as New York, as few as 6 percent of those eligible to be drafted ever served. One small measure of working-class pressure was found in military command. Popularly elected "political generals" often led northern soldiers rather than those trained at West Point.

Until the mid-20th century, the United States had a small peacetime military whose ranks were filled by volunteers. Officers usually came from the upper and upper middle class and recruits from society's lower ranks, but there was little public discussion of military recruiting until the United States entered World War I in 1917. A new draft was instituted and, again, protests greeted it. The war was not immediately popular and various **anarchist, socialist**, and radical groups opposed it, though the **American Federation of Labor** (AFL) supported U.S. involvement and the socialist movement eventually split over the issue. A 1918 Supreme Court upheld the constitutionality of conscription, while the U.S. government launched propaganda campaigns in support of the war and passed laws to quash dissent such as the Espionage Act of 1917. Leftists such as **Eugene V. Debs**, **William Haywood**, and members of the **Industrial Workers of the World** were prosecuted for impeding the war effort and for (allegedly) encouraging workers to evade the draft. More than 65,000 individuals declared themselves conscientious objectors (COs) to the war, and an estimated 300,000 evaded the draft. The AFL found it expedient to support the war and wrangled over promising wartime concessions that failed to survive the return to peace.

Upon the war's completion, voluntary service remained in effect until the 1940 Selective Training and Service Act (STSA) was passed. It was, technically, the first peacetime conscription act, though it came on the eve of World War II. Initially a lottery system determined service, but it became universal when the United States entered the war in December 1941. Both the AFL and the **Congress of Industrial Organizations** (CIO) supported the U.S. war effort, and all but a handful of unions—most notably the **United Mine Workers of America**—took **no-strike pledges** for the duration of the war in exchange for **National War Labor Board** promises to protect labor rights. Workers in defense industries were exempt from the draft, though thousands volunteered for military service. Wartime production, which was tremendously aided by the introduction of women defense industry workers, achieve soaring productivity levels that were instrumental in securing the Allied victory. The STSA expired in 1947, but was renewed in 1948.

During World War II, just 12,000 individuals filed for exemption from service as COs. There was, however, racial, gender, and class tension associated with military service. African Americans served in segregated units until 1953, despite an order from President Harry Truman to integrate the military six years earlier, and women remained excluded from combat units until the 1980s. As for whites, the lower one's socioeconomic status, the more likely one was to be assigned to the infantry and the less likely one was to be promoted. The outbreak of a postwar **Red Scare** and the emergence of the **Cold War** blunted opposition to peacetime conscription. In like fashion, organized labor fell under the sway of Cold War unionism and many labor leaders touted military service as the patriotic duty of workingmen. The STSA was expanded by the 1951 Universal Military and Service Act, a more aggressive draft aimed at meeting personnel needs during the Korean War. Most labor unions unflinchingly supported the United States' entrance into the Korean conflict, the building of overseas military bases, and U.S. involvement in defense alliances such as the North Atlantic Treaty Organization. Although unions were already under pressure from the 1947 **Taft-Hartley Act**, most AFL and CIO affiliates needed little prompting to adopt anticommunist measures.

During the postwar period, the U.S. military also became associated with hope for material prosperity. The 1944 Servicemen's Readjustment Act, better known as the G.I. Bill, linked military service with benefits such as educational training, medical care, and low-interest home loans. These measures dovetailed with the expansion of consumer society that emerged in the post-World War II period. In addition, rapid growth of the sector of the economy that, in 1961, President Dwight Eisenhower famously dubbed the "military-industrial complex" created thousands of high-paying jobs in factories that produced weaponry and military hardware. High-profile tours of duty by popular-culture icons such as baseball player Ted Williams and singer Elvis Presley removed some of the perception that the military was stratified by social class, and by the late 1950s military service was widely accepted as a rite of passage for boys on the cusp of adulthood. The reality, however, was more complex. The poor and members of the working class often saw military service as an avenue for upward social mobility, whereas middle-class males were far more likely to enroll in officer training programs and thus maintain greater control over their destiny. The Marine Corps and Army received recruits that were, on the average, poorer and less educated than those of the Navy or Air Force, and the latter two services tended to offer training skills more adaptable to civilian life.

Built-in inequities would become problematic during the **Vietnam War** (1964–1973). The percentage of African Americans and Latinos serving in the military in Vietnam was roughly equal to their overall representation in American society, but such troops—as well as poor whites—were far more likely to engage in direct combat. Occupational exemptions and student deferments meant that affluent whites found it easier to avoid service. In one New Mexico Congressional district, not a single draftee came from a family with a net worth of more than $5,000, while the 1970 Harvard graduating class of 1,200 men saw just 56 of its members enter the military and only two of them serve in Vietnam, neither in combat. There were 248 sons of Congressional representatives who came of age during the Vietnam conflict; only 28 served in Vietnam.

The Vietnam War proved a tremendous challenge for organized labor. Much of the leadership of the merged **American Federation of Labor-Congress of Industrial Organizations** (AFL-CIO), including President **George Meany**, supported the war and continued to do so long after U.S. efforts soured and public support for the war waned. As labor leaders such as **Walter Reuther** turned against the war and younger workers influenced by the **counterculture** expressed reservations, the AFL-CIO was torn asunder by debate over Vietnam. The situation was particularly acute among black workers, especially those associated with black nationalist groups such as the **Dodge Revolutionary Union Movement**. Many black activists included opposition to the war in their critique of American society.

As the Vietnam War grew more unpopular, draft resistance and desertion rates skyrocketed. According to Howard Zinn, the number of college students enrolled in the Reserve Officers Training Corps (ROTC) dropped from nearly 192,000 in 1966 to just 72,459 in 1973, and many universities threw the ROTC off campus. More than 170,000 Americans obtained CO status, as many as 100,000 Americans fled the country to avoid the draft, and many times that number simply refused to register or show up for induction. Anti-Vietnam protests increasingly turned into broader attacks on the military-industrial complex, a direct challenge to unions in industries dependent upon military contracts. By 1970, organized labor was so badly divided by the Vietnam War that some commentators began to speak of rising **blue-collar** conservatism, and the several **hard hat riots** in which union members attacked counterculture protestors seemed to confer that trend.

Protests did, however, bring needed attention to inequities within the military. The draft was scaled back and a lottery system prevailed between 1969 and 1973, when conscription ended and an all-volunteer military went into effect. The post-1973 recession actually exacerbated inequality in the short term. As **deindustrialization** turned older manufacturing centers into rust belts marked by high unemployment, de facto economic conscription emerged in hard-hit areas. Increased military spending under Presidents Jimmy Carter and **Ronald Reagan** leveled the recruitment field to some degree. First, military pay rose. Second, generous recruitment packages proved attractive, especially to cash-strapped college-bound students, and thus brought increasing numbers of **middle-class** recruits into the military. By the 1980s, ROTC was back on most campuses, especially at taxpayer-funded state universities.

Labor unions faced a dilemma when the Cold War ended in the late 1980s. Politicians began to discuss a possible "peace dividend" that would result in cuts in military spending. The AFL-CIO often vigorously resisted such plans, as they would result in lost jobs for union members. It proved successful in lobbying politicians in potentially affected areas and, in the end, there was no "peace dividend." Unions such as the **United Auto Workers of America** had also lobbied against environmental laws deemed detrimental to job retention. In the midst of battles over **concessions** and **downsizing**, it is easy to understand organized labor's fears, but the cost of such rearguard actions was to cast some unions in the public eye as resistant to progressive change. The peace dividend debate ended with the terrorist attacks of September 11, 2001. American labor responded with great patriotism that sometimes veered toward xenophobia.

Many liberals retain notions of the military as a repository for those who come from the lower and working classes. These views are largely holdovers from the

Vietnam era. The 21st-century profile of the U.S. military roughly parallels the country's overall social demographics. The annual family income of recruits has risen steadily and is now nearly on par with the national average. That same recruit also has more education and a higher IQ than the aggregate public at large; 93 percent of all military personnel have obtained a high school diploma or its equivalency, and 90 percent of all officers have some college education.

Likewise, it is not entirely true that the post-2007 recession reinstated de facto economic conscription. An uptick in enlistment was noted among lower-income individuals, but not among the poorest families. The increasing unpopularity of the ongoing wars in Iraq and Afghanistan has hampered recruitment among the poor. There are also higher levels of distrust for the military among African Americans than among whites. In 1996, African Americans made up 18 percent of all recruits; by 2005, that figure was less than 13 percent.

It is difficult to predict future trends in military service given the uncertainty of future employment opportunities in the United States. The American public currently supports the idea of military service, but the historical contempt for compulsory service remains, as evidenced by recent failures of conscription bills to advance through Congress. Observers continue to debate the degree to which the American working class has become conservative, but at present there is little doubt that support for the military is very high. A 2008 Gallup poll revealed that 71 percent of the American public view the military favorably, a figure that places it atop the public confidence scale and dwarfs the favorable rating for the police (58 percent), churches (48 percent), newspapers (24 percent), and Congress (12 percent).

Suggested Reading

Christian Appy, *Working-Class War: American Combat Soldiers and Vietnam*, 1993; Tod Ensign, Christian Appy, and Martin Binkin, *America's Military Today*, 2006; Maria Kefalas, *Working-Class Heroes: Protecting Home, Community, and Nation in a Chicago Neighborhood*, 2003.

MILLER, ARNOLD. *See* Bituminous Coal Strikes of 1974 and 1977–1978; United Mine Workers of America; Yablonski, Joseph A.

MINER STRIKES. *See* Anthracite Coal Strike of 1902; Bituminous Coal Strikes of 1974 and 1977–1978; Coal Miners Strike of 1943; Colorado Labor Wars; Copper Miners and Strikes; Lewis, John Llewellyn; United Mine Workers of America.

MINIMUM WAGE

The minimum **wage** is a federally mandated floor for compensating workers paid by the hour. Minimum wage laws apply to most labor, with some exceptions for agricultural work. In addition, restaurants and some other **service-industry** jobs are allowed to factor employee tips into compensation calculations and also pay less than the minimum rate. Effective July 24, 2009, that rate became $7.25 per hour. Employers are free to pay wages higher than that rate, and several states have statutes that mandate higher compensation, but no employer can legally offer less than $7.25 per hour other than in the few excluded job categories. Workers living in states with minimum wage laws are entitled to the higher of the two wages. This consideration applied to 18 states by 2012, with rates ranging from $7.40 in Michigan to $9.04 per hour in Washington.

Labor unions lobbied for minimum wage laws well in advance of the first federal law, which was established in 1933 as part of the **National Industrial Recovery Act** (NIRA). The NIRA put in place a $0.25 per hour standard, but a 1935 Supreme Court decision struck down the NIRA as unconstitutional and thus abolished the minimum wage. The impact of this was less than one might assume, as New Deal programs and codes had made the $0.25 floor standard practice, and that rate was enshrined anew in the 1938 **Fair Labor Standards Act**.

Since 1938, organized labor has consistently lobbied for a higher minimum wage, though it has been increased only nine times since 1938. In the 1950s, the strong U.S. economy eventually raised the federal minimum wage to $1.00 per hour. The problem with the minimum wage has been that it is a floor whose level has seldom kept pace with inflation. For example, although the 2001 rate of $5.15 was more than five times higher than it had been in 1960, a rate of $5.90 per hour would have been needed to give a wage-earner the equivalent buying power of the rate 40 years earlier. The current rate of $7.25 would yield a full-time worker an annual income of just $15,080. Such a sum would place a family of two just $510 above the 2009 official federal poverty line, and a family of three would fall short by $3,230.

Some economists, small-business owners, and retailers claim that raising the minimum wage causes unemployment to rise, as employers are forced to lay off workers when their payrolls increase. They also argue that minimum wage laws prevent the poorest individuals from entering the job market, especially teenaged and entry-level workers with few skills, who need low-level jobs to break into the labor force. Other arguments against the minimum wage include the belief that there are more effective ways to fight poverty, including the Earned Income Tax Credit and other tax benefits for those in the lowest income brackets.

Organized labor generally takes the view that employers that cannot afford sums as trifling as the minimum wage are not financially stable enough to be in business in the first place, and that most arguments against the minimum wage come from large corporations such as McDonald's and Wal-Mart that simply seek to pad their profits at the expense of America's most vulnerable workers. The record indicates that most minimum wage workers are adults, not new workers; that they are heavily concentrated in the retail trade industry; and that they work in establishments not represented by unions. To date, very little research indicates that job loss occurs when the minimum wage rises, and quite a bit suggests that job losses due to minimum wage laws are minimal, if not nonexistent. Data also show that states with higher minimum wage rates generally have higher levels of economic growth than those that do not. In 2001, journalist Barbara Ehrenreich's sensational and contro-versial participant-observation study demonstrated how difficult it is to survive on the minimum wage.

Organized labor does agree with the business community that a higher minimum wage is unlikely to alleviate poverty. Although most unions continue to support increases in the minimum wage, many unions have shifted their focus to a **living wage** campaign.

Suggested Reading

Barbara Ehrenreich, *Nickel and Dimed: On (Not) Getting by in America*, 2001; Paul Krugman, *The Conscience of a Liberal*, 2007; "Minimum Wage," U.S. Department of Labor, http://www.dol.gov/dol/topic/wages/minimumwage.htm, accessed March 16, 2011; "The Minimum Wage: Information, Opinion, Research," http://www.raiseminwage.org/, accessed March 16, 2011.

MINORITY LABOR

Minority labor has had an ambiguous and sometimes troubled relationship in both the workforce and within the organized labor movement. This is due in part to larger social patterns within the United States, where minority status is defined by access to power, not raw numbers. Historically, Protestant white males of western and northern European backgrounds have disproportionately held power. Although that pattern has changed somewhat, male WASPs (white Anglo-Saxon Protestants) retain many of the privileges of the past across society's class, income, and occupational barriers. For example, white males made up just 32 percent of the 2010 population, yet just 15 chief executive officers of *Fortune* 500 firms were women and only 8 were African American. In like fashion, 83 percent of all *Fortune* 100 board members are male and 71.5 percent are white, though whites make up just 65.1 percent of the total U.S. population. More equality exists the fur-ther one goes down the economic scale, but by 2011 just 5.2 percent of all busi-nesses, large or small, were owned by African Americans and an even smaller percentage were owned by **Latinos**. Income for women, who make up nearly 51 percent of the U.S. population, continues to average just 77 percent of what white males are paid.

These data indicate that members of minority groups suffer discrimination at the hands of the dominant group, whether directly or as an offshoot of institutionalized power arrangements reinforced by social custom or statute. Race and gender have historically been major determinants of minority status vis à vis males of western European ancestry, who have been the defined majority power group, though they have never been numerically so. Other factors, including religion, education, and family background, further constrict entry into the majority. Within the labor move-ment, skill has also stratified workers, with trained **artisans** generally ranked at the top of **blue-collar** pay and prestige scales.

The historical record of many labor unions is less than exemplary in combating discrimination. **Labor federations** such as the **Knights of Labor** (KOL), the **Industrial Workers of the World** (IWW), and the **Congress of Industrial**

Organizations (CIO) made some attempts to combat racism and sexism, but each also had blind spots. The KOL, for example, made valiant efforts to overcome the legacy of **slavery** and ongoing practices of Jim Crow labor in organizing African American workers, but fell prey to the vicious anti-Chinese hysteria of its time. In like fashion, the IWW sometimes turned a blind eye to the popular racism of many of its Western members; the CIO acceded to New Deal provisions that denied work to married women and some members were involved in anti-Mexican incidents in the 1940s. The record of the **American Federation of Labor** (AFL) was grim over-all, except in isolated cases. Numerous AFL **craft unions** banned women and non-whites from membership. Until the 1980s, very few labor unions could boast of a long or distinguished record in advancing minority labor.

The WASP identity present since the early days of North American colonization inexorably made its way into work patterns. Racism has been a key factor in the exploitation of **Native Americans**, African Americans, Asians, and Latinos. Transplanted sexism also placed female workers in a subordinate status. The imprecision in defining minorities means that many other groups also suffered discrimination. Catholic workers, for example, were barred from many jobs in the 19th and early 20th centuries, and discriminatory patterns against southern and eastern European immigrants during the same period parallel those later borne by Latino and Asian immigrants. Prior to the **Civil War**, most northern workers were profoundly racist, and free black laborers experienced great diffi-culty in securing decent jobs. In the postwar period, groups such as the **National Labor Union** and the KOL did organize African Americans, but they often met resistance from their own white members. With the decline of the KOL, few black workers were organized, as most AFL unions banned black membership. Employers often exploited labor's own racism and employed black or Asian **scabs** during strikes. The Colored NLU formed in the 1870s, but the 1925 **Brotherhood of Sleeping Car Porters** was the first independent black union to enjoy more than momentary success. Black union membership did not rise significantly until after 1935, with the emergence of the CIO. Several unions, including the **United Auto Workers of America**, the **United Mine Workers of America**, and the **United Packinghouse Workers of America** took tentative steps in combating union racism, and the **civil rights** movement forced the entire labor movement to reevaluate its position on black workers. The 1950s through the 1970s saw numerous vitriolic battles to dismantle discrimina-tory practices within organized labor's ranks. Although the contemporary **American Federation of Labor-Congress of Industrial Organizations** (AFL-CIO) is committed to racial equality, there are still clashes within the rank-and-file over issues such as seniority and **affirmative action** hiring. In some cases, these conflicts have grown more acute since the 1980s given the **downsizing** of many American industries. Since the turn of the 21st century, however, the AFL-CIO's record on race has been considerably more progressive than that of *Fortune* 500 companies.

Women have also battled for equal recognition in the workplace and within the labor movement. This fact is ironic given that women were the earliest industrial workers in America and made up the bulk of line workers in antebellum textile manufacturing. Women were also heavily represented in the needle trades, shoe and cigar making, clerical and sales positions, domestic service, and in teaching. The **Lowell Female Labor Reform League** may have been the first women's labor union. The KOL organized female workers under the leadership of **Leonora Barry**, and women have been proactive in forming their own unions. Among the groups in which women played central roles are the **Women's Trade Union League** and the **International Ladies' Garment Workers' Union**. The 1930s and 1940s eroded some of their gains made in the early 20th century, although women played a militant role in labor struggles during the period. As noted, both the AFL and the CIO supported bans on employment of married women during the Great Depression, and both labor federations called for replacing women workers with returning male veterans after World War II. By the 1950s, women began to press unions to redress their sexism, a process that accelerated when the women's movement emerged with new vigor in the 1960s. Several labor union women were involved in the founding of the National Organization for Women in 1966. Soaring numbers of women in low-wage retail and office positions also stimulated militancy and led to the creation of groups such as **9 to 5**. Recessions in the 1970s and 1980s led more women into the workplace and laid to rest sexist myths that women worked only to secure discretionary funds. The AFL-CIO and the **Change to Win Federation** now actively address issues related to women's labor and are aided by groups such as the **Coalition of Labor Union Women**. Seniority, affirmative action hiring, **comparable worth**, child care, **equity pay**, women's health, and sexual harassment are among the issues with which women workers are currently concerned.

Problems facing Latino workers were widely ignored until the 1960s. The Mexican War (1846–1848) led to the first large absorption of Latino workers into the U.S. workforce, and the opening of the Great Plains to white ranchers led to another increase. Many "American" **cowboys** were actually Mexican *vaqueros*. The borders between the United States, Mexico, and the Caribbean have long been porous. By the 20th century, many Latino workers were located in Florida, the Southwest, New York, and California, where they worked in cigar making, agricultural labor, the garment trades, railroads, the canning industry, and other occupations. During World War I and again in the 1940s and 1950s, the federal government sponsored the **Braceros** program to recruit contingency agricultural workers. Since the 1950s, Mexicans, Puerto Ricans, Jamaicans, and other Latinos have picked much of the American harvest. (Filipinos and other Asians also played a large role.) Abuses within agriculture led to the formation of the **United Farm Workers of America**, the best-known predominately Latino union. Today Latinos work in all sectors of the American economy, though they are disproportionately concentrated in low-wage **service-industry** jobs. Latinos join blue-collar unions at a higher rate than most Anglo workers. They have also been leaders in advancing the concept of international organizing and have been better attuned to the implications of **runaway shops**, movable capital, and economic **globalization** than many Anglos.

A group of miners pose in Las Animas County, Colorado. Hispanic workers from Mexico emerged as an important component of the labor force for the mining industry. (Courtesy History Colorado. Trinidad Collection, Scan #20004917. All rights reserved.)

America's demographic profile is changing. According to the U.S. Census Bureau, by 2050 non-Hispanic whites will be a numerical minority within the overall population. Although it is too soon to project what will happen to male WASP dominance, it seems likely that it will face steep challenges in the forthcoming decades.

Suggested Reading

Eric Arnesen, *The Black Worker: Race, Labor, and Civil Rights Since Emancipation*, 2007; Evelyn N. Glenn, *Unequal Freedom: How Race and Gender Shaped American Citizenship and Labor*, 2004; Edwin Melendez, Clara Rodriquez, and Janis Figueroa, eds., *Hispanics in the Labor Force: Issues and Policies*, 2007; U.S. Census Bureau, http://www.census.gov/ipc/www/usinterimproj/, accessed March 21, 2011.

MITCHELL, JOHN

John Mitchell (February 4, 1870–September 9, 1919) was the president of the **United Mine Workers of America** (UMWA) from 1899 to 1908 and is remembered for his leadership in the **anthracite coal strike of 1902**. To his many defenders, Mitchell was the very model of a responsible labor leader, one who was driven by pragmatism rather than ideology. To his critics, including future UMWA president **John L. Lewis**, Mitchell was overly cautious and was too willing to make compromises.

For much of his tenure, Mitchell was a beloved leader. Part of his popularity rested upon the fact that he came from the background of the men he represented and knew firsthand the hard work and poverty that confronted coal miners. Mitchell was born in the tiny coal patch of Braidwood, Illinois, the son of Robert Mitchell, a coal miner and farmer, and Martha (Halley) Mitchell. He left school when he was orphaned at the age of six and needed to work to help support his stepmother and siblings. Some sources say that Mitchell entered the mines when he was 12, though some claim he was younger. His regimen of self-education was aided by joining the **Knights of Labor** (KOL) in 1885, as the organization placed high value on literacy and intellectual improvement. The KOL's Trade District 135 functioned as a national trade union for coal miners and was a direct predecessor of the UMWA. Membership in the KOL provided Mitchell with a travelling card that enabled him to secure work at KOL-organized mines, a necessary item for the youthful Mitchell, who spent several years as an itinerant miner in the Southwest and West before drifting back to Illinois.

When the KOL began to decline, Mitchell was among those miners who helped found the UMWA in 1890. He showed an affinity for organization and rose quickly through the UMWA ranks. Mitchell also continued his self-education, was a voracious reader, and joined numerous debating societies and social organizations to develop his communication skills. He worked as a UMWA organizer in Illinois, and made an effort to visit every coal-mining village in the state. Mitchell realized early on that ongoing **immigration** constantly changed the composition of the American **working class**, and he labored diligently to ease ethnic divisions between Irish miners and more recent immigrants from Germany and Poland. He was elected secretary-treasurer of UMWA District 12 (Illinois) in 1895. Two years later, he was appointed as an international organizer and worked in southern Illinois and West Virginia with **Mary "Mother" Jones** and John H. Walker.

In 1897, Mitchell became UMWA vice president. He assumed the role of acting president when UMWA president Michael Ratchford resigned in 1898, and was elected in his own right to that position the next year. He also became a vice president in the **American Federation of Labor** (AFL) in 1898, a role he would fill for the next 10 years. Mitchell took over the UMWA at a difficult time. The **Lattimer Massacre** had occurred a year earlier, mine disasters were commonplace in the poorly regulated industry, **strikes** rocked mine regions, and conditions were so bad that most coal miners died before they reached their mid-40s. Mitchell used his organizational skills to increase UMWA membership from approximately 34,000 to more than 300,000 by the time he left office in 1908.

Mitchell achieved his greatest public notoriety during the anthracite coal strike of 1902. In 1900, he helped create the **National Civic Federation** (NCF), a **Progressive Era** consortium of business and labor leaders that sought to **arbitrate** labor disputes and rationalize business operations. Mitchell would call upon his NCF contacts to mediate the 1902 strike. As he had done as an Illinois organizer, the 32-year-old Mitchell also traveled throughout the strike region, an action that earned the trust and respect of miners, who referred to him as "Johnny d'Mitch."

Mining families placed Mitchell's photograph in their homes next to religious icons and prints. In the end, though, Mitchell's NCF connections were less instrumental in settling the strike than the intervention of President Theodore Roosevelt, who acted in response to a developing coal shortage. Mitchell and the leading coal operators were summoned to the White House for a negotiating session in which Mitchell's courteous conduct stood in sharp contrast to the arrogance of the operators and disposed Roosevelt to favor the miners. The settlement of the strike was much hailed, though some UMWA officials felt that Mitchell capitulated too easily. Miners got **wage** increases, but only limited **union recognition**. The strike also took a toll on Mitchell's health and personal life.

In 1906, Mitchell's AFL vice presidency made him a target in the lawsuit related to the AFL's **boycott** of the **Buck's Stove and Range Company** and Mitchell found himself facing possible jail time for contempt of court. His case would eventually be dismissed, but Mitchell increasingly mired himself in UMWA bureaucracy and distanced himself from the rank-and-file. Just six years after being lionized by UMWA members, he was voted out of the presidency; he was succeeded in that position by Thomas L. Lewis.

Mitchell continued his involvement with NCF, which gave ammunition to opponents who charged he had grown conservative and conciliatory. He served as chairman of the Trades Agreement Department of the NCF from 1908 to 1911, was a member of the New York State Workmen's Compensation Commission from 1914 to 1915, and was the chairman of the New York State Industrial Commission from 1915 until his death from pneumonia in 1919. Mitchell is buried in Scranton, Pennsylvania, where a statue in his honor stands in Courthouse Square. Many miners still celebrate the second Monday in April as John Mitchell Day.

Suggested Reading

Robert Cornell, *The Anthracite Coal Strike of 1902*, 1957; Elise Glück, *John Mitchell, Miner: Labor's Bargain with the Gilded Age*, 1985; Craig Phelan, *Divided Loyalties: The Public and Private Life of Labor Leader John Mitchell*, 1994.

MOHAWK VALLEY FORMULA

The Mohawk Valley Formula is a strike- and union-busting tactic that evolved in the 1930s. It is named for the Mohawk River Valley of New York State, where the Remington Rand Company, a typewriter manufacturer in Ilion, used a systematic plan to battle the **American Federation of Labor** (AFL). The AFL had a very weak **federal union** that sought to organize Remington and several other typewriter factories. It nonetheless launched a **strike** against Remington in 1934 and won a contract in 1936. Remington President James Rand, Jr., then launched a program designed to discredit the union. His pre- and post-contract efforts became the Mohawk Valley Formula, which so impressed the business community that it was endorsed by the **National Association of Manufacturers** (NAM) as a blueprint for resisting and discrediting unions. Modernized versions of the formula remain standard practice in resisting union campaigns.

The central features of the Mohawk Valley Formula are slander, rumor, community pressure, and company resistance. Every effort is made to depict labor leaders as outside agitators bent upon spreading discord and overthrowing local customs. Union leaders are portrayed as dangerous radicals, perhaps even **communists**. Radical threats justify the formation of "citizens' committees" of concerned locals bent upon protecting community values and preserving "law and order." These committees—which are largely company creations—engage in publicity campaigns to rally support for the company and opposition to the union. At the same time, rumors circulate—planted by the firm—that the company might be forced to consolidate its operations or move the plant. The creation of a large security force of private guards or police (or a combination thereof) then harass union **pickets** and make a display of force in **working-class** neighborhoods. In some cases, paramilitaries act as **agent provocateurs** who incite violence, which in turn justifies using greater force against the union. Careful media management and the hiring of **scabs** are used to try to convince workers that the union's cause is lost and that they should return to work. In many cases, organized **company unions**, "back-to-work," committees, and "loyal" employee committees are formed. Staged return-to-work days add to an impression-management scheme that strikers are a minority group of troublemakers.

If a union does manage to win, the Mohawk Valley Formula shifts to rumor and resistance. More innuendo circulates about impending plant closure that is designed to scare workers into abandoning the union. The company also uses its considerable resources to delay signing a contract in hopes that workers will grow discouraged. In Remington's case, nearly two years passed between strike victory and the signing of a contract. In some cases companies openly defy rulings by bodies such as the National Labor Relations Board and allow lawsuits to go forth. While a case is pending, either awaiting judgment or on appeal, the company imposes its own conditions. It took another two years of court rulings and negative publicity from the **La Follette Committee** before the AFL was able to implement the terms of its contract with Remington, and the cost of lawsuits had a detrimental effect on union treasuries. Even then Remington attempted to maintain its company union into 1940.

Many of the tactics and methods involved in the Mohawk Valley Formula are **unfair labor practices** as defined by the **National Labor Relations Act**. That is of secondary concern to NAM firms resistant to unionization, many of which see the struggle as a war of attrition rather than one based in legal principles. Although the Mohawk Valley Formula is the product of another era, its central features endure and modern anti-union consulting firms often adapt and update those features. The "outside agitator" image had become a staple in labor relations and rumored plant closures a potent weapon in an increasingly postindustrial society. Moreover, legal proceedings are now much slower and far more expensive than during the 1930s. Numerous capital/labor battles have been abandoned because the union affected ran out of resources.

Suggested Reading

Stephen Norwood, *Strike-breaking and Intimidation: Mercenaries and Masculinity in 20th-Century America*, 2002; Robert G. Rodden, *The Fighting Machinists: A Century of Struggle*, 1984.

MOLLY MAGUIRES

The Molly Maguires ("Mollies") were an alleged Irish and Irish American terrorist organization active in the anthracite coal region of Carbon, Columbia, Luzerne, Northumberland, and Schuylkill Counties of Pennsylvania from 1870 to 1876. It remains an open question as to whether the Mollies were real, or a chimera created by coal and railroad companies to justify their crackdown on labor unions. Most scholars agree that anti-unionism and anti-Irish nativism heightened fears of the Molly Maguires.

Between 1846 and 1854, more than 1.2 million Irish immigrated to the United States, where they were subjected to discrimination. Popular anti-Irish and anti-Roman Catholic sentiments were widespread in the mid- and late 19th century, and fierce debate raged over questions of where Catholic loyalty lay and whether parochial schools should be allowed. To cope with discrimination, Irish immigrants often concentrated their homes in ethnic enclaves where the church, saloons, and fraternal organizations such as the Ancient Order of Hibernians (AOH) offered solace. In addition to discrimination, Irish miners faced harsh working conditions, low **wages**, and long hours. Many mine hamlets were **company towns** in which corporate will was reinforced through a combination of **paternalism** and authoritarianism. The isolated coal-mining villages of northeastern Pennsylvania also bred ethnic rivalry between largely Irish workers and their Welsh- and English-heritage supervisors. Violence and unsolved murders abounded. In 1870, John Siney organized the Workingmen's Benevolent Association (WBA), which launched **strikes** against area mines and raised the ire of the Philadelphia, Reading, and Lehigh Valley Railroad (PRLVR), which controlled many of the area's mines.

By 1873, the region was rife with rumors that Irish miners belonged to the Molly Maguires, a clandestine terrorist group. The origin of the term *Molly Maguire* is obscure. It was alleged that Molly Maguire was an Irish woman who rallied opposition to British landlords in Ireland, but there is no direct evidence that such a person existed and some historians believe the term derives from popular protest traditions in which men disguised themselves as women. In 1873, PRLVR President Franklin Gowen hired **Pinkerton** Agency detective James McParlan to infiltrate the Mollies. Posing as James McKenna, McParlan—who also spelled his name McParland—claimed to have unearthed a labyrinthine conspiracy across the region involving the AOH, saloon keepers, and miners. The Mollies supposedly operated independent cells headed by a "bodymaster." The cells coordinated plans via interlocking membership, furtive meetings, and a complex network through which they threatened, harassed, and murdered opponents. McParlan blamed the Mollies for numerous murders of mine superintendents, police officers, and local citizens. The first arrests came in May 1876, and by 1879, 19 alleged Mollies had been hanged, including "Black Jack" Kehoe, whom McParlan claimed was a major ringleader.

Evidence for the Molly Maguires conspiracy rests mostly on rumor, innuendo, and McParlan's testimony. Siney and other Irish Americans accused Gowen and

McParlan of inventing the Molly Maguires as an excuse to crush the WBA, whose five-month "Long Strike" in 1875 vexed Gowen. They also charged anti-Irish xenophobia, a theme trumpeted by the newspaper *The Irish World and Industrial Liberator*. All those arrested as Mollies were Irish, most had participated in mine strikes, and several were members of the AOH and the Irish Land League, a group active in Ireland and North America that sought to liberate Ireland from the control of British landlords. The WBA declined after 1876, and recruitment for heavily Irish organizations such the **Knights of Labor** was hampered by Molly Maguire associations. Molly Maguire references fueled anti-Irish discrimination and were used to justify crackdowns against radicals throughout the Gilded Age.

The term "Molly Maguire" was so cavalierly applied throughout the latter part of the 19th century that is often difficult to determine the boundaries between truth and rumor. There were those who declared the Mollies a myth, but also those that claimed they survived the crackdown and continued to dispense vigilante justice throughout the region, the latter charge supported by the fact that the region remained violence-prone for decades to come. Franklin Gowen's fate added to the mystique of the Mollies. He was forced out as PRLVR head in 1886 and died of a gunshot wound in 1889. It was ruled a suicide, but rumors persisted that the Mollies exacted a revenge killing. By then, however, the term Molly Maguire had lost much of its shock value and terms such as "tramp," "communist," and "anarchist" were more effective for those seeking to slander the organized labor movement.

Suggested Reading

Anthony Bimba, *The Molly Maguires*, 1970; Wayne Broehl, Jr., *The Molly Maguires*, 1964; Kevin Kenny, *Making Sense of the Molly Maguires*, 1998.

MOORE, MICHAEL FRANCIS

Michael Moore (April 23, 1954–) is an independent filmmaker, author, blogger, and media personality known for his provocative critiques of corporations, political malfeasance, and what he sees as assaults on **working-class** America. Moore is an unabashed supporter of labor unions, popular democracy, and a regulatory state. For many Americans on the political left, Moore is their analog to right-wing commentators such as Rush Limbaugh and Glenn Beck. Not surprisingly, Moore is anathema to conservatives, who view him as an egotistical polemicist and denounce his work as propaganda. Although Moore has been known to manipulate time sequences in his documentary films and to indulge in sensationalism, for the most part his projects have proved to be factually sound.

Moore was born in Flint, Michigan. His father, Frank, was an automobile **assembly-line** worker, and his mother, the former Veronica Wall, a secretary. Moore was raised Catholic, is a graduate of Flint public schools, and attended the University of Michigan-Flint for one year before dropping out. He left college and began editing a progressive regional magazine that was eventually titled *The Michigan Voice*. His work attracted the attention of *Mother Jones*, and he moved to San Francisco to assume the editorship of that magazine. He lasted just four months before being fired for refusing to run a story critical of Nicaragua's leftist government, which he felt was factually unsound. He also battled the magazine over a story about **deindustrialization** in Flint, which the publishers did not wish to run. Moore returned to Flint and won a small wrongful dismissal suit against *Mother Jones* that underwrote his early filmmaking career. In 1990, Moore married producer Kathleen Glynn, with whom he has a stepdaughter.

The story that *Mother Jones* refused to run became Moore's first documentary film, *Roger & Me* (1989), a poignant and sometimes humorous look at what happened to Flint when General Motors (GM) **downsized** and closed the plant that was the site of the famed 1936–1937 **General Motors sit-down strike**. In the film Moore dogs the steps of GM Chairman Roger Smith and seeks to engage him in discussing GM's impact on Flint. He also showed Flint's brutal descent into a postindustrial nightmare.

The guerilla filmmaking style of *Roger & Me* became Moore's trademark, which he applied to subsequent documentary projects such as *The Big One* (1997), in which he skewered **runaway capital** as practiced by firms making record profits; *Bowling for Columbine* (2002), which critiqued America's obsession with guns; *Fahrenheit 9/11*, a look at the political uses of fear; *Sicko* (2007), a searing indictment of the American health care system; and *Capitalism: A Love Story* (2009), in which Moore blamed the financial crisis that began in 2007 on corporate greed and the policies of President George W. Bush that allowed malfeasance to go unchecked and unpunished. Moore also directed a fictional film, *Canadian Bacon* (1995), whose premise was that of an unpopular president seeking to bolster his ratings by fomenting a war against Canada. That film anticipated Hollywood's 1997 *Wag the Dog*, which most critics see as a superior film, but *Canadian Bacon* also anticipated much of Moore's judgment of President Bush and his handling of the September 11, 2001, terrorist attacks on the United States.

Moore's unapologetic criticism of corporate capitalism and conservative-politics films has made him a target of the right, but his films have been very popular, especially given that he mostly works in a documentary style that generally does not attract large audiences. Moore, however, won an Oscar for *Bowling for Columbine*, and *Fahrenheit 9/11* has grossed more than $200 million, making it the most successful documentary film of all time. Many of Moore's film themes are present in best-selling books such as *Downsize This!* (1996), *Stupid White Men* (2001), and *Dude, Where's My Country?* (2007). As of 2011, Moore had published seven nonfiction books. He has also made television series, including *TV Nation* and *The Awful Truth*, and several short films, each of whose approaches were creative mixes of investigative journalism, humor, and agit-prop documentary style.

Republicans often accuse Moore of being a shill for the **Democratic Party**, but Moore has been equally scathing in his criticism of both parties and supported Ralph Nader's mercurial presidential bid in 2000. He has been active in getting young people to register to vote—the subject of *Slacker Uprising* (2004)—and he supported Barack Obama in his presidential bid in 2008, though he has been critical of President Obama since his election. Moore is motivated mainly by what he sees as a class war launched by wealthy elites against working people and the poor. He supports a regulated economy, a single-payer national health care program, the reindustrialization of the United States, an expansion of personal freedom, and the revitalization of organized labor. He often uses his fame—or notoriety, as critics would have it—to be a public spokesperson for progressive causes. His March 2011 speech at a Madison, Wisconsin, rally against Governor Scott Walker's plan to strip public employees of their **collective bargaining** rights was an Internet sensation.

Suggested Reading

Michael Moore, *Downsize This! Random Threats from an Unarmed American*, 1996; Michael Moore.com, http://www.michaelmoore.com/, accessed March 25, 2011; Roger Rapoport, *Citizen Moore: The Life and Times of an American Iconoclast*, 2006.

MULLANEY, KATE

Kate Mullaney (1845?–August 17, 1906) was the founder of the Collar Laundry Union (CLU) in 1864, which became a model for subsequent women's labor unions. Mullaney was also the first woman to be appointed to a male-dominated national union office when, in 1868, she became assistant secretary and women's organizer for the **National Labor Union** (NLU).

Very little is known about Mullaney's early life or her formal education. She was born in Ireland, and her family emigrated when she was a teen. Like many Irish Catholics, the Mullaneys were destined for a **working-class** life. Her family settled in Troy, New York, an industrial city that featured numerous iron foundries as well as commercial laundries that cleaned detachable shirt collars and cuffs. (These items were first developed in Troy in 1827, and the city manufactured approximately 90 percent of the nation's stock by the 1860s. In the 19th century, one usually laundered collars and cuffs far more frequently than entire shirts.) Her father died when Mullaney was 19, and her mother's delicate health required that Kate become the family breadwinner. More than 3,000 women toiled in Troy's 14 commercial laundries, often working up to 14 hours per day for as little as $3 per week. In addition to the long hours, caustic chemicals, hot water, bleach, and the rapid pace of work exposed laundry workers to burns and other dangers. Newly developed starch machines were especially infamous for inducing horrifying burns.

Mullaney entered this world to provide for her mother and four siblings. Troy was a strong union town, anchored by the Iron Molders Union (IMU) and its dynamic president and future NLU leader **William Sylvis**. Inspired by the molders and by unions like the Cigar Makers International Union that had begun to accept female members, Mullaney decided to organize Troy's laundresses into the CLU. Some sources credit this as the first women's labor union in the United States, though the **Lowell Female Reform Association** formed by **Sarah Bagley** in 1845 predates it. On February 23, 1864, Mullaney, aided by the IMU, led a

strike of approximately 300 women. In just a week's time, 14 Troy laundry establishments granted pay rises of more than 20 percent and agreed to address safety concerns. In 1866, Mullaney led another successful strike that raised laundress's **wages** to about $14 per week. In that same year, Sylvis and other labor activists formed the NLU. Sylvis launched a rhetorical call to organize women based on the CLU's success. In 1868, Mullaney attended a New York City labor congress and was elected as second vice president of the NLU. She declined that honor, but Sylvis appointed her as an NLU assistant secretary and organizer for women's work.

Mullaney showed acumen in building up the collar union's treasury, whose resources she occasionally used to show **solidarity** with other New York workers. In 1868, for example, the CLU donated $500 to striking New York City bricklayers. In March 1869, Mullaney helped CLU starchers win a strike. The CLU's phenomenal success ended later that year, however. When the CLU struck again in May, laundry owners decided to break the union. Workers received substantial financial assistance from the IMU and moral support from the NLU, but Troy laundry owners offered wage increases only to women who agreed to quit the CLU. Mullaney was briefly the president of the Union Line Collar and Cuff Manufactory, an attempt at a worker-owned **cooperative**. The cooperative landed a major contract to supply A. T. Stewart, then New York City's largest department store, only to run afoul of technological change. The development of paper collars altered the equation, and both the CLU and Troy quickly faded as suppliers of collars, cuffs, and shirts. The CLU was also damaged by the death of William Sylvis in July 1869. Sylvis was a champion of women's rights, and with his death, both financial support from the molders' union and the NLU's rhetorical commitment to working women declined. Both the CLU and the NLU faded from view shortly after Sylvis's death. In February 1870, Mullaney dissolved the CLU, and she and other women returned to work according to pre-May 1869 wage scales.

The CLU was an important forerunner and model for subsequent efforts at organizing women, especially those of the **Knights of Labor**. Not much is known about Mullaney's career after 1870. She eventually married a worker named John Fogarty and died in 1906. For many years her body lay in an unmarked grave in Troy. In the 1990s, Mullaney was belatedly recognized for her precocious accomplishments. Her Troy home became a National Historic Landmark in 1998, with Hillary Rodham Clinton adding her voice to those praising Mullaney. In 1999, local labor leaders and Irish cultural organizations adorned Mullaney's grave with a suitable monument.

Suggested Reading

"Kate Mullaney: A True Labor Pioneer," http://pef.org/katemullaney.htm, accessed March 23, 2011; David Montgomery, "William Sylvis and the Search for Working-Class Citizenship," in *Labor Leaders in America*, Melvyn Dubofsky and Warren Van Tine, eds., 1987; Carole Turbin, *Working Women of Collar City*, 1992.

MULLER V. OREGON

Muller v. Oregon was a landmark 1908 Supreme Court decision that upheld the right of states to pass legislation limiting the conditions of women's employment based upon their sex. The *Muller* decision created a dilemma for organized labor: On the one hand, it granted female workers the shorter workday that unions had long advocated; on the other hand, it was a form of **protective labor legislation** rooted in the assumption that women were an inherently "weaker" sex.

Progressive Era reformers sought to ameliorate the worst effects of industrial labor through laws designed to ensure safe and humane working conditions, but some of these ran afoul of the U.S. Supreme Court. In 1905, the Supreme Court's ruling in **Lochner v. New York** struck down a recently passed New York state law that limited the workday to 10 hours for male bakery workers. The court opined that the law was unconstitutional because it violated workers' freedom of contract rights, and that longer hours adversely impacted neither the health of the bakers nor the health of the consumers of their bread. Three years later, Oregon business owners challenged a state law limiting the hours of women working in laundries and factories, cited *Lochner*, and argued that no threat posed to workers' health. Oregon secured the services of activist attorney Louis Brandeis, who, along with his sister-in-law Josephine Goldmark, presented more than 100 pages of evidence and convincingly argued that women's physical differences justified special protection. They specifically argued that that long hours of work jeopardized women's abilities to bear and raise children.

In *Muller v. Oregon*, the U.S. Supreme Court upheld the Oregon law, though the court went out of its way to insist that it was not reversing the *Lochner* decision. Writing for the majority, Justice Brewer argued that the physical health of potential mothers was a matter of public interest, and that special protection was needed to "preserve the strength and vigor of the race." The *Muller* decision cleared the way for a wave of protective labor legislation that allegedly sought to ensure the health of women workers. By the mid-1920s, all but five states had passed some form of law restricting the number of hours women could work in industrial settings. (Women in domestic service and agricultural work were exempt.)

Each piece of protective legislation posed dilemmas for organized labor and women's rights advocates. To argue against the then-prevailing view of essentialism—the belief that men and women are inherently different biologically and, therefore, more naturally suited to some social roles but not others—was a risky strategy given that *Lochner* had not been reversed. The *Muller* ruling suggested that freedom of contract was not an absolute right and that future limits might benefit male workers as well. Reversing *Muller* ran the risk of making freedom of contract inviolable in all cases. Women were also in a bind, as to accept the very conditions that many male workers desired entailed explicitly or implicitly accepting female inferiority.

The 1938 **Fair Labor Standards Act** posed the first serious challenge to the *Muller* decision, in that it included a federal, maximum-hour law for both men and women in most categories of employment. Moreover, other New Deal legislation enshrined the eight-hour workday as the norm in most cases. The role of women workers in the defense industry during World War II also challenged notions that women were incapable of certain types of work. Nonetheless, the sex-based protective ideals established in the *Muller* decision endured, and many types of work remained male-only preserves until challenged by second-wave feminism in the 1960s and beyond. Although women's wages are, in theory, protected by the 1963 **Equal Pay Act** and women have made tremendous strides in reversing many forms of employment discrimination rooted in essentialism, an Equal Rights Amendment to the U.S. Constitution failed. As a consequence, gender inequities have been addressed piecemeal on a case-by-case basis, with women looking to both federal and state governments to address workplace issues. In this sense, aspects of the *Muller* decision remain in place.

Suggested Reading

Nancy Erickson, "*Muller v. Oregon* Reconsidered: The Origins of a Sex-Based Doctrine of Liberty of Contract," *Labor History* 30 (1989): 228–250; Julie Novkov, *Constituting Workers, Protecting Women: Gender, Law, and Labor in the Progressive Era and New Deal Years*, 2001; Nancy Woloch, *Muller v. Oregon: A Brief History with Documents*, 1996.

MULTICULTURALISM AND LABOR. *See* Minority Labor. *See also* Asian American Labor; *Braceros*; Chinese Exclusion Act; Civil Rights and Labor; Immigrants and Labor; Latino Labor; Native Americans and Labor; Nativism and Labor; Slavery.

MURRAY, PHILIP

Philip Murray (May 25, 1886–November 9, 1952) was an important leader of the **United Mine Workers of America** (UMWA), an organizer for the group that eventually formed the **United Steelworkers of America** (USWA), and was the second president of the **Congress of Industrial Organizations** (CIO). Murray is best remembered for his efforts to reconcile the union movement with Roman Catholicism and for his fierce opposition to **communism**.

Murray was born in Blantyre, Scotland, on May 25, 1886, the eldest of five children to William Murray, a coal miner and local union official, and Rose (Layden) Murray, a weaver. The Murrays were Irish, but immigrated to Scotland before Philip's birth. Mrs. Murray died when Philip was just two, and the elder Murray remarried and fathered eight more children. The elder Murray took an active role in instructing his son on pressing social questions, the importance of labor unions, and the Catholic faith. Family poverty interrupted Philip's formal education after just a few years and, at the age of 10, he began working in Scottish coal mines. The 16-year-old Murray joined his father in immigrating to the United States in 1902. They worked in mines in southwest Pennsylvania, saved money, and brought the rest of the family to the United States in 1903. Although Philip had very little formal education, he studied math and science through correspondence courses. In 1910, he married Liz Lavery, a miner's daughter whose father had been killed in a mining accident. The next year Murray became a U.S. citizen.

His father's lessons on unionism took hold, and Murray joined the UMWA shortly after arriving in the United States. In 1905, he was elected president of his UMWA **union local** in Horning, Pennsylvania. In 1912, Murray was chosen to fill a vacant seat on the UMWA national executive board and, in 1916, he became president of the UMWA's District Five, which covered all of western Pennsylvania. Murray's rise within the UMWA paralleled that of **John L. Lewis**, who would at various times be Murray's mentor, friend, confidant, and adversary. Murray supported Lewis's candidacy for UMWA vice president in 1917 and president in 1920. In turn, Lewis appointed the 33-year-old Murray as the UMWA's vice president in 1920. Murray would remain Lewis's able lieutenant until the two split in 1940.

Although the UMWA was affiliated with the **American Federation of Labor** (AFL), Murray did not share the AFL's principles of government non-interference in capital/labor relations and came to believe that government could become a guarantor of labor union rights. He also supported the ideal of cooperative industrial relations advanced by Monsignor John A. Ryan. Father Ryan asserted that the interests of owners and workers were mutual—principles that were enshrined in Catholic teaching by the 1891 papal encyclical *Rerum Novarum* (and would be reaffirmed by *Quadregisimo Anno* in 1931). During World War I, Murray served on the National Bituminous Coal Production Committee and on the Pennsylvania Regional War Labor Board. In accord with Father Ryan's ideals, these agencies were composed of labor, management, and government representatives who sought to arbitrate labor disputes. Murray's faith in such arrangements would be severely challenged after World War I, when **Republican** administrations and the business community abandoned tripartite boards and launched anti-union campaigns that eroded UMWA strength.

Murray's patience was rewarded when Franklin Roosevelt assumed the U.S. presidency in 1933. Roosevelt's New Deal included many bills—most importantly for labor, the **National Labor Relations Act** (Wagner Act) in 1935, which helped the UMWA regain vibrancy and which provided federal government support for **collective bargaining** rights. Murray served on several New Deal boards, including an advisory panel for the **National Industrial Recovery Act**. The UMWA was never a comfortable fit within the **craft union** dominance of the AFL. Thus Murray aided UMWA president John Lewis in creating the **industrial union** committee within the AFL that eventually split the **labor federation** and became the rival Congress of Industrial Organizations. In 1938, Murray became a CIO vice president and Lewis appointed him to chair the Steelworkers Organizing Committee (SWOC). This was a big challenge, as the steel industry was mostly unorganized and had a record of brutally crushing union movements in high-profile clashes such as the 1892 **Homestead Steel lockout and strike**, the **McKee's Rock** battle of 1909, and the nationwide **steel strike of 1919**. To the surprise of many, SWOC had won a contract with industry giant U.S. Steel in 1937. By comparison, a Murray-led **strike** in 1937 against non-union firms collectively known as **Little Steel** proved more difficult. This clash was violent and left more than a dozen strikers dead. Little Steel finally capitulated in 1941, and the next year Murray stepped down as SWOC chair when the USWA formed.

Murray's long alliance with Lewis unraveled in 1940 when Lewis repudiated President Franklin Roosevelt's reelection bid and backed his Republican rival, Wendell Wilkie. Murray felt that Roosevelt was labor's greatest ally and disagreed with Lewis's assessment that government had come to play too big a role in capital/labor relations. Lewis, as he pledged he would do if Roosevelt was reelected, resigned as CIO president. Murray was chosen to replace him and thereby earned Lewis's enmity. In 1942, Lewis engineered Murray's expulsion from the nonaligned UMWA. When Murray took over the CIO, he was surprised to find its finances in shambles. Murray moved decisively to return the CIO to solvency, only to see Lewis submit a bill for past UMWA subsidies of the CIO. He also sought to browbeat Murray. In turn, Murray authorized the charter of the USWA, a group Lewis hoped to incorporate into the UMWA. In addition, he led the CIO to accept a **no-strike pledge** during World War II, which the UMWA refused to endorse. In the short term, Murray's support of federal-government involvement proved fruitful. Through the help of the federal government, the Little Steel companies signed contracts. In like fashion, Ford Motor Company finally settled with the **United Auto Workers of America** union. As he had done during World War I, Murray served on wartime tripartite industrial councils such as the **National War Labor Board**.

As had happened after World War I, however, the permanent industrial councils Murray sought once again failed to materialize. The years following World War II were difficult for Murray. The passage of the anti-union **Taft-Hartley Act** in 1947 was especially dispiriting to him, even though he shared its anticommunist sentiments. Bowing to the postwar **Red Scare**, in 1949 and 1950 he spearheaded efforts to expel 11 CIO unions that were allegedly dominated by communists. He would also give support for **Cold War** foreign policy objectives and for the Korean War. These measures did little to silence labor union critics, and they severely weakened the CIO.

Murray had led national USWA strikes in 1946 and 1949, but a 1952 strike tested the aging leader. He enlisted the aid of the federal government, through the Wage Stabilization Board, and sought the personal involvement of President Harry Truman. Although the USWA gained a satisfactory contract, it came with significant costs. More than any other CIO leader, Murray had cultivated direct government involvement in labor relations. When the Republicans gained control of the White House for the first time in 20 years in 1952, however, organized labor was perhaps too closely associated with the **Democratic Party**. Murray himself exacerbated that perception; in the wake of the passage of the Taft-Hartley Act, he prodded the CIO to set up a Political Action Committee to raise money for labor-friendly candidates; most of that support went to Democrats.

Murray would not live to see how these matters played out. Just five days after Dwight Eisenhower was elected as president and Republicans won control over both houses of Congress, Murray died of a heart attack.

Suggested Reading

Pat Angelo, *Philip Murray, Union Man: A Life Story*, 2003; Paul F. Clark, Peter Gottlieb, and Donald Kennedy, eds., *Forging a Union of Steel: Philip Murray, SWOC, and the United*

Steelworkers, 1987; Ronald Schatz, "Philip Murray and the Subordination of the Industrial Unions to the United States Government," in *Labor Leaders in America*, Melvyn Dubofsky and Warren Van Tine, eds., 1987: 234–257.

MUSIC AND LABOR

Working people have long used music as a weapon in their fight for social justice. Most labor songs were written as spontaneous responses to immediate conditions, not with an eye toward posterity. They were created in the hope that mutual singing would build **solidarity** among workers and strengthen them in their struggles. Only a select few have endured. Many labor songs put new words to well-known tunes to facilitate their use in a **strike**, **boycott**, or protest. A prime example is "Solidarity Forever," the song now considered the anthem of American workers. The words were written in 1915 by **Industrial Workers of the World** (IWW) songwriter Ralph Chaplin, who set the lyrics to the well-known tune "John Brown's Body," which also lent its tune to "The Battle Hymn of the Republic."

"The Marseillaise" and "The International" are popular labor songs worldwide, though less so in the United States; instead, most American labor songs are part of an indigenous protest tradition. Common themes include lampoons of privilege, exposés of harsh conditions, pleas for social justice and civil rights, political commentary, and parodies of labor's enemies. Many occupations also created music designed to keep cadence with work patterns or to while away long hours. Miners, sailors, cattle drovers, and textile workers are among those with strong work-song traditions. North American **slaves** created extraordinarily rich songs to help ameliorate their harsh conditions, encode protest messages, set the pace of work, and build community. In Colonial America, workers parodied both the British and their bosses. **Journeymen** used music to protest against **master craftsmen** before and after the American Revolution, but organized labor's song tradition developed in earnest when journeymen's organizations became full-fledged trade unions in the 1820s. **Labor journalism** helped popularize protest songs, with papers associated with the **Workingmen's movement** publishing songs in the 1830s. Factory conditions led to labor protest songs. Lowell women sang "I Will Not Be a Slave" during an 1836 strike, and other songs appeared in the pages of the *Lowell Offering* and *The Voice of Industry*. Both the ten- and **eight-hour movements** produced songs to rally supporters, as did reactionary nativist and antiabolitionist groups with large **working-class** followings. Irish and German immigrants brought musical traditions that they adapted to American conditions. German *turnverein* groups often functioned as a hybrid gymnastics club, singing society, and impromptu labor organization.

In the 19th century, trade unions created more songs than **labor federations**, until the rise of the **Knights of Labor** (KOL), which produced hundreds of songs. One KOL song, "Storm the Fort Ye Knights of Labor" was reworked as "Hold the Fort" and is still sung. The KOL also popularized I. G. Blanchard's "Eight Hours," the rallying song of the eight-hour movement. Followers of both **Henry George** and **Edward Bellamy** produced numerous songs, as did the **Populist** and **socialist** movements. In the late 19th century, it was rare to encounter a picnic, parade, strike, rally, or protest at which workers did not sing.

Labor singing declined in the late 1890s, as the **American Federation of Labor** (AFL) lacked the musical vibrancy of preceding labor groups. But music was revived with enthusiasm by the IWW, which nurtured skilled songwriters like Ralph Chaplin, "Haywire" Harry McClintock, T-Bone Slim, and **Joe Hill**. The last contributed songs such as "The Preacher and the Slave," "Mr. Block," "The Rebel Girl," and "There Is Power in a Union." Although the IWW is now a small organization, it continues to publish its *Little Red Songbook*, copies of which have helped perpetuate songs such as "The Popular Wobbly," "Hallelujah, I'm a Bum," and "Solidarity Forever." Also popular is "Bread and Roses," a James Oppenheim song-poem that honors women's participation in the 1912 **Lawrence textile strike**.

Repression of labor marked the 1920s and early 1930s, and that, too, was enshrined in music. The violent Gastonia-Loray textile strike of 1929 claimed the life of North Carolina songwriter Ella May Wiggins, whose songs subsequently gained wider currency than they might have had she not been murdered. In like fashion, Appalachian balladeer Aunt Molly Jackson was forced to flee Kentucky for New York, where she sang of the miners' plight and influenced Woody Guthrie. The bloody Harlan County, Kentucky, coal strike of 1932 influenced Florence Reece, whose "Which Side Are You On?" is now a labor standard. Socialist and communist groups introduced songs such as "We Shall Not Be Moved," whose theme of class struggle found receptive audiences among the victims of 1920s repression and 1930s depression, and was subsequently appropriated by **civil rights** organizers in the 1950s and 1960s. Many left-wing organizers were found in the **Congress of Industrial Organizations** (CIO), especially during the **Popular Front** period. Union singing generally peaks during crisis periods or when a movement struggles to gain recognition; thus the 1930s was a fruitful period for music. Labor-themed radio stations such as WCFL in Chicago and WEVD in New York played labor songs, and both the labor and left-wing press printed them. The CIO and the Communist Party each sponsored folk-music concerts at which labor songs were sung. Old and new songs such as "Step by Step" and "Sit Down" found their way into labor's repertoire.

The flurry of left-wing and labor activity in the 1930s also attracted professional musicians who brought labor songs into the musical mainstream. This group included Woody Guthrie, Lee Hays, Millard Lampell, Huddie Ledbetter (Leadbelly), Earl Robinson, and Pete Seeger. Guthrie's "Dust Bowl Ballads" have been hailed as a musical snapshot of rural America during the Great Depression. He also penned famed offerings such as "Union Maid," "Pastures of Plenty," "You Gotta Go Down," and "This Land Is Your Land," the last a satire written to protest the discrepancies between rich and poor during the Great Depression. Robinson co-wrote "Joe Hill," which became a classic, while Leadbelly, Josh White, Bill Broonzy, and Paul Robeson added powerful black voices to the working-class struggle. In 1940, Guthrie, Hays, Lampell, and Seeger formed the Almanac Singers. The Almanacs became a changing musical lineup that brought labor songs to the masses. Their repertoire included their 1941 composition "Talking Union," written to assist

CIO organizers. In 1945, Seeger formed People's Songs, Inc., whose *People's Songs Bulletin* and *People's Songsters* publicized labor music. In 1950, People's Songs gave way to *Sing Out! Magazine*, which continues to publish labor-themed songs, though it is now also a general folk-music publication. Among the important labor songs distributed by these sources are "Banks of Marble," "Roll the Union On," and "If I Had a Hammer" (whose copyrighted title is "The Hammer Song.")

"The Hammer Song" and left-wing political associations brought problems for Hays and Seeger during the post-World War II **Red Scare**. Right-wing thugs broke up labor rallies featuring leftist performers, most infamously at a 1949 Peekskill, New York, concert in which Seeger and Paul Robeson narrowly escaped lynching. The folk-music revival of the early 1950s had popularized labor songs, but within a few years numerous leftist singers were blacklisted, radio was reluctant to play controversial songs, and organized labor was actively expelling leftwing activists. Labor music suffered during the remainder of the decade, though a few noteworthy performers came hit their stride, including the AFL's Joe Glazer.

The folk-music revival of the 1960s pumped new life into labor songs, with artists such as Seeger, Bob Dylan, Joan Baez, Tom Paxton, and Phil Ochs performing old and new tunes. Members of the **counterculture** often embraced labor radicalism as part of their critique of American society and sang labor songs as a political statement. Protest music was en vogue during the early 1960s. It was a staple at yearly Newport Folk Festivals, and ABC even televised a show titled *Hootenanny* during 1963 and 1964—the very name evoking 1930s parties at which music was sung and which often evolved into labor rallies. Joan Baez sang "Joe Hill" at the Woodstock music festival in 1969.

By the 1970s, however, music's importance as a labor-organizing tool was in deep decline, a victim of changing popular culture tastes shaped by television and Top 40 radio, as well as competing social concerns such as civil rights and the Vietnam War. The earlier popularity of labor songs came with associated problems. As professionals and recording artists embraced social protest singing, the songs became passively consumed by listeners rather than a tactic used by mobilized masses. **Deindustrialization** and declining union membership further reduced the blue-collar workforce that nurtured much of labor's singing tradition. Music retained its greatest vitality within newer movements, such as **United Farm Workers of America** campaigns during the 1970s. Women also used music to call attention to inequity in the workplace; Dolly Parton's 1980 hit "9 to 5" inspired a movement, and Fred Small's "Fifty-Nine Cents" addressed gendered wage differentials. For the most part, however, labor songs began to address the disappearance of work, with songs such as "Aragon Mill," "The L & N Don't Stop Here Anymore," and "The Run Away Shop Song" expressing that theme.

Currently, labor songwriting is less noticeable. Occasionally, popular recording artists such as Bruce Springsteen, Billy Joel, U2, Willie Nelson, Henry Rollins, Jello Biafra, and Rage Against the Machine address working-class concerns, but only as a small part of their total repertoire. Very few current performers write or perform labor songs, including folk musicians. Among those who do are Billy Bragg, Pete Seeger, Tom Juravich, Si Kahn, Jeni and Billy, Larry Long, John McCutcheon,

Ani DiFranco, and Peggy Seeger. With the death of Joe Glazer in 2006 and Bruce "U. Utah" Phillips in 2008, labor song lost two of its most prolific singers.

This does not, however, mean that labor singing is dead. In some respects, it has returned its roots and is an immediate and spontaneous response to local concerns—a rallying tool rather than a musical performance. When Wisconsin Governor Scott Walker announced his intention to strip public employees of their **collective bargaining** rights in 2011, many of the protestors sang both labor standards and impromptu compositions to express their outrage. Such actions are typical and are quickly forgotten unless someone happens to record the songs, as happened with Harvard clerical workers during their union organizing drive in 1988. It is important to remember that preservation for posterity is seldom the purpose of labor music. Music has been a useful tool for social reformers, but few believe that song alone changes society.

Suggested Reading

Ronald Cohen, *Work and Sing: A History of Occupational and Labor Union Songs in the United States*, 2010; R. Serge Denisoff, *Great Day Coming: Folk Music and the American Left*, 1971; Lawrence J. Epstein, *Political Folk Music in America from Its Origins to Bob Dylan*, 2010; John Greenway, *American Folksongs of Protest*, 1953; Pete Seeger and Bob Reiser, *Carry It on! A History in Song and Picture of America's Working Men and Women*, 1985.

MUTUALISM. *See* Anarchism.

NATIONAL ASSOCIATION OF MANUFACTURERS

The National Association of Manufacturers (NAM) has been one of the most influential business organizations in American history. For more than a century, it has promoted the values of free-market **capitalism** by lobbying politicians for pro-business legislation and by conducting public-relations campaigns. To that end, the NAM frequently has been at the forefront of fighting labor unions and has been accused—rightly in many cases—of exploiting American workers and riding roughshod over labor laws in the pursuit of corporate profits. At its core the NAM opposes a regulatory state. It sees organized labor as an impediment to economic growth and management prerogative.

The NAM was formed in 1895, when more than 500 manufacturers gathered in Cincinnati, Ohio, to discuss ways of responding to the Panic of 1893 and the overall instability of the Gilded Age economy. At the time, American capitalism was marked by boom-and-bust cycles in which 16 of the 25 years between 1870 and 1895 saw various forms of recession, depression, and economic upheaval. The founders of the NAM discussed ways of establishing new markets for their goods. Throughout the **Progressive Era**, the NAM lobbied the government for such pro-business policies as higher tariffs and low-inflationary monetary policies based on maintaining the gold standard. It also helped create numerous business-friendly political organizations such as the National Industrial Council and the National Council of Commerce, the predecessor of the U.S. Chamber of Commerce.

A consistent theme was the NAM's position that labor unions and the political influence they wielded were antithetical to free-market capitalism and the expansion of trade. The NAM opposed the **Clayton Act** and supported legal challenges to efforts to curtail **child labor** and reduce the workday. In many locales, NAM members helped organize vigilante groups—often disguised as "citizens councils"—to battle radical challenges from the **Industrial Workers of the World**, but it found even the moderate policies of the **American Federation of Labor** (AFL) distasteful. For instance, NAM played a key role in breaking the AFL **boycott** of Danbury hat manufacturers that led to the U.S. Supreme Court's decision in *Loewe v. Lawlor*, which almost led to the imprisonment of AFL President **Samuel Gompers**. It was widely regarded at the chief union-busting vehicle of the early 20th century. Although the NAM accused labor unions of having too much political influence, it held so much of its own that many labor reformers saw it as a veritable "invisible" government. NAM leaders promoted the idea of the **open shop**, which would allow employers to decide the terms of workplace relations without organized labor's influence.

NAM principles ran counter to the **welfare capitalism** policies advocated by social reformers, benevolent capitalists, and some union leaders. Its demeanor often contrasted markedly with that of the **National Civic Federation** (NCF), which was also pro-business but far less strident in tone. The NAM even opposed the capital/labor accords created during World War I because they encouraged union growth, set price controls, and stipulated production goals. After the war, the NCF declined and NAM ideals prevailed. The open-shop movement gained traction during the 1920s and membership declined in many unions; in fact, the only organizations to demonstrate robust growth were **company unions**, a NAM-designed dodge that gave workers the illusion of **collective bargaining** within corporate-controlled bodies.

To the NAM, the 1930s and New Deal labor legislation were setbacks. It responded to the emergence of the **Congress of Industrial Organizations** (CIO) and the pro-labor policies of the New Deal by launching campaigns to educate workers about the virtues of free-market capitalism compared to state control. The organization produced corporate-friendly radio shows, newspaper columns, and movie shorts. It also produced anti-Franklin Roosevelt propaganda and supported **Republican** presidential candidates. During the Great Depression, NAM's efforts mostly failed to change popular opinion; large numbers of Americans greeted the growth of organized labor and political liberalism with enthusiasm. As it had done in World War I, the NAM also opposed many World War II capital/labor agreements, especially the granting of union **maintenance of membership** rights.

The NAM succeeded in reestablishing its pre-New Deal influence after World War II. Troubled by the numerous **strikes** during the 1930s and the 1935 **National Labor Relations Act**, it lobbied Congress to limit the scope of labor laws. It was also able to seize upon events such as the **United Mine Workers of America's** refusal to take a **no-strike pledge** during the war to present itself as a responsible organization fighting the abuses of organized labor. The NAM lobbied for the **War Labor Disputes Act (Smith-Connally Act)** and scored a major victory when Congress passed the **Taft-Hartley Act** in 1947, which placed limits on the power of organized labor by barring certain types of strikes, prevented foremen from joining trade unions, and forced trade unionists to sign anticommunist affidavits. Most importantly, the Taft-Hartley Act gave workers the right *not* to join labor unions. It generally seized upon the climate of the **Cold War**, fears of **communism**, and the tensions of the postwar era to trumpet the marvels of capitalism, portray labor unions in a negative light among the general public, and lobby politicians for the expansion of trade. In the 1950s, the NAM produced short television programs on the triumphs of industry.

Throughout the century's last decades, the NAM has sought tax breaks for business and supported **deregulation**. It found sympathetic ears in the administrations of Jimmy Carter, **Ronald Reagan**, George H. W. Bush, George W. Bush, and even Bill Clinton, who signed the **North American Free Trade Agreement**. It demonstrated great lobbying power during the Reagan presidency and was at the fore of the **concessions** and **decertification** movements that have contributed to precipitous declines in union membership from the late 1970s to the present.

The NAM represents mostly manufacturing interests and is based in Washington, D.C.; it also maintains 10 regional offices. It remains a powerful pro-business organization that retains its antilabor union bias, though it and the **American Federation of Labor-Congress of Industrial Organizations** (AFL-CIO) occasionally cooperate on issues such as oversight of the **Occupational Safety and Health Act**. In a new twist, the NAM may find itself fighting for relevance in the future in many of the same ways that labor unions are now doing. Many analysts speak of a postindustrial economy that sometimes exaggerates the importance that manufacturing continues to have in the United States, but industrial contraction is nonetheless the overall trend. As of 2011, the NAM represented approximately 11,000 manufacturers, down from 14,000 less than a decade ago.

Suggested Reading

"About NAM: Manufacturing in America," http://www.nam.org/About-Us/About-the-NAM/US-Manufacturers-Association.aspx, accessed March 30, 2011; Robert Collins, *The Business Response to Keynes, 1929–64,* 1981; Elizabeth Fones-Wolf, *Selling Free Enterprise: The Business Assault on Labor and Liberalism,* 1994; Howell Harris, *The Right to Manage: Industrial Relations Policies of American Business in the 1940s,* 1982.

NATIONAL CIVIC FEDERATION

The National Civic Federation (NCF) was founded in 1900 and sought to reconcile capital/labor disputes through reason, discussion, and **arbitration**. Its heyday was the period between 1900 and 1917. It was a classic **Progressive Era** body in terms of the faith it placed in experts and its belief that social cohesion could be attained through pragmatism. The NCF was created by reformist newspaper editor Ralph Montgomery Easley, who envisioned it as being an alternative to the acrimonious and often violent industrial conflict of the Gilded Age. Easley hoped that business, labor, and civic leaders could jointly attack disagreements and hammer out mutual accords. His wife, Gertrude Beeks Easley, directed **welfare capitalism** programs for the International Harvester Corporation in Chicago. Although most NCF members were unabashed supporters of **capitalism**, they hoped to negotiate with labor unions, humanize the industrial system, and reduce class conflict. Their goals and tactics differed markedly from those espoused by the aggressively anti-union **National Association of Manufacturers** (NAM).

Prominent NCF members included industrialist and Republican strategist Mark Hanna, banker Lyman Gage, former President Grover Cleveland, social reformer Jane Addams, and George W. Perkins, a partner of J. P. Morgan. Labor representatives included **American Federation of Labor** President **Samuel Gompers**, **United Mine Workers of America** President **John Mitchell**, and International Longshoremen's Association President Daniel Keefe. NCF members shared the belief that extremists in both the business and labor realms disrupted social harmony and were injurious to their respective causes. They hoped to mediate disputes through reform and discussion, rather than via **strikes**, political radicalism, or repression. NCF business leaders promoted measures as **workman's compensation** laws, profit sharing, **child labor** laws, and welfare capitalism programs as ways to improve the workplace, and some even entertained beliefs that stronger antitrust laws and business regulations were needed to moderate the excesses of the modern industrial world.

The NCF helped settle the **anthracite coal strike of 1902**, but that was among the few disputes in which it played a key role. Ultimately, the NAM's ideology proved more persuasive within the business community. The Progressive Era saw vicious crackdowns on radical groups such as the **Industrial Workers of the World** (IWW), and courts seldom favored organized labor. Even Gompers and Mitchell were arrested in 1911 for their roles in a **boycott** against the Buck's Stove and Range Company. Terrible incidents such as the 1914 **Ludlow Massacre** led many labor leaders and rank-and-file members to criticize those labor leaders who cooperated with the NCF. Both the IWW and the Western Federation of Miners were scathing in their criticism of labor cooperation with the NCF and saw Gompers as his ilk as traitors.

The NCF turned more conservative during World War I. It fully supported America's war effort and viewed **socialists**, pacifists, and critics of the war as disloyal. The Bolshevik Revolution in Russia made Easley fearful of **communism**, and he was fed information from the Justice Department's Bureau of Investigation both during the war and during the postwar **Red Scare** on alleged radicals in the labor movement. The failure of Progressives to pass meaningful labor legislation other than the **Clayton Act** also dulled labor's enthusiasm for the NCF, as did the attacks on unions during the 1920s.

The NCF did not formally disband until 1950, but by the early 1930s it had largely lost its reason for being. New Deal labor legislation led most labor unions to place their faith in the government and the **Democratic Party** rather than business interest groups such as the NCF. Moreover, the creation of the National Labor Relations Board provided a formal government mechanism for handling labor-management strife and superseded the NCF's mediation role.

Suggested Reading

Christopher Cyphers, *The National Civic Federation and the Making of a New Liberalism, 1900–1915*, 2002; Marguerite Green, *The National Civic Federation and the American Labor Movement, 1900–1925*, 1956; John Zerzan, "Understanding the Anti-radicalism of the National Civic Federation," *International Review of Social History* 19, no. 2 (1974).

NATIONAL EDUCATION ASSOCIATION

The National Education Association (NEA) is the United States' largest union; it represents public school teachers, support staff, and college professors. Its 3.2 million members are drawn from all levels of public and private education, although the U.S. Supreme Court's decision in *National Labor Relations Board v. Yeshiva University* limits its ability to engage in **collective bargaining** in private schools.

The NEA was founded in Philadelphia, Pennsylvania, in 1857, but did not engage in collective bargaining until after 1962. For much of its history, it functioned more as a teachers' guild and trade association than as a trade union. It often drew leaders from among university presidents concerned with issues such as teacher preparation, curriculum development, college-entrance standards, and technical education. The NEA also operated as an effective lobbying organization for educational reform, supporting such important bills as the Morrill Act (1862) and various bills in state legislatures that protected teacher tenure. The group's relationship to classroom teachers was more amorphous than its commitment to professional standards, however, and by 1920, it was losing members—especially in higher education—to other organizations. The NEA began to revive when it adopted a more aggressive stance toward issues affecting individual instructors. Its 1928 resolution "Freedom of the Teacher" marked its entrance into the issue of academic freedom. In 1934, the NEA moved its offices to Washington, D.C., from whence it tackled emergent issues such as teacher loyalty oaths and ideological biases in the awarding of teacher contracts. In 1941, the NEA Defense Commission (later the DuShane Fund for the Defense of Teacher Rights) was set up to assist legal battles over academic freedom. In the 1950s, the NEA was among the few labor organizations to oppose censorship and **Red Scare** tactics such as red-baiting and enforced conformity. It did participate in programs such as the G.I. Bill of Rights, the Fulbright Programs, and the National Defense Education Fund. In the 1950s, the NEA undertook its first comprehensive study of teacher salaries and had grown to have more than 700,000 members by 1957.

Nonetheless, it was the **American Federation of Teachers** (AFT) that took the lead in collective bargaining rights for teachers. The NEA did not even explore the issue until 1962. It was only in 1966 that an NEA junior-college affiliate won a **union contract**; a university first did so in 1969. Growth came slowly, with several groups designed to organize colleges and universities declaring independence from the NEA, which was viewed as insufficiently attentive to grassroots organizing. In 1974, the NEA restructured its efforts under the National Council for Higher Education.

The organization enjoyed far greater success among elementary and secondary teachers, who spurred much of the NEA's dramatic growth from the mid-1970s onward. Once the NEA shifted its focus, it became outspoken in defending public school teachers against attacks on education during the 1980s, and it offered tactical and logistical support to numerous locals engaging in tough bargaining situations and job actions. The NEA's various state affiliates were given wide latitude to bargain and set policy, a structural arrangement that encouraged growth on the local level, while freeing the parent organization to lobby for teacher rights and teacher-friendly educational reforms. The NEA was particularly effective at warding off attacks on educators related to the 1983 report *A Nation at Risk*. The administration of President **Ronald Reagan** had hoped to parlay that report into a restructuring of American education, but the NEA took the lead in revealing the report's deep flaws and inaccuracies. It also engaged in a 1974 battle, eventually decided by the Supreme Court, that made it illegal to fire female teachers who became pregnant.

Ten years later, the NEA backed lawsuits that protected the **pension** rights of women. It has been at the vanguard of many issues related to racial and gender equity.

Local control has allowed the national NEA to heal the rifts between this group and the AFT, as well as settle **jurisdictional** disputes between the two unions. The NEA and the AFT have cooperated since 1998, and numerous merger discussions have been undertaken, but such mergers have occurred in only a few states. The AFT is affiliated with the **American Federation of Labor-Congress of Industrial Organizations** (AFL-CIO), whereas the NEA is part of an international federation of educators known as Education International.

The NEA has become aggressive in its defense of teacher rights and has been, since the 1980s, a target of the political right, especially conservative **Republicans**. Critics charge that the NEA protects incompetent teachers, is interested in preserving the status quo, and reflexively opposes programs such as school choice, voucher programs, **merit pay**, teacher testing, competency exams for students, and the No Child Left Behind Act. The NEA responds that mandatory testing of veteran teachers and other imposed standards should be bargained collectively, not imposed unilaterally. It also asserts that many ideas purporting to be reforms are, in fact, are a combination of nostrums and ideologically driven private agendas. The NEA points out, for instance, that the United States has no national curriculum and that local control over educational funding means that the gap between rich and poor districts is so wide that it is patently unfair to hold both ends of the spectrum to the same standards. It also points to the fact that educational cuts in the past decades have come during a period in which politicians have demanded that educators take on more tasks and be held accountable for social and cultural issues beyond their control. Congressional demands are often de facto unfunded mandates.

The NEA is currently pressing for major changes in the No Child Left Behind Act. It accuses politicians of abrogating their responsibility to the poor and minorities, and of seeking to implement a two-tiered educational system that favors those with economic resources. Some within the NEA charge that the United States is moving in a direction that would gut public education and make it a second-class system for those who cannot afford private education.

In 2011, several states—including Wisconsin and Ohio—stripped public employees, including teachers, of their collective bargaining rights. The NEA has been actively battling those actions and has initiated legal challenges that are likely to linger in the courts for years. It is also involved in seeking to change the political equation and is likely to become aligned even more closely with the **Democratic Party**.

Suggested Reading

Marjorie Murphy, *Blackboard Unions*, 1990; National Education Association, http://www.nea.org/, accessed April 5, 2011; Bob Peterson and Michael Charney, eds., *Transforming Teacher Unions: Fighting for Better Schools and Social Justice*, 1999; Joel Spring, *Conflict of Interests: The Politics of American Education*, 2004.

NATIONAL FEDERATION OF FEDERAL EMPLOYEES. *See* American Federation of Government Employees; International Association of Machinists and Aerospace Workers.

NATIONAL INDUSTRIAL RECOVERY ACT

The National Industrial Recovery Act (NIRA) was an important early New Deal program. Although it would be struck down as unconstitutional, it served to cement emerging **working-class** loyalty to the **Democratic Party**, and many of its features were included in the **National Labor Relations Act** (NLRA) and the **Fair Labor Standards Act**, which succeeded it. The NIRA was designed to stabilize American industrial and work patterns during the Great Depression by reducing destructive competition and by protecting working people. The NIRA created the National Recovery Administration (NRA), whose two-year mandate gave the president of the United States great leeway in developing industrial codes regulating prices, working hours, and **wages**.

Although much of the business community came to resent the NIRA, part of its intent was to satisfy demands from industrialists to stabilize the economy and relieve it from recurring boom-and-bust cycles. The first serious attempt to regulate trusts came via the 1890 **Sherman Antitrust Act**, which was strengthened by the 1914 **Clayton Act**. Neither these laws nor various trade associations managed to restore competitive balance or predictability to the economy. At the onset of the Great Depression, numerous business and labor leaders turned to the federal government in the hope that national planning could achieve business stability. Some business leaders also hoped that such planning would involve self-regulation and a relaxation of antitrust laws. In fact, the NIRA was modeled in part on the **National War Labor Board** (NWLB) from World War I, which did rely to some extent on industrial cooperation and self-regulation. Nevertheless, the NIRA, as it began to take shape, went beyond the NWLB's scope. Business leaders were particularly alarmed by early proposals from Alabama Senator Hugo L. Black, which would have reduced unemployment by imposing a 30-hour work week. Black's bill passed the Senate on April 6, 1933, but President Franklin Roosevelt asked Secretary of Labor **Frances Perkins**, U.S. Senator Robert Wagner, and eventual NRA director Hugh Johnson to craft the less rigid alternative that became the NIRA.

The NIRA was signed into law on June 16, 1933. It provided for mild relaxation of antitrust regulations, but it mostly featured wage and-price stabilization efforts, a regulation of work hours, and public-works funding to provide immediate employment. Organized labor cheered Section 7(a) of Title I, which included guaranteed **collective bargaining** rights for workers "free from the interference, restraint, and coercion of employers." It also outlawed **company unions** and **yellow-dog contracts**, and legislated a $0.40 per hour **minimum wage** and a 35-hour work week. Equally important for hard-hit workers was Title II's establishment of the Public Works Administration (PWA). Its $3.3 billion budget provided work on projects such as highways and federal buildings. NIRA codes did not apply to **agrarian** production, which fell under the Agricultural Adjustment Act (AAA).

The NIRA generated controversy among employers who did not share the president's views on organized labor, but its public relations campaign produced even greater resentment. The NIRA code was, in theory, voluntary. In practice, NIRA codes often encouraged **boycotts** of noncompliant industries and employers. Those who acceded to NIRA standards were given the right to display a blue eagle graphic, the official symbol of the NRA. The presence or absence of that logo came to be seen by consumers as an indicator of fair and unfair employment practices. Moreover, the NIRA placed too much faith in self-policing, and many industrialists found ways to duck the codes. Many small-business owners complained that the NIRA favored the interests of big business. Even some labor leaders greeted the NIRA with skepticism, especially those inside the **American Federation of Labor** (AFL). Although unions took full advantage of Section 7(a) to replenish membership rolls ravaged by the anti-union policies of the 1920s, labor had little input in crafting the codes. In addition, those AFL leaders devoted to the principle of **voluntarism** were troubled by the implication of government intervention in labor relations. Disputes also arose over the interpretation of the law, especially regarding the **closed shop**, and some unions launched **strikes** to force employer compliance to NIRA codes.

The NIRA ended when the business community challenged its legality. In May 1935, the Supreme Court's decision in *Schecter Poultry Co. v. U.S.* struck down the bill as unconstitutional on the grounds that the NIRA vested too much legislative authority in the executive branch. President Roosevelt had anticipated the decision and quickly replaced the NIRA with the National Labor Relations Act, which was passed by Congress in July 1935 and withstood subsequent constitutional challenge. Roosevelt was able to secure support from Congress when the 1934 elections gave the Democratic Party a massive 313–117 advantage in the House of Representatives, a clear indicator of the popularity of the New Deal among **blue-collar** voters. The NLRA included many of the same provisions as the NIRA; still others would be legislated through the 1938 Fair Labor Standards Act.

Despite its limited lifespan, the NIRA was of great advantage to organized labor. It spurred unprecedented levels of organization that both replenished the AFL and gave rise to the **Congress of Industrial Organizations**, which would bring unionization to heavy industries previously resistant to collective bargaining. The NIRA also ushered in enduring changes in working conditions, including the enactment of minimum wage laws, the regulation of work hours, and the curtailment of **child labor**.

Suggested Reading

Bernard Bellush, *The Failure of the NRA*, 1975; Colin Gordon, *New Deals: Business, Labor, and Politics in America, 1920–1935*, 1994; Charles Morris, *The Blue Eagle at Work: Reclaiming Democratic Rights in the American Workplace*, 2004; Fiona Venn, *The New Deal*, 1998.

NATIONAL LABOR RELATIONS ACT

The 1935 National Labor Relations Act (NLRA) is generally viewed as the single most important piece of pro-worker labor legislation in American history. It is often known as the Wagner Act after its sponsor, New York Senator Robert Wagner. The NLRA replaced the **National Industrial Recovery Act** (NIRA), which had been struck down as unconstitutional, but a version of the NLRA was first introduced in 1933. President Franklin Roosevelt originally supported the NIRA over the NLRA in the hope that the business community would be more willing to accept the former, but when it launched a constitutional challenge to the NIRA, Roosevelt became convinced that a stronger bill was necessary to compel employers to adhere to fair treatment of workers.

Roosevelt was in a stronger position in 1935 when the NIRA was struck down and he sought to advance the NLRA. The 1934 Congressional elections saw Roosevelt's **Republican Party** opponents lose 14 seats, leaving the **Democratic Party** with a massive 322-seat to 103-seat advantage. Part of this landslide was due a surge in **blue-collar** voting. Organized labor had begun to recover from the anti-union sentiment of the 1920s, and Roosevelt's New Deal initiatives were popular among workers reeling from the effects of the Great **Depression**. The NIRA was struck down by the U.S. Supreme Court in May 1935, but the NLRA sailed through Congress quickly and was signed into law by President Roosevelt on July 5, 1935.

The NLRA put the power of the federal government behind several key principles that had relied upon goodwill under the NIRA. For instance, the NIRA gave workers **collective bargaining** rights, but enforcement of them was uncertain. The NLRA created the National Labor Relations Board (NLRB), a body designed to apply the NLRA impartially. One of the main charges of the NLRB was to establish procedures through which workers can form unions. It allows workers to petition the NLRB for a secret-ballot election to determine whether they wish to form a union bargaining unit. If a majority of workers vote for a particular union, the NLRB grants **certification**, and employers are then required to engage in good-faith negotiations with that union. If necessary, the NLRB can compel employers to do so and impose fines and other sanctions. Employees can also petition the NLRB to hold **decertification** votes if they choose to abandon their union.

Fairness and non-intimidation are central to the NLRB's certification (or decertification) process. Past intimidation practices such as threats, the hiring of spies and stool pigeons, firing union activists, offering bribes, and the use of company **goons** are expressly forbidden under the NLRA. So, too, are management union smashing tactics such the creation of **company unions** and **yellow-dog contracts**. The NLRA requires both sides to bargain in good faith, defined as reaching a signed contract that specifies the particulars of the agreement reached and that has the force of law. The NLRA preserves the right of workers to **strike**, and of unions and employers to file an **unfair labor practice** claim in the case of bad-faith bargaining or violations of the terms of the contract. When such a complaint is filed, the NLRB must investigate the claims. The NLRB has the power to dismiss such claims and to rule on them. If it issues a ruling that either side ignores, the NLRB can request action by the federal courts.

The NLRA was passed at a difficult moment in capital/labor relations and was bitterly opposed by the business community, even though its provisions apply equally to both sides. Business leaders immediately challenged the NLRA, and its fate remained uncertain until the 1937 Supreme Court decision *National Labor Relations Board v. Jones and Laughlin Steel Corporation*. By a 5–2 vote, the court ruled the NLRA was constitutional. Most scholars point to two external factors that swayed the court. First, President Roosevelt had attacked the court for being tone-deaf to the economic crisis gripping the nation and the legitimate need to protect the American people from corporate abuses. The president unveiled a plan to expand the size of the Supreme Court. Though his proposal was unwise and ultimately determined to be unconstitutional, Roosevelt's threats may have played a role in making the Supreme Court more open to the logic of the NLRA. The rise of labor activism was likely a more significant factor, however. Organizing drives led by the **Congress of Industrial Organizations** (CIO) and by the resurgent **American Federation of Labor** (AFL) led to an increase in strikes. Much of what was enshrined in the NLRA had already been won at the point of production, but at the cost of considerable social unrest. The NLRA appeared to offer a way to settle union recognition struggles with less social upheaval.

Both the AFL and the CIO initially hailed the NLRA because it gave legitimacy to the union movement and culminated a century-long struggle to win collective bargaining rights in an atmosphere free from intimidation and constraint. A majority of early NLRB rulings went in favor of organized labor, which led the business community to charge that the body was biased. Historians largely disagree with that assessment and view the pro-labor rulings of the NLRB as redressing longstanding abuses. Nonetheless, those rulings were politically charged and compromised perceptions of the NLRB's impartiality. As political winds shifted, the NLRA has been amended, generally in ways that have weakened the rights of organized labor in favor of management rights. Two revisions in particular—the 1947 **Taft-Hartley Act** and the 1959 **Landrum-Griffin Act**—dramatically shifted the emphasis of the original NLRA and led to a surge of employers filing unfair labor practice charges against unions. Those revisions, especially the Taft-Hartley Act, have been the source of union rancor and opposition, but many labor analysts believe that a far greater threat has been the politicization of the NLRB, whose members are appointed. In the 1980s, President **Ronald Reagan** appointed staffers with decided pro-business and anti-union biases.

Numerous observers believe that the NLRB is no longer impartial or effective. Its legal machinery dates from 1935, another problem for the union movement. Anti-union employers often take advantage of the complexity and slowness of the American legal system and refuse to bargain in good faith or pay attention to NLRB rulings. Their objective is to engage unions in a war of attrition. To pick just one example, **Fieldcrest** workers voted to unionize in 1995, but did not win a contract until 2000. This agreement culminated a 15-year struggle that involved numerous tactics that the 1935 NLRB likely would have viewed as unfair labor practices, including firings and relocation threats, slurs against the union, and the casting of illegal votes.

In recent years, a growing number of labor reformers have sought to circumvent the NLRA in organizing campaigns that put direct economic and community pressure on employers. Some reformers have even gone so far as to call for the dismantling of the NLRA and all other labor laws. They argue that the NLRB, the courts, and the federal government are not impartial and that the only settlements that can be enforced are those won in the workplace. Such views are deemed extreme by most organized labor leaders, but the critique points to a larger concern: The NLRA was passed in 1935 and, more than 75 years later, remains the most significant guarantee of the rights of American workers. It is the product of a very different political and economic climate, and it is uncertain as to how well it can protect workers in the postindustrial and **globalized** future.

Suggested Reading

James B. Atleson, *Values and Assumptions in American Labor Law*, 1983; Melvyn Dubofsky, *The State and Labor in Modern America*, 1994; National Labor Relations Board, http://www.nlrb.gov/, accessed April 15, 2011; David E. Strecker, *Labor Law: A Basic Guide to the National Labor Relations Act*, 2011.

NATIONAL LABOR RELATIONS BOARD V. JONES AND LAUGHLIN STEEL CORPORATION. See National Labor Relations Act.

NATIONAL LABOR RELATIONS BOARD V. YESHIVA UNIVERSITY

National Labor Relations Board v. Yeshiva University, 444 U.S. 672 (1980), was a U.S. Supreme Court decision that makes it exceedingly difficult for faculty at private colleges and universities to unionize. By a 5–4 decision, the Court ruled that faculty members in private schools are managers, not employees. Its decision was hailed by trustees of private and religious colleges, but has been assailed by labor unions and professors.

The original case involved full-time faculty members at Yeshiva University, a private, Jewish university in New York City. In 1974, faculty in 10 of Yeshiva's 13 undergraduate and graduate schools sought representation for the Yeshiva University Faculty Association (YUFA) and petitioned the National Labor Relations Board (NLRB) for certification as a bargaining unit. The NLRB granted that petition, and in 1975 the faculty voted to unionize. Yeshiva University refused to recognize the election and ignored a NLRB order to open negotiations with the union, choosing instead to file a lawsuit challenging the legitimacy of the YUFA. In 1978, the Court of Appeals for the Second Circuit denied the NLRB's petition to force Yeshiva University to bargain with the YUFA. In 1980, the Supreme Court upheld the university's position.

Writing for the majority, Justice Lewis Powell asserted that no evidence was given to prove that Congress ever intended faculty to be covered by the **National Labor Relations Act** or the **Taft-Hartley Act**. Moreover, the court ruled that faculty were substantially independent decision makers who determined matters related to curriculum, admission policies, grading standards, graduation requirements, the academic calendar, and numerous other matters. It also advised university administration on such things as hiring, promotion, tenure, and sabbaticals. By Powell's reckoning, this meant that faculty were essentially management rather than employees, as few of the latter have such broad autonomy. Justice William Brennan wrote a blistering dissenting opinion endorsed by three fellow justices, the essence of which was a rebuttal of the idea that faculty members could be considered part of the very group charged with their supervision. Both sides agreed that current statutes are unclear in the matter of university faculty.

Since the 1980 decision, groups such as the **American Federation of Teachers**, the **National Education Association**, and the American Association of University Professors (AAUP) have called on Congress to amend labor laws to include faculty members at private colleges and universities. To date, Congress has failed to act on this proposal, other than in a vague component of the unsuccessful 1994 Teamwork for Employees and Managers Act, which organized labor opposed as a backdoor attempt to reintroduce **company unions**; President Bill Clinton vetoed the so-called TEAM Act. The *Yeshiva* decision has been consistently upheld in private religious colleges. In 1995, faculty at the University of Great Falls (in Montana), a Roman Catholic school, were denied the right to organize, even after several previous decisions found the university's mission to be primarily secular. Efforts at the University of St. Francis in Chicago were similarly frustrated. The *Yeshiva* decision has not been a universal precedent, however. Faculty at state colleges and universities—many of whom are unionized—have not been deemed management, raising the question of how their duties differ in substantive ways from those of their counterparts at private institutions. Further muddying the waters is the fact that some private colleges are organized, their administrations having chosen not to challenge the legitimacy of faculty to unionize. It is also unclear as to what degree the *Yeshiva* decision applies to nonreligious private schools.

In recent years, potent challenges have arisen to the *Yeshiva* ruling. In 2001, part-time and adjunct faculty at Emerson College in Boston were organized by the AAUP, with their part-time status insulating them from being considered management. Other questions have arisen as to whether faculty at institutions without tenure who are classified as "employees at will" can reasonably be considered as management. Currently, most teachers' unions seek changes to labor laws and steer clear of attempting to organize faculty at private schools. Faculties at private colleges have begun to explore ways of circumventing the *Yeshiva* decision. The court decision does not forbid faculty from creating unions; it merely says that said bodies are not under the jurisdiction of the NLRB.

Suggested Reading

"Faculty Sidestep the *Yeshiva* Decision," http://www.aaup.org/AAUP/pubsres/academe/ 2001/JF/NB/yeshiva.htm, accessed April 7, 2011; *NLRB v. Yeshiva Univ.*, 444 U. S. 672 (1980), http://supreme.justia.com/us/444/672/, accessed April 7, 2011; Susan Palmer, "A Brief History of Collective Bargaining in Higher Education," http://www .newfoundations.com/History/HECollectBar.html, accessed April 7, 2011.

NATIONAL LABOR UNION

The National Labor Union (NLU; 1866–1873) is sometimes regarded as the first national **labor federation**, though some scholars give that honor to the **National Trades' Union** (1834–1837). Those who credit the NLU note that the National Trades' Union was mostly a pressure group formed by shipyard workers to lobby for a 10-hour workday and made little effort to evolve a permanent bureaucratic structure. Neither it nor the NLU is considered a successful attempt at federation.

The NLU was the brainchild of Baltimore iron molder **William H. Sylvis**, an activist in the **eight-hour movement**. In 1866, 70 union activists and seven leaders from Eight-Hour Leagues announced the formation of the NLU, whose vague goal was to supplant **capitalism** with **cooperative** ventures. A loose federation was set up in which yearly labor congresses planned an agenda relevant to all constituent unions and Eight-Hour Leagues. In 1867, farmer organizations were added to the eligibility list. Affiliates received one delegate per 500 members. In addition to a call for an eight-hour workday and the creation of cooperatives, NLU congresses fashioned a general reform platform that embraced land and currency reform, a ban on the sale of prison-made goods, mandatory **arbitration** laws, women's suffrage, and an end to **child labor**. There were also rhetorical calls for gender and racial equality (except for the Chinese). **Kate Mullaney**, a Troy, New York, laundress, was an NLU vice president, and the organization also had loose links with the **Colored National Labor Union** (CLNU) led by Isaac Myers.

The NLU issued numerous resolutions that summed up many of the agendas and principles that working people held in common, but its rhetorical thrust far surpassed its organizational prowess. The yearly congress format was more meaningful to union leaders and reformers than to rank-and-file workers, many of whom had little idea that they were represented in the NLU. Groups attending NLU congresses did all the grassroots organizing, and there is little way of determining exactly how many individuals the NLU actually represented. Estimates run from as few as 60,000 to as many as 800,000 members. Very few were actively involved in the NLU, however, and the vast majority of NLU members had little grasp of the organization's activities.

Members and leaders were deeply divided ideologically, fractures that widened upon Sylvis's premature death in 1869. Rural members were devoted to the **greenback** cause, but less interested in unionization—the opposite of how many urban workers felt. Relations with the CNLU cooled when that group remained devoted to the **Republican Party** because of the party's association with the abolition of **slavery** and its leadership in the ongoing debate over **Reconstruction**. By contrast, the NLU gravitated toward third-party politics and the formation of a **labor party**. It was dominated by trade unionists, but also contained numerous **Lassallean** socialists who favored political agitation. Politics proved the NLU's undoing. In 1872, the NLU became the National Labor Reform Party (NLRP) and nominated Illinois judge David Davis as its presidential candidate. He was an uninspiring candidate who withdrew from the race weeks before the general election. The NLU held its final congress in September 1872, with only seven delegates showing up. In a twist of fate, the NLU collapsed on the eve of its greatest success. In 1872, President Ulysses Grant granted most federal workers an eight-hour day, but the NLU failed to survive the Panic of 1873.

The NLU's greatest legacy is what it inspired rather than what it did. The tumult of Gilded Age capital/labor relations drove home the need for a permanent labor federation, and the **Knights of Labor** (KOL) would fill the void left by the NLU. When the KOL held its first convention in 1878, many of the principles adopted were those previously endorsed by the NLU. The NLU's uncertain structure also provided a negative example for **Samuel Gompers**, who would later articulate a strong bureaucracy to sustain the **American Federation of Labor** when it came to life 14 years after the NLU's demise.

Suggested Reading

Foster Dulles and Melvyn Dubofsky, *Labor in America*, 1993; Gerald Grob, *Workers and Utopia: A Study of Ideological Conflict in the American Labor Movement 1865–1900*, 1961; George McNeill, *The Labor Movement: The Problem of To-Day*, 1887.

NATIONAL TRADES' UNION

The National Trades' Union (NTU) was formed in New York.City in 1834 and is sometimes cited as the first attempt at forming a nationwide **labor federation**, although its loose structure and focus on general reform render such a claim problematic. The NTU is perhaps best viewed as an outgrowth of social strains associated with Jacksonian democracy. The NTU drew upon a variety of **Jacksonian-era** reformers, including those associated with 10-hour societies, the **Workingmen's movement**, land reform, and trade unions. Key labor leaders included John Ferral, a Philadelphia weaver; William English, a radical Philadelphia shoemaker; Seth Luther, a well-known New England labor activist; and Charles Douglas, a labor editor and Workingmen's advocate. Its first president was Ely Moore, a **journeyman** printer.

The NTU emerged at a time when journeymen's associations were evolving into trade unions and **strikes** were widespread. NTU leaders hoped to form a federation that could amass a strike fund from national contributions that could assist workers during walkouts of constituent unions. That idea showed promise during an 1836 strike of Philadelphia bookbinders, who won their struggle with the help of financial aid from New York City's General Trades' Union, a body that resembled a prototype **central labor union**. The NTU, however, never forged strong ties with trade unions and mainly held an annual congress in which delegates debated the pressing issues of the day and issued resolutions stating the NTU's positions. It also sought to exert political influence, though it was officially nonpartisan. In the sense that its rhetorical force exceeded its concrete actions, the NTU presaged the **National Labor Union**, though the latter clearly built itself around trade unions, which the NTU did not.

The American **Industrial Revolution** was in its infancy when the NTU formed. Although many NTU advocates understood manufacturing's implications for the future, the NTU often appeared as more of a general reform society than as an advocate for the **working class**. Those scholars who say that the NTU was not a true labor federation also note that it is often conflated with the Workingmen's movement, with which it had ties but with which it was not synonymous.

The NTU—like the Workingmen and numerous trade unions—failed to survive the severe economic downturn known as the Panic of 1837. Although its accomplishments were modest, the NTU was an early forum in which labor reformers from across the nation gathered and discussed mutual interests. For decades after its demise, labor leaders held periodic congresses that kept alive the dream of a national organization to represent labor. Those ideals gave rise to the NLU in 1866, which in turn gave way to more powerful federations such as the **Knights of Labor** and the **American Federation of Labor**.

Suggested Reading

Bruce Laurie, *Artisans into Workers: Labor in 19th-Century America*, 1989; Edward Pessen, *Most Uncommon Jacksonians*, 1967; Paul R. Taylor, *The ABC-CLIO Companion to the American Labor Movement*, 1993.

NATIONAL UNION OF HOSPITAL AND HEALTH CARE EMPLOYEES LOCAL 1199

The National Union of Hospital and Health Care Employees Local 1199 is part of America's largest organization of health care workers. Local 1199 is noted for its historic connections to the **civil rights** movement and for its efforts to bring women, **Latinos**, and **minority** workers into the labor movement. Most branches are affiliated with the **American Federation of State, County, and Municipal Employees** (AFSCME), but because its membership base is broad, some are affiliated with the **Service Employees International Union** (SEIU). Local 1199 has been one of the few American labor organizations to enjoy growth over the past three decades, though in recent years it has been under assault by budget-cutting politicians and by "Tea Party" ideologues within the **Republican Party**.

Local 1199 was founded in New York City in 1932 and was originally known as the Drug, Hospital, and Health Care Employees Union (DHHCEU), a collection of pharmacists, clerks, and soda fountain workers. Its first president was Oscar Lerner, but its guiding spirit was Leon Julius Davis, who took over the presidency in 1934 and would remain active with the union for nearly 50 years. In 1932, Davis, who attended Columbia University's School of Pharmacy, was among a small group of mostly Jewish pharmacists and clerks who organized with the help of the

Communist Party's Trade Union League. The DHHCEU adopted as its motto, "An Injury to One Is an Injury to All"—a slogan used by the **Industrial Workers of the World**, which had modified the rallying cry of the **Knights of Labor**. Like those organizations, the DHHCEU was committed to organizing broadly. Davis and his Jewish cohorts were at the vanguard in battling racial discrimination and actively sought to end discriminatory hiring in Harlem and elsewhere in New York City. As an **industrial union**, the DHHCEU represented not only pharmacists, but also clerks, porters, "soda jerks," and cosmeticians. In 1936, the union joined the **American Federation of Labor** and acquired the designation Local 1199. In that same year, Davis became the union's first full-time organizer and oversaw a **strike** in Harlem that lasted for seven weeks and won the right for African Americans to serve as pharmacists. Local 1199 would subsequently give logistical and financial support to numerous civil rights battles, including the 1954–1955 Montgomery bus boycott.

Local 1199 came under attack for its activism and its left-wing politics during the post-World War II **Red Scare**, but it remained defiant and, in 1958, began to take shape as a larger union. By 1959, Local 1199 had organized approximately 90 percent of pharmacy workers in New York City and turned its attention to organizing workers in the city's voluntary, nonprofit hospitals that were excluded by the **National Labor Relations Act** and hence not subject to basic **wage**, hour, and **collective bargaining** guarantees. In 1959, Davis and organizer Elliot Godoff led a strike of 3,500 hospital workers in defiance of New York State laws forbidding such an action. Local 1199 won concessions, but not **union recognition**. Davis led another defiant strike—this one against Beth El Hospital—in 1962 and spent 30 days in jail for refusing to call off the strike. The strike ended with Governor Nelson Rockefeller's promise to secure unionization rights for hospital workers. This concession fueled substantial growth for Local 1199, which was also aided by its 1959 decision to drop ties to the Communist Party.

The union expanded throughout the 1960s, and extended its organizing efforts to hospitals, nursing homes, eye clinics, and mental health facilities in other sections of the country. When nurses' aides in Charleston, South Carolina, sought to address their **grievances** in 1969, they turned to Local 1199 for help. The organizing drive stimulated by events in Charleston led to the creation of the National Union of Hospital and Health Care Employees in 1973. Local 1199 fought hard battles for recognition. It weathered opposition in the form of the National Guard during the Charleston strike and, in 1972, Philadelphia organizer Norman Rayford was killed by a hospital guard during a strike against the city's Metropolitan Hospital. By the 1970s, however, Local 1199 had branches in Pennsylvania, West Virginia, Kentucky, Ohio, South Carolina, and other states.

In 1981, Davis retired as Local 1199 president; he was succeeded in that role by Henry Nicholas. The change in leadership had little bearing on the union's commitment to social and economic justice for all workers and to the civil rights movement. It also maintained its progressive political stance. The union protested the involvement of the United States in Vietnam during the 1960s and would voice opposition to South African apartheid and U.S. activities in Central America during the 1970s and 1980s. In 1988, Local 1199 endorsed the Reverend Jesse Jackson for president. Factional fights within the union occurred during the 1980s, but these were eventually settled everywhere except New York City, whose Local 1199 branch remained independent until 1998. Local 1199 enhanced its strength by devoting more funds to organizing unorganized workers and through affiliation with other unions. In 1984, it received a direct charter from the **American Federation of Labor-Congress of Industrial Organizations** (AFL-CIO).

In 1989 moves aimed at increasing its political strength, various Local 1199 branches affiliated with either AFSCME or SEIU; the latter affiliation strengthened Local 1199's efforts to bring Head Start, library, and higher-education workers into the union. In 1998, New York City Local 1199 workers also joined SEIU. Another indication of the union's efforts to include new industries and workers came in 2001, when members of the Social Agencies Employees Union (SAEU) merged with Local 1199.

Local 1199 is often cited as a model of militancy, flexibility, and adaptation to the changing workplace of postindustrial America. Today it represents workers such as nurses, clinicians, nursing home employees, home health care providers, pharmacists, and human services workers. Roughly 13,000 workers belong to Local 1199 directly, but its AFSCME connection gives it the combined clout of more than 300,000 workers. In addition to workplace issues, Local 1199 has led high-profile battles against anti-union governors in Washington and Florida. It also advocates putting an end to tax loopholes for corporations and creating a single-payer national health care plan. Its activist stance has made it the target of political conservatives, but the union has been aggressive in striking back at its critics.

Suggested Reading

Leon Fink and Brian Greenburg. *Upheaval in the Quiet Zone: A History of Hospital Workers' Union, Local 1199*, 1989; www.nuhhce.org/about.html, accessed April 11, 2011; www.1199seiu.org/, accessed April 11, 2011.

NATIONAL WAR LABOR BOARDS: WORLD WAR I AND WORLD WAR II

During both world wars, special boards were set up to mediate capital/labor disputes in an attempt to avoid interruption in wartime production. The boards included representatives of organized labor, the business community, and—in the case of World War II—the public. They often granted gains to labor as a whole that would have been difficult to obtain through individual actions. They also represented a less-confrontational solution to workplace disputes than **strikes**, **lockouts**, or **boycotts**. Because **arbitration** had long been the goal of many unions, much of organized labor sought to continue the work of the boards during peacetime, but business groups such as the **National Association of Manufacturers** and the Chamber of Commerce saw them as emergency measures and sought to dismantle them as quickly as possible once overseas hostilities ceased. In this sense, the national war labor boards represent a promising path not taken in settling workplace disputes.

The United States entered World War I in 1917, an action that required increasing industrial output and retooling some plants to produce military materiel. This ramp-up was not accomplished easily, as many young men went into military service. To meet their production targets, many factories introduced **overtime** and **speedups**, some of which led to resistance and strikes. In April 1918, President Woodrow Wilson created the National War Labor Board (NWLB), a 12-member body that consisted of five labor and five business representatives, plus two co-chairs, one from each group. The NWLB sought to ban strikes and lockouts and to maintain productivity levels. It did not have enforcement power for its decisions, but President Wilson's active support for the NWLB ensured that most disputes were settled amicably. Between April 1918 and March 1919, the NWLB rendered decisions in approximately 500 disputes. In many cases workers gained an **eight-hour** workday, women achieved rates of pay that were comparable to men's wages, and some workers gained **collective bargaining** rights for the first time. (Wilson had signed into law the **Clayton Act** in 1914, which exempted unions from antitrust laws.) The **American Federation of Labor** saw its membership soar from 2 million to 3.2 million by the war's end. It and other unions wanted to continue wartime arrangements, but the NWLB was discontinued in March 1919. The ensuing **Red Scare**, the **open-shop** movement, and a general assault on organized labor during the 1920s eroded many of the gains made by labor during World War I.

The attack on Pearl Harbor, on December 7, 1941, drew the United States into World War II. On January 12, 1942, President Franklin D. Roosevelt reactivated the NWLB and asked representatives of labor and business to arbitrate wartime disputes. The composition of the World War II NWLB was altered slightly from the World War I version. The World War II board consisted of four labor representatives and four employer representatives, plus four members representing public interests. Most unions signed **no-strike pledges** and won **maintenance of membership** guarantees and a prohibition of employer lockouts in exchange for their cooperation. Unlike the World War I NWLB, the World War II board had the power to impose settlements in any conflict that would interfere with the "effective prosecution of the war." During World War II the board handled 1,425 cases, of which it imposed a settlement in just 520. Even so, the World War II NWLB encountered more challenges than its World War I counterpart. The **Little Steel Formula** was used as a guidepost for **wage** disagreements, and many unions complained that the formula inadequately addressed inflation. Even more problematic was the refusal of the **United Mine Workers of America** to place itself under the NWLB's authority. World War II officially ended in August 1945, and the NWLB was discontinued on December 31, 1945.

The war labor boards were successful in limiting the number of workplace interruptions during wartime. They also gave workers a voice in determining federal policy and unions generally found that their participation provided great advantages. Increases in union recognition, pay, reduced hours, and equalizing women's pay met with stiff opposition from employers, many of which wished to terminate the NWLBs as quickly as possible and return to business as usual. The effectiveness of the boards is easily seen when one looks at the increased levels of capital/labor conflict that ensued once the boards were dissolved. Numerous strikes took place in 1919 as workers tried to improve upon the gains they had made during World War I. In several cities, including Seattle, **general strikes** were called when employers sought to roll back wartime gains. In like fashion, 1946 was one of the most strike-torn years in all of American history. A total of 4,985 strikes took place, idling more than 4.6 million workers, who collectively lost 116 million workdays. Although NWLB arbitration was by no means a panacea to labor/capital strife, wartime boards are an intriguing model of what could have been an alternative way of settling such disputes.

Suggested Reading

James B. Atleson, *Labor and the Wartime State: Labor Relations and Law during World War II,* 1998; Valerie Jean Conner, *The National War Labor Board: Stability, Social Justice, and the Voluntary State in World War I,* 1983; Marc Allen Eisner, *From Warfare State to Welfare State: World War I, Compensatory State Building, and the Limits of the Modern Order,* 2000.

NATIVE AMERICANS AND LABOR

It is difficult to make definitive remarks about Native Americans. Scholars have identified roughly 500 separate nations in North America at the time of European contact, and currently the U.S. government recognizes 310 official reservations that are considered sovereign nations. There are also 562 officially recognized tribes. Even the term "Native American" is problematic; many modern-day groups and individuals prefer the term "Indian," the label attached to these peoples by the earliest European explorers, who mistakenly thought they had sailed to the East Indies. Still other peoples today are identified by terms that were imposed upon them by outsiders who misheard languages (or arbitrarily assigned descriptors). Terminology problems extend to the very use of terms such as "tribe" to describe groups that often shared little more than linguistic similarity to others bearing the same label. Moreover, more than six centuries of contact with Europeans and European-Americans has resulted in extensive interbreeding, miscegenation, cultural diffusion, and social adaptation.

A few things do (mostly) hold true for all Native Americans. First, pre-contact native peoples generally engaged in subsistence economics and localized trade; hence they seldom depleted resources in the commercial manner in which European settlers would do. Although many peoples did connect the natural world with spirituality, it is a romantic stereotype to see all natives as mystical stewards of the environment; natives routinely burned forests, started grassfires, and engaged in other actions that were not ecologically sound, such as stampeding herds of animals over cliffs.

Second, although some groups—including the Iroquois, Winnebago, Chippewa, and Creeks—were matriarchal and gave women great decision-making power, most scholars caution against exaggerating the agency of women. Nearly all pre-Columbian North Americans had clear **divisions of labor** according to gender (as well as age).

Navajo miners work at the Kerr McGee uranium mine on the Navajo reservation in Cove, Arizona, May 7, 1953. (AP/Wide World Photos)

Third, recent research indicates that Native America was far more complex than previously realized. It was also more densely settled. Older studies often claim that as few as 10 million indigenous peoples lived in North and South America, but many scholars think that this number may have been closer to 75 million. Nearly all scholars agree that native cultures rivaled those of Europe in complexity and, in many cases, surpassed them in this sense.

Finally, the lifestyles and work habits that evolved in the pre-Columbian period were radically altered by European contact. Very few modern-day cultural practices, production methods, or labor patterns exist as uncorrupted pre-1492 practices.

Anthropologists identify eight (or nine) distinct cultural traditions in the future United States during the late pre-Columbian period before 1492. Those practices, in conjunction with geographical conditions, shaped the labor that took place among the populations.

Eastern Woodlands peoples extended from (roughly) the Atlantic Ocean to the Mississippi River and southward into present-day North Carolina; they include groups such as the Abenaki, Iroquois, Hurons, Foxes, Shawnees, Winnebago, and various Algonquin peoples. Work patterns varied by group, with two major systems prevailing: **agrarianism** and hunting-gathering. Squash, beans, and maize were grown by groups who led a more settled existence, while those who led semi-nomadic lifestyles exploited the abundant forests for animal protein and gathered berries and plant foods. Fishing was an important activity throughout the region, especially along the Atlantic seaboard and Great Lakes region. For the most part, hunting and fishing were male pursuits. In some tribes women were responsible for farming. Other important work tasks included processing furs, making pottery, building shelter, and manufacturing weapons, tools, and utensils.

Southeastern peoples such as the Cherokees, Choctaws, Chickasaws, Seminoles, and Yamasees tended to live more settled lives; hence their labor patterns often revolved around farming, with hunting and fishing supplementing diets. For the most part women were responsible for growing, preparing, and storing plant foods, and for the rearing of children. Among the crops grown were cotton, maize, tomatoes, and sweet potatoes. A few tribes along the coast sustained themselves largely through fishing and led nomadic lives.

Most native peoples in the *Plains* region lived very different lifestyles. This sparsely populated region stretched from west of the Mississippi River to the Rocky Mountains, extending north into the Canadian prairies and south to Texas. Many of the peoples who lived there were formerly Eastern Woodlands tribes pushed westward by enemies. For peoples such as the Blackfeet, Cheyenne, Sioux, Kiowa, and Comanche, sustenance and subsistence were highly dependent upon the buffalo. Men generally hunted buffalo, but villages were veritable buffalo-processing centers, with the meat consumed; hides made into clothing, containers, blankets, and teepee shelters; sinew made into bow strings; hooves rendered for glue; bones fashioned into tools; and hair used for everything from headdresses to pillows. Some agriculture took place in the Plains, but because most tribes were nomadic, the crops grown—such as pumpkins—were ones that grew quickly and with minimal care.

Natives in the *Southwest* generally lived quite differently from those in the adjacent Plains region. The arid climate of the Southwest made subsistence more precarious and there were fewer animals to hunt or foodstuffs to gather. Hence, many groups, such as those collectively known as Puebloan peoples, lived sedentary lifestyles in meticulously constructed villages. Some, such as the Tewa and Zunis, lived in multilevel complexes. Maize, beans, and squash were staples for Pueblo dwellers. Because storage of food was crucial, many Southwestern tribes made ornate pottery. A few Southwestern groups, notably the Navajo, were hunter-gatherers before Europeans arrived and lived in round dwellings (hogans) that could be easily dismantled if need be.

Plateau and Basin tribes—sometimes viewed as distinct cultural regions because the former was dramatically transformed by the introduction of horses after 1700—tended to be more nomadic than those in the Southwest. Tribes such as the Flatheads and Nez Perce, whose range was proximate to the Columbia River, fished for salmon and ventured east to hunt buffalo, according to seasonal cycles. Camassia quamash, a wild herb with an edible onion-like bulb, was also gathered and incorporated into the diet. Tribes residing farther south, such as the Shoshone, also hunted buffalo and caught freshwater fish; those bordering the Southwest such as the Paiutes settled near scarce water sources where they fished and hunted fowl, rabbits, pronghorn deer, and other animals.

California natives generally had greater access to food than peoples east of the Sierra Nevada range. Most were hunter-gatherers in the pre-European period, with those living closer to the mountains relying more on hunting and those along the coast more on fishing. Coastal Chumash peoples, for example, built sturdy canoes suitable for offshore whaling. They also produced skillfully made basketry.

Northwest natives—including Chinooks, Nootka, Haida, and Tlingits—lived along a thin coastal slice stretching from present-day northern California and into Alaska. They fished for salmon in rivers and exploited the abundant marine life of the Pacific for food. They also hunted game in the rain forest and harvested wood for shelter, fuel, and practical and ceremonial objects such as carved storage boxes and totem poles.

A small number of indigenous peoples in the future United States—such as Inuits—can be classified as *Arctic* peoples. They dwelled in harsh climates that discourage farming, though they gathered wild berries and grasses in the short Arctic summer. For the most part, however, those in the pre-Columbian period hunted and fished. Animals such as seals, walrus, and polar bears occupied the same importance among them as the buffalo among Plains tribes.

The coming of European explorers and settlers disrupted cultures and populations so profoundly that some scholars use the term "holocaust" to describe the impact. Even before permanent European settlements arose, casual contact with traders and fishermen introduced diseases against which natives had few natural immunities. The Pilgrims and Puritans who settled Massachusetts, for example, found relatively large tracts of abandoned land left by decimated populations. The economic phenomenon often called the "transatlantic exchange" further disrupted work and social patterns in North America. For Europeans, goods such as fur, tobacco, indigo, wild rice, fish, precious metals, and forest products had exchange as well as use value. In some cases Europeans simply seized what they desired, but even when they traded with natives, they often did so in ways that placed environmental strain on resources. Fur trading, for instance, depleted the immediate supply of animals, forcing native and European traders to venture deeper into the interior in search of trade goods. In many cases, this trend caused the additional problem of bringing once-peaceful native groups into conflict with one another. In another example, extensive tobacco cultivation exhausted minerals in the soil, causing settlers to move farther from the coast, where they came into conflict with natives. The Colonial period was marked by numerous wars between Europeans and natives, with the latter usually faring badly in the long term. Warfare also had an impact on daily life among natives, in that it placed more pressure upon women. Many of the warriors were also hunters and/or fishermen, and their removal from everyday patterns of life led women to assume a greater role in providing sustenance.

Perhaps the ultimate disruption was the emergence of the reservation system. Although many Europeans, including those Jamestown settlers associated with **Bacon's Rebellion**, advocated annihilation of natives, most Colonial leaders embraced the seemingly more pragmatic position that natives should be confined to special areas "reserved" for their use. As early as 1658, Virginians established the Mattaponi and Pamunkeg reservations. In like fashion, Massachusetts placed numerous Nipmuck peoples on reservations in the 1680s. Such systems were fraught with problems, not the least of which was the coerced consent of natives that often forced them upon poor land and into nonfamiliar work patterns. An even larger issue was the Europeans' inability to abide by their own treaty provisions. The Ohio Valley, for instance, was the source of great conflict in the 18th century, as settlers illegally moved into areas allegedly set aside for natives. In fact, the attempt of the British government to stymie settlement in the region is generally enumerated among the grievances that precipitated the American Revolution.

The newly created United States inherited the legacy of wars against Eastern tribes and the problems associated with moving them onto reservations. The nascent U.S. government initially considered forfeit the lands of all tribes that sided with Britain during the American Revolution, though it eventually provided for reservations for some groups. It also created the controversial 1819 Civilization Fund, which set up Indian schools and missions whose aim was to assimilate native peoples. Five years later, the U.S. government created the Office/Bureau of Indian Affairs to administer treaties and oversee Indian lands. In some cases, especially among Cherokees, Creeks, and several other tribes, assimilation took tenuous hold. In western Georgia, some natives had converted to Christianity, received Western-style education, intermarried with Caucasians, and established themselves as **yeomen** and businessmen. Some even held African American **slaves**. Assimilation was seldom sufficient to overcome racism or forestall the demand for land, however. As the United States grew and whites moved west of the Appalachian Mountains, new conflict arose. In 1830, for instance, Congress passed the Indian Removal Act. Cherokee Chief John Ross—who was only one-eighth native and a product of assimilation efforts—spearheaded a legal challenge upheld by the U.S. Supreme Court. Despite this ruling, President Andrew Jackson engaged in subterfuge that justified ordering the removal of more than 46,000 natives from lands desired by white settlers and their resettlement on reservations in modern-day Oklahoma. Thousands of natives died en route to these reservations, and thousands more perished when plopped onto lands that bore little resemblance to those that had sustained them hundreds of miles to the east.

The 1851 Indian Appropriations Act formalized the 1830 bill and established Oklahoma as a repository for Native Americans whose lands would be seized in the next four decades. It most profoundly impacted Plains Indians, whose lands came under U.S. control as a result of the 1803 Louisiana Purchase and the 1846 Mexican War. What history books glibly call "Western expansion" was disastrous for Plains Indians, many of whom fought losing wars against the U.S. government between 1860 and 1890. In many cases, tribes that once sustained themselves by hunting were thrown onto Oklahoma and expected to become farmers. The 1887 Dawes Act sought to expand yeoman ideals even further by largely dissolving the tribal system. It granted 160 acres of land to individuals. The land was held in trust for 25 years, at which time deeds were granted and holders were granted full citizenship rights. The Dawes Act also allowed the government to sell "unclaimed" land. The combination of farm failures, unclaimed tracts, resistance to government policy, and enticements to sell land meant that more than half of the lands set aside by the 1887 bill ultimately fell into the hands of non-natives. The Dawes Act failed so spectacularly that the 1934 Indian Reorganization Act restored the right for tribal land to be owned collectively. Indians had been granted full citizenship rights 10 years earlier, and the 1934 bill also granted tribes sovereignty in most matters occurring on the reservation.

The end of the Indian wars in the Plains ushered in a system in which the majority of natives were ensconced upon reservations and placed under the authority of the Bureau of Indian Affairs (BIA), which assumed most of the responsibility for job creation on the reservations. It was not a salutary situation. Reservation Indians topped most lists of negative social indicators, including having the country's highest rates of **unemployment**, infant death, alcoholism, and serious diseases. The BIA was chronically understaffed and underfunded, and it proved incapable of creating enough jobs to allow native communities to rise to material levels comparable to the rest of society. Many reservations were marked by such crippling poverty that their residents were virtual welfare clients of the U.S. government. The situation was exacerbated by cases of corruption and sweetheart deals with non-natives, such that in some cases white contractors and crews were given contracts to complete tasks that natives could have done. A handful of success stories were observed prior to the 1930s, including a successful timber business operated by the Menominees in Wisconsin, and salmon canneries operated by natives in the Pacific Northwest, but such ventures were rare. On a more ambiguous note, some Indians enjoyed success in arts and crafts production, though many of these cottage industries were actually begun by non-native railroad and hospitality entrepreneurs seeking to promote tourism. This trend did, however, give rise to the development of a fine arts tradition that persists to the present, and some Indian artists now produce museum-quality works that command high prices. The flip side to this tradition has been the proliferation of schlocky tourist goods—often made abroad—that trade in stereotypes and cultural insensitivity.

A particularly pernicious ancillary problem was that any native or mixed-blood individual who chose to live off the reservation was ineligible for BIA support and was expected to compete in the **capitalist** market like any other worker. Indians could be found as Midwestern factory workers, West Coast **longshoremen**, and as **oil workers** in the Plains. A handful of Indians and mixed-blood individuals joined labor unions, but most of the latter emphasized their white identity. Among the few who touted his native roots was Frank Little of the **Industrial Workers of the World** (IWW). Little helped organize copper workers in the West and was lynched by a mob in 1917 for urging workers to avoid volunteering for World War I.

Ironically, World War II altered the place of Native Americans in society. Tens of thousands of natives served in the armed forces and were not placed in segregated units, as African Americans would be. The assistance of Navaho "code talkers" proved valuable in transmitting undecipherable military data. Military service led many returning veterans to seek employment off the reservation, a pattern that accelerated the number living on such lands. In the early 1940s, roughly half of all natives lived on reservations; today about three-fourths live amidst the general population.

Also instrumental in spearheading change was native involvement in the **counterculture** of the 1960s and 1970s. High-profile protests during the period and a handful of violent clashes between natives and government officials led to further examination of the role of Indians in American society. The 1975 Indian Self-Determination and Education Assistance Act was aimed at lessening the power of the BIA and other government agencies, and a 1996 bill gave Indians more control over construction and housing projects on tribal lands. The tension between self-determination and BIA control remains a thorny one. In some cases the government has moved toward terminating its role for tribes that are deemed self-sufficient, or that do not meet federal guidelines for official recognition. Conversely, many tribes fear the withdrawal of federal support, though the continuing role of the BIA in administering more than 55 million acres of Indian land remains a contentious issue. In some cases, the BIA has vetoed projects such as building toxic waste storage projects or opening uranium mines, which tribe dwellers in high-unemployment areas favor.

Reservation sovereignty has long fostered small-scale enterprises run by natives. Gasoline and tobacco sales on reservations, for instance, are not subject to federal taxes; thus some Indians earn their livelihood by selling to individuals who visit the reservation to buy commodities at lower prices. Throughout the Southwest, Indians have sold silverwork, clothing, and lower-cost handicrafts both on reservations and through shops in nearby towns and cities. They also operate low-stakes bingo parlors and other gambling games. In 1988, the last activities were changed dramatically when a nearly two-decades-old legal challenge led Congress to enact the Indian Gaming Regulatory Act. This bill allowed Indian reservations to operate casinos. By 2002, Indian casinos were generating nearly $4 billion of annual revenue and a few reservations, including those operated by the Pequot and Mohegan tribes in Connecticut, the Chumash and Pechanga peoples of California, and the Tiwa and Apaches of New Mexico, have been awash in cash. Tribes such as the Mashuntucket Pequot have wisely reinvested revenues and have created many new enterprises, both in the hospitality industry and in the small business sector.

The success of a handful of casinos has led to new problems for Indians. With large amounts of revenue to be shared from such ventures, the problem of defining Indians reemerged; it is a sometimes-difficult task given centuries of miscegenation. An additional issue is the false perception that all Indians are now financially solvent. Although several tribes have generated high revenue, numerous Indian reservations continue to suffer unemployment rates exceeding 50 percent, with all the incumbent social problems that come with this phenomenon. Nor should the **wages** of casino workers be conflated with the profits made by casino shareholders.

Native Americans are today found in all walks of life. Their number includes high-profile sports, music, and acting stars as well as workers found in **blue-collar** and **white-collar** jobs. Overall, however, the situation among Native Americans is analogous to that of other **minority** workers in America: Much progress has been made, but social justice and financial security continue to elude a disproportionate percentage of the overall native population.

Suggested Reading

Thomas Barker and Marjie Britz, *Jokers Wild: Legalized Gambling in the 21st Century*, 2000; William Bauer, Jr., *We Were All like Migrant Workers Here: Work, Community, and Memory on California's Round Valley Reservation, 1850–1941*, 2009; Dee Brown, *Bury My Heart at Wounded Knee*, 1970; William Cronon, *Indians, Colonists and the Ecology of New England*, 1983; David Getches, Charles F. Wilkinson, and Robert A. Williams, *Cases and Materials on Federal Indian Law*, 4th ed. 1998; Brian Hosmer, *Persistence and Innovation among the Menominees and Metlakatians*, 2009; Alvin Josephy and Frederick Hoxie, eds., *America in 1492: The World of the Indian Peoples before the Arrival of Columbus*, 1993; Charles Mann, *1491: New Revelations of the Americas before Columbus*; Jack Weatherford, *Indian Givers: How Native Americans Transformed the World*, 2010.

NATIVISM AND LABOR

The United States is a nation of **immigrants** and one of the most heterogeneous nations in human history. One of the enduring conundrums is why the citizens of such a nation so often fall prey to nativism, a dislike and distrust of recent arrivals. There is, technically speaking, no group that can truly claim to be "native" to North America. This includes **Native Americans**, whose ancestors migrated to the continent roughly 12,000 years ago—probably from Eurasia—though they are the only group that has a legitimate claim to being indigenous. Nativism is not rooted in anthropological reality, but rather in the belief that certain ethnic groups are more "American" than others. Nativism has been a particular challenge for the **working class** and the unions seeking to organize the members of this class. Although **wage** labor and social class ought to unite working people, the reality is that ethnic differences have often divided them.

Colonial North America saw Europeans from Spain, France, the Netherlands, and Great Britain conquer Native Americans. British settlers would eventually dominate the lands that would become the United States and Canada, and they installed an ideology in which white males with an Anglo-Saxon and Protestant background were deemed superior to all others. This view—often called the WASP mentality—would become the basis for both racism and nativism. Racist logic lay behind wars against Native Americans and the decision to implement **slavery**. It was also used to blunt the social class implications of **indentured servitude**. Although white indentures were often treated deplorably during the Colonial era, they were given a modicum of privileges not accorded to those with black or red skin.

Whiteness as a source of power went unchallenged for much of the Colonial and early Republican periods. Although immigrants came to North America, land was plentiful and the largest numbers of immigrants came from Britain and the German states—peoples whose Anglo-Saxon credentials were intact. The coming of industrialization led to a demand for labor, however. By the late 1830s, large numbers of Irish immigrants fleeing famine arrived in North America, the bulk of whom were Roman Catholics and of non-Anglo Saxon stock. The Irish would be the first group to experience nativism on a broad scale. Vicious anti-Irish propaganda was commonplace prior to the **Civil War**, much of which portrayed the Irish as neither white nor fully human. The same fate befell numerous **Latinos**, whose population surged due to the annexation of Texas and U.S. seizure of Western lands after the conquest of Mexico in 1848.

After the Civil War, the **Industrial Revolution** took off in earnest and brought with it an insatiable demand for labor. The period between 1870 and 1920 saw nearly 26 million immigrants come to the United States, the bulk of whom became industrial workers. Low wages, long hours, dangerous conditions, and economic insecurity within an economy prone to boom-and-bust cycles were widespread. New **craft unions** and **labor federations** emerged in response to the plight of the working classes. As they sought to unite workers in common cause, however, they often ran into—and sometimes encouraged—nativist impulses that made **solidarity** more difficult to secure. Many of the post-1870 immigrants were non-WASP émigrés from eastern and southern Europe. The overall unevenness of the American economy encouraged better-established ethnic groups to see newer ones as economic competition and as cultural threats to their own perceived Americanism. Historians of American immigration often speak of an "immigrant cycle" in which the most recent arrivals were viewed pejoratively and were placed at or near the bottom of the social scale. They stayed there until new groups pushed them up the social ladder. As labor historian Herbert Gutman famously observed, the very composition of the American class was constantly replenished during the 19th century. Although the exploitation of, say, Italians and Slavs paralleled the discrimination experienced by the Irish, their respective experiences were disconnected in time. By the 1870s, for instance, the rise in social status among Irish Americans on the West Coast was such that they were often at the fore of agitation in favor of the **Chinese Exclusion Act**, with an Irish immigrant, Denis Kearney leading this campaign in California. The **Knights of Labor** (KOL) also fell prey to anti-Chinese sentiment, though the group managed to avoid nativism in most other cases. Nativism proved so potent, however, that the **American Federation of Labor** (AFL) had fewer qualms about supporting the call for immigration restriction and some of its constituent unions openly practiced nativist discrimination. Even **Terence Powderly**, the son of Irish immigrants, fell victim to popular nativism. Powderly, the former head of the KOL, worked for the Bureau of Immigration from 1897 and 1902, and again from 1907 to 1921. He, too, became a champion of immigration restriction.

Members of the North American working class were so susceptible to nativism that some employers found it to their advantage to encourage it as a way of dissuading unionization. Favored tactics included paying newer immigrants lower **wages**, importing immigrant **scabs** during **strikes**, creating work teams composed of feuding ethnic groups, and encouraging their workforces to see immigrants as competition for their jobs. Once strikes broke out, labor unions had some success in breaking down nativist barriers, but these alliances often proved temporary and old animosities returned once disputes were settled.

Nativism did not decline significantly until the 1930s, and for ironic reasons. Those clamoring for immigration restriction gained political clout and, in 1924,

Congress enacted reforms that slowed the pace of immigration and reduced the number of non-WASP immigrants to a trickle. Five years later, the Great Depression began and the United States had a labor surplus. By the time labor activism was revived in the 1930s, spurred by New Deal reforms and the emergence of the inclusive **Congress of Industrial Organizations**, most of the groups that had arrived prior to World War I had become established in North America. Scholars speak of the emergence of hyphenated identities (e.g., Polish-American, Greek-American) in which "American" had come to soften previous divisions. This phenomenon was of great value to AFL and CIO organizers during the 1930s.

The word "nativism" made its debut in 1845 and was on the wane by the 1930s, but its discriminatory practices made a comeback during World War II and beyond. The Japanese bombing of Pearl Harbor in 1941 led to the internment of more than 110,000 Japanese and Japanese Americans between 1942 and 1946, a harbinger of the way in which nativism would find new targets in the postwar world. **Cold War** unionism largely removed organized labor's last stigmas against southern and eastern Europeans, but the treatment of Asians from the Philippines, Korea, and Southeast Asia sometimes paralleled the experience of the Chinese in the 19th century. A bigger challenge still has been immigration from the Caribbean, Central America, and Mexico. Haitians, for example, have suffered the double blow of racism related to their dark skin and nativism because of their language and cultural backgrounds. Puerto Ricans—who are U.S. citizens—have been targeted because of their Spanish heritage, as have Latinos in general. In the 1960s, unions such as the **United Farm Workers of America** made strides in securing rights for Asian and Latino workers, but Latinos, especially those from Mexico, have been the target of 21st-century nativists and immigration restriction advocates. Although the **American Federation of Labor-Congress of Industrial Organizations** (AFL-CIO) maintains a progressive attitude about immigration, including calls for a generous amnesty program for illegal immigrants, much of its rank-and-file often disagrees with that stance. As has been the case since the 1870s, uncertain economic development marked by periodic recessions encourages many workers to see new immigrants as undeserving competition rather than as groups seeking to replicate older immigrant success stories.

Suggested Reading

David Gordon, Richard Edwards, and Michael Reich, *Segmented Work, Divided Workers: The Historical Transformation of Labor in the United States*, 1982; Herbert Gutman, *Work, Culture, and Society in Industrializing America*, 1977; Noel Ignatiev, *How the Irish Became White*, 1995; Immanuel Ness, *Immigrants, Unions, and the New U.S. Labor Market*, 2005.

NEW BEDFORD TEXTILE STRIKE

The six-month-long New Bedford strike of 1928 was the longest textile **strike** in New England's history. It stands as an example of organized labor's inability to reconcile divisions between **artisan** and unskilled labor, the pitfalls associated with nativism, the outmoded ideals of **craft unionism**, and the perils of red-baiting. The fate of New Bedford mills also ultimately presaged the coming of **deindustrialization** to New England.

New Bedford was comparable to other eastern Massachusetts seaport cities such as Fall River, Newburyport, and Salem, in that it was a city whose initial wealth was built upon maritime enterprises—whaling in New Bedford's case. That industry was in steep decline by the early 19th century. In 1814, Joseph Whelden, a retired sea captain, constructed what was probably the first cotton textile plant in Massachusetts. His example was quickly emulated, so that on the eve of the **Civil War**, New Bedford had transformed itself from a seaport city to a cotton textile center. The discovery of oil in Pennsylvania provided the energy source that allowed even greater expansion of manufacturing enterprises after the war. The city's population nearly doubled in size during the 1870s and increased even more dramatically from the 1880s on. The lure of manufacturing jobs drew **immigrants**, especially French Canadians and Poles, who intermingled with the Portuguese, Cape Verdeans, and Azoreans who originally came to work in the fishing industry. By 1905, less than 20 percent of New Bedford's population consisted of native-born New Englanders.

Although immigrants made up the bulk of the population, the textile mills were stratified, with those of Anglo-Saxon background holding most of the skilled jobs and immigrants toiling in skilled and semiskilled positions. By the time of the 1928 strike, there were approximately 30,000 textile workers in New Bedford, but they were dispersed between two non-cooperating unions. Skilled craft unionists belonged to the Textile Council (TC), a division of the Amalgamated Textile Workers Union, which was affiliated with the **American Federation of Labor** (AFL). It represented only a small percentage of workers, as mechanization advances had deskilled much of the production process. The TC had led a successful strike in 1920, but the situation was quite different in 1928. Despite the post-World War I **Red Scare**, **communist** organizers gave logistical support through the party's Trade Union Educational League (TUEL) and New Bedford's immigrant textile workers formed the Textile Mill Committee (TMC) to represent their interests.

The immediate cause of the 1928 strike was rooted in an overproduction crisis endemic to New England textiles. Instead of cutting production or streamlining management, New Bedford manufacturers unilaterally imposed a 10 percent wage cut on April 9, 1928. This move led to a walkout by both the TC and the TMC. The strike call from the TC was a gamble on the part of its president, William Batty, as the TC represented only a small fraction of the workforce. Batty needed TMC support for the strike, but he hoped to direct the strike on his own terms. The TC's modest demand—rescinding the wage cut—proved unacceptable to TMC firebrands such as Fred Beal, Joseph Figueiredo, and Jack Rubenstein. The TMC had little incentive to yield to TC demands—it was far larger and felt little kinship with the TC. In keeping with AFL principles, the TC had long excluded unskilled immigrant workers from membership. The TMC responded with its own demands: a 20 percent wage increase, the implementation of a 40-hour work week, an end to **child labor** in the mills, equal pay for equal work, and a vow of non-retaliation against union members.

The strike began with great promise, as city officials, local newspapers, and the police force opposed wage cuts. Only TC members were permitted to set up **pickets** or hold public meetings, however, and TMC members were beaten and jailed on a regular basis. More than 2,000 would be arrested before the strike ended. Moreover, the New Bedford Manufacturers' Association (NBMA) announced it would bargain only with the TC, an arrangement the TC readily accepted as it engaged in red-baiting with equal fervor to that of the manufacturers. The NBMA initially overplayed its hand, however; a July attempt to reopen the factories with the wage cuts in place was met by a protest of more than 20,000 workers. Local officials and the NBMA blamed the protest on the TMC and began to pressure the police department to crack down on the organization. They were tacitly aided by the TC, which proceeded to negotiate with the NMBA without input from the TMC, even though the NMBA hardened its stance by announcing its intent to put a **speedup** in place on the line, as well keeping the wage cuts.

The strike came to an inglorious end when, in September, the TC agreed to accept an offer in which wages would be cut by just 5 percent. The TMC vigorously opposed the deal, but on October 6 the TC agreed to return to work. When the TMC attempted to renew the strike, it was met by force that included beatings and the deportations of several strikers.

The TC and the AFL soon found out they had signed a bad bargain. Most workers saw wage cuts far in excess of 5 percent; in some cases, wages fell by as much as 20 percent. The coming of the Great Depression brought even greater hardship. The AFL soon lost its dominance in textile unions, as the **industrial unionism** model of the **Congress of Industrial Organizations** proved a more pragmatic alternative to the AFL's antiquated craft union principles. Also lost in the 1928 strike was attention to a TUEL contingency plan that would have taxed company property in the event that jobs were moved to the low-wage South. Such a plan would have provided income for the city to hire displaced workers. New Bedford and other New England towns would soon wrestle with precisely the problems predicted by the TUEL. New Bedford would hemorrhage 21,000 jobs by 1937, mostly because of plants relocating to the South rather than the effects of the depression. Just 13 mills remained in the city when World War II ended.

The 1950s is often portrayed as a period of economic boom and prosperity. This was not the case in New England, where plant closings anticipated what would happen in the rest of the nation in the 1970s and 1980. New Bedford's population fell from 130,000 in 1924 to 105,000 in 1955, the year when another unsuccessful textile strike rocked the city's remaining plants. Most of those plants would close before the decade ended. Today the city has just 90,818 residents and a few specialty textile plants, each with a small workforce.

Suggested Reading

Philip Foner, *History of the Labor Movement in the United States, Volume 10: The T.U.E.L 1925–1929,* 1994; Daniel Georgiana and Hazen Aaronson, *The Strike of '28,* 1993; S. L. Wolfbein, *Decline of a Cotton Mill City: A Study of New Bedford,* 1944.

NEW DEAL AND LABOR. *See* Congress of Industrial Organizations; Democratic Party and Labor; Depression-Era Strikes; Fair Labor Standards Act; Federal Emergency Relief Act; General Motors Sit-down Strike; La Follette Committee; National Industrial Recovery Act; National Labor Relations Act; Perkins, Frances Coralie; Social Security Act.

NEW LEFT AND LABOR. *See* Counterculture and Labor.

NEW SOUTH AND LABOR. *See* Reconstruction and Labor.

NEWSPAPER BOYS

Newspaper boys—popularly called "newsies"—were a common phenomenon on metropolitan streets in the late 19th and early 20th centuries. They were street peddlers whose job it was to sell newspapers; in some cities, they were the only major distribution network for newspapers. They were poorly paid, and the bulk of them were independent contractors who bought the papers from the publishers. Because their **wages** depended upon how many units they sold, most newsies developed creative methods of hawking their wares, often resorting to sensationalist claims that rivaled those of yellow journalism.

The newsies were a product of the converging forces of industrialization, urbanism, **immigration**, and **social Darwinism**. American industry expanded dramatically after the **Civil War**, which caused ripple effects across U.S. society. Cities grew rapidly in the latter part of the 19th century as former rural dwellers and immigrants poured into urban areas seeking jobs. Many cities grew much faster than the infrastructure needed to deliver basic services such as communications, education, and social welfare systems. It was not until 1918 that school attendance became mandatory in all states. Prior to that time, even states that had mandatory attendance allowed children to leave school at early ages—generally around 14 years. Nor was school attendance strictly enforced in the 19th century, especially in the case of immigrant families. **Child labor** was a common feature among financially strapped immigrant households. Social agencies were rare in the 19th century, and the very concept of social welfare was frowned upon; the dominant social Darwinian views of the time held that personal and familial misfortune and poverty resulted from flawed character, not flawed social structures. Nearly all aid was in the hands of private charities and philanthropies, which proved wholly inadequate to address the needs of growing cities marked by wide gulfs between the small moneyed classes and the struggling masses.

Collectively, these factors resulted in large numbers of children roaming American streets, many of whom were homeless by reasons such as being abandoned, being runaways, or being left to fend for themselves due to family

A six-year-old newspaper boy working the streets of Los Angeles, 1915. (Library of Congress)

misfortune. New York City alone had at least 10,000 homeless children by the early 1880s. Although there were numerous employment opportunities for children, even street urchins could peddle newspapers. Given the sentiments of the day, ragged newsboys attracted more complaints and derision than public sympathy.

The story of child labor generally casts underage workers in the victim role. That is undoubtedly true, but children were not entirely without agency—and this was especially true of newsies. Technological changes made newspapers easier to mass-produce and growing cities created larger markets. Most cities had numerous multiple-edition journals, competition among them was fierce, and newsies could sometimes negotiate better rates on papers, though they often had to toil well into the night just to earn an average of approximately $0.30 per day. Although newsies had to buy their papers and could not return them, they also realized that most papers would sell very few copies without their efforts. Although newsies competed against one another, they also managed to cooperate. New York City newsies led brief strikes in 1884, 1886, and 1887, usually in response to attempts of publishers to raise the price of the 100-paper bundles purchased by the newsboys.

Those strikes went largely unnoticed, but an 1899 strike captured the public's imagination. During the Spanish-American War, New York City publishers raised the bundle price from $0.50 to $0.60. Newsies absorbed the immediate price rise as sales boomed during the war, but the end to hostilities reduced their volume and New York's largest papers refused to roll back their prices. Legend holds that New York City's strike began spontaneously when the newsies who sold William Randolph Hearst's *New York Journal* found that a particular deliveryman had cheated them and responded by tipping over his wagon and simply appropriating his papers. Word spread of the rebellion, which proved the catalyst for some 5,000 newsies to take on Hearst and his equally powerful rival, Joseph Pulitzer of the *New York World*. It is unclear who, if anyone, actually coordinated the strike, though papers of the day mention a child named Morris Cohen and note fiery speeches from a boy allegedly blind in one eye and known simply as Kid Blink. A union was formed on July 19, 1899, and announced a strike for July 22, unless Hearst and Pulitzer rolled back costs. Neither took the boys seriously, and newspaper van drivers were shocked to encounter mass protests, banners, and blockades. Attempts to use force against the boys built public sympathy for their cause and emboldened the newsies, who used tactics such as pelting delivery vans with stones and destroying papers the moment they were tossed onto the street. Within days the newsies had shut down much of the newspaper distribution in New York, Brooklyn, and immediate environs. The strike ended after two weeks when Hearst and Pulitzer agreed to a compromise that allowed them to save face while granting the newsies a victory—the price rise remained in effect, but the publishers agreed to reimburse the newsies for all unsold papers at 100 percent of their value.

New York City newsies dissolved their impromptu union, though their publicized example inspired newspaper boys elsewhere to lead strikes of their own. Boston newsies formed a union in 1901 and even received a charter from the **American Federation of Labor**. Similar actions took place in Chicago in 1912, Detroit in 1914, and in Seattle and Minneapolis in 1916 and 1917. A Minneapolis strike during 1917 left that city with virtually no news for several days and the boys won their strike. New York and Brooklyn saw a repeat of the 1899 strike in 1918.

The early 20th-century battles were largely the last gasp of the newsies. **Progressive Era** reformers sought to end child labor. Although legislation designed to achieve that goal was struck down as unconstitutional, mandatory school attendance laws greatly reduced the number of children on the streets. Newspapers looked for ways to reduce their reliance on the newsies, a search that led to the development of adult-staffed newsstands, subscription services, and home delivery. Newsies could be seen into the 1930s but the practice faded away quickly when social mores changed, social agencies emerged, and public schools expanded. In retrospect, the newsies played a key role in making child labor more visible and in exposing the underlying cruelty of unexamined social Darwinism.

The Walt Disney Corporation made the events of the 1899 strike the subject of a 1992 musical film in 1992. It did poorly at the box office, perhaps another indication of society's evolving revulsion for child labor.

Suggested Reading

Susan C. Bartoletti, *Kids on Strike!*, 2003; David Nasaw, *Children of the City*, 1985; J. S. Reiner, P. Ferguson, and E. West, *Boyhood in America: An Encyclopedia*, 2001.

NEW YORK CITY TEACHERS STRIKE

The New York City teachers strike of 1960 was a landmark event that led to the first **collective bargaining** agreement for public schoolteachers in a major U.S. city. It provided inspiration for teachers in other regions of the United States, and over the next several decades teachers across the nation unionized for the first time. Teachers, like other public-sector employees, were excluded from protection under the **National Labor Relations Act** of 1935. The **American Federation of Teachers** (AFT) had sought to organize teachers much earlier, but by the late 1950s its efforts had stalled. It would take several illegal strikes to revitalize AFT efforts.

Former educator and union strategist David Selden cofounded a New York City teachers' union called the United Federation of Teachers (UFT), which launched a campaign to organize the city's 50,000 public school teachers. Teachers were restive, as the city school board and local politicians had largely ignored long-standing complaints of low **wages**, poor fringe benefits, large classes, and student unrest in the classroom. In March 1960, Charles Cogen, the first president of the UFT, threatened to call a teachers' strike. The New York Board of Education responded by agreeing to allow a certification election if 30 percent of the city's teaching staff requested one. It also agreed to offer a higher **salary** scale and increased sick leave. The UFT quickly concluded that the board was simply stalling, and it called a strike vote in the fall of 1960.

On November 7, 1960, more than 5,000 teachers participated in a one-day strike to demand collective bargaining rights. They walked out in defiance of the 1947 Condon-Wadlin Act, which expressly forbade New York State public employees from striking, but the very size of the protest led Democratic Mayor Robert F. Wagner, Jr., to pressure the New York Board of Education to authorize a union-recognition election. In June 1961, New York teachers overwhelmingly voted for collective bargaining rights; in December, they designated the UFT as their sole bargaining agent. Contract negotiations over salaries bogged down in April 1962, prompting the UFT to call another strike. More than 20,000 teachers walked off the job, though they returned after one day when the New York State Supreme Court declared the action illegal. Once again, however, the size and **solidarity** demonstrated during the walkout prompted officials to take notice. New York's **Republican** governor, Nelson Rockefeller, agreed to increase city aid to meet the UFT's salary demands, and the union successfully negotiated the first comprehensive collective bargaining agreement between teachers and any major U.S. city. In addition to a substantial salary increase, New York City teachers won improved working conditions and the establishment of a **grievance** procedure.

New York City's achievements galvanized teachers across the United States. Emboldened by its own success, the AFT voted, in 1963, to repeal its no-strike pledge. The AFT's decision to do so was motivated in part by its recognition that teachers elsewhere lacked the political clout of those of New York City. Between 1963 and 1974, more than 1,000 teacher strikes idled more than 800,000 teachers. These actions forced states to adopt legislation allowing public-sector collective bargaining agreements. By the end of the 1970s, more than 70 percent of public schoolteachers were covered by such agreements, and AFT membership soared from 59,000 in 1960 to more than 200,000 in 1970, and again to more than 900,000 by 2000. Its activism also inspired the **National Education Association** to abandon its guild-like practices and evolve into a fully functioning collective bargaining unit in its own right. Both it and the AFT are affiliated with the American Federation of Labor-Congress of Industrial Organizations. Until his death in 1997, **Albert Shanker**—who headed the AFT from 1974 onward—was a powerful union leader who wielded formidable political clout. He was also a sought-after expert on education.

The growing power of teachers' unions after 1963 became a *bête noir* for conservatives, who view them as special interest groups that block desired conservative reforms such as competency testing, voucher systems, support for private education, **merit pay**, textbook content, sex education, school prayer, and local control over education. Well-publicized battles between conservative groups and teachers' unions have raged for decades. In 2011, conservative governors in Wisconsin and Ohio took preliminary steps to strip teachers and other public employees of their collective bargaining rights. It remains to be seen if these efforts will withstand legal challenges and labor unrest.

Suggested Reading

Robert Braun, *Teachers and Power: The Story of the American Federation of Teachers*, 1972; Marjorie Murphy, *Blackboard Unions: The AFT and the NEA, 1900–1980*, 1990; Philip Taft, *United They Teach: The Story of the United Federation of Teachers*, 1974; United Federation of Teachers, http://www.uft.org/, accessed April 27, 2011.

NEW YORK CITY TEXTILE STRIKES, 1909–1910. *See* Uprising of the 20,000.

9TO5: NATIONAL ASSOCIATION OF WORKING WOMEN

9to5: National Association of Working Women (9to5) is a lobby and pressure group with chapters in several cities and a presence in all 50 states. It focuses on issues of concern to working women, including sexual harassment, employment discrimination against women, pay inequity, **glass ceiling** impediments to women's advancement in their jobs, and antifamily business practices. Since its birth in 1973, the organization has been a major force in helping **minority labor** groups assert their rights. Its major focus is on low-wage female workers.

9to5 began life in 1972 as the newsletter *9 to 5 News*, published by disaffected Boston office workers. The organization's founder was Harvard University clerical worker **Karen Nussbaum**. Clerical workers at Harvard launched a creative campaign—including the adoption of the slogan "You Can't Eat Prestige"—to call attention to the substandard **wages** paid by the world's wealthiest university. Their efforts shamed the university and brought it to the bargaining table, which led to substantial gains for the workers. The efforts in Boston resonated with women's experiences elsewhere, and a national organization soon evolved. The organization's high public profile spawned a fanciful namesake Hollywood film in 1980 and a song from country/pop artist Dolly Parton. Neither was directly about 9to5, and some critics complained that these popular-culture expressions trivialized women's work issues, but they also engendered publicity that aided the organization.

9to5 emerged as a full-fledged lobbying group in response to the slowness of some employers to grasp the new realities of an increasingly female American workforce, and the reluctance of others to make financial concessions to women. Women's participation in the workforce has increased dramatically since World War II, but progress in combating gender discrimination has not proceeded apace. In 1970, 43 percent of all women worked; a decade later, that percentage had climbed to more than 50 percent. It is now more than 60 percent, and the overall American workforce is approaching a 50/50 gender split. Despite this fact, women's wages are, on average, only about 77 percent of those of men. By 9to5's reckoning, despite the 1963 Pay Equity Act, the gap between male and female wages has closed by less than one-half penny per year. 9to5 has been very active in trying to get more women into labor unions, as the union wage differential between men and women is far better than that in non-union workplaces.

In addition, 9to5 has been at the fore of many social justice issues. It has been a champion of **affirmative action** policies, has fought for better conditions and pay for **contingency labor**, supports nonpunitive welfare reform, and has been a leader in a broad-based civil rights agenda. It was a major supporter of the **Family and Medical Leave Act**, though it maintains that the program's limited scope needs to be expanded. It is currently embroiled in efforts to assist low-wage workers, to develop an amnesty program for illegal immigrants, to turn back budget cuts that hurt working families, and to end discrimination based upon sexual preference. Of particular interest to the group is a desire to make family leave and sick leave available to low-wage workers, as well as attempts to address serious inequities in Social Security benefits for workers who were trapped in low-paying jobs for most of their careers. It maintains the Job Problem Hotline, through which women can request assistance in dealing with workplace discrimination.

9to5 operates regional offices in Atlanta, Denver, Los Angeles, and Milwaukee, with the last city also being the home of its national office. 9to5 has cordial relations with the **American Federation of Labor-Congress of Industrial Organizations**, the **Change to Win Federation**, and other workplace reform groups.

Suggested Reading

Ellen Bravo, *The Job/Family Challenge: A 9 to 5 Guide—Not for Women Only*, 1995; "9to5, National Association of Working Women," http://www.9to5.org/, accessed April 27, 2011; John Sweeney, Karen Nussbaum, and Eli Ginzberg, *Solutions for the New Workforce*, 1989.

NON-WAGE LABOR

Non-wage labor is a self-defining term that refers to uncompensated work. There are large numbers of people whose work is important to society, but who receive little or no compensation for their efforts. Some engage in volunteer work and consider their toil to be a form of direct philanthropy. Of growing concern, however, are forms of uncompensated labor that replicate or replace paid jobs, work that perpetuates social stereotypes, coerced work, and volunteer labor done by those who would prefer to be paid.

Non-wage workers are not covered by labor laws and few of them are organized. For the most part, unions have ignored or made half-hearted attempts to represent non-wage workers. In some cases—such as court-ordered community service work, prison labor, and volunteer work—unions interpret non-wage labor as a threat to worker wage security. This is especially the case when non-wage workers take on tasks such as street cleaning, building and street maintenance, or teacher's aide positions that replicate jobs that usually pay **wages**. Some states ban the sale of prison-made goods, as they are viewed as unfair competition for firms paying employees to produce similar goods.

Historically, the largest group of non-wage laborers has been domestic homemakers, a trade customarily dominated by women. During the Colonial and Early Republic periods, **agrarianism** dominated and wage-earners were relegated to minority status. This situation began to change with the advent of the **Industrial Revolution**, a phenomenon that upset customary economic relations. The **yeoman** ideal held that agrarian workers were independent and self-employed; hence each family member was simultaneously a producer and a consumer. This relationship made the work of each family member integral to the financial security of all, even when jobs were not valued equally. ("Women's work" associated with child-rearing and food production was generally viewed as less prestigious.) Workers who did not own farms might receive a wage, but this condition was viewed as temporary; even **artisans** were presumed to be working toward a goal of land ownership.

Under industrialization, more workers became lifelong wage-earners and the family economy gave way to ideals of a **family wage** in which a single wage-earner would be able to support all family members. Prevailing gender notions were such that the family wage usually accorded the breadwinner role to male heads of households and, in turn, confined women to domestic duties. This had a profound impact on women. By the mid-19th century, dominant social ideals held that men should have public roles, while women ought to assume only private ones associated with their households. Because men received payment for their work, it was viewed as more important. In effect, this system made males producers and relegated the rest of the family to the consumer role. Even when women worked—a necessity for most 19th-century **working-class** families—their work was denigrated. Women generally received lower wages in the belief that they were not as capable as men, and that they would soon return to their homes to take up their "natural" roles—unpaid household labor. During economic downturns, laws sometimes forbade married women from wage work on the assumption that jobs should be reserved for male breadwinners. Propaganda supplemented social custom in reinforcing the idea that women belonged in the home.

Occasionally—including World War I and World War II—equally powerful propaganda was used to convince women they could temporarily assume wage-earner roles, but mostly women were told that they *should* be performing domestic duties and that these tasks were not as valuable as male wage work. Women nonetheless entered the workforce in increasing numbers, especially in the latter half of the 20th century. Even as women worked for wages and the family wage ideal eroded, women were still expected to perform the bulk of nonpaid domestic chores.

The rebirth of the feminist movement in the 1960s challenged the way in which non-wage work for women was valued. Women complained of the "double shift," as studies revealed the expectation that women would continue assuming the bulk of domestic chores meant many working women held the equivalent of two full-time jobs. There were even proposals to pay women for housework, an idea that was much ridiculed in popular culture, but which was based on sound economic calculations of the true value of women's unpaid labor and the potential cost to society if it were to be withdrawn. Advocates also pointed out that homemakers and other non-wage laborers have no health care benefits, **workman's compensation**, sick leave, or **pensions**; they do not even accrue Social Security benefits unless they take paid positions. The rising divorce rate—which has stood at 50 percent since the 1990s—made homemakers especially vulnerable to economic pressure. Feminists pointed out that many American women were but one death or divorce away from poverty. To date, not much progress has been made on compensating homemakers for their labor and not much is anticipated, as the full-time homemaker is an ever-shrinking group.

In recent years, concern over non-wage labor has shifted to other fronts. Many artists, writers, musicians, and performing artists often donate work and services. When they do not get paid for their work, they fall prey to many of the same problems as full-time homemakers. For example, online publications often pay nothing to publish the work of non-established writers. Many writers, in fact, are pressured to donate their work in exchange for publication credits they hope will give them the credibility to parlay future assignments into paid work. Unions such as the National Writers Union (NWU), a local of the **United Auto Workers of America**, have pushed for standards that would require payment for published work, but have not made much headway to date. In the early 21st century, the NWU enjoyed modest success in getting print publications to compensate writers for reprint of their work on the Internet, but many of those gains have been reversed and this form of non-wage work has grown more popular recently. In effect, some publications generate repeat revenue from writers, but pay them just once.

Even more troublesome is labor that some unions dub coerced volunteering. The push to move welfare to workfare has, in some cases, forced individuals into job training or educational programs for which they might not be compensated; some programs require volunteer work in exchange for benefits. In some cases, welfare recipients even work **apprenticeships** in which they produce goods and services, but receive no pay. Unions such as the **American Federation of State, County, and Municipal Employees** have complained that some workfare programs are abused by cost-cutting towns and cities seeking to trim budgets by replacing paid workers with coerced volunteers. Nonpaid internships are another source of contention, as recent college graduates and trainees are often asked to assume tasks that others get paid to do. Some critics now complain that many internships have long ceased to be mentoring programs and are simply a source of free labor for parsimonious employers.

Volunteerism in the larger sense will likely remain a contentious issue in the future. Teachers, nurses, social workers, and others complain that an influx of well-meaning individuals into nonpaid positions has led schools, hospitals, and agencies to rely upon volunteers while laying off paid aides and counselors. In an interesting twist, the rise of non-wage labor has fueled the campaign for a **living wage**, which would link wages to local indices of what it actually costs to survive in a particular locale.

Suggested Reading

Jane Collins and Martha Gimenez, eds. *Work without Wages: Comparative Studies of Domestic Labor and Self-Employment*, 1990; Michael Hinton and Jean Bloch, *What Is a Wife Worth*, 1984; Susan Strasser, *Never Done: A History of American Housework*, 1982.

NORRIS-LAGUARDIA ACT

The Norris-LaGuardia Act is also known as the Anti-Injunction Act of 1932. It was an important piece of pro-labor legislation that set the tone for the coming New Deal, though it was actually introduced during the waning days of President Herbert Hoover's administration and he signed it into law on his last day in office. The law was named for the bill's sponsors, Senator George Norris, a Nebraska **Republican**, and Representative Fiorello LaGuardia, a New York Republican. The **American Federation of Labor** (AFL) lobbied energetically for the passage of the bill.

The Norris-LaGuardia Act is notable mostly for curtailing abuses rather than for establishing new precedents. Its two major features involved forbidding the use of judicial **injunctions** and restraining orders during nonviolent labor disputes, and an unambiguous ban on **yellow-dog contracts**. These seemingly small measures provided labor unions with greater freedom to organize, **strike**, **picket**, and use other forms of leverage against management, and it cast the federal government as a neutral party in capital/labor disputes. Prior to the Norris-LaGuardia Act, federal courts often ruled that unions were unlawful combinations and that strikes were illegal conspiracies and restraints of trade. Based on this logic, courts routinely issued injunctions and restraining orders to limit the activities of unions, union members, and their supporters. Workers came to view federal courts as allies of anti-union employers. After passage of the Norris-LaGuardia Act, federal courts were allowed to use injunctions only if strikers broke or threatened to break the law, engaged in personal violence, or committed irreparable property damage. Even in these cases, injunctions required a five-day waiting period and public hearings before they could take effect. Under the act, courts could no longer be the first resort of employers, and injunctions were allowed only after attempts at negotiation and mediation had failed. For a court to issue an injunction, hard evidence had to support the claim that illegal acts had occurred or had been threatened, that irreparable harm would occur, that law enforcement was unable to maintain public order, and that there were no remedies at law for threatened illegal actions.

The bill was a boon to unions, which gained the right to organize workers, go on strike, publicize their disputes, and induce others to support them without the interference of courts. The AFL hailed the law as one of its greatest accomplishments. Alarmist antilabor members of Congress described the law as nothing less than an intrusion of **communist** ideals that threatened American society. The critics fought a losing cause, as subsequent New Deal acts reinforced key aspects of the Norris-LaGuardia Act.

Suggested Reading

Douglas L. Leslie, *Labor Law in a Nutshell*, 2000; Richard Lowitt, *George W. Norris: The Persistence of a Progressive, 1913–1933*, 1971.

NORTH AMERICAN FREE TRADE AGREEMENT

The North American Free Trade Agreement (NAFTA) is an economic treaty between the United States, Canada, and Mexico that eliminates barriers to trade and investment between the three nations. It went into effect in January 1994, after a bitter political battle. It is very unpopular among organized labor, and many unions have called for its repeal. That is unlikely to occur in the near future.

Both independent unions and those affiliated with the **American Federation of Labor-Congress of Industrial Organizations** (AFL-CIO) have opposed NAFTA from its inception and see it as a particularly egregious example of allowing the economics of **globalization** to affect adversely environmental, workers' rights, and living standards in the United States. Labor largely sees NAFTA as an agreement that has enriched international corporations at the expense of U.S. workers. The idea behind NAFTA was to launch a North American free trade zone akin to that represented by the European Union. The original proponents of NAFTA asserted that the agreement would create jobs in all three nations by raising Mexican living standards and enlarging markets, which would in turn lead to an increase in demand for goods, higher production, and more jobs. To date, critics of NAFTA have more economic data on their side, as NAFTA's most tangible effect has been the creation of **runaway shops**.

According to the Economic Policy Institute, 766,030 U.S. jobs were lost from 1994 to 2000 alone; as of 2010, 879,280 jobs had disappeared. Of these, 78 percent came from the **blue-collar** manufacturing sector. Numerous American manufacturers closed factories—many of which were profitable—and relocated their operations in *maquiladoras* facilities, shops located in Mexican cities that border the United States, but in which the **wage** structure is considerably lower and where environmental standards are lax. The AFL-CIO contends that NAFTA has been little more than an assault on blue-collar union workers. Although the United States added 709,488 jobs to its economy in the period between 1993 and 2007, very few of them are connected to NAFTA, and the bulk of new jobs have appeared in

service industries, which are mostly non-unionized and which pay on average 20 to 25 percent lower wages than the manufacturing jobs that were lost. The AFL-CIO also contends that NAFTA has had a negative effect even on those manufacturing jobs that remain in the United States and Canada. Employers often wring economic **concessions** from their workforce and avoid serious **collective bargaining** by threatening to move their plants to Mexico.

Some analysts also argue that NAFTA has been a bad deal for Mexico as well. There is little evidence of improved conditions in most *maquiladora* communities and, in some cases, local wages have actually declined by more than 20 percent. Nonetheless, since the passage of NAFTA, other free trade and **fast-track** agreements have been signed. A Free Trade Area of the Americas (FTAA) proposal seeks to extend NAFTA to an additional 31 countries and 400 million people. The AFL-CIO, the **Change to Win Federation**, and most other American and Canadian unions strenuously oppose this idea.

NAFTA has hurt the **Democratic Party** as well. Although the idea originated among **Republican** policymakers and was made possible by changes in business regulations and the tax code enacted by **Ronald Reagan**, it was the Democratic President Bill Clinton who signed NAFTA into law. The biggest job losses in U.S. industries have come in automotives, electronics, textiles, and lumber and wood products concerns. This trend has weakened labor unions in those industries— and unions collectively form an interest group more likely to support Democrats. California and New York have lost the most jobs, but there has also been significant contraction in Michigan, Ohio, and parts of Texas that historically supported Democratic candidates. Some organized labor advocates argue that the Democratic Party has abandoned workers and is as firmly under the control of business interests as its Republican rival. They argue that labor should stop supporting the Democrats and shift its financial resources to grassroots organizing. The battle over NAFTA and other free trade agreements has resulted in unorthodox political swings in which the call for **protectionism** is now confined to figures who disagree on most other matters, such as the independent socialist Senator Bernard Sanders and ultraconservatives such as Patrick Buchanan.

Those who assert that the two major parties largely agree on the importance of free trade are, at present, correct. For that reason it is unlikely that the United States will abrogate NAFTA, though there is some sentiment for Canada to do so. In recent years, the overall passion of businesses to relocate in Mexico has cooled considerably due to violence associated with drug trafficking in Mexico and the reality that employers now have the flexibility to move to even lower-waged nations. The cooling of ardor for Mexico notwithstanding, it seems likely that progress toward realizing an FTAA agreement will continue. The long-term implications of such a scenario are uncertain, though current trends do not give hope to those calling for a "reindustrialization" of the United States.

Suggested Reading

David Bacon, *The Children of NAFTA: Labor Wars on the U.S./Mexico Border*, 2004; Maxwell Cameron and Brian W. Tomlin, *The Making of NAFTA: How the Deal Was Done*, 2002;

Economic Policy Institute, "NAFTA's Impact on the States," http://www.epi.org/pages/briefingpapers_nafta01_impactstates/, accessed April 30, 2011.

NO-STRIKE PLEDGE

A no-strike pledge is a self-defining term that refers to an agreement not to engage in work stoppages. No-strike pledges are generally linked to peaceful dispute resolutions. Under this type of agreement, **strikes** are usually deemed illegal, though there is a more limited form of no-strike pledge that stipulates the conditions that must be met before a strike is justified.

In U.S. history, the term is generally associated with an accord reached between labor unions and the **National War Labor Board** (NWLB) during World War II. The **American Federation of Labor**, the **Congress of Industrial Organizations**, and most of their constituent members agreed to no-strike agreements to ensure that wartime production would not be interrupted. In exchange for their pledge, the NWLB granted unions key concessions over **wages**, **fringe benefits**, the length of the workday, the creation of formal **grievance** procedures, and other matters. Unions benefited greatly from **maintenance of membership** clauses that compelled workers to remain in their unions during the life of a **contract**. Many also applauded **arbitration** provisions that set up formal mechanisms for settling capital/labor disputes. Even **communist** organizations agreed to no-strike pledges during the war. Among the few exceptions was the **United Mine Workers of America** (UMWA), which withdrew its adherence to the pledge and staged walkouts. UMWA President **John L. Lewis** claimed that employers violated their part of the bargain, though his critics charged that Lewis was merely exploiting the war to advance UMWA demands he could not have negotiated during peacetime. Some historians believe that the UMWA's wartime strikes were a tactical mistake that served to justify anti-union legislation during and after the war. Most unions enjoyed the industrial peace that the pledge assured under the NWLB. When the war ended, it was employers—not unions—who pushed for termination of NWLB programs. The end of agreements associated with the pledge touched off intense conflict: 1946 was one of the most strike-torn years in American history.

No-strike pledges are rare today, though some construction unions agree to them as part of a strategy to win contract bids. Municipal governments and others seeking to build large-scale projects such as stadiums and convention centers desire no-strike agreements as a way to keep costs predictable and finish projects on time. Unions agree to them to allay employer fears. Public employees are often required to take no-strike pledges as well. In the current climate, however, strikes of all sorts are rare.

Suggested Reading

Nelson Lichtenstein, *Labor's War at Home*, 1987; "Padres Ballpark Work to Proceed Uninterrupted; No-Strike Clause Part of 'Historic Agreement,'" *San Diego Union-Tribune*, January 15, 2000; Robert Zieger, *John L. Lewis*, 1988.

NUSSBAUM, KAREN

Karen Nussbaum (April 25, 1950–) is the founder of **9to5: National Association of Working Women** (9to5), has served as an officer in the **Service Employees International Union** (SEIU), headed the Women's Bureau at the **Department of Labor**, led the Working Women's Department of the **American Federation of Labor-Congress of Industrial Organizations** (AFL-CIO), and currently leads Working America, an agency that works with non-unionized workers.

Nussbaum was raised in Chicago, Illinois, and attended the University of Chicago, before dropping out and eventually finishing her bachelor's degree at Goddard College in 1975. After leaving the University of Chicago, she moved to Boston and took a clerical job at Harvard University. Even by the standards of the early 1970s, her $2 per hour pay was too low to allow a decent standard of living. Nussbaum began to meet with other female Harvard workers and, in 1972, began publishing a newsletter to draw attention to their situation. That newsletter became the genesis for 9to5, an organization formed in 1973 that expanded its reach throughout the greater Boston area. Its campaign against Harvard embarrassed the university but resulted in higher **salaries** and improved working conditions for working women. Nussbaum was aided by SEIU, which chartered office workers as a **local**; in 1981, this organization became the national District 925 of the SEIU. Nussbaum served as executive director of 9to5 from 1977 to 1993, and was president of SEIU District 925 from 1981 to 1993. (The two are allied, but distinct.) Nussbaum also served on SEIU's executive board and headed its Office Workers Division, which served more than 170,000 members.

Nussbaum left both 9to5 and SEIU District 925 in 1993, when President Bill Clinton appointed her to head the Women's Bureau at the **Department of Labor**, a post she held through 1996. She helped rebuild the Women's Bureau, which had been downsized by President George H. Bush, of whom Nussbaum was a harsh critic. She was especially scornful of Bush's decision to close numerous Women's Bureau regional offices. Nussbaum is also credited with the survey "Working Women Count!," a comprehensive study of working women in the 1990s. She supported President Clinton's initiative that led to passage of the **Family and Medical Leave Act**. In 1995, SEIU national president **John Sweeney** became the president of the AFL-CIO, and he convinced Nussbaum to direct the AFL-CIO's Working Women's Department (WWD), an initiative that began in 1997. Nussbaum was placed in charge of overseeing policy, outreach, political activity, and organizing efforts for the WWD.

In 2003, the AFL-CIO helped create Working America, a nonprofit, nonpartisan lobby group that engages in grassroots organizing and voter education campaigns. It officially works with non-unionized workers, though it is allied with the AFL-CIO and part of its charge is to advance AFL-CIO issues and initiatives. Nussbaum currently heads Working America, and the organization has been active in mobilizing voters. It claims to represent some 1 million non-unionized working people and lobbies for reforms in health care, **living wage** legislation,

pension protection, workplace rights, educational reform, and curtailment of corporate abuses.

Suggested Reading

Ellen Cassedy and Karen Nussbaum, *Nine to Five: The Working Woman's Guide to Office Survival*, 1983, 1989; Mary Hartman, ed., *Talking Leadership: Conversations with Powerful Women*, 1999; "Working America," http://www.workingamerica.org/, accessed April 28, 2011.

O

OCCUPATIONAL SAFETY AND HEALTH ACT (1970)

The 1970 Occupational Safety and Health Act (OSHA) is the major piece of federal legislation assuring that workers are protected from occupation and health hazards in their workplaces. It was the culmination of a long campaign to alleviate structural and environmental dangers associated by work. Although OSHA is by no means a perfect law and it has many critics, most American jobs are considerably safer now than before OSHA went into effect.

The American **Industrial Revolution** produced a dizzying array of new goods that brought wealth to society as a whole, but the toll it exacted on the **working class** was often appalling. In the largely unregulated business environment of the 19th century, factories often lacked such now-standard protections as safety guards for machines with sharp blades, shields to prevent hair and clothing from getting caught in gears, protective clothing for workers, or rules for how underground mines should be shored to prevent cave-ins or how poisonous gases were to be dispersed. Stonecutters and textile workers toiled in nonventilated rooms and developed complications such as pneumonia, silicosis, and **black lung disease** at early ages. Most stonecutters, for instance, died in their early forties. Iron puddlers and steelworkers worked in rooms at temperatures of more than 100°F and handled molten metals that could result in instant death if spilled. In the 1890s, railroad work was so dangerous that one of every 306 employees was killed on the job and one in 30 suffered a serious injury.

The deaths of 146 women during the 1911 **Triangle Factory Fire** fueled **Progressive Era** plans to regulate the workplace and address some of the more horrifying conditions, but American jobs remained largely unhealthy, unsanitary, and dangerous. In the 1920s, roughly 20,000 workers were killed and 2.6 million were injured each year. In 1945, 16,500 workers were killed and 2.6 million were injured.

Despite nearly a century of agitation for government safety regulations, it was not until the 1960s that the movement to legislate worker safety began to gather force. During that decade, approximately 14,000 workers died each year and injury rates began to climb after a dip during the 1950s. Greater public awareness certainly contributed to the push for OSHA, and the emerging environmental movement may have also played a role. The greatest call for change came from the workers themselves, who voiced concerns to their unions and their employers about unsafe working conditions and occupational diseases, some of which were not officially recognized at the time. The slowness of businesses and unions alike to recognize the need for improved standards led to a spate of **grievances** and **wildcat strikes** that hastened Congressional action. A milder health and safety bill was passed at the behest of President Richard Nixon in 1968, but Senator Harrison Williams and Representative James O'Hara advanced a stronger bill that had first been discussed during Lyndon Johnson's presidency. That bill became OSHA, which President Nixon signed in 1970. Organized labor hailed it a veritable safety bill of rights.

The OSHA legislation created three permanent agencies that are under the auspices of the **Department of Labor**: (1) the Occupational Safety and Health Administration (also known as OSHA), which administers and enforces the bill, and creates workplace health and safety standards; (2) the National Institute for Occupational Safety and Health, the research arm of OSHA; and (3) the Occupational Safety and Health Review Commission, which decides cases in which employers are alleged to be out of compliance with the law. The law requires employers to adhere to its standards and to maintain careful records of injuries, employee illnesses, and exposure to toxic materials. OSHA is expected to investigate allegations that workplace safety has been compromised and it has the right to undertake periodic inspections. Its standards are considered to be the minimum guidelines—states may, if they wish, enact stronger standards.

Many observers consider OSHA to be the most significant piece of pro-labor legislation since the New Deal. It was the first federal legislation in U.S. history to grant the government the right to inspect workplaces and punish employers who made people work in unsafe and unhealthy environments. When first enacted, it covered 56 million workers at 3.5 million workplaces. It now covers nearly all American workers and workplaces.

OSHA faces critics on both sides. Its regulatory and punitive powers have engendered some resentment within the business community, with critics regarding it as a special interest arm of organized labor, though others hail it for reducing lost production due to injury and illness. Small businesses have complained that they are forced to make changes in their operations that they cannot afford. (In truth, OSHA standards differ according to the size of the workplace.) Labor unions and other worker organizations also have complaints. Some accuse OSHA of being obsessed with inspection and data collection to the detriment of enforcement and drafting new regulations. Penalties for OSHA violations are relatively mild, and labor advocates point to the fact there have been only 12 criminal violations in the 40-plus years of OSHA's existence. Labor also contends that too many OSHA posts involve political appointments and that **Republican** administrations have weakened OSHA by placing biased pro-business advocates in key positions.

The hue and cry of critics notwithstanding, OSHA's very existence has had a dramatic impact on workplace safety. There has been a 60 percent decrease in workplace deaths since the law went into effect, and a 40 percent drop in injury rates. OSHA also operates training programs and partners with companies that seek to improve their safety records. It has also led the way in producing breakthroughs in areas such as ergonomics, regulation of the handling of pesticides and hazardous materials, and ways to curtail repetitive strain injury—the prevalence of the last condition has skyrocketed with the **computer revolution**. Recent data indicate continuing progress in the effort to make American workplaces safer. OSHA cites a

22 percent decrease in workplace injuries between 2005 and 2009. In 2004, some 5,724 workers died on the job; by 2009, that figure had dipped to 4,340 out of a workforce of 154.7 million. This is still a high figure, but OSHA attributes progress to increases in inspections. In 2010, the agency handed out 96,742 citations, a 15.3 percent increase since 2006.

Suggested Reading

Department of Labor, "Occupational Safety & Health Administration," http://www .osha.gov/index.html, accessed May 2, 2011; Thomas Mcgarity and Sidney A. Shapiro, *Workers at Risk: The Failed Promise of the Occupational Safety and Health Administration*, 1993; United States Department of Labor, *Reflections on OSHA's History*, 2009.

OIL WORKERS

Petroleum was not widely used in the United States until after 1857, when Edward Drake drilled the first successful oil well in Titusville, Pennsylvania. Most of the early oil deposits were refined into kerosene. Larger deposits found in Oklahoma in 1859, in California in 1875, and in Texas in 1887 hastened the development of new uses for "black gold," as oil was dubbed. It also led to the emergence of a Gilded Age monopoly. In 1865, John Rockefeller and his partner, Henry Flagler, established Standard Oil; within 12 years, their company produced one-tenth of the nation's oil and would soon become so powerful that it would overwhelm most of its competitors. By 1890, it controlled nearly 90 percent of all oil refining, a stranglehold it held until antitrust legislation broke it into 34 separate firms in 1911.

Lost in the story of Standard Oil's rise is the plight of oil workers, nicknamed "wildcatters," perhaps because many wells were located in remote areas. Drillers, pumpers, carpenters, and pipe fitters worked long hours for low **wages**. Sudden explosions, fire, fractured pipe, and other hazards made oil work among the most dangerous jobs in America. Oil drillers attempted to organize in 1889, but it took another 10 years before the Brotherhood of Oil and Gas Well Workers formed a national union and received a charter from the **American Federation of Labor** (AFL). It lasted just a few years and folded in 1904. Low wages, a 1905 **wildcat strike**, and rising demand for petroleum associated with the development of the automobile industry assured that new unionization efforts would emerge. Standard Oil of New Jersey attempted to stave off oppositional unionization in 1918 by setting up a **company union**. That so-called Employee Representative Plan survived into the 1930s, when New Deal legislation expressly forbade company unions.

A more important union emerged among oil-rig workers in California's San Joaquin Valley in 1917, where workers demanded an **eight-hour** workday. In early 1918, the AFL charted the International Association of Oil Field, Gas Well and Refinery Workers of America (OFGWRWA) as one of its few **industrial unions**. The OFGWRWA engaged in a strike during 1918, which forced companies to abandon the 12-hour workday and establish a $4 per day minimum wage. At the time, Gulf Coast oil workers were engaged in their own battles for better conditions, but they largely failed to achieve their goals. They and others soon turned to the OFGWRWA, whose membership rose from approximately 4,000 in 1918 to more than 40,000 two years later. That figure plummeted to just 3,000 after a failed California strike in 1921, and by 1926 the OFGWRWA had shrunk to 700 **dues**-paying members; its membership subsequently fell to just 300 in 1933. The weakened union quit the AFL in 1937, changed its name to the Oil Workers International Union (OWIU), and joined the **Congress of Industrial Organizations** (CIO). The OWIU engaged in several unsuccessful strikes against Mid-Continental Petroleum Company, a firm notorious for flaunting labor laws, between 1938 and 1940, but it gained new strength under the **National War Labor Board** (NWLB) during World War II. The attempt of several companies to abrogate NWLB standards led to a brief strike in 1945, which was settled by a government board that imposed an 18 percent pay increase and confirmed the OWIU as a contending force within the oil fields.

The 1955 AFL-CIO merger led to consolidation between the OWIU and several other unions and a rechristening of the organization as the Oil, Chemical, and Atomic Workers Union (OCAW). The name change also reflected the growing importance of energy in the United States. The World War II Manhattan Project, which developed the atomic bomb, also led to production of electricity from fissionable materials. The first U.S. application of atomic energy occurred in Idaho in 1951; in 1957, the first U.S. commercial power plant opened in Shippingport, Pennsylvania. World War II also gave birth to the plastics industry; plastics are petroleum-based products whose manufacture also entails the use of chemicals. Chemicals were already important in industries such as fertilizer production, but it was not until 1944 that American workers formed the International Chemistry Workers Union.

Given the volatility and toxicity of substances handled by workers, safety and health concerns became a major focus of OCAW activity. This often meant taking on government boards such as the Department of Energy, which licenses power plants; the Nuclear Regulatory Agency, which is responsible for safety in nuclear power plants; the Department of the Interior, which approves most onshore oil drilling; and the U.S. Minerals Management, which oversees offshore drilling. The OCAW was among the leaders in lobbying for the passage of the 1970 **Occupational Safety and Health Act** and, by 1973, all OCAW **collective bargaining** agreements included specific health and safety clauses. The last holdout against such clauses was the Shell Oil Company, and a four-month strike against that company in 1973 drew support from unions around the world and from a wide coalition of environmental activists.

Among OCAW's most prominent fights was the tragic case of Karen Silkwood, a worker for the Kerr-McGee Nuclear Corporation in Oklahoma. Silkwood was exposed to massive plutonium radiation in 1974. In turn, she revealed lax practices in the nuclear power industry, including the disappearance of 44 pounds of enriched uranium. She died in a mysterious car crash that many people believe was a company-directed assassination. That allegation was never proved, but Silkwood's heirs sued; they reached a $1.38 million settlement with

Kerr-McGee. Long-time OCAW official Tony Mazzocchi (1926–2003), a personal friend of Silkwood, pressured the OCAW to lobby even harder for improved work-place safety standards. Silkwood's death galvanized many OCAW members, and some of its rank-and-file, already influenced by the **counterculture**, moved sharply to the left politically.

The BASF **lockout** of the 1980s further radicalized OCAW members. The more than five-year lockout of 1,200 chemical workers at BASF's Geismar, Louisiana, facility began in 1984. It occurred during the brutal **concessions and downsizing** campaigns of the 1980s, but the OCAW was able to win a partial victory through a creative international **corporate campaign** against the German-based BASF. The experience also led Mazzocchi and other OCAW activists to lose faith in conventional politics and contemplate the need for a **labor party**. In 1990, Mazzocchi announced the formation of Labor Party Advocates (LPA) to explore that possibility. In 1991, he quit as secretary-treasurer of the OCAW to devote his energy to the LPA. The LPA reformed as the Labor Party in 1996. The party has mostly been a moral voice, has not enjoyed electoral success, and was moribund as of 2011.

The OCAW found itself at the fore of battles to stop **runaway shops**. In 1992, it won a $24 million settlement against American Home Products, which misused the U.S. tax code to relocate profitable plants to tax havens in Puerto Rico and other Caribbean islands. Ironically, the OCAW became a victim of the offshore economy.

An oil slick is seen as the *Deepwater Horizon* oil rig burns in the Gulf of Mexico on April 21, 2010. The oil platform sank on April 22 after it burned for 36 hours following a massive explosion. Eleven oil workers were killed. (AP/Wide World Photos)

It lost nearly half of its membership between 1980 and 1995 as offshore oil drilling shifted farther out to sea, sometimes beyond the reach of U.S. labor laws. The union nearly merged with the **United Mine Workers of America** in 1988, but remained a separate entity until 1999, when it merged with the United Paperworkers to form PACE, the Paper Allied-Industrial, Chemical, and Energy Workers International Union, which represented more than 300,000 workers in the pulp, paper, chemical, petroleum, nuclear, and pharmaceutical industries. PACE, in turn, merged with the **United Steelworkers of America** (USWA) in 2005. It is estimated that approximately 80,000 of the USWA's 860,000 members come from occupations once represented by the OCAW. The USWA continues the OCAW's emphasis on environmental action, workplace safety, and employee health issues.

On April 20, 2010, an explosion at British Petroleum's Deepwater Horizon oil platform, located 41 miles off the Louisiana coast, sent billions of gallons of oil gushing into the Gulf of Mexico. Much of the media focus concentrated on the environmental degradation of the region; less discussed was the fact that 11 workers died in the accident. They are a poignant reminder that oil work remains a dangerous occupation.

Suggested Reading

Ray Davidson, *Challenging the Giants: A History of the Oil, Chemical and Atomic Workers*, 1988; Matthew Yeomans, *Oil: Anatomy of an Industry*, 2004; Daniel Yergin, *The Prize: The Epic Quest for Oil, Money, and Power*, 1991.

OPEN SHOP

An open shop is a workplace that does not require employees to join a union, even if one represents other employees. Numerous **right-to-work** states legally enforce the open shop, but most places in the country allow individual employers to institute an open-shop policy unless a union specifically negotiates a contract stipulating a **union shop**. Such clauses are relatively rare in the contemporary job market, though unions routinely negotiate the right to collect an **agency fee** from workers who choose not to join the bargaining unit. Such workers do not pay **dues**, but because they enjoy all the privileges that union workers receive under a contract, they reimburse the union for **wages**, **fringe benefits**, and improved working conditions that they enjoy because of the union's efforts. Whenever they can, however, unions oppose both open shops and agency fees. In their view, even those paying agency fees are "free riders" to a large extent, as they enjoy all contract provisions but pay for only a fraction of them.

The open-shop movement dates from a 1903 plan developed by the **National Association of Manufacturers**. It was designed as an indirect antilabor ploy to discourage union membership. The **American Federation of Labor** spoke out vociferously against the movement. The **Industrial Workers of the World** (IWW) saw open-shop employees as akin to **scabs** and encouraged its members to dispense workplace justice against workers who refused to join the union—mostly in the form of petty harassment that included calling the workers names such as "Scissor

Bill" and "Mr. Block." IWW workers also refused to cooperate with open-shop advo-cates on the job and encouraged the community to ostracize them. The post-World War I **Red Scare** led to a resurgence of open-shop schemes, especially those associ-ated with the **American Plan** of the 1920s. The American Plan equated the open shop with patriotism, self-reliance, and individualism, and accused unions of coercing membership.

Many of the methods used under the American Plan were deemed **unfair labor practices** under the **National Labor Relations Act**, but the 1947 **Taft-Hartley Act** opened the door for right-to-work legislation that most unions regard as the open-shop movement under a new guise.

Suggested Reading

Irving Bernstein, *The Lean Years*, 1960; Mike Davis, *Prisoners of the American Dream*, 1988; Joan Pynes, *Human Resources Management for Public and Nonprofit Organizations*, 2004.

OPERATION DIXIE

Operation Dixie was an unsuccessful attempt by the **Congress of Industrial Organizations** (CIO) to unionize southern states during the years 1946 through 1953. The CIO's failure to reverse the historical animus against labor unions in the South resonates to the present day.

By the end of World War II, the CIO had more than 250,000 southern mem-bers, largely in textiles, mining, and the steel industry. Nonetheless, CIO leaders worried that the spread of **right-to-work** laws in the South would accelerate an ongoing trend in which cost-conscious and/or anti-union northern capitalists relo-cated their operations in the region. The CIO's response to this fear was an attempt to advance unionization to the South and thus level the playing field. Affiliated unions donated more than $1 million to support the efforts of more than 400 organizers.

Operation Dixie began to unravel quickly. The CIO's commitment to racial equal-ity faced stiff opposition from southern segregationists. The depth of opposition they faced in the South also surprised CIO organizers. They were often the targets of threats and violence, and the region's employers, newspapers, politicians, law enforcement officials, white-supremacy groups, and churches launched vicious propaganda campaigns to discredit the CIO. Accusations that federation leaders were **communists** proved especially damaging. In cases that presaged the tactics that would be used against the **civil rights movement**, local elites and the police made alliances with the Ku Klux Klan to harass, threaten, and beat CIO organizers. Especially shocking was the vehemence with which many southern churches opposed the CIO. The union attempted to compensate by adding evangelical Protestant organizers, but made only modest gains through this tactic. Against all odds, though, organizers managed to found more than 300 new unions and enjoyed modest success among timber workers, especially among African Americans.

In the end, however, the opposition proved too powerful and the passage of the 1947 **Taft-Hartley Act** signaled political hostility toward organized labor. Most CIO regional offices closed before the end of 1949, at which point only some 400,000 CIO members remained in the South. Subsequent organizing campaigns ceased in 1953, with the union admitting that its efforts were a failure. The collapse of Operation Dixie was among the factors that inspired the 1955 merger between the **American Federation of Labor** (AFL) and the reeling CIO, but the newly created AFL-CIO proved no more capable of organizing the South than the CIO alone. By the mid-1950s, most of the northern textile industry had fled to the low-**wage** South and New England experienced widespread **deindustrialization** and economic hardship that served as a poignant counterpoint to the postwar economic boom that flourished in other parts of the nation. By then, most southern states had right-to-work laws and union membership in the South has declined to less than pre-1946 levels.

The implications of the collapse of Operation Dixie would resonate in the auto industry in later decades. When foreign auto manufacturers such as Nissan, BMW, and Volkswagen began to build plants in the United States beginning in the 1970s, most of them located in the South, where wages were lower and unions weaker. The wage differential between the North and South also touched off a competitive battle between the regions for new businesses, with northern states offering tax incentives and other inducements to offset its higher wage scale.

Moreover, ill will exists in some circles. When southern textile firms began to suffer the effects of **globalization** and move offshore, some northern union activists saw this as rudimentary justice and issued only mild protest over the region's job losses. To this day, wages are, on the average, higher in the North, and the South remains a more sparsely organized region.

Suggested Reading

Elizabeth and Ken Fones-Wolf, "Sanctifying the Southern Organizing Campaign: Protestant Activists in the CIO's Operation Dixie," *Labor* 6, no. 1 (2009), 5–32; Barbara Griffith, *The Crisis of American Labor: Operation Dixie and the Defeat of the CIO*, 1988; William Jones, "Black Workers and the CIO's Turn Toward Black Liberalism: Operation Dixie and the North Carolina Lumber Industry, 1946–1953," *Labor History* 41, no. 3 (August 2000): 279–306; Robert Zieger, *The CIO, 1935–1955*, 1997.

O'REILLY, LEONORA

Leonora O'Reilly (February 16, 1870–April 3, 1927) was a labor organizer, reformer, and feminist. She was born in New York City, the daughter of Irish immigrants John and Winifred (Rooney) O'Reilly. Her father, a printer, died when Leonora was only one, forcing her garment-worker mother to work longer hours to support Leonora and her brother. Leonora was forced to leave school at age 11 to work in a collar factory. She joined the **Knights of Labor** (KOL) when she was 16 and participated in the Comte Synthetic Circle, a Lower East Side self-education group. There she met Victor Drury, a French-born intellectual, **anarchist**, and KOL activist, who became her mentor. Drury tutored her in French and exposed O'Reilly to books and ideas that more than compensated for her interrupted formal education.

The KOL organized women, a cause that became O'Reilly's lifelong endeavor. In 1886, she cofounded the Working Women's Society and caught the attention of philanthropist and activist Louise Perkins, who introduced her to the Social Reform Club, a New York gathering devoted to discussions of the political economy. O'Reilly supported herself in the garment industry. In 1897, she set up a **cooperative** shirtwaist shop at the Henry Street Settlement House, but the project faltered. With Perkins's help, she began taking art courses at Brooklyn's Pratt Institute in 1898 and obtained a degree from that institution in 1900.

O'Reilly served as the head resident at the Asacoq House settlement from 1902 through 1909, a time during which she also supported herself by teaching sewing at the Manhattan Trades School for Girls. A tireless worker and organizer, O'Reilly achieved her greatest fame came after 1903, when she cofounded the national **Women's Trade Union League** (WTUL), a coalition of middle- and **working-class** women devoted to bringing women into the fold of organized labor. In 1909, she became a full-time WTUL organizer, and the vice president of New York City's WTUL. As a WTUL activist, O'Reilly helped organize the 1909 New York City **strike** nicknamed the **Uprising of the 20,000**, and she galvanized protests following the **Triangle Factory Fire of 1911**. O'Reilly also became involved in the fights for women's suffrage and civil rights; she joined the National Association for the Advancement of Colored People (NAACP) in 1909. Like many on the political left, she was a peace activist and was highly critical of the United States' entry into World War I. The ravages of the war deepened her opposition to war and military preparedness.

In 1915, O'Reilly attended the International Congress of Women (ICW) at The Hague. A weak heart curtailed both her ICW and WTUL efforts after that point, and she resigned from the latter organization upon returning home. She retained enough strength to care for her old friend Victor Drury, whom she nursed in her own home before he passed away in 1918. In 1919, she attended the International Congress of Working Women, but her own fragile health reduced her role in the venture. She was able to teach labor history courses for the New School for Social Research in 1925 and 1926 before dying of heart disease in 1927.

Suggested Reading

Domenica Barbuto, *American Settlement Houses and Progressive Social Reform: An Encyclopedia*, 1999; Edward James, Janet James, and Paul Boyer, eds., *Notable American Women 1607–1950*, 1971; *Women's Trade Union League Papers: Leonora O'Reilly File*, Radcliffe University.

O'SULLIVAN, MARY KENNEY

Mary Kenney O'Sullivan (January 8, 1864–January 18, 1943) was a labor organizer and social reformer best known for her sympathy for the **working class** and her proto-feminist views on the right of women to organize for self-protection and social justice.

She was born in Hannibal, Missouri, the daughter of Irish **immigrants**, Mary Kelley and Michael Kenney. Her father was a railroad machinist who participated in the **railroad strikes of 1877**. He imparted the wisdom from his experience to his 13-year-old daughter, which formed the early core of Mary's **class consciousness**, as did the fact that she received just a fourth-grade education before being **apprenticed** to a dressmaker. Her labor awareness deepened further in 1878, when her father died and she became a bookbinder's apprentice to support for her widowed mother. Over the next decade, Mary Kenney worked in bookbinderies in Hannibal and Keokuk, Iowa, before moving to Chicago in the late 1880s. She became a highly skilled **artisan** in her craft, but grew frustrated by the fact that men routinely held the highest-paying jobs within binderies. This inequity led her to contemplate an organization for **wage**-earning women. In Chicago, Kenney organized Women's Bindery No. 1 and accepted the invitation of Jane Addams to use her recently opened settlement, Hull House, as a meeting place. Like many others, Kenney soon fell under the charismatic sway of Addams. Kenney secured an adjacent apartment building and started the Jane Club, a **cooperative** living space.

Kenney's efforts on behalf of working-class women attracted notice and, in 1892, **American Federation of Labor** (AFL) President **Samuel Gompers** appointed her as the AFL's first woman organizer. She spent several months organizing women workers in the greater Boston region, but she soon grew frustrated with the AFL. Unlike the **Knights of Labor**, which it was coming to supplant, many AFL affiliates excluded women from membership. Indeed, the prevailing view among **craft union** men was that women were unskilled workers who worked mostly for discretionary spending funds or to build up dowries in advance of marriage. Although the AFL terminated her after just six months, Kenney holds the distinction of being the AFL's first paid female official. Such was the depth of her commitment to labor that she organized on the AFL's behalf even after her dismissal.

Kenney returned to Chicago briefly before returning to Boston in 1894 and marrying local labor leader John F. O'Sullivan. In the next eight years, she continued to organize women workers, even though she gave birth to four children during the period. One of her children died in infancy, and her husband was killed in trolley accident in 1902. She compensated for her grief by immersing herself in local settlement house and labor movements. She was a mainstay at Denison House, a settlement in Boston's South End. In 1903, O'Sullivan was among the cofounders of the **Women's Trade Union League** (WTUL), a cross-class alliance of women wage-earners and their middle- and upper-class allies that agitated for **protective labor legislation** and organized women into AFL-affiliated unions. During the next decade, Kenney O'Sullivan was a leader in the WTUL on both the national and regional levels, but she quit in protest during the **Lawrence textile strike** of 1912. Neither the AFL nor the WTUL supported the mass strike because of its association with the radical **Industrial Workers of the World** (IWW). O'Sullivan, in contrast, was far more concerned with justice for the many immigrant women on strike. She was a central figure in negotiating an end to the conflict on terms favorable to workers, and she stayed on in the city for a time to direct post-strike relief efforts.

O'Sullivan was leery of the IWW's ideology, though the Lawrence strike made her even more suspicious of the AFL's commitment to women workers. For most of the rest of her life, she maintained a guarded stance toward the AFL. In 1914, O'Sullivan was appointed a factory inspector for the Massachusetts Board of Labor and Industries, a post she held until her retirement in 1934. She died at her West Medford home in 1943.

O'Sullivan was also devoted to the causes of pacifism and women's suffrage, but she was first and foremost an advocate of the rights of wage-earning women, especially their right to organize.

Suggested Reading

Robin Miller Jacoby, *The British and American Women's Trade Union Leagues, 1890–1925*, 1994; Kathleen Banks Nutter, *The Necessity of Organization: Mary Kenney O'Sullivan and Trade Unionism for Women, 1892–1912*, 2000; Meredith Tax, *The Rising of the Women: Feminist Solidarity and Class Conflict, 1880–1917*, 1981.

OUTSOURCING

Outsourcing is the practice of contracting work once handled in-house to another company. It is has proved a major threat to **blue-collar** labor in contemporary society, and has increasingly displaced **service industry** and **white-collar** work as well. Outsourcing is an intentional corporate strategy to reduce costs associated with **wages** and **fringe benefits**. It is often a major component of corporate **downsizing** plans that include business consolidation, store and plant closings, and implementation of technology to replace workers. American business leaders claim that outsourcing is necessary to remain competitive in the age of **globalization**, whereas labor unions and social activists charge that this claim is often a ruse for shedding well-paid workers and increasing stockholder profits. When work is outsourced, employers pay only for the product or services and the outside firm is responsible for paying employees' wages and benefits. Jobs can be outsourced to American-based firms, though increasing numbers are going to companies outside U.S. borders.

In the past, American industries produced most products on site. They often even manufactured the parts that went into the finished product and maintained their own service staff to take care of physical facilities and equipment. To highlight how the outsourcing trend changed just one industry, by the 1990s, auto manufacturers routinely outsourced more than 70 percent of the goods and services needed to create an automobile. Many contracted with outside firms to clean and service the factories, and some even outsourced accounting and other office work In most cases, contracted workers made far less than members of the **United Auto Workers of America** union or white-collar **salaried** staff.

In some cases, entire industries have been outsourced—a phenomenon that is especially noticeable in appliances and electronics. At the end of World War II, U.S. manufacturers dominated the global market in these products. By the 1980s, however, nearly all electronics and appliances manufacturing had been outsourced to low-wage countries in Latin America and Southeast Asia, and only wholesaling, retailing, and repairs remained in the United States. Even repair work jobs have declined, as those products have come to be seen as "disposables" whose repair costs approximate the cost of replacement. Part of that perception is due to the collapse of domestic parts manufacturing.

Marxists and other **socialists** argue that it is the nature of **capitalism** to reduce costs and increase profits without regard to its social toll. Many economists believe that charge is overstated, though the historical record certainly suggests that cost cutting at the wage level has long been a feature of American capitalism. Today's outsourcing is, in many ways, the logical extension of earlier **runaway shop** practices of relocating businesses to low-wage, non-unionized locales. The **film** industry, for example, left the East Coast in the early 20th century as much in an attempt to lower wages and flee unions as a move to take advantage of Hollywood's weather. In like fashion, shoe and textile manufacturers developed in New England in the 19th century, but fled to **right-to-work** states in the South throughout the 20th century. By the late 20th century, large numbers of manufacturing jobs in those industries had been outsourced to nations such as Brazil, China, Taiwan, India, and Korea. Treaties such the **North American Free Trade Agreement** facilitated the relocation of more than 800,000 U.S. manufacturing jobs to Mexico between 1980 and 1995. The granting of most-favored-nation trade status to China and other low-wage nations has also exacerbated outsourcing problems. Once-dominant U.S. industries such as apparel, electronics, glass, rubber, steel, and textiles are now considered **sunset industries** that have disappeared entirely or have been relegated to niche markets and are no longer mass-production industries.

Although outsourcing has always been a feature of U.S. business, its pace and strategy accelerated in the 1970s in response to soaring oil prices, aging factories, and hyperinflation. Corporate greed also played a major role. Workers and labor unions have sometimes been forced to accept **concessions**, **downsizing** plans, and outsourcing in the name of making employers more competitive in the global market. Between 1969 and 1976, more than 22 million manufacturing jobs disappeared in the United States. Workers were promised that savings would be reinvested to prevent future job loss, but this did not occur. During the anti-union presidential administrations of **Ronald Reagan** and George H. Bush during the 1980s, it became clear that breaking labor unions and cutting wages was the real goal of some firms. Workers fought back in bitter **strikes** during the 1980s and 1990s against firms such as Caterpillar, Eastern Airlines, Fieldcrest, Hormel, International Paper, Phelps Dodge, Pittston Coal, Ravenswood Steel, and Staley. A few strikes were won, but most ended badly. By the 21st century, it was standard practice to outsource jobs even in highly profitable firms. Executive office complexes, for example, found it more profitable to lay off their cleaning staff and hire outside contractors, many of whose workers are poorly paid and have no benefits.

The **middle class** has begun to pay more attention to outsourcing as now many **white-collar** jobs are now fleeing U.S. borders. Publishers, for example, now routinely outsource copyediting and printing. The computer industry has seen many of its semiconductor design and manufacturing functions shift overseas, information technology services now reroute calls to low-wage workers in India and Pakistan, and hospitals outsource such basic functions as lab analyses and the reading of x-rays. Even engineers have seen work outsourced to planners located offsite or overseas. Outsourcing and downsizing are two of the biggest challenges facing American workers in the immediate future. A few alarmists have raised the specter of a post-work society developing the United States as a result of this trend.

Suggested Reading

Donald Barlett and James Steele, *America: What Went Wrong?*, 1993; Pete Engardio, "Outsourcing: Job Killer or Innovation Boost?" *Business Week*, November 6, 2006; Michael Moore, *Downsize This!* 1997; Allison Stanger, *One Nation under Contract: The Outsourcing of American Power and the Future of Foreign Policy*, 2011; Edward Yourdon, *Outsource?: Competing in the Global Productivity Race*, 2004.

OVERTIME

Overtime refers to hours spent at work that exceed the normal workday and/or work week. Those employees who are paid an hourly **wage** are entitled to extra compensation for overtime in accordance with federal and state laws. If the workers have a union **contract**, that compensation rate might be higher than what laws stipulate.

The battle to shorten the workday was long and bitterly contested. When the first factories appeared in the 19th century, 12- to 14-hour days were the norm, and workers were sometimes required to toil even longer. Early labor organizations put forth demands to reduce time at work to 10 hours. By the time of the **Civil War**, an **eight-hour** movement had emerged. Some workers succeeded in getting their hours reduced, but few laws existed to compel employers to grant shorter hours to all workers, and those who had won them complained bitterly that their employers routinely ignored agreements and forced them to work overtime. Another favorite business ploy was to deter the shorter hours movement by threatening to reduce workers' wages in proportion to the number of fewer hours they would work. Given that most 19th-century workers already earned less than a **family wage**, such reductions would have caused further hardship.

When the 20th century opened, only federal workers had consistent standards on what constituted a workday or work week. Many other workers had won reduced hours, but these privileges existed only as long as a contract was in place. Employers routinely sought to lengthen the workday when new negotiations took place; in many cases they simply imposed longer hours in mid-contract. In almost no cases did employers pay higher wages to compensate for the longer hours.

It was not until the New Deal that the eight-hour workday and 40-hour work week became widespread. The **Fair Labor Standards Act** (FLSA) of 1938 established **minimum wages** and maximum hours beyond which overtime pay is mandatory, setting a weekly threshold of 40 hours before overtime **premiums** must be paid. Hours in excess of the standard are generally paid at one and one-half times the normal rate, though local or state standards may be higher. In all cases employers are required to pay workers for all time worked, whether the employer requested the work or not. The FLSA placed the burden of regulating excess work upon management.

The FLSA applies only to workers drawing wages. An ongoing problem in the American workplace is the number of hours worked by those who draw a **salary**. Although job descriptions generally state how long a salaried employee is expected to work, those descriptions are often more theoretical than real. Many **white-collar** jobs are built around task completion rather than repetition of daily routines, and employers expect staff to take as long as is needed to finish their work. Professionals such as lawyers, medical interns, and information technology workers are notorious for working exceedingly long hours, and much of the business world valorizes long workdays. Business often assign bonuses and **merit raises** to workers who put in long hours, but they are not paid overtime and no additional compensation of any sort is required. In the late 20th century a dramatic lengthening of the average workday occurred, as businesses argued that **globalization** was driving them to be more competitive.

Although some workers thrive on long hours, many others complain that their jobs leave them little time for family or personal life. Sociological and economic data also indicate a negative correlation between longer hours and production; that is, workers driven too hard become inefficient and cost employers more than they earn. In cases such as the medical profession, fatigued staff can make clouded decisions that are life threatening.

In recent years trends have emerged to reduce the workday and to offer compensation (comp) time to workers forced to labor extra hours during a busy period. Some employers even impose time off. These, however, are merely trends and are not backed by statute. Some reformers argue that forcing employers to pay overtime to salaried workers would ensure that white-collar workers are not abused, but low unionization rates among such workers make that scenario unlikely in the immediate future.

There is also ongoing concern about how overtime has been abused among workers for whom the FLSA does apply. Wal-Mart and Food Lion are among the many businesses that have been cited for forcing employees to work "off the clock." A favorite ploy among unscrupulous employers is to coerce employees to sign out for meals and other breaks that they do not actually take. Employees themselves sometimes abuse overtime laws. Police officers, for example, often take on extra duties such as monitoring construction sites, which pay them generous overtime benefits. Some citizens complain that, because of this extra work, they become too fatigued to perform their expected duties. Unions sometimes battle their own rank-and-file on the overtime issue. Workers enjoy the extra money in their paychecks, but continuing to accept overtime assignments works against union demands that management expand the workforce.

Suggested Reading

Robert A. Hart, *The Economics of Working Overtimes*, 2004; Juliet Schor, *The Overworked American: The Unexpected Decline of Leisure*, 1993; United States Department of Labor, "Overtime Pay," http://www.dol.gov/dol/topic/wages/overtimepay.htm, accessed May 6, 2011.

OWEN, ROBERT; OWEN, ROBERT DALE

Father and son Robert (May 14, 1771–November 17, 1858) and Robert Dale Owen (November 9, 1801–June 24, 1877) were important **utopian** thinkers whose experiments inspired the early labor movement.

Robert Owen was born in Newtown, Wales, the sixth of seven children. His father was a saddler and ironmonger, and his mother came from a well-do-do **yeoman** family. Owen was formally schooled until he was 10 years old, at which time he took up a draper's trade. He lived in London and Manchester, England, and steadily rose in society because of his innate business acumen. By the time he was 21, Owen was managing a Manchester textile mill. During a visit to Glasgow he met Caroline Dale, the daughter of mill owner David Dale. The couple married in 1799 and eventually had eight children.

Owen's father-in-law owned a mill in New Lanark, Scotland, which he had begun with Dale and Richard Arkwright, the latter of whom is credited with perfecting a textile spinning frame. Owen developed an interest in a bourgeois form of reformist and electoral **socialism** that anticipated Fabianism. He eventually convinced Dale to help underwrite a radical experiment at New Lanark, a community of approximately 2,500 people, of whom one-fifth were children. Owen had spent time among the working poor of Glasgow and had grown troubled by the manner in which the British **Industrial Revolution** had bred poverty, unhealthy cities, and social misery. New Lanark offered a different model. Owen envisioned industrial villages as an alternative to sprawling cities, and he sought to empower rather than disenfranchise workers. He eliminated the "truck system" at New Lanark, an oppressive practice in which workers were paid partly or entirely in script redeemable only at company stores and establishments. New Lanark workers not only received **wages**, but also participated in corporate profit sharing. The local store and bakery were run on a **cooperative** basis and offered goods below market rates. Owen also outlawed **child labor** for those younger than age 10, a radical idea for its day. Even more advanced was the tuition-free school he established to educate **working-class** offspring, and the various dances, concerts, and recreational opportunities he provided. New Lanark also offered free health care. New Lanark is often cited as having the first infants' school in Great Britain.

Productivity at New Lanark outpaced that of similar communities, but investors nonetheless complained of the expense of maintaining Owen's social experiments. After 1828, New Lanark operated more in accordance with other textile villages, but Owen's legacy was such that it remained a more desirable place to live and work than most comparable places. Owen was disappointed by decisions to transform New Lanark, and he purchased land in Indiana in the United States in 1824, with the idea in mind of continuing his utopian experiments there. The community was named New Harmony, as the site of "Harmony" was purchased from the religious Rappite community that was already established there. By then Owen was enamored with the ideas of French utopian socialist Charles Fourier (1772–1837). Fourier envisioned a cooperative community of precisely 1,620 individuals.

Work and society would be organized into occupational groups called "phalanxes," and community members would live in four-story *phalanstéres* in which social status was conferred by literally moving up until one reached the top floor. Fourier also placed great emphasis on education, work incentives, and the virtues of village life. His ideals won popularity among **anarchists**, and American-born anarchist Josiah Warren was among New Harmony's residents.

Owen planned to build a *phalanstére* at New Harmony, but the community never advanced much beyond the cabins originally constructed by the Rappites. Internal squabbles, including complaints over Owen's **paternalism**, which clashed with the individualism of anarchists in residence, doomed the experiment. It lasted from just 1825 to 1829. Robert Owen's ideals inspired numerous other experiments, however, including the Forestville Commonwealth of Earlton, New York, and several other industrial villages in Great Britain. Moreover, his vision of a cooperative society formed one of the touchstone values for millions of workers throughout the 19th century.

Robert Owen's legacy also lived on in the person of his eldest son, Robert Dale Owen, who lived briefly at New Harmony. He was also aligned with New York's **Workingmen's movement**, primarily using it as a vehicle to advance a plan for state-funded public education he developed in conjunction with Frances Wright. Robert Dale met the Scottish-born Wright at New Harmony and traveled with her to Wright's controversial experimental community in Nashoba, Tennessee. Nashoba was biracial and sought to prepare **slaves** for freedom, though many of the black residents there also complained of paternalism. Robert Dale Owen co-edited newspapers with Wright at New Harmony and Nashoba, Owen followed her to New York City in the spring of 1829, where they started a new journal, the *Free Enquirer*. Wright was notorious in the early 19th century not only for her racial views, but also for her support of free love and feminism, and her blistering attacks on **capitalism** and organized religion. She and Owen held public lectures at a converted church—renamed the Hall of Science—and advocated public education plans first advanced by the elder Owen. Public education would also become a working-class cause célèbre.

Robert Dale Owen supported education, the New York City Workingmen's Party, and laws to make 10 hours the legal workday. In addition to the *Free Enquirer*, Owen also edited the *Daily Sentinel*, a **labor journal**, and contributed to the *Working Man's Advocate*, a paper edited by George Henry Evans. In December 1829, Owen helped oust radical agrarian **Thomas Skidmore** and his backers from the Workingmen's party, only to suffer the same fate in the spring of 1830, when political opportunists gained control over the party. Owen went on to serve three terms in the Indiana legislature and two terms in the U.S. House of Representatives. In each position, he advocated free public education, abolition of slavery, and women's rights. Although he was never again directly associated with labor organizations, his ideals—like those of his father—continued to capture working-class imaginations.

Suggested Reading

Ian Donnachie, *Robert Owen: Owen of New Lanark and New Harmony*, 2000; Carl Guarneri, *The Utopian Alternative: Fourierism in 19th-Century America*, 1991; Richard Leopold, *Robert Dale Owen: A Biography*, 2007; Celia Morris, *Fanny Wright: Rebel in America*, 1984; Sean Wilentz, *Chants Democratic: New York City and the Rise of the American Working Class, 1788–1850*, 1984.

PAPERMAKERS

The United States has a long tradition of papermakers—those workers who process wood pulp, animal skins, or cloth or linen rags into materials suitable for bags, wrapping, wall coverings, writing, or receiving typographical print. Papermaking dates at least as far back in antiquity as ancient Egypt. In Europe, the first water-powered paper mills appeared in the late 13th century, but it was the 15th-century application of movable type by Johann Gutenberg that turned paper into a commodity that was in widespread use.

Paper was still mostly **artisan**-made in Colonial America and was a relatively rare and expensive item. Newspapers, for instance, were often shared and carefully passed from user to user rather than cavalierly discarded. Paper was still enough of a luxury item that the majority of Colonists were unaffected by the special tax that the 1766 Stamp Act placed on printed documents.

As an industrially produced product, papermaking came into its own in the early 19th century when advances in France and England led to the development of machines capable of making paper in a continuous roll rather than one sheet at a time. Of particular note was the Fourdrinier Machine, which features wire frames that help process wood pulp into paper. Variants of this 19th-century machine continue to be used today.

The first organizational efforts of papermakers date to 1765, but significant unionization efforts came with the advent of industrial-style papermaking. Industry scholars generally credit a group of paper workers in Holyoke, Massachusetts, with organizing a local in 1884 that gave birth to the International Brotherhood of Paperworkers (IPB). From there, union organization spread throughout New England and then throughout the United States and Canada. Although paper was made industrially, parts of the trade remained in the hands of highly skilled **craft** workers. IPB membership was initially restricted to the upper echelon of skilled papermakers who passed the secrets of production from generation to generation, with fathers often introducing sons both to the craft and to the union. The IPB zealously guarded knowledge of the technological complexities of sophisticated papermaking machines as well as various tricks of the trade such as exactly when raw materials were properly mixed.

As a result of the IPB's exclusivity, in 1906 a rival organization, the International Brotherhood of Pulp, Sulphite, and Paper Mill Workers (IBPSPMW) formed to represent skilled, semiskilled, and unskilled workers in the mills. The IBPSPMW also served as a response to changing realities within the industry. Although paperworkers sought to maintain papermaking as a skilled craft, technological advances and the desire of manufacturers to reduce labor costs inevitably led to an overall deskilling of paper production.

The IPB endured a bitter strike in 1912 in an attempt to secure the **eight-hour** day and, in an infamous five-year strike that began in 1921, papermakers fought the International Paper conglomerate. The battle against International Paper saw strikers and sympathizers evicted from their homes in various **company towns**, machine guns erected on company property, and the shooting of strikers by company guards. The strike did, however, lead to accords with International Paper that brought industrial peace to the company for decades to come.

During the 1930s, the **Congress of Industrial Organizations** (CIO) established its own organizing committee for paperworkers, which resulted in the formation of the United Paperworkers of America. In the 1930s and 1940s, paperworker unions enjoyed great success in gaining improvements in **wages** and **fringe benefits**. In 1957, following the merger of the **American Federation of Labor** and the CIO, the United Papermakers and Paperworkers (UPP) emerged from the combination of various **craft** and **industrial unions** in the industry. In 1972, UPP merged with the IBPSPMW to form the United Paperworkers International Union (UPIU). It, in turn, merged with the **Oil, Chemical, and Atomic Workers' Union** in 1999 to form the Paper, Allied-Industrial, Chemical and Energy Workers International Union (PACE). In 2004, PACE formed an alliance with the **United Steelworkers of America**. It was not a full merger, rather a working agreement to coordinate efforts on issues of mutual concern.

Modern papermaking is quite different from both the days of handmade paper and the early days of factory production. Paperworkers now tend sophisticated multi-million-dollar machines that mix, measure, calibrate, and manufacture various paper products. While technology would seem to have given management more power in labor-management relations, the UPIU successfully battled industry giant International Paper in 1983 when, after 50 years of what the union termed "enlightened cooperation," International Paper hired anti-union consultants and sought to **decertify** the UPIU. Paperworkers responded by forming **Corporate Campaign, Inc**. (CCI). CCI used public relations techniques to alert International Paper stockholders, government regulators, investors, and influential business allies to the potential cost of full-scale disclosures of labor, environmental, and tax violations that the union had unearthed. At International Paper's annual stockholder meeting in 1983, activists raised questions that proved so embarrassing to the company and to individual executives that International Paper backed down. At the time it was hailed as a successful battle against the **concessions** wave that decimated other unions during the 1980s, but it proved a temporary measure. In 1987–1988, a strike in Jay, Maine, resulted in the loss of 1,200 union jobs when International Paper replaced them with **scabs**. That loss led many within the UPIU to revive plans first contemplated in 1979 of merging with other unions to form a more powerful counterforce to corporate power, discussions that anticipated the formation of PACE. The PACE/United Steelworkers alliance has shown some promise, including the signing of a four-year contract with International Paper in 2008.

Suggested Reading

Harry E. Graham, *The Paper Rebellion: Development and Upheaval in Pulp and Paper Unionism*, 1970; "History of a Great Union: PACE," http://www.usw.org/our_union/who_we_are ?id=0004, accessed December 27, 2010; Peter Kellman, *Divided We Fall: The Story of the Paperworkers' Union and the Future of Labor*, 2004.

PARSONS, ALBERT RICHARD; PARSONS, LUCY ELDINE

Albert Richard Parsons and Lucy Eldine Parsons were American **anarchists** and champions of the **working class**. Albert (June 24, 1848–November 11, 1887) was hanged for his alleged role in the 1886 **Haymarket bombing**. Upon his death in 1887, his widow Lucy (c. 1853–March 7, 1942) supported radical causes with even greater fervor.

Albert was born in Montgomery, Alabama, one of 10 children born into a family that owned and operated a small shoe factory. His parents died when he was young and he was sent off to Tyler, Texas, to live with an older brother who owned a newspaper. Details of Albert's childhood are sketchy, but he appears to have very little formal education beyond an **apprenticeship** to his brother, whose care he fled in 1859. Albert then apprenticed at the *Galveston News*, where he began to learn the printers' trade before the **Civil War** erupted. Although he was just 13, Albert Parsons willingly left the *News*, a situation he felt was exploitative. Parsons saw action in an irregular Confederate militia, and then joined the regular Confederate Army, despite the objection and ridicule of his employers. When the war ended, he took up farming and printing in Waco, hired ex-**slaves** to work his fields, and took classes at the forerunner of Baylor University. He also had deep misgivings about the recently ended war and came to regret his role in fighting for slaveholder rights. Albert became an enthusiast of **Reconstruction** and joined the **Republican Party**—actions that made him very unpopular in the Waco area. His paper soon foundered and he was forced to work as a traveling correspondent for Houston's *Daily Telegraph*. It was through those journeys that he met his future wife, Lucy Gonzalez, probably around 1870. The two married in either 1871 or 1872.

Lucy Eldine Gonzales—who may have been christened Lucia—was born to mixed-race parents. Although her ancestry was African American, **Native American**, and Mexican, under the South's "one-drop" rule she was considered black. Little is known of her childhood, but in all likelihood she was born a slave. For a time after their marriage, Albert and Lucy tried to advance the fiction that she was entirely of Mexican descent. This attempted ruse fooled very few and served to make Albert even more despised by intolerant Texans and white supremacy groups.

Albert held several Republican Party civil service patronage jobs, but his deepening radicalism led him to flee Texas. In 1873, Albert and Lucy settled in Chicago, where Albert took a job with the *Chicago Times*. They arrived in a city that was in the throes of reinventing itself after the disastrous 1871 fire that destroyed about a third of it. Meatpacking, steel, farming equipment, and railroad concerns made Chicago into an industrial giant and a magnet for job-seeking **immigrants**. Within

20 years, the city's population soared to more than 1 million, but expansion also brought labor strife, poverty, and social stress.

In 1875, Albert Parsons cast off his allegiance to the Republican Party and became a **socialist**. He ran for alderman twice and for U.S. Congress once on the Social Democratic ticket. Parsons also took an interest in the labor movement, first with the **National Labor Union** and then with the **Knights of Labor** (KOL). Albert cofounded one of Chicago's first KOL assemblies and agreed with the KOL's view that wage labor should give way to **cooperation**. In 1884, he broke with trade unionists and quit the Typographical Union because he felt craft unions were exclusionary, though he continued his association with the German and socialist-dominated Central Labor Union. By then, however, Albert had grown too radical for most unions, including the KOL. The **railroad strike of 1877** affected him deeply. By the late 1870s, he was known as a fiery street orator and was considered an agitator by Chicago police.

By 1880, Albert Parsons had come to doubt the likelihood of ballot-box reform and was drifting toward anarchism. Both he and Lucy participated in radical gatherings and, in 1883, Albert attended a conference in Pittsburgh, Pennsylvania, that gave birth to the anarchist International Working People's Association, nicknamed the "Black International" because of its willingness to entertain the use of violence to overthrow bourgeois **capitalism**. In 1884, Albert began publishing the anarchist weekly *The Alarm*, a paper to which Lucy also contributed. Both were involved in protests, **strikes**, and local conflicts with authority figures.

The Parsons came to national attention in May 1886, when Albert was among the eight men charged for the bombing in Chicago's Haymarket Square that rocked the city on May 4. He had been part of a call for a nationwide **general strike** on May 1 to force employers to grant an **eight-hour** workday. That had movement fizzled in most cities, partly because the KOL refused to endorse the anarchist-led action. In Chicago, however, the eight-hour movement coincided with a strike against the McCormick Harvester Corporation, where strikers clashed with **scabs**. When police fired upon and killed several workers, anarchists called for revenge and a May 4 protest rally took place. It was there that a bomb exploded, killing eight police officers. Four workers also died when police opened fire on the crowd. Parsons was not present in Haymarket Square when the bomb went off, nor was he in Chicago when seven anarchists were arrested and charged with criminal conspiracy. He dramatically walked into the courtroom and presented himself for arrest when trials began on June 21, 1886. In proceedings most legal experts consider deeply flawed and unfair, Parson and six of his seven codefendants were convicted and sentenced to hang.

Albert remained defiant on death row and refused to write a letter asking for clemency that might have spared his life. Lucy shocked authorities by "confessing" her own role in Haymarket and demanding that she, too, be hanged. Illinois authorities declined to act on her demand, but it deeply embarrassed and troubled them as she severely undermined both their credibility and prevailing gender stereotypes. Lucy directed the Haymarket clemency movement until her husband's execution on November 11, 1887.

In the years to come, Lucy Parsons would offer challenges to authority that made some wish they had taken up her offer to be hanged. She continued to work for labor and the socialist cause and published a biography of her husband's life in 1889, which included a brief essay on the labor movement. She also briefly edited *Freedom: A Revolutionary Anarchist-Communist Monthly* in 1892. Lucy Parsons was present at the 1905 organizing convention of the **Industrial Workers of the World** and is considered a cofounder of that group. Although she supported women's suffrage and was a devout feminist, Parsons linked women's rights to the liberation of the working class as a whole and refused to take part in groups that decoupled class and gender rights. Lucy was so radical that she even split with **Emma Goldman**, whose involvement with free love and birth control causes Parsons considered frivolous and inattentive to class conflict. Details of her personal life are largely speculative, though she was said to have taken numerous lovers after Albert's execution. Her public life was, however, an open book. During the 1910s, she directed her energies toward alleviating poverty, and she directed a massive 1915 anti-hunger demonstration in Chicago that she largely shamed the **American Federation of Labor**, the Socialist Party, and reformers such as Jane Addams into supporting. She spent increasing amounts of her time working on causes in conjunction with **communists**, though she appears not to have joined the Communist Party until 1939. Whether a communist or not, Chicago police considered Lucy Parsons one of the most dangerous radicals in the land. She also tackled race in the era of Jim Crow and made her voice heard in the famed Scottsboro Boys trial of 1931.

Lucy Parsons remained a radical until the end. She died in a house fire and was thought to be approximately 90 years old at time. She was laid to rest in Waldheim Cemetery in Chicago, near her husband and a monument erected to the Haymarket martyrs.

Suggested Reading

Carolyn Ashbaugh, *Lucy Parsons: American Revolutionary*, 1976; Paul Avrich, *The Haymarket Tragedy*, 1986; Mari Jo Buhle, Paul Buhle, and Dan Georgakas, *Encyclopedia of the American Left*, 1992; Alan Calmer, *Labor Agitator: The Story of Albert R. Parsons*, 1937; Albert Parsons, *Life of Albert R. Parsons with Brief History of the Labor Movement in America*, 1889.

PART-TIME LABOR

Part-time labor is, according to the **Bureau of Labor Statistics** (BLS), any job in which an employee works fewer than 35 hours per week. As of May 2011, more than 26.8 million Americans worked on a part-time basis, more than 8.6 million of whom did so involuntarily because they could not find full-time work. Thus 17.4 percent of the nation's total workforce of 153.4 million is officially engaged in part-time employment. (Some analysts place the actual proportion of part-time workers at closer to 25 percent.) Disagreement rages over whether involuntary part-timers constitute a social problem. The Employment Policy Foundation claims that the percentage of part-time workers has remained around 18 percent of the total workforce since the 1970s, and that only one-fifth of these workers remain unwilling part-timers for more than a year.

Part-time work has always been a feature of American labor, but it has taken on new urgency in recent years. Although the BLS argues that the job market has begun to stabilize, rising numbers of part-time workers jeopardize the overall standard of living in the United States. Put starkly, workers must be able to afford goods and services, or demand for those items will fall and cause ripple effects across the economy. Growing numbers of critics charge that part-time employment is due more to corporate greed than to structural problems with the economy. They assert that companies could afford to hire more full-time workers, but choose not to because part-time labor pays less and many less-than-full-time workers receive few or no **fringe benefits**. The money saved on **wages** and benefits often goes to stockholders and corporate officials—payouts that do not generate as much overall social benefit as workers' wages.

Critics and defenders of contemporary hiring practices agree that there are more voluntary than coerced part-time workers. By BLS reckoning, in May 2011 nearly 18.3 million part-time workers were in that status for "noneconomic reasons." Students, retirees, parents seeking flexible hours, and individuals making lifestyle choices make up 68.2 percent of all part-time workers. Their numbers are highest in the retail, food, and service industries, where more than 30 percent of the workforce is part-time. They are also found in large numbers in manufacturing and farming. Increasing numbers are also found in higher education; at some colleges and universities, graduate students or adjunct faculty teach more than half of all courses. In 1960, 75 percent of all college faculties consisted of full-time employees; by 2010, that figure had fallen to just 27 percent. Those persons teaching on a part-time basis average slightly less than half of what a full-time professor makes when broken down per course, and very few part-time faculty receive fringe benefits.

Most part-time workers are younger than age 24 or older than age 55. They are also disproportionately female. By 2011, more than 60 percent of all part-time workers were women. Feminists take issue with those who claim that part-time employment levels have remained constant. They note that fewer women worked in the early 1970s and that today there is a glaring gender discrepancy in part-time work. They also point out that women are far more likely to head single-parent households today than when data first started to be collected. That critique has gained potency due to welfare reforms that require part-time "workfare" as a precondition for drawing benefits. Social reformers also sometimes point to educational inequities and assert that the less education a worker has, the more likely he or she is to be an involuntary part-time worker. This, too, may be antiquated thinking given the growing number of professionals and highly educated individuals who now work part-time. Many physical and occupational therapists, for example, now involuntarily work as part-time contracted workers, whereas they were once full-time staff members at hospitals and clinics. In fact, according to the BLS, 20 percent of all health care workers are part-timers.

Unions note that part-time workers average just 55 percent of what full-time workers earn. Their diminished earnings exacerbate the national health care crisis, as skyrocketing medical costs often make quality care and insurance difficult to afford. Labor organizations also charge that employers use part-time work to discourage unionization.

The current debate over part-time work is likely to continue into the near future. Although the recession that officially began in 2007 had eased somewhat by 2011, economists spoke a "jobless recovery" in which hiring and investment levels are expected to remain tepid. Some economists believe that full job recovery might not happen until 2020.

Suggested Reading

Kathleen Barker and Kathleen Christensen, eds., *Contingent Work: American Employment Relations in Transition*, 1998; "Labor Force Characteristics," Bureau of Labor Statistics, http://www.bls.gov/cps/lfcharacteristics.htm#fullpart, accessed May 8, 2011; Cynthia Negrey, *Gender, Time, and Reduced Work*, 2009.

PATERNALISM

Paternalism refers to a relationship in which an employer exercises power over employees akin to that of a father over his children. That power can be benevolent and caring or autocratic and impulsive, though outward caring is generally more prevalent. Although some workers like paternalist bosses because they appear to be motivated by something other than company objectives, paternalism is generally controversial because it tends to infantilize adult workers.

The term as applied to work probably dates from an 1881 *Chicago Times* article, though the practice predates it. Paternalism was a central feature of many antebellum businesses of the pre-**Industrial Revolution** era and is a relic of the guild system. In the latter, children were taken on as **apprentices** by a **master craftsman**, who was responsible for their room, board, training, and discipline until they obtained **journeyman** status and could negotiate their own **wages** and leave the master's home. Paternalism was a standard feature of shops during the Colonial and Early Republic periods, and its practices were easily transferred to the first American factories. When Samuel Slater opened his first mills in the Blackstone River Valley of Rhode Island and Massachusetts, he constructed self-contained communities that included churches, shops, schools, and other necessities for families. Slater, in fact, preferred to hire entire families to work in his mills because he felt they were easier to obtain, retain, and control.

Textile production set the early standard for industrial paternalism. In small towns, the mill owner was often a town resident, employees were neighbors, and decision making took place in a face-to-face context. Many mills, for example, operated on a seasonal basis and were closed during busy agricultural periods. Even industrial giants such as the Lowell mills featured paternalist elements. Because their workforce consisted of many girls and single young women, large mills provided supervised dormitory accommodation for their female workforce, maintained strict moral codes of behavior, and provided what mill owners deemed to be suitable recreational and educational activities. These features aided in recruitment and served to assure fathers that the company would act *in loco parentis*.

Paternalism has always been a double-edged sword, however, as the line between benevolent control and tyranny is ambiguous, as is that between concern and masked self-interest. In the South, for instance, paternalism was used to justify **slavery**, with chattel servants said to benefit from, and even enjoy, their status. In many cases, adult slaves were literally described as children in need of the father's firm hand. The same logic was often used by northern industrialists, especially those overseeing large numbers of **immigrant** workers in isolated regions, such as coal patch villages.

The **Civil War** destroyed the illogic of slave-based paternal systems at roughly the same time that industrial expansion in the North ushered in forms of industrial **capitalism** controlled by absentee owners, corporate boards, and far-off investors. In investment capitalism, the corporate "bottom line" generally takes precedence over community standards, and workers are valued solely for their productivity while on the job. Urbanization and the influx of large waves of immigrants also eroded older paternal ideals; by the 1870s, paternalism was largely a rural phenomenon. When it resurfaced in urban settings—as in Homestead, Pennsylvania, or the utopian experiment of Pullman, Illinois—its creators were hailed as visionary by some reformers, but as foolish dreamers by many of their capitalist peers. Both Homestead and Pullman suffered chaotic **strikes** that put an end to many paternalist practices, as among the workers' **grievances** were complaints of excessive control over their lives.

Paternalism did not disappear, however. During the **Progressive Era** some business and political leaders concluded that American capitalism had become too rapacious and had caused too much economic disparity. In that spirit, some businesses instituted **welfare capitalism** plans designed to humanize the workplace, make workers feel as if they had a stake in the company, and give them access to educational opportunities for their children, company-sponsored recreation, profit sharing, and negotiated **fringe benefits**. A handful of early 20th-century entrepreneurs, most notably chocolate baron Milton Hershey, built paternal-style industrial towns that managed to avoid many of the problems associated with earlier enterprises such as Homestead and Pullman. Groups such as the **National Association of Manufacturers** viewed these reforms as fanciful and wasteful, but paternalism proved to be a profitable model in some locales. This was particularly the case in southern textile towns. In the 20th century, numerous northern concerns relocated to the South, where the **wage** structure was lower and where unions had to compete with state **right-to-work** laws. Some of the mills were located in remote areas, where owners replicated early 19th-century paternalism; others simply dominated the towns in which they located. Through a combination of economic dominance, paying attention to local preferences, and doling out a modicum of paternalism, mill owners and investors successfully cast themselves as community pillars and unions as self-interested outsiders.

Paternalism's fatal flaw is that it is more costly to maintain than disinterested capitalism. Paternalist benefits take money out of the corporation that could otherwise go to stockholders or be reinvested. Many paternal and welfare capitalist benefits are put into place during flush times, but when sales lag or a recession hits, pressure is great to reduce operating costs. In such situations, paternalism is often viewed as a "luxury" that can be sliced or eliminated. By the 1970s, paternalism was on the wane and was viewed by many as an artifact unlikely to survive the postindustrial era. It is premature to reach this conclusion, however. Paternalism is also a central feature of many Asian firms, which some American capitalists view as models for revamping the American workplace.

By the end of the 20th century, a "caring capitalism" trend had emerged in which some firms sought to demonstrate their concern for their employees and for global issues such as the environment and social justice. Caring capitalism has many of the same virtues and drawbacks as earlier paternalist models. Employees do, however, seem to respond to caring capitalism with more enthusiasm than to the *faux* paternalism of firms seeking to piggyback on the trend. Business seminars routinely emphasis "team building," and many companies have launched public relations programs that tout their employees as "family." Employees often view such efforts negatively and see them for what they are: smokescreens built upon rhetoric rather than substance. Administrators often fail to understand that employees' outward enthusiasm for corporate image making is merely a modern form of the **stint**.

Suggested Reading

Lee Alston and Joseph P. Ferrie, *Southern Paternalism and the American Welfare State: Economics, Politics, and Institutions in the South, 1865–1965*, 1999; Ronald Garay, *U.S. Steel and Gary, West Virginia: Corporate Paternalism in Appalachia*, 2011; Tamara Hareven, *Family Time and Industrial Time: The Relationship between Family and Work in a New England Industrial Community*, 1982; Phillip Scranton, "Varieties of Paternalism: Industrial Structures and the Social Relations of Production in American Textiles," *American Quarterly* 36, no. 2 (1984): 235–257.

PATTERN BARGAINING

Pattern bargaining is a form of sequential **collective bargaining** in which a union determines the order in which it hopes to negotiate a contract with employers within an industry. The idea is to strike an agreement with a key employer and then use that contract as a template, a "pattern," through which agreements with other employers can be reached. If done properly, pattern bargaining establishes regional or industry-wide standards that take **wages** out of competition between employers, and results in comparable contracts within the region or industry.

The key to collective bargaining is to begin with an employer that both is likely to settle with the least resistance and is of sufficient magnitude within the industry to be viewed as a trendsetter. From there, the union negotiates with others in the order in which it anticipates meeting resistance, saving the difficult negotiations for last. Once the pattern has been established, a union can, if need be, present its offer to a recalcitrant employer on a take-it-or-leave-it basis. It is more difficult to resist settling if one's peers have already done so, as there is little incentive for other companies to break their agreements and interrupt productivity to help a competitor. The **United Auto Workers of America** (UAW) used that strategy to win its first contract with Ford. After the **General Motors sit-down strike** of 1937 won a UAW contract with that company, Chrysler quickly settled with the UAW as well. Ford held out until 1941, but eventually found that it could not afford labor strife that allowed its competitors to seize its market share while its plants were idle. The **International Brotherhood of Teamsters** was also quite successful in establishing pattern bargaining in the 1950s and 1960s.

Over time, some companies came to like pattern bargaining because it stabilized their workforce. When most firms within an industry had comparable contracts, retention rates tend to stabilize and costs were more predictable.

Unions favor pattern bargaining because it dissuades management from using regional wage differentials to undercut what all workers get paid. In addition, it acts as a safeguard against rogue employers that pay substandard wages and place unionized workers at a competitive disadvantage. Nevertheless, not all unions like pattern bargains precisely because they collapse regional differences. The Canadian branch of the UAW, for example, disaffiliated from the parent group in 1984 when the UAW accepted a **profit sharing** plan and wage structure that was not acceptable to higher-paid Canadian workers.

Pattern bargaining reached its peak in the period between 1977 and 1983. With the onset of **globalization** and the weakening of the labor market, wages in most industries have been put back into competition. The UAW, for example, found itself in a condition that some have dubbed "reverse pattern bargaining" in that it agreed to **concessions** packages that set the standard across the automotive industry. The Teamsters lost considerable pattern bargaining power when **deregulation** of the trucking industry undercut industry standards.

Unions also lost pattern bargaining clout due to U.S. Supreme Court rulings on "whipsaw strikes," so dubbed because their quick duration. When an employer in a pattern bargain sought to break the template, unions sometimes called selective strikes to discipline that employer. In many cases, not all workers struck—just enough to disrupt operations. In 1957, however, the court ruled that employers could issue a **lockout** in such a circumstance. A 1965 decision said that employers could even lock out nonstriking employees during a whipsaw strike and replace them with **scabs**.

Pattern bargaining still occurs. Federal government employees, for instance, negotiate contracts whose wage scales and **fringe benefits** apply to all workers. Overall, though, pattern bargaining has declined.

Suggested Reading

John W. Budd, "The Internal Union Political Imperative for UAW Pattern Bargaining," *Journal of Labor Research*, 16, no. 1 (Winter 1995); Kathryn Ready, "Is Pattern Bargaining Dead?," *Industrial and Labor Relations Review* 43, no. 2 (January 1990): 272–279; Gary Samuels, "Bargaining in Detroit: One Size No Longer Fits All," *Business Week* 30 (September 1996).

PENSIONS

Pensions are private retirement plans, primarily employer sponsored, that are intended to supplement the **Social Security** benefits. They are an important feature of American labor because Social Security benefits in the United States are low in comparison to government-funded pensions in other Western nations. Social Security operates as supplemental—not maintenance—funding for retirees. In recent years pensions have become hotly contested, with some employers seeking to cut costs by backing out of pension agreements reached in the past.

Pensions are a **fringe benefit** that can be negotiated as part of a union **contract**, or may be granted as a free-will offering by the employer. In most cases an employer makes contributions, usually a fixed amount or percentage, to retirees or their beneficiaries based on the worker's years of service to the company. Few standards exist as to how employers configure pensions, though company contributions are usually invested either with an outside fund or within an internal pension service. Employees are entitled to draw upon these funds upon reaching a certain age, after working a number of years for the same employer, or a combination of the two. The formula used to derive the compensation generally takes into consideration the years of service and the employee's previous compensation. Several types of qualified pension plans are allowed under the law, though all share a general restriction that their formulas cannot discriminate in favor of management.

The American Express Company is credited with establishing the first private pension plan in 1875. Five years later, the Baltimore and Ohio Railroad set up a plan, and by 1930, more than 400 pension plans were in place. Unions were initially hesitant to embrace employer-managed pensions, with many voicing concern that they were forms of **paternalism**. Labor unions have a long history of offering their own pension plans. In fact, many 19th-century unions began life as mutual aid societies and some, including railroad brotherhoods, retained pension benefits.

Most unions embraced the 1935 Social Security Act, but soon realized that it fell considerably short of retirement plans in Europe and Australasia. In 1946, the **United Mine Workers of America** negotiated the first employer-financed pension program that was jointly administered by employers and the UMWA. In 1948, the National Labor Relations Board ruled that pensions could be negotiated through **collective bargaining**. The U.S. Supreme Court affirmed that right in the 1949 decision *Inland Steel v. the National Labor Relations Board*. Since then, pensions have become a standard negotiating item.

In recent years great controversy has erupted over how employers administer pension funds and the length of time they should be compelled to honor pensions. Companies have, in some cases, moved pension funds into other accounts, shifts that threaten the solvency of pension systems. Pensions are also among the first **concessions** that employers seek to negotiate. For example, auto manufacturers and mine operators have argued that they can no longer afford the generous pension plans negotiated with the **United Auto Workers of America** (UAW) and the UMWA. The UAW and UMWA take the position that companies must honor their commitment to current retirees.

The 1974 Employee Retirement Income Security Act (ERISA) established the standards with which employers must comply, but debates continue to rage over whether ERISA is a floor or a ceiling for responsibility. ERISA also set up the Pension Benefit Guaranty Corporation, an insurance plan that pays benefits to retirees when plans are terminated because funds are exhausted or firms or unions go out of business. Bankruptcy and reorganization generally do not exempt a company from its pension responsibilities, but they do make claims harder to press. Ironically, the decline of labor unions has also placed them in the same position of employers; those that operated pension plans are subject to ERISA standards.

Many employers now seek to impose "defined" pension plans rather than the generous and open-ended plans of the past. Another trend is to encourage employees to invest in individual retirement accounts, especially 410(k) plans that place most or all of the responsibility for savings to the employee. As of 2011, roughly 60 percent of workers nearing retirement in the United States had 401(k) plans. The pension debate is likely to be heated and divisive in the near future as some politicians call for cuts to Social Security and companies seek greater relief from pension burdens. Many retirees have found that their 401(k) plans are as inadequate as Social Security. The future of American retirees is in great flux at present. Rising life expectancy and the retirement of "Baby Boomers" (those persons born between 1946 and 1964) have placed a strain on both private and public pensions.

Suggested Reading

Gordon L. Clark, *Pensions and Corporate Restructuring in American Industry: A Crisis of Regulation*, 1993; Jay Conison, *Employee Benefit Plans in a Nutshell*, 3rd ed., 2003; Roger Lowenstein, *While America Aged: How Pension Debts Ruined General Motors, Stopped the NYC Subways, Bankrupted San Diego, and Loom as the Next Financial Crisis*, 2008.

PERKINS, FRANCES CORALIE

Frances Perkins (April 10, 1880–May 14, 1965) was a social reformer and the first female Cabinet officer. She served as the secretary of labor under President Franklin Roosevelt.

Perkins was born in Boston, the only daughter of Frederick W. and Susan (Bean) Perkins. The family eventually moved to Worcester, where Perkins attended Worcester Classical High before going on to Mount Holyoke College, from which she received a bachelor of arts in chemistry and physics in 1902.

A speech by Florence Kelly of the National Consumers League (NCL) inspired Perkins toward social service. She taught at several New England girls' schools from 1902 through 1904, and then at Ferry Hall in Chicago from 1904 through 1907. While in Chicago, Perkins also worked for both Hull House and Chicago Commons, which were settlement houses. She then moved to Philadelphia, where she became the executive secretary of the city's Research and Protective Association, a social agency aimed at protecting **immigrant** women and recent African American arrivals from the South. She also studied economics and sociology at the Wharton School of Finance and won a Russell Sage Foundation fellowship that took her to the New York School of Philanthropy in 1909. She obtained her master of arts degree from Columbia University, her thesis dealing with malnutrition among slum children.

In 1910, Perkins became NCL executive secretary and was mentored by Kelly. Perkins investigated safety and health conditions in **sweatshops** and bakeries and was profoundly affected by the **Triangle Factory Fire of 1911**. That tragedy led to the creation of the New York State Investigating Commission, for which Perkins served as executive secretary from 1912 through 1917. On September 26, 1913, she married economist Paul C. Wilson; in 1916, the couple had a daughter, Suzanne. In a move quite unusual for the time, Perkins not only retained her maiden name, but also defended her right to do so in court.

Perkins's passion for reform drew the attention of New York Governor Al Smith, whom Perkins advised on progressive factory legislation. Smith's successor, Franklin Delano Roosevelt,

Frances Perkins became the first woman in U.S. history to serve as a member of the Cabinet when she was appointed Secretary of Labor by Franklin D. Roosevelt. (National Archives)

appointed her state industrial commissioner in 1929. When Roosevelt was elected president in 1932, he asked Perkins to serve as his secretary of labor, and she became the first woman to hold a Cabinet post. She advised the president during a chaotic period for organized labor that saw such events as the **sit-down strikes**, the birth of the **Congress of Industrial Organizations**, and the passage of the **National Labor Relations Act**. She was also instrumental in incorporating into the **Department of Labor** key New Deal programs such as the Civilian Conservation Corps, the Civil Works Administration, the **Federal Emergency Relief Administration**, and the Public Works Administration. Perkins was also at the forefront of advising Roosevelt on issues such as the **minimum wage**, **child labor**, and public-works projects. In addition, she reorganized both the Bureau of Immigration and the **Bureau of Labor Statistics**. Perkins pushed Roosevelt to sign both the **Social Security** Act of 1935 and the **Fair Labor Standards Act** of 1938.

During World War II, Perkins oversaw the Department of Labor's efforts to shift the economy from domestic to military production. She also thwarted Federal

Bureau of Investigation (FBI) Director J. Edgar Hoover's plan to keep dossiers on all American citizens. Perkins resigned her post when Roosevelt died in 1945, but President Harry Truman appointed her to the Social Security Commission in 1946, and asked her to attend the International Labor Organization's founding meeting in Paris. Perkins championed the creation of the Federal Mediation and Conciliation Service—an agency that helps **arbitrate** labor disputes—in 1947. She also found time to pen *The Roosevelt I Knew*, a memoir of her service with the deceased president.

Perkins retired from government service in 1952, the same year in which her husband died. She taught at the University of Illinois until 1954, when she joined the industrial and labor relations faculty at Cornell University. At the time of her death, she was working on a biography of Al Smith, which became the basis for a book by historians Hannah and Matthew Josephson.

In addition to offering her service to the labor movement, Perkins and First Lady Eleanor Roosevelt served as role models for young women. Her alma mater, Mount Holyoke College, named a program for her—one that helps nontraditional students attend college. The U.S. Department of Labor headquarters in Washington, D.C., also bears her name. In her lifetime, Perkins was known for her patrician bearing, for remaining cool under pressure, and for not knuckling under to pressure from conservatives. Conservatives demanded her resignation when, in 1939, she refused to deport **Harry Bridges**, head of the West Coast **longshoremen's** union, who was accused of being a **communist**. As it transpired, Perkins was correct not to do so, as Bridges won his long deportation battle. Perkins was the center of a posthumous battle with right-wing **Republicans** when, in 2011, Governor Paul LePage of Maine ordered a mural depicting Perkins removed from Maine's Department of Labor.

Suggested Reading

George Martin, *Madame Secretary: Frances Perkins*, 1976; Naomi Pasachof, *Frances Perkins: Champion of the New Deal*, 1999; Frances Perkins, *The Roosevelt I Knew*, 1946.

PESOTTA, ROSE

Rose Pesotta (November 20, 1896–December 7, 1965) was an important activist in the **International Ladies' Garment Workers' Union** (ILGWU). Her career illustrates both the militancy of Jewish women in organized labor and the problems encountered by **immigrant** and **minority labor** within unions.

Pesotta was born Rakhel Peisoty in Derazhyna, Ukraine (then part of Russia), the daughter of grain dealers. She embraced **anarchism** as a teenager and received a good education before fleeing Russia when she was 16 to avoid an arranged marriage. She immigrated to New York City in 1913 and became known as Rose Pesotta due to a clerical error at Ellis Island. In New York, Pesotta resided with her older sister, Esther. Like many Jewish women, she found employment in the city's garment industry and took a sewing job in a shirtwaist factory. Her work in the garment industry came at a tense time. A fragile "protocol of peace" had been forged between the ILGWU and the city's major employers, but many employees remembered the 1909 **Uprising of the 20,000** and several smaller **strikes** in 1910. The tragic **Triangle Factory Fire of 1911** also remained a raw wound.

Pesotta joined a heavily Yiddish ILGWU local and quickly rose through the ranks, despite her involvement with the anarchist and free-love movements, and her outspoken opposition to World War I. Pesotta befriended **Emma Goldman** and, like her, was arrested and marked for deportation during the postwar **Red Scare**. Unlike Goldman, Pesotta retained her citizenship and remained in the country, though her fiancé was deported to Russia and they never met again. Pesotta was elected to the ILGWU's executive board in 1920, and also served as a national organizer. She continued her education and graduated from Brookwood, a **labor college**, in 1926. The following year she joined the unsuccessful clemency campaign for Sacco and Vanzetti, activism that led to her second arrest.

The ILGWU sent Pesotta to Los Angeles in the late 1920s, where she enjoyed success in bringing **Latinas** into the ILGWU. In 1933, new ILGWU president David Dubinsky promoted Pesotta to a union vice presidency and encouraged her work in Los Angeles, where she helped around 7,500 women spread among 200 **sweatshops** develop a Spanish/English bilingual **labor journal**. Pesotta also assisted them in a 1933 cloakmakers' strike that was almost broken when men broke ranks and returned to work. The fiery Pesotta used creative tactics to maintain **solidarity** among the women, including broadcasting strike messages from Mexico when a local station refused to air coverage, and holding a mock fashion show on a **picket** line outside a Los Angeles hotel where new spring fashions were being unveiled. Her persistence helped the women win a union contract despite a lack of support from male cloakmakers.

From 1934 through 1942, Pesotta traveled across the United States, Puerto Rico, and Canada organizing women garment workers. She took part in **sit-down strikes** conducted by Akron, Ohio, rubberworkers and Flint, Michigan, autoworkers. As in the case of the cloakmakers' strike, Pesotta made enemies as well as friends. She was badly beaten by **goons** during several strikes, and suffered permanent hearing loss as a result. Although she was a skillful organizer, her personal and political views made her controversial in union circles as well. She complained bitterly of sexism within the ILGWU, a charge made manifest by the fact that she was the only woman officer for an organization whose membership was 85 percent female. Moreover, her advocacy of anarchism and free love troubled Dubinsky, who desired to purge the union of **communists** and other radicals.

In 1942, Pesotta helped Los Angeles workers win a contract against several dress retailers, but her tactics and combative personality led to conflict with the ILGWU's male West Coast director, Louis Levy. When Dubinsky sided with Levy and removed Pesotta from the very local she founded, she defiantly resigned her ILGWU vice presidency and returned to work as a sewing-machine operator. She also opposed the ILGWU's decision to sign a **no-strike pledge** during World War II. In 1944, she quit the ILGWU executive board. Although she continued to be active on the local level, Pesotta never again held an ILGWU post.

World War II served to rekindle Pesotta's Jewish identity. She toured Europe after the war, was deeply moved by what she witnessed, took up the cause of refugees, and became a Zionist. Pesotta won acclaim for two autobiographical books, *Bread upon the Waters* (1944), which recounted her union organizing efforts, and *Days of Our Lives* (1958), the story of her Ukrainian childhood. Throughout the 1950s and into the 1960s, she spoke out against anti-Semitism and against racism directed at African Americans.

Pesotta's clashes with the male leadership of the ILGWU underscored the sexism inherent in much of the organized labor movement, an issue not fully addressed until second-wave feminists challenged unions in the 1960s and 1970s. Her battles also highlight organized labor's discomfort with radical activism even before the **Taft-Hartley Act** was signed into law in 1947. Numerous labor analysts believe that unions would have done better to encourage the sort of grassroots activism that Rose Pesotta represented. Pesotta died in Miami in 1965, having retired from the dressmaker profession several years earlier.

Suggested Reading

Elaine Leeder, *The Gentle General: Rose Pesotta, Anarchist and Labor Leader*, 1993; Ann Schofield, *"To Do and To Be:" Portraits of Four Women Activists, 1893–1986*, 1997; Naomi Shepherd, *A Price below Rubies: Jewish Women as Rebels and Radicals*, 1998.

PHELPS DODGE STRIKE

The Phelps Dodge strike was a brutal struggle between **copper miners** and corporate interests in Arizona during 1983 and 1984. It ended in a complete rout of more than 2,000 strikers and the 30 local unions that represented them. The **strike** is viewed as one of the worst **downsizing, decertification, and concessions strikes** of the 1980s. Evidence suggests that the Phelps Dodge Corporation's intent from the start was to break its unions. The strike had a devastating effect on **Latino** communities such as Ajo, Clifton, and Morenci, Arizona.

Long before the 1983 strike, Phelps Dodge was infamous for its poor labor relations. In 1903, the company rounded up and deported Mexican activists attempting to unionize, and in 1917, a company-sponsored vigilante committee in Bisbee, Arizona, herded members of the **Industrial Workers of the World** into unventilated railroad boxcars and transported them into the desert. In 1941, the company was forced to rehire 35 members of the **International Union of Mine, Mill, and Smelter Workers** (IUMMSW) when U.S. Supreme Court Justice Felix Frankfurter blasted Phelps Dodge's union-busting record in his brief in *Phelps Dodge v. National Labor Relations Board*. Conditions remained tense, and in 1953 a strike broke out among largely Hispanic miners. It was immortalized in the documentary *Salt of the Earth*, a classic **labor film**.

The IUMMSW also had to endure red-baiting, as it contained **communist** members objectionable to both the company and the **Congress of Industrial Organizations**. The IUMMSW was eventually forced to purge its left-wing members. In 1967, it merged with the **United Steelworkers of America** (USWA), which became the dominant union in the copper fields. Copper production boomed in the late 1960s, when the USWA negotiated **pattern bargaining** agreements with most producers in the Southwest. Phelps Dodge was forced into pattern bargaining by a USWA-led strike in 1967. The next year, the company began a relationship with the University of Pennsylvania's Wharton School of Business, which was in the process of developing strategies for businesses wishing to break unions. (Today, the Wharton School's methods are considered the definitive way to defeat unions.)

Pattern bargaining held at Phelps Dodge into 1983, and the USWA and other unions succeeded in getting **wages** raised to an average of $12 per hour. Although copper field wages were slightly lower than those paid to many other miners, most copper workers had obtained contracts providing for periodic **cost-of-living adjustments** (COLAs). Phelps Dodge officials complained that high wages and COLAs made the firm uncompetitive against imported copper, a disingenuous claim given that the company actually owned copper mines in Chile, Peru, and the Congo and was competing against itself. Phelps Dodge demanded **concessions** from various unions, including the right to pay new hires lower starting wages.

When the contract with the company expired on June 30, 1983, and no progress emerged in negotiations, Phelps Dodge workers authorized a **strike**. The two locales most affected were the adjacent towns of Morenci and Clifton, the former a virtual **company town**, and the latter a union stronghold with a heavily Hispanic population. It soon became apparent that Phelps Dodge intended to break its unions. It pulled out of pattern bargaining agreements with other producers, won **injunctions** to limit the number of **pickets**, threatened union workers, and began to recruit **scabs**. The company even tried to get courts to ban the word "scab," though it was rebuffed in that effort. It did, however, take full advantage of the current political climate. In the wake of the **Ronald Reagan** administration's firing of **Professional Air Traffic Controllers Organization** workers, unions found themselves on the defensive. Court rulings that allowed firms to hire replacement workers during economic strikes gave Phelps Dodge the opening it wanted, and Arizona's **right-to-work** laws allowed the firm to replenish its workforce quickly.

During the months that ensued, Phelps Dodge resorted to brutality seldom seen since the 1930s. Spies infiltrated **union locals**, and company **goons** precipitated violent clashes with strikers. That violence, in turn, was used to convince Arizona's Democratic Governor Bruce Babbitt to call in the National Guard on August 19, 1983. The Guard was also involved in violence—in some cases precipitating it—and several communities were transformed into armed camps, with tanks, helicopters, and camouflaged troops patrolling company property and town streets. Phelps Dodge also exerted influence on media reportage of the strike, and it rebuffed all attempts at **arbitration**. The company even exacerbated ethnic and religious tensions by hiring mostly Protestant Anglos to take the places of striking Catholic Hispanics.

The affected towns suffered tremendously. Some strikers broke ranks and returned to work, raising tensions considerably. The Morenci Miners Women's

Auxiliary set up food banks, day-care centers, clinics, and other community services, but it suffered from inadequate capital and supplies. The women did, however, demonstrate more militancy than many of the men. They constantly harassed scabs, confronted police and National Guard members, and pressured local merchants and doctors to aid strikers. The unions seemed powerless to offer much more, however, and some strikers complained that leadership was out of touch. The USWA brought in consultant Ray Rogers to launch a **corporate campaign** against Phelps Dodge. An attempt to pressure Manufacturers Hanover Investment Company—which dealt with Phelps Dodge and held union **pension** funds—yielded only minor results. Singer Bruce Springsteen donated $10,000 to strikers, but deprivation raged.

In the end, Governor Babbitt's decision to use the National Guard doomed the strike. With strikers unable to disrupt production, Phelps Dodge had little incentive to negotiate. Unions filed numerous complaints of **unfair labor practices**, but given that the regional director of the National Labor Relations Board (NLRB), Milo Price, had once clashed with unions, they stood little chance of succeeding. By September 1983, the strike was largely broken. Production was near capacity despite ongoing protests, and Phelps Dodge had put into place all of its demands, including a two-tier wage system and an end to COLAs. Price called an October 9, 1984, union **decertification** vote. Because strikers could not cast ballots, company scabs easily voted out all 30 unions. Price announced the official results on January 24, 1985, and appeals lingered until February 19, 1986. As expected, the NLRB ruled against the unions, officially ending the strike.

One study calculated that Phelps Dodge invested approximately $92,000 per scab worker rather than negotiate with union workers earning roughly $26,000 annually. The firm lost money during 1983, but copper prices quickly rebounded, and it began to realize large profits. In 1988, it paid workers an $8,000 bonus, after posting a profit of more than $420 million. The company could not buy goodwill, however, and it was cited for an environmental record that was as troubled as its labor relations. Nor did Phelps Dodge remain union free: The USWA rebuilt part of its base, and both the International Brotherhood of Electrical Workers and the Office and Professional Employees International Union gained toeholds.

In 1996, unionized workers in Chico, New Mexico, found themselves without a contract. Rather than replay the events of 1983, workers stayed on the job while their unions applied pressure through community groups, filed NLRB complaints, and exposed company environmental violations that stood to cost Phelps Dodge tens of millions in fines. Phelps Dodge again tried hardball tactics, threatening to lay off more than 300 workers, but in the end was forced to capitulate. On November 19, 1998, the company signed a four-year contract with several unions.

The Phelps Dodge strike is now viewed as an example of corporate arrogance and of the unequal power relationship between capital and labor in the 1980s and beyond. Some observers draw other conclusions as well. The actions of Governor Babbitt led some to argue that labor's historic alliance with the **Democratic Party** had outlived its effectiveness. (President Bill Clinton appointed Babbitt to be secretary of interior in 1993, further angering activists.) Moreover, the NLRB's role suggested that the board had become tainted by partisan politics and abrogated its original purpose of operating as a neutral body to safeguard the rights of workers and employers. Critics of **deregulation** point to the Phelps Dodge struggle as an example of the abuse potential of laissez-faire economic policies. Optimists viewed strikes in the 1980s as a wake-up call for organized labor to renew grassroots organizing, but to date those efforts have not reversed the decline of labor unions.

The 1983–1984 events devastated several small Arizona communities in ways not fully repaired even three decades later. In 2006, Phelps Dodge's mining operations were purchased by Freeport-McMoRan, the world's largest private copper concern. Few workers mourned the passing of Phelps Dodge.

Suggested Reading

James Byrkit, "The Bisbee Deportation," in *American Labor in the Southwest*, James C. Foster, ed., 1982; Barbara Kingsolver, *Holding the Line: Women in the Great Arizona Mine Strike of 1983*, 1989; Jonathan Rosenblum, *Copper Crucible: How the Arizona Miners' Strike of 1983 Recast Labor-Management Relations in America*, 1999.

PHILADELPHIA CARPENTERS' STRIKE (1791)

The Philadelphia **carpenters'** strike of 1791 is often cited as the first strike to occur in the new United States of America. That is probably not the case, but it was certainly the first to attract widespread notice and is one of the earliest known **strikes** in the building industry. The strike of **journeymen** carpenters demanding a 10-hour workday also signaled the manner in which older forms of work and deference were eroding even before the **Industrial Revolution** took effect.

After the American Revolution, wageworkers began to exercise independence in employment decisions by becoming more mobile and, in some instances, opening their own businesses in new locations. Necessity factored into many of those decisions, as lost trade with Great Britain and the economic uncertainties of the new nation rendered old work patterns problematic. Philadelphia's master carpenters formed the Carpenters' Company in 1724 and created a book of prices to regulate their income and the **wages** paid to **journeymen**. In 1786, **master craftsmen** drafted a new rulebook, changing how journeymen's wages were determined. In particular, journeymen began to draw a daily wage rather than being paid by **piecework**. For a skilled carpenter, this represented a wage cut during summer months. It also involved a longer workday.

In 1791, journeymen carpenters—already pressed by rising costs—formed a temporary union to confront their eroding conditions of employment. Though they were disgruntled over their wages, the major issue leading to the strike was the length of the workday, more than 12 hours in many cases. The journeymen resolved to work from 6:00 in the morning until 6:00 in the evening, with two hours allocated for meals and **overtime** pay for more than 10 hours of work. Master carpenters dismissed the strikers' complaints as unfounded, though they had, in fact, been engaged in the subterfuge of paying piecework rates during the shorter days of the winter and a flat daily wage during the longer summer days. Because journeymen were denied access to their employers' rulebook, they could not estimate the value of their work. They countered by demanding a standard workday regardless of the season. Workers also argued that they were not at their masters' bidding like **slaves** or **indentured servants**.

Master carpenters refused to meet the strikers' demands and painted the journeymen as lazy agitators and themselves as victims of an insecure trade. The journeymen lost the 1791 strike, but it proved merely to be round one of a protracted struggle. Carpenters eventually abandoned the idea of a "temporary" union, and **craft unions** evolved from the journeymen's associations formed by carpenters and other skilled workers. In 1827, Philadelphia's journeymen carpenters joined with other trade unions to form the Mechanics' Union of Trade Associations, an organization important in the **Workingmen's movement**. This citywide coalition of workers again raised the 10-hour issue and, in 1835, won a strike for a 10-hour strike and both higher daily and piece-work rates.

While the journeymen carpenters lost their 10-hour strike in 1791, they set in motion a chain of events that altered the relationship between laborers and employers. American wageworkers began to reject the **paternalism** embedded within work based on outmoded guild structures. They also demonstrated how ideals from the American Revolution had democratized American society. In particular, old systems of deference began to wither and workers no longer believed that employers were, by nature, their social superiors. This important and necessary shift in worldview allowed carpenters and other workers to create centralized, politically vital organizations that eventually became full-fledged labor unions.

Suggested Reading

David Brody, *In Labor's Cause: Main Themes on the History of the American Worker*, 1993; Philip S. Foner, *History of the Labor Movement in the United States, Vol. 1: From Colonial Times to the Founding of the American Federation of Labor*, 1947; Sharon V. Salinger, "Artisans, Journeymen, and the Transformation of Labor in Late 18th-Century Philadelphia," *William and Mary Quarterly* 3 (January 1983): 62–84.

PHILADELPHIA SHOEMAKERS' STRIKE (1805). *See* Federal Society of Journeymen Cordwainers.

PICKETING

Picketing is an organized protest often associated with a **strike** in which workers air **grievances** against their employer in public. It is generally a peaceful form of protest in which employees carry signs and banners emblazoned with slogans and/or charges against their employer. It is considered a form of free "speech" protected under the First Amendment, though picketers are also subject to public safety laws and other restrictions that sometimes allow employers to win **injunctions** limiting the scope of picketing.

The main ideas behind picketing are to publicize employee concerns and to cast the employer in a negative light. It is hoped that negative publicity will force the employer to the bargaining table, and that the presence of pickets will deter **scabs**

A striking member of the United Financial Employees Union heckles a businessman who crossed the picket line in New York City in 1948. (National Archives)

from taking the jobs of strikers. Not all picketing is associated with a strike, however. Some pickets are informational in nature, with the goal of bringing public attention to a situation perceived to be unfair, dangerous, or capricious on the part of a business. Informational pickets are often set up in advance of contract negotiations, in response to a perceived violation of an existing contract, or during a stalemate in the **collective bargaining** process. Pickets might also be used to encourage a **boycott** of a business in conflict with its employees. Unions seeking to gain a certification vote can also use pickets.

Pickets are one of the oldest forms of public protest in North American history and have been used by virtually every social movement in Colonial and United States history. Labor unions, however, have had an ambiguous relationship with picketing. Although pickets have been a common feature before and during strikes, the uncertain legal status of unions throughout the 19th and early 20th centuries placed picketers in jeopardy. First, weak labor laws made it easy for employers to retaliate against identified picketers simply by firing them. Second, manipulation of the court system by powerful business interests often led to injunctions forbidding pickets, or the application of criminal conspiracy, antitrust, or restraint of trade laws against pickets. In some cases—most infamously the *Loewe v. Lawlor* case of 1908—courts even held unions responsible for reimbursing companies' lost revenue associated with a strike and picket. Picketing was difficult even in states that theoretically gave workers the right to do so. Few laws existed to constrain employers from intimidating picketers. In many cases, company **goons** beat up picketers;

violence, in fact, was a common feature on picket lines. Strikers frequently used petty violence to intimidate nonstrikers and scabs, whereas employers used **agent provocateurs** to precipitate violence so that the company could request the intervention of police, the National Guard, or the U.S. military.

It was not until the passage of the 1935 **National Labor Relations Act** (NLRA) that organized labor won a clear right to picket, which was affirmed by the 1940 U.S. Supreme Court decision in *Thornhill v. Alabama*. The NLRA specifically protects the rights of striking workers to picket to gain public support and identifies intimidation of picketers as an **unfair labor practice** potentially punishable by civil or criminal prosecution. The NLRA did, however, set limits on picketing. Pickets may not intimidate others, deliberately misinform the public, or inflict more economic harm on an employer than is necessary to achieve their goals. The last of these conditions has proved controversial due to its inherently ambiguous nature. **Corporate campaigns** have come under scrutiny for causing excessive economic harm, but it has been difficult for anyone to determine the definition of excessive harm. It is also illegal for a union to picket for recognition if there is already a certified union in place.

Most **secondary boycotts** are now also illegal, though they were commonplace before 1935. This, too, is an ambiguous issue, as the line between an informational picket and a secondary boycott is unclear. The **United Farm Workers of America**, for instance, launched successful boycotts in the 1960s and 1970s in which picketers urged consumers entering grocery stores to avoid buying table grapes. Because they did not urge a boycott of the store itself, the protesters were viewed as engaging in informational picketing rather than a secondary boycott. Picketers must be very careful in such an activity, as they tread upon contested legal terrain and may not enjoy NLRA protection. Another tricky situation occurs when unions attempt to apply force to the struck employer by picketing businesses that have no direct dispute with the union, but whose relationship is important enough that the protest might encourage a third party to intercede. In some cases—as in direct subsidiaries supplying necessary materials or to which work has been shifted during a dispute—picketing is considered legal; in others it is an illegal secondary boycott.

Public safety laws are often used to limit where pickets may be deployed, how many picketers can be present, and what they are allowed to do. They remain a common feature of capital/labor conflict, though in recent years some activists have questioned whether they remain an effective tactic given the constraints placed on picketing.

Suggested Reading

Douglas Leslie, *Labor Law in a Nutshell*, 5th ed., 2008; *Thornhill v. Alabama*, http://www.law.cornell.edu/supct/html/historics/USSC_CR_0310_0088_ZO.html#310_US_88n2, accessed May 12, 2011.

PIECEWORK

Piecework is a self-defining term that refers to a pay scale linked to production. Piecework can be paid in lieu of **wages** or it can be paid as a bonus that rewards workers for output above an established quota. It has been a familiar practice in many sectors of American manufacturing, although it is most commonly associated with the garment industry.

Workers generally have an ambivalent attitude toward piecework. On the one hand, enterprising workers can sometimes earn more money than they might on an hourly basis; on the other hand, to do so often entails working much harder. Skilled **master craftsmen** such as tool-and-die workers and machinists once favored piecework because they could set their own pace and their production commanded high prices. The overall deskilling of work has removed much of that bargaining power, however, and with it the enthusiasm for piecework. Historically, piecework systems have often been exploitative. Within the garment trades, for example, they have been associated with **sweatshop** production.

Employers have long favored piecework as it directly links production to pay. Such a system has been used as an enticement when implementing **Taylorism** and related efficiency programs, though these have also led to resistance from workers as they are predicated upon increasing the amount of work by a greater percentage than the percentage of increased compensation. On **assembly lines**, for example, a **speedup** might double production in exchange for a 20 percent piecework bonus. Textile workers from the 1830s onward have resisted **stretch-outs** in which the workers were offered small increases and piecework rates in exchange for tending more machines. The very attempt to implement piecework has led to **strikes** and protests in that industry and others, though the garment industry has constantly sought to implement piecework because changing fashions and their ephemeral nature make production time-sensitive.

Piecework as a stand-alone payment remained in effect through the 1940s, but then went into decline in the 1950s. It was often made more palatable by combining it with a base pay rate. In general, this payment scheme has met the least amount of resistance in **homework**, sales commission work, and other jobs in which isolated individuals are responsible for production. It is more difficult to implement in factories, where the collective workforce often imposes informal **stints**.

After years of decline, piecework has made a comeback in non-industrial settings. The pay of telemarketers, for example, is often linked to their success in attracting accounts. In like fashion, maintenance and cleaning staff are sometimes paid per unit maintained regardless of how long it takes them to complete a job. Piecework also remains a staple in some **agrarian** jobs such as fruit picking. In addition, some small assembly jobs pay per piece. Even companies such as Amazon and Google employ piece rate workers. In theory, the Fair Labor Standards Act regulates all forms of employment, though many unions complain that compliance is easily avoided and loosely enforced.

Suggested Reading

Kathleen Barker and Kathleen Christensen, *Contingent Work: American Employment Relations in Transition*, 1998; David Montgomery, *Workers' Control in America*, 1979; Gus Tyler, *Look for the Union Label: A History of the International Ladies' Garment Workers' Union*, 1995.

PINK-COLLAR LABOR. *See* Blue-collar Labor; Glass Ceiling; Minority Labor.

PINKERTONS

The Pinkerton National Detective Agency was the most notorious of numerous private companies contracted by **capitalists** to sabotage the efforts of labor unions. It was so hated among 19th-century workers that the very word "Pinkerton" was used generically to refer to almost any squad of **goons** or union-busters. The Pinkertons were frequently compared to Russian Cossacks in the **labor press**.

The agency was founded by Scottish immigrant Allan Pinkerton in 1850 and is often considered the first modern American detective agency. Its earliest days were devoted to investigating counterfeit rings, train robberies, and outlaw gangs. The Pinkertons achieved their greatest acclaim for their effectiveness as spies for the Union cause during the American **Civil War**. After the **railroad strikes of 1877** and the passage of state laws giving corporations the power to hire private militias, the Pinkerton agency expanded its activities to include union-breaking. Between 1875 and 1877, Pinkerton spy James McParlan allegedly infiltrated the **Molly Maguires** and gave testimony that sent 10 men to the gallows. McParlan's exposure of this supposed Irish American terrorist group in Pennsylvania's anthracite coal region led to an increase in demand for Pinkerton services. The company's anti-union strategy took two main forms: (1) planting labor spies within unions to identify activists or expose their tactics and (2) providing private armies for employers seeking to guard company property, engage **scabs**, or **lock out** their employees.

Pinkerton's success spawned competitors such as the Burns Detective Agency, the Thiel Detective Service, and the Baldwin-Felts Detective Agency, as well providing the template for corporations setting up their own security forces. Groups such as the **Knights of Labor** lobbied for the passage of laws to curtail the hiring or creating private industrial armies and argued that such groups operated as veritable extralegal vigilante groups. The Pinkertons gained special notoriety when they precipitated violence during the 1890 New York Central strike, and again during the 1892 **Homestead Steel lockout and strike**. At Homestead, Pinkertons traded gunfire with workers that left more than a dozen people dead. Labor groups complained that the agency routinely employed thugs and ex-criminals, a charge that had considerable merit. The firm's reputation was further tarnished when **William Haywood** and several associates were acquitted of murder charges stemming from the 1903–1904 coal strikes associated with the **Colorado labor wars** brought forth by none other than James McParlan. The trial revealed that McParlan blatantly lied under oath and that he had falsified evidence. He was so discredited that some historians now doubt his Molly Maguires testimony as well.

The role of Pinkerton and other such agencies in industrial disputes slowly diminished as a result of poor public relations, a public outcry against private industrial armies, and the formation of federal agencies such as the forerunner of the

Federal Bureau of Investigation. Pinkerton agents did provide information used to repress the **Industrial Workers of the World**, a campaign that employed future author Dashiell Hammett, but public outrage from the 1914 **Ludlow Massacre** and the 1920 shootout at **Matewan**, though neither involved the Pinkerton Agency, gave impetus to movements seeking to limit the power of private industrial armies. The National Labor Relations Act expressly forbade many of the worst practices, and revelations from the 1937 **La Follette Committee** led to aggressive regulation of private security forces. Although the Pinkerton Agency and its rivals engaged in many worthy law enforcement activities—including the apprehension of Western outlaws—they became visible symbols of the oppression of the **working class**. In the period between 1875 and 1940, the very name "Pinkerton" aroused hatred and fear.

The Pinkerton agency still exists, though it no longer calls itself a "detective" agency. In 2003, it was combined with the Burns Agency and purchased by Securitas AB. Its employees are mainly engaged in building security, conducting employee background checks, providing personal-protection services, and investigating fraud. In a stunning and ironic turnaround, Securitas agents have lodged complaints against the parent company and have discussed the possibility of joining the **Service Employees International Union**.

Suggested Reading

Jeremy Brecher, *Strike!*, 1997; Frank Morn, *The Eye That Never Sleeps: A History of the Pinkerton National Detective Agency*, 1982; Stephen Norwood, *Strikebreaking and Intimidation: Mercenaries and Masculinity in 20th-Century America*, 2002.

PITTSTON COAL STRIKE

The Pittston Coal strike was a successful 10-month **strike** during 1989–1990 led by the **United Mine Workers of America** (UMWA) against the United States' second-largest coal exporter. It was an important victory for organized labor, as it came after nearly a decade of lost **downsizing, decertification, and concessions strikes**. To many analysts, it also suggested that labor unions should engage in militant actions and ignore labor laws tilted in favor of employers. It touched off a debate among unions that continues to the present.

The strike began on April 5, 1989, and involved miners employed by the Pittston Coal Group in Virginia, West Virginia, and Kentucky. Workers had already labored without a contract for 14 months. At the heart of the dispute were working conditions and benefits. Pittston sought to operate its mines on an around-the-clock basis, abolish the **eight-hour** workday, and require Sunday labor. One company official even claimed that workers merely feigned interest in church to avoid work. Matters came to a head when the company announced plans to eliminate medical benefits for more than 1,800 individuals, including widows, disabled miners, and those on **pensions**. The company's arrogance led 1,700 miners to walk out on April 5. Eventually nearly 9,000 miners took part in the strike. Because the National Labor Relations Board (NLRB) ruled Pittston guilty of **unfair labor practices**, the company could not hire permanent replacement workers, though it did import more than 1,000 temporary **scabs**. Aside from the initial NLRB ruling, most other official actions went in favor of the company. Virginia state police were used to escort scabs to the mines, and employees of Vance Security—a firm evocative of the **Pinkertons** that specialized in anti-union activity—patrolled company property. Numerous court rulings went against the UMWA, including **injunctions** limiting **picketing**. At one point, strikers attempted to bottleneck roads leading in and out of Pittston mines by driving slowly. Slow driving was ruled a violation of federal injunctions, and drivers were arrested; several spent as long as 90 days in jail, and the UMWA was slapped with fines.

Strikers and the UMWA responded with a variety of tactics. Some militants tossed jackrocks (a welded assemblage of spikes designed to flatten tires) on the roads, while others pelted scabs with rocks. The UMWA did not sanction acts of violence, but was nonetheless fined because a decision had been reached early in the strike to engage in acts of civil disobedience. When UMWA officials told a Virginia judge, Don McGlothin, Jr., that the strike was a "class war," he slapped more than $30 million in fines on the union. The UMWA responded with roving pickets and public demonstrations. It also briefly sanctioned **wildcat** and **sympathy strikes**, which broke out in 11 states and idled 46,000 miners. Because these actions were illegal, the UMWA called them memorial strikes. The UMWA quickly retreated from this tactic, however, and withdrew its official sanction for impromptu actions, though it did little to discourage **solidarity** initiatives. It also authorized a **corporate campaign** against Pittston Coal that led to picketing of the Shawmut Bank in Boston and prompted the Boston City Council to remove city funds from the bank. (Shawmut later went out of business.)

Key to winning the strike was the remarkable level of unity sustained. A sympathetic council in New Jersey petitioned the **American Federation of Labor-Congress of Industrial Organizations** (AFL-CIO) to call a one-day sympathy strike by all AFL-CIO members. That request was turned down, but more than 30,000 supporters went to the UMWA's Camp Solidarity in Virginia between June and September 1989, including the Reverend Jesse Jackson. Jackson's presence symbolized the unity of black and white miners during the strike. Strikers also received assistance from the International Confederation of Free Trade Unions, which convinced Secretary of Labor Elizabeth Dole to visit Camp Solidarity. In a movement reminiscent of the 1937 **General Motors sit-down strike**, 99 individuals illegally occupied Pittston's Moss Number 3 Mill between September 17 and September 20. Miners and the UMWA ignored an NLRB order to vacate Moss and the $13.5 million fine it levied; occupiers left after 77 hours on their own accord, defiantly waiting until an NLRB-imposed deadline had passed.

Also key to the strike was the role of women. Wives, daughters, and sympathizers of the mostly male strikers formed the Daughters of **Mother Jones** (DMJ) to offer strike support. Unlike women's auxiliaries in previous eras, the DMJ went well beyond support that extended traditional domestic roles to strikers. In addition to supplying food and child care, women helped plan and participate in militant tactics. Many of them were among the more than 4,000 individuals arrested for acts of civil disobedience, and women played the central role in planning public demonstrations and in taking charge of public relations. Several newspapers and television stations gave positive coverage of the strike, a rarity for the time. Women also helped get out the vote. The UMWA rejoiced when one of its members upset 22-year incumbent Don McGlothin, Sr.—father of the judge who had fined the union—for a seat in the Virginia state legislature after a three-week write-in campaign.

Pittston Coal lost more than $25 million in the last quarter of 1989, and it was clear the firm was losing the strike as well. Secretary Dole appointed a federal mediator, and West Virginia Senator Jay Rockefeller introduced successful legislation to protect miner pensions. An agreement was hammered out on December 31, 1989, that gave Pittston the right to operate its mines 24 hours per day, but did not allow the company to make miners work during daylight hours on Sundays. The UMWA also won preservation of health and pension benefits, and a guarantee that laid-off miners would be the first to be offered jobs when openings occurred in Pittston's non-union mines. The 1992 Coal Act went a step further and required coal mine operators to provide health care benefits and pensions for miners. Most of the fines levied against the UMWA were eventually rescinded. UMWA officials such as **Richard Trumka** received praise from many rank-and-file members for their willingness to sanction militant tactics evocative of the days when **John L. Lewis** headed the union.

The rank-and-file insisted on several minor changes in the December settlement before ratifying a new contract on February 19, 1990. Three days later, miners returned to work. The Pittston strike was an important symbolic, as well as actual, victory for organized labor. After years of anti-union activity sanctioned by **Ronald Reagan**'s administration, labor's victory during his successor George H. W. Bush's tenure signaled the possibility of reversing the downward trend. Many came away from the Pittston strike convinced that militancy led to success. Some activists openly advocated ignoring U.S. labor laws in favor of **direct action** at the point of production. Few AFL-CIO officials shared such views, but **John Sweeney** did make renewed militancy a component of his successful bid for the AFL-CIO presidency. In 1995, documentarian Anne Lewis recounted the strike in the **film** *Justice in the Coalfields*; it has proved popular among union advocates.

The strike contained notes of irony. By 1995, only one-third of the strikers still had union jobs. Technological change and a declining demand for coal led to layoffs in the Pittston Coal Group. In December 1997, the UMWA reopened a contract with the Bituminous Coal Operators Association nine months early and signed a new five-year agreement with operators, which included Pittston. Union militants protested the UMWA's agreement to work rules that allow workers to be scheduled two Saturdays out of every three, as well as a requirement that they must continue operating equipment until relieved by the incoming shift. Some complained that Trumka had become a **business unionist** and had quashed rank-and-file militancy. Overall, UMWA strength declined from around 120,000 members in 1982 to approximately 40,000 in 1998. It is not clear that militancy is truly the answer to organized labor's declining strength. Nearly 15 percent of American workers were unionized at the time of the Pittston victory; two decades later, that share had fallen to less than 12 percent. In 2003, Alpha Natural Resources, now the nation's largest coal supplier, purchased Pittston.

Suggested Reading

Adrienne Birecree, "The Importance of Women's Participation in the 1989–90 Pittston Coal Strike," *Journal of Economic Issues* 30, no. 1 (March 1996): 187–211; Richard A. Brisbin, Jr., *A Strike like No Other Strike: Law and Resistance during the Pittston Coal Strike of 1989–1990*, 2002; James Green, *Taking History to Heart: The Power of Building Social Movements*, 2000; John H. Laslett, *The United Mine Workers of America: A Model of Industrial Solidarity?* 1996.

PLANTATION ECONOMY. *See* Slavery.

POLITICS AND LABOR. *See* Democratic Party and Labor; Labor Party; Populism; Republican Party and Labor.

POPULAR FRONT

The Popular Front was an alliance of moderate and left-wing political and social reform activists that was active between 1935 and 1939, and lingered into 1949. It was formed in reaction to the rising specter of fascism in Europe and included **communists**, **socialists**, labor activists, and reformers. In addition to seeking to counter fascism, the Popular Front sought to create "social democracy" in the United States, the term denoting a form of ballot-box socialism in which **capitalism** coexists (at least temporarily) in a state that is dedicated to workers' rights, promotes the general welfare, and establishes economic justice. The Popular Front was very influential in promoting the revival of labor unions during the 1930s, though nearly all of its support was thrown to the newly created **Congress of Industrial Organizations** (CIO). Popular Front members tended to see the **American Federation of Labor** (AFL) as both outmoded and reactionary.

Before the 1930s, communists had some success in organizing workers, but mostly endured a troubled relationship with American labor unions. Shifting directives from the Communist International (Comintern) were partly to blame for the Communist Party's weak presence in the United States. Between 1920 and 1929, communists sought to work within AFL unions as the Trade Union Educational League (TUEL). In 1929, the Comintern directed American communists to dissolve the TUEL and form separate communist labor unions under the banner of the **Trade Union Unity League** (TUUL). The U.S. Popular Front was one of numerous organizations formed worldwide; it emerged from Soviet leader Josef Stalin's concern over fascist movements in Germany, Italy, and Spain. Stalin called for a counterbalancing alliance of communists, socialists, and bourgeois reformers. In France, socialist and communist workers cooperated in defeating an attempted fascist coup in 1934. At a 1935 meeting in Moscow, Georgi Dmitrov proclaimed the new policy of the Popular Front as a bulwark to defeat fascism. This constituted a change in policy, as communists and socialists had long battled each other and communists called for the overthrow of the bourgeoisie. Stalin and the Comintern, however, saw the Popular Front as a much-needed united front to combat fascism. In the United States, the TUUL was dissolved and the Popular Front proclaimed.

Reformers and leftists did not universally embrace Stalin's call. Leon Trotsky denounced it and Trotsky-influenced unions such as the **Teamsters** of the Upper Midwest were suspicious of the Popular Front. In like fashion, the Comintern's previous denunciations of socialists as "social fascists" made them ill disposed to trust the Popular Front. In 1936, Socialist Party leader Norman Thomas rebuffed the Comintern's call for cooperation. He, like many others on the left, was horrified by Stalin's purges and oppression inside the Soviet Union.

The Popular Front did, however, enjoy success within the emerging **industrial unionism** movement in the United States. The effects of the Great Depression had led many young activists to reconsider traditional modes of organizing, and some idealized the Soviet Union, which appeared to avoid the worst ravages of the worldwide economic downturn. Young **Walter Reuther** and his brothers, though they were not communists, even went to the Soviet Union and worked in a Gorky truck plant between 1933 and 1935. The Popular Front, as it existed in the United States, comprised an assortment of dedicated organizers, leftists, and communists. It also contained moderate voices, such as future CIO President **Philip Murray** and **James B. Carey**, the future head of the **International Union of Electrical, Radio, and Machine Workers** union, who was anti-communist. At the same time, the organization included numerous communists and **anarchists**, as well as a smattering of socialists and Trotskyists.

To a large degree, the labor movement's embrace of the Popular Front was tactical. New Deal reforms were under attack by conservatives and the business community, CIO industrial unionists were struggling to establish a separate identity, and the nation was riven by capital/labor clashes, many of them violent. This unsettled condition led numerous labor leaders to seek new alliances and to rethink former positions. **John L. Lewis** had actually banned communists from membership in the **United Mine Workers of America** in 1927. In like fashion, **Sidney Hillman** of the **Amalgamated Clothing Workers of America** fought battles with the communists during the 1920s. Yet both men embraced their former opponents during organizational campaigns during the 1930s. Communists had already shown their ability to galvanize support on the grassroots level through campaigns such as rent strikes and hunger marches, and they proved equally adroit at signing up new union members. They were especially good rabble-rousers.

The actual number of communists involved in the labor movement was small, however, and the party likely contained just 100,000 members nationwide at its height around 1938. (It claimed twice that number.) Communists did, however, create sympathy for labor's cause and, by extension, their own. Sympathetic individuals dubbed "fellow travelers" were an important part of the CIO's success. At the national level, several communists gained prominence. Lee Pressman became the CIO's general counsel. He not only negotiated and drew up **contracts** with employers, but also brokered affairs between the differing factions. Leonard De Caux, a former member of the **Industrial Workers of the World**, assumed the editorship of the *CIO News*. Among national unions, Mike Quill of the Transport Workers Union and Joseph Curran of the National Maritime Union maintained alliances with the Popular Front that enabled their unions to make major gains. **Harry Bridges**, an influential leader among the **longshoremen**, was reputed to be a communist, a charge he denied and one never proven.

At its most influential, American labor's Popular Front alliance provided a united, powerful, and more radical counterpart to the New Deal. Some scholars credit it with pushing New Deal reforms further to the left than President Franklin Roosevelt and his advisors originally intended. One of the great ironies of the Popular Front was that its communist members also proved good at getting out the vote. **Working-class** voters delivered Roosevelt and the **Democratic Party** a huge victory during the 1936 elections.

The Popular Front largely disintegrated due to another shift in Comintern policy. In August 1939, the Molotov-Ribbentrop Pact was signed and the Soviet Union and Nazi Germany briefly became allies. That agreement, combined with the decision to invade and divide Poland between the two aggressors, and the assassination of Leon Trotsky in 1940, horrified many American reformers and destroyed the credibility of the American communist movement. Loyal communists hewed the party line, but many quit in disgust. Germany's 1941 invasion of the Soviet Union rebuilt some of the Popular Front's support, and communist unionists heartily endorsed **no-strike pledges** during the war. U.S. Communist Party head Earl Browder even dissolved the party in 1944 in favor of a Communist Political Association that endorsed Roosevelt's reelection. Although Browder declared, "Communism is 20th-century Americanism," neither the U.S. government nor the mainstream labor movement viewed the alliance with communists as anything other than one of convenience to defeat fascism.

In the immediate aftermath of World War II, the rump of the Popular Front supported both the creation of the United Nations and organized labor's involvement in the World Federation of Trade Unions (WFTU). Soon, however, the emergence of **Cold War** unionism and conservative backlash at home shattered what was left of the Popular Front. In 1946, Walter Reuther assumed the presidency of the **United Auto Workers of America** (UAW) and quickly purged its communist members. Policy within the entire CIO shifted as well. Philip Murray, a devout Catholic who was troubled ideologically by communism, headed the CIO after 1940. Moreover, the 1947 **Taft-Hartley Act** forbade union leaders from having Communist Party affiliations. The postwar **Red Scare** accelerated the activities of congressional committees investigating alleged communist subversion, and CIO leaders greatly feared a spillover effect in which conservatives would tar the labor movement with disloyalty and seek to overturn gains made in the previous decade. In February 1948, the CIO sought to enforce loyalty among its unions by demanding that they support the Marshall Plan and that they renounce the presidential ambitions of progressive candidate Henry Wallace. The following year, the CIO withdrew from the WFTU and began expelling unions it deemed unduly influenced by communists. Nearly one-third of the CIO's total membership was purged. This put an official end to the Popular Front and communist influence within organized labor was thoroughly eradicated. But along with it, the progressive nature of American unions suffered, and militancy declined.

Suggested Reading

Michael Denning, *The Cultural Front: The Laboring of American Culture in the 20th Century*, 1996; Maurice Isserman, *Which Side Were You On?: The American Communist Party during the Second World War*, 1987; Harvey Klehr, *The Heyday of American Communism: The Depression Decade*, 1984; Joseph Starborin, *American Communism in Crisis, 1943–1957*, 1972.

POPULISM

Populism is the informal name associated with the People's Party of America. Although the People's Party of America existed for only a few years, it represented one of the most successful third-party political movements in U.S. history. It found its greatest strength among **agrarian** reformers in the South and Midwest. Populists sought to expand and become a de facto **labor party** as well, an effort that met with limited success due in part to the unstable American monetary system that tended to place the interests of producer farmers at odds with consumer industrial workers, much as the earlier **greenback** movement had done.

The Populists shared the same roots as the greenback movement and emerged from the Grange (Patrons of Husbandry) and the Farmers' Alliance, rural movements that began life as social organizations seeking to alleviate the isolation often experienced by rural dwellers. Both groups began to take on political dimensions when farmers gathered and shared common complaints such as abuses associated with the monopolistic practices of railroads, grain elevators, banks, and middlemen. As commodity producers, farmers were entirely at the mercy of others to store and deliver their products, and had no control over market prices or the interest rates on mortgages or loans needed each year to buy seed, tools, and supplies. The Grange enjoyed some success in advancing state regulations that helped farmers, particularly in the West and Midwest, while southern Farmers Alliance groups focused on declining cotton prices during **Reconstruction** occasioned by reduced world demand. Southern farms were particularly hard hit and numerous former landowners found themselves reduced to becoming sharecroppers or tenant farmers. The Farmers Alliance, in fact, first put forth the "subtreasury" plan to stabilize commodity prices that became a centerpiece of the Populist platform. This complex scheme called for the government to control prices by either buying crops or advancing loans to farmers at set rates. The government would then release or withhold the stored supply based on market prices. Populists came to advocate running this program through postal savings banks, as the post office was the one government agency found in most rural areas.

The money supply itself was of utmost concern to farmers, as highlighted in both the greenback and the free silver movements. The gist of the problem was expressed as a debate between "hard" and "soft" money. The government's devotion to the gold standard resulted in a hard money system that put relatively little money into circulation. This kept prices low, but it meant that loans were harder to negotiate and that interest rates were high. Farmers saw this situation as inherently unfair; the prices of their products were completely determined by market supply-and-demand cycles, whereas banks manipulated the supply of money. In years in which farm prices were low, many farmers failed to make enough to meet their costs and were in danger of foreclosure or falling into debt peonage. Greenbacks, or the introduction of more silver into circulation—trading at a ratio of roughly 16 ounces of silver to 1 ounce of gold—would increase the money supply and drive down interest rates. It would, however, cause an inflationary rise in prices that benefited farmers, but not consumers.

By the 1880s, various state and regional People's Parties had formed. Some of them became acutely aware of the disconnect between farmers and industrial workers and sought to develop pro-labor agendas that could break down those barriers. A major area of agreement, as demonstrated dramatically during the **Great Upheaval**, was that both **Democrats** and **Republicans** sided with elites and businesses at the expense of the **working class**. A national People's Party (Populists) formed in Omaha, Nebraska, on July 4, 1892. The platform adopted was an intriguing mix of reforms desired by farmers and those favored by the labor movement. It called for the enactment of a subtreasury plan, the abolition of national banks, the elimination of absentee land ownership, and the establishment of **cooperatives**, but also the enactment of an **eight-hour** bill to limit the workday and the nationalization of railroads, telegraphs, and telephones. Of great interest to organized labor was the Populist call to enact a graduated income tax that would force wealthy Gilded Age elites to turn over some of their profits to government coffers, with these funds then being used to promote the general welfare of all American citizens. Labor also applauded the Populist political reforms aimed at advancing direct democracy: initiative, referendum, and recall rights for voters; adoption of the Australian ballot in all elections; and direct election of U.S. Senators. For these reasons and others, the Populists attracted great support among the **Knights of Labor**.

The party did very well in the 1892 elections. Its presidential candidate, James Weaver, got more than 1 million votes (9 percent of the total votes cast) and won 22 electoral votes by virtue of winning in Kansas, Colorado, Nevada, and Idaho, and splitting the electoral votes in North Dakota and Oregon. Weaver's modest achievement somewhat obscures the success of the Populists in Congress; between 1892 and 1902, the party elected 45 members to the House of Representatives and 6 to the Senate. During the same period, eight states elected Populist or Populist fusion governors. It did even better on the local level and left a legacy of farmer political power, particularly in midwestern states such as Minnesota and North Dakota.

The Populists challenged many of the prevailing views of American society at the time: **social Darwinism**, laissez-faire economics, the view that government was not responsible for social reform, and the very basis of the two-party political system.

They promoted reforms that anticipated the **Progressive Era** and laid to rest stereotypes of farmers as bumbling hayseeds. The Populists' urban agenda served to reinforce organized labor's critique of the abuses of the **Industrial Revolution** and of unregulated **capitalism**. In fact, the message of the Populists so resonated with some members of the working class that, contrary to popular view, the Knights of Labor did not wither away in the 1890s; in many parts of the country, especially in rural areas, it simply fused with the Populist movement.

The Populists' day as a contending major party was brief, but important. The party suffered a double blow in 1896, when it endorsed Democrat William Jennings Bryan for president. (It also rather perversely nominated the Populist Thomas Watson as vice president rather than endorsing Bryan's chosen running mate, Arthur Sewall.) The Populists were enamored by Bryan's outward support for Populist goals and saw him as having the best chance of winning. Bryan, however, saw much of the Populist platform as **socialism** and did not support the party's entire agenda. More serious was Bryan's loss to Republican William McKinley, who convinced large numbers of urban workers that Bryan's views were antithetical to their own. McKinley used the specter of rising bread and food prices to his advantage and defeated Bryan first in 1896, and then again in 1900. With his victory, the free silver movement faded.

So, too, did the Populist Party, though it did not die before leaving a negative legacy in the South. The party reorganized in 1904 and nominated Georgian Thomas Watson for president. Earlier Watson had called upon southern tenant farmers and sharecroppers to set aside their racial differences in the name of class **solidarity**. This made southern Populists subject to race-baiting, and they often lost outright or to fusion candidates for their advocacy of biracial cooperation. Numerous states erected electoral barriers designed to disenfranchise black voters and prevent biracial class coalitions. When the Populists reorganized, Watson and other southern Populists embraced racism. Watson, in particular, became an ardent segregationist. When the party finally withered for good, many of its standard bearers drifted into the Democratic Party.

On a more positive note, the Populist movement also began the transformation of the Democratic Party in progressive ways. The party became more attentive to the concerns of rural and industrial workers. Democrats jettisoned many of Populism's more controversial and socialist ideals, but incorporated liberal ideas such as adopting a graduated income tax and expanding popular democracy. Many political scholars credit Populism with preparing Democrats to embrace the **Progressive Era** politics of Woodrow Wilson and the future urban reformism of Al Smith and Franklin Roosevelt.

Suggested Reading

Edward Ayres, *The Promise of the New South: Life after Reconstruction*, 1992; Lawrence Goodwyn, *The Populist Moment: A Short History of the Agrarian Revolt in America*, 1976; Matthew Hild, *Greenbackers, Knights of Labor, and Populists: Farmer-Labor Insurgency in the Late-19th-Century South*, 2007; C. Vann Woodward, *Tom Watson: Agrarian Rebel*, 1963.

POSTAL WORKERS AND THE STRIKE OF 1970

The postal strike of 1970 began as a **wildcat strike** and became the first successful nationwide strike of federal employees. It started on March 18, 1970, when the Manhattan Bronx Postal Union (MBPU) walked out over long-simmering disputes, and the job action quickly spread to more than 200,000 letter carriers, clerks, and mail handlers nationwide. At the time, it was illegal for postal workers to strike; in the end, the postal workers forced a reexamination of the relationship between government and federal employees.

The United States Post Office Department (USPD) is one of the oldest institutions in the nation. The Second Continental Congress established it in 1775, and Benjamin Franklin served as the first Postmaster General. Post Office employees, however, have not always enjoyed harmonious relations with the government. The 1792 Postal Service Act placed the USPD in an ambiguous situation in that it gave Congress responsibility for regulating the USPD but placed it under the supervision of the executive branch. In 1829, President Andrew Jackson elevated the Postmaster General to a Cabinet-level position, one of the last significant changes in the USPD until after the 1970 strike.

Early postal workers often traveled long distances to deliver mail. Improved transportation such as the development of canals, steamships, and railroads cut delivery times in many parts of the country, but also exacerbated ongoing funding problems because it meant contracting delivery services with private companies. In 1845, for example, the USPD ran a $30,000 deficit, the equivalent of more than $693,000 in 2010 terms. The expansion of railroads worsened the organization's deficit problems. By an 1860 estimate, the USPD was paying $175 per mile to railroads for its mail contracts. In areas of the country such as the Trans-Mississippi West, where rail service was nonexistent, mail was delivered by horseback. In 1860, the Pony Express, as it was dubbed, became a staple of American lore and romance, but it was a very hard and dangerous job that required carriers to ride through difficult terrain—often through areas controlled by nonfriendly **Native American** and bandits—and the system took its toll on workers and horses. The building of transcontinental railroads reduced the need for such services, as did their expense. The Pony Express, for example, was disbanded in 1861, after it lost numerous riders and more than $110,000 in less than two years. After the **Civil War**, Congress grappled with high railroad rates on numerous occasions, and the 1887 Interstate Commerce Act outlawed price-fixing.

The very cost of operating the USPD meant that Congress was notoriously parsimonious in compensating employees. It also exempted USPD employees from laws that granted federal employees an **eight-hour** workday. Invariably workers sought to unionize. The National Association of Post Office Workers (NAPOC) was created in 1890 and barred supervisors from the union to get around Congress's argument that postal clerks were not "laborers" subject to eight-hour regulations. In 1891, NAPOC merged with a **Knights of Labor** affiliate to form the United National Association of Post Office Clerks (UNAPOC). UNAPOC soon found its efforts throttled by restrictions placed on federal employees' rights to lobby; in 1902, in fact,

Postmaster General Henry Payne put in place a gag order that forbade federal employees from airing **grievances** publicly. In an effort to resist this restriction, UNAPOC allied with the **American Federation of Labor** in 1906, some UNAPOC members split off and reorganized as the National Federation of Post Office Clerks (NFPOC). It, too, met with stiff resistance and the USPD was marked by extraordinarily high turnover rates. It was not until the 1912 Lloyd-La Follette Act that civil servants gained a clear right to form and join unions, though the bill did not come with full **collective bargaining** rights, nor did it provide for the right to **strike**. The UNAPOC, in fact, called for its repeal.

Very little progress was made in the 1930s, though a rival organization, the National Association of Letter Carriers (NALC), formed under the aegis of the **Congress of Industrial Organizations**. NALC forbade racial discrimination, a proviso that was resisted by the rank-and-file in both the North and South. Many NALC locals retained either de jure or de facto segregation as late as 1963. The USPD did, however, take in larger numbers of women after President John F. Kennedy issued an executive order mandating it. The 1964 Civil Rights Act forced postal unions to end racial discrimination in hiring.

By the mid-1960s, post office work was known for its long hours and poor pay. Clerks and carriers started at $6,000 per year and it took 21 years to obtain the top grade of $8,442, a **salary** that was nearly $3,000 below what the federal government deemed necessary for a family of four to live in "moderate" comfort. Moreover, increased mechanization in processing and sorting divisions did not always make work easier; many employees complained of mind-numbing **speedups**. USPD workers were divided among numerous unions, none of which had the right to strike, but several of which came very close to defying this edict in 1968. In that year, both the United Federation of Postal Clerks (UFPC) and the NALC, the two largest of seven national unions representing post office workers, deleted **no-strike clauses** from their constitutions. Both unions warned of worker discontent and the impossibility of keeping their members on the job without significant improvements. Under prevailing federal law, however, strikes were illegal, unions could not bargain directly with USPD management, and they had to ask Congress for pay increases. A strike was narrowly averted, but the issues surfaced again in 1970.

The immediate cause of the walkout related to poor pay earned by urban postal workers, especially the differences in pay rates between government and private-sector employees. Those differences were made all the more apparent by inflation unleashed by the **Vietnam War**, which made workers' real wages even lower. The **counterculture** and the 1960s climate of social protest also influenced the 1970 walkout decision, as did provocative action on the part of the U.S. government. On March 12, 1970, the House of Representatives' Post Office and Civil Service Committee offered a pay raise deemed so insulting that postal workers immediately rejected it. New York City workers were equally angry with Congress, President Richard Nixon, and their own union leaders. When President Nixon announced that the next scheduled wage increase would be postponed for six months, Local 36 workers rejected pleas for calm—at one point they hanged NALC President James Rademacher in effigy—and voted to strike. Their action was officially a wildcat strike because they had no legal right to walk out, but the city's UFPC members and other New York locals quickly joined them. Within two days, postal workers in Buffalo, Boston, Pittsburgh, Detroit, and other locales walked off the job in **solidarity** with the New Yorkers and in hopes of winning improved wages.

At the height of the walkout, approximately 25 percent of the nation's postal employees were on strike. The one-week action shut down New York-based financial and business centers and caused delays in national mail delivery. Rademacher blamed the strike on Students for a Democratic Society infiltration of the NALC, a charge that had some merit, but that overlooked the overall desperation of postal workers and years of government inaction in redressing their grievances. The *New York Times* blamed Congress and the White House, and public sentiment was generally favorable toward the strikers. The government's response was heavy-handed rather than conciliatory. The White House sought and obtained a court **injunction** requiring postal unions to compel their members to return to work. When the unions found Postmaster General Winton Blount unwilling to concede any issue that would encourage workers to abandon the strike, representatives from the seven unions asked Secretary of Labor George Shultz to intervene. Shultz pressured Blount to meet with union officials on March 20, the day the NALC was meeting to decide whether to make the strike official. When union members rejected Blount's compromise, President Nixon demanded that the strike end on March 23. Workers ignored the order and Nixon declared a state of national emergency. He sent 25,000 soldiers and National Guardsmen to New York City to sort and move mail, though he stipulated that troops be unarmed, dress in uniforms without battle gear, and avoid confrontations with strikers. The troops provide unable to replace all of the 57,000 striking New Yorkers, so they concentrated on moving mail vital to business interests and did not make home deliveries. The administration won additional injunctions that threatened crushing fines on locals remaining on strike after March 25, and these promised penalties forced most strikers back to work.

Although the strike ended within a week, it led to a dramatic overhaul of the relationship between the federal government and organized federal employees. A new contract provided an immediate 6 percent wage increase, with a larger increase coming after congressional approval. It also reduced the time necessary to achieve top pay from 21 years to 8 years and granted amnesty to strikers. The Postal Reorganization Act was passed, which transformed the USPD into an autonomous and self-supporting government corporation. In exchange, postal employees gave up the right to strike and agreed to binding **arbitration**. The latter point relieved Congress of the responsibility for USPD wage negotiations. Congress quickly approved the agreement, and Nixon signed the bill into law on April 15, less than one month after the strike began.

The 1970 strike marked the beginning of a long process that brought a living wage to postal workers. In 1971, several unions merged to form the American Postal Workers Union (APWU). It has been effect in that by 1990, the value of USPD wages and **fringe benefits** quadrupled.

The gains made by postal workers reverberated among other federal workers, including truckers, who engaged in their own wildcat strike, and the **Professional Air Traffic Controllers Organization** (PATCO), which held a **sick-out** to achieve higher pay. (PATCO would suffer a crippling blow in 1981, when President **Ronald Reagan** fired air traffic controllers during a strike.) It is also important to note that the 1970 post office strike did not resolve all of the issues inside the USPD. It remained (and remains) underfunded. ZIP codes were introduced in 1972 as yet another plan to streamline operations and make the USPD self-sufficient. Just four years later, the USPD ran a $4 billion deficit and nearly 2,000 post offices closed in the next 15 years as the organization tried to close the budget gap. During the same period (1976 to 1990), however, postal workers handled nearly twice as many letters and packages. Postal workers, like other workers, found little support for their requests for increased workforces during the anti-union climate of the 1980s. Indeed, the APWU had numerous acrimonious exchanges with White House officials during the 1980s. Postal workers' unions did, however, make great strides in gender and racial equity. (By the early 1990s, APWU membership was more than 40 percent female.)

The USPD was reorganized as the United States Postal Service (USPS) in 1971 and has been revamped several times since then. It faces stiff compensation from private parcel carriers such as Federal Express, DHL, and United Parcel Service. The **computer revolution** and the introduction of email have also cut into USPS revenues, resulting in higher postal rates, more post office closings, and reduction of staff. The drive to cut costs and increase efficiency has taken a major toll in the workplace. In the 1990s, the phrase "going postal" gained traction in popular culture after several high-profile shootings took place in USPS facilities. Several were perpetrated by laid-off or dismissed former employees, or by workers driven beyond their capacity. The future of post office work is uncertain at the present, and many observers argue that the government-sponsored service has outlived its usefulness and should be completely privatized. An unclear future, trite popular culture slogans, changing technology, and gains since 1970 should not serve to obscure the fact that contemporary postal work remains a demanding and stressful job.

Suggested Reading

Vern Baxter, *Labor Politics in the U.S., Postal Service*, 1994; Postal Employee Network, http://www.postalemployeenetwork.com/postal-employee-salary-history.htm, accessed May 16, 2011; Carl Schele, *A Short History of the Mail Service*, 1970; John Walsh and Garth Magnum, *Labor Struggle in the Post Office: From Selective Lobbying to Collective Bargaining*, 1992.

POSTINDUSTRIALISM. *See* Deindustrialization.

POST-WORLD WAR I STRIKES. *See* Boston Police Strike of 1919; General Strike; Red Scare; Steel Strike of 1919.

POST-WORLD WAR II STRIKES. *See* Cold War and Labor; National War Labor Board; Red Scare; Reuther, Walter; United Auto Workers of America.

POWDERLY, TERENCE VINCENT

Terence V. Powderly (January 22, 1849–June 24, 1924) was the national leader of the **Knights of Labor** (KOL) from 1878 through 1893. He later served as commissioner general of **immigration** and in the **Department of Labor**.

Powderly was born in Carbondale, Pennsylvania, the son of Terence and Margery (Walsh) Powderly. He attended Carbondale schools until age 13, at which time he became a railroad worker. In 1866, he **apprenticed** as a machinist and worked at various shops in the greater Scranton area until 1877. He married Hannah Dyer on September 19, 1872. The couple had a child who died in infancy.

In the early 1870s, Powderly got caught up in the various causes that defined his life: Irish nationalism, temperance, politics, and labor. As the son of an Irish immigrant father, Powderly was deeply interested in Irish politics. He was an active member of the Irish Land League, supported Irish independence, and was an outspoken critic of British policy toward the Irish. Powderly was also a teetotaler and an ardent supporter of temperance causes. During his tenure as leader of the KOL, the organization established a working relationship with the Women's Christian Temperance Union, even though the KOL organized **brewery workers**.

The exploitation of labor after the **Civil War** had a profound effect on young Powderly. Though he later denounced radicalism and supported the **Republican Party**, for a brief period he paid **dues** to the Socialist Labor Party. He was also caught up in the **Greenback** Labor movement and in 1878 rode that ticket to victory as mayor of Scranton, serving three 2-year terms.

Portrait of Terence Powderly, leader of the Knights of Labor (1879–1893). (Library of Congress)

Ultimately, Powderly achieved his greatest fame as a labor leader. He joined the Machinists and Blacksmiths Union in 1871. Like many **craft unions**, the machinists were badly hurt by the panic of 1873. Powderly gravitated toward the ultra-secret Noble and Holy Order of the KOL and probably joined it in 1874. He was appointed an organizer in 1876, and he helped expand the KOL westward from its Philadelphia base. In that same year, he became master workman (president) of his **union local** and corresponding secretary for his district assembly. In 1879, Powderly became the general master workman of the entire KOL when founder Uriah Stephens resigned to run for Congress on the Greenback Labor ticket.

Powderly led the KOL from secrecy and obscurity to national prominence as an open organization. The group had fewer than 10,000 members in 1878; by mid-1886, it had perhaps 1 million. Powderly lectured and organized tirelessly on behalf of the Knights and managed administrative affairs admirably given the KOL's clunky and inchoate bureaucratic structure. He supported the inclusion of both women and African Americans in the KOL, and he oversaw the KOL's greatest triumph: its 1885 strike victory over Jay Gould's Southwest railway conglomerate. Powderly also called for an end to the **wage** system and its replacement by producer and distributor **cooperatives**.

By the mid-1880s, Powderly was the nation's most famous labor leader. Politicians and reformers sought his advice, and local assemblies, retail products, children, and a suburb of Birmingham, Alabama, were named for him.

Another major milestone was Powderly's success in getting the Roman Catholic Church to remove its condemnation of the labor movement. Powderly sometimes clashed with anti-union clerics, but he was a faithful Catholic and worked with James Cardinal Gibbons, who convinced Pope Leo XIII to issue the 1891 encyclical *Rerum Novarum*, which gave the Vatican's sanction to unions.

Powderly's KOL tenure was controversial as well. Despite the victory over Gould, Powderly was bitterly opposed to **strikes** and called for mandatory **arbitration**, a position that angered many trade unionists and radicals. He was also lukewarm toward the idea of independent labor parties and, after the **Haymarket bombing** of May 4, 1886, an outspoken critic of **anarchism**, **socialism**, and radicalism. His many enemies also claimed he was vain, argumentative, petty, and self-serving. Some accused him of trying to turn the KOL into a personal power machine, while others said he was part of an internal conspiracy that was opposed to trade unions.

When the KOL began to decline after the **Great Upheaval** collapsed, Powderly often bore the brunt of criticism for the KOL's declining strength. The Knights also faced competition from the **American Federation of Labor** (AFL) after 1886, and battles between the two organizations were exacerbated by the mutual hatred between Powderly and AFL head **Samuel Gompers**. In 1893, a coalition of urban socialists and agrarian radicals forced Powderly to resign as KOL leader. He appears to have become more bitter and conservative after his ouster. He battled the KOL over back pay, spouted allegations and engaged in plots against KOL leaders, and wrote voluminous defenses of his tenure as KOL head. He quarreled with the organization so bitterly that the KOL briefly expelled him. For a time he worked as a lawyer, a profession ineligible for KOL membership.

In 1897, President William McKinley appointed Powderly U.S. commissioner general of immigration. He took over the post at a time in which immigration faced intense scrutiny, procedures at Ellis Island were under attack, and sentiment was high to restrict immigration to the United States. Powderly's xenophobic, anti-immigrant diatribes did little to distinguish him, and his battles with other officials made him unpopular. He was removed from his post in 1902 in the midst of a dispute in which Powderly (correctly) accused high-ranking officials at Ellis Island of corruption. He went on to hold several posts with the Department of Labor.

Powderly's wife, Hannah, died in 1901, and on March 31, 1919, he married Emma Fickenscher, his former secretary. He died in Washington, D.C., on June 24, 1924. At the time, he was nearly forgotten, but in many respects, Terence Powderly was the first prominent leader of an American **labor federation**. In January 2000, he was inducted into the Labor Hall of Fame. For a time Powderly stood accused of leading the KOL to ruin and of being too conservative. More recently historians have reevaluated Powderly, as his views on the futility of strikes and some of his critiques of the AFL now appear prescient.

Suggested Reading

Craig Phelan, *Grand Master Workman: Terence Powderly and the Knights of Labor*, 2000; Terence V. Powderly, *The Path I Trod: The Autobiography of Terence V. Powderly*, Harry Carman, Henry David, and Paul Guthrie, eds., 1968 (reprint of 1940 edition); Robert E. Weir, *Knights Unhorsed: Internal Conflict in a Gilded Age Labor Movement*, 2000.

PRE-COLUMBIAN LABOR. *See* Native Americans and Labor.

PREFERENTIAL PAY. *See* Overtime.

PREVAILING WAGE

The prevailing wage refers to the pay standards for construction workers within a given geographical territory. Under legislation specifying enforcement of a prevailing wage, employers must meet that minimum standard whether or not the workforce is unionized, though they may pay more.

The prevailing wage is an outgrowth of the 1931 **Davis-Bacon Act**. The 1936 Walsh-Healy Public Contract Act officially made the prevailing wage the federal **minimum wage** for construction projects. In addition, 35 states have some form of prevailing-wage law; these are sometimes dubbed "little Davis-Bacon Acts." In each case, an employer is required to pay **wages** in line with local custom on any job open to public bid or involving state or federal **contracts**. The term "wage" is used loosely to refer to all forms of compensation, which allows contractors to count **fringe benefits** toward meeting prevailing-wage standards.

Prevailing-wage laws are designed to protect local wage structures. They apply mainly in the building industry where large public projects are put out for competitive bids. The purpose of such laws is to prevent nonlocal firms from obtaining contracts funded by local taxpayers, then importing low-wage workers who would undercut local pay rates. Employers must pay prevailing wages if they accept a contract, even if their workers customarily work for lower rates. States publish the prevailing wage for various regions and that information is available to contractors before they put in bids. The **Department of Labor** also maintains current data on prevailing wages. In addition, some nonprofit agencies, such as the Prevailing Wage Contractors Association, assist firms in complying with existing laws.

In 1985, the Department of Labor defined the prevailing wage as the amount paid to at least 50 percent of workers within a job classification. This somewhat clarified questions as to whether the amount was calculated based on average or median wages, but disputes still arise on how to determine the prevailing wage and there is no standard formula used by all states. Some states establish thresholds that stipulate the total value of a contract before prevailing wages must be paid, though eight states have no minimum threshold whatsoever. This figure is usually low, though it is $400,000 for new construction in Connecticut and $500,000 in Maryland.

The construction and business communities are generally opposed to prevailing-wage laws and have funded expensive campaigns to overturn them. They argue that prevailing-wage laws lead to "pork barrel" projects in which politicians waste taxpayer money by rewarding friends, unions, and campaign contributors. Unions and most construction workers counter that opponents of prevailing wages are a collection of ideologues and greedy construction barons seeking to enrich their own profit margins, not protect taxpayers. They also argue that many are modern-day "carpetbaggers"—outsiders with little connection to the communities funding their projects and disrespectful of local cultures, customs, and standards of living.

With the exception of New Hampshire, all of the states without prevailing-wage laws are located in the South, or west of the Mississippi River. Of the 15 states that do not have prevailing-wage laws, just seven have never had one. Seven states repealed their prevailing-wage laws between 1979 and 1987 during the presidencies of Jimmy Carter (two states) and **Ronald Reagan** (five states), whose administrations were generally viewed as hostile toward labor unions and business regulations. Studies reveal that those states experienced an immediate 2 to 4 percent decline in construction industry wages and approximately a 10 percent decline in wages for unionized workers. In recent years, unions have done a better job of fending off attacks. Since 1987, only Oklahoma has repealed its law, which occurred when its Supreme Court ruled that the state's prevailing-wage law was unconstitutional. Efforts to do so in Oregon were turned aside in 2005. Nevertheless, there are well-financed efforts to get rid of the prevailing-wage, and the **Republican Party** supports such efforts. As of 2011, there were efforts to overturn laws in Ohio and Michigan. Opposing these efforts, a growing movement has sought to link prevailing wage and **living wage** campaigns, and a grassroots movement has denounced the "race to the bottom" on wages. Workers' wages are likely to be a contentious issue for some time to come.

Suggested Reading

Lambert Surhone, Mariam Tennoe, and Susan Henssonow, eds., *Prevailing Wage*, 2010; U.S. Government Planning Office, "Davis-Bacon Wage Determinations," http://www.gpo.gov/davisbacon/, accessed May 17, 2011; U.S. Government Planning Office, "Davis-Bacon Wage Determinations by State," http://www.gpo.gov/davisbacon/allstates.html, accessed May 17, 2011.

PROFESSIONAL AIR TRAFFIC CONTROLLERS ORGANIZATION STRIKE

The Professional Air Traffic Controllers Organization (PATCO) strike was a 1981 job action that pitted the administration of President **Ronald Reagan** against one of the few labor unions that had endorsed his election. It ended in a complete rout of the union and is now viewed by scholars as a pivotal moment in the precipitous decline of organized labor in the United States. The loss of the PATCO strike and the firing of air traffic controllers opened the door for a full-scale assault on unions by pro-business and anti-union forces.

Air traffic controllers had (and have) one of the most stressful jobs in the United States—monitoring the safety of the nation's airspace and making certain that planes landing, taking off, and flying do so within specific air corridors. At busy facilities, such as Atlanta's Hartsfield-Jackson International Airport, a plane lands or takes off roughly every 30 seconds. Air traffic controllers sit behind radar and computer terminals and direct the flow of traffic in and out of airports. Intense concentration, precise communication with pilots, excellent short-term memory, and an ability to react quickly are prerequisites for the job, and controllers are considered highly skilled professionals who must meet exacting physical and mental standards. It is a job in which a single mistake could result in mass tragedy. Because of the stress involved and the need to maintain mental acuity, most air traffic controllers are required to take a 30-minute break after each 90-minute or 2-hour stretch behind the monitors. In some nations, they are allowed to work only 4 days out of 7 and, in the United States, they must retire at age 56.

PATCO formed in 1968 to call attention to the demands on air traffic controllers. At first it was considered a professional association, but after a series of slowdowns that resulted in flight delays, it was declared a union in 1969. Because air traffic controllers are federal employees, they are forbidden to **strike**. In 1970, PATCO conducted a **sick-out** to dramatize the need for higher pay and increased staff. An **injunction** was secured that ended the job action, but more air traffic controllers were hired.

The immediate cause of the 1981 strike was a demand for better **wages** and a call for a reduced work week. On August 3, 1981, roughly 13,000 air traffic controllers employed by the Federal Aviation Administration (FAA) refused to report for duty in airport control towers and in the control centers that managed traffic between air hubs. The walkout was technically a **wildcat strike**, but nearly 80 percent of the FAA's air traffic control personnel responded to PATCO's call. Their absence seriously damaged the flow of air traffic. PATCO President Robert Poli called for a

32-hour work week, improved retirement benefits, and an immediate $10,000 per year raise. At the time Poli hoped he would be able to strike a quick deal with President Reagan, who had seemed sympathetic to PATCO during his candidacy. PATCO, in fact, endorsed Reagan over Jimmy Carter, who was running for reelection.

In retrospect, the seemingly exorbitant **salary** demand was a public relations mistake. The United States was still mired in the worst recession since the Great Depression of the 1930s, and was suffering from high unemployment and stagflation occasioned by various oil **boycotts** staged by the Organization of Petroleum Exporting Countries. Poli intended the $10,000 figure to be a bargaining chip, but the media seized upon it and the general public was largely unsympathetic to PATCO, a **white-collar** union. The wage issue also obscured PATCO's central complaint: the need to reduce the stress of air traffic controllers lest public safety be jeopardized by impaired judgment. Nor was it widely reported that PATCO's action was neither impulsive nor spontaneous; it had been negotiating with the FAA for months before the strike. In July 1981, the PATCO rank-and-file had actually rejected an FAA offer that would have granted significant wage increases, because the offer largely ignored core **grievances** concerning working conditions. Moreover, because of the nature of air traffic controllers' work, PATCO announced its intention to walk out in advance of actually doing so. President Reagan declared a national emergency under conditions outlined by the **Taft-Hartley Act** and responded with an ultimatum: He gave air traffic controllers 48 hours to return to work or they would be fired.

Reagan proved true to his word; the 11,350 controllers who ignored the ultimatum were fired on August 5. With a sweep of a pen, Reagan replaced 70 percent of the nation's air traffic controllers and hired **scabs** to take their places. Military controllers and FAA supervisors had manned terminals during the brief strike, and they hastily trained replacement workers. Reagan signed an executive order banning fired air traffic controllers from future federal employment. Reagan's actions made him popular not just with the business community and political conservatives, but also with the public at large, which admired his decisive leadership in the wake of the political malaise of the 1970s. At a time when labor union strength was already on the wane due to **deindustrialization**, much of the public also bought into conservative attacks on unions that blamed their alleged greediness for making businesses less competitive in the global marketplace and retarding recovery from the recession.

In addition to Reagan's action of firing the workers, federal judges issued costly **injunctions** that assessed PATCO for damages resulting from the strike. These penalties quickly bankrupted the organization. Numerous strike leaders were arrested and jailed for defying injunctions, and newly hired air traffic controllers held a swift **decertification** vote that, in October 1981, removed PATCO as their bargaining unit.

The **American Federation of Labor-Congress of Industrial Organizations** (AFL-CIO) publicly supported PATCO and organized nationwide grassroots **solidarity** protests to express collective outrage at Reagan's anti-union tactics. Although

Reagan's decision was popular in the United States, PATCO received support from outside U.S. border, and the Canadian Air Traffic Controllers Association even staged a limited **sympathy strike** in solidarity with PATCO. However, the failure of other airline unions to honor PATCO **picket** lines contributed to the union's resounding loss.

The lost PATCO strike emboldened the American business community and signaled that the Reagan administration would not intervene in private-sector union-busting. That belief proved largely true. The PATCO fiasco touched off a new wave of **downsizing, decertification, and concessions strikes**. Within a few years, private employers had opted to hire scabs to replace strikers at Phelps Dodge, International Paper, Hormel, and other major companies, contributing to a dramatic drop in strike rates in the United States that has not been reversed.

For conservatives, the 1981 PATCO strike is a defining moment of the Reagan presidency. Few accounts bother to reveal the next chapter in the story, however. The quality and availability of skilled air traffic control suffered in the years to come and, in 1986, the Reagan administration quietly reversed course and allowed some of the fired controllers to reapply for jobs. In 1993, President Bill Clinton rescinded Reagan's non-hire order altogether. Moreover, new hires soon discovered the legitimacy of PATCO's grievances concerning working conditions and formed a new union in 1987. Most air traffic controllers are once again unionized, either with a body affiliated with the **American Federation of State, County, and Municipal Employees** or by a reorganized and independent PATCO.

Suggested Reading

Willis Nordlund, *Silent Skies: The Air Traffic Controllers' Strike*, 1998; Michael Round, *Grounded: Reagan and the PATCO Crash*, 1999; Arthur Shostak and David Skocik, *The Air Controllers' Controversy: Lessons from the PATCO Strike*, 2006.

PROFIT SHARING

Profit sharing is a plan that links a portion of a worker's yearly compensation to the company's profitability. Instead of—or in addition to—an annual pay rise, the employee receives a bonus when the company meets or exceeds its financial target, but not if the company fails to achieve expected goals. Profit sharing has been a standard feature in American corporations since the **Progressive Era** and was a key component of **welfare capitalism**. It is allied with the concept of "stakeholding"—that is, making workers feel that they have a vested interest in the continued success of the business. By the late 1920s, more than 1 million workers were enrolled in profit-sharing plans, though many of those systems collapsed during the Great Depression.

Profit sharing has both defenders and critics. Supporters argue that profit sharing makes workers more attentive to issues such as efficiency, waste, and cost cutting. Critics counter that it can be used to justify **speedups** and **Taylorism**. The latter charge is sustained by the fact that employees seldom have access to employer accounts; hence they cannot assess how much profit their diligence is worth. If, for instance, they work harder in the course of a normal workday and increase output by 50 percent but receive a small percentage of that increased productivity in profit sharing, it might be economically advantageous to work at a less physically demanding pace and collect **overtime** pay instead of profit sharing. Labor unions also charge that profit-sharing plans are sometimes a dodge designed to avoid giving raises. Moreover, making pay raises contingent can also harm employees' long-term buying power, especially when deferred compensation causes **wages** to lag behind the inflation rate. Most profit-sharing plans pay bonuses as a lump sum, which does not have the same cumulative effect as an annual raise, because the base wage remains stagnant. Moreover, profit sharing cannot be relied upon for long-term financial planning.

Unions have long claimed that profit sharing and welfare capitalism plans deter unionization by creating the false impression that management will take care of workers without being pressured to do so. They point to the plans from the 1920s and 1960s as cases in point. Profit sharing can be sustained only during flush economic times, as defined by the employers. When profits dip, employee profit sharing is one of the first benefits to be cut. Modern corporations pay dividends to stockholders before they give bonuses to employees. There is great pressure to maintain dividend value even when profits decline; in such cases employers often artificially maintain dividends by reducing or eliminating profit sharing. In some cases employees do not get a pay bump, even though the company is highly profitable.

Despite problems associated with profit sharing, such plans have gained in popularity since the 1970s. Numerous employers enlist them as means to encourage employees to be more competitive in an era of **globalization**. They are relatively common among **white-collar** workers. Many **contracts** contain profit-sharing language, despite union skepticism of this approach's merits. Whenever they can, unions seek to negotiate profit sharing as a supplement to, rather than in lieu of, annual pay rises. Some also prefer stock options to profit sharing. "Gain sharing" is also becoming more popular; this type of plan directly returns cost savings to the employees who initiate them.

Suggested Reading

Douglas Kruse, Richard B. Freeman, and Joseph Blasi, eds., *Shared Capitalism at Work: Employee Ownership, Profit and Gain Sharing, and Broad-Based Stock Options*, 2011; Michael Poole and Glenville Jenkins, *The Impact of Economic Democracy: Profit-Sharing and Employee-Shareholding Schemes*, 2011.

PROGRESSIVE ERA AND LABOR

The Progressive Era was the first of three great government-directed reform movements of the 20th century. Progressive Era reformers enacted legislation to regulate trusts, make food and drugs safer, curtail municipal corruption, encourage direct democracy, stabilize finance, enact fair trade standards, conserve public lands, and attack social problems. The end of the period saw the enactment of a graduated income tax, women's suffrage, and **Prohibition**. Scholars agree that an impressive array of long-overdue reforms were enacted and that the first decade and a half of the 20th century was remarkably forward looking when compared to the late Gilded Age, especially the 1890s, which were marked by class conflict and economic hardship. Scholars disagree, however, on most other aspects of the Progressive Era, including when it took place. The period is conventionally dated as beginning with Theodore Roosevelt's ascension to the presidency in 1901 and ending with the United States' entry into World War I in 1917. Conversely, some scholars date it as beginning as early as the 1870s and/or extending into the late 1920s. From the standpoint of the **working class** and organized labor, there is considerable debate as to whether there was a "progressive" period at all. A few reforms such as the **Clayton Act** notwithstanding, much of what occurred in the early 20th century mirrored the capital/labor conflicts of the Gilded Age.

Progressivism was a broad and complex phenomenon that defies easy generalization. For the most part, its leaders came from **middle-class** and upper-class backgrounds. They included anticorruption mayors and city councilors, as well as U.S. presidents such as Theodore Roosevelt, William Howard Taft, and Woodrow Wilson. Most Progressives came from the private sector; their number included journalists, college professors, settlement house workers, sociologists, artists, economists, philosophers, women's suffrage advocates, temperance campaigners, and members of women's clubs and professional associations. Relatively few Progressives were labor leaders. Progressives were obsessed with expertise, so reform was often imposed from the top of the social hierarchy rather than bubbling up from grassroots social movements. Those historians who attempt to locate the Progressive Era's origins in the 19th century invite considerable disagreement from colleagues who point out the considerable differences in social class and organizational strategy between elitist Progressive Era reformers and plebeian-based Gilded Age social movements such as the **eight-hour movement**, the **Knights of Labor**, or the **Populists**.

Most Progressives embraced at least four major ideals: opposition to monopolies, the importance of social cohesion, desire for social efficiency, and a belief in industrial progress. They shared with working people the belief that unregulated **capitalism** had created unacceptable levels of social misery. Although the extent of the era's trust-busting activities is often exaggerated, most working people applauded efforts to regulate business and restore competition. The highly publicized breakup of trusts such as Standard Oil and the Northern Securities Company met with public acclaim, though they frightened many in the business community. In like fashion, the general public approved of laws aimed at assuring the quality and safety of food and drugs. They were also gratified to see a general rejection of **social Darwinism** and an acceptance of the reality of social problems. There was, however, very powerful opposition to attempts to regulate business, including that coming from the Chamber of Commerce and from the **National Association of Manufacturers**.

Progressives were reformers, not radicals. Their emphasis on social cohesion led them to seek change in presumptions of social consensus rather than social conflict. Working-class movements such as the **International Ladies' Garment Workers' Union** (ILGWU) engaged in intense internal debates over whether it was possible for the "respectable" middle class to understand working people and whether it could be trusted to ally itself with working-class struggle. Social cohesion led Progressives to tout the virtues of education, pragmatism, education, and accountability—positive values, but not necessarily those central to the immediate shop-floor struggles of working people. ILGWU spokeswomen such as **Rose Pesotta** and **Rose Schneiderman** repeatedly made the point that the middle class often offered nostrums rather than substance in the wake of chaos and tragedies such as the **Uprising of the 20,000** or the **Triangle Factory fire**.

Progressives saw American industrial democracy as flawed, but fixable. To working-class critics, Progressives were willing to tinker, but not to enact systemic change. They solicited advice from labor leaders such as **John Mitchell** and **American Federation of Labor** (AFL) President **Samuel Gompers**, both of whom joined the **National Civic Federation** (NCF), but they did not hesitate to turn against them when self-interest was at stake. Mitchell and Gompers found themselves facing possible jail sentences for supporting the **boycotts** of Danbury hat makers and the stove company that brought suit in *Loewe v. Lawlor*. In like fashion, industrialist John Rockefeller was an NCF member, but he vigorously defended corporate rights and attacked unions when responding to the 1914 **Ludlow Massacre**.

If social cohesion-minded Progressives sometimes found the AFL too radical, they had little tolerance whatsoever for groups espousing revolutionary ideology such as the **Industrial Workers of the World** (IWW). The period's mainstream newspapers and opinion-makers portrayed the IWW as dangerous and violent; in reality, nearly all of the violence associated with the IWW was done *to* IWW members, not *by* them. Crackdowns on the IWW during its West Coast free speech campaigns, the **Lawrence textile strike**, the Paterson silk strike, and the **Centralia Massacre** were, again, more in keeping with Gilded Age conflicts than with a reform spirit.

Progressives believed that too many resources and too much human talent were being squandered. Their view of social efficiency relied heavily on the opinions of professional experts such as those who populated licensed boards, law offices, planning commissions and professional associations. As such, they frequently distrusted grassroots movements. At precisely the time that old Populist demands such as petition, referendum, recall, primaries, and direct election of U.S. Senators were being enacted, voter participation dropped dramatically. Many political scientists attribute this decline to the fact that many Progressive Era political reforms actually took decision-making power away from voters and elected officials, and placed it in the hands of expert-staffed boards and commissions. Some critics suggest that Progressive reform ultimately paved the way for special interests to eclipse public interest in power and influence.

Views of efficiency also extended to the industrial and business sector. Progressives and working-class movements alike believed in "progress," but they meant very different things when they used this term. The workplace mirrored the stark contrasts in their definitions of "efficiency" and "progress." In the vision of

19th-century grassroots reformers such as **Edward Bellamy**, efficiency was achieved through the creation of an "industrial army" in which all citizens were producers within a state-controlled economic structure that equalized access to wealth. This gave way to the mass **assembly-line** system of Henry Ford and his imitators, and to the corporate-controlled time-motion efficiency of **Taylorism**, a system designed to trick workers into dramatically increasing output in exchange for small increases in pay. Progressives accepted without question the merits of private capitalism, which led them to countenance repression of **socialists** such as **Eugene Debs** and **anarchists** such as **Emma Goldman**. They demonstrated equal intolerance for those whose social views of progress violated middle-class norms, such as birth control advocates.

It is important also to recognize also that Progressive Era reforms were limited by a conservative judicial system that was largely constituted in the Gilded Age. Those courts often thwarted changes that would have benefited working people. **Child labor** laws, for example, were struck down an unconstitutional, as were laws that would have limited the workday. The same courts routinely issued **injunctions** against **strikes**, sided with employers in labor disputes, allowed weaker federal workplace safety laws to supersede tougher state regulations, upheld discriminatory "Jim Crow" laws, gave support for gathering **immigration** restriction regulations, and issued perplexing rulings on **protective labor legislation**.

The Progressive Era was a needed first step in reforming American society, but its scope was limited insofar as social change came to working people. There would not be comprehensive "progressive" change for laborers until the New Deal, and even it fell substantially short of the protections and guarantees of other industrial democracies.

Suggested Reading

John D. Buenker and Joseph Buenker, eds., *Encyclopedia of the Gilded Age and Progressive Era*, 2005; Melvyn Dobofsky, *The State and Labor in Modern America*, 1994; Richard Hofstadter, *The Age of Reform*, 1960; Michael McGeer, *A Fierce Discontent: The Rise and Fall of the Progressive Movement in America, 1870–1920*, 2003; David Montgomery, *The Fall of the House of Labor*, 1987; Robert Wiebe, *The Search for Order, 1877–1920*, 1967.

PROHIBITION AND LABOR

The labor movement has had a mixed relationship with alcohol. Most labor groups have supported temperance—moderating one's consumption of alcohol—but few have been comfortable with an outright prohibition of alcoholic beverages. Prohibition—a ban on the sale, manufacturer, and consumption of alcoholic beverages—was in effect in the United States from January 1919 to December 1933. In the immediate aftermath of World War I, six other nations also enacted prohibition laws.

In the early industrial age, workers routinely consumed alcohol on the job. Workers generally carried a tin container called a growler with them to work. It was common for workers to consume its contents—roughly 30 ounces—before and during their lunch break and pay young boys to have it refilled at a local pub so that they could imbibe before their workday concluded. Beer, in particular, was heavily consumed for several reasons. First, alcoholic beverages were brewed at a time in which very few water sources were treated. This made beer a safer alternative to water. Second, beer was a considerably different product in the 19th century and contained more nutrients than contemporary brews. Nicknamed "bottle of bread," beer was an important part of a worker's diet, and hard work easily burned off the calories consumed. Finally, tavern life was an important part of working-class culture for males.

The antebellum **middle class**, inspired by the religious revivals known as the Second Great Awakening, led the charge to eliminate drinking from the workplace, a campaign that met with great resistance from workers in the 1830s and 1840s. By the time of the **Civil War**, however, workplace drinking had generally disappeared, though the war also served to weaken the push for greater restrictions on alcohol.

Gilded Age labor movements mostly supported temperance as an ideal, as most unions saw drunkards as unreliable comrades. Some groups, most notably the **Knights of Labor** (KOL), embraced temperance as official policy. Those selling and manufacturing alcohol were banned from KOL membership, though the KOL paradoxically organized **brewers**. The KOL also forged an alliance with the Women's Christian Temperance Union (WCTU), a group that formed in 1873 and became the leading moral force behind the move to restrict alcohol. Few 19th-century labor groups went as far as the KOL, but the avoidance of drunkenness was closely aligned with concepts of "manliness" and **working-class** "respectability," and most union members outwardly acceded to the need to regulate one's alcohol consumption. The historical record suggests, however, that temperance was more easily articulated than practiced. Alcohol abuse was widespread and came with concomitant social problems such as spousal abuse, family neglect, addiction, and crime. Women were disproportionately represented in the prohibition movement because they were disproportionately victimized by alcoholism. Women's rights advocates such as Susan B. Anthony and Frances Willard supported prohibition efforts; they were also involved in the labor movement.

Immigration complicated movements to curtail alcohol consumption. Irish and German immigrants had a long brewing tradition and generally opposed attempts to regulate the alcohol trade. The Irish Knights of Father Mathew made some inroads among immigrants, but also met resistance from the Irish and Irish American working class. By contrast, many French Canadians and Swedes supported prohibition movements. In many cities, then, prohibition was likely to involve as much interethnic as interclass conflict. Religious and urban/rural splits on the issue also occurred. Temperance and prohibition found allies among Protestants, especially Methodists and Lutherans, but Catholics and Jews were less supportive. Although most cities had active temperance and prohibition societies, it was harder for those movements to gain traction than in the countryside. This was especially true in port cities and heavily industrialized cities such as Boston, Chicago, New York, and Philadelphia, whose cosmopolitan natures made alcohol such a divisive issue that local politicians and labor leaders alike treaded lightly before embracing restrictions more strict than controlling the distribution of liquor licenses.

Prohibition found its greatest strength in rural America, but it was a considerable force given that rural dwellers outnumbered those in cities until 1920. Prohibition also enjoyed great support among the middle class and had become the majority view by the time the Eighteenth Amendment was ratified on January 17, 1919. It is important to remember that the Eighteenth Amendment merely nationalized the crusade against alcohol. Local option laws had led to "dry" towns and counties as early as the 1830s, and prohibition was in place in 13 states before the amendment was ratified. By 1869, there was even a national Prohibition Party. Though it did not do well in presidential elections, it sent members to Congress and elected state and local officials.

In retrospect, Prohibition was a failure, though it was originally intended to be a great humanitarian advance. Relatively few labor leaders supported an outright ban on alcohol—**American Federation of Labor** (AFL) Vice President Matthew Woll was a rarity—but many agreed with reformers who believed that society would be greatly improved if workers gave up drinking. Some echoed 19th-century teetotalers such as **Terence V. Powderly** in predicting great improvements to working-class family and financial life because of prohibition. For the most part, though, the AFL was strongly opposed to prohibition. Not surprisingly, its brewers' unions spoke out against it; other AFL members claimed that the movement was controlled by middle-class bigots, who were also anti-Catholic and anti-Semitic. In the South, at least, that charge had merit; the Ku Klux Klan enthusiastically supported Prohibition and attacked Catholics and Jews in its defense of it. AFL President **Samuel Gompers**, who was Jewish, opposed Prohibition.

Prohibition supporters failed to anticipate how unpopular statutory elimination of alcohol would become. Estimates from some cities indicated that drinking among the working classes actually increased during Prohibition; indeed, the AFL advised a 1926 Senate committee that 90 percent of working-class homes were involved in home brewing and that wine was being made out of everything from parsnips to dandelions. Organized crime certainly benefited from the ban and did a brisk business in bootlegging and illegal distilling. It did not lack for customers. An inkling of the opposition of working Americans came in Al Smith's unsuccessful 1928 presidential campaign. Although Republican Herbert Hoover won the election and supported the Eighteenth Amendment, Smith drew great support from urban America, though he was a Roman Catholic and a "wet" favoring repeal of Prohibition. In one of the few times in American history in which this was true, the upper class allied with the working class in seeking an end to Prohibition. Four years later, **Democrat** Franklin Roosevelt pledged to repeal Prohibition. He kept his promise and, on December 5, 1933, the Twenty-First Amendment overturned the Eighteenth Amendment. Workers greeted the news by singing Roosevelt's campaign song "Happy Days are Here Again," and hailing the president as "the man who saved the workingman's beer."

Prohibition was not completely defeated, however. Local option laws remain in effect and, as of 2011, some 18 million Americans lived in dry counties where alcohol cannot be legally sold, purchased, or served in public. Many of them are located in areas of the South and Southwest that were once hotbeds of support for the Eighteenth Amendment. Mississippi was the first state to ratify this amendment; today nearly half of its counties are dry. Alabama has 24 dry counties, Arkansas 42, Texas 45, Kentucky 55, and Kansas 69.

Suggested Reading

Jon M. Kingsdale, "The 'Poor Man's Club': Social Functions of the Urban Working-Class Saloon," *American Quarterly* 25 (October 1973): 472–489; Catherine Gilbert Murdoch, *Domesticating Drink: Women, Men, and Alcohol in America, 1870–1940*, 1998; Daniel Okrent, *Last Call: The Rise and Fall of Prohibition*, 2010; Thomas R. Pegram, *Battling Demon Rum: The Struggle for a Dry America, 1800–1933*, 1998; John Rumbarger, *Profits, Power, and Prohibition: Alcohol Reform and the Industrializing of America, 1800–1930*, 1989.

PROTECTIONISM

Protectionism is an economic practice in which one nation uses tariffs, incentives, regulations, and quotas to give goods and services produced domestically an advantage over imported goods. It is often presented as the opposite of free trade, though neither protectionism nor free trade tends to be a pure model in practice.

Protectionism is generally presented in a negative light in modern-day **capitalism**, though many workers and unions favor some degree of protectionism because it preserves jobs that might otherwise be shipped to nations that pay lower **wages**. Free trade benefits consumers and investors, but can do tremendous harm to job markets as well as a nation's balance-of-trade ledger, gross domestic product, and overall standard of living. Many economists argue that protectionism harms a country's ability to distribute goods and services effectively in the long term, though most concede that protectionism is beneficial to "infant industries," many of which simply could not survive if thrown into the market in competition with similar products or services produced by mature providers. Trade regulations are sometimes used when a concern arises regarding the quality of imports, such as automobiles. Consumers sometimes wonder why particular automobiles appear to be "cheaper" abroad. Some of the difference is due to differing wage structures, but the price differential also exists because the United States requires safety and pollution-control devices that are not required elsewhere.

Working people and their unions often favor some form of protectionism and bemoan the way that cheap imports have reduced quality and endangered American jobs. Occasionally they find allies among manufacturers seeking alleviation from foreign competition to their products. Today's free trade versus protectionism debate is merely the latest chapter in a dispute that has raged since the Colonial era. Protectionism was a key component of the "American System" of the early 19th century, and a clarion call from manufacturers during the early **Industrial Revolution**. After the **Civil War**, the dominant **Republican Party** took up protectionism and pushed for high tariffs. The **Democratic Party** lobbied for reduced tariffs, in part because its rural base produced farm goods that could not compete globally because of export duties.

Past and present advocates of free trade argue that this policy benefits workers as both consumers and producers by providing low-cost goods for purchase while opening markets for the goods and services workers create. That claim has generally fallen upon deaf ears. A handful of labor activists, most notably **Henry George**, were dedicated to free trade, but most 19th-century workers zealously favored protectionism, and George's vigorous defense of free trade is among the factors that cost him his bid for New York City's mayoralty in 1886. By contrast, the **Knights of Labor** maintained a paid lobbyist in Washington, D.C., to pressure Congress to support protectionist legislation. The **American Federation of Labor** (AFL) also tended to support protectionism as a way to protect the wages and jobs of **craft unionists**. A call for high tariffs was routinely listed among the AFL's principles.

In the 20th century, Democrats and Republicans alike became more receptive to free trade principles, a luxury afforded by the maturing of manufacturing and America's growing dominance of international trade. They also embraced free trade when leading economists cited the protectionist Smoot-Hawley Tariff Act as one of the causes that set off the economic depression of the 1930s. Free trade ideals became the political consensus after World War II, when the United States emerged with its infrastructure intact and was the world's undisputed leader in making consumer goods, providing military hardware, energy production, and services distribution. Even then, however, the majority of working people supported protectionism. The decline of American dominance, **deindustrialization**, the **globalization** of the economy, and the American public's desire for cheap consumer goods from the early 1970s on have fueled the free trade movement. Investors, commodities traders, importers, retailers, and financial-sector advisors have come to see free trade as a veritable cornerstone of capitalism.

Most labor groups continue to advocate protectionism, and the **American Federation of Labor-Congress of Industrial Organizations** (AFL-CIO) sees some measure of it as necessary to "reindustrialize" the United States. Workers have adamantly opposed the **General Agreement on Tariffs and Trade**, the **North American Free Trade Agreement**, and attempts of groups such as the World Trade Organization to knock down international trade barriers. They also oppose **fast-track legislation** that would streamline free trade agreements. The AFL-CIO and other labor groups note the way that free trade ruined industries once touted as replacements for the smokestack industries lost by previous abandonments of protectionism, including high-tech jobs in the computer industry and biomedical research.

Worldwide, anti-globalization movements are highly critical of free trade. They note that the abrogation of protectionist policies has led to a "race to the bottom" in regard to workers' wages, environmental quality, and human rights standards. They also note, correctly, that under current free trade standards goods and services can move across national borders easily, but labor cannot. In addition, they point to the numerous hidden costs involved in free trade, including turning a blind eye to child labor and, in some cases, have documented actual cases of **slavery**. One of the more potent critiques of free trade is the argument that in many cases free trade has been a one-way street. In the 1980s, allegations swirled that Japan demanded free trade from its trading partners, but practiced protectionism at home. More recently, the same charges have been leveled against China. Critics also note that authoritarian governments, including that of **communist** China, create de facto protectionist markets by highly regulating their economies. This creates conditions antithetical to free trade in which free-market goods from abroad cannot compete with those created by state-run monopolies posing as individual enterprises.

Great uncertainty over the future of work in the United States is likely to rekindle demands to add protectionist layers to the U.S. economy.

Suggested Reading

William Burris, *Protectionism and Anti-globalization*, 2009; Douglas A. Irwin, *Peddling Protectionism: Smoot-Hawley and the Great Depression*, 2011; Anne Krueger, ed., *The Political Economy of Trade Protection*, 1996; Paul R. Krugman, "Is Free Trade Passé?," *Journal of Economic Perspectives* 1, no. 2 (1987): 131–144.

PROTECTIVE LABOR LEGISLATION

Protective labor legislation refers to laws designed to protect laborers from the potentially damaging effects of work demands by their employers or inherent within the work itself. It has proved problematic when designating special categories of workers as more deserving or needy of protection than others. Such legislation has been most often applied to children and women.

Protective labor legislation evolved out of Colonial debates about free labor versus the reality of the changing nature of work. In theory, each Colonial worker was free to negotiate **wages**, hours, and working conditions according to the best bargain he or she could fashion. Custom generally dictated said terms, and a guild-like closed economic system reinforced them. In an increasingly **capitalist** economy, however, competition rendered customary practices less viable. One of the first groups to push for work regulations was **journeymen**. After the American Revolution, journeymen carpenters led the move to regulate the number of hours that constituted a legal workday. Courts often declared journeymen associations illegal, but journeymen's efforts nonetheless inspired, first, the 10-hour movement and, later, the **eight-hour movement**. Women textile workers, including those in the **Lowell Female Labor Reform Association**, also played an important role in both movements. One of the earliest versions of protective labor legislation was an 1840 10-hour bill for federal employees.

After the **Civil War**, the push for protective labor legislation took on more pronounced gender characteristics, with state and federal courts playing a pivotal role in associating protective legislation with women. Courts routinely struck down laws regulating hours and conditions for male workers, but left them intact for women. Those decisions dovetailed with Victorian social and cultural mores that assumed women to be inferior to men in physical strength and intelligence. Victorians advocated separate spheres for men and women, with males viewed as suited for the public world of business, commerce, and work, while women's "natural" roles were those of homemaker and mother. Ideally, a male worker would earn a **family wage** sufficient to support his spouse and children. Few **working-class** males actually earned that amount, however, and women usually did not have the luxury of confining themselves to the private realm. Nevertheless, Victorian customs excluded women from many jobs, especially those involving heavy toil, or those that exposed women to moral dangers, such as bartending or night work. Courts also opined that special protections for women were necessary to protect their presumably fragile reproductive systems and their delicate psychological health.

Ironically, 19th-century women were often better protected than children, as **child-labor** laws were notoriously lax throughout the century. This situation changed somewhat during the **Progressive Era**; by 1912, 38 states had adopted rudimentary child-labor laws. (Many of them, including a national law, were struck down as unconstitutional.) Progressive Era legislation and court decisions had far different implications for women, however. By 1900, numerous states regulated the number of hours women could work, and many male workers had won reduced hours through agitation and **strikes**. In 1905, though, the U.S. Supreme Court ruling in *Lochner v. New York* declared unconstitutional a New York state law regulating bakers' hours. Subsequent rulings stripped male workers of hard-fought reduced hours, but left shorter hours in place for women. Practice was cloaked in law in 1908, when the Supreme Court's *Muller v. Oregon* decision upheld shorter hours for women. Justice Louis Brandeis's majority opinion relied heavily on Victorian assumptions about women's health. By 1917, 19 states had fashioned laws based on the *Muller* decision.

Women's-rights activists faced a dilemma. On the one hand, women were granted reduced hours, weight-lifting restrictions, hazardous-waste-handling safeguards, and other protections that male workers still struggled to obtain through **collective bargaining**. To accept these without challenge, however, meant acceding to notions of women's inferiority, which feminists found objectionable. Groups such as the **Women's Trade Union League** and the **International Ladies' Garment Workers' Union** became embroiled in hot debates over whether to acquiesce to gender-based protective legislation. Feminists correctly asserted that in lieu of an Equal Rights Amendment, women workers were vulnerable to unfavorable protective labor legislation.

New Deal legislation in the 1930s resolved some protective labor issues, but created new ones. Programs such as the **National Industrial Recovery Act** and the **Fair Labor Standards Act** instituted the eight-hour workday, **minimum-wage** laws, **overtime** rules, and child-labor laws without regard to gender. Even so, job shortages during the Great Depression led numerous states to enact laws forbidding married women from holding most wage-earning jobs. New Deal job programs largely left that custom intact and excluded married women from employment. Labor shortages during World War II led to overturning of many bans on married-women's work, though wartime workplaces continued to mandate rest periods for women, pay them lower wages, and restrict women from certain jobs.

In the post-World War II period, protective labor legislation expanded, but for most workers, not just female employees. Feminists in the 1960s began to challenge social customs, especially as they extended to the workplace. The 1963 **Equal Pay Act** outlawed differing wage scales for the same work, and Title VII of the 1964 Civil Rights Act referred sexual discrimination allegations to the Equal Employment Opportunities Commission (EEOC). Other bills and executive orders dismantled numerous discriminatory barriers as well. Greater awareness of workplace safety issues culminated in the 1970 **Occupational Safety and Health Act**, child-labor laws were tightened, and gender-neutral **workman's compensation**, **minimum wage**, and **overtime** laws were periodically updated.

By the 1970s, women were found in numerous occupations once thought the preserve of men, but customary gender biases persisted, with entire categories of work being considered as gender specific. Secretarial work, for example, was so heavily female (and so poorly compensated) that commentators spoke of it as a "pink-collar ghetto." Full equality was dealt a blow in 1982, however, when a proposed Equal Rights Amendment to the U.S. Constitution failed to achieve ratification.

Many women complain that de facto protective legislation continues. Some jobs, most notably in the construction and parcel-post industries, continue to limit the amount of weight that women can lift, and custom continues to dictate that certain jobs are inappropriate for women. Critics also note that EEOC equal-pay provisions are circumvented by manipulating job titles instead of actual duties—complaints that have fueled the call for **comparable worth** legislation. Women also assert that in many workplaces their representation is mere tokenism and that a **glass ceiling** prevents them from advancing.

Race has proved another sticking point in protective labor legislation. **Affirmative action** programs have led to complaints from white male workers that women and people of color are given unfair preference in hiring and promotion. The logic behind defending affirmative action often implies the same dilemmas as early 20th-century feminists faced. On the one hand, past discrimination is obvious; on the other hand, defense of race- or gender-based affirmative action rests upon seeing certain categories of workers as "different," and perhaps not able to fend for themselves. Hiring quotas have been especially controversial, though rigid quotas were struck down by the Supreme Court's 1978 decision in *University of California Board of Regents v. Bakke*. Labor unions also oppose any affirmative action programs when they conflict with negotiated seniority systems.

In 1973, the term "sexual harassment" was introduced to describe unwanted and unwarranted attention of a sexual nature. Since the mid-1970s, the number of workplace sexual-harassment complaints has skyrocketed. The call for and enactment of special rules to reduce sexual harassment have rekindled Progressive Era dilemmas. Most sexual harassment complaints have been lodged by women, which has led some males to question women's ability to cope in competitive and pressure-packed work environments. The same charges are leveled when women lobby for flexible hours, job sharing, increased medical coverage for women's health issues, or expansion of the **Family and Medical Leave Act**. Employers often struggle to adopt rules that protect workers, but couch their policies in gender-neutral ways.

Overall, the track record of protective labor legislation is mixed. Obtaining it in some form or another is central to the mission of organized labor. Few observers would argue the wisdom of implementing child-labor laws, minimum-wage protection, and workplace-safety provisions, but laws that apply only to certain categories of workers have proved controversial.

Suggested Reading

Rosalyn Baxandall and Linda Gordon, *America's Working Women: A Documentary History*, 1995; Alice Kessler-Harris, *Out to Work: A History of Wage-Earning Women in the United States*, 1982; Susan Lehrer, *Origins of Protective Labor Legislation for Women, 1905–1925*, 1987; Christine Stansell, *The Feminist Promise: 1792 to the Present*, 2010.

PULLMAN STRIKE/LOCKOUT

The Pullman strike/lockout of 1894 is one of the most infamous labor stoppages in American history. It is often invoked as the embodiment of many of the social ills and injustices of the late Gilded Age. Despite the crushing defeat dealt to the **American Railway Union** (ARU), the strike catapulted **Eugene Debs** to national prominence, focused attention on the woes of the laboring classes, contributed to political realignment, and paved the way for needed reforms during the **Progressive Era**.

The events of 1894 took place against a backdrop of deep conflict and a serious recession. The crushing of the nationwide **railroad strikes of 1877** did little to bring quiescence to an industry marked by numerous subsequent **strikes**, especially during the **Great Upheaval** of the mid-1880s. Because rail workers were split into six brotherhoods, and the **Brotherhood of Locomotive Engineers** was particularly loath to cooperate with other groups, rail workers achieved only modest gains in their working conditions through the 1880s.

The **Knights of Labor** (KOL) proved more successful than any of the brotherhoods, but its decline in urban America after losing the 1890 New York Central strike again left rail workers in a weak position. In 1893, Debs formed the ARU, an attempt that expanded the KOL's efforts to encourage **industrial unionism** among railroad workers. His fledgling union won a victory against the Great Northern Railroad in 1893, but was so ill prepared to tackle the Pullman Palace Car Company in 1894 that Debs cautioned workers not to strike.

Industrialist George Pullman held a monopoly share of the lucrative sleeping-car industry. In 1880, Pullman purchased land 12 miles south of Chicago's central business district and constructed a new manufacturing facility. Pullman also responded to the growing urban social problems of the day by constructing what he hoped would be a utopian industrial town around his factory: Pullman, Illinois. Pullman's wide streets, sturdy homes, manicured lawns, and city services stood in marked contrast to Chicago's slums—but Pullman was a **company town** and workers' lives there were highly regulated. Saloons and labor unions were banned from

Pullman, and the town library did not even carry information on union organizing. In addition, rents and utilities cost more in Pullman, such that the company actually turned a profit on rent and services.

George Pullman's utopian vision was challenged by the collapse of financial markets in 1893. Tension between workers and employers was already high, and memories of the **Haymarket bombing** of 1886 remained vivid. The Panic of 1893 led to wide-scale business failures, bank closings, and layoffs. The Chicago area was hit even harder, as it had attracted numerous temporary laborers lured to construction jobs in preparation for the World Columbian Exposition that opened in 1893. Pullman exacerbated the region's unemployment by laying off nearly half of his 5,500 workers in 1893. His workforce rose to more than 3,300 by April 1894, but Pullman slashed the **wages** between 25 and 40 percent without lowering rents, utilities, or prices at company stores.

The immediate catalyst for the work stoppage came in May, when Pullman rejected the pleas of a **grievance** committee that approached him for relief on rents. Despite a promise not to seek reprisals against the committee, he fired three members of it, possibly with the knowledge that all three belonged to the ARU. At the time, the ARU had a very small presence at Pullman. Somewhat oddly, Pullman himself had violated the town's no-union proviso by allowing a small **company union** to form; some of its members also joined the ARU. Pullman refused to submit the firings to **arbitration**, and on June 21, ARU locals in Pullman voted to issue a **boycott** of Pullman Palace cars unless he reconsidered. Rather than wait, Pullman preemptively closed his factory, thereby officially making the events of 1894 a **lockout**. A consortium of railroad executives known as the General Managers Association (GMA) backed Pullman's actions, as they, too, were anxious to cripple the ARU.

The ARU officially issued its boycott on June 26, with union members staying on their jobs but refusing to handle Pullman cars. (ARU crews "made up" trains by coupling cars.) When companies attempted to fire those individuals who refused to work with Pullman cars, entire crews walked off the job. Within days, the ARU boycott tied up much of the freight traffic from Chicago to the West Coast, and the boycott threatened to expand to East Coast lines. At the height of the strike at the end of June, more than 25,000 workers were out on strike. Public opinion was initially on the side of the workers, and Republican leaders such as Mark Hanna called upon Pullman to arbitrate the dispute. The GMA, however, secretly schemed to create legal conflicts and incite violence to justify crushing the strikers and boycotters. This was accomplished largely through the importation of **scabs** from Canada and by attaching mail cars to Pullmans. The GMA also convinced Attorney General Richard Olney—a board member and stockholder in several railroads—to deputize more than 3,400 agents to make sure trains ran. Mainstream newspapers began to feed the public a steady diet of anti-strike propaganda.

Predictably, strikers clashed with scabs and deputies, and railroad property was destroyed. These activities prompted Olney to request that President Grover Cleveland send federal troops to protect the mails. Four divisions were dispatched over the protests of Illinois Governor John P. Altgeld. The provocation of federal troops initially energized strikers, but on July 2, Olney used several obscure **Civil War**-era laws and the recently passed **Sherman Antitrust Act** to obtain a court **injunction** from Judge Peter Grosscup, who would later stand accused of illegally ruling on railroad cases in which he was a stockholder. The injunction expressly forbade interference with mail delivery and interstate commerce. By early July, strikers faced more than 6,000 federal and state militia troops, in excess of 5,000 marshals, and some 3,100 police officers. Debs and the ARU contemplated a **general strike**, but those hopes were dashed when the **American Federation of Labor** (AFL) refused to sanction **sympathy strikes**. Despite support from the KOL and several unions that defied AFL leadership, the Pullman action was doomed.

Several strike leaders, including Debs, were arrested for conspiracy to obstruct the mails, made bail, and were rearrested for contempt of court. The strike was officially raised on August 2, though troops had been withdrawn several weeks earlier. Judge Grosscup sentenced Debs to six months' imprisonment; an experience that Debs later claimed converted him to **socialism**. Twenty-five workers died during the Pullman conflict, and 406 were seriously injured. Railroad losses totaled more than $5.3 million, and workers lost more than $1.7 million in wages. Many workers were **blacklisted**, and those who got their jobs back were forced to accept their employers' terms. The ARU quickly collapsed. More damaging still was the widespread use of court injunctions during future strikes, with the Pullman incident supplying the model for their issuance.

Despite the rout, not all was lost. The Pullman strike, plus other traumatic events like the **Homestead Steel lockout and strike** and the march of **Coxey's Army** convinced many Americans that reform was needed. The Panic of 1893 lingered into 1898, another indicator that industrial **capitalism** needed to be regulated. Even Attorney General Olney became a reluctant convert to that conclusion. In 1898, the Erdman Act corrected some railway abuses. President Cleveland's decision to send troops to put down the strike was a factor in the decision of **working-class** voters to repudiate the **Democratic Party** in the 1896 election. No Democrat would occupy the White House until 1913, after party officials reevaluated the party's overt pro-business biases. That reevaluation paved the way for the election of a series of pro-labor Democratic governors and legislators. Eugene Debs emerged from prison as a heroic figure and rallied tens of thousands to the socialist cause before his death in 1926.

Suggested Reading

James Gilbert, *Perfect Cities: Chicago's Utopias of 1893*, 1991; Almont Linsey, *The Pullman Strike*, 1964 (reprint of 1942 original); Richard Schneirov, Shelton Stromquist, and Nick Salvatore, eds., *The Pullman Strike and the Crisis of the 1890s*, 1999.

PURE AND SIMPLE UNIONISM

Pure and simple unionism refers to the idea that a labor union's primary task is the pursuit of higher **wages**, shorter hours, and better working conditions for its members. The concept derives from **Adolph Strasser** and **Samuel Gompers**, officials in the Cigar Makers International Union (CMIU). Gompers made it a central principle of the **American Federation of Labor** (AFL), the first important **labor federation** to embrace that ideal. It was a direct repudiation of the reform unionism of the **Knights of Labor** (KOL), which Strasser and Gompers saw as unrealistic **utopianism**.

Capitalism was still a contested concept in the 19th century, and most labor federations spoke of supplanting it with a more just economic system. By the 1880s, the KOL was the nation's largest labor federation and the CMIU was affiliated with it. Like most groups of the time, the KOL embraced a broad reform agenda whose ultimate goal was a remaking of the nation's cultural, economic, political, and social systems. Instead of capitalism, the KOL called for **cooperation**. **Socialist** and **anarchist** groups also called for the dismantling of capitalism and proposed equally idealistic agendas. Socialist cigar makers in New York City quarreled with the CMIU in the early 1880s and formed a rival organization. When the KOL backed the challengers, Strasser and Gompers led the CMIU out of the KOL. Gompers, who claimed to have been a socialist in his youth, grew disenchanted with he perceived to be their naïve and utopian views. He reached similar conclusions about the KOL and most other versions of reform unionism. To both Gompers and Strasser, too much energy was siphoned off in pursuit of unobtainable goals, and both men believed the KOL's opposition to **strikes** was wrongheaded. They saw the strike as labor's primary weapon to force employers to grant what they did not wish to give. They further concluded that only individuals within the same trade unions would be able to maintain sufficient levels of **solidarity** to sustain strikes. Gompers also rejected popular sentiments to form a **labor party**, as he felt the two-party system was too entrenched and that politics merely diverted energy from the workplace. Both he and Strasser distrusted government and felt that workers needed to win rights at the point of production lest they become overly dependent upon government, which they perceived to be an unreliable ally of labor.

When the AFL was founded in 1886, Gompers and Strasser effectively pared labor's agenda to that of wages, hours, and conditions. Many workers, reformers, and labor advocates of the time found the AFL's modest goals too narrow, though its view ultimately prevailed. By stripping the AFL of partisan politics and social agitation, the organization gave implicit acceptance to the legitimacy of capitalism. That perspective, plus its exclusionary membership policies, earned it the opprobrium of the **Industrial Workers of the World** (IWW), which called the AFL the "American Separation of Labor." In fact, the IWW was the last important labor federation to call for the dismantling of capitalism. Since the early 20th century, most labor unions have accepted the permanence of the capitalist system. Today unions lobby for government-directed reforms and hold lofty visions of the future akin to those of their 19th-century forbearers. Nonetheless, the pure-and-simple approach is the everyday operating philosophy of most unions.

Suggested Reading

Julie Greene, *Pure and Simple Politics: The American Federation of Labor and Political Activism, 1881–1917*, 1998; Bruce Laurie, *Artisans into Workers*, 1989; Nick Salvatore, ed., *Seventy Years of Life and Labor: An Autobiography of Samuel Gompers*, 1984.

Q

QUALITY CIRCLES

Quality circles are production units in which small groups of managers and laborers work in tandem to plan and accomplish tasks. They are an alternative to **assembly-line** production. Unlike the mind-numbing specialization and repetitiveness of **Fordism**, or the relentless drive for efficiency of **Taylorism**, quality circles stress task diversity and cooperation between management and labor. Instead of individual workers performing a single task, each member of a quality-circle team performs multiple, changing tasks and sees the product or service through from planning to completion. The goal is to make workers feel less alienated toward the workplace, thereby ensuring high quality and happier employees.

Quality circles originated in Japan, though in many ways their central tenets hark back to human-relations theories developed in the 1930s by organization theorists such as Elton Mayo, and the Plan-Do-Check-Act work theories of consultant W. Edwards Deming. They began to catch on in the United States in the 1980s, especially in the automotive industry, which had been hard hit in the 1970s by foreign imports and declining consumer confidence in domestic auto quality. Honda Motors was the world leader in using quality circles, with General Motors being the first U.S. domestic auto manufacturer to adopt the method. By the 1990s, more than 90 percent of all *Fortune* 500 corporations used quality circles to some degree. Some unions remain suspicious of quality circles, seeing them as a way for management to change work rules without negotiating such changes, though two National Labor Relations Board decisions in the early 1990s ruled that quality circles were subject to the **National Labor Relations Act**. An attempt by conservative **Republicans** to circumvent those decisions (the "TEAM Act") was vetoed by President Bill Clinton in 1996.

By the 21st century, the idea of diversifying work tasks has become standard in American workplaces as diverse as the fast-food industry and library staffing. An ongoing complaint, however, is that management no longer shares planning decisions or takes part in the tasks assigned. Cooperation has given way to a surge in top-down management with an emphasis on providing information to staff on a "need-to-know" basis.

Suggested Reading

Steve Babson, *The Unfinished Struggle: Turning Points in American Labor, 1877–Present*, 1999; Richard Florida and Martin Kennedy, "Transplanted Organizations: The Transfer of Japanese Industrial Organization to the US," *American Sociological Review* 56 (1991): 381–398; David C. Hutchins, *The Quality Circles Handbook*, 1985.

QUICKIE

A quickie is another name for an unauthorized **wildcat strike**. As its name suggests, it seeks to be sudden, unexpected, and of short duration. Like any **strike** that occurs without notice or approval by union officials, quickies are generally viewed as troublesome. In some cases they violate **collective bargaining** agreements and can be illegal under the **National Labor Relations Act**, especially if a contract is in effect. They are seldom prosecuted vigorously, however, because they tend to be very short. Many represent spontaneous outbursts of anger over a perceived injustice in which workers seek to dramatize the need for immediate redress rather than seeking a resolution through slower **grievance** procedures. In some cases quickies are more strategic and are called to demonstrate worker strength and warn employers.

During the 1930s and 1940s, quickies occurred quite frequently, despite opposition to them from both management and union officials. During World War II, unions sometimes used quickies to get around **no-strike pledges**. By the 1950s, one-third of all strikes were quickies, and rank-and-file unionists used them to force companies to renegotiate workplace-rights provisions. Even when seemingly successful in securing **wage** increases or changed working conditions, very few quickies shifted the balance of power of production and workplace issues to the employees. In many cases, these actions led employers to seek retaliation during subsequent contract negotiations. **Business unionism** discourages unilateral actions such as quickies because it weakens the credibility of business agents in the eyes of management.

Quickies fell from favor in the 1970s, but some unions have revived them. Long-term strikes are hard to sustain and even harder to win in the current labor environment. Groups such as the **Hotel Employees and Restaurant Employees International Union** find that the strategic use of quickies is more effective, as even short-term disruption of **service-industry** employers causes enough disruption to make management more prone to bargain. The **United Auto Workers of America** has also experimented with quickies as an alternative to a long strike: A six-hour walkout against Chrysler in 2007 led to a settlement.

Suggested Reading

Stephen Franklin, "Quickie Strikes Puzzling: Are Unions Ready to Revive Tactic or Is It Process Posturing?," *Chicago Tribune*, October 11, 2007; Martin Glaberman, *Wartime Strikes*, 1980; David Moberg, "Hotel Quickie Strikes Build Union, Workers' Determination for Contract Battles," *In These Times*, September 11, 2010.

R

RACKETEER INFLUENCED AND CORRUPT ORGANIZATIONS ACT

The Racketeer Influenced and Corrupt Organizations Act (RICO) is an act of Congress designed to help the federal government prosecute organized crime. RICO is often referenced as shorthand for attempts to break crime syndicates though, technically speaking, the actual RICO bill has been in place only since 1970. Although RICO is not aimed at organized labor specifically, some unions have been prosecuted because they were riddled with internal corruption and had ties to organized crime. The fact that labor unions have been pursued as aggressively under RICO as groups such as the Mafia and drug cartels has prompted some observers to charge that RICO has been used as much for political and ideological reasons as for actual corrupt practices inside unions. Alarmists may have a valid point. During the 1980s employers sought to invoke RICO so often that, in 1988, even U.S. Supreme Court Chief Justice William Rehnquist, a conservative, opined that the law was being used in ways that Congress never intended. Most of the recent charges brought against unions have proved frivolous or unfounded. The **American Federation of Labor-Congress of Industrial Organizations** (AFL-CIO) asserts that recent allegations of union violations of RICO are little more than blatant attempts at union-busting.

The federal government has long found it difficult to break crime syndicates. Merely arresting corrupt individuals often does little to lessen crime; intact organizations simply replace them. The Federal Bureau of Investigation (FBI) was created in 1924 to replace a less-effective federal anticrime unit, and turned its attention to organized crime activities such as bootlegging, gambling, extortion, and prostitution. The FBI and other federal agencies have also investigated labor unions. A variety of pre-RICO federal laws were put into effect to deal with possible union corruption. The 1935 **National Labor Relations Act** offers protection for union members from both employers and abusive union officials. Those rights were greatly enhanced by the 1946 **Taft-Hartley Act**, which also enhanced employers' prerogatives. The Hobbs Act was passed in 1946 to curtail union racketeering and to protect employers during negotiations; this legislation made it a federal crime to attempt robbery or extortion in activities that involve interstate or foreign commerce—provisions later directly incorporated into RICO. The 1959 **Landrum-Griffin Act** contained a union members' "bill of rights," as well as provisions requiring unions to disclose their internal procedures and explain how they use union funds. It also placed limits on an **international union**'s rights to place **union locals** in trusteeship. In the past, some international unions sought to silence reform movements and whistleblowers exposing unethical conduct by high-ranking union officials by placing their locals in receivership and exercising direct control over them.

These actions became necessary because, unfortunately, some unions have been guilty of corrupt practices. The International Brotherhood of Teamsters forged an alliance with organized crime that dates to the early 1950s, if not before. Some **longshoremen's** unions were so infamous for their connections to the criminal underworld that their practices formed the basis of the 1954 Hollywood **film** *On the Waterfront*. Smaller unions—such as unions of bakers, laundry workers, and hotel and restaurant employees—have come under scrutiny. So, too, did the **United Mine Workers of America**, which was rocked by a 1969 scandal in which the reform candidate for its presidency, **Joseph Yablonski**, was murdered by henchmen working for the incumbent. It was the **Teamsters**, though, whose activities most served to associate "Big Labor" with organized crime. Beginning in 1957, the Senate Select Committee on Improper Activities in the Labor Management Field— better known as the McClellan Committee—investigated the Teamsters and other unions. Eventually, Teamster boss **James Hoffa** went to prison, as did several of his successors.

The government's long-running battles with the Teamsters were among the factors that led to writing RICO laws. RICO largely strengthened the Hobbs Act and other measures aimed at curtailing organized crime. This act makes it a federal crime punishable by up to 20 years in prison—or life, if the crime is one for which a life sentence can be imposed—to "conduct or conspire to conduct an enterprise whose activities affect interstate commerce by committing or agreeing to commit a pattern of racketeering activity." To be convicted under RICO, an individual must be proven to be a part of an organization whose history includes two or more racketeering episodes. RICO prosecutions take place for crimes such as murder, extortion, jury tampering, gambling, mail fraud, counterfeiting, distributing pornography, drug trafficking, and a host of other activities. Usually, government agents are given wide leeway in investigating potential RICO violators.

One problem with RICO has been its ambiguity. Terms such as "enterprise," "conspiracy," "pattern," and "racketeering" are subject to overly broad interpretation. Soon after the act's passage, some employers saw RICO as a potential weapon to counter the power of unions. A few attempted to use RICO to revive pre-**Clayton Act** practices that interpreted unions as criminal conspiracies. A **strike**, for example, might affect interstate commerce, and a union doing so more than once could be viewed as having demonstrated a racketeering pattern. A 1973 Supreme Court decision clarified this point by exempting labor unions from prosecution if their activities were related to legitimate union objectives. One controversial section of that ruling extended protection to illegal acts committed by members when the union itself was pursuing legitimate goals. RICO could not, for example, be used against an international union merely because some members of a union local conspired to commit acts of vandalism.

RICO has been applied against unions on numerous occasions. The two best-publicized cases involved the Teamsters in 1988, and the longshoremen two years later. Both unions were placed under federal trusteeship until rank-and-file reform groups could reorganize the unions along democratic lines. Nevertheless, there have also been many misapplications of RICO. Many of these were countenanced during the anti-union climate of the **Ronald Reagan** presidency and continued into the 1990s. Between 1983 and 1989, RICO charges against labor unions increased eightfold, though there was little cause for this trend. Still another conservative, Samuel Alito, a current Supreme Court justice, also agreed that RICO was being abused, and coauthored a book outlining his views. In the late 1990s, for example, California building trades unions began setting up protect-labor agreements (PLAs) that required contractors to sign **contracts** with at least one union on public works projects. Contractor groups tried to sabotage PLAs by bringing RICO suits against the unions. None was successful.

Congress took up possible amendments to RICO in 1986, but these failed in the Senate. Based on several Supreme Court decisions, though, labor unions have been given mild relief from RICO abuses. As noted, unions are exempt from commerce clauses in RICO, if the damage they do is related to the pursuance of legitimate union goals, such as strikes, seeking **collective bargaining** rights, or redressing **grievances** against an employer. Employers also sought to bring racketeering charges against unions engaged in **corporate campaigns**, which led courts to narrow the definition of extortion. Courts also ruled that, in most cases, unions do not obtain an employer's property; hence damage to a business during a labor action is (usually) not extortion.

RICO nonetheless remains a weapon used by employers. In 2000, for example, AK Steel brought suit against the **United Steelworkers of America** (USWA) and numerous union officials, including then USWA (now AFL-CIO) President **Richard Trumka**, charging them with RICO violations ranging from extortion and threats to attempted murder of AK Steel families. In 2002, those suits were dismissed as having no merit. In 2001, unions won a major concession on RICO in the case of *Petrochem Insulation v. Labor Unions of Northern California*. Based on the 1981 decision in *United States v. Turkette*, which opened the door for corporations to be charged under RICO as well, the court ruled in the *Petrochem* case that the company, which failed to lodge National Labor Relations Board (NLRB) charges, was guilty of **unfair labor practices** and RICO violations. Petrochem Insulation was ordered to reimburse unions for their legal costs plus expenses.

Defending RICO lawsuits is a very expensive proposition. The AFL-CIO maintains that many charges are filed with the sole intention of diverting union resources. In 2011, Sodexo USA filed RICO complaints against the **Service Employees International Union** (SEIU). The specifics of the charges appeared to many observers to be more petty than criminal. Nonetheless, SEIU now faces a long and expensive legal battle.

Suggested Reading

James Brudney, "Collateral Conflict: Employer Claims of RICO Extortion against Union Comprehensive Campaigns," *Southern California Law Review* 83, no. 731 (2010): 731–796; Gary McDowell, ed., *The RICO Racket*, 1989; Frank Shanty and Patit Paban

Mishra, *Organized Crime: An International Encyclopedia*, 2005; U.S. Department of Labor, "Employment Law Guide," http://www.dol.gov/compliance/guide/index.htm, accessed May 20, 2011.

RAIDING

Raiding occurs when one union seeks to steal members from a rival union. It can occur between **labor federations** or between **international unions**. For raiding to occur, though, workers must already be represented by a union; unorganized workers are generally considered fair game, though unions may squabble over **jurisdiction** rights.

Sometimes raiding occurs for ideological reasons. In the 19th century, for example, the **Knights of Labor** (KOL) and the **American Federation of Labor** (AFL) disagreed over the importance of **craft unions**. The AFL sought to get trade unionists to quit the KOL and organize according to their profession, whereas the KOL sought to convince workers that craft unionism was exclusionary and that they should unite under KOL principles. That drama would be played out anew in the 1930s, when the newly formed **Congress of Industrial Organizations** (CIO) raided AFL unions of workers they convinced that **industrial unionism** was a better organizing model.

Since the 1955 **American Federation of Labor-Congress of Industrial Organizations** (AFL-CIO) merger, most raiding has occurred when a union sought to bolster its membership to gain bargaining power. A precondition of the AFL-CIO merger was a 1954 no-raiding agreement by existing AFL and CIO affiliates. Unions agreed not to organize or represent employees where "an established bargaining relationship" already existed between the employer and another union. The agreement was effective for four years and, in 1958, was incorporated in Article II, Section 8 and Article III, Section 4 of the AFL-CIO constitution, making the no-raiding agreement mandatory for all affiliates.

That article proved easier to write than to enforce. Although the AFL-CIO could and can discipline affiliates that do not comply, there are numerous independent unions over which it has no control. The AFL-CIO's **American Federation of Teachers** has clashed with the independent **National Education Association**, for example, though the two have enjoyed amicable relations since the 1990s. More troublesome are unions that are expelled from or quit a labor federation. In 1967, the International Brotherhood of Teamsters sought to raid Chicano workers allied with **César Chávez** and the **United Farm Workers of America**. It took many years before the two unions could cooperate or trust each other. In like fashion, the **United Auto Workers of America** (UAW) quit the AFL-CIO in 1968 and did not rejoin the federation until 1982. During that period the UAW organized workers who were not autoworkers, sometimes using raiding to accomplish that task. In 2005, seven unions quit the AFL-CIO to form the **Change to Win Federation**, which has also led to clashes. The **Teamsters**, for example, have organized workers who bolted the AFL-CIO's **United Steelworkers of America** union, and Change to Win's **UNITE-HERE** also engaged in raiding. Discussions are afoot about a possible merger—especially given the 2009 decision of the **United Brotherhood of Carpenters** to rejoin the AFL-CIO—but ill will exists because of mutual raiding.

Raiding and jurisdictional issues have surfaced again recently in the wake of union mergers and the expansion of older industrial unions into workplaces outside their traditional constituencies. Although many unions recognize the need to merge in an effort to regain bargaining strength, weaker unions are sometimes raided as a prelude to merger.

Suggested Reading

Steve Early, "The AFL-CIO Debates Union Raiding," *Monthly Review*, September 19, 2009, http://mrzine.monthlyreview.org/2009/early190909.html, accessed May 20, 2011; Susan Ferriss, Ricardo Sandoval, and Diana Hembree, eds., *Fight in the Fields: Cesar Chavez and the Farmworkers Movement*, 1998.

RAILROAD STRIKE OF 1877

The railroad strike of 1877 is sometimes called the Great Labor Uprising because it was so extensive and, in many locales, evolved into **general strikes**. It is widely regarded as the first nationwide industrial strike and remains one of the most chaotic labor actions in all of American labor history. The strike lasted for more than six weeks in some areas of the country, but its most dramatic and violent phase unfolded during the last two weeks of July 1877. It left more than 100 people dead, caused millions of dollars in property damage, and planted fears among the **middle class** and elites that American society was besieged by **communists**, tramps, **anarchists**, and foreign-born radicals.

The strike began on July 14, when railroad workers in Martinsburg, West Virginia, spontaneously walked off their jobs and refused to allow any rolling stock to leave the rail yard when they discovered that the Baltimore & Ohio Railroad (B & O) had slashed their **wages**. From there, the strike quickly spread and evolved into a popular revolt against the economic might of railroads, the excesses of corporate power, and the mistreatment of industrial workers. As the first major strike to sweep from coast to coast, the uprising was both a turning point for American labor and a harbinger of things to come. The same tracks that carried goods across the nation and connected the trans-Mississippi West to the East also carried work stories that fostered a sense of **class consciousness** among workers who felt mistreated by their employers. Coming just 12 years after the end of the **Civil War**, only six years since workers in Paris, France, declared the city an independent commune, and during the fourth year of a devastating depression, the strike's anger and violence shocked business leaders and politicians and confirmed the fears of labor activists that industry and the state cared little for working people.

The seeds of the strikes were sown in the Panic of 1873 and the ensuing five-year-long depression. Unemployment levels soared and railroad workers lucky enough to keep their jobs saw their wages slashed. Firemen, conductors, and train operators had unions, but only the **Brotherhood of Locomotive Engineers** (BLE) had much vitality and most railroad workers found that companies simply ignored their **grievances**. What rail workers could count upon, however, was that a sizable portion of the general public shared their views that railroad firms were arrogant and that they operated in ways that were not always in the greater public interest. Farmers complained of high costs associated with storing and shipping their commodities to market, merchants in large cities criticized discriminatory railroad rates, and city and town dwellers across the nation resented the encroachment of dangerous and inconvenient railroad lines into public spaces.

The 10 percent wage cut imposed upon B & O workers on July 14 turned out to be the event that triggered an outpouring of pent-up frustration. The BLE urged its members to show restraint when previous wage cuts were incurred and argued that employers and workers shared common interests. Its cautious approach and exclusive nature stimulated the formation of a new association in June 1877, the Trainmen's Union (TU). Neither it nor the BLE proved able to stave off the new wage cuts, and the B & O had taken steps to deter TU organizers. Although some texts discuss the role of the TU in Martinsburg, for the most part the actions taken on July 14 were spontaneous and uncoordinated. This would prove to be true in many locales, and a lack of central control ultimately made the strikes easier to contain. Railroad companies did, however, commit a tactical error by using telegrams to relay instructions, oblivious to the fact that telegraphers considered themselves to be members of the working class.

Although no central union was involved, gangs of workers stopped trains in both Baltimore, Maryland, and Martinsburg, West Virginia, on July 16. Firemen, brakemen, and engineers acted unilaterally to express their dissatisfaction. This led to a showdown between workers, employers, and elected officials that yielded surprising results and revealed the depth of discontent with the railroads. When state governors ordered troops to restore service, they found local militia soldiers in sympathy with fellow workers. In Martinsburg, several stripped off their uniforms and joined the strike. Their defection prompted President Rutherford B. Hayes to send federal troops to protect the B & O lines on July 18—the first known incident of an American president using federal force to put down a labor insurrection. Although federal troops would ultimately prevail, their very presence—as well as that of state-controlled militias—served mainly to precipitate the violence they were allegedly supposed to prevent. (The National Guard can be called into service by a state's governor, whereas the president of the United States is commander and chief of all U.S. military troops.)

The decision to send National Guard troops from Baltimore to Martinsburg touched off both a walkout and riots in Baltimore, where crowds surged toward the B & O's Camden Station. The Maryland National Guard had to fight its way to the station and numerous strikers were killed. The Guardsmen also battled angry mobs in Cumberland, Maryland, and a total of 11 people lay dead even before the first outside militia troops reached Martinsburg on July 19. President Hayes was forced to dispatch federal troops to Baltimore, where angry mobs destroyed railroad stock and set fire to Camden Station.

News of the uprising made its way to workers on Pennsylvania Railroad (PRR) lines. The PRR had an unsavory reputation for being among the most ruthless of

Destruction of the Union Depot and hotel in Pittsburgh during the railroad strike of 1877. Major riots occurred in Pittsburgh and several other cities during the strike, which shut down two-thirds of the U.S. rail system and resulted in the deaths of almost 100 people. Despite a nearly crippling loss for workers, the 1877 strike magnified the gap between capital and labor and eventually inspired stronger labor organization. (Library of Congress)

railroad employers, and its employees had numerous unresolved complaints. Some of the very worst violence occurred along PRR lines, especially in Pittsburgh. When trainmen in Pittsburgh blocked the railroad lines leading out of the city, Pennsylvania Governor John Hartranft ordered National Guard troops from Philadelphia to clear the way for rail traffic. Governor Hartranft sent the troops at the urging of PRR President Thomas Scott, who did not trust Pittsburgh-based militiamen and was anxious to avoid a repeat of the events in Martinsburg. Nevertheless, the use of troops from Philadelphia—and Scott's own reputation for being a robber baron—was viewed as deliberate provocation. On July 21, 20 strikers were killed by National Guardsmen, and the city erupted into a general strike as miners, glassworkers, and others joined the railway men. Enraged mobs destroyed 39 PRR buildings and torched more than 1,000 train cars and engines. Another 20 workers died in clashes with troops. So intense was anger among Pittsburgh citizens that the city was one of the last holdouts once the strikes were broken. President Hayes was forced to send federal troops to assist the National Guard. There were also violent confrontations in Reading, a city on the main rail line between Philadelphia and Pittsburgh.

The struggles in Martinsburg, Baltimore, Cumberland, Reading, and Pittsburgh spread both westward and northward. Most cities that had rail yards experienced unrest, including large cities such as Boston, Chicago, Cincinnati, Louisville, New York, St. Louis, and San Francisco, as well as smaller ones such as Terre Haute, Indiana, Steubenville, Ohio, and Illinois towns such as Bloomington, Decatur, and Urbana. In several places in Illinois, miners joined the strikes. In most cases, the rail strikes served to magnify local grievances that often expressed themselves violently. In Chicago, workers battled an assortment of police officers, militia soldiers, federal troops, and private security forces. St. Louis saw the outbreak of a general strike aimed at establishing an **eight-hour** workday. In San Francisco, 8,000 workers gathered to show **solidarity** with workers in the East, but also to assault the city's Chinese population. At the height of the uprising, more than 100,000 workers were on strike and rumors began to circulate that a full-fledged revolution was under way.

Such claims were fanciful nonsense, but they provided fodder for railroad officials and elites, who stirred up fear to justify harsh crackdowns on strikers. Their efforts were aided by the presence of the Workingman's Party of the United States, a loose confederation of **Marxists** and **Lassallean** socialists in Cincinnati, Chicago, Louisville, New York, and St. Louis, who tried to coordinate strike activities. These **socialist** groups commanded very few members and had little overall impact on the strikes, but their presence stoked charges that the strikers were revolutionaries. In truth, the patterns in most places were quite similar—the strikes were spontaneous, undirected, and peaceful until militia or military troops arrived. The introduction of armed forces against workers sparked most of the violence associated with the strikes, and was often started by those forces. Nonetheless, many journalists described the strikes as if they were a contagious disease threatening to infect the entire nation. Militias, police, private forces, vigilantes, and federal troops managed to regain control of city streets and rail yards, and by August 1, most railroad traffic had resumed.

The strikes left a mixed legacy for American labor. Strikers were partially successfully in the sense that their outburst frightened employers enough that wage cutting was temporarily curtailed, and some companies sought to appease workers with newly created life insurance and medical programs. Other lines, such as the PRR, responded in the opposite direction and strengthened private security forces. PRR President Thomas Scott also lobbied government officials to provide greater federal protection for railroads and private property. One manifestation of that effort was that a spate of National Guard armories rose in American cities, ostensibly to protect the middle class from impending civil insurrection. For the most part, the mainstream press blamed the strike on **communists**, **Molly Maguires**, tramps, and immigrant radicals. Those terms became convenient specters that could be invoked by business leaders and conservative politicians hostile to organized labor.

The most immediate effect of the rail strikes was the temporary decline of **craft unions**. Negative publicity, fear, and the ongoing effects of the depression proved too much for many unions to endure and only a handful of national organizations survived. In the longer term, however, 1877 served as a wakeup call that working people needed stronger organizations to do battle with industrial **capitalism**. The **Knights of Labor** (KOL) held its first national convention one year later in

Reading, Pennsylvania, where a dozen strikers had died in 1877. The strike forced some American workers to see themselves as a class with common interests and needs. The 1877 strikes ended in a rout, but the conditions and complaints of working people did not disappear in a fusillade of militia bullets, nor would labor struggles in the following decades be any less bloody. By the 1880s, trade unions were undergoing a revival, the KOL was gathering in strength, and **class consciousness** would find new expression during the **Great Upheaval**.

Suggested Reading

Michael Bellesiles, *1877: America's Year of Living Violently*, 2010; Robert V. Bruce, *1877: Year of Violence*, 1959; Philip S. Foner, *The Great Labor Uprising of 1877*, 1977; David O. Stowell, *Streets, Railroads, and the Great Strike of 1877*, 1999.

RAILROAD STRIKE OF 1922

The railroad strike of 1922, also known as the Big Strike or the Great Railroad Strike of 1922, is often considered the largest **strike** in U.S. history. Between July and September of 1922, some 400,000 skilled craft workers, known as shopmen, walked off their jobs to protest **wage** cuts and work-rule changes. This incident saw the most widespread use of **injunctions** in American labor history and resulted in a loss for the six unions involved.

The strike was a direct result of the breakdown of the National Agreement, a measure set up during World War I. The National Agreement created the Railroad Labor Board (RLB) to mediate wage and work disputes that might otherwise lead to stoppages that would jeopardize the movement of troops and war materiel. The RLB included representatives from the government as well as from railroad carriers and unions. Vague promises of future **cost-of-living adjustments** were made, and the tripartite RLB resolved most wartime disputes peacefully.

In 1920, the government's direct role in the RLB ended and power shifted to private carriers. A postwar economic slump and a desire to break the power of **craft unions** led carriers to slash wages on July 1, 1921. Several lines, led by the Pennsylvania Railroad, also announced intentions to cease paying **overtime** rates for work on Sundays and holidays, and to change how seniority was calculated. The Pennsylvania Railroad added insult to injury by cutting more than 8,000 jobs during the winter of 1922, largely by **subcontracting** work once done by shopmen. Many of the railroad's actions were inspired by the **National Association of Manufacturers**, which had launched an **open-shop** drive to break the power of unions. In all, companies foisted approximately $60 million in wage cuts upon their employees. Because most of the company's actions were in violation of the National Agreement, craft unionists appealed to the RLB, but it acquiesced to carrier demands.

As conditions deteriorated in 1922, unions and carriers alike readied themselves for confrontation. Shopmen had the potential to inflict severe economic damage to both railroads and the nation at large. Because automobiles were not yet a fixture of American society, a sizable percentage of the nation's mail, commerce, and passengers was transported by rail. Rail carriers depended on skilled carpenters, machinists, welders, repairmen, and others to keep the railroads running smoothly.

The first workers to leave their jobs were those employed in Pennsylvania Railroad shops, but the walkout soon spread to other lines. Discontent among rail workers was so widespread that the July 1 strike vote received the approval of 97 percent of rank-and-file union members, even though the RLB declared the impending strike illegal. Within days, as many as 400,000 rail workers walked off the job.

When the **American Railway Union** became defunct after the **Pullman strike/lockout**, railroad workers were left without an **industrial union**. As a consequence, the 1922 strike was confined to skilled shopmen dispersed among six unions, including the **International Association of Machinists**. Although those six unions negotiated through a joint Railway Employees' Department, railroad brotherhoods like the carmen, firemen, and the **Brotherhood of Locomotive Engineers** were covered by separate agreements and continued to work during the strike. This allowed the railroads to operate by recruiting **scabs** from among management, the unemployed, college students, clerks, and those ideologically opposed to labor unions. The RLB authorized the hiring of scabs, and it turned a blind eye as machine guns and hired guards appeared in rail yards across the East and Midwest. The scabs proved unable to take on such highly skilled work, which led railroad officials across the United States to seek injunctions to force workers back to work. Thousands faced arrest rather than yield. On July 28, President Warren G. Harding tried to broker an agreement that would have done little except protect seniority rights. The Railroad Employees' Department reluctantly accepted Harding's modest proposal, but railroad executives rejected it out of hand.

The unions and President Harding were undermined by Harding's own attorney general, Harry Daugherty, who played much the same role during the 1922 strike as Attorney General Richard Olney had assumed during the Pullman struggle 30 years earlier. Daugherty sought broad injunctions against strikers, partly to protect his own investments, and partly because he had a pathological fear of **communism**. The Bolshevik Revolution had taken place in Russia five years earlier, and Daugherty claimed that railroad workers sought to emulate it. His interpretation was ludicrous, but his fear mongering proved a successful strategy in the wake of the postwar **Red Scare**. Daugherty convinced Federal District Judge James Wilkerson to issue restraining orders on September 1, based on rather convoluted interpretations of the **Sherman Antitrust Act**, and as if the **Clayton Act** had never been passed. As in the Pullman dispute, alleged interference with the U.S. mail was cited as one justification for injunctions.

Wilkerson's restraining order involved the broadest application of injunction powers in U.S. labor history. He placed a total gag order on the unions, officials, and the rank-and-file. Strikers were forbidden to **picket**, hold strike meetings, issue press releases, or in any manner encourage the strike. Wilkerson's orders even forbade use of the mail or telegrams; in essence, the judge outlawed free speech. Wilkerson's temporary restraining order also contained his defiant defense of open shops. Hundreds of union members were jailed as a result of the injunction. In San Francisco, a $9 million judgment was ordered against striking unions; elsewhere, even individuals filed lawsuits against the strikers. There was little unions could do in the face of such opposition except surrender. On August 25, 1922, less intransigent employers of the New York Central and Baltimore and Ohio Railroads settled with their workers. The resulting "B & O Plan" retained seniority systems and rehired most of the strikers at existing wage rates. It became the blueprint by which disputes on other lines were settled. Most strikes were over by mid-September, though some Pennsylvania Railroad workers remained on strike for more than two years.

In the short term, the strike was a disaster for unions. Unions were weakened to the point where they could not muster opposition even when promises on seniority were broken. Tens of thousands of railroad workers were forced to quit their organizations and join **company unions**. The 1922 strike stands as the most dramatic example of the fate that befell most strikers in the 1920s. Union membership across the nation plummeted in the wake of a full-scale assault on the part of aggressive anti-union employers. But rail carriers also paid a heavy price. The Daugherty/Wilkerson injunctions were so outrageous than even some conservatives saw them as unreasonable. Daugherty's subsequent role in the Teapot Dome scandal crippled his credibility and, in 1924, forced him to resign as attorney general. Some awards against unions were either overturned or drastically reduced. Many workers responded to the political heavy-handedness of the strike by supporting the 1924 Progressive Party campaign of Robert La Follette, who garnered more than 4.8 million votes, more than half as many as **Democratic** challenger John Davis. In 1926, Congress passed the **Railway Labor Act of 1926** to correct some of the problems within the industry. In 1935, the **National Labor Relations Act** outlawed many of the abusive injunction methods used in 1922.

Suggested Reading

Irving Bernstein, *The Lean Years*, 1960; Colin J. Davis, *Power at Odds: The 1922 National Railroad Shopmen's Strike*, 1997; Foster Rhea Dulles and Melvyn Dubofsky, *Labor in America: A History*, 1984.

RAILROAD UNIONS. *See* American Railway Union; Brotherhood of Locomotive Engineers; Knights of Labor.

RAILWAY LABOR ACT OF 1926

The Railway Labor Act (RLA) of 1926 is the federal law that governs labor relations and **collective bargaining** in the U.S. railroad and airline industries. It is a direct outgrowth of the **railroad strike of 1922**, which was the latest in six decades of bitter capital/labor conflicts in the railroad industry. The RLA's objective is to curtail **strikes** and other disruptive conflicts that interrupt interstate commerce and weaken the economy. The act guarantees the right of employees to form labor unions, and it set up a federal agency to mediate disputes.

The railroad industry was wracked by constant tension from the **railroad strike of 1877** onward. Many of the strikes were violent and resulted in the loss of life and destruction of property. Rail workers, with the exception of those affiliated with the **Brotherhood of Locomotive Engineers**, were notoriously underpaid, worked long hours, and labored under dangerous conditions. At the turn of the 20th century, one of every 306 railroad workers died on the job, and one in 30 was injured. A series of laws, the first of which appeared in 1888, sought to achieve industrial peace in the railroad industry. Most were ineffective as they relied upon voluntary compliance; the RLA mandated mediation. The abusive use of **injunction** power against workers during 1922 was another impetus for the RLA.

The act promotes **collective bargaining** and is administered by the National Mediation Board (NMB). The NWB does not possess binding **arbitration** power, but strikes over pay and working conditions are illegal unless the NMB releases the parties from mediation. Should a strike occur, the RLA allows employers to hire **scabs** during the dispute, but they cannot fire strikers unless they commit a crime or other major infraction. The RLA also allows the president of the United States to delay a strike by creating a Presidential Emergency Board to investigate the dispute. More than 230 such boards have been convened since 1934. There are also provisions to prevent work stoppages over other **grievances**.

The RLA authorizes secret-ballot elections and union **certification** votes conducted by the NMB. If a majority of workers vote for union representation, employers must bargain with it. Initially, the RLA applied only to the railroad industry; airlines were added to the legislation in 1934. Ironically, the NLA came about at precisely the time at which railroads began to wane in importance due to the rise of the automotive industry. The RLA is significant for its implication for airline workers, however, and because it influenced the framing of the 1935 **National Labor Relations Act**.

Suggested Reading

Douglas Leslie, ed., *The Railway Labor Act*, 1995; Charles Rehmus, ed., *The Railway Labor Act at Fifty: Collective Bargaining in the Railroad and Airline Industries*, 1977; Frank Wilner, *Understanding the Railway Labor Act*, 2009.

RANDOLPH, ASA PHILIP

A. Philip Randolph (April 14, 1889–May 16, 1979) was a trade unionist and social activist regarded by many as the bridge between earlier reform efforts and the modern civil-rights movement. He was the son of the Reverend James William and Elizabeth (Robinson) Randolph, and completed high school in Jacksonville, Florida. In 1914, he married Lucille Greene. Shortly thereafter he moved to the Harlem section of New York City, and worked as an elevator operator while taking classes at City College of New York.

Randolph's arrival in New York coincided with a flowering of political and cultural activity within the black community known as the Harlem Renaissance. He became a **socialist** and, in 1917, set up the mostly African American United Brotherhood of Elevator and Switchboard Operators union. That same year, he and Chandler Owen began publication of *The Messenger*, an independent socialist journal. That paper was sympathetic to the **Industrial Workers of the World** and critical of African American involvement in World War I. Randolph was arrested as a suspected **communist** in 1918, was briefly jailed, and then was drafted into military service, but the war ended and charges against him were dropped.

The Messenger advocated that African Americans join labor unions—important advice at the time. The decline of the race-neutral **Knights of Labor** created a crisis for black workers, as many affiliates of the **American Federation of Labor** (AFL) were racist and banned black members. Some black leaders saw organized labor as so mired in racism that they said it was acceptable for blacks to **scab** on white workers during industrial disputes. Randolph was no accommodationist, however: He was highly critical of both **capitalism** and the National Association for the Advancement of Colored People (NAACP)—the latter he deemed too conservative and conciliatory. In 1919, Randolph served on

A. Philip Randolph won respect for his quiet dignity and his firmness in a lifelong commitment to racial justice. A union organizer and socialist early in life, he became the country's best-known African American trade unionist and a nationally prominent leader in the struggle for civil rights during the early to mid-20th century. (Library of Congress)

the executive board of the National Brotherhood Workers of America and, in 1920, he set up Friends of Negro Freedom, an organization to protect migrant and tenant rights. Randolph also quit the Socialist Party when it moved too slowly on civil rights issues. In 1925, he founded the **Brotherhood of Sleeping Car Porters** (BSCP) and commanded its 12-year struggle to obtain a contract with the Pullman Corporation. In 1936, the BSCP became affiliated with the AFL. Randolph continued as president of the BSCP until his retirement in 1968.

Randolph was one of the most important civil rights advocates of the 20th century. He served on numerous commissions on race and, in 1936, co-founded the National Negro Congress to promote black job opportunities under the New Deal and protect the rights of black workers. His threat to organize a march of black workers on Washington, D.C., prompted President Franklin Roosevelt to establish the **Fair Employment Practices Committee** in 1941. During and after World War II, Randolph was an outspoken critic of military segregation. He was equally vocal when confronting racism within the labor movement. As a delegate to the International Confederation of Free Trade Unions in 1951 and a member of the executive council of the **American Federation of Labor-Congress of Industrial Organizations** (AFL-CIO) after its 1955 merger, Randolph forcefully argued for full inclusion for people of color. In 1960, he founded the Negro American Labor Council to advance black union members. His militancy led to numerous clashes with cautious AFL-CIO leaders and, in 1961, the executive council censured Randolph. His relationship with AFL-CIO **George Meany** was especially contentious. Randolph often allied with **Walter Reuther** to press the AFL-CIO on issues of race; Meany considered both men to be troublemakers.

Randolph was the national director of the 1963 March on Washington for Jobs and Freedom and addressed the rally just before the Reverend Martin Luther King, Jr., delivered his iconic "I Have a Dream" speech. By the time of Randolph's death in 1979, the AFL-CIO had adopted many of the protections for black workers that he advocated. Since 1965, the **A. Philip Randolph Institute** has operated as a constituency group within the AFL-CIO. In 1989, Randolph was posthumously inducted in the **Department of Labor**'s Labor Hall of Fame.

Suggested Reading

Jervis Anderson, *A. Philip Randolph: A Biographical Portrait*, 1972; Andrew Kersten, *A. Philip Randolph: A Life in the Vanguard*, 2006; Cynthia Taylor, *A. Philip Randolph: The Religious Journey of an African American Labor Leader*, 2006.

RATE CUTTING

Rate cutting refers to an employer's attempt to extract more work and higher production rates from workers by reducing their pay. This tactic is used mostly in jobs in which overall pay is tied to **piecework** rates, as direct cuts to **wages** sometimes backfire and make workers feel disinvested in whether a company does well or poorly. In extreme cases, rate cutting can breed so much resistance that workers will engage in **sabotage** as once defined by the **Industrial Workers of the World**—"the systematic withdrawal of efficiency."

Rate cutting generally occurs in enterprises such as brick making, textiles, the garment trades, or semiskilled assembly work in which the quantity of goods produced is essential to the firm's overall profit margin. Trade unions usually oppose piecework payment because this practice is so open to rate cutting. It often leads to a de facto **speedup** in which workers push themselves harder simply to retain a comparable level of pay, though almost always their increased efficiency and production far outstrip their remuneration. Unions also charge that employers, in effect, punish employees who have mastered their skill; instead of rewarding them for efficiency, they seek to work them harder.

Rate cutting is primarily associated with jobs that pay a fixed sum for each article produced. It is a key component in scientific management principles associated with **Taylorism** and has often generated fierce opposition from workers. For example, the demand for production of wartime supplies in the early 1940s generated conflict and safety concerns at automotive plants such as Chrysler and Packard Motors.

Even though the **United Auto Workers of America** had signed a **no-strike pledge**, workers challenged management consistently over rate cutting and forced plants to maintain production standards and enact incentive pay rates instead. On a less formal level, veteran workers on most jobs develop internal ideas about what constitutes a "fair" day's labor. Part of the initiation of new workers consists of learning the **stint** from peers, who apply direct or indirect pressure to enforce it.

Rate cutting was more common during the industrial than the postindustrial era. Today, slashing wages directly is the preferred way of imposing cost cutting, and is often imposed under the rubric of becoming leaner to compensate for **globalism**'s competitive pressures. However, rate cutting still occurs in fields such as product assembly, sales, and telemarketing in which commissions and incentive pay are based on output.

Suggested Reading

H. Dean Smith, ed., *Source Book on Collective Bargaining*, 2011; Frederick Winslow Taylor, *The Principles of Scientific Management*, 1911.

RAVENSWOOD LOCKOUT

The Ravenswood lockout was a protracted struggle between the **United Steelworkers of America** (USWA) and the Ravenswood Aluminum Company (RAC). To some observers, the USWA's partial victory in 1992 signaled an important reversal of union fortunes in the 1980s and served as a portent of organized labor's potential for renewal. Thus far those predictions have proved overly optimistic.

Problems at Ravenswood stemmed from the merger mania that marked American corporate culture in the 1980s. The aluminum reduction and fabrication plant in this small West Virginia town on the Ohio River opened in 1954, as part of the Kaiser Aluminum Company (later known as ALCOA). In 1958, the USWA organized plant workers in local 5668. For many years, capital/labor relations were marked by **paternalism**, which took the shape of union/management cooperation and civic benevolence on the part of the corporation. By the 1970s, however, ALCOA's market share had declined in the face of competition from imports and decreased efficiency due to the antiquated nature of its manufacturing facilities. Jobs were eliminated in Ravenswood and other facilities. ALCOA management forced Local 5668 to accept deep **concessions** in 1984. By 1986, though, ALCOA was still deeply in debt. Two years later, Ravenswood was part of an ALCOA sell-off that placed the RAC under the control of an international holding company clandestinely financed by corporate raider and tax-evader Marc Rich.

Safety conditions and morale were already in decline at the RAC. They were made worse by new plant management that was openly hostile to the USWA. The on-the-job deaths of several Ravenswood workers brought matters to a head in 1990, when the USWA declared that those deaths were due in large part to the company's refusal to upgrade facilities and implement safety procedures. On November 1, RAC management issued a **lockout** of the plant's 1,700 workers, declared it a non-union facility, and began hiring **scabs** to replace USWA members. For the next 18 months the USWA battled the company on the **picket** line, in domestic and international courts, before the National Labor Relations Board, in the political arena, and on the public relations front. The USWA launched an especially effective **corporate campaign** that exposed Ravenswood's ties to Marc Rich, by then an international fugitive from justice living in Switzerland. The USWA also showed how cost-cutting measures took place in violation of the 1970 **Occupational Safety and Health Act** and how the firm routinely violated the Clean Air and Clean Water Acts. RAC workers also maintained inspiring levels of **solidarity** throughout the struggle. Even more impressively, Local 5668 built bridges with overseas union movements that collectively placed pressure on Rich, banks doing business with Ravenswood, and politicians who coddled questionable corporate practices. The union also convinced important RAC clients—such as Coca Cola and Anheuser-Busch—to stop purchasing scab-made cans. The union's anti-Rich campaign took it to Australia, England, Finland, France, the Netherlands, Romania, Russia, Spain, Switzerland, and five other nations. The USWA successfully linked Rich's consortium to labor struggles around the globe and pressured Rich holdings worldwide.

Faced with international pressure, mounting legal bills, and overwhelmingly negative public opinion, the RAC settled its dispute with USWA Local 5668. On June 12, 1992, members ratified a new contract and, on June 29, jubilant workers marched into the plant singing "Solidarity Forever." For many observers, the Ravenswood events—like 1990s victories by United Parcel Service workers, NYNEX workers, **Fieldcrest** employees, and others—showed that organized labor was on the cusp of a renewal. Ravenswood workers received high praise for their creativity, their international organizing efforts, and their steadfast refusal to cave in. The Ravenswood lockout was also viewed as proof that modern labor conflicts needed to go beyond traditional trade union reliance on **strikes**.

The final settlement was not a complete victory for the USWA, however. In the short term, Ravenswood nearly went bankrupt during the lockout and its uncertain financial future delayed promised safety improvements, job guarantees, and pension schemes. The $2,000 in back pay given to each worker hardly compensated for their losses, and several hundred workers failed to get their jobs back when the RAC reopened with a reduced workforce. Moreover, the USWA had to welcome into the union more than 300 **scabs** who took vacant positions. In 2001, President Bill Clinton granted a presidential pardon to Marc Rich, an act seen by many USWA members as an insult.

Two decades later, Ravenswood looks to be considerably less than the victory the USWA and labor analysts had hoped it would be. Labor union membership has continued to plummet in the private sphere, and a 2010 *USA Today* article dubbed Ravenswood as a "new ghost town." Ravenswood has long been a classic **company town** whose 4,000 residents were either directly or indirectly linked to the fate of the old Kaiser Aluminum complex. In 1995, the RAC was purchased by the Swiss-based firm Glencore International, which reorganized it as part of Century Aluminum in 1997. Two years later, it sold Ravenswood's fabrication facilities—which makes plate aluminum—to a French film. Alcan, in turn, purchased it in 2003.

The Century plant, which smelts aluminum, struggled to maintain profitability and, in 2009, closed most of its smelters at Ravenswood and laid off 651 workers. Century sought to cancel the **pensions** of retirees in 2011, and made vague promises of returning work to Ravenswood, but the U.S. Senate rejected that plan as a violation of pension reform laws. Alcan continues to employ approximately 1,000 workers in Ravenswood, but Rio Tinto absorbed Alcan in 2007 and the future of the Ravenswood facility is uncertain. Some more somber observers now view aluminum production and fabrication as a **sunset industry**.

Suggested Reading

Steve Early, "Lessons from the Last Twenty-Five Years: Walking Out and Winning," *Solidarity*, http://www.solidarity-us.org/node/113, accessed May 23, 2011; Rick Hampson, "New Ghost Towns: Industrial Communities Teeter on the Edge," *USA Today*, March 1, 2010; Tom Juravich and Kate Bronfenbrenner, *Ravenswood: The Steelworkers' Victory and the Revival of American Labor*, 1999.

REAGAN, RONALD, AND LABOR

The presidency of Ronald Reagan (1981–1989) is one that continues to perplex scholars and labor activists. The Reagan administration was the most pro-business and anti-organized labor presidency since that of Calvin Coolidge (1923–1929). By objective standards, the vast majority of Reagan-era tax cuts and economic initiatives favored large corporations and wealthy individuals, yet Reagan was popular among the **middle class** and among **blue-collar** voters. The latter point was particularly vexing for labor leaders, as the Reagan presidency saw the acceleration of **deindustrialization**, the weakening of labor laws, support for the **right-to-work** movement, the smashing of the **Professional Air Traffic Controllers Organization** (PATCO) **strike**, changes in the tax code that aided **runaway shops**, and explicit support for employers during **downsizing, decertification, and concessions strikes**. Scholars generally cite the malaise of the 1970s, a reaction against the 1960s **counterculture**, personal charisma, and clever politicking as among the reasons for Reagan's popularity among the **working class**.

Reagan swept to the presidency by trouncing the **Democratic** incumbent, Jimmy Carter. In a three-way race that also featured independent John Anderson, Reagan took nearly 51 percent of the popular vote to Carter's 41 percent, and swamped Carter in the Electoral College 189 to 49. When Reagan ran for reelection in 1984, his Democratic challenger Walter Mondale won only the electoral votes of Minnesota and the District of Columbia. The latter election prompted a study by Stan Greenberg of a blue-collar Detroit suburb in which two of every three voters in traditionally Democratic Macomb County cast a ballot for Reagan. Greenberg's use of the term "Reagan Democrats" to describe the transference of power caught on with the media, though it is unclear whether Greenberg actually coined it.

The stagflation and political malaise of the 1970s played a key role in Reagan's election. A series of **boycotts** launched by the Organization of Petroleum Exporting Countries (OPEC) oil cartel beginning in 1973 unleashed soaring energy costs whose effects rippled across through the economy in the form of oil shortages, layoffs, and a wave of high inflation paired with stagnant economic growth for which economists coined the term "stagflation." By 1980, the United States was mired in year seven of the worst economic downturn since the Great Depression of the 1930s. Presidents Richard Nixon, Gerald Ford, and Jimmy Carter each sought, but failed, to reduce stagflation and unemployment. The ruined economy was exacerbated by blows to American prestige and confidence occasioned by events such as Nixon's resignation because of the Watergate scandal, the defeat of South Vietnam by the **communist** forces of North Vietnam, a botched attempt to rescue the crew of the U.S. merchant ship *Mayaquez* from Cambodia's communist government, the Three Mile Island nuclear mishap, Carter's signing of an unpopular treaty giving Panama control over its namesake canal, and a crisis in Iran in which Americans were held hostage by revolutionaries for 444 days.

Reagan appeared as the antidote to the malaise of the 1970s. His decisive firing of PATCO workers during their illegal 1981 **strike** appeared an act of bold leadership to Americans frustrated by the events of the previous decade. Many also bought into Reagan's explanation that the turmoil of the 1970s had been occasioned by the chaos of the 1960s. Reagan consciously evoked the boom economy of the 1950s and linked it to the "family values" he insisted reigned during that decade. (He conveniently ignored the fact that the 1960s economy was more prosperous, and that 1950s society countenanced racism, sexism, nativism, and a **Red Scare**.) Reagan's "blame the 1960s" strategy resonated with many blue-collar workers who were uncomfortable with the Democratic Party's perceived coddling of the political left. Many had viewed opposition to the **Vietnam War** as unpatriotic and, in 1970, several hundred New York City construction workers clashed with antiwar demonstrators during what was dubbed the **hard hat riots**. Other social issues also arose. Reagan's outward support for the antichoice, pro-life movement appealed to evangelicals and Catholics troubled by the 1973 *Roe v. Wade* Supreme Court decision that legalized abortion. In like fashion, many white male workers made fearful by deindustrialization and runaway shops blamed **affirmative action** for their precarious economic status and applauded Reagan's attacks on feminism and "social engineering."

Reagan exuded personal charm, a skill he and his handlers used to frame an economic program based on tearing down **protectionism**, **deregulating** American business, cutting social programs, increasing military spending, and enacting massive tax cuts. Nearly all of the tax cuts benefited the wealthy, but Reagan vigorously defended them as the key to a "supply-side" economic program that would revitalize the American economy. The administration argued that stagflation had resulted from "unearned sufficiencies" such as welfare and social programs that drained revenue and were economically nonproductive and could be sustained only via high taxes. Those high taxes, however, discouraged investors, so that both prices and unemployment rose. According to the supply-side philosophy, tax cuts for the wealthy would free up capital to be invested in the economy; such investments would, in turn, create a trickle-down effect in which jobs would be created. Under Reagan, the tax rate for the top income bracket was lowered from 70 percent to just 38 percent, and more than $12 billion per annum was lopped from the tax rolls.

The promises of the tax cuts did not match the reality. Two million jobs disappeared within the first six months of tax cuts enacted in August 1981. Housing markets and the construction industry listed dangerously when the prime rate—the amount the Federal Reserve System charges commercial banks to borrow—soared above 20 percent. The Reagan administration touted growth, but nearly 90 percent of all Reagan-era tax cuts accrued to the richest 1 percent of the population, and just 1,700 companies collected 80 percent of the savings in corporate taxes, though they created only 4 percent of all the new jobs created before 1990. Cuts in federal support for state and local government and programs led to rising state, local, property, and sales taxes. Once adjusted for inflation and new taxes, Americans making between $30,000 and $50,000 per year saved just $84 in taxes, while those earning less than $30,000 got no tax relief whatsoever. The situation was particularly dire for the working poor, who had no tax shelters or write-offs, and for whom half of their income went to taxes of some sort. Cuts to job-training programs, food stamps, Medicare, and other poverty-oriented programs served to widen the gulf between rich and poor. Corporate executive officers, by contrast, did exceedingly well. In 1980, the average CEO made 40 times more than the average worker; by 1990, they made 93 times more. In his eight years in office, Reagan oversaw the creation of 16 million new jobs, but the vast majority of these gains came in the **service industry** sector, or were created by small businesses that benefited very little from Reagan's economic policies.

The Reagan administration was, however, masterful at manipulating political perception. By 1982, the official unemployment rate stood at 10.8 percent; by November 1984, it had dropped to 7.6 percent. Reagan seized upon this trend and insisted that his economic plan was working, even though the unemployment rate was actually 0.2 percent higher in 1984 than it had been under Carter. Inflation did decline significantly during Reagan's time in office and the gross national product increased nearly 4 percent per year, but unemployment did not tumble to less than 6 percent until 1987. That same year a stock market crash occurred—one that many economists attributed to deficit spending by the Reagan administration. Under Reagan, the United States' national debt spiraled upward from $997 billion to $2.85 trillion. The lingering effects of the recession touched off by the country's enormous debt load and the stock market crash soon caused unemployment to rise anew. This rate stood at 7.4 percent in 1992—the same level as it had been in 1980—and was a major factor in denying a second term to Reagan's successor, George H. W. Bush. Unemployment did not dip below 5 percent until 1997, after President Bill Clinton raised taxes on the wealthy and balanced the federal budget.

Reagan often spoke of his admiration for working people and touted the virtues of the Polish trade union movement Solidarity, which sought to cast off the yoke of Poland's communist government. Somewhat oddly, given his antilabor stance, Reagan was the only president who had been a union official, having served seven terms as president of the Screen Actors Guild. Nonetheless, the Reagan years saw numerous bitter capital/labor conflicts, including the PATCO strike, a walkout by Arizona copper workers in 1983, and battles involving Hormel workers in 1985, the *Chicago Tribune* in 1986, the United Steelworkers in 1986, and International Paper in 1987. The **American Federation of Labor-Congress of Industrial Organizations** (AFL-CIO) co-sponsored and took part in several mass public protests against Reagan's policies, including a 1981 Solidarity March of more than 250,000 people that registered disagreement with Reagan's handling of the PATCO strike, and a 1982 protest in New York in opposition to the administration's stance on nuclear power, foreign policy, and labor standards. That event was attended by as many as 1 million people and occurred at the time the largest protest rally in American history. The AFL-CIO also complained bitterly that Reagan politicized both the **Department of Labor** and the National Labor Relations Board by appointing pro-business/anti-union members to what were designed to be impartial organizations. There can be little doubt that the Reagan years were unkind to organized labor. In 1980, 23 percent of American workers were unionized; when Reagan left office in 1989, just 16.4 percent belonged to unions, which Reagan routinely characterized as outmoded and impediments to economic growth.

The standard **Marxist** explanation for Reagan's appeal to the masses is that they were duped. The reality is more complex than that dictum, just as the assertion that 1980 was a realigning election is overly simplistic. During the 1930s, President **Franklin Roosevelt** crafted what came to be known as the "New Deal Coalition," a voting bloc that helped Democrats dominate politics for much of the next five decades. It consisted of long-time Democratic groups such as southern farmers and Irish Catholics, plus urban blue-collar voters, naturalized **immigrants**, African Americans, and Jewish Americans. The New Deal Coalition was by no means an airtight alliance, as seen by the Dixiecrat rebellion of 1948 and the fierce opposition of southern Democrats to the **civil rights** movement from the 1910s through to the 1980s, when many bolted and joined the Republican Party. Numerous Democrats were also found among the **right-to-work** movement.

Reagan capitalized on long-term Republican strategies to develop "wedge" issues to divide the New Deal Coalition. Although Lyndon Johnson won the presidency easily in 1964, his Republican opponent Barry Goldwater cracked the "Solid South" by winning five states in the region. In the 1968 election, five southern states supported George Wallace's segregationist third party, and the Democratic candidate for president, Hubert Humphrey, won only Texas in the South. Republican policymakers such as Lee Atwater and Karl Rove became adroit at developing code words to play on the racial and economic fears of white voters without sounding overtly racist or alarmist. Opposition to school busing to achieve racial balance proved a powerful "wedge" issue to win suburban middle- and working-class class voters. Republicans also became adroit at packaging tax and spending cuts as "jobs" programs. In each case, organized labor's support for Democrats also made unions vulnerable targets for disgruntled Americans.

Some political scientists argue that the Reagan Democrats phenomenon is exaggerated and that the fracturing of the New Deal Coalition represents an outgrowth of American multiculturalism and uncertainty over the shape of the postindustrial economy. The height of the Reagan Democrat wave came in 1984, but even then just 30 percent of Democrats switched their loyalty. It is also unclear whether blue-collar voters actually became Reagan Democrats. The AFL-CIO is among those organizations arguing that union families did not support Reagan, and that most continue to cast Democratic votes. The growth of American multiculturalism might also signal that social class is not necessarily the primary factor in determining voting patterns. Republicans, for example, have done very well among voters identifying themselves as evangelicals, even when those voters also support unions. Democrats, by contrast, have enjoyed success in courting economic conservatives who support a liberal social agenda. Nearly one-fourth of all voters are now registered as independent; by 2010, those voters outnumbered Republicans and Democrats in 11 states.

More than three decades after Ronald Reagan's election, it now seems hyperbolic to call 1980 a realigning election. Two Republicans and two Democrats have been elected president since Reagan; in the 11 Congresses since Reagan left office, Democrats and Republicans each controlled five Senates and one was split 50-50; Republicans have enjoyed a six-to-five hold on the House of Representatives. It is probably wiser to see an American society evenly split over social and economic changes rather than a realignment in which the New Deal Coalition was supplanted by a Reagan-inspired alliance. Many of the current worries over jobs and the future of the American economy would probably have occurred even if Reagan had lost. Still, organized labor's erosion was accelerated by Reagan's policies and it has not yet reversed that decline.

Suggested Reading

Philip M. Dine, *State of the Unions*, 2008; Samuel Freedman, *The Inheritance: How Three Families and America Moved from Roosevelt to Reagan and Beyond*, 1998; Ronald Radosh, *Divided They Fell: The Demise of the Democratic Party, 1964–1996*, 1998; Michael Schiavone, *Unions in Crisis? The Future of Organized Labor in America*, 2008; Lowell Turner, Harry C. Katz, and Richard Hurd, *Rekindling the Movement: Labor's Quest for Relevance in the 21st Century*, 2001.

RECONSTRUCTION AND LABOR

Reconstruction refers to the period between 1865 and 1877 in which the United States sought to rebuild after the **Civil War**. Reconstruction had a profound effect on the shape of future race and capital/labor relations.

The Civil War disrupted American society in many ways, and the labor movement was not immune to the upheaval. The **Lynn shoe strike of 1860** took place on the eve of the war, and the conflict itself forced a reassessment of race and power. The northern **working classes** largely supported the preservation of the Union, but commitment to **free labor** ideals did not always translate into sympathy for ending **slavery** or supporting ideals of black citizenship, issues over which white workers divided. In fact, Lincoln's decision to sign the Emancipation Proclamation dampened the enthusiasm for war of many northern workers. As the war wore on, some northern workers supported the idea of letting the South secede; others rioted over conscription laws seen as violations of personal liberty in defense of slave emancipation. There was also widespread resentment against northern merchants perceived (rightly in many cases) of war profiteering through the production of substandard ("shoddy") goods. Although they are not widely recorded in history texts, several **strikes** occurred during the war, including ones involving Chicago bricklayers, female garment workers in New York, and St. Louis printers. Northern **craft unions**, in fact, gained in strength during the war—increasing in number from 79 such organizations in 1862 to 270 in 1863. Among the bodies to form or gain strength during the war were the **Brotherhood of Locomotive Engineers**, the Cigar Makers' International Union, and the Iron Molders' Union.

The end of the war rekindled disputes between capital and labor. Workers also faced the prospect of taking sides on the important issues of the day: the fate of freed slaves, the definition of a fair day's labor, the integration of **immigrants** into American society, the emergence of monopoly **capitalism**, and the instability of the nation's money supply. In the North, some workers—both as voters and as union members—cast their fate with Radical Republicans, a faction that emerged to challenge President Andrew Johnson's lenient plan for allowing former Confederate states to rejoin the Union. In 1866, Radical Republicans gained control of Congress and enacted a harsher reconciliation plan. Northern workers largely acceded to the idea that the South had to accept the Thirteenth Amendment officially abolishing slavery, though they split on the Fourteenth and Fifteenth Amendments, which guaranteed citizenship and voting rights for black men but withheld suffrage from women.

The popularity of Radical Republicans reached its apex in 1868, when they came within a single vote of removing President Johnson from office, and declined rapidly after 1873, by which time the nation was thrust in economic distress resulting from the Panic of 1873. Some workers, including those active in the **eight-hour movement**, saw Radical Republicans as allies, especially figures such as Massachusetts Congressman Benjamin Butler. On the local and state levels, ties were even stronger. The most pronounced links between labor activists and Radical Republicans were evident in Massachusetts, but similar alliances emerged in Kansas, Illinois, and elsewhere. Some Radical Republicans also expressed support for Fenianism, an Irish nationalist movement popular among Irish American workers.

An extensive alliance between Radical Republicans and labor never materialized, however, and even before the former movement faded, many northern workers had grown distrustful of it. Sentiment built in favor of the creation of a **labor party**, and new movements, such as **greenbackism**, emerged to advance causes for which Republican support was tepid. As Radical Reconstruction unfolded, new labor organizations emerged. In 1866, **William Sylvis** and 77 other labor reformers created the **National Labor Union** (NLU), an attempt to unite unions in a **labor federation**. The Knights of St. Crispin formed in 1877 and soon became the largest trade union in the United States. Two years later the **Knights of Labor** (KOL) formed. Both the NLU and the KOL accepted the principle of fellowship with black workers; the KOL would actively recruit African Americans. On a less savory note, some workers west of the Rocky Mountains severed ties with Republicans seen as unsympathetic to the growing anti-Chinese movement.

The situation in the South differed markedly from that in the North. Long before Henry Grady coined the phrase "the New South" in 1886, Southerners realized the need to diversify the region's economy. That remained a future task during Reconstruction, as the region struggled to rebuild its **agrarian** base. This struggle took place against a backdrop of intense racism and resistance to northern-directed Reconstruction including, initially, an attempt to industrialize the South. Immediately after the Civil War, southern legislatures sought to reestablish the pre-conflict power structure and enact Black Codes that were little more than slavery under a new guise. Those efforts pushed Radical Republicans into power. So, too, did 1866 race riots in Memphis and New Orleans that left scores of black people dead, and black churches, homes, and businesses ruined. The rise of racist paramilitary groups, the failure of white law enforcement to protect black communities, and the attempt of former Confederate leaders to take seats in Congress led Radical Republicans to demand stricter federal oversight over the South. Radical Reconstruction divided the South into five military districts with federal troops deployed until each state submitted a new constitution that included adoption of the newly crafted Fifteenth Amendment.

Reconstruction was highly unpopular in the South. Under federal protection, black men voted in greater numbers, numerous black officials won election to political office, and freedmen flocked to newly opened schools. It was even possible for black washerwomen in Memphis and Atlanta to unionize to secure higher rates. By the end of the 1870s, however, nearly all of those gains had been swept aside, African Americans were becoming disenfranchised, "Jim Crow" labor and social systems were on the verge of becoming entrenched, and the northern public had lost interest in Reconstruction. Reconstruction's demise was partly due to external distractions such as the Panic of 1873, internal corruption in the Ulysses S. Grant administration, an outbreak of strikes in industrial cities, and battles over the banking system—but the biggest sticking point was plans to redistribute land.

Very few ex-slaves had non-agricultural skills or formal education, the latter of which was forbidden by law during the antebellum period. As a consequence, the immediate postwar challenge for them was to determine a way to make freedmen self-sufficient. Radical Republicans debated the possibility of seizing the plantations of rebellious white southerners, subdividing the estates into smaller plots, and distributing those lands to former slaves. Such plans had, in fact, gone into effect during the war. In 1862, the Union's Confiscation Act allowed for the seizure of Confederate lands and Union commanders such as Benjamin Butler and Benjamin Grierson sometimes gave liberated lands to slaves. In January 1865, General William T. Sherman transferred 400,000 acres of Sea Island land off South Carolina and Georgia to approximately 40,000 freedmen. Later that summer, General Rufus Saxton pursued land division as a means of creating a new society of independent farmers. Saxton headed the postwar Freedmen's Bureau work in this region, and his policies gave rise to the freedmen's strongly held conviction that the federal government would provide "40 acres and a mule" to black families. By the end of the summer of 1865, however, President Andrew Johnson had rescinded Sherman's order and ordered federal troops to wrest land from reluctant freedmen.

The Freedmen's Bureau was ordered to promote labor contracts between freedmen and landowners. Congress debated, but ultimately rejected, land redistribution plans as too extreme. Stripped of the ability to achieve true financial independence, most freedmen were forced to become tenant farmers or sharecroppers, often upon the very land upon which they had been slaves and often under the aegis of their former masters. The loss of political, social, and economic power set the stage for a racially divided society in which African Americans were relegated to second-class citizenship marked by disenfranchisement, poverty, and terror at the hands of white supremacy groups.

Reconstruction officially ended in March 1877, when Rutherford B. Hayes assumed the presidency after the disputed election of 1876, in which Hayes was proclaimed the victor over **Democratic Party** challenger Samuel J. Tilden by a single electoral vote. Most observers (then and now) attributed Hayes's victory to political trickery of the worst magnitude, but the South agreed to allow Hayes to take office in exchange for removing the remainder of federal troops from the former Confederacy and allowing "home rule" in the region. In truth, Reconstruction was already a dead issue. Among white working people, the **railroad strike of 1877** signaled a new chapter of capital/labor conflict. As was true for the rest of the nation, for organized labor race became an unresolved issue over which intense struggles would take place.

Suggested Reading

Eric Foner, *Reconstruction: America's Unfinished Revolution, 1863–1877*, 1988; Tera W. Hunter, *To 'Joy My Freedom: Southern Black Women's Lives and Labors after the Civil War*, 1997; Russell L. Johnson, *Warriors into Laborers: The Civil War and the Formation of Urban-Industrial Society in a Northern City*, 2003; Jacqueline Jones, *Labor of Love, Labor of Sorrow: Black Women, Work, and the Family, from Slavery to the Present*, 2001; David Montgomery, *Beyond Equality: Labor and Radical Republicans 1862–1872*, 1981.

RED SCARE

The Red Scare refers to periods of repression and fear following both World War I and World War II. Much of the repression was directed against **communists**—hence the use of the modifier "Red"—but in each case progressive groups of all sorts were targeted. The Red Scares proved particularly damaging to organized labor and **socialist** groups, many of whom actually shared a dislike of communists. Originally the term "Red Scare" was applied solely to the crackdown on radicals following World War I, but it has since been applied to post-World War II repression and has largely supplanted "McCarthyism" as a shorthand for post-1945 paranoia, as that term is too narrow and neglects fears that both predate and postdate the period in which Senator Joseph McCarthy dominated public discourses on Americanism. Both Red Scares rested upon the manufactured assumption that the American way of life was narrowly defined and that all who failed to conform were dangerous, unpatriotic, and disloyal. In each case, the Red Scare found its greatest support among **middle class**, the business community, and social elites.

The Red Scares would be used as an excuse to call into question the patriotism of bohemians, **immigrants**, racial minorities, and **working-class** labor activists. In some cases these individuals *were* communists, but more often they were just individuals who were singled out for their unpopular views. Because the accusers came from the upper strata, they generally controlled institutions with great political power such as the police, the government, and the courts, or those that shaped public opinion, such as newspapers, radio, and other media outlets. Those accused of disloyalty were subject to **blacklists**, public humiliation, imprisonment, beatings, fines, and, in the case of immigrant radicals, deportation. Some were executed. Due process was often abused but, as in the case of most forms of social hysteria, the Red Scares often enjoyed popular support.

Although the term "Red Scare" refers specifically to 20th-century phenomena, the 19th century also saw outbreaks of paranoia directed at labor organizations. The highly publicized **Molly Maguires** trials of the 1870s led to outbreaks of fear, and accusations of "Molly Maguirism" became an effective tool with which employers could tar labor activists as dangerous and violent when, in most cases, they were neither. The 1871 Paris Commune also provided early opportunities to whip up fears of communism, and the term "tramp" also engendered fear.

Anarchism, however, was the label that most struck fear into elites during the late 19th century. The **Haymarket bombing** of May 4, 1886, led to a mass crackdown on the anarchists and, by extension, any group even remotely open to being smeared as having associations with them. The **Knights of Labor** (KOL) was suppressed, even though KOL officials bitterly renounced both the Haymarket incident and anarchism. Alexander Berkman's attempt to murder Henry Clay Frick following the collapse of the 1892 **Homestead Steel lockout and strike** also piqued fears of anarchism. Berkman was the lover of famed anarchist **Emma Goldman**, and his attempt coincided with a worldwide wave of anarchist bombings and assassinations, including President William McKinley's death at the hands of an anarchist gunman in 1901.

The first events specifically dubbed "the Red Scare" occurred between 1917 and 1920. They represented a direct outgrowth of American involvement in World War I. During the war, government officials narrowly redefined patriotism and suppressed dissent through legislation. War broke out in Europe in 1914 and, initially, American public opinion favored neutrality. The United States entered the conflict in April 1917 and, in June, Congress passed the Espionage Act, which made it illegal to interfere with the war effort. Free speech was greatly curtailed, and speeches protesting U.S. entry in the war were interpreted as impeding the war effort. The October Bolshevik Revolution in Russia served to heighten fears, and the 1918 Sedition Act strengthened the Espionage Act. Both proved dangerous for the Socialist Party (SP) and for the **Industrial Workers of the World** (IWW), as each organization viewed the European conflict as a war among **capitalists** and urged the working class to avoid it. Crackdowns on both the SP and the IWW took place during the war. IWW offices were ransacked and IWW leader Frank Little was lynched by a Butte, Montana, vigilante group with ties to local copper barons in August 1917. Popular SP leader **Eugene V. Debs** was arrested and jailed in

September 1918. The **American Federation of Labor** (AFL), by contrast, supported both the repression of the IWW and the war effort. The AFL willingly complied with **National War Labor Board** (NWLB) efforts to maintain production during the war.

The NWLB enforced numerous provisions favorable to organized labor, but business leaders sought to discontinue these measures when the war ended in 1919. That year saw a massive **strike** wave—including a **general strike** in Seattle and the **Boston police strike**—as workers sought to preserve wartime gains. 1919 was also marked by a recession, race riots, and a wave of anarchist bombings. Federal officials argued that the bombs were part of a coordinated communist attack. That fear was rekindled in September 1920, when a bomb exploded on Wall Street, killing 40 and injuring 300. This incident was cited to justify an ongoing campaign against anarchists, communists, foreign-born activists, and labor union liberals spearheaded by Attorney General Mitchell Palmer. During what were dubbed the "Palmer raids," police and federal investigators raided homes and offices, intercepted mail, shut down objectionable newspapers, stopped speeches, and deported 600 foreigners, including Emma Goldman. The IWW was effectively eviscerated during the period. The climate of fear and nativism led to a rise in vigilantism. In addition, law enforcement officials often overstepped their authority. Many of those who were arrested and/or deported were innocent, and many of those targeted for investigation were labor activists seeking to enhance the position of unions, not overthrow the government. Even AFL organizers were harassed, the union's wartime loyalty notwithstanding.

The Red Scare crippled the Socialist Party, which had increased its membership from 75,000 members in 1918 to 108,000 in 1919. Although Debs attracted nearly 1 million votes in a 1920 presidential bid conducted from his cell in a federal penitentiary, the SP had just 26,000 members in 1920; eight years later, only 8,000 remained. The Communist Party of the United States (CPUSA) formed in August 1919, and had 27,000 members just two months later. After the Palmer raids, its membership dipped to just 8,200 by April 1920. The Red Scare also provided ammunition for groups such as the **National Association of Manufacturers**, which packaged its **open shop** drive as the patriotic antidote to unions. Employers used labor spies and fired union activists to roll back gains made by labor unions.

The Red Scare dissipated in intensity by the end of 1920, its decline hastened by Palmer's absurd prediction that a communist revolution would begin on **May Day**, the dismissal of charges against more than 1,000 immigrants, and warnings by legal scholars that much of the activity associated with the Palmer raids was unconstitutional. Nonetheless, the ripple effects of the Red Scare, such as nativism and distrust of unions, dominated the 1920s. Congress enacted a harsh immigration restriction law in 1924, and hate groups such as the revitalized Ku Klux Klan added communists, immigrants, and labor activists to their enemies lists. Most scholars also link the flawed 1927 trial and executions of Sacco and Vanzetti to the climate of fear stemming from the Red Scare.

During the Great Depression, several radical movements—including the CPUSA—rebuilt their strength. The economic crisis led legions of Americans to question long-held political and economic assumptions. It also led groups seeking to redress the crisis to form alliances based upon effectiveness, not ideology. In that spirit, the newly formed **Congress of Industrial Unions** (CIO) counted communists among its members. Communists, in fact, proved to be adroit union organizers. Those connections would make the CIO vulnerable after World War II, even though the United States was allied with the Soviet Union during the conflict, and the CPUSA urged workers to take **no-strike pledges** during the war. The United States/USSR alliance was merely one of convenience, and the House Un-American Activities Committee (HUAC) had held three investigations into alleged communist subversion between 1930 and 1945 that presaged a new Red Scare.

The second Red Scare began in 1947 and stretched into the 1960s. It was a key component of the early **Cold War** and prompted many labor organizations to embrace Cold War unionism. In 1947, President Harry Truman adopted a strong anti-communist foreign policy and introduced a Federal Employee Loyalty Program. That program caused hundreds of federal workers to be fired and thousands of others to resign because they had been sympathetic to leftist ideas. The signal event of the fear that would follow was the 1947 Hollywood Ten case, an extension of the HUAC's investigation into alleged communist subversion of the motion picture industry. Although its first victims were writers and directors, the Hollywood Ten case led to a general blacklist of actors, writers, directors, and industry personnel that included hundreds of names. The **United Electrical, Radio, and Machine Workers of America** was one of several unions with ties to Hollywood that suffered as a result of the blacklist. The investigation of Hollywood also indirectly launched the political career of **Ronald Reagan**, who was serving as president of the Screen Actors Guild at the time. Reagan was among several "friendly witnesses" before the HUAC and he supported efforts to ferret out Hollywood radicals.

Labor was also weakened when the **Republican Party** gained control of Congress in 1946 and directed a conservative backlash against both domestic New Deal policies and the gathering Red Scare. Union power was greatly curtailed by the 1947 **Taft-Hartley Act**, which was enacted despite President Truman's veto. International tensions exacerbated the intensity of the second Red Scare, including the Soviet Union's postwar occupation of Central Europe, the communist revolution in China in 1949, the Soviet Union's successful test of an atomic bomb in 1949, and the invasion of South Korea by communist North Korea in 1950. Red Scare leaders claimed that the federal government was infiltrated by communist spies, a charge kept alive by a handful of high-profile espionage arrests, such as that of atomic spy Klaus Fuchs and allegations that high-ranking government officials such as Alger Hiss were disloyal. In retrospect, most of these fears were unfounded, but a national climate of fear ensued. The CIO's **Operation Dixie** fell prey to red-baiting and pressures to conform to the Taft-Hartley Act were so great that, in 1950, the CIO expelled 20 percent of its membership rather than defend radical unionists.

Unions and the white public at large felt great pressure to conform to perceived social, cultural, and political norms associated with "Americanism" throughout the 1950s, but especially during the inflamed period between 1950 and 1954, when Senator Joseph R. McCarthy held Senate hearings on disloyalty and alleged communist subversion. McCarthy also tarred the New Deal era with the sobriquet "20 years of treason." Although McCarthy never unmasked a single communist, he gained popular support and perpetuated a climate of fear that led thousands of government employees, teachers, scholars, media figures, and others to lose their jobs. McCarthy was censured by the Senate in 1954 and lost influence, but the fear he engendered persisted. Individuals lost their jobs because of rumors, casual acquaintance with unorthodox individuals, suspicion of insufficient patriotism, or refusal to cooperate with investigators. Those who had a radical past, such as artists, musicians, and labor and **civil rights** officials, were especially vulnerable. Pete Seeger, an important figure in labor **music**, was blacklisted in 1952, hauled before the HUAC in 1955, slapped with a contempt of Congress citation, suffered legal woes until 1962, and continued to be blacklisted into the late 1960s.

Although seldom discussed, Congressional hearings on internal subversion continued through the 1960s, though they failed to excite the passion they had generated in the 1950s. The repercussions of the second Red Scare lingered even longer, especially for labor unions. When the AFL and the CIO merged in 1955, one precondition was that the CIO would continue to purge radicals from its ranks. Most labor leaders embraced **business unionism** with new fervor in the 1950s. In practice, this often meant cracking down on rank-and-file rebellion, an action that disempowered the rank-and-file and discouraged grassroots organizing. It also led the **American Federation of Labor-Congress of Industrial Organizations** (AFL-CIO) to link its internal agenda to U.S. foreign policy objectives. Although many leaders, including AFL-CIO President **George Meany**, touted labor's patriotism and boasted of workers' material gains during the postwar economic boom, the disconnect between labor's activist past and its emerging moderation made it ill prepared to adjust to social changes looming on the horizon. Organized labor would split badly on its responses to the civil rights movement and the rise of the **counterculture**. Although it may be overblown, some analysts trace the roots of working-class conservatism to the second Red Scare.

In the early 21st century, journalists and political scientists noted that domestic responses to the September 11, 2001, terrorist attacks on New York and Washington, D.C., paralleled those of the Red Scares. The AFL-CIO largely supported initiatives such as the Homeland Security Act and sought to organize workers in security professions.

Suggested Reading

Robert W. Cherney, *American Labor and the Cold War: Grassroots Politics and Postwar Political Culture*, 2004; Philip S. Foner, *History of the Labor Movement in the United States. Vol. 8: Postwar Struggles, 1918–1920*, 1988; Robert K. Murray, *Red Scare: A Study in National*

Hysteria 1918–1920, 1964; Richard G. Powers, *Not without Honor: A History of American Anti-communism*, 1997; Shelton Stromquist, ed. *Labor's Cold War: Local Politics in a Global Context*, 2008.

REEVES V. SANDERSON PLUMBING PRODUCTS, INC.

Reeves v. Sanderson Plumbing Products, Inc. is a U.S. Supreme Court decision rendered in June 2000 that makes it easier for employees to file bias lawsuits against their employers. The plaintiff, Roger Reeves, was a supervisor in the Sanderson Plumbing Products firm of Columbia, Mississippi. In 1995, he was fired after working for the firm for 40 years. The company alleged that Reeves was dismissed for poor record keeping and lax supervisory skills, but Reeves maintained that he was fired because of his age. A company manager told the 57-year-old Reeves that he was "too damn old" several months before his dismissal. This incident followed a similar slight delivered several months before.

Reeves's job reviews were exemplary, and he filed suit alleging that he was a victim of age discrimination. Reeves won, but the original verdict was overturned by a federal appeals judge who ruled that Reeves failed to demonstrate discrimination, even though the company's stated reasons for firing him were untrue. In June 2000, the Supreme Court unanimously sided with Reeves and reinstated the original verdict, noting that Sanderson Plumbing had violated Title VII of the 1964 Civil Rights Act. The 1967 Age Discrimination in Employment Act also protects employees from dismissal based solely on age unless mandatory retirement is specifically stipulated in a job description. In its decision, the court noted that employees need only demonstrate that an employer's explanation for a hiring or promotion decision is false, and that it is the task of the jury to determine whether discrimination occurred.

Unions and worker advocates hailed the decision, which had the practical effect that employees no longer have to provide concrete evidence of discrimination to win suits against their employees. Legal scholars predicted that the ruling would dramatically increase discrimination suits against employers. That has not proved to be the case thus far, though some employment analysts believe this has been true largely because employers have become more adroit at hiding age discrimination in the wake of the *Reeves* verdict.

Suggested Reading

Facts about Age Discrimination, http://www.eeoc.gov/facts/age.html, accessed May 25, 2011; Marcia McCormick, "*Reeves v. Sanderson Plumbing*, Turning back the Tide on Summary Judgment in Federal Employment," *Washington Post*, June 13, 2000; *Reeves v. Sanderson*, http://www.law.cornell.edu/supct/html/99-536.ZS.html, accessed May 25, 2011.

RELIGION AND LABOR

Sociologists and political analysts have observed three salient features about American religious practices that shape social movements.

First, religion is deeply ingrained in American political discourse. Whether Americans are actually more pious than citizens of other Western democracies is debatable, but religion is certainly a powerful symbol in American public life. More than eight of 10 Americans belong to a religious group, and four of 10 claim to attend weekly religious services, though a recent Harris poll indicates the actual number is closer to half of that. Religion, however practiced, plays an important role in American society, despite constitutional provisions for the separation of church and state.

The second important observation insofar as working people are concerned is that the centrality of religion in American life weakens **Marxist** assumptions that the exploitation inherent in **capitalism** and the material conditions of **working-class** life will invariably lead to the formation of **class consciousness**. Many sociologists who study social class argue that one's material condition in society is only one factor in shaping one's politics, social behavior, or class identification. American labor movements that have defined class solely or primarily in economic terms have had a mixed record of success.

A final codicil about American religion is that Protestant Christianity has been dominant since the founding of the first English colonies. Many of the colonies were founded by particular Protestant sects, though Maryland's George Calvert was a Catholic and Georgia's James Oglethorpe was said to have Jewish ancestry (though he did not emphasize it). John Winthrop, who founded Massachusetts Bay Colony in 1630, referenced the New Testament and referred to his colony as a holy "city upon a hill," a metaphor that stuck and has been central to political discourse ever since. Though many of the leaders of the American Revolution had been shaped by Enlightenment thought and held skeptical or deist beliefs, they nonetheless used religious metaphors in public to connect with the Protestant populace.

So, too, did the earliest leaders of the labor movement. **Journeymen**'s associations and the **Workingmen's movement** often used Biblical language in their pleas for social justice, and much was made of the fact that Jesus had been a carpenter—hence he endorsed a life of noble toil. The Workingmen freely mixed religion and principles of **republicanism**. New York Workingmen, for example, tried to rally support for **labor party** candidates by imploring voters to "send a carpenter to Albany." Another measure of the power of religion in American civic life is that in the three decades preceding the **Civil War**, religion was used not just to advance abolitionism and **free labor** ideology, but also to defend **slavery** or slave revolts.

Antebellum religion was greatly shaped by the Second Great Awakening, a series of Protestant religious revivals that began in the early 19th century, crested in the North in the 1840s, and lingered in the South into the 1860s. Denominations such as the Baptists, Congregationalists, Episcopalians, Lutherans, and Methodists experienced explosive growth, but they disproportionately appealed to the rising **middle class**. The revivals set a pattern that persisted in American society in that religiously oriented elites sought to impose their morality upon the **masses**. Workers long accustomed to drinking on the job, for instance, faced off against employers who wished to stop the practice, and witnessed the emergence of a **prohibition** movement. The nascent labor movement found itself badly divided between free-thinking radicals, traditionalists, and zealous evangelicals.

For working people, the post-Civil War years were marked by struggles to define the social purpose of religion. The central question was whether religion would become a tool of social control or would be used to advance social justice. That debate was greatly complicated by **immigration**. More than 30 million Europeans immigrated to the United States between 1836 and 1914. The first large wave of immigrants, the Irish, were predominately Roman Catholic. Their presence challenged Protestant hegemony, especially in urban areas; within two generations, the Irish had gained political control in several cities. In general, post-1836 immigrants were more religiously diverse than earlier arrivals. Large numbers of Jewish, Roman Catholic, and Eastern Orthodox believers were numbered among the newcomers, and there were also smatterings of Muslims and atheists.

Negotiating this diversity proved challenging to labor movements. Unity proved more difficult to establish among working classes whose religious beliefs often landed them on different sides of issues such as temperance, the swearing of secret oaths, the political authority of religious leaders, the morality of **strikes**, and the proper place of women in society. Even debates over tariffs or the money supply could take on religious overtones. More challenging still were the gathering **anarchist** and **socialist** movements, some of whose members denounced religion as superstitious and oppressive. Karl Marx famously called religion an "opiate" that served to dull the masses and deflect them from their "historic task" of uniting as a class and casting off their bourgeois capitalist masters. It was, however, another measure of religion's power in America that many devoted socialists rejected Marx's atheism and defined socialism in religious terms. The speeches of **Eugene V. Debs**, for example, were peppered with Biblical verses and metaphors.

Many labor organizations tried to dodge religious disagreement by banning discussions of religion from their lodges and assemblies. That proved hard to 'do, as Gilded Age elites sought to appropriate religion in their defense of **social Darwinism**. That mix of perverted biological theory and determinist religion proved unpalatable to workers; in some cases, it struck individuals as akin to blasphemy. They pointed out, with considerable merit, that the Bible did not sanction the accumulation of capital, heap blessings on the wealthy, or countenance cruelty toward the poor. The **Knights of Labor** (KOL), the period's largest **labor federation**, seized the initiative and challenged social Darwinism at its core. Knights positioned themselves as "True Christians" and attacked their opponents as heretics and hypocrites. The KOL also distinguished between Christianity and "Churchianity," defining the latter as simply another repressive institution in the service of elite masters. Other Gilded Age workers weighed in by staying away from churches in droves, or by attending non-aligned churches sympathetic to the poor. Street churches cropped up with names such as the Workingman's Church and Church of the Carpenter—bodies that anticipated the rise of independent and evangelical churches in the 20th century. The late 19th century also witnessed the convening of Protestant conferences devoted to the theme of "Why do workingmen distrust the church?"

The answer to that query was obvious and fueled the rise of the **Social Gospel** movement. By the 1890s, social Darwinism's defense of constituted wealth and authority was in retreat, and the notion that organized religion should play an active role in alleviating poverty and effecting social reform was on the rise. Such ideas were old news to black churches, which had long linked religion to the battle for **civil rights** and justice, but numerous white Protestant churches rethought their social views and realigned their domestic views to conform to ideals practiced in foreign missionary work. Mainline Protestant churches were also motivated by the fact that evangelicals such as Dwight L. Moody and Billy Sunday seemed to have more success at attracting working-class followers than they did. The Catholic Church, though never a defender of social Darwinism, was also forced to rethink its relationship with labor unions, an effort that led to the 1891 papal encyclical *Rerum Novarum*.

The **American Federation of Labor** (AFL), which supplanted the KOL as the nation's leading labor federation, sought to heal rifts between organized religion and the union movement. A particularly creative effort in that regard was the AFL's Labor Forward initiative between 1910 and 1920, a program that took place in more than 150 cities. Labor Forward sought to reassure church leaders that workers remained devoted to Christianity. In keeping with **Progressive Era** values, the AFL also affirmed its belief in the mutualism of capital/labor interests. Efforts such as these were scorned by the **Industrial Workers of the World** (IWW), whose leaders were often dismissive of organized religion, but the IWW was equally naïve in underestimating the power of religion. Many radicals mirrored the AFL's efforts at fusing religion with a labor agenda. Social Gospel figures such as Walter Rauschenbush, W. D. Bliss, and George Herron advanced notions of Christian socialism. The popularity of **Edward Bellamy** also fueled the movement. In the early 20th century, Christian socialism ideals were advanced by individuals such as the theologian Reinhold Niebuhr, journalist Vida Scudder, settlement house pioneer Jane Addams, and Eugene Debs.

Efforts to heal the breech between labor and organized religion were made throughout the 20th century. In 1908, the Federated Council of Churches (FCC) announced its support for labor unions and its commitment to a **living wage**; both principles remain intact. Two years later, Presbyterians set up a Labor Temple in New York City and worked directly on social reform campaigns. Churches also responded to the economic depression of the 1930s by distributing direct relief to distressed workers, and by joining efforts to improve conditions. Ministers and rabbis were found on the faculties of **labor colleges** and new organizations emerged. The FCC set up the Religion and Labor Council of America in 1932, which sought to reconcile Christian theology and economic theory. It worked closely with both the AFL and the **Congress of Industrial Organizations** (CIO). The **International Ladies' Garment Workers' Union** created the Jewish Labor Committee in 1934.

Catholics were especially active in labor organizing from the 1930s onward. Peter Maurin and Dorothy Day founded the socialist-tinged Catholic Workers Movement in 1933. Three years later, the **Association of Catholic Trade Unionists** emerged. Catholics also sponsored a labor school movement, which operated from 1936 to

1956. The infusion of greater numbers of **Latinos** into the U.S. population also led the Catholic Church into greater involvement with the labor movement; the church played a key role in the organizing efforts of **César Chávez** and the **United Farm Workers of America**. It has also reaffirmed its commitment to *Rerum Novarum* on several occasions, most notably in the 1931 encyclical *Quadragesimo Anno* and in 1981's *Laborem Exercens*.

By the middle of the 20th century, labor leaders proudly asserted their religious beliefs rather than seeking to justify them. By then, most religious bodies recognized labor's right to organize. Prominent Jewish labor leaders included David Dubinsky and **Sidney Hillman**; Catholic leaders included **Philip Murray**, **George Meany**, **John Sweeney**, and César Chávez. In like fashion, **Walter Reuther**, **Lane Kirkland**, and **A. Philip Randolph** openly professed their Protestant faith.

The central role of religion in the civil rights movement is well known, but less often told is the part played by labor unions. The **Brotherhood of Sleeping Car Porters** was crucial in planning events that forced President Franklin Roosevelt to set up the **Fair Employment Practices Commission**, the **United Auto Workers of America** supported the Montgomery bus boycott, Reuther and Randolph pressed the **American Federation of Labor-Congress of Industrial Organizations** (AFL-CIO) to endorse civil rights, and the Reverend Martin Luther King, Jr., became an ardent supporter of labor. King was, in fact, in Memphis to lead a sanitation workers' strike when he was assassinated in 1968. King's murder did little to diminish the resolve of black churches to continue their quest for social justice—campaigns that included labor rights.

Pockets of religion-based resistance to labor appeared in the 20th century and persist to the present. In the South, **paternalism** reigned in many areas and Protestant leaders often tarred labor unions as anti-Christian and anti-American. During **Operation Dixie**, CIO leaders were stunned by the zeal of anti-union church leaders. Many white Protestants also resisted the civil rights movement, and some shifted rightward politically. In a similar fashion, since the culture wars of the 1920s, evangelical Christianity has tended toward association with political conservatives. The **Republican Party** began to court evangelical Christians in the 1960s, and the 1980 election of Ronald **Reagan** brought them to political prominence. At present the conservative/evangelical alliance promotes numerous positions antithetical to organized labor, including **right-to-work** legislation, the elimination of **collective bargaining** rights for public employees, the elimination of **protectionist** trade barriers, and a social agenda that includes restoration of school prayer, the abolition of gay marriage, and a prohibition against abortion. There has also been a revival of religion-based defense of wealth and attacks on anti-poverty programs and government taxation policies that some observers have dubbed a return to social Darwinism.

Labor unions take the position that American society is multicultural and diverse. They argue that free religious expression is a vital right, but that barriers should remain between church and state if only because no clear consensus on belief and values exists. They accuse religious conservatives of acting as if their particular religious tenets were shared by all Americans. Christians continue to be in the majority in modern America, with approximately 76 percent of Americans claiming Christianity as their faith. Of these, however, 25 percent are Catholic and the remaining 51 percent are spread across dozens of denominations and sects. Baptists are currently the largest Protestant denomination in the United States, but they are split into several competing factions and collectively account for fewer than 16 percent of all Protestants. Advocates of secularism point out that within a given area, religious diversity is so great that any public policy based in the specifics of any faith would be patently unfair. To pick just one example, in the city of Lowell, Massachusetts, once the crown jewel of the American **Industrial Revolution**, Buddhism now has the largest number of adherents in the city.

Such data notwithstanding, religion outwardly remains very important to Americans. It would be naïve to predict it will diminish in political importance in the near future. There is, however, a perplexing conundrum that churches and labor unions will share in the future: Both mainstream churches and conventional unions have seen steep declines in their memberships in the past several decades.

Suggested Reading

Ken Fones-Wolf, *Trade Union Gospel: Christianity and Labor in Industrial Philadelphia, 1865–1915*, 1989; Joseph McCartin and Leon Fink, "Labor and Religion," *Labor: Studies in Working-Class History of the Americas* 6, no. 1 (2009); Jarod Roll, *Spirit of Rebellion: Labor and Religion in the New Cotton South*, 2010; Mark Zwick and Louise Zwick, *The Catholic Worker Movement: Intellectual and Spiritual Origins*, 2005.

REPLACEMENT WORKERS. *See* Scab.

REPUBLICANISM

Republicanism is often cited as the foundational ideology around which core American political beliefs and institutions formed in the years preceding and following the American Revolution. It is, however, an imprecise term whose meaning varied depending upon who used it and in which context. It is probably more accurate to view republicanism as an array of ideas and principles from which individuals and groups selectively chose. Among the tenets of republicanism were virtue, citizenship, community, liberty, and equality—all high-sounding but vague concepts open to interpretation. Many of these also held meanings that are different from the way those terms are understood today. Equality, for instance, was often expressed as a belief in "equal rights." In that sense, it referred more to a criticism of privilege and aristocratic pretense than to a desire to engage in social leveling. Those evoking equality mainly objected to unfair advantages and advocated what today might be called meritocracy, a society in which individuals rise according to ability rather than family connections, inheritance, or other unearned benefits. Few who evoked equality believed that hierarchy was, by nature, unnatural; rather, they suggested only that all individuals should have equal opportunity. In like fashion, many 18th- and 19th-century individuals denounced the inequalities of colonialism, **slavery**, and industrialization, but did not necessarily see them as interconnected. Some critics of industrial abuses, for example, also defended the existence of slavery.

Republicanism was important in the early labor movement. Workers embraced iconic figures of the American Revolution such as George Washington. Thomas Jefferson was even more popular among laborers of the early 19th century because of his strong advocacy of **agrarianism** and his perceived radicalism. Few figures, however, inspired as much passion as Thomas Paine, the British labor agitator who emigrated to America and, in 1776, penned the pamphlet *Common Sense*. Paine sought to recruit farmers and **artisans** to the cause of American independence, and they responded to his proclamation that "the floor of Freedom is as level as water." Many workers identified with Paine's challenges to authority and his insistence that true liberty was radically democratic. Among antebellum **masters** and **journeymen** alike, Paine's birthday (February 9) was the de facto **Labor Day** and a holiday from work. Republicanism also found expression in several slave rebellions, most notably that led by Gabriel Prosser in 1800, who echoed revolutionary orator Patrick Henry's "Death or Liberty" slogan.

Prior to the 1820s, many Americans associated republicanism with forms of economic individualism. In the late 1820s and into the 1830s, however, the **Workingmen's movement** used republicanism to critique industrial abuse and wealth accumulation. The "Workies," as they were nicknamed, consciously drew upon the Declaration of Independence and the Bill of Rights to denounce emerging power systems that they believed endangered liberty and independence. Their call for equal rights included a blistering criticism of social and economic elites, and challenged American society to honor the democratic ideals embedded within its founding documents. Those ideals formed the basis for specific demands such as the regulation of banks, land reform, the enactment of mechanics' lien laws, shorter workdays, the reform of inheritance-tax laws, universal public education, the abolition of debtor prisons, an end to laws requiring males to drill in local militias, and the elimination of monopolies. The Workingmen also supported continuing expansion of suffrage rights. Prior to the War of 1812, most states restricted voting to property holders or had plural voting systems that gave more weight to the votes of elites. By 1840, however, a one-man, one-vote system prevailed. Some Workies even supported women's right to vote—a call that did not come to pass in their time but was one of the inspirations for the women's suffrage movement.

The coming of industrialization disrupted tradition-based **divisions of labor**. In particular, the erosion of the household economy and the emergence of a distinct **working class** placed more emphasis on **wage** labor. New England women working in textile mills used republican language to denounce class and workplace injustices. **Sarah Bagley**, for instance, used the term "wage slavery" to characterize the debased status of working women. Republicanism also provided the rhetorical framework for workers that embraced the abolition movement and **free labor** ideology.

After the **Civil War**, workers involved with the **eight-hour movement** sought to link a shorter workday with civic virtues. Some argued that relief from toil would unleash greater democracy by giving workers more time to engage in community service. In the 1880s, the **Knights of Labor**'s motto, "An injury to one is the concern of all," tapped into workers' republican idealism. Knights, in fact, regarded themselves as "True Republicans" whose duty it was to rescue democracy from erstwhile plutocrats. When Knights and other unionists participated in **labor parties** and ran for political office, **labor newspapers** routinely touted them as saviors of the Republic.

By the end of the **Great Upheaval**, though, labor republicanism had lost much of its luster. By the time the 20th century dawned, older republican ideals had largely fused with resurgent liberalism, which had begun to jettison laissez-faire economics and call for regulation of **capitalism** to curtail the activities of trusts and robber barons. After 1900, republicanism was associated more with ideals of serving the nation and purifying its civic life. It remains important in that regard, but has lost most of its association with **working-class** movements.

Many political scientists and historians argue that republicanism, though often vague, played a very important role in the development of American political views. In the United States, republicanism predated **socialist** forms such as **Marxism**, **anarchism**, and **Lassalleanism**. Thus a strong indigenous radical tradition was already present when those later philosophies arrived. Native-born workers, in fact, often associated socialism with **immigrants** and were suspicious of both. Proponents of "American exceptionalism" sometimes evoke republicanism to explain why American workers were less susceptible to socialism than those in other Western democracies. They argue that the rhetorical force of republicanism was made manifest in the nation's political life; in essence, American workers had already achieved suffrage rights, guarantees of personal liberty, and basic freedoms that Europeans were struggling to obtain. The claims of American exceptionalism are often overblown, but there is little doubt that imported socialism was forced to compete with a broad array of political thought in the United States.

Suggested Reading

Leon Fink, *Workingmen's Democracy: The Knights of Labor and American Politics*, 1983; Eric Foner, *Tom Paine and Revolutionary America*, 1976; Sean Wilentz, *Chants Democratic: New York City and the Rise of the American Working Class, 1788–1850*, 1984.

REPUBLICAN PARTY AND LABOR

Although individual Republican Party ("Grand Old Party" [GOP]) politicians have been sympathetic to working-class movements, the Republican Party has followed, since the 1870s, an overtly pro-business agenda. In the late 19th century, the GOP embraced laissez-faire principles that remain part of its platform, though it has changed its stance on protectionism. Since the end of World War I, Republicans have generally supported deregulation and free-market capitalism. The party's relationship with organized labor frequently has been contentious.

The Republican Party was formed in response to the 1854 Kansas-Nebraska Act, a bill that hastened the coming of the **Civil War**. It was widely perceived to be a party that called for the abolition of **slavery**, though its original purpose was to prevent its expansion, not dismantle it; that did not become a party goal until President Abraham Lincoln's Emancipation Proclamation went into effect in 1863. Even then, the party's position on abolition remained ambiguous; the Emancipation Proclamation applied only to areas "in rebellion," not slaves in areas under federal control. During **Reconstruction**, a faction known as the "Radical Republicans" gained control of Congress and directed a reunification plan for the Union that briefly advanced black political enfranchisement and citizenship rights. This made the GOP popular among African Americans, and they remained loyal to the party into the 1930s, far longer than other groups of farmers and wage-earners.

In the mid-1870s, however, Reconstruction weakened; in some places Republican retreat from Reconstruction was so pronounced that black leaders lost hope and joined third-party movements. As the party's commitment to Reconstruction declined, its tilt toward the business classes became more obvious. The **Democratic Party** was not a pro-labor party either, although it did tend to favor white **agrarian** interests more than the Republicans. Post-Civil War labor unions generally distrusted both major parties, and many workers saw a need for a **labor party** to represent their interests. By the 1870s, the leaders of both major political parties either publicly supported or privately acceded to the ideals of **social Darwinism**, including its defense of wealth accumulation and its explanations for poverty. Politicians took full advantage of the unregulated business environment of the day and enriched themselves through practices such as insider trading, awarding contracts to supporters, and sponsoring bills for private economic advantage that would today be illegal. Political machines often ran growing industrial cities, and bribery and corruption were commonplace. Railroad and banking interests wielded far more political influence than labor and farmer movements, and many elected officials were also major stockholders in large corporate concerns. Corporations, especially railroads, had so much power that bad (or crooked) stock deals could send the entire nation into recession.

The presidency of Republican Ulysses S. Grant (1869–1877) was rocked by the crippling Panic of 1873, which stretched into 1877. It also suffered through so many financial scandals involving key administration and Congressional figures that Grant often neglected Reconstruction. The public's interest in Reconstruction also flagged in the face of soaring unemployment and hardship. The disputed election of 1876 put an official end to Reconstruction; southern Democrats demanded home rule in exchange for accepting Republican Rutherford B. Hayes as president. Hayes holds the dubious distinction of being the first American president to sanction the use of federal troops to break up a **strike**; he used federal militia to subdue the **railroad strike of 1877**.

Republican and Democratic politicians alike made free use of **injunctions** and criminal conspiracy laws to favor business in capital/labor conflicts, but several factors shifted the GOP more strongly toward business and, over time, made the

Democratic Party appear more sympathetic to laboring people. First, from 1861 to 1913, Grover Cleveland (1885–1889 and 1893–1897) was the only Democrat to serve as president. Although Cleveland was generally conservative, the GOP's policies had higher public visibility, given that the party occupied the White House for 44 years of the 52-year period. Cleveland also favored lowering export tariffs, a position favored by farmers seeking new markets for their goods, but opposed by Republicans. Second, the Democrats courted **immigrants** to a greater degree, a strategy that (eventually) bolstered the Democratic Party's profile among the working class. Third, the Republican Party openly advanced legislation favorable to business and banking interests. Republicans supported the gold standard and rebuffed the efforts of the Greenback Labor movement, free-silver activists, and advocates of bimetallism to enact monetary reform that would help borrowers.

Republicans took an equally uncompromising stand on the tariff issue. From 1861 to 1913, the GOP advocated high tariffs designed to protect development during the American **Industrial Revolution**. Industrial workers generally supported high tariffs, while southern and midwestern farmers opposed them. Tariffs often determined the fate of elections. President Cleveland, for example, lost his reelection bid in 1888 when he denounced the high McKinley tariffs as a violation of **republicanism**. He recaptured the White House in 1892 by attacking President Benjamin Harrison's support for high tariffs, but his own 1894 reform left intact protectionist rates favored by industrialists and factory workers.

The election of 1896 proved pivotal in clarifying the differences between Republicans and Democrats. The Populist Party's ability to make inroads in the South and Midwest had stung Democrats. In 1896, Democrats nominated William Jennings Bryan for the presidency, and he also garnered the **Populist** nomination. Bryan attacked the GOP as the party of big business—a charge that proved largely true. Ohio industrialist Mark Hanna ran Republican challenger William McKinley's campaign, but McKinley cleverly blamed Grover Cleveland's lower tariffs for prolonging the Panic of 1893. He also promised that preservation of the gold standard and support for the banking industry would bring "a full dinner pail" to all workers, including immigrants, and warned that a Bryan victory would lead to higher bread prices. McKinley lost most of the rural South and Midwest, but easily won the presidency by sweeping the growing urban population. He defeated Bryan again in 1900, but the Democrats began to alter their platform to adopt parts of the Populist agenda that appealed to farmers and wage-earners, including direct democracy, the **eight-hour** workday, and a graduated income tax.

The GOP dominated national politics during the **Progressive Era**. It was, however, the last time that the party made substantive overtures to working people. President Theodore Roosevelt earned an exaggerated reputation as a trust buster who was willing to take on monopoly capitalists, and won admiration from workers for his handling of the **anthracite coal strike of 1902**. Although Roosevelt was not overly enamored with unions, he found **John Mitchell**, president of the **United Mine Workers of America**, more conciliatory than coalmine operators and threatened to use the U.S. Army against the latter. Republican progressives also introduced bills that regulated railroads, food and drug purity, and interstate commerce. Overall, though, the Progressive Era saw as many setbacks as advances for working people. **Child labor** laws were struck down as unconstitutional; **protective labor legislation** for women, however, passed legal muster. Republican-dominated courts also took pro-business stances that included issuing **injunctions** against labor strikes, assessing punitive damages against unions, and sanctioning crackdowns against politically left groups such as the **Industrial Workers of the World** (IWW), **socialists**, and **anarchists**. Even the moderate **American Federation of Labor** (AFL) suffered political and legal woes during the period; in 1908, the AFL accused the GOP of using federal courts to bludgeon organized labor. The major pro-labor law of the period, the **Clayton Antitrust Act**, was signed into law by Woodrow Wilson, a Democrat. Wilson also advanced the 1913 Underwood Tariff, which dramatically reduced the GOP's 1909 Payne-Aldrich Tariff. This move met with the approval of farmers; most laborers also hailed the graduated income tax enacted by the Sixteenth Amendment, also on Wilson's watch. The GOP's support for African American **civil rights** was its one consistent position that benefited the working classes; it proved controversial, as much of the white working class of the day was racist.

Organized labor's relationship with both parties remained contentious overall. The AFL applauded gains made under the **National War Labor Board** during World War I, but these measures proved temporary and a massive wave of strikes broke out in 1919 when employers sought to reverse wartime concessions made to labor. The government also approved a wartime suppression of civil liberties that further devastated the IWW and other leftist organizations. The postwar **Red Scare** began during the Wilson administration, though Republican elected officials often embraced it with even more fervor than the Democrats. The **Boston Police strike of 1919** was subdued by Republican Governor Calvin Coolidge, while Ole Hanson, Seattle's Progressive Republican mayor, used police and federal troops to suppress the city's **general strike** in 1919, though strikers had not engaged in violence.

Republican presidential administrations throughout the 1920s pursued an overtly pro-business agenda. President Warren G. Harding reinstituted a high protective tariff in 1922; the next year AFL President **Samuel Gompers** charged that the GOP was supporting the **open-shop** movement. Harding's successor, Calvin Coolidge, announced, "The chief business of the American people is business," and was widely perceived to be a supporter of laissez-faire economics. During the 1980s, Ronald Reagan expressed his admiration for Coolidge and some scholars reassessed the thirtieth president, but Coolidge did not aggressively enforce business regulations and pursued tax cuts that anticipated the supply-side economics of Reagan. By 1927, only the richest 2 percent of Americans paid any income tax.

Coolidge was succeeded by Herbert Hoover in 1929, the Republican with the misfortune of seeing the Great Depression begin under his watch. Although it was not his fault, Hoover was widely chastised for his ineffectiveness stemming from ideological blindness in responding to the crisis. Hoover, an admirer of **Fordism** and **Taylorism**, looked to business to solve the panic and directed reforms at business rather than supplying relief to individuals. His 1932 order to remove petitioning World War I "bonus marchers" from Washington, D.C., was regarded as an act of callousness, and his signing of the 1930 Smoot-Hawley Tariff perhaps worsened the financial crisis.

In many ways, the 1932 election redefined American politics in ways that are still being worked out. The winner, Democrat Franklin D. Roosevelt, was as experimental as Hoover had been cautious. Historians may debate the depth of Roosevelt's pro-labor sympathies, but there can be little doubt that his New Deal policies enacted significant protections for working people, including the **National Industrial Recovery Act**, the **National Labor Relations Act**, the **Fair Labor Standards Act**, and the **Social Security Act**. Labor unions expanded dramatically during his four presidential terms. **Industrial unionism** was firmly established with the rise of the **Congress of Industrial Organizations** (CIO), and unionization came to basic industries such as auto, rubber steel, and textiles. Roosevelt also raised taxes and was anathema to the business community and the wealthy. They spent large amounts of money trying to defeat Roosevelt, but he enjoyed such popularity among **blue-collar** voters, farmers, urban dwellers, and ethnic minorities that he easily deflected Republican challengers. Labor solidified its support for the Democratic Party during the New Deal, and African Americans also abandoned the GOP. At the same, the New Deal served to expand the business community's support for Republicans.

Since Roosevelt, a substantial part of the business community and Republican Party have sought to weaken or dismantle the New Deal, organized labor, demand-side economics, and the income tax structure. Roosevelt's death in 1945 provided an opportunity for GOP operatives to begin doing so. World War II ended in August of that year, and Republicans used labor unrest such as strikes by railroad workers, the **United Auto Workers of America** (UAW), and the **United Mine Workers of America** to argue that unions had grown too powerful. They also asserted that New Deal had been a failure and that only World War II had ended the Great Depression. The GOP regained control of Congress in 1946; the next year Congress passed the **Taft-Hartley Act**, a bill despised by unions, but enacted through an override of President Harry Truman's veto. Although Truman surprised many by winning the presidency in 1948 and Democrats regained control of Congress in the same election, the battle lines were drawn. For the next 32 years, elections often hinged on how voters viewed business regulation, social programs, and labor unions. Republicans would also enlist a new weapon in battling Democrats and unions—namely, fear of **communism**. The 1947 **General Agreement on Tariffs and Trade** (GATT), an international accord, also removed an old GOP burden and allowed Republicans to flip their position on tariffs; by the 1970s, Republicans had become ardent supporters of free trade. (GATT was replaced by the World Trade Organization in 1995.)

In 1952, Democratic presidential candidate Adlai Stevenson charged that Republicans were "the enemy of labor." That assertion did not enable him to claim victory in a political climate shaped by a new Red Scare, the **Cold War**, and pent-up consumer demand. Labor purged leftists from union ranks and, in 1955, the AFL and the CIO merged to try to overturn the Taft-Hartley Act. Republican

President Dwight Eisenhower was so opposed to altering this legislation that his secretary of labor resigned in protest. Eisenhower also signed into law another bill that troubled many union supporters—the 1959 Labor-Management Reporting and Disclosure Act. Labor's support for Democrats meant, however, that Congress remained under Democratic control except for a brief period between 1953 and 1955 in which the GOP held the edge in the Senate.

The New Frontier and Great Society programs of Democratic presidents John Kennedy and Lyndon Johnson served to push labor further into alliance with the Democrats. The 1964 election did, however, plant the seed for a new Republican strategy. GOP tactician Lee Atwater used the unpopularity of **civil rights** legislation among white voters to make a dent in the Democrats' control of the South; in the 1980s, many Southern politicians and voters—especially "Dixiecrats" opposed to both the civil rights and labor movements—shifted their allegiance to the Republican Party. Republicans also attacked social programs passed by Democrats, such as **affirmative action** and expansion of welfare programs. Richard Nixon made use of these positions during his successful 1968 presidential campaign and, in addition, accused Democrats of coddling the **counterculture**. In like fashion, the GOP linked the Democratic Party to controversial court rulings such as those banning school prayer, legalizing abortion, and limiting the use of capital punishment.

Nixon fell from power due to the Watergate scandal, but the economic woes of the 1970s coupled with the loss of American prestige owing to the **Vietnam War**, the Iran hostage crisis, and Cold War impasses paved the way for **Ronald Reagan**'s election in 1980. President Reagan was charismatic and successfully drove a wedge in the Democrats' New Deal coalition. During his eight years in the White House, he fashioned an agenda that forms the parameters of the present-day GOP platform: fiscal and social conservatism, unflagging support for the military and U.S. foreign policy objectives, an appeals to "family values," tax cuts, free trade, deregulation of business, **right-to-work** laws, and attacks on special interest social groups such as civil rights and gay rights organizations, the women's movements, and organized labor. The Reagan years were disastrous from the standpoint of labor unions. Reagan met with public approval for his tough handling of the **Professional Air Traffic Controllers Organization** strike and was hailed by the business community for his support during the **downsizing, decertification, and concessions strikes** of the 1980s. The GOP successfully changed the public perception of unions, tarring them as antibusiness, outmoded, and impediments to job creation. Unions, already reeling losses related to **deindustrialization**, slipped further into a downward spiral that has yet to be reversed. Republicans also revived Coolidge-era beliefs in supply-side economics and pushed for massive tax cuts that precipitated cuts in social spending.

Much of the Republican agenda is antithetical to the self-interest of working people, but the GOP has been more successful at controlling perceptions and political rhetoric than Democrats. In fact, so many Democrats have embraced fiscal conservatism that many union activists have called upon the labor movement to sever its ties to the party. Republicans and Democrats have alternated occupancy of the White House since Reagan's presidency, with each occupying it for 12 years through 2012.

Nevertheless, the GOP agenda—to which a war on terrorism was added in 2001—often generates more passion among voters. Republicans captured control of the House of Representatives in 2010 and have called for deeper tax cuts, reduced social spending, and greater control over labor unions. Highly publicized GOP efforts in Wisconsin, Ohio, and Maine to strip public employees of their **collective bargaining** rights during 2011 showed that labor unions are still very much on the defensive.

Some cracks in the current Republican coalition have emerged that opponents may be able to exploit. The GOP's call for **immigration** restriction and a roundup of illegal aliens resonates among many voters, but is out of touch with changing demographics that will make white, Anglo-Saxon Protestants a numerical minority in the United States by the middle of the 21st century. The GOP has also made appeals to the **middle class**, but its policies have led to a widening gap between rich and poor that has contracted the middle class. The Republican Party has become allied with evangelicals, a segment of the population whose views alienate many voters. In addition, the party's devotion to conservative social issues troubles fiscal conservatives, including business interests. Many see social issues as divisive, doubt that most Americans agree with the GOP's stance, and believe that the controversy is bad for business. The GOP's current devotion to budget cutting includes calls to scale back popular programs such as Social Security, Medicare, and Medicaid, which have already engendered voter backlash. Moreover, serious efforts to pare the budget will almost certainly entail deep cuts in military spending, which would cause serious tension within the GOP ranks.

Perhaps the biggest challenge derives from fiscal conservatism itself. It is clear that wealthy individuals and corporate interests have benefited handsomely from laissez-faire policies, deregulation, and **runaway capital**. To date, average Americans largely have not benefited from GOP fiscal policies, the future of American work is uncertain, and American standards of living are slipping. Whether these factors will engender a revival of demand-side economics and resurgent labor union growth remains to be seen. At present, though, groups such as the American Federation of Labor-Congress of Industrial Organizations (AFL-CIO) have a lot of history on their side to bolster claims that the Republican Party is unfriendly to working people.

Suggested Reading

Michael Bowen, *The Roots of Modern Conservatism: Dewey, Taft, and the Battle for the Soul of the Republican Party*, 2011; Mary C. Brennan, *Turning Right in the Sixties: The Conservative Capture of the GOP*, 1995; Thomas Frank, *What's the Matter with Kansas? How Conservatives Won the Heart of America*, 1995; Nelson Lichtenstein, *State of the Union: A Century of American Labor*, 2003; Reihan Salam, *Grand New Party: How Republicans Can Win the Working Class and Save the American Dream*, 2009.

RERUM NOVARUM

Rerum Novarum was an 1891 encyclical issued by Pope Leo XIII. Among other things, it removed the Roman Catholic Church's blanket condemnation of secret societies and recognized the legitimacy of labor unions. It offered critiques of both **socialism** and **capitalism** and asserted that capital and labor needed to recognize that their interests were inextricably linked.

Prior to *Rerum Novarum*, Catholic workers faced a dilemma. In the wake of the anti-Masonic agitations in the early 19th century and violence associated with the clandestine **Molly Maguires** in the 1870s, the Catholic Church reaffirmed views against secret societies that dated to the Middle Ages. It took a similarly dim view of burgeoning socialist movements, both in Europe and in the United States. Catholics joining any sort of secret order faced the threat of excommunication. In the United States, however, the church's position ran afoul of other social trends. First, the post-Civil War period saw a proliferation of fraternal orders, most of which practiced some degree of ritual secrecy. Second, many labor unions also maintained levels of secrecy. In the absence of labor laws protecting **collective bargaining** rights, workers faced severe sanctions merely for associating with a labor union. To protect membership, many unions chose to operate clandestinely. For Irish, German, and French Canadian Catholic immigrants, the church's condemnation imposed a special burden: Obeying the church's prohibition meant avoiding fraternal groups and labor unions important to helping **immigrants** assimilate into American society. In that regard, church condemnation fueled already deep nativist suspicions of foreign-born workers. Moreover, many workers were attracted to socialism, and many immigrants had been involved in movements prior to arriving in America.

The Catholic Church's position became untenable with the growth of the **Knights of Labor** (KOL) in 1880s. Because the KOL operated in complete secrecy until 1882, it was roundly condemned by Catholic clerics. In Canada, especially Quebec, Catholic workers were forbidden to join the KOL; those in America faced church discipline for doing so. The KOL's leadership, however, was heavily Roman Catholic and, at least until 1886, so was the bulk of its membership. Forced to choose between their church and their union, many chose the latter. The KOL took the lead in attempting to ameliorate disputes with Rome. In 1879, Knights changed wording in their ritual to allow communicants to reveal parts of it to their priests, and KOL head **Terence Powderly**, a practicing Catholic, led the move to make the KOL a public organization in all but the practice of its ritual. He also forged an alliance with the powerful James Cardinal Gibbons of Baltimore, the de facto archbishop of the United States at a time in which Catholicism was still a missionary effort in many parts of the country. Gibbons admired the KOL, saw no threat to the faith in its precepts, and lobbied the Vatican to make policy changes. At first he was rebuffed, but after 1885, so many workers joined the KOL that Gibbons successfully argued that the Church would be irreparably harmed by continuing a blanket ban against secret orders and labor unions.

Catholics were still suspect in the predominately Protestant United States, and outbreaks of anti-Catholic discrimination were common, especially against Irish and Irish American populations. Powderly himself came under intense criticism from self-proclaimed "antipapists" for making efforts to placate Rome. Gibbons parlayed all of this upheaval into a successful plea in Rome. Canadian parishes were ordered to cease excommunicating KOL members and, in 1891, Pope Leo XIII issued *Rerum Novarum*.

Rerum Novarum pales in terms of its fervor when compared with pronouncements emanating from the **Social Gospel** movement. The document offers only tepid acceptance of labor organizations, though it did recognize unions' struggles for social justice and placed the blame for industrial strife upon the shoulders of capital rather than labor. It also valorized manual labor and the dignity of toil, echoing sentiments present in labor manifestos. Officially, it endorsed neither capitalism nor socialism, but instead upheld a vague mutualism rooted in principles of Christian fraternity and charity.

Despite these factors, *Rerum Novarum* had a profound impact on the American labor movement. The KOL was in deep decline by 1891, however, and the encyclical did little to revive its sagging fortunes. Nevertheless, many future labor leaders—including **Philip Murray**, the second president of the **Congress of Industrial Organizations**, were Roman Catholics, and the encyclical allowed Catholic workers to join unions with a clear conscience. Rome's periodic reaffirmations of *Rerum Novarum* also insulated it from charges of complicity with the forces of oppression. The most significant reaffirmation was *Quadragesimo Anno*, issued by Pope Pius XI in 1931, which contained blistering condemnations of unemployment in the midst of a worldwide depression. As an ironic footnote, *Rerum Novarum* also led to the founding of a large Catholic fraternal order that uses secret rituals: the Knights of Columbus.

Suggested Reading

Sidney Ahlstrom, *A Religious History of the American People*, 1975; Henry Browne, *The Catholic Church and the Knights of Labor*, 1949; Robert E. Weir, *Beyond Labor's Veil: The Culture of the Knights of Labor*, 1996.

RETAIL WORKERS

Retail workers include cashiers, merchandisers, customer assistance workers, and stock handlers. Retail work is one of the fastest-growing parts of the **service industry** sector of the economy; it is also among the most poorly paid. Many retail workers earn **minimum wage** or slightly above it, and they generally have few **fringe benefits**. According to the U.S. **Bureau of Labor Statistics**, there were 7.6 million retail workers in the United States in 2010—a figure many economists believe is understated.

The retail industry expanded in tandem with the **Industrial Revolution**. Prior to industrialization, production and retailing were conducted from the homes of **master craftsmen** and there was little separation between producers, wholesalers, and retailers. Dry goods merchants were a notable exception, but even then hired help often did auxiliary tasks such as basting shirtwaists, sewing buttonholes, and manufacturing garments for sale in the store. Retailing, as it is now understood, presupposes the production of surplus goods. Once economies of scale emerged in which surpluses were generated, retailing became a distinct economic function. The extent of retail activity varied depending upon location, but generally found its fullest expression in cities. Alexander Stewart's New York City dry goods store opened in 1848 and is widely regarded as the template for department stores. Well into the 20th century, though, most retailing took place in small shops.

Retail clerks then, as now, were viewed as unskilled labor, worked long hours, and were poorly paid. The first known attempt to organize these workers came in 1835, when some Philadelphia clerks joined a city movement to establish a 10-hour workday. That effort failed, and many retail workers routinely began work at 6 A.M. and labored 14 hours or more. By the 1890s, a practice had evolved in which workers lived in rooms above the shop; it was not uncommon for workers to exceed 100 hours of labor per week. The **Knights of Labor** led an "early closing" movement on behalf of shopkeepers, but its efforts proved more successful abroad than in the United States. The **American Federation of Labor** (AFL) also organized come clerks; in 1890, they combined to form a body that, after several names changes, was called the Retail Clerks International Union (RCIU).

Among the challenges facing retail workers was the assumption that they were **white-collar** laborers. Such employees were often viewed with suspicion and contempt by industrial workers, who unfairly associated clerks with their employers and blamed them for high prices. This was especially true for retail workers in **company towns**. Many 19th-century workers supported the principles underlying **cooperatives** and urged **boycotts** of private establishments. Employees were also hampered by the fact that from the 1880s onward, women made up a large part of retailing workforce. Domestic ideology made all female wage-earners suspect, and labor organizations fiercely debated questions of whether women should be organized and whether they should be paid at rates equal to those paid to male workers.

The RCIU remained a small organization that seldom called **strikes**; it preferred boycotts and moral suasion campaigns to make advances. A notable exception occurred in Lafayette, Indiana, in 1912. The RCIU sought a $5 per week minimum wage for female retail workers and early closing during slow periods; union members held out for 17 months and eventually proved victorious. The RCIU enjoyed growth until the end of World War I, when the **Red Scare** successfully (and absurdly) associated the union with communism. Historians generally associate the attack on the RCIU with an effort by rising corporate interests to control costs; chain stores had begun to drive smaller establishments out of business, and by 1929, about 22 percent of all retailing took place inside corporate chains. Weak labor organizations made it easier for retail giants to implement **Taylorism** and other scientific management regimens.

The **National Industrial Recovery Act** and other New Deal programs were a boon to retail workers, as the federal government defined the workday and set wage floors. These policies greatly reduced the number of hours that retail workers toiled. Those wishing to organize also had a choice between the AFL's RCIU and groups associated with the **Congress of Industrial Organizations** (CIO) such as the Retail Employees of America and the Department Stores Organizing Committee.

Retail clerks even conducted **sit-down strikes** in Detroit, New York, Philadelphia, and Providence.

The next great change for retail workers came in the 1950s, when pent-up demand created by the Great Depression and World War II led to a surge in retail sales, an expansion of the sales industry, sharp growth in the U.S. population associated with the Baby Boom, and population shifts into growing suburbs. New shopping malls emerged, which posed a challenge for union organizers, as most were located on private property. The RCIU, a combined organization after the **American Federation of Labor-Congress of Industrial Organizations** (AFL-CIO) merger of 1955, managed to set up 450 **union locals** by 1957, but its 300,000 members—concentrated mostly on the West Coast, the Midwest, and in Eastern Seaboard cities—represented only a small fraction of those working in the trade. The union added another 100,000 members by 1960, but most retail workers remained unorganized.

Large discount retailers first emerged in the late 1950s, but did not play a major role within the national economy until the 1960s. By 1965, however, "big box" stores had surpassed old-line retailers such as J.C. Penney in total sales. The growth of discounters was driven by the lower prices they offered to consumers, a feat they accomplished by buying in volume and by ensuring that their labor costs were 15 to 20 percent lower than those of other retailers. Workers employed by chains such as Kmart, Jamesway, Ames, and Zayre seldom paid more the federal minimum wage, and some stores were organized physically in ways that made it difficult for employees to communicate with one another. Discounters were, for the most part, actively opposed to unions and used other tools to discourage organization, including surveillance of employees, dividing different stores into different companies, and implementing vague employment guidelines that gave managers discretionary power to dismiss employees deemed troublesome. Still another tactic was to hire employees likely to be short-term workers or those thought less likely to agitate, such as students, married women, and the elderly. These strategies remain staple methods used by discounters to thwart organizing to the present day.

Many labor analysts believe that the RCIU did not respond well to changes wrought by the rise of discounters and new emphasis on volume and speed occasioned by the introduction of Universal Product Codes and self-service shopping. As an organization rooted in AFL models of **craft unionism**, the RCIU was slow to realize that customer-service models of retailing were obsolete and that retailing had, indeed, become a semiskilled job. In 1979, the RCIU combined with a **butchers** union to form the **United Food and Commercial Workers** (UFCW) union. A 1985 strike of 5,000 grocery workers in Oregon established the UCFW in supermarkets and the union generally has a far greater presence in grocery stores than among retailers and discounters.

The dominance of Wal-Mart has proved an even greater challenge to attempts to organize workers. Wal-Mart is now the world's most profitable public corporation and has more than 2 million employees. It has been, and remains, rabidly anti-union, to the point that the parent company has closed stores whose employees sought to unionize. Wal-Mart has been cited for untold numbers of labor law violations, but persists on its path of keeping prices low by cutting costs. In 2006, the state of Connecticut was among those in which Wal-Mart cost taxpayers more money than it generated because it provided no health care benefits for its employees.

The fate of retail workers is of vital interest to the future of the American economy. In 2001, the number of people employed in manufacturing and those employed in retail had equalized; retail workers have since surpassed manufacturing workers.

Suggested Reading

Charles Fishman, *The Wal-Mart Effect: How the World's Most Powerful Company Really Works —and How It's Transforming the American Economy*, 2006; Walter Galenson, ed., *The Retail Clerks*, 1962; Caitlin Kelly, *Malled: My Unintentional Career in Retail*, 2011; Nelson Lichtenstein, ed., *Wal-Mart: The Face of 21st Century Capitalism*, 2006; "Retail Clerks," UCFW, http://www.ufcw.org/about_ufcw/ufcw_history/industries/retail.cfm, accessed June 1, 2011.

REUTHER, WALTER

Walter Reuther (September 1, 1907–May 9, 1970) was an activist in the **United Auto Workers of America** (UAW) union, the final president of the **Congress of Industrial Organizations** (CIO), an architect of the **American Federation of Labor-Congress of Industrial Organizations** (AFL-CIO), a supporter of the **civil rights** movement, and one of the most important liberal reformers of the mid-20th century. His premature death in a 1970 plane crash robbed organized labor of an important voice at a crucial moment in history.

Reuther was born in Wheeling, West Virginia, the son of German immigrant parents. His father, Valentine, was a brewery-wagon driver, insurance agent, and trade union and **socialist** activist. Walter and his two younger brothers, Roy (1909–1968) and Victor (1912–2004), absorbed their father's working-class idealism and commitment to social justice. In 1923, Walter dropped out of high school to work as an **apprentice** die maker; in 1927, he moved to Detroit, where he worked as a die maker for Ford Motor Company. While working full-time at Ford, Reuther finished high school and enrolled at Detroit City College (later Wayne State University). He was involved in campus politics and worked actively for the 1932 presidential campaign of socialist Norman Thomas. He also joined the Auto Workers Union and became affiliated with the communist **Trade Union Unity League**, but lost his job when the Great Depression set in.

In 1933, Walter and his brother Victor went to Europe, where they witnessed the Nazis' rise to power and briefly worked with the underground resistance. The Reuthers then made their way to the Soviet Union, where they worked in a Gorki automotive factory. Enemies later charged that Walter was a **communist**, but he admitted only to being a socialist. He also claimed that he and Victor left the Soviet Union in 1935 because they found the regime of Josef Stalin oppressive.

Walter Reuther became involved in the labor movement when he returned to the United States. He attended the 1935 **American Federation of Labor** (AFL) convention, where **John L. Lewis** pressed for **industrial unionism** and argued that industry-wide organization made more sense in mass-production industries. Although Reuther was between jobs, he obtained a UAW union card from a small local of General Motors (GM) workers in Detroit. He served as a delegate at the UAW's South Bend, Indiana, convention in 1936, where his ambition, self-confidence, oratory skills, and reputation for activism propelled him to a position of leadership.

Reuther became president of Local 174, a **union local** of just 100 members. He and his brothers nonetheless led a successful **strike**, in December 1936, against Kelsey-Hayes Corporation, a brake and wheel supplier for Ford. That victory spurred tremendous growth for Local 174. Immediately following the Kelsey-Hayes settlement, the Flint, Michigan, **General Motors sit-down strike** began. Walter and his brothers were deeply involved in the Flint strike and sought to expand the battle against GM to Ford. Walter was involved in a violent episode known as the Battle of the Overpass. On May 26, 1937, Ford Service Division **goons** viciously attacked Reuther and other UAW organizers at an overpass outside Ford's River Rouge plant. Newspapers throughout the nation published lurid photographs of Reuther, Richard Frankensteen, and other bloodied UAW organizers. Reuther was badly injured, but the incident confirmed his reputation a fearless crusader for labor rights. It also hastened his rise within the UAW.

Between 1936 and 1939, the UAW was torn by internecine factionalism that pitted communists against conservatives, and spilled over into clashes between leadership and the rank-and-file over tactics, strategy, and organization. At this stage of his life, Reuther had no qualms about working with communists, who proved capable organizers. In 1939, he became the head of the UAW's potentially important GM Department, which he transformed from a paper organization into a critical part of the UAW by organizing the tool and die makers. Reuther knew that without the output of the tool and die makers, GM could not roll out its 1940 models. Brief clashes occurred, but GM capitulated and bargained with the UAW.

As the United States entered World War II, Reuther proposed converting auto plants to military production, with the goal of producing 500 aircraft per day. He presciently saw the war as an opportunity for labor to achieve a greater voice in workplace management and pushed the UAW to cooperate with the **National War Labor Board**. Reuther served on the War Manpower Commission, the Office of Production Management, and the War Production Board during the war and proposed ideas that gained him national attention. Like many employers, auto manufacturers sought to reinstate prewar conditions once the war ended and conversion to peacetime production began. When Reuther pressed General Motors for **wage** increases for UAW members, GM argued it could not afford them without steep increases in the cost of automobiles. In a bold move, Reuther challenged GM to "open the books" to prove the company's contention. He asserted that GM could offer a 30 percent raise without a price hike and put forth a plan in which plants would be co-managed by GM and the UAW. The **United Auto Workers of America strike of 1945–1946** lasted for 113 days and resulted in a lucrative **contract** for UAW members. Workers at the time hailed Reuther's rich settlement, though some labor analysts later asserted that dropping the demand for co-management was a missed opportunity for organized labor that could have reshaped American economic and industrial history.

In 1946, Reuther defeated R. J. Thomas and became UAW president. Because Thomas and George Addes, the UAW's secretary-treasurer, had been among Reuther's staunchest opponents, he purged the UAW leadership cadre of all remnants of their caucus.

In 1948, a shotgun blast ripped through his home that struck Reuther in the right hand and left it paralyzed. The next year he weathered another assassination attempt, though the next evening, his Victor was shot in the head and lost an eye. No assailants were ever arrested. Speculation ran wild, with communists, Ford, and Detroit police all coming under suspicion—the last group because neither they nor the FBI investigated a 1949 bombing of the UAW's Detroit headquarters. The allegations against Ford stemmed from the 1937 beating that Reuther had suffered from Ford security guards, and his ongoing acrimonious relations with the auto manufacturing concern. Reuther beefed up personal security for the remainder of his life.

Reuther was fiercely anticommunist by the end of World War II and an early proponent of **Cold Wear** unionism. He accused former UAW secretary-treasurer Addes of being a communist, and he pressured the CIO to rid itself of communist influences. In 1949, the CIO expelled 11 communist-dominated unions and Reuther emerged as the most prominent anticommunist leader in the labor movement. This was not a sudden change of heart on Reuther's part; like other men of the left, he came to admire President Franklin Roosevelt. During the 1930s, Reuther abandoned the Socialist Party and became a stolid supporter of the New Deal. In another strategy whose wisdom continues to spark debate, Reuther came to believe that alliance with the **Democratic Party** was the only practical way for labor to achieve national political influence. Reuther harbored hopes that labor could become the left wing of the party and transform it along the lines of European social democratic parties. Reuther would later emerge as a force within the Democratic Party, solidly backing John F. Kennedy and Lyndon B. Johnson in their presidential bids and enthusiastically supporting Democratic programs on civil rights and the Great Society.

As UAW president, Reuther shifted his strategies in a manner reminiscent of a high-stakes version of **pattern bargaining**. Rather than negotiate with Chrysler, Ford, and GM simultaneously, the UAW targeted a single firm that would bear the brunt of strike actions. Reuther then made the settlement with that firm the basis for bargaining with the other two auto giants. It proved a successful a tactic; autoworkers made tremendous gains in the postwar era. By 1955, UAW members had negotiated **cost-of-living** increases, employer-funded **pensions**, employer-paid medical insurance, supplemental unemployment benefits, and job security guarantees. Reuther's critics charged that he accomplished these feats by weakening the rank-and-file and by sacrificing militancy in ways that turned the UAW into the disciplinary arm of the auto companies' personnel departments.

Reuther did, however, transform the UAW into the largest union in the CIO. When CIO President **Philip Murray** died in 1952, Reuther succeeded him.

Reuther started the negotiations that led to the merger of the AFL and CIO in 1955, as he believed that industrial unionism had established itself, that most of the disagreements between the two **labor federations** had disappeared, and that they needed to combine their strength to seek repeal of the **Taft-Hartley Act**. When the AFL-CIO formed in 1955, Reuther served as a vice president under President **George Meany** and headed the federation's Industrial Unionism Department.

Reuther miscalculated the similarities between the AFL and the CIO. Although he had moderated his views considerably since his socialist youth, he was a staunch progressive and he found Meany overly cautious, combative, and stubborn. Meany, in turn, was troubled by the UAW's embrace of the civil rights movement. Although Meany was a moderate on civil rights, several AFL affiliates excluded black workers; he was also troubled by what he saw as the militancy of the movement. Reuther ignored Meany and became an ardent supporter of civil rights. Reuther was among the speakers at the 1963 March on Washington at which the Reverend Martin Luther King, Jr., delivered his most famous speech. Meany and Reuther also clashed over the emerging **counterculture** in the 1960s. Meany seethed when the UAW supported the formation of Students for a Democratic Society, and was furious when Reuther spoke out against U.S. involvement in the **Vietnam War**. Reuther, in turn, disapproved of the AFL-CIO's slowness to embrace the **United Farm Workers of America** (UFWA).

In 1968, Reuther withdrew the UAW from the AFL-CIO and announced the formation of the Alliance for Labor Action, a rival federation that included the UAW, the UFWA, and the **Teamsters**. The Alliance never really established a foothold and faded away after Reuther and his wife were killed in a small plane crash in Pellston, Michigan, on May 9, 1970. Reuther's brother Roy predeceased him. Victor quit the UAW in 1971, when he grew disaffected with the union's leadership; he devoted the rest of his life to labor education. Reuther died before the full brunt of **deindustrialization** ravaged American industry. Speculation rages over what his response would have been, but many observers believe his leadership of the UAW would have been more decisive than that of his successors. In 1990, Walter Reuther was posthumously inducted in the **Department of Labor**'s Hall of Fame. The library at Wayne State University now bears his name.

Suggested Reading

John Barnard, *American Vanguard: The United Auto Workers during the Reuther Years, 1935–1970*, 2004; Kevin Boyle, *The UAW and the Heyday of American Liberalism, 1945–1968*, 1995; Nelson Lichtenstein, *The Most Dangerous Man in Detroit: Walter Reuther and the Fate of American Labor*, 1995; William Serrin, *The Company and the Union: The "Civilized Relationship" of the General Motors Corporation and the United Automobile Workers Union*, 1973.

RIGHT-TO-WORK

States that have right-to-work laws make it illegal to force a worker to join a union or pay union **dues** as a condition for employment. In essence, such laws forbid

union shops. In states that do not have right-to-work laws, unions sometimes successfully negotiate a closed union shop in which all employees must join a union to continue their employment; those who refuse can be summarily dismissed. Opponents argue that compulsory unionism violates their individual freedom of choice; some also disapprove of the way that unions spend their money, particularly in the area of political contributions and lobbying. The 1947 **Taft-Hartley Act** expressly forbade forced joining of a union as a condition of employment, but left in place the possibility of requiring employees to pay union dues after a certain period of time. Section 14(b) of the bill, however, allowed states to pass right-to-work laws that make union shops illegal in any form.

Unions, not surprisingly, strongly oppose right-to-work legislation. They argue that they represent all employees when they negotiate a contract and that non-union members are "free riders" who get the same **wages**, **fringe benefits**, and other privileges as union members paying for those services. Depending upon the wording of state laws, unions in right-to-work states generally seek contract language that allows them to collect an **agency fee** from non-union members that is, in essence, payment for the part of union services negotiated on their behalf. Individuals are not allowed to refuse payment—which is deducted from their checks—if an agency fee is in place. In cases where an agency fee is not required, unions attempt to negotiate less inclusive "fair share" payments. In extreme cases, unions can refuse to deliver any services whatsoever to non-union members and can, if they wish, seek two-tier wage structures that pay less money to non-union employees and give union members privileges that do not apply to nonmembers such as **bumping** rights and recall from layoff priority.

The National Right to Work Committee lobbies for the extension of right-to-work legislation beyond the 22 states that currently have such laws, and the National Right to Work Legal Defense Foundation provides legal representation for workers trying to challenge union membership requirements. Unions see right-to-work campaigns as little more than thinly disguised attacks on the entire **collective bargaining** process. They assert (correctly) that the modern right-to-work movement is simply the **closed shop** movement of the early 20th century in a new guise. Far from being a campaign to protect individual freedom, the phrase "right-to-work" is used to mask union-busting efforts on the part of unscrupulous employers and ideological conservatives.

Nearly all of the states that currently have right-to-work laws are located in the South, Southwest, and Plains states. Unions have a much more difficult time in organizing in such states, though both Nevada and Iowa have substantial numbers of union members. Unions seek the overturn of right-to-work laws, but have made little headway in accomplishing that goal. In more positive vein, no new states have passed right-to-work laws since 2001; a 2011 attempt to introduce such a law in New Hampshire was vetoed by the state's governor.

The right-to-work battle has taken on distinct ideological dimensions, with the **Republican Party** in favor of expanding right-to-work legislation and much of the **Democratic Party** opposing it. Not surprisingly, there is also widespread disagreement over the impact of right-to-work laws. The business community touts the fact that 10 of the 15 states deemed most friendly to business have right-to-work laws in place. The **American Federation of Labor-Congress of Industrial Organizations** counters that being "business friendly" does not mean that a state actually prospers. It has presented data that purport to show that right-to-work laws drive down wages and reduce the number of jobs available.

Right-to-work laws do not apply to railroad or airline employees, who must belong to unions regardless of the state in which they reside.

Suggested Reading

American Federation of Labor-Congress of Industrial Organizations, Washington, DC, 1995; Michael Mauer, *The Union Member's Complete Guide: Everything You Want—and Need—to Know about Working Union*, 2001; National Right-to-Work Committee Legal Defense Foundation, http://www.nrtw.org/rtws.htm, accessed May 31, 2011.

ROBOTICS. *See* Automation.

RUNAWAY CAPITAL/SHOPS

The terms "runaway capital" and "runaway shops" refer to the business practice of moving operations in whole or in part to another locale, state, or country. This step is most often taken to lower costs by relocating production and/or services in places with lower **wages** and fewer labor unions and government regulations. Businesses justify the practice by claiming that the pressures of **globalization** force them to be more competitive, while unions counter that too many companies are more interested in stockholder profits than in the welfare of workers, communities, or the United States. Many observers see runaway capital as among the biggest threats to the future of work in the United States. In recent years, a whole host of jobs once thought secure have been **outsourced** or located offshore.

The Northeast and northern tier of the Midwest were the first regions of the United States to feel the brunt of **deindustrialization** and runaway shops. These regions were once heavily industrialized. Over time, they also became hotbeds of labor union organizing. Even before the 1935 **National Labor Relations Act** secured **collective bargaining** rights for organized labor, a custom had emerged in which some business owners moved (or threatened to move) their operations to non-union regions. At first, employers moved to the South, where unions were weak and wages were lower.

The 1947 **Taft-Hartley Act** allowed state legislatures to pass **right-to-work** laws that prohibited compulsory union membership, thereby accelerating the move of manufacturing operations to the South, West, and Plains states. The Northeast saw most of its textile, shoes, and machine tool industries leave the region and relocate in the South.

Since the 1970s, however, runaway shops have tended to leave the United States altogether. Changes in the tax code under President **Ronald Reagan** made it much easier for corporations to write off U.S. investments; in many cases, U.S. taxpayers subsidized companies that chose to close their U.S. operations and shift production to low-wage operations such as Mexican *maquiladoras*. That trend was greatly accelerated when President Bill Clinton signed into law the controversial **North American Free Trade Agreement**, which removed many tariff barriers between the United States, Canada, and Mexico. It became the model for knocking down **protectionist** barriers elsewhere in the Latin America and around the globe. This philosophy has proved so popular,in the business community that it takes the lead in lobbying for **fast-track legislation**. It has, however, led to tremendous economic and social dislocation in cities and states that have lost once-lucrative businesses. The city of Detroit and the state of Michigan, for example, have yet to adjust from lost employment in the auto industry; both have unemployment and poverty rates in excess of the national average.

The debate over runaway shops has become ideological and is seen by opponents of unions as a way to curb their political influence and power. Unions counter that proponents of current trends are content to divide the United States into a society in which a small number of haves rule over a nation of have-nots. Both **Republicans** and **Democrats** tend to embrace free-market **capitalism**, and unions currently have little clout in preserving American jobs. Ironically, it is often the extreme right of conservative movements that now call for an end to practices that benefit runaway shops.

Economists now routinely speak of the United States as having a postindustrial economy. The advance of runaway capital has, however, thrown the very future of American labor into doubt. The **computer revolution**, for example, now allows **service industry** and professional jobs such as those involving data entry, sales, and medical diagnoses to move offshore. In doing so, these jobs join industrial production that long ago moved out of the United States and contribute to a severe balance-of-trade deficit for the country. A growing number of economists warn that the current standard of living in the United States cannot be sustained by current trends of low-wage labor, high unemployment, and deficit spending. Runaway capital greatly exacerbates all of these problems.

Suggested Reading

Marc Cooper, "Runaway Shops," *The Nation*, March 16, 2000; Richard Donkin, *The Future of Work*, 2009; Gary C. Hufbauer and Jeffrey Schott, *NAFTA Revisited: Achievements and Challenges*, 2005; Thomas Kochan, *Restoring the American Dream: A Working Families' Agenda for America*, 2006.

S

SABOTAGE

Sabotage is a social protest tactic designed to interrupt work and production. It is commonly (or deliberately) misunderstood when applied to labor relations. In common parlance, it refers to wanton destruction of property resulting from a dispute between two parties. It is often used to refer to damages inflicted by workers on the property of recalcitrant employers, especially during a **strike** or **boycott**. That is sometimes true, but most labor unions adhere to a definition of sabotage developed by the **Industrial Workers of the World** (IWW): a systematic withdrawal of worker efficiency. The IWW calls it "striking on the job."

Sabotage as today practiced is quite different from the past. Scholars generally link the term to the French word *sabot*, meaning "wooden shoe," but its precise origin is shrouded in legend. One school of thought credits the term to a 1910 French rail strike in which workers damaged the shoes (*sabots*) holding rails together. Still others claim it comes from the practice of disgruntled machine tenders hurling their *sabots* into machines in the early days of the French Industrial Revolution. The latter claim seems more probable, as the practice of both wanton and passive forms of sabotage assuredly predates 1910. As numerous IWW supporters were fond of pointing out, the act of ancient Hebrew slaves spoiling Egyptian bricks was a form of sabotage, as were acts of antebellum **slaves** filling the bottoms of cotton bags with stones.

American workers have, on occasion, engaged in direct destruction of property, though most such actions have come from desperate individuals rather than carrying the official sanction of a labor union. Destructive sabotage was quite common during the **railroad strike of 1877**. Workers have long understood, however, that destruction of property is an invitation to use force to break strikes and unions. When several hotheaded strikers derailed a train during an 1890 strike against the New York Central Railroad, for example, the railroad used the incident to justify the hiring of **Pinkerton** guards (which was actually done before the incident) and to convince reluctant state governments to send National Guard troops into numerous locales. Likewise, striking miners who dynamite pits or commit other acts of destructive sabotage have often found themselves subject to state repression in the wake of their sabotage. Some ideological radicals have, nonetheless, called upon workers to destroy property. **Anarcho-syndicalists**, including some IWW leaders, believed that destruction could be used as part of a larger **direct action** program aimed at disrupting **capitalism**.

For the most part, destructive sabotage has been less common than striking on the job. IWW leader **William Haywood** once remarked, "The manager's brains are under the workman's cap." It is often more advantageous and effective for employees to use their superior knowledge of the work process to demonstrate how jobs simply cannot get done without the cooperation of workers. For example, **assembly-line** workers might engage in a "slowdown" in which they deliberately and collectively reduce the pace of their work so they barely meet production quotas, or fail to meet them altogether. Workers can disrupt work processed by withholding specialized knowledge they possess that management does not. A group of workers might, for instance, feign ignorance of how to repair a broken machine, thereby slowing production.

This sort of sabotage can be so effective that management exaggerates or invents physical sabotage threats to justify heavy-handed crackdowns. In the past, some companies hired **agent provocateurs** to either incite strikers to commit property damage or make it appear that unions did damage that was done by company thugs. The 1936 **La Follette Committee** revealed that this was a widespread tactic. The use of agent provocateurs, like destructive sabotage itself, is illegal, but both continue to occur occasionally. For the most part, however, destructive worker sabotage has been an act of frustration, not a tactic authorized, endorsed, or condoned by unions. **Picketing** strikers angered by **scabs** taking their jobs have, for example, engaged in acts of petty vandalism such as smashing windows, slashing tires, or throwing "jack rocks," improvised tire-piercing spikes, on roads leading in and out of a picketed business.

In the current labor environment, which makes it easy to hire scabs to replace strikers, striking on the job is a more effective tool. One variant of sabotage is the "work-to-rule" campaign in which workers perform only tasks stipulated in their **contracts** and no others. Truckers in the International Brotherhood of Teamsters have several times won employer concessions simply by driving the speed limit at all times, taking breaks exactly as mandated in the contract, and refusing to do any loading or unloading of cargo not specifically mandated. Teachers and other public employees have had success with "work-to-rule" campaigns. Few contracts, for instance, require teachers to stay after hours to tutor students, monitor lunchrooms, meet with parents, volunteer for school events, advise clubs, make photocopies, grade homework at night, supervise bus loading, assume extra duties during an emergency, informally deal with discipline problems, or coach sports teams—yet schools would be hard-pressed to operate efficiently without such assistance. Work-to-rule campaigns have proved effective in forcing school boards to negotiate with teachers and, in many cases, staved off strikes.

Because of the negative associations it carries, few contemporary workers use the term "sabotage." Given the disproportionate power between management and employees, however, sabotage remains part of the American workplace. An ironic by-product of declining union strength is that sabotage incidents are likely to increase. Union contracts stipulate work conditions and **grievance** procedures that unions expect members to honor; without a contract, employees have fewer restraints.

Suggested Reading

Frank Bohn, "Some Definitions: Direct Action—Sabotage," and Ben William, "Sabotage," in Joyce Kornbluh, ed., *Rebel Voices: An I.W.W. Anthology*, 1968; Martin Sprouse, ed., *Sabotage in the American Workplace: Anecdotes of Dissatisfaction, Mischief and Revenge*, 1992.

SALARY

Salary is a marker of **white-collar labor**. It refers to an employee's compensation for work. Unlike **wages**, however, salaries are not pegged to an hourly rate; instead, they are either based on a yearly amount to be paid or linked to a limited-term **contract**. As long as salaried workers perform the tasks specified by their job descriptions, they receive the agreed-upon amount irrespective of the number of hours they work. A salaried employee making $52,000 per year would be paid $1,000 per week (before taxes) whether that person worked 30 hours or 50 hours. By contrast, a wage-earner making $25 per hour would have to work 40 hours to receive $1,000; if that individual worked only 30 hours and could not apply agreed-upon leave time to his absence—such as sick leave, personal leave, or vacation time—that worker would receive just $750.

The 1938 **Fair Labor Standards Act** (FSLA) governs most employer/employee compensation, but exempts six major categories of employees from its span of control: executives, administrators, workers in professions, elected officials, agricultural employees, and those working in entertainment and recreational fields. Those exemptions generally cover types of work that are salary based, and for which employees receive a fixed payment for any pay period without regard to the number of days or hours worked. Unless union or non-union contracts specify otherwise, salary deductions theoretically can be made for all such work absences as personal reasons, illness, or disability, though in practice more salaried employees enjoy compensation protection than those working for wages. The FSLA forbids deductions of salaries or wages for employees called for jury duty, court service, or temporary military leave.

Salaries generally serve as another distinction between jobs that society sees as "professional" employment requiring more education and specialized training, and those seen as manual, **blue-collar**, semiskilled, or unskilled labor. The expansion of **service industry** work has blurred traditional distinctions somewhat, but salaries continue to carry social class implications, with many Americans associating a salary with solidifying middle-class identity, whereas wages continue to be associated more with the **working class**. Salaries do not, however, mean that white-collar employees are necessarily better off than blue-collar workers. In many cases, skilled blue-collar workers such as **master** plumbers or unionized **assembly-line** workers may make more money than teachers, nurses, or journalists. Moreover, because salaried workers are not "on the clock" and cannot command **overtime** pay, many complain of long work hours and burdensome job duties. Some without union contracts often lack formal **grievance** procedures and are at the whim of employers;

complaints against abusive supervisors have risen, but because many salaried workers are considered "employees at will," it is harder for salaried employees to prove abuse. Many labor observers believe that professional and white-collar workers are ripe for union-organizing drives.

Suggested Reading

Richard Ford, ed., *White Collar, Blue Collar, No Collar: Stories of Work*, 2011; Juliet Schor, *The Overworked American: The Unexpected Decline of Leisure*, 1993; Robert Sutton, *Good Boss, Bad Boss*, 2010.

SAN FRANCISCO GENERAL STRIKE (1934). *See* Depression-Era Strikes.

SCAB

Scab is the term used to refer to workers who refuse to participate when their colleagues **strike**, or to workers who are hired by management to replace strikers. The term is purposely offensive and is applied with contempt. To loyal union supporters, there is no greater insult than to be dubbed a scab.

The exact origin of the term is disputed. Its first known use in English occurred in 1529 as a synonym for moral decay. By 1590, it was used generally to refer to persons of low character. Its first recorded use as referring to strikebreakers occurred during a 1777 cordwainers' strike in Bristol, England, though it is likely the term was in currency long before then. The term appeared in the United States as early as 1806 during a bootmakers' and shoemakers' strike. For much of the 19th century it vied with "blackleg" as the favored term of abuse, though the latter has fallen from popular use. Printers also commonly used the terms "fink," "rat," and "ratfink" to refer to strikebreakers.

Imported scabs have long been a staple during capital/labor disputes, with management attempting to maintain production and thus break strikes. Until recently, most scabs have been recruited from among the ranks of **immigrants**, itinerant laborers, and the unemployed. In some cases, workers were unaware that they were strikebreakers until they arrived at their jobs and faced **pickets**. Some of the tension between African American and Caucasian labor can be traced to the deliberate importation of black workers into strike-torn situations. Nineteenth-century employers also used Chinese scabs, another factor in fueling hysteria that resulted in the **Chinese Exclusion Act**. In most strikes, the introduction of scabs intensifies the conflict; in some cases, this practice has led to violence. Assaults upon scabs have occurred often during labor conflict though it is far more common for strikers to be beaten or killed than scabs. A rare example of scabs faring worse than strikers was during the 1922 **Herrin Massacre** in Illinois, in which outraged strikers killed 19 scabs.

The 1938 **Mohawk Valley Formula** established a blueprint whereby employers sought to hire scabs as a new and permanent workforce. In most cases, though, the usual practice was that most or all scabs would be dismissed once a dispute was settled; public contempt for scabs was generally so fierce that companies found it easier to make peace with previous strikers than to integrate scabs into the community. Since the late 1970s, however, employers have turned increasingly to professional strikebreaking firms during conflicts. These firms are often called upon to procure "replacement workers." Court cases and policy shifts have made it easier to apply the logic of the Mohawk Valley Formula, declining union strength has weakened the ability to resist scabs, and successful public relations campaigns have succeeded in changing the public's perception of unions. The very term "replacement worker" is a measure of this trend; it is now the term normally used in the media to describe scabs and many of those taking jobs from strikers defend their actions by appealing to individualism, freedom of contract, and desire for self-betterment. The rhetoric has shifted to the degree that "replacement workers" have sought court relief banning the use of the term "scab" as libelous. They have not been successful. A 1999 11th Circuit ruling in *Dunn v. ALPA* stated that the use of word "scab" to describe pilots who crossed picket lines was accurate and nonlibelous. That ruling has withstood subsequent challenge.

Suggested Reading

Stanley Aronowitz, *From the Ashes of the Old*, 2000; Archie Green, *Wobblies, Pile Butts, and Other Heroes*, 1993; Stephen Norwood, *Strikebreaking and Intimidation*, 2002.

SCHNEIDERMAN, ROSE

Rose Schneiderman (April 6, 1884?–August 11, 1972) was an important leader of the **Women's Trade Union League** (WTUL), the **International Ladies' Garment Workers' Union** (ILGWU), and numerous other organizations. Schneiderman was an important voice for **immigrant** women workers in the first half of the 20th century. She may have been the first person to use the term "bread and roses" to describe the **Lawrence textile strike of 1912**, a phrase that was probably never used by Lawrence workers.

She was born in either 1882 or 1884 in Saven, Poland (then Russia), the daughter of Samuel and Deborah (Rothman) Schneiderman. Her Jewish parents immigrated to the United States in 1890, and settled in New York City's Lower East Side. Soon after their arrival, Schneiderman's father, a tailor, died of influenza, and the Schneiderman children were dispatched to orphanages and to the homes of relatives. Rose's public school education ended when she was 13, and she went to work in a department store. She left for a factory job stitching cap linings, but the brutal conditions of factory work led Schneiderman to convert to **socialism** and to join the trade union movement. She helped form New York Local 23 of the United Cloth Hat and Cap Makers of North America (UCHCM), and was elected the union's first secretary. That was a remarkable achievement because, at the time, the UCHCM did not even officially admit women, a policy Schneiderman helped reverse. She also helped direct a successful 1905 strike that increased **wages** for city hat makers.

Despite being raised in poverty and having only a grammar school education, Rose Schneiderman became a well-known trade unionist in the United States. She was a founding member of the American Civil Liberties Union and served as president of the Women's Trade Union League. (Library of Congress)

Schneiderman's efforts attracted notice among labor activists and, in 1907, she was elected as vice president of the New York Branch of the WTUL. She also received a scholarship to attend classes at a preparatory school while working as an East Side organizer. She and **Leonora O'Reilly** were key figures in organizing a 1908 strike against the Cohen Company that secured higher wages for workers and put an end to the **piecework** system. The successful strike also led the dressmakers' union to affiliate with the ILGWU. Schneiderman also played an active role in 1909 **Uprising of the 20,000**, a strike that made the ILGWU a powerful union.

Schneiderman came to national public attention following a rousing speech she gave after the **Triangle Factory Fire of 1911**, in which she excoriated the **middle class** for its half-hearted support for the **working class**. She delivered her remarks at a funeral held by the city for the unclaimed dead and marched in the procession to represent the WTUL. After the fire, Schneiderman organized workers with increased vigor. She was an ILGWU organizer from 1914 to 1916, duties that took her across the country. She unionized workers in Boston, Philadelphia, Cleveland, and Chicago. In Chicago, she assisted in the successful Herzog glovemaker strike of 1915.

Schneiderman continued to rise in WTUL ranks; she served as WTUL vice president from 1919 to 1926, and as its president in 1918 and again from 1926 to 1947. Although sympathetic to all immigrant groups, she spent much of her time organizing Jewish and Italian workingwomen in the garment industry of the Lower East Side. She repeatedly claimed that Eastern European Jewish women were the most loyal union members.

Schneiderman was a devoted suffragist and campaigned vigorously for women's right to vote. In 1920, the year the Nineteenth Amendment secured the right for women to vote, Schneiderman attended the International Congress of Working Women, and ran a quixotic campaign for the U.S. Senate on the Socialist Labor

Party ticket. She was also interested in workers' education and served as a trustee of Brookwood Labor College from 1924 to 1929. She was an early supporter of Franklin Roosevelt and, in 1933, became the sole female labor unionist on the board of the National Industrial Recovery Administration. She also served as secretary to the New York Department of Labor from 1937 to 1944. Her friendship with Eleanor Roosevelt provided Schneiderman with White House access, and some scholars assert that Schneiderman was among the brain trust that helped Franklin Roosevelt formulate his New Deal policy.

By the 1940s, Schneiderman's influence had waned and the WTUL was in severe decline. Some critics link the WTUL's disintegration to Schneiderman's decision to distance the WTUL from the **Congress of Industrial Organizations**. Others blame her for holding on to the WTUL's reins for too long. Schneiderman dismantled the national WTUL in 1949 and retired, though she continued to make occasional speeches on behalf of the labor movement.

Suggested Reading

Gary E. Endelman, *Solidarity Forever: Rose Schneiderman and the Women's Trade Union League*, 1981; Philip S. Foner, *Women and the American Labor Movement: From the First Trade Unions to the Present*, 1980; Alice Kessler-Harris, "Rose Schneiderman and the Limits of Women's Trade Unionism," in *Labor Leaders in America*, Melvyn Dubofsky and Warren Van Tine, eds., 1967; Rose Schneiderman, *All for One*, 1967.

SCIENTIFIC MANAGEMENT. *See* Taylorism.

SECOND GREAT AWAKENING AND LABOR

The Second Great Awakening was a series of Christian religious revivals that engulfed the United States in the early 19th century. It is best known for its emphasis on perfectionism, millennialism, and emotionalism, and the founding of new sects and denominations such as the Seventh-Day Adventists, the Mormons, and the Church of Christ. The revivals began in upstate New York in the 1820s and were still in effect in some parts of the South on the eve of the **Civil War**. The Second Great Awakening was linked to moral reform in the North and to the greater articulation of emotion-based religious practices in the South and the frontier. The revivals also contributed to social and political changes during the period that affected working people such as northern wage-earners and southern **slaves**.

For the most part, Second Great Awakening preachers rejected or deemphasized predestination, a doctrine that was foundational for the 17th-century architects of the First Great Awakening. Central to the Second Great Awakening was the idea that individuals could break the power of sin and make themselves worthy of salvation; some even believed that moral perfection was possible. The notion that individuals were complicit in their own salvation found resonance with the growing northern **middle class**, especially those small merchants embracing emergent **capitalism**. In essence, some individuals came to believe that they determined their own fate in the here and the hereafter. Because many converts were also millennialists who thought they were ushering in the thousand-year rule of Christ in advance of the final judgment, they felt called upon to reform society. Northern converts could be found in such moral reform movements as temperance, prohibition, abolitionism, the public school movement, missionary tract societies, anti-prostitution crusades, women's rights, and asylum and prison reformation. Working people would also take part in the revivals, but not to the degree with which their middle-class employers embraced them. In some cases, the moral zeal of middle-class employers clashed with the time-honored customs of workers. This was especially the case in alcohol reform aimed at discontinuing the practice of drinking on the job; workers could countenance voluntary temperance, but many resented and resisted **prohibition** campaigns.

Northern moral reform also occasionally took on anti-immigrant and anti-Catholic undertones that distressed Irish workers. The workforce of the 1830s and 1840s also contained substantial numbers of itinerant workers. Canal workers in particular had little interest in the revivals; Sunday was a rare day of rest for them, and the social lives of single males often revolved around saloons, gambling dens, and brothels. The revivals also met with disinterest from those radicalized by early trade unions or the **Workingmen's movement**. Eventually a segment of the working class was also caught up in the new religious spirit, but these "revivalists" had to compete for working-class hearts and minds with "radicals" and "traditionalists" keen on preserving old customs. Many of the revivalists joined cause with moral reformers.

One of the most enduring effects of the revivals on working-class life was the articulation of what is sometimes called "working-class respectability." It is frequently confused with an aping of the middle class, and the line between the two is occasionally hard to delineate. Generally speaking, though, working-class respectability involved the cultivation of character and refinement, but within an ethos that stressed the dignity of honest toil and was critical of idleness, hypocrisy, moral smugness, and autocracy. It also emphasized mutualism and community rather than the excessive individualism of the middle class. After the Civil War, working-class respectability shaped the public demeanors of labor leaders, especially **William Sylvis** and **Terence Powderly**. Many late-19th-century workers also saw themselves as the preservers of Christian morals corrupted by greedy **social Darwinists**.

The Second Great Awakening also had an impact in the frontier and in the South and West. Much as in northern cities, many frontier converts sought to redeem and purify society. Although Baptists, Methodists, and Presbyterians took the lead during the revivals, the movement's overall character was nondenominational and nontheological. In many cases revivals were led by those who felt they had received the "call" to preach—a phenomenon that made southern and frontier revivals more democratic in character than those in the North. The revivals also penetrated the lower ranks of society more thoroughly, in part because both the middle class and the wage-earning **working class** were smaller and weaker outside of the Northeast and Midwest. Even greater emphasis was placed upon emotion than in the North, and the Second Great Awakening left behind a legacy of backwoods and rural preaching that often deemphasized reason and intellectualism in favor of Biblical literalism and personal piety. In the post-Civil War era, the same regions often spawned particularly strong reactions against new ideas such as **Marxism**, Darwinism, and Freudianism. They were hotbeds for prohibition, however, and the South departed dramatically from the North in that post-Awakening support for abolitionism declined rather than expanded. Southern whites often appealed to religion to justify slavery before the Civil War, and to "Jim Crow" systems after the conflict. Religion was often at the heart of opposition to **Reconstruction** in the 1860s and 1870s, and to resistance to **civil rights** movements thereafter. As labor unions would often discover to their horror, religion was also often used to promote individualism and to tar unions as anti-American and immoral. In the South, preachers and nondenominational churches frequently led opposition to unions.

The postwar opposition to civil rights is ironic, as the Second Great Awakening found willing converts among southern slaves. Prior to the revivals, slave owners debated whether slaves should be evangelized in hopes of making them compliant, or if Christianity should be withheld for fear that slaves would desire liberation. The end of the overseas slave trade after 1808 meant that within a generation most legally traded slaves were domestically born African Americans, not African immigrants. Many within the new generations of slaves embraced emotional forms of Christianity arising from the Second Great Awakening. Much as some earlier masters had feared, however, black Christianity picked up upon liberation themes that some earlier converts had embraced. Nat Turner, a Virginia slave and bush preacher, led a bloody rebellion in Virginia during 1831 that prompted calls to tighten controls on African American religion. These laws proved easier to issue than to enforce. Although outright rebellions were rare (and suicidal), scholars have long appreciated the myriad ways in which slaves used religion to support freedom movements. Hymns and Biblical texts, for instance, often carried coded messages for runaways. The longest-lasting effect of the Second Great Awakening among black converts was the establishment of a link between Christianity and social justice that was less pronounced in white churches. Christian-based activism was and remains central to African American civil rights activism.

The lingering effects of the Second Great Awakening serve as reminders that a thorough understanding of American society requires attention to religious expression. Social movements, including the labor movement, have often advanced or stumbled according to how well or how poorly they reconciled their goals with religious ideals.

Suggested Reading

Sydney Ahlstrom, *A Religious History of the American People*, Vols. 1 and 2, 1975; Nathan O. Hatch, *The Democratization of American Christianity*, 1989; Paul Johnson, *A Shopkeeper's Millennium: Society and Revivals in Rochester, New York, 1815–1837*, 2004; Bruce Laurie, *Working People of Philadelphia, 1800–1850*, 1980; Liston Pope, *Millhands and Preachers: A Study of Gastonia*, 1942.

SENATE CIVIL LIBERTIES COMMITTEE. *See* La Follette Committee.

SERVICE EMPLOYEES INTERNATIONAL UNION

The Service Employees International Union (SEIU) represents more than 2 million workers, most of whom are employed in the **service industry**, though the union specializes in three employment categories: health care workers, public employees, and workers who maintain properties. Its members range in occupation from custodians and nurses to taxi drivers and window washers. At a time in which many unions have struggled to maintain their strength, the SEIU has more than doubled its ranks since 1980. It is also one of the most diverse unions in the United States. More than 30 percent of its rank-and-file consists of **minority labor**, and more than 50 percent is female. The SEIU is so aggressive in organizing that it has become embroiled in controversy over its methods. Unlike most contemporary unions, however, the SEIU seeks to encourage rather than contain grassroots activism.

The SEIU was founded by a group of Chicago janitors in 1921 and was chartered by the **American Federation of Labor**. It was known as the Building Service Employees International Union (BSEIU) until 1968, when it changed its name to SEIU. Although the BSEIU has not received the attention from scholars that the **industrial unions** of the 1930s have, it organized hospital workers and public employees during the 1930s, when few other unions were attempting to do so. It was most active in large cities, including New York, where Local 32B won several strikes that resulted in **wage** increases for members.

The BSEIU began to grow in the 1960s, due in part to shifts in the American economy that led to an expanded service industry sector. Its growth coincided with the resurgence of feminism and the union found itself inexorably drawn into the organization of women, especially in the health care industry. In 1974, the SEIU was one of the major supporters of the **Coalition of Labor Union Women**, a group that seeks to address women's issues and place more women in union leadership roles. In 1975, the SEIU chartered **9to5**, a union of women clerical workers. Although 9to5 has since evolved into a separate organization, the SEIU maintains a strong presence among clerical workers.

The SEIU was also deeply affected by the **civil rights** movement and took part in the 1965 march from Selma to Montgomery, Alabama, despite the refusal of the **American Federation of Labor-Congress of Industrial Organizations** (AFL-CIO) to endorse the protest. The SEIU's District 1199 has a distinguished record of organizing minority workers, as many custodians and office support staffers have been (and are) African American and Latino. In 1985, SEIU members in Denver created Justice for Janitors (JfJ), a campaign to organize office cleaners and custodians. Since its inception, this movement has spread to other cities, including Los Angeles and Boston, where heavily non-English-speaking **immigrant** workforces have won wage and benefit concessions from the 1990s onward. Such gains are no small accomplishment as the workers targeted by JfJ are often among the working poor, a sector of the workforce too often ignored by other unions.

The SEIU enjoyed a reputation for being among the more democratic unions in the AFL-CIO. The AFL-CIO recognized this fact when, in 1995, it tapped SEIU President **John Sweeney** to head the **labor federation**. Sweeney promised to bring SEIU-like grassroots organizing models to the entire AFL-CIO and allocated more resources for doing so. His own union, however, grew disenchanted with his results and criticized the AFL-CIO as a **business union** that is too conciliatory toward employers and too focused upon bureaucracy. The SEIU suffered a setback in 2000, when its Canadian affiliates representing 30,000 workers disaffiliated. Publicly, Canadian leaders claimed a desire for a more uniquely Canadian perspective, but most observers cited dissatisfaction with lower wage rates in negotiated settlements in the United States. Privately, the SEIU agreed that U.S. rates were too low. Under the leadership of Andrew Stern, the SEIU healed its breach with Canadian workers, dramatically increased in size, and pushed a reform agenda inside the AFL-CIO. When the SEIU grew dissatisfied with the slow pace of change, it disaffiliated from the AFL-CIO in 2005 and co-created the **Change to Win Federation**, an AFL-CIO rival.

The SEIU has been aggressive in protecting its membership, and has engaged in high-profile battles with state and local governments seeking to cut costs in the wake of the recession that began in 2007. It successfully staved off cuts in California, a major coup. The SEIU has stood accused of **raiding** AFL-CIO unions as well as coercing workers to vote for it during several recent **certification** drives. It has been embroiled in several bitter struggles against the food services corporation Sodexo, which filed **Racketeer Influenced Corrupt Organizations** charges against the SEIU. The union responded, among other ways, by underwriting campaigns that exposed Sodexo overcharges in New York State—a finding that resulted in a $30 million judgment against the company.

The SEIU maintains that militancy is the key to revitalizing the labor movement. Some analysts temper SEIU's claims by pointing out that much of the union's success is due to the fact that it represents workers who are less susceptible to **outsourcing** and **runaway shops**. They also point out that Change to Win has not fared any better than the AFL-CIO in recent years and that there is now discussion afoot of dissolving it and reuniting with the AFL-CIO. Nonetheless, amidst an overall portrait of organized labor gloom during the past three decades, the SEIU offers a rare glimmer of hope.

Suggested Reading

Thomas Beadling, Grace Palladino, Pat Cooper, and Peter Pieragostini, *A Need for Valor: The Roots of Service Employees International Union 1902–1992*, 1992; Leon Fink and Brian Greenberg, *Upheaval in the Quiet Zone: 1199/SEIU and the Politics of Healthcare Unionism*, 2009; Bill Fletcher and Fernando Gapasin, *Solidarity Divided: The Crisis in Organized Labor and a New Path toward Social Justice*, 2008; Service Employees International Union, http://www.seiu.org/, accessed June 7, 2011.

SERVICE INDUSTRY

The service industry is the part of the American economy in which customers, clients, and businesses are assisted. Also called the "tertiary" sector, this industry is characterized by workers who provide direct knowledge, help, or duty. They do not produce tangible products, though their actions often make production possible or more efficient. Examples of service industry jobs include those in **retail**, repair, health care, financial services, entertainment, advertising, communications, wholesaling, valet service, restaurant work, and tourism and hospitality trades. The service industry is both the largest and the fastest-growing sector of the U.S. economy. More than three-fourths of the nation's 2009 gross national product came from the service sector. Services are equally valuable as exports; in 2010, the United States exported services valued at nearly $543 billion.

The service sector will continue to play an important part in American economic life. According to the **Bureau of Labor Statistics**, an additional 1.2 million manufacturing jobs will disappear by 2018, whereas roughly 14.5 million service-sector jobs will appear. Another 17 million professional **white-collar** jobs are projected to be created. Gains are anticipated in fields such as health care, customer service, food services, retail teaching, landscaping, construction, and office work, whereas steep declines are anticipated in textiles, shoes, the needle trades, and most production jobs. More than 80 percent of all American workers are now employed in the tertiary sector and that percentage will certainly increase in the near future, though there is great debate over whether a service-based economy is sustainable in the long term.

Critics of the service industry express doubts that the United States can sustain an economy in which the bulk of finished goods are imported. In 2008, the country suffered a $690 billion balance-of-trade deficit, a figure than consumed nearly 5 percent of the nation's gross domestic product. The United States remains deeply in debt to foreign powers, especially China. Some observers believe that the United States must reverse its trend toward **deindustrialization** and some reformers, including those inside the **American Federation of Labor-Congress of Industrial Organizations**, have called for **protectionism** to help American manufacturing reindustrialize. To date, neither **Democratic** nor **Republican** politicians have shown any inclination to abandon free trade principles or slow the pace of economic **globalism**.

The service industry is more complex than many individuals appreciate. Critics also charge that service industry jobs are occupational and financial dead ends. As they see it, the decline of manufacturing has saddled millions of Americans with low-**wage** jobs that widen the gap between rich and poor, threaten to shrink the **middle class**, and will ultimately transform the United States into a two-tier society defined by haves and have-nots. The service sector is, however, often viewed as synonymous with retailing, which is often a poorly paid occupation. Many service-sector employees are, in fact, specially trained, highly educated, **salaried**, professional workers. The postindustrial economy has also resulted in a high degree of romanticism regarding lost manufacturing jobs. Although unionized workers in the boom economy following World War II often earned high wages, the longer history of American industrial work has been marked by the same two-tier system that alarmists fear the future will bring. This suggests that the underlying problem may be related more to how **capitalist** society constructs and maintains **social class** than to the nature of work itself. Put simply, the problem may not be too many service industry jobs, but rather that too many service industry jobs are poorly compensated.

Nonetheless, there is adequate cause for concern over the dominance of the service sector, if for no other reason that it has not been stable. The computer industry, for example, has seen great fluctuation as data processing, hardware production, and customer service have been subject to **outsourcing**. The health care industry, though growing, is also saddled with soaring costs that have made it unaffordable for millions of Americans. Hospitals and medical facilities sometimes seek to contain costs by laying off nurses, converting staff specialists into fee-for-service workers, and reducing levels of client care. As noted, there is also the lingering question of how competitive the United States can be in the global export market by relying on tertiary services.

Suggested Reading

Benjamin Cheever, *Selling Ben Cheever: Back to Square One in a Service Economy*, 2001; Occupational outlook handbook, 2010–2011 edition, http://www.bls.gov/oco/oco2003.htm, accessed June 12, 2011; U.S. Census, Service Annual Survey, http://www.census.gov/svsd/www/services/sas/sas_summary/summaryhome.htm, accessed June 12, 2011; Laurie Young, *From Products to Services: Insights and Experiences from Companies Which Have Embraced the Service Economy*, 2008.

SHANKER, ALBERT

Albert Shanker (September 14, 1928–February 22, 1997) is considered the architect of effective teachers' unions in the United States. He served as the president of the **American Federation of Teachers** (AFT) from 1974 until his death in 1997.

Shanker was born in New York City to Mamie and Morris Shanker, Jewish **immigrants** from Poland. His father delivered newspapers and his mother was a garment worker who was active in the **Amalgamated Clothing Workers of America** (ACWA) and took part in ACWA campaigns against **sweatshops**. The Shanker household embraced the moderate **socialism** of Norman Thomas, but came to support Franklin Roosevelt's **New** Deal. Albert graduated from high school in 1946, and went on to obtain a B.A. in philosophy from the University of Illinois and a M.A. in mathematics and philosophy from Columbia University. He entered a Ph.D. program at Columbia, but began teaching mathematics in New York City public schools and never completed his dissertation

When Shanker began his teaching career in the 1950s, some teachers were unionized, but their organizations were more akin to professional associations than to labor unions; New York public laws also forbade public employees from going on **strike**. Shanker became active in a teachers' **union local** called the Teachers' Guild. He organized his own school and, in 1959, became a full-time union organizer. The next year, the Teachers' Guild merged with the High School Teachers' Association to form the United Federation of Teachers (UFT).

Shanker and the UFT challenged New York State law when, on November 7, 1960, more than 5,000 UFT members walked off the job to demand **collective**

bargaining rights. They were successful and, in a 1961 **certification** vote, New York teachers chose the UFT as their bargaining agent. This marked the first time in which teachers in a major city negotiated a comprehensive collective bargaining agreement. The 1960 New York City action became the template for teachers across the nation to negotiate their own collective bargaining rights. It also thrust Shanker into the national limelight. He was elected UFT secretary in 1962, and in 1964, he succeeded Charles Cogen as the second UFT president, a position he held until 1986.

In the 1960s, Shanker was twice jailed for violating New York law barring public employee strikes. The first time came in 1967 during a strike held to demand smaller class sizes and increased public spending on public education. His second arrest came during the **New York City teachers' strike** of 1968. The latter involved an issue near and dear to Shanker's heart: **civil rights**. Shanker was an ardent supporter of civil rights and among the most hotly debated issues in 1968 was the African American community's desire to replace white schoolteachers in the city's Ocean Hill-Brownsville neighborhood. Shanker's arrests served to heighten his public profile and steel his resolve. During the 1970s, Shanker was one of America's most widely recognized labor leaders.

In 1972, Shanker helped effect a merger between the New York State AFT affiliate and the state chapter of the rival **National Education Association** (NEA). The resulting New York State United Teachers became the largest and most influential statewide union in the country, and Shanker served as its executive vice president from 1973 to 1978. Shanker sharpened his public profile through a *New York Times* column titled "Where We Stand." He also appeared on so many radio and television programs that director Woody Allen satirized him in the 1973 futuristic **film**, *Sleeper*. In 1974, Shanker both was elected AFT president and became a member of **American Federation of Labor-Congress of Industrial Organization** (AFL-CIO) executive council. In 1975, New York City experienced a financial crisis so severe that the city teetered on bankruptcy; Shanker won acclaim for helping the city avoid insolvency by using the UFT's **pension** money to buy city bonds.

Shanker was strongly anticommunist. He used his position with the AFL-CIO executive council to promote **Cold War** unionism policies that sometimes stood in stark contrast to his social progressivism. Shanker supported U.S. involvement in the **Vietnam War** and used autocratic methods to prevent the UFT and AFT from debating U.S. foreign policy. He headed the AFL-CIO's International Affairs Committee, and pushed the AFL-CIO to offer financial backing for pro-American labor unions around the world. In 1993, Shanker became the founding president of Education International, a pro-Western worldwide teacher-union federation formed through a merger of the International Federation of Free Teachers' Unions (IFFTU), to which the AFT belonged, and the NEA-affiliated World Confederation of Organizations of the Teaching Profession.

Shanker's support for Cold War unionism is one of several issues that continue to baffle scholars seeking to pin down Shanker's ideological identity. On the one hand, he zealously defied politicians when he felt that teacher rights were jeopardized, and he tried to use insider pressure to derail the efforts of the **Ronald Reagan** administration to **decertify** the **Professional Air Traffic Controllers Organization**. On the other hand, Shanker was an early convert to conservative calls for national educational standards and teacher testing. He also embraced a call for greater classroom discipline and evoked a family values agenda to blame parents for student failures. Although from 1976 to 1996 he was a regular delegate to the **Democratic** National Convention, and was an education advisor to U.S. presidents from Jimmy Carter through Bill Clinton, he was also a member of the conservative Competitive Policy Council, a board established by President George H. W. Bush in 1991.

Shanker was married twice and fathered four children. He died of cancer in 1997.

Suggested Reading

Richard D. Kahlenberg, *Tough Liberal: Albert Shanker and the Battles over Schools, Unions, Race, and Democracy*, 2007; Dickson Mungazi, *Where He Stands: Albert Shanker of the American Federation of Teachers*, 1995; Philip Taft, *United They Teach: The Story of the UFT*, 1974.

SHAPE-UP

A shape-up is a much-resented form of hiring short-term laborers. It originated among **longshoremen** but applies to other situations in which daily laborers are chosen. Often the workers involved are unskilled or semiskilled laborers.

A shape-up occurs when more workers than are needed gather at a designated spot and hope that a foreman, supervisor, union officer, or company official will choose them for a short-term job assignment. Common shape-up locations include work sites, union halls, or streetscapes such as bus stops and shelters known by both workers and employers as places where job-seeking men and women gather. Shape-up workers make up part of what economists call the "casual labor market." They may be laid-off workers, chronically unemployed individuals, or those trapped in the secondary labor market seeking a short-term boost in their **wages**.

Typically workers in a milling crowd are chosen during a morning shape-up, though sometimes—particularly during peak production periods or if there is a rush order—the event can take place during other times of the day. Shape-ups were used extensively during the Great Depression, when employment needs were uncertain and the labor market was glutted due to high unemployment. Politicians often sought preferential hiring for particular ethnic groups. Employers saw the system as a way to prevent casual workers from gaining strength in the workplace; shape-up hiring is discretionary on the part of the person selecting workers. The system encouraged kickbacks, favoritism, and graft. Sometimes the arbitrary method of selecting workers encouraged autocracy on the part of the hiring agent; even more often it allowed that person to pander to individual prejudices. **Minority labor** was particularly ill served during many shape-ups. The inequities of the shape-up system gave rise to repeated resistance such as **strikes** and **boycotts**, but unless backed by a union most protests had limited success given that workers seeking shape-up employment seldom had much clout or organizational strength.

A bad situation was made worse in some industries when union officials sometimes cooperated with employers and politicians. Unions sought to use the shape-up to secure jobs for hard-pressed rank-and-file union members. In some cases, though, union officials proved as susceptible to graft as those outside of organized labor. This was a constant complaint among the rank-and-file within several longshoremen's unions, as immortalized in the classic Hollywood **film** *On the Waterfront*. Longshoremen fought a long struggle to change or eliminate shape-ups.

Reform came on a piecemeal basis. On the West Coast, a 1939 **arbitration** decision, written by future U.S. Senator Wayne Morse, replaced the shape-up system with union hiring halls that still required workers to assemble, but offered work opportunities on a fair rotational basis for all union members seeking work. The International Longshore and Warehouse Union (ILWU) operated union hiring halls in which elected dispatchers assigned work according to posted rules; employers were forbidden to bypass the hiring hall. On the East Coast, however, arbitrary dockworker shape-ups persisted into the 1950s.

In recent years, shape-ups have become common in hiring agricultural workers and day laborers for factories and retail work. Sometimes this approach is used by employers seeking to avoid workplace health and safety regulations, or to avoid paying **Social Security** taxes by paying day laborers "off the books." The practice also thrives among **immigrant** laborers, illegal aliens, and homeless individuals anxious to secure employment, but wishing to avoid public scrutiny. According to the General Accounting Office, **contingent workers** make up nearly 30 percent of the American workforce. Although most contingent laborers do not face shape-ups, they are disproportionately susceptible to them. Representative Luis Gutierrez (Democrat-Illinois) has been at the forefront of championing reforms aimed at protecting day laborers from the abuses of the contemporary shape-up system.

Suggested Reading

"Boss of the Waterfront," Wayne Morse Center for Law and Politics, University of Oregon, http://libweb.uoregon.edu/speccoll/exhibits/morse/, accessed June 10, 2011; Howard Kimledorf, *Reds or Rackets?*, 1988; Charles P. Larrowe, *Shape-up and Hiring Hall: A Comparison of Hiring Methods and Labor Relations on the New York and Seattle Waterfronts*, 1955.

SHERMAN ANTITRUST ACT

The Sherman Antitrust Act was passed by Congress in 1890, ostensibly to curtail monopolistic business methods. In practice, the act was applied more vigorously against labor unions than against monopolists. It stands as an example of how courts and laws operated with a pro-business bias that often showed little regard for the content or spirit of statue law.

The bill was drafted by Senator John Sherman of Ohio in response to the rise of trusts and monopolies in the 25 years after the **Civil War**. The Sherman Act outlawed combinations deemed a restraint of trade or commerce, including cartels, price-fixing schemes, and other impediments to competition. The act allowed the federal government, as well as private parties, to initiate restraint-of-trade lawsuits.

It was enforced by the Department of Justice, and violators could be fined and/or imprisoned. If the courts so desired, triple damages could be levied against violators.

From the law's inception, organizations such as the **National Association of Manufacturers** opposed applying the Sherman Act to regulate business practices, but saw it is a useful weapon against labor unions. The act was invoked during the 1894 **Pullman strike/lockout**, when courts obliged the company by issuing **injunctions** against the **American Railway Union** (ARU). ARU President **Eugene Debs** spent six months in prison for violating court injunctions. By contrast, the 1895 Supreme Court ruling in *United States v. E. C. Knight* asserted that manufacturing was not covered by the commerce clause of the Constitution. This effectively eviscerated much of the act's original intent and opened the door for broader use of the Sherman Act against labor. President Theodore Roosevelt used the Sherman Act against the Standard Oil Corporation and several other trusts, but government pursuit of business monopolies remained rare.

The **American Federation of Labor** (AFL) made reform of the Sherman Act a high priority for its legislative lobbyists. This stand later caused tension within the **National Civic Federation**, a labor/management board on which AFL President **Samuel Gompers** sat, but the importance of reform was obvious to most working people. By 1901, 18 suits had been brought under the Sherman Act, but half of them were against labor. The following year saw the D. E. Loewe Company of Danbury, Connecticut, bring suit against the striking United Hatters, Cap, and Millinery Workers International Union. The courts awarded Loewe $240,000 in damages and declared most secondary **boycotts** illegal. Liens were placed on both union bank accounts and the homes of individual hatters. The AFL was stunned when the Supreme Court upheld the awards. In 1903, the Kellog Switchboard and Supply Company and the American Anti-Boycott Association brought a successful suit against the International Brotherhood of Teamsters, which had urged a boycott to support Kellog strikers. The AFL included the misuse of the Sherman Antitrust Act among the list of wrongs it presented to Congress in its 1906 Bill of Grievances. In that same year, however, an AFL boycott of the **Buck's Stove and Range Company** of St. Louis led to injunctions against the AFL. Gompers was sentenced to a year in jail for contempt of court, though the conviction was later overturned and Gompers never served the sentence. The Sherman Act remained a thorn in labor's side until most labor activity was placed beyond "restraint of trade" interpretations by the 1914 **Clayton Antitrust Act**.

Suggested Reading

Ronald Filippelli, *Labor in the USA: A History*, 1984; Philip Foner, *History of the Labor Movement in the United States*, Vol. 3, 1964; Sherman Antitrust Act Text, http://www.stolaf.edu/people/becker/antitrust/statutes/sherman.html, accessed June 10, 2011.

SHOP STEWARD

A shop steward—also called union steward—is the individual who represents workers in the workplace. Stewards are the first tier in a union's bureaucracy.

They handle **grievances**, make certain that **dues** are collected, recruit new members, and communicate with the local **business agent** and other higher officials. Shop stewards are usually elected by the rank-and-file members of the workplace, though some are appointed by upper-level union officials. Most shop stewards continue their employment within the workplace they represent and perform union duties on a part-time or release-time basis. Quite a few shop stewards perform their tasks on a volunteer basis.

Most unions operate according to the same representative democracy principles as the U.S. government. In this regard, individual members elect individuals to represent their interests. Most of the union business that happens within a specific workplace begins with the union steward. If, for example, a group of factory workers felt that they were being asked to perform tasks that were not part of their job, the first step would be to bring the matter to their union steward. The steward would decide whether the matter could be resolved informally, whether to discuss it with management, or whether it needed to be brought to the attention of higher union officials. Because stewards are usually face-to-face peers encountered on a daily basis by other workers, they seek to process complaints and requests quickly. A good union steward often resolves petty matters before they escalate into major conflicts.

The position of shop steward has evolved over time. Before labor laws assured unions a legal right to exist, the steward had to fight the employer as well as wrangle dues from colleagues. Stewards were often physically imposing males who could, when necessary, intimidate employer and coworker alike. Since the passage of laws such as the **National Labor Relations Act** and the Labor Management Disclosure Reporting Act, unions have been legitimated, procedures such as dues **checkoff** have been put in place, and relations between workers, their representatives, and management are regulated. These factors have transformed the shop steward from a physical enforcer to a legal enforcer, as well as a generalist whose major role is perform services and represent his or her peers.

Suggested Reading

David Prosten, *The Union Steward's Complete Guide*, 2nd edition, 2006.

SICK-OUT

A sick-out is a self-defining term that refers to a decision by large numbers of workers to call in sick on a predetermined day. Some professions, such as police and firefighters, self-mockingly call such an action the "blue flu." It is a form of protest that may be sanctioned by a union, though sick-outs are quite frequently unauthorized **wildcat strikes** born out of frustration. The purpose of such a job action is to force concessions from an employer without resorting to a formal **strike** or other action that would negatively affect workers' **wages** or threaten their jobs. It is designed to disrupt work, but only for a short period of time; in essence, workers send a message of discontent to management. In many respects, a sick-out is a form of non-physical **sabotage** that the **Industrial Workers of the World** once defined as a "systematic withdrawal of efficiency."

Although the term "sick-out" did not first appear until 1951, these labor actions have been used since Colonial times and have been an occasionally effective tactic since then. They must be used sparingly, however, as in many cases they are actionable. Some **contracts**, for example, provide workers with sick leave but allow management to discipline workers who abuse the system and are not actually sick. Workers in critical services, such as nurses or police, must make sure that a "skeleton crew" reports to work, lest their unions be held liable for harm that occurred during the sick-out. Unions such as the **United Mine Workers of America** have used sick-outs to showcase workers' resolve and hasten stalled contract negotiations. Sick-outs have also been used when a **no-strike pledge** or contract language disallows a formal work stoppage. Some public employees, for instance, have limited strike rights, but have used sick-outs to lash out against unfairness and force management to pay attention to their **grievances**. Teachers in Wisconsin held a massive sick-out in 2011 to protest the passage of a law that stripped them of **collective bargaining** rights. They gained tremendous public sympathy and have spawned movements to repeal the law and recall officials who voted for it.

Sick-outs have gained in popularity since the 1980s, given the relative ease with strikes are now broken and **scabs** secured. The **Professional Air Traffic Controllers Organization** set the standard in that union members forbidden to strike won past concessions through sick-outs, but were fired when they actually struck in 1981. Sick-outs, even when they violate existing labor laws, are often safer than formal actions, and they frequently generate publicity for worker grievances. Moreover, these actions are relatively easy to organize. Some sick-outs, in fact, take place among non-unionized employees. Those individuals must be careful, however, as workers not in unions are much easier to fire.

Suggested Reading

Nancy Bupp, "Big Brother and Big Boss Are Watching You," *WorkingUSA: The Journal of Labor and Society* 5, no. 2 (September 2001): 69–81; Bruce S. Feldacker, *Labor Guide to Labor Law*, 2000.

SILKWOOD, KAREN. *See* Oil Workers.

SIT-DOWN STRIKES

Sit-down strikes occur when workers refuse to leave their place of employment or continue production until a **grievance** or contract is settled. Sit-down actions have been very powerful in the past. In a conventional **strike**, employers can use management personnel or import **scabs** to continue operations, even if on a limited basis. During a sit-down, however, protestors physically occupy a facility, thereby making it impossible to conduct business until they leave or are removed.

The first known use of a sit-down strike in industrial relations came in 1906, when the **Industrial Workers of the World** (IWW) coordinated a sit-in of some 3,000 workers at a General Electric plant in Schenectady, New York. Nevertheless, the IWW tactics did not catch on more broadly until a generation later during the

Great Depression of the 1930s. The **Congress of Industrial Organizations** (CIO) split from the **American Federation of Labor** (AFL) in this period, and workers committed to **industrial unionism** found that a well-coordinated sit-down strike could completely handcuff an employer. The CIO employed a number of IWW labor-action methods, especially the sit-down strike.

The most famous example of this type of protest occurred during the **General Motors sit-down strike** in Flint, Michigan, during 1936–1937. Although it was not the first time the CIO had used the tactic, the incident garnered national attention, established the credibility of the **United Auto Workers of America** (UAW) union, and touched off what was dubbed "sit-down fever" in which laborers ranging from rubber workers to Woolworth's clerks engaged in sit-downs. In 1937, some 477 sit-down strikes collectively idled more than 400,000 workers; the next year there were 52 more such labor actions, though by then a backlash had set in and steps had been taken to curtail the practice.

The seizing of facilities by workers claiming "sweat equity" in production units clashed with the sanctity with which private property is regarded in the United States, as well as with the free enterprise mentality. In some cases, strikers misjudged local sentiment; in 1937, for instance, non-striking chocolate workers in Hershey, Pennsylvania, cooperated with local authorities in removing sit-down strikers. The U.S. Supreme Court outlawed the practice in 1939, a decision reinforced by the 1948 passage of the **Taft-Hartley Act**. Sit-downs nonetheless have occurred on occasion—usually in the context of a **wildcat strike**—and have proved popular outside the United States in nations with less restrictive labor laws.

The sit-down strike was very important in the 1930s, as it forced numerous reluctant employers to negotiate with unions lest they too suffer sit-down disruptions akin to those at Flint. The most enduring legacy of the sit-downs was the inspiration they provided for the **civil rights** movement and to the **counterculture**. Neither of those groups was constrained by labor laws. Sit-downs and sit-ins proved a powerful civil disobedience tactic for African Americans battling "Jim Crow" laws. The famed 1960 sit-in by black students at a Greensboro, North Carolina, Woolworth's lunch counter was one of many such actions used to challenge segregation laws. Campus protestors associated with Students for a Democratic Society (SDS) also used tactics such as taking over administration buildings or occupying public parks to rally support for their causes. Not coincidentally, both the civil rights movement and SDS received logistical, tactical, and financial support from unions such as the UAW.

Suggested Reading

Irving Bernstein, *The Turbulent Years: A History of the American Worker, 1933–1941*, 1970; Jeremy Brecher, *Strike!*, 1997; Sidney Lens, *The Labor Wars: From the Molly Maguires to the Sit Downs*, 1974.

SKIDMORE, THOMAS

Thomas Skidmore (August 13, 1790–August 7, 1832) was an important early labor radical and a member of New York's Workingmen's Party. Skidmore is an example of how an indigenous form of American radicalism rooted in **republicanism** took hold long before **Marxism** and other forms of European **socialism** made their way to the United States. His career is also a reminder of the emphasis that 19th-century labor activists placed on land reform.

Skidmore was born in Newtown, Connecticut, the eldest John and Mary Skidmore's 10 children. He was a precocious and brilliant child who, at the age of 13, became a teacher in the Newtown school district. He taught there for five years before moving on to teach in Connecticut, New Jersey, Virginia, and North Carolina. Skidmore left teaching in 1815 to pursue an interest in the chemical properties of gunpowder. He moved to New York in 1819 and married Abigail Ball two years later.

Skidmore held exceedingly progressive views for his day. He advocated free, universal education; the 10-hour workday; racial equality; property redistribution; and equal rights for women. He worked for the presidential campaign of John Quincy Adams in 1828, and was a cofounder of the New York Workingmen's Party in 1829. Although Skidmore was largely responsible for writing the party platform, he is best known for his 1829 book, *The Rights of Man to Property*, which stands as a radical testament to his views on land reform. In it, Skidmore advocated the abolition of inheritance rights, the nationalization of all property, and land redistribution by lottery. His proposal that no property could be bequeathed to heirs horrified conservatives, but at a time in which **agrarian** ideals dominated but many individuals lacked property, his views attracted notice and followers. He narrowly lost an 1829 bid for the New York legislature. Skidmore then published a short-lived labor paper, *The Friend of Equal Rights*.

Skidmore was a temperamental man who quarreled with other leaders. As the Workingmen began to splinter and falter, he tried to salvage a radical wing that he called the Original Workingmen, or the Poor Men's Party. In 1832, he was ousted from the very party he founded, and he died that summer of cholera.

Suggested Reading

Edward Pessen, *Most Uncommon Jacksonians*, 1967; Ronald Walters, *American Reformers 1815–1860*, 1978; Thomas Skidmore, *The Rights of Man to Property*, http://www.ditext .com/skidmore/property.html, accessed June 11, 2011.

SLAVERY

Slavery was the forced labor system involving Africans and African Americans that persisted in English-speaking North America from 1619 to 1865. Slavery has existed since antiquity, but the variety found in the United States traced its roots to Portuguese explorers whose explorations of the West African coast during the late 1400s involved them in the slave trade. Both Portugal and Spain used African slave labor in their various colonies to produce cash crops such as sugar and in mining precious metals. There were already approximately 130,000 African slaves in North America by the time the first slaves arrived in the English colony of Jamestown in 1619. Slavery would quickly become an institution both in the English colonies and in the United States. Although slavery would prove more important to the economy of the American South than in other regions, it was legal in all states immediately after the American Revolution and persisted in many northern states well into the 19th century.

Although some owners held slaves for status and prestige reasons, slavery was primarily a labor system. Demand for slaves rose in English North America when tobacco emerged as a valuable export during the 17th century. The demand for labor was high in the Chesapeake colonies, **Native Americans** proved difficult to enslave, and **indentured servants** became less profitable when the colonies' death rates dropped and more indentured individuals lived to claim their promised lands. Indentured servants rose up against Virginia's elites during Bacon's Rebellion in 1676, an event that led to a dramatic increase in demand for slaves and a corresponding decrease in indenturehood. By 1700, Virginia alone had more than 6,000 slaves. The American Revolution did nothing to decrease the expansion of slavery; it was, in fact, the British who offered slaves freedom during the war, not Colonists.

Slaves on the J. J. Smith plantation in Beaufort, South Carolina, in 1862. A small minority of plantation owners (perhaps 15 percent) relied upon slave labor, a condition that led to further stratification of Southern society. (Library of Congress)

In 1790, there was nearly 700,000 slaves in the newly created United States. Eli Whitney's perfection of the cotton gin, which removed seeds and stems from cotton fibers, led to an explosion in demand for slaves; by the time of the **Civil War** there were nearly 4 million slaves in the country, concentrated most densely in the South. American slaves toiled as domestic servants, **agrarian** laborers, **longshoremen**, carpenters, draymen, and many other jobs; some even worked in manufacturing and turned over their **wages** to their masters.

One of the many peculiar aspects of American slavery was that it was so thoroughly racialized. Racial stereotypes led to social policies in which literacy, liberty, and wage labor came to be seen as the domain of whites. Caucasian laborers complained bitterly when forced to toil beside blacks, or when they received poor treatment they felt should be reserved for slaves. The term "wage slavery" was coined to express the latter sentiment; it was at once a complaint against autocratic bosses and an assertion of perceived racial superiority. In a similar vein, the very **free labor** ideology used by northern elites to whip up public support for the Civil War often worked against them after the war began; some northern workers had come to see slavery as so debased that they had little desire to fight for slavery's end and thereby create a secondary labor force that could compete for wages. Racism was the norm in all parts of the United States by 1860, even though nearly 500,000 free blacks lived in the nation by then. Even abolitionist ranks were dominated by racism; many called for freed slaves to be sent to Africa—an absurdity for most slaves as the African slave trade had ended in 1808, and nearly all slaves had been born in the United States when the Civil War began.

Slavery was a complex and horrific system on many levels, not the least of which involved its social class dimensions. Plantation slavery stamped southern society with characteristics that persisted long after emancipation, such as the influence of planters in politics and a presumption of racial hierarchy. White racism had so thoroughly penetrated the region that it became a powerful tool for social control. The South was, in fact, a pyramidal civilization with a small elite planter class on top, former slaves on the bottom, and a middling stratum of whites whose families had never owned slaves. At most, one-third of Southern families had slaves during the antebellum period; most estimates place the figure at less than 20 percent. The presumption of white racial superiority was used to recruit Confederate soldiers during the war and led to resistance during **Reconstruction**. Many southern whites allied themselves with elites and paramilitary racist organizations rather than with freed African Americans, who were closer to them in economic and social status. Their offspring would come to romanticize the Civil War, exaggerate the abuses of Reconstruction, and resist **civil rights** movements from the 1870s on. Labor movements from the **Knights of Labor** through the **Congress of Industrial Organizations** wrestled with the conundrum that white southern workers often seemed more devoted to maintaining Jim Crow and racism than to bettering their own economic conditions.

Nevertheless, slavery also left a racist stain in the North. Northern merchants profited mightily from the pre-1808 slave trade and the early **Industrial Revolution** was fueled by cotton picked by southern slaves and manufactured into textiles by northern workers. Slave-produced rice, sugar, indigo, and other products made their way onto northern tables and store shelves. Popular racism allowed northern workers and the middle class to be critical of the South yet simultaneously embrace the indirect advantages brought by slavery. Southern slavery apologists often argued that slaves were treated better than northern wage-earners—a charge that was true in some cases. Northern elites rallied support for the preservation of the Union, but were unable to dodge social inequalities when the war began. The North saw draft riots involving members of the **working class** who resented exemptions for the wealthy. Many workers also disagreed with President Abraham Lincoln's issuance of the Emancipation Proclamation in 1862, which redefined the war as one to end slavery rather than preserve the Union. Resentment was particularly high among Irish **immigrants**, many of whom were conscripted and saw the end of slavery as imperiling what little social status they held.

In the postwar North, class tensions erupted with renewed vigor and made their way into the labor movement. The northern working class lost interest in Reconstruction in the early 1870s and turned its attention to issues concerning white workers. The Knights of Labor organized African Americans during the 1880s, but in so doing the organization often faced resentment from white workers. It did not help matters that freed African Americans sometimes served as the wage-containing secondary labor force that prewar critics had feared they would be. The use of African American **scabs** during **strikes** bred particular resentment. As in the South, racism would prevail in the North, including within the organized labor movement. Numerous crafts represented by the **American Federation of Labor** excluded African Americans from their number. Although many unions dedicated themselves to racial equality far in advance of the rest of American society, the labor movement as a whole would not confront slavery's legacy until the post–World War II civil rights movement forced it to do so.

Suggested Reading

Ira Berlin, *Many Thousands Gone: The First Two Centuries of Slavery in North America*, 1998; Robert W. Fogel, *Without Consent or Contract: The Rise and Fall of American Slavery*, 1989; Eric Foner, *Free Soil, Free Labor, Free Men: The Ideology of the Republican Party before the Civil War*, 1995; William H. Harris, *The Harder We Run: Black Workers since the Civil War*, 1982.

SLOWDOWN. *See* Sabotage; Stint.

SMITH-CONNALLY ACT. *See* War Labor Disputes Act.

SOCIAL CLASS. *See* Middle-Class Ideology; Working Class.

SOCIAL DARWINISM

Social Darwinism was a philosophy embraced by the business community and many members of the **middle class** and upper class in the middle and late

19th century. It sought to apply Charles Darwin's evolutionary models to society, particularly his assertion that within nature a struggle for existence rages, and that survival of the fittest dictates which species gets access to limited resources. Proponents of social Darwinism such as William Graham Sumner, Herbert Spencer, and Francis Galton (Darwin's half-cousin) perverted Darwin's biological findings to argue that wealth and poverty were natural products of social struggle and, therefore, that those who made great fortunes were more "fit" than those who lived in poverty. Quite conveniently, social Darwinists ignored factors such as inherited wealth, corrupt financial and political practices, and exploitation. In their eyes, entrepreneurs of the emerging business class, investors, and the rich were a more completely evolved species than the toiling masses. Eugenicists, nativists, and racists also cast these principles in ethnic and racial terms.

Social Darwinism was, in some respects, a logical outgrowth of the underlying principles of **capitalism**. In his classic treatise *The Wealth of Nations*, Adam Smith argued that economic activity ought to be free of external regulations and controls and subject only to the natural laws of supply and demand. Those views found few adherents among Colonial American **artisans**, and were roundly challenged by workers after the American Revolution. Many advocates of the **Workingmen's movement** of the 1830s offered devastating **republicanism**-based critiques of an unregulated economy and lambasted any attempts to institute special privileges or class legislation.

Capitalism expanded during the antebellum period, but did not reach its take-off phase in most industries until after the **Civil War**. The introduction of mass industry, the birth of modern corporate structures, and the advent of new managerial techniques gave rise to manufacturers, investors, and business owners who had fewer ties to local communities and the customary social arrangements of the past. With profit as the driving motive for many such individuals—who were dubbed "robber barons" by their critics—business competition was often cutthroat and the exploitation of workers brutal. Yet these same ruthless forces helped the national economy expand exponentially, pushing the United States to first-tier status among the world's economic and military powers. Enormous fortunes were made in the last third of the 19th century, and they were used to buy political influence. Economic expansion also led to more complete articulation of the middle class, which was small by contemporary standards but more stratified. Its upper echelon consisted largely of the nouveau riche who were wealthy, but who lacked the social pedigrees of long-standing elites. New industrialists, managers, and professionals tended to identify with the social and cultural practices of the elites but, like the working classes, had to work for their compensation. Social Darwinism thus served to both justify amoral business practices and confer social status on the upwardly mobile.

The primary theorists of social Darwinism were English philosophers Herbert Spencer and Walter Bagehot, and American sociologist/economist William Graham Sumner. Industrialists such as John Rockefeller and Andrew Carnegie also sprinkled social Darwinian thought throughout their many speeches and essays. By the 1870s, social Darwinism was the hegemonic social philosophy within the United States. Ministers, mainstream newspapers, orators, and writers praised its virtues and lampooned its critics. In practice, social Darwinism was a marriage between laissez-faire economics and conservative politics, with courts routinely turning aside legal challenges to limit wealth, regulate business, or legitimize labor unions seeking to force businesses into **collective bargaining** agreements. Social Darwinists justified their great wealth and power by arguing that their alleged virtues—such as sobriety, thrift, investment acumen, and hard work—were hallmarks of being more highly evolved than those who failed to attain their levels of success. Such thinking was in accord with late Victorian beliefs. The concept of social problems had not yet been articulated; rather, misfortune was associated with sin and personal moral failings.

Not surprisingly, the American working class begged to differ with the social Darwinists. Trade unions and the **Knights of Labor** mounted powerful rhetorical challenges to their practices, with the labor press churning out stories of exploitation, graft, and illegalities on the part of allegedly moral and upright social Darwinists. Among workers, the writings of **Henry George**, Victor Drury, David Ricardo, Karl **Marx**, and other social critics were widely discussed, as were various forms of **anarchism**, **communism**, **socialism**, **Edward Bellamy**'s nationalism, **cooperation**, and other ideas that challenged capitalism and social Darwinism. More than rhetoric, however, it was workers' direct challenges to social Darwinism that loosened its grip. So many workers boycotted social Darwinian churches that conferences were held to discuss ways to win them back to the pews. The Vatican summoned American cardinals and priests to Rome because many Catholics were giving up the church for their unions. In 1891, Pope Leo XIII issued the encyclical *Rerum Novarum*, which both removed the Vatican's objections to organized labor and strongly condemned unbridled capitalism (as well as most forms of socialism). By the 1890s, many Protestant churches had abandoned social Darwinism in favor of the Social Gospel movement, which was characterized by messages about alleviating poverty and warnings against materialism.

Even more powerful were the challenges to social Darwinism that occurred in the workplace and in the voting booth. **Strikes** were frequent and violent after the Civil War, including the **railroad strikes of 1877** and the voluminous number of work stoppages that occurred during the **Great Upheaval** of 1885 through 1890. Labor- and **agrarian**-based third parties dislodged numerous Republicans and Democrats on the local and state levels, and threatened to do so nationally when the Populist Party unified in 1892. The social Darwinian cause was hurt further by the numerous panics and recessions that threw the nation into economic turmoil. Ultimately, the late 19th century proved so chaotic that even members of the middle class—especially those of moderate wealth or less—concluded that reform was necessary. The Gilded Age gave way after 1901 to the **Progressive Era**, the first significant reform movement that also involved local, state, and federal governments. Most of that period's leading reformers were members of the middle class. Unions and labor advocates continued to press for economic and social changes, though social Darwinism's grip remained powerful enough to keep them on the political fringe.

The American labor movement deserves credit for exposing the inequities, flawed logic, and ruthlessness of social Darwinism. The development of modern sociology also helped reveal the naiveté of attributing social problems to individual weakness. By the early 20th century, social Darwinism had lost its moral force and was widely viewed as morally suspect. The business community contained numerous individuals who were as heartless as their Gilded Age predecessors, but social Darwinism was no longer the dominant social or cultural philosophy within the United States. Those who openly practiced its precepts were roundly criticized by many of the same forces that once defended its practices—namely, the church, the media, and liberal politicians. Most people in the business community gave at least rhetorical support to philanthropy and moderate reform; some even experimented with **welfare capitalism**.

It is a mistake, however, to assume that social Darwinism passed from the American scene. Its major assumptions continue to be held by many conservatives and some modern business practices are as cruel as those of an earlier age. Though social Darwinism is no longer the prevailing philosophy, it retains so much vigor that in the early 21st century numerous articles and books appeared touting the premise that social Darwinism has returned and that the United States is entering a new Gilded Age. Unlike its counterpart from the 19th century, organized labor possesses less clout to oppose the imposition of this view.

Suggested Reading

Paul Crook, *Darwin's Coat-Tails: Essays on Social Darwinism*, 2007; Richard Hofstadter, *Social Darwinism in American Thought*, 1955; Robert McCloskey, *American Conservatism in the Age of Enterprise 1865–1910*, 1951; John G. West, *Darwin Day in America: How Our Politics and Culture Have Been Dehumanized in the Name of Science*, 2007.

SOCIAL GOSPEL

The Social Gospel was a religious movement of the late 19th and early 20th centuries that emphasized the church's responsibility to the poor and called for social reform. It was concentrated in Protestantism, but echoes of it were also found in Catholicism and Judaism. The antithesis of **social Darwinism**, the Social Gospel represented a reaction against religious leaders, denominations, sermons, and theology that upheld the virtues of **capitalist** accumulation and blamed the poor for their own misery. Whereas social Darwinians enumerated labor unions as among the forces that threatened social order, Social Gospel adherents often allied themselves with unions.

The Social Gospel—also known as "social Christianity" or expressed as Christian **socialism**—rejected the radical individualism and laissez-faire economic and social policies supported by numerous mainstream denominations after the **Civil War**. Industrial expansion, urbanization, and **immigration** prompted several influential clergymen to place less emphasis on creeds, doctrine, and the private, individual salvation of the soul, and more emphasis on charity to address the nation's growing social problems. Followers of the Social Gospel drew inspiration from Jesus's earthly ministry among commoners and from Biblical injunctions to honor the poor and reject material wealth. Some Protestants were also motivated by the desire to make inroads in large cities where the Catholic Church was popular among the growing immigrant population. Social Gospel ministers and laymen also sought to address declining church attendance among the **working class**, which charged (with considerable merit) that religious organizations were more sympathetic to capital than to labor.

The Social Gospel began as an intellectual movement among liberal church leaders seeking to apply the teachings of Jesus to the social and economic questions of the day. The poverty resulting from the Panic of 1873 and violent **strikes** such as the **railroad strikes of 1877** concerned church leaders, though many viewed trade unions with suspicion and feared state interference in the economy. The opening salvo of the Social Gospel movement was a moderate call for change in *Working People and Their Employers* (1876), written by Washington Gladden (1836–1918). The Reverend Gladden called upon workers to unify under Christianity and hoped that the application of the Golden Rule would bridge the growing divide between capital and labor. Views such as this found resonance among liberal union workers. Members of the **Knights of Labor** (KOL) fashioned themselves as "True Christians" and used religious imagery to rally workers. Gladden soon came to believe that stronger measures were needed to correct social abuses, and he advocated state-regulated capitalism well in advance of the **Progressive Era**.

Another important work came from Josiah Strong. Although Strong was a xenophobe whose own Social Gospel credentials were sometimes suspect, his book *Our Country: Its Possible Future and Present Crisis* (1885) encouraged Protestants to engage in missionary work in the nation's cities and in the American West. Storefront churches appeared in working-class neighborhoods and figures such as the Episcopal minister James O. S. Huntington (1854–1935), Jesse Jones (1836–1904), and William D. Bliss (1835–1911) sought souls and succored the poor in precincts such as New York's Lower East Side, Boston slums, and Chicago's stockyards. Both James and Bliss encountered and joined the KOL in the 1880s. James set up a popular church for workers in Boston, the city in which Bliss first embraced the Social Gospel. Bliss was so moved by the poverty of workers that he quit his job as pastor of a well-heeled Congregationalist church, moved to Chicago, and set up the Mission of the Carpenter to minister to workers. Bliss was also deeply influenced by **Edward Bellamy** and joined the Nationalist movement. Bliss became a socialist, founded the Society of Christian Socialists, and served as the editor of its publication, *The Dawn*. The magazine was a crusading voice on issues such as the abolition of **child labor**, higher **wages**, a shorter work week, a **living wage**, and prison reform.

Another important Social Gospel convert was Professor Richard Ely (1854–1943). Ely expressed his admiration for unions in his 1886 book *The Labor Movement in America* and, in 1891, became the secretary of the Christian Social Union, a group that sought to apply religious precepts to social problems. Ely's advice and policy decisions found great expression during the Progressive Era.

Also influential was Congregationalist minister George Herron (1862–1925), who won acclaim for an 1890 sermon titled "The Message of Jesus for Men of Wealth." Herron excoriated the acquisition of wealth in the United States. Eventually, he completely lost confidence in industrial capitalism and established "The Kingdom Movement," a brand of social Christianity aimed at establishing "the Kingdom of God" on earth. During the early 20th century, Herron was active in the Socialist Party and was an ardent supporter of **Eugene Debs**. He eventually split from the party when it opposed World War I.

The Social Gospel reached the height of its influence during the Progressive Era, by which time it had come to supplant social Darwinism among religious thinkers. Social Gospel ministers found allies among social workers, muckraking journalists, settlement house workers, and reformers. This movement deserves great credit for helping establish the very concept of social problems —that is, the idea that individuals can be victimized by social and economic environments that deny them opportunities and condemn them to degraded life chances. By then, however, the Social Gospel movement was moving toward a middle-class base. The Depression of 1893, strikes, and **direct action** troubled those adherents who favored working within the political system. Before the Social Gospel became passé, however, its strongest voice emerged—Baptist minister Walter Rauschenbusch (1861–1918). Rauschenbusch worked in one of New York's toughest neighborhoods, Hell's Kitchen, where he put into practice the ideal of trying to live a Christ-like life. He also gained a reputation as one of America's greatest theologians. *Christianity and the Social Crisis* (1907) sought to define the role of the church in American society and, among other things, advocated public ownership of utilities and transportation and redistribution of land to improve housing conditions for workers. In works such as *A Theology for the Social Gospel* (1917), Rauschenbusch insisted that concern for the downtrodden and action on their behalf was a command to believers, not an option. His work would resurface among black ministers involved in the **civil rights** movement.

The Social Gospel declined when Progressive Era gave way to World War I and both Rauschenbusch and Gladden died in 1918. It left behind an unambiguous message that religious duty required concern for those at the bottom of society. Organized labor and other reform movements found it much easier to find allies among religious leaders courtesy of the Social Gospel. Modern religious thought often replicates the debates of the late 19th century between latter-day social Darwinists and Social Gospel followers.

Suggested Reading

Susan Curtis, *A Consuming Faith: The Social Gospel and Modern American Culture*, 2001; Donald K. Gorrell, *The Age of Social Responsibility: The Social Gospel in the Progressive Era, 1900–1920*, 1989; Benjamin Hartley, *Evangelicals at a Crossroads: Revivalism and Social Reform in Boston, 1860–1910*, 2011; Charles Howard Hopkins, *The Rise of the Social Gospel in American Protestantism, 1865–1915*, 1940; Walter Rauschenbusch, *Christianity and the Social Crisis*, 1964 (reprint).

SOCIALISM

Socialism is one of the most misunderstood terms in all of American political discourse. It is often used as a synonym for **communism**, when the latter is simply one variant of socialism. The term is a general one whose meaning, akin to a term such as "Christianity," depends on the group and/or adherents to which one is referring. Socialist ideology runs the gamut from religious communalism at one end of the spectrum to revolutionaries at the other end. As a rule, socialists reject the individualism associated with **capitalism** and believe that the collective needs of society should take priority over individual desires. In regard to industry and business, most socialists argue that work should be controlled collectively and its fruits should be channeled into social programs and public works projects that benefit the larger society rather than serving the narrow interests of a restricted group of individuals. For these reasons, many labor unions, past and present, have espoused socialist ideals in some form or other; most American unions have preferred moderate versions of this philosophy. Most socialists believe that citizen-controlled governments should direct how goods and services are produced and distributed, though variants such as communists and **anarchists** distrust the state and disagree with this position. Most socialists agree that wealth should not be accumulated or hoarded by single individuals. They reject the capitalist logic that links **wages**, prices, and the supply of goods and services to market forces.

Radical socialists have suffered repression, whereas moderates have exerted some influence on American society. Because socialist ideals run counter to those of hegemonic capitalism, socialism's overall impact on U.S. society has been less than its influence in most other industrial societies. At various moments, though, socialism has resonated with sizable segments of the population. Numerous religious groups, such as the Shakers, German Pietist groups, monastic orders, and **counterculture** religious communes practiced rudimentary socialist collectivism. As noted earlier, many labor activists and organizations have also supported at least limited forms of socialism.

Socialism is an ancient ideal—the 1st-century Christian community operated according to socialist ideals—but socialism as understood and practiced in the United States is largely a 19th-century European import, arriving with **immigrants** whose **class consciousness** was piqued by evolving intellectual currents in their homelands. Some—such as Germans fleeing from the failed social revolutions of 1848—had been socialist activists before emigrating. The popularity of the *Manifesto of the Communist Party* (1848) penned by Karl Marx and Friedrich Engels stimulated discussions about socialism in the United States. In the antebellum period, German immigrants such as Herman Kriege and Wilhelm Weitling sought to organize workers in accordance with socialist ideas. In New York City, Joseph Wedemeyer organized the Proletarian League, an organization that lasted until 1854. After the **Civil War**, new writings from Karl Marx and Ferdinand Lassalle inspired American socialists to organize new socialist associations.

From the start, however, American socialism has been marked by its diversity. Two consistent themes run through the history of American socialism. First, socialist groups that attract large numbers of native-born individuals often (though not always) fared better than those associated with immigrants. In like fashion, socialist groups most attuned to older forms of American radicalism linked to **republicanism** found more welcoming audiences than those espousing ideals hitherto absent from American society. That is, perhaps, one reason why revolutionary socialism has fared less well than evolutionary socialist variants that stressed the use of ballot-box politics to reform society. It also helps explain why socialists have been among the most rabid anticommunists in American history. Numerous socialist groups have formed and fallen apart since the middle of the 19th century, but the Socialist Labor Party (founded in 1877) and the Socialist Party (SP; formed in 1901 when the Social Democratic Party absorbed several smaller groups) have been the foremost organized political expressions of American socialism.

Throughout the late 19th and early 20th centuries, socialists wrestled with internal and external challenges. On the one hand, the influx of new immigrant groups—especially Germans, Yiddish-speaking Jews, and Finns—brought zeal to the socialist movement. On the other hand, they rekindled debates over tactics, ideology, and culture.

American-born socialists such as **Eugene V. Debs** did not always agree with immigrant radicals such as **Daniel DeLeon**. Although **Marxism** commands more scholarly attention, **Lassallean** ballot-box socialists proved more enduring than revolutionary Marxism. Modified Lassallean ideals showed up in the writings of **Henry George** and in *Looking Backward*, **Edward Bellamy**'s enormously popular utopian novel, which spawned a nationwide movement. Socialists frequently spoke out against anarchists emanating from socialism's far left wing. Some, for instance, refused to endorse clemency movements for the eight men accused of the 1886 **Haymarket bombing**; still others viewed anarchists such as **Emma Goldman** as dangerous fanatics whose rhetoric harmed the labor movement.

Despite disagreements, the economic decline that occurred in the 1890s and the repression of labor movements helped socialism gain supporters. After the brutal suppression of the 1894 **Pullman strike/lockout**, Eugene Debs emerged as the leading socialist spokesperson in the United States. Debs became the leading SP politician of the day. In 1912 and again in 1920, he collected nearly 1 million votes for president. The first two decades of the 20th century saw numerous socialists win political offices on the local level; these "municipal socialists" (often derisively nicknamed "sewer socialists") often spearheaded civic improvements such as the building waste treatment facilities, sidewalks, parks, and municipal power plants. In addition, more than 300 socialist newspapers were in circulation during this era, and independent socialist Victor Berger was elected to the U.S. Congress in 1910. The SP reached its high-water mark in 1918, when it had more than 100,000 dues-paying members and many more supporters.

World War I did great damage to the socialist movement. Although **Industrial Workers of the World** (IWW) cofounder **Bill Haywood** belonged to the SP and Eugene Debs was an IWW cofounder, the two groups parted ways; IWW **anarcho-syndicalists** rejected the SP's program of state-sponsored reform, while

SP followers were uncomfortable with the IWW's revolutionary agenda. Both groups, however, viewed the coming war in Europe with skepticism; each saw World War I as a war brought on by corrupt aristocrats and opportunistic capitalists and urged workers to avoid it. This stance rendered the SP and IWW vulnerable to wartime laws stifling dissent and to the postwar **Red Scare**. The 1917 Bolshevik Revolution also complicated matters. Many left-wing socialists saw the events in Russia as ushering in the long-awaited workers' state and bolted their organizations in favor of communist groups such as the Communist Party of the United States (CPUSA). During the Red Scare, authorities seldom bothered to make the doctrinal distinctions that often preoccupied the political left—socialists were often persecuted just like anarchists, anarcho-syndicalists, and communists.

As socialists sought to rebuild the movement in the 1920s, they faced three pressing challenges: electoral politics, bourgeois reform, and ideological squabbles. Much as had happened with the Populists, socialists who embraced electoral politics saw **Republicans** and **Democrats** co-opt many of their more moderate ideas. Party activists also divided over municipal socialism, with many coming to doubt that socialism could emerge one city at a time, and still others seeing urban reform as simply bourgeois reform masquerading as socialism. That charge was fueled by the fact that the line between moderate socialism and liberalism was thin and indistinct. The 1924 presidential campaign embodied that confusion, with many socialists backing Progressive Party candidate Robert La Follette, Sr., because of his strong pro-labor and pro-business regulation views. But La Follette was not really a socialist; he also carried the endorsement of the **American Federation of Labor**, a far more moderate group than the SP. Increasing numbers of socialists looking for more comprehensive change gravitated to the CPUSA, and SP numbers dwindled. By 1929, when the Great Depression ravaged the U.S. economy, communists held a higher profile than the SP.

The SP was revived under the leadership of Norman Thomas, who garnered 800,000 votes for president in 1932. In like fashion, socialist Upton Sinclair polled well in his bid to become governor of California in 1934, but the SP continued to suffer from doctrinal discord, and it could not compete with Franklin Roosevelt's popularity among **working-class** voters. Roosevelt's New Deal undermined SP strength by adopting watered-down socialist ideals in programs such as **Social Security** and unemployment compensation. Socialism achieved its greatest success in the 1930s in the form of labor leaders who embraced its precepts and found communism too radical. Prominent socialist labor leaders included **Walter Reuther**, **A. Philip Randolph**, and **Sidney Hillman**.

Few radical groups weathered the post-World War II Red Scare well, though socialists inside the **Congress of Industrial Unions** (CIO) fared better than communists. Many, in fact, became ardent anticommunists during the **Cold War**. Even so, socialism's overall influence declined, especially in organized labor. During the 1950s, labor unions increasingly embraced **business unionism** and distanced themselves from leftist ideologies of all sorts. Socialist advocates such as Michael Harrington and the League for Industrial Democracy (LID) served left-labor interests well into the 1960s, and "Old Left" socialists played a role in advising the New Left **counterculture** of the 1960s. LID, for example, helped organize Students for a Democratic Society. By then, however, socialism existed more as a set of ideals than as a strong movement. Socialist principles found expression in both New Frontier and Great Society programs between 1961 and 1968, after which idealism waned. Some unions continue to espouse socialist collectivist principles, but the term "socialism" now carries negative connotations and is often avoided in favor of "softer" labels such as "progressive."

Scholars from the 1920s onward have pondered why socialism was weak in the United States, though in recent years their assumptions have been called into question. The debate hinges on the failure of U.S. socialists to form independent **labor parties** such as those established in other Western industrial democracies. While it is true that many peer nations enacted social legislation that is far in advance of the laws passed in the United States, labor parties abroad have been social democratic movements whose overall impact on transforming society is usually one of degree rather than substance vis-à-vis the United States. Some scholars argue that today's labor parties are not substantially different from American political parties; some suggest that moderate American socialists created a de facto labor party by becoming the left wing of the Democratic Party. Moreover, it is a mistake to view the United States as devoid of socialism. Ill-informed individuals continue to use the term to engender fear, but there are many programs in the United States that are inherently socialist in that they are run by the state, are funded by taxpayers, and operate for the benefit of all society. These include public education, police and fire services, Social Security, Medicare, Medicaid, banking regulations, the interstate highway system, welfare programs for the disadvantaged, environmental protection rules and agencies, national and state parks, municipal water supplies, the postal service, student loan programs, and the U.S. military. Whether labor unions are comfortable with the term or not, their collectivist **solidarity**-based organizations are inherently socialist as well.

The future of American socialism as an organized political movement is, at present, uncertain. Socialism continues to provide an ideological critique of capitalism, potential exists for an international workers' movement, and socialism has provided conceptual and tactical tools for leftist opponents of **deregulation** and **globalization**. A substantial number of Americans now identify themselves as "independents" in political terms, and an independent socialist, Bernard Sanders, serves in the U.S. Senate. Numerous grassroots political and labor groups are socialist in spirit, if not in name.

Suggested Reading

Mari Jo Buhle, Paul Buhle, and Dan Georgakas, *Encyclopedia of the American Left*, 1922; Albert Fried, ed., *Socialism in America: From the Shakers to the Third International, A Documentary History*, 1992; Seymour Martin Lipset and Gary Marks, *It Didn't Happen Here: Why Socialism Failed in the United States*, 2000.

SOCIALIST LABOR PARTY. *See* Labor Parties; Socialism.

SOCIALIST PARTY OF AMERICA. *See* Debs, Eugene Victor; Labor Parties; Socialism.

SOCIAL REFORM UNIONISM

Social reform unionism is an organizational principle that links union gains to larger issues of social change. It is the antithesis of **pure and simple unionism**, which confines union goals to the ideas of securing higher **wages**, better working conditions, and shorter workdays for members. Social reform unionists want these things as well, but they also wish to reform society. Some, in fact, believe that working people will not secure justice until significant social change occurs, and that there are some issues that cannot be secured through **collective bargaining** and require legislation to redress. Social reform unionists see society as a whole as their arena of struggle, not just individual workplaces. Social unionism runs the gamut from socially sanctioned reform efforts to revolutionary ideology.

Government authorities and business leaders have historically viewed organized workers with suspicion and treated them with antagonism—except during wartime when labor peace is deemed necessary to maintain uninterrupted production. Because of this "us versus them" mentality, labor's agenda has often moved beyond pure and simple principles and has tackled larger social problems and broad-based reform efforts. In fact, until the 1880s, nearly all unions adhered to social reform unionism ideals. The **Workingmen's movement** of the 1830s combined demands for shorter hours and higher wages with a political program that included a call to end **child labor**, a crackdown on municipal corruption, reform of inheritance laws, demands for free public education, and ending property requirements that disqualified working men from voting in some states. This sort of agenda remained the norm for the next 50 years. Both the **National Labor Union** and the **Knights of Labor** (KOL) called for wholesale revamping of political and economic conditions. The KOL, in fact, developed an extensive social reform agenda and advocated changes as sweeping as the enactment of mandatory **arbitration** laws to settle strikes, the abolition of the wage system, racial and gender equality, temperance, and land reform.

The first major **labor federation** to adopt pure and simple unionism was the **American Federation of Labor** (AFL), which organized according to **craft unionism** principles. The AFL was more exclusive, and sought to match up a skilled worker monopoly against corporate trusts. The AFL largely rejected the KOL's social reform advocacy as a form of **utopianism**, insisted that workers should not depend upon government, and argued that change came only from workers at the point of production. AFL affiliates often won wage increases and **fringe benefits** for their members, but critics decried that such gains did little to assist the **working class** as a body.

In the early 1900s, an insurrectionary version of social unionism found expression in the **Industrial Workers of the World** (IWW), which called for the overthrow of the free-enterprise system. The AFL outlasted its union and corporate foes by maintaining its focus on everyday working conditions and by using tactics that did not threaten the larger political framework. This evolutionary approach brought the AFL through the depression of 1893 and helped it gain acceptance among some employers as the safe alternative to the IWW during World War I. Although the AFL survived the postwar **Red Scare**, even it declined in the 1920s, when businesses returned to their prewar hostility toward unions and eviscerated organized labor by the time of the stock market crash and the onset of the Great Depression.

Economic collapse rekindled social reform unionism, especially in the unskilled and semiskilled ranks of the new **Congress of Industrial Organizations** (CIO), the most creative mainstream union since the KOL. The upsurge in labor militancy dovetailed with (and in some cases inspired) sweeping social reform associated with President Franklin Roosevelt's New Deal. Labor's changing rank-and-file—swelled by previously ignored **immigrants**, women, and people of color—became both devoted Roosevelt voters and an army for social change. Leftists were instrumental in fashioning this alliance, though their **socialist** and **communist** ties later haunted the labor movement. The CIO did, however, cement an enduring link between labor and the **Democratic Party** that had implications for the future of social reform unionism.

After World War II, tensions developed between the United States and the Soviet Union. Much of organized labor embraced **Cold War** unionism, a set of ideals that included strident anticommunism. Left-wing radicals were isolated or purged from the labor movement—actions that often served to discourage the sort of grassroots activism that fueled social reform unionism. The climate of fear in the 1950s made some labor leaders suspicious of social change movements, including African American **civil rights**. It also left some unions ill prepared to engage the **counterculture** of the 1960s. Although the AFL and the CIO merged in 1955, social reform remained a sticking point within the combined organization. In many cases, former AFL unions remained cautious in the face of social movements, whereas former CIO affiliates such as the **United Auto Workers of America** and the United Packinghouse Workers were more willing to endorse, underwrite, and support them. The AFL-CIO also split badly over whether to support the U.S. role in the **Vietnam War**. Organized labor did, however, strengthen its ties to the Democratic Party.

Labor was a house divided when the 1970s brought challenges such as the energy crisis, **runaway shops**, and the pressures of **globalism**. The conservative forces of **business unionism**, confronted by economic change and a hostile political environment, discovered that labor was, at best, a junior partner in a corporate-dominated society. **Deindustrialization** led to massive job losses in former union strongholds such as steel mills, automobile factories, and machine shops. Sophisticated human relations programs also undercut the appeal of unions, as management practiced enlightened policies during flush economic times. Those labor activists hoping that the Democratic Party would help them weather the anti-union policies of presidents **Ronald Reagan** and George H. W. Bush were often disappointed. Many unions lamented their lost militancy and questioned their acceptance of prevailing economic and political arrangements. They also noticed that those unions that maintained a militant spirit, such as the **American Federation of Teachers** and the **Service Employees International Union** (SEIU), fared better than those following a more conciliatory path. In 1995, SEIU President **John Sweeney** was elected to head the AFL-CIO, largely on his promise to reinvigorate the federation with social reform unionism principles. By 2003, however, Sweeney's efforts had yielded so little fruit that his own union, the SEIU, bolted the AFL-CIO and helped create the rival **Change to Win Federation**.

To date, neither Change to Win nor the AFL-CIO has induced levels of social unionism or activism comparable to that demonstrated by the KOL, IWW, or early CIO, but recent efforts suggest a promising revision of business unionism. **Richard Trumka**, who became AFL-CIO president in 2009, has pledged to advance social reform unionism, and the AFL-CIO has already made strides in sharpening its political agenda, advancing the interests of **minority labor**, and leading the charge on progressive social change. It would seem that pure and simple unionism—not reform unionism—is on the wane.

Suggested Reading

Simeon Larson and Bruce Nissen, eds., *Theories of the Labor Movement*, 1987; Kim Moody, *An Injury to All*, 1989; The New Unionism Network, http://www.newunionism.net/ accessed June 12, 2011.

SOCIAL SECURITY ACT

The Social Security Act of 1935 (SSA) was a centerpiece of President Franklin Roosevelt's New Deal. The bill provided **pensions** for workers older than the age of 65 years and was (and is) funded by employee and employer contributions. The act also provided federal funds for unemployment compensation, aid to families with dependent children, and other health and welfare programs. In 1939, benefits for dependents and survivors of workers who died before retirement were added to the program, and a 1956 revision included benefits for disabled workers.

The Social Security Administration now oversees a welter of complex programs, but the original SSA had more modest aims. Millions of Americans now depend on Social Security as their sole source of income during retirement, but the program was originally intended to supplement private insurance for retirees or the temporarily unemployed and, as a consequence, benefits were set at a low level. In 1937, just 53,236 individuals received a combined $1.2 million in Social Security funds. Although passage of the original bill entailed a fierce political battle, most parts of the SSA—especially its Federal Old-Age, Survivors, and Disability Insurance provisions and unemployment benefits—proved so popular that Congress has been pushed to expand coverage rather than diminish it. In 1950, for example, Congress enacted **cost-of-living adjustments** that raised retiree benefits. It also added coverage for workers excluded from the original bill, such as public employees, farm workers, domestic workers, the self-employed, and those working in small firms. Federal civilian employees were added in 1983, though many state and local governments, private schools, and others have alternative retirement programs. New programs were also added during the 1960s.

Conservatives often argue that SSA is too expensive and that parts or all of it should be privatized, but by 2008 nearly 51 million Americans collected more than $615.3 billion in Social Security benefits. Moreover, parts of the program are so popular that the SSA is often considered a "third rail" issue that can lead to the political death of politicians who seek to alter it. Current **Republican Party** policy—bitterly opposed by the **American Federation of Labor-Congress of Industrial Organizations** (AFL-CIO) and nearly every labor union and progressive group in America—nonetheless calls for massive scaling back and privatization of the SSA.

Privatization schemes face the additional obstacle of swimming against the tide of history, in the sense that SSA was born out of the failure of private and individual plans to protect workers. The **Industrial Revolution** hastened the shift from **agrarianism** and independent **yeomanry** to a society of consumer wage-earners within a money-based **capitalist** economic system. The Industrial Revolution also helped create two new classes, the **middle class** and a permanent **working class**, which faced new challenges, such as the need for a steady income throughout one's life, threats of unemployment, and debilitating injuries. Workers became more mobile and more likely to establish lives independent of their birth families. As society grew more complex, customary family and community patterns eroded and individuals' lives were governed by the logic of the marketplace. The introduction of tens of millions of **immigrants** into American society also sounded the death knell for traditional ways of caring for the elderly and the economically disadvantaged. Although **journeymen**'s associations and mutual aid societies sometimes set up insurance schemes for their members, these piecemeal efforts had little effect on society as a whole, and often provided little more than stop-gap relief; few beneficiaries could be sustained for more than a brief period.

By the 1870s, industrial workers across the globe pressed for old-age pensions, unemployment benefits, and compensation for on-the-job injuries. Germany introduced the first government-run social insurance program during the 1880s. It was funded by payroll taxes paid by the employer and employee and by contributions from the government. Subsequently, most developed countries have initiated some form of social security system based on the German model. An 1898 pension program enacted in New Zealand attracted notice in the United States and was much discussed by **Progressive Era** reformers. By the early decades of the 20th century, most U.S. states provided compensation for injured workers, some cities funded unemployment relief programs, and veterans received pensions from the federal government, but most down-on-their-luck workers depended on private charity for assistance. Numerous civic-spirited companies enacted **welfare capitalism** programs for employees that sometimes included pensions and health and safety insurance, but most employers were neither that enlightened nor that generous. The reality for legions of workers was that they needed to borrow, rely on charity, or live by their wits during times of distress.

The inadequacy of the U.S. system of social security was exposed during the Great Depression of the 1930s. During this decade, approximately one in four workers was unemployed, thousands of companies went out of business, wages were slashed for those lucky enough to remain working, and private philanthropy simply could not cope with the magnitude of the crisis. Municipal authorities, state governments, charities, churches, and families all looked to the federal government for relief. President Roosevelt sought advice from his aides, and Secretary of Labor **Frances Perkins** provided valuable input for the bill that eventually became SSA. The final bill, although assailed by critics as a form of **socialism**, was far less sweeping than labor unions and pension crusaders such as Francis Townshend had hoped for, but the 1935 SSA did build the initial framework upon which much of today's social security, unemployment compensation, and welfare systems rest.

After World War II, many Western democracies enacted complex government-funded social welfare legislation, but because of opposition from private insurance companies, the medical profession, and conservatives, health remained a private concern in the United States. Unions were often successful in negotiating **contracts** that offered employee health insurance and pensions, but coverage was by no means universal. In 1965, Congress created the Medicare program, which provides federally funded health care for the elderly and disabled. It also established Medicaid, which disburses federal funds to the states to pay the medical expenses of the poor. In 1974, the Supplemental Security Income program was added, which gives additional income to the elderly poor, the blind, and disabled individuals. Family assistance was revamped in 1997 by the Temporary Assistance for Needy Families Act, and children's health care was expanded by a separate piece of legislation. The Social Security Administration also oversees the Patient Protection and Affordable Care Act, enacted by President Barack Obama's administration in 2010, which seeks to protect health insurance holders and contain health care and prescription drug costs. President Obama also extended unemployment benefits to those displaced by the 2007 recession.

Compared to other industrialized countries, American social security provisions are neither generous nor extensive. Unemployment laws vary from state to state and are generally restricted to 26 weeks of coverage, unless Congress authorizes extension of benefits such as it did in 2010. The **Family Leave and Medical Act** is also quite weak and allows workers to take only unpaid leave, whereas many other Western nations supply government-funded maternity and family emergency leave. The private health care system in the United States leaves millions unprotected or confined to subpar plans, whereas most peer nations provide state-funded universal health care. The AFL-CIO has long called for a revamping of the SSA that would expand virtually every aspect of it, including more benefits for retirees, longer periods of unemployment compensation, and the enactment of a single-payer health care plan. This call has taken on new urgency as in recent years Social Security and Medicare have increasingly become the primary or sole pension package and health insurance for retired workers as corporations discontinue employee pension plans and medical insurance. Employers cite the pressures of **globalization** and the need to be competitive as reasons for ditching these benefits. Unions, social activists, and other retort that globalization is being used as a smokescreen to mask greedy desires to pocket greater profits. Still other observers see current pension and health care problems as analogous to the 1930s in that they are so large that the private sector is incapable of coping with them.

Government spending poses a major roadblock to SSA reform. At present the political will exists to cut unpopular programs, but not to authorize expansion of any program that would entail increasing taxes on individuals or corporations. In 1996, for example, President Bill Clinton, a **Democrat**, imposed time limits on how long benefits could be received from aid to families with dependent children programs. Republicans are even more eager to slice money from the SSA budget and cite figures purporting to prove that Medicare will be bankrupt by 2024 and that the Social Security Trust Fund for retirees will be depleted in 2036. They propose privatizing and investing the funds, as well as raising the retirement age to 70 years. (It is currently 67.5 years for most workers wishing to collect full benefits.) Labor unions and social reformers reply that Republicans and Democrats alike are hiding from the simplest solution for funding Social Security: removing the income cap and imposing the current 6.2 percent tax on all individual and corporate income. At present only the first $106,800 of income is subject to Social Security taxes and everything above it is exempt. This has the unintended effect of making Social Security a regressive tax in the sense that those with high incomes end up paying a much smaller portion of their total income for Social Security taxes than a worker making **minimum wage** would pay.

The battle over Social Security is likely to become more intense in the immediate future. Although many analysts see some form of pension privatization as necessary and nearly everyone agrees that SSA benefits are inadequate as a sole source of retirement income, the track record of the private sector in managing such funds gives pause. In 2005, President George W. Bush proposed partial privatization of Social Security that would allow citizens to invest some of their contributions in the stock market. Bush's plan met with stiff opposition from unions, senior citizens, and social activists. Had Bush's proposal been enacted, Social Security would have lost tens of billions of dollars in the stock market crash and recession that began on the heels of his proposal. The same recession also witnessed hard-pressed families paying stiff penalties and withdrawing funds from individual retirement accounts, an indicator of the risk involved in giving individuals access to funds designed to be used in the long term. Large government deficits have recently led Republicans to renew their call for reinvestment of Social Security funds, privatization, and tightened restrictions for using various programs. As of 2011, the public's reception of the GOP plans was quite negative, thereby giving more credence to the notion that for all its faults, the SSA is a popular program with which one tinkers at one's peril.

Suggested Reading

Edward D. Berkowitz, *America's Welfare State: From Roosevelt to Reagan*, 1991; Jeffrey R. Brown, Jeffrey B. Liebman, and David A. Wise, *Social Security Policy in a Changing*

Environment, 2009; Marie Gottschalk, *The Shadow Welfare State: Labor, Business, and the Politics of Health Care in the United States*, 2000; "Historical Background and Development of Social Security," http://www.ssa.gov/history/briefhistory3.html, accessed June 13, 2011; Social Security Administration, http://www.ssa.gov/, accessed June 13, 2011.

SOLIDARITY

Solidarity is a term that encapsulates the central organizing principle of most labor unions. It denotes the collective ideal that only in unity can working people attain their objectives and goals. It implies mutualism and community and entails both rights and responsibilities for individuals. Solidarity unionism, as ideally practiced, educates and supports individuals and their families, but individuals are expected to forgo private goals if doing so would better serve the union. Solidarity can express itself in classic **Marxist** perspectives on social class, or in less precise notions of interdependence, fellowship, or comradeship.

The goal of most unions is to foster solidarity among the rank-and-file, though, in practice, solidarity is usually strongest in moments of struggle and challenge, such as **strikes**, contract negotiations, and external oppression. This term derives from the French *solidarité* and was used by those intellectuals and workers who formed the short-lived Paris Commune in 1871. It probably came to the United States via immigrant **anarchists** and **communists** shortly after 1871. The term was used in the late 19th century, but greater popularity came after 1915, when **Industrial Workers of the World** songwriter Ralph Chaplin penned "Solidarity Forever." That song became the unofficial anthem of the American labor movement for workers of all ideological dispositions and is so much a part of labor **music** that most modern-day unionists have forgotten its radical roots.

Since 1915, the term "solidarity" has passed into general usage and has become a shorthand phrase for organizers and unionists expressing the need for unity. Appeals to solidarity are used to mute internal union bickering, justify coalitions with other groups, and substantiate calls for greater rank-and-file involvement in their unions. The term has also come to imply a near-mythic ideal of unity, harmony, and strength. In 1980, unionized Polish workers opposed to the ruling Soviet-style government dubbed themselves *Solidarność*. Their struggles revitalized use of the term "solidarity" within the United States. In 1981, the **American Federation of Labor-Congress of Industrial Organizations** called a Solidarity Day to oppose the economic policies of President **Ronald Reagan**. An estimated 500,000 people rallied in Washington, D.C., perhaps the largest labor protest in American history. That same year, Pope John Paul II defended the concept of solidarity in the papal encyclical *Laborem Exercens*. Despite the imprecision of the term and the abstractions for which it sometimes stands, solidarity remains the highest ideal of the labor union movement.

Suggested Reading

Jeremy Brecher, *Strike!*, 1997; Bang Jee Chun, *The Impact of Solidarity or Conflict on Participation in a Labor Union*, 1997; Simeon Larson and Bruce Nissen, eds., *Theories of the Labor Movement*, 1987.

SOUTHERN TENANT FARMERS' UNION

The Southern Tenant Farmers' Union (STFU) was a rare pre-World War II interracial workers' organization. It began life in Tyronza, Arkansas, in 1934, when a black/white coalition of small farmers, tenant farmers, and sharecroppers united in response to dire economic conditions during the Great Depression. The STFU's biracial makeup and its criticisms of economic privilege upset the presumptions of the Jim Crow South, frightened white southern landholders, and provoked occasional violence. The STFU set up **cooperatives**, fought legal battles, lobbied Congress, and engaged in **strikes**, all with the goals of protecting members from forced evictions, improving daily **wages** for farm laborers, and obtaining a fair share of crop reduction payments from the federal government. The STFU had limited success, but it did serve to draw the nation's attention to the plight of impoverished southern farmers. It also served as a role model for future interracial labor organizing.

The failure of **Reconstruction** to enact meaningful land reform left much of the rural South saddled with a rigid class system in which much of the profitable land was in the hands of a small landholding elite. African Americans had been thoroughly disenfranchised politically, and the bulk of the black population was landless and forced to eke out subsistence as tenant farmers or sharecroppers. More whites owned land than blacks, but many of them were hard-pressed small farmers seeking to sustain themselves on small or marginally profitable acreage. The livelihood of much of the South's **agrarian** population was threatened when the depression drove down commodity prices. Cotton—the staple crop of much of the Deep South—was particularly hard hit, and New Deal programs designed to help farmers had the unintended effect of making conditions worse for small producers. The 1933 Agricultural Adjustment Act (AAA) attempted to apply a demand-side solution to sinking commodity prices up by paying farmers to plow under or leave fallow a portion of their acreage. In theory, reduced supply would lead to price rises. Although AAA crop reduction contracts stipulated that farm owners had to make strong efforts to keep tenants on the land and to split the crop reduction payments with them, few landowners complied, and many landowners evicted tenants and sharecroppers and hired day laborers instead.

Norman Thomas, a perennial **socialist** candidate for president, visited Tyronza in 1934 and was appalled by the poverty he witnessed. He urged impoverished farmers to form a union to address these problems. Thomas joined forces with local Socialist Party members Harry Leland Mitchell and Clay East, and with black preachers E. B. McKinney and Owen Whitfield, in seeking relief for Arkansas farm workers. They petitioned New Deal officials to enforce AAA contracts on behalf of tenant farmers and sharecroppers. The STFU sued Arkansas plantation owner Hiram Norcross for evicting tenants in violation of AAA policies. Norcross, however, represented entrenched landowning interests, and the STFU lost the court case. The STFU expanded it base and extended into five additional states, but hoped-for support from Washington, D.C., was seldom forthcoming. Secretary of

Agriculture Henry Wallace sympathized with the STFU, but he also knew that the success of President Roosevelt's New Deal required the compliance of southern **Democrats**, some of whom were themselves large landowners. Wallace fired Jerome Frank, the General Counsel to the AAA, and a number of other government officials that supported the STFU.

Parts of the AAA were struck down as unconstitutional in 1936. The act was rewritten in 1938 and rural relief also came through the Farm Security Administration (FSA), created in 1936, which provided loans to small farmers. While helpful to a small number of farmers, the FSA did not restore farms to evicted tenant farmers, or assist farm laborers whose daily wages were abysmally low. The STFU did, however, convince U.S. Senator Joseph Robinson, who also happened to be a large Arkansas landowner, to give the group tepid support. Nonetheless, across the South many sharecroppers lost control over their lands and were forced to become day laborers working for low wages. When it could, the STFU led strikes to force landowners to raise daily wages. A 1935 action that led to wage increases for cotton farmers led to a surge in membership; by 1936, the STFU had approximately 25,000 members in six southern states.

STFU strikers sometimes met with violence, and several died. In 1936, Mitchell and East moved the STFU to Memphis, Tennessee, in part to isolate activists from gathering violence in Arkansas. The union was able to build **solidarity** through methods that combined union activism, a vibrant labor **music** tradition, reliance upon **labor college** volunteers, and close alliances with religious institutions, especially in black communities.

The STFU avoided the **communist**-dominated Share Croppers Union, which had formed in Alabama, but it did join forces with the **Congress of Industrial Organizations** (CIO) in 1937. The STFU aligned with the CIO's United Cannery, Agricultural, Packing, and Allied Workers of America (UCAPAWA). another farm worker-based union, until a 1939 ideological squabble led to a split. When the STFU left the UCAPAWA, it lost support from some black union members who preferred to remain linked to UCAPAWA, and who had also come to question the commitment of white STFU leaders to interracial cooperation. The desertion of the Reverend McKinney proved a crippling blow, and the union quickly contracted from its 1938 height of 35,000 members.

The STFU continued to battle on behalf of small farmers, sharecroppers, and day laborers, though the organization's focus shifted during the 1940s and it also took up the light of migrant workers. After World War II, the STFU changed its name to the National Farm Labor Union, later known as the National Agricultural Workers' Union. It faded from existence shortly after Harry Mitchell died in 1960.

The STFU's actual successes were modest, but it provided an inspirational model for the early **civil rights** movement, which was also interracial in makeup and relied upon some of the same organizational methods.

Suggested Reading

Jerold S. Auerbach, "Southern Tenant Farmers: Socialist Critics of the New Deal." *Labor History* 7 (Winter 1966): 3–74; Donald H. Grubbs, *Cry from the Cotton: The Southern*

Tenant Farmer's Union and the New Deal, 1971; Howard Kester, *Revolt among the Sharecroppers*, 1997 (reprint of 1936 original).

SOUTHWEST RAILWAY STRIKES OF 1885–1886

In 1885, a **strike** victory against railroad interests controlled by robber baron Jay Gould led to an enormous surge in membership for the **Knights of Labor** (KOL). One year later Gould exacted revenge, and the KOL lost many of the new members it had gained. The two strikes against Gould's Southwest system exemplify both the militancy of American workers in the late 19th century and the limits of worker gains in a political climate in which few laws protected **collective bargaining** rights, enforced **contracts**, or regulated business practices.

Few figures were as despised by Gilded Age workers as Jay Gould. He was one of the richest individuals in the United States, having made a fortune by owning and operating the elevated railway system of New York City, Western Union Telegraph, and many of the rail lines west of the Mississippi River. His Southwest conglomerate consisted of major lines such as the Missouri Pacific, the Wabash, the Texas and Pacific, the Union Pacific, and dozens of trunk roads. In total, Gould held controlling interest in approximately 12 percent of all U.S. rail mileage. He also controlled several eastern railroads, had major interests in leather goods, and speculated in commodities such as grain and gold. Gould was known as a brutal employer, for which he made no apologies; he bragged that, if necessary, he could hire one half of the **working class** to kill the other half. Gould had clashed with the KOL before, including several nasty incidents involving KOL telegraphers in the early 1880s.

The first Southwest strike had its origins in one of Gould's periodic **wage** cuts, a 10 percent slash imposed on workers on the Missouri Pacific, the Wabash, and the Missouri, Kansas, and Texas lines in October 1884. When Gould enacted an additional 5 percent cut in February 1885 and several KOL workers were fired, workers walked out. Union Pacific (UP) workers also struck out of fear that the cuts and firings would extend to them. Many UP workers were organized in KOL assemblies that were prototypical **industrial unions**, and they maintained remarkable levels of **solidarity** that made it difficult for Gould to hire **scabs**—the one exception being the **Brotherhood of Locomotive Engineers** (BLE), which refused to honor any of the KOL strikes. (BLE members fit the profile of **aristocrats of labor** and clashed so often with the KOL and other railroad brotherhoods that they often scabbed against the BLE during its strikes.) By March 1885, much of Gould's rail traffic was tied up and workers along many lines **boycotted** Gould trains and refused to handle or service them. KOL leader **Terence Powderly** finally convinced Gould to negotiate with the men. In October, Powderly called off the strike when Gould agreed to raise wages and to end discrimination against KOL members.

The gains were actually rather modest, but forcing the hated Jay Gould to the bargaining table had an electrifying effect on American workers. Hundreds of thousands rushed to take out KOL membership in the hope that the union was the long-awaited savior for the impoverished working class. Official membership soared from 111,395 in July 1885 to 729,000 one year later, and hundreds of thousands of other workers claimed KOL affiliation. (Applications came in so quickly that the KOL's administration could not process them fast enough.)

Rapid growth was not necessarily a good thing for the Knights. Although the first Southwest strike gave the KOL a high public profile and made Powderly a media sensation, many of the new members badly misunderstood the organization's principles and values. Scholars often reference the post-Gould victory as an example of the perils facing social movements whose rank-and-file holds expectations inconsistent with the overarching organizational principles and obtainable goals. New members failed to understand several things. First, Gould's capitulation was strategic. Unknown to most Knights, Gould had over-leveraged himself in several other speculative ventures and needed an infusion of cash lest his holdings became vulnerable to even richer opponents such as William Vanderbilt or John Rockefeller. Second, the Southwest strike was inconsistent with KOL principles. The Knights generally sought alternatives to strikes such as boycotts, **arbitration**, or political intervention. Most of the KOL's principles required political and social reform, not point-of-production activism. Finally, many KOL, including members of the Southwest system, were unskilled and semi-skilled workers from heavy industries controlled by some of the most powerful individuals in the United States. Although the KOL engaged in industrial unionism experiments, its membership was far more vulnerable to employer retaliation than the skilled workers to which the future **American Federation of Labor** (AFL) and its **craft union** affiliates would confine themselves.

That vulnerability was exposed in the second Gould strike in 1886. Historians have debated whether the strike was provoked by Gould for the purpose of smashing the KOL, whether Powderly betrayed strikers, or whether strike leader Martin Irons—who was scapegoated when the action collapsed—led his charges into an ill-advised and unauthorized strike. The event began in March 1886 when Irons called for a strike vote after a KOL leader on the Texas Southern line was fired for calling a meeting on company time. Powderly would subsequently argue that he could have arbitrated this dispute and that Irons acted rashly. Soon, more than 200,000 workers in Texas, Arkansas, Illinois, Kansas, and Missouri were on strike. Once again the BLE refused to honor it. This time Gould acted quickly; he hired scabs, brought in **Pinkerton** guards, and possibly **agent provocateurs**. Violence and property damage provided a pretext for requesting troops in Missouri and Texas, though several other governors turned down Gould's requests, having found no evidence of KOL involvement in violence. Meetings with Gould, political officials, and Powderly failed to result in an agreement. Texas Rangers helped smash the strike in that state, and hired gunmen did the same elsewhere. By summer, the KOL was in retreat. The strike was officially called off in September, an act that angered many of the strikers. Irons was suspended from the KOL, was **blacklisted** from railroad employment, and struggled to earn a living. He died in 1900.

By the time of Irons's death, the KOL was also gasping for life. The organization bickered bitterly over the second Gould strike, with some members taking Powderly's side and others viewing Irons as a martyr. The collapse of the second Gould strike destroyed much of the KOL's presence among western railroad workers—who quit the KOL in droves—and the lost New York Central strike of 1890 had the same effect among easterners. Some historians prematurely write off the KOL after the second Gould strike. It would be more accurate to say that by 1890 the organization had contracted to its pre-1886 levels and to view the explosive growth after the first strike as anomalous. The KOL retained some level of influence throughout the **Great Upheaval** and, in the 1890s, switched its emphasis from industrial organizing to rural campaigns; in the countryside, the KOL was often indistinguishable from **Populism**.

The two strikes against Gould do, however, offer several important lessons. First, industrial unionism models appear to have been prematurely birthed in the late 19th century, a lesson also embodied in the demise of the **American Railway Union**, which absorbed many of those workers who quit the KOL. In retrospect, Powderly appears to have been correct in his assessment that the second strike should not have been called. (Whether he communicated that message effectively is debatable.) Workers organized in mass industries simply did not have the resources or strength sufficient to do battle with men as powerful as Gould or the New York Central's William Vanderbilt. Second, social movements need to find ways to make certain that members act in accordance with official directives and in ways consistent with organizational goals. That was also a problem for the ARU. Third, the second strike serves as a reminder that one should exercise caution before romanticizing strikes and militancy. Militancy is important in maintaining solidarity, but it can also precipitate rash actions. KOL leader Joseph Buchanan maintained that no job actions should be taken unless they met two criteria: The cause is just, and the action taken has a reasonable chance of succeeding. Finally, one should not view the working class as monolithic or assume that all workers sympathized with one another. The actions of the BLE throughout the 19th century indicate that some workers placed self-interest above class interest.

The AFL was founded just months after the second Gould strike failed. It did not survive because its principles were superior to those of the KOL, but because it, like the BLE, did not attempt to do as much as the KOL. By jettisoning **social reform unionism**, confining itself to skilled workers, and maintaining a smaller presence in some of the large industries tackled by the KOL—railroads, meatpacking, textiles, and steel—the AFL gained the time to solidify its base in ways denied to the KOL. When it became feasible to organize basic industry, it would be the **Congress of Industrial Organizations**, not the AFL, that finished the job begun by the KOL.

Suggested Reading

Ruth Allen, *The Great Southwest Strike*, 1942; Shelton Stromquist, *A Generation of Boomers: The Pattern of Railroad Labor Conflict in 19th-Century America*, 1987; Robert E. Weir, *Knights Unhorsed: Internal Conflict in a Gilded Age Social Movement*, 2000.

SPEEDUPS

A speedup is a self-defining term that refers to an imposed requirement for increased work and productivity without a parallel increase in pay or

fringe benefits. Management often impose speedups in the name of being more competitive or efficient, but those actions are generally resented by workers. The fact that speedups are implemented without discussion with employees means that, technically speaking, they are not a form of **Taylorism**, though the goal of getting more work out of employees is the same in each case. In many cases, workers resist speedups either formally or informally.

Speedups tend to be associated with manufacturing, though they are common in all sorts of work. A common form occurs on **assembly lines**, where the very pace of the movement of parts and goods is accelerated so that the finished product reaches completion more quickly. In a **service industry** scenario, delivery routes might be increased, or office personnel could be assigned a larger number of tasks. The speedup was once a standard feature in industries such as textiles and automobiles, with companies often using it to build up excess inventory prior to contract negotiations as a hedge against possible **strikes**. Such unilateral work changes occur most frequently in non-union settings, however, because **collective bargaining** agreements have provisions blocking such management practices without prior negotiations. Moreover, any dramatic change in work requirements during a period in which a contract is in place would be considered an **unfair labor practice** and expose the company to possible sanctions. Today, many multinational corporations with labor-intensive operations avoid negotiations over speedups by relocating production plants to developing nations where unions are weak.

Speedups were once optimistically thought to be on the wane, but they seem to be making a comeback. Computers can be used to monitor and time employee tasks, according to quotas set by management. These quotas are often changed with little or no employee input—a complaint that resonates among data entry personnel, telephone operators, mail sorters, and telemarketers, among others. Informal speedups occur when companies **downsize** their workforces but expect the same output; this goal can be achieved only by forcing existing workers to do the jobs once performed by former staff. The speedup has also made its way into **white-collar** jobs. Many workers on **salary** now complain that they can finish tasks only by working longer hours and/or taking work home with them.

Management often congratulates itself for thinking that it is getting more work out of employees. Studies reveal, however, that speedups often provide only a short-term boost in productivity. Fatigued employees produce less in the long run, plus workers often find ways around speedups, even if the workplace is not unionized. Employees might agree, for instance, upon a **stint** and sanction workers who do not adhere to it. They might also engage in subtle acts of **sabotage** such as slowdowns, seeking management input on tasks they already know how to perform, inventing "problems" that disrupt the workflow, or producing poorer-quality work.

Suggested Reading

Ash Amin, ed., *Post-Fordism: A Reader*, 2000; Robert Asher and Ronald Edsforth, *Autowork*, 1995.

STALEY LOCKOUT

The Staley lockout took place between June 1993 and November 1995. It was one of three major labor disturbances in Decatur, Illinois, during the 1990s that transformed the once-proud **blue-collar** city of 85,000 into a veritable capital/labor war zone. In addition to the A. E. Staley Manufacturing Company (a corn processor), local facilities of Caterpillar Tractor (**Caterpillar strike**) and Bridgestone-Firestone Tires (**Bridgestone-Firestone strike, 1994–1995**) were involved in clashes that pitted multinational corporations against labor unions. The **lockout** in Decatur drew comparisons to the infamous 1892 **Homestead Steel lockout and strike**. Parallels between the actual events of the two lockouts are overdrawn, but in each case an entire community was traumatized and a climate of distrust, resentment, and economic dislocation was left behind. Observers who question whether organized labor remains relevant also point to the Staley lockout as an exemplar. A better comparison, however, would be between Staley and Hormel workers in the 1980s (**Hormel strike and lockout**), as Staley workers also had to battle their own union as well as management.

Decatur's troubles began in the fall of 1991, when members of the **United Auto Workers of America** (UAW) struck Caterpillar factories in Decatur and Peoria, and the company responded by locking out union workers at four Illinois plants. Caterpillar sought a six-year contract that would break UAW **pattern bargaining** in the tractor industry and create a two-tier **wage** system with a lower scale for new hires. The issues remained unresolved when, in the spring of 1992, Caterpillar threatened to hire **scabs**. That threat prompted the UAW to end the **strike**, but workers returned to their jobs without a new contract. The next several years were marked by tense shop-floor relations, including frequent disputes between UAW members and managers, and firings of union activists.

Also in 1992, Tate & Lyle, a London-based multinational corporation that had purchased the Staley company in 1988, sought to cut labor costs and increase management flexibility. Management insisted on a new work rules, including 12-hour, rotating shifts. Workers affiliated with the Allied Industrial Workers Union (AIW) rejected the proposal. Although the plant employed as many as 2,300 workers in the late 1960s, the 1992 workforce was down to just 740 individuals when the company indicated its intent to make further reductions. A brief walkout by AIW workers in early June 1993 prompted a company lockout several weeks later. Staley workers retained the services of labor consultant Ray Rogers and launched a **corporate campaign** against Tate & Lyle, hoping to bring public and financial pressure on the company and soften its contract demands.

Confrontation also brewed at the Bridgestone/Firestone plant, located on Decatur's east side. Bridgestone, a Japanese firm, purchased venerable Firestone in 1988. Six years later, Bridgestone/Firestone sought a new contract with the **United Rubber Workers of America** (URW) that also included 12-hour, rotating shifts. Bridgestone also sought productivity-linked wage hikes, cuts in vacation time, and a two-tiered wage system. When the URW struck in July 1994, the company hired **scabs** at 30 percent lower wages. Efforts by the Bill Clinton administration to withdraw government contracts from the tire maker in response to its hiring of scabs failed.

During the various troubles in Decatur, massive demonstrations and acts of civil disobedience took place across the city, including the arrest of a priest and several nuns in June 1994. Police used pepper gas against lawful and peaceful demonstrators at Staley. Rogers kept up the pressure, however, and organized Staley "road warriors," who traveled about the United States to solicit support from other unions. Hunger strikes also kept the focus on Staley, and Rogers opened negotiations with Pepsi, a firm that purchased about 30 percent of the corn sweetener produced by Staley. In 1994, Staley lost a major contract with the brewing giant Miller. Rogers also spearheaded a drive to have consumers pressure Pepsi to use leverage against Staley.

Despite the fact that Staley workers had been locked out for more than a year and a half, optimism ran high among Staley workers. New **American Federation of Labor-Congress of Industrial Organizations** (AFL-CIO) President **John Sweeney** pledged support for both Staley and a renewed commitment to grassroots labor militancy. The problem was that not all AFL-CIO unions supported Sweeney, and both he and Staley workers ran into **business unionism** at its worst. During the lockout, the AIW had been reorganized under the United Paperworkers International Union (UPIU). It Local 7837 was led by Dave Watts, who had done a remarkable job of maintaining **solidarity**. The Staley rank-and-file had twice rejected contracts negotiated by the UPIU **international union**, viewing each as unacceptable. In November 1995, just days after local activist Dan Lane ended a 65-day hunger strike, the UPIU's international president Wayne Glenn announced he was taking charge of the strike. Glenn also took credit for Staley's lost contract with Miller, even though the UPIU had little to do with it. Glenn and the UPIU executive council negotiated a settlement with Staley and voted not to send it to the local for acceptance. In what most labor analysts see as an in-house coup d'état, Watts was unseated as Local 7837 president and a Glenn loyalist took his place. On December 22, 1985, the newly reconstituted Local 7837 accepted a new contract with Staley. The UPIU had to ask police to remove its own dissident members from the hall during the vote.

The new contract—the UPIU's spin on it notwithstanding—was little more than a total surrender. Staley got all that it asked for, plus seniority rights were lost, and major changes were made to the **grievance** procedure. All of this happened despite the fact that word on the street held that Pepsi planned to stop buying from Staley if it did not reconcile with workers by January 1. Of the 740 workers employed at the time of the lockout, just 146 returned to work. As the decade ended, the plant employed only 270 laborers. The UPIU also faltered and, in 1999, merged with the **papermakers** and several petrochemical workers' unions. Its death went unmourned in many Decatur homes.

The Staley debacle was just one of several travails for Decatur workers. UAW Caterpillar workers were saddled with a contract similar to that found at Staley. An even worse fate befell Bridgestone workers. Their 1996 agreement included 12-hour, rotating shifts, acceptance of scabs as permanent workers, and other distasteful measures. In 2001, just as labor relations were beginning to improve, the plant closed in the wake of negative publicity involving tire problems in Ford vehicles that used tires during the period in which scab labor ran the production lines. Approximately 1,500 men and women were left unemployed.

It is hard to put a positive spin on any of the events in Decatur, least of all the Staley lockout. Neither the UPIU nor the AFL-CIO handled the lockout well. Critics of business unionism interpreted the strike as a loss that did not need to happen and an early warning sign that John Sweeney would not be successful in dislodging AFL-CIO bureaucrats. Many believe that Ray Rogers was far more capable of directing the Staley campaign than the AFL-CIO. Rogers continues to launch corporate campaigns, but he is often *persona non grata* vis-à-vis the AFL-CIO. To workers and students of labor history, the Decatur disputes stand as a testament to the failure of traditional organized tactics in the late 20th century. Many wonder if labor has not yet fashioned an adequate response to the aggressive demands of multinational corporations.

Suggested Reading

Steven Ashby and C. J. Hawking, *Staley: The Fight for a New Labor Movement*, 2009; Stephen Franklin, *Three Strikes: Labor's Heartland Losses and What They Mean for Working Americans*, 2001; C. J. Hawking, "Snatched from the Jaws of Victory? Staley Workers End Lockout," http://www.illinoislaborhistory.org/staley-lockout.html, accessed June 15, 2011.

STEEL STRIKE OF 1919

The steel strike of 1919 was one of the many labor stoppages that erupted in the years following World War I. Like most of the other labor actions during this era, it was precipitated by the attempts of employers to reverse agreements made during the war and enforced by the **National War Labor Board**, wherein workers agreed to keep production levels high in exchange for improved **wages** and working conditions.

The steel industry was notoriously union averse and organizers took full advantage of the war to attempt to reestablish organized labor's presence in the mills. The National Committee for Organizing Iron and Steel Workers (NCOISW) was led by John Fitzpatrick of the Chicago Federation of Labor and by former **Industrial Workers of the World** (IWW) activist **William Z. Foster**, who started recruiting steelworkers nationwide in 1918. Steel producers reluctantly turned a blind eye to those efforts, as they were aware that President Woodrow Wilson would tolerate no disruption of wartime production. Producers underestimated worker resentment, however, and NCOISW quickly signed up thousands of workers in the war's waning days. Its unionizing drive was the first sustained effort to organize steelworkers since the **Homestead Steel lockout and strike** of 1892, a traumatic loss that had largely driven unions from the industry.

When the war ended, NCOISW leaders sought to open negotiations with industry executives in the hope of securing **collective bargaining** rights and securing a **contract**. They encountered a unified wall of resistance; steel producers refused to

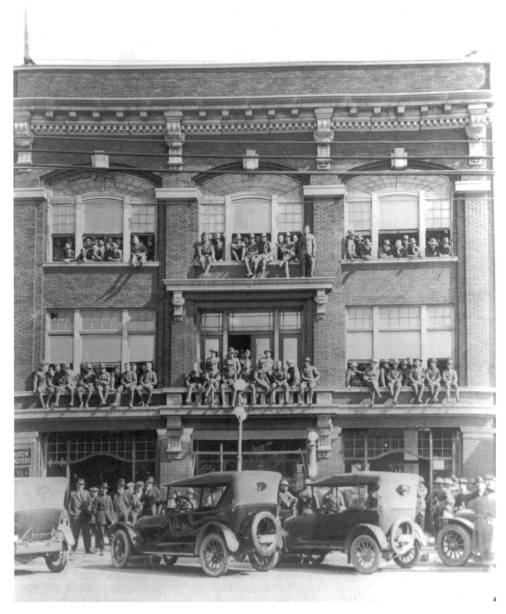

Opposition to unionization led to a strike of steel workers in Gary, Indiana, in 1919 and 1920. (Calument Regional Archives, Indiana University N.W.)

even meet with them. NCOISW leaders sought more time to organize, but an angry rank-and-file pressured leaders to issue a call for a nationwide steel **strike**, which began on September 22, 1919. The workers' demands were modest: union recognition and a reduction in working hours from 12 to 10 hours per day.

The strike affected firms differently. Most of the facilities owned by industry-giant U.S. Steel were shut down. By contrast, Bethlehem Steel, U.S. Steel's main competitor, experienced only scattered disruptions. Most sources claim that 250,000 steelworkers walked out, representing approximately half the industry's workforce.

Steel producers defeated the strike by using three strategies. First, they immediately hired **scabs** to replace as many strikers as possible, an easy task given that the NCOISW had signed up large numbers of unskilled workers. Second, management deliberately inflamed racial and ethnic tensions in the workforce. For example, U.S. Steel paid African Americans in Gary, Indiana, to march through the streets rather than to make steel, thereby fanning fear among white strikers that blacks would take their jobs. Finally, the industry publicized the political views and pasts of strike organizers, especially Foster, whose previous career with the IWW afforded opportunities to tar the NCOISW as a radical organization at a time in which a postwar **Red Scare** was gathering steam.

The strikers held out hope when President Wilson convened an industrial conference in October, and they tactfully offered to submit the dispute to government **arbitration**. That hope vanished when U.S. Steel chairman Elbert Gary refused to discuss the dispute and there were no U.S. laws that compelled him to submit to arbitration. Striking workers gradually returned to their jobs—without union contracts. The NCOISW formally called off the strike on January 8, 1920, although production had returned to normal levels weeks before. Steel remained largely non-union until the **Congress of Industrial Organizations** won major victories for labor in the 1930s. Much as had happened with **Eugene Debs** a generation earlier, the lost strike further radicalized Foster. He resigned from the NCOISW and became active an active **communist**.

Suggested Reading

Robert Asher, "Painful Memories: The Historical Consciousness of Steelworkers and the Steel Strike of 1919," *Pennsylvania History* 45 (January 1978): 61–86; David Brody, *Labor in Crisis: The Steel Strike of 1919*, 1987; David Brody, *Steelworkers in America: The Nonunion Era*, 1969.

STEEL STRIKE OF 1959–1960

The steel strike of 1959–1960 was the last nationwide walkout of steelworkers and one of the last major work stoppages in the heavy manufacturing sector that had made the United States a world power during the **Industrial Revolution**. One of the largest and most successful strikes in U.S. history, it took place within an industry that had seen such past turmoil as the **Homestead Steel lockout** and lockout of 1892, the **steel strike of 1919**, and the efforts of the **Congress of Industrial Organizations** (CIO) to win **collective bargaining** rights for steelworkers in the 1930s.

More than 500,000 steelworkers represented by the **United Steelworkers of America** (USWA) began their **strike** on July 15, 1959. Twelve firms were struck, including U.S. Steel. In all, the strike disrupted production in roughly 85 percent of the industry, idled nearly 1 percent of the nation's entire labor force, and represented the single-largest number of collective lost work hours in U.S. history. Strikers held out for 116 days and returned to work on November 7 under a "cooling off" provision authorized under the **Taft-Hartley Act**. Before the strike could be renewed, steel companies capitulated and an agreement was signed in January 1960.

The troubles began when steel companies actively sought a strike in the hope of forcing the USWA to make **concessions** on gains won in previous contracts. Management gambled that a long strike would cause the rank-and-file to abandon their USWA leaders. Ultimately, the companies wanted to reduce union and worker power on the shop floor. Section 2(b) of the steelworkers' contract forced company management to negotiate with the union over work processes, which the firms saw as an infringement of management rights and which the USWA interpreted as drawing upon the expertise of workers to make certain that jobs were done safely and efficiently. Thus the strike was an anomaly in that it was not initially over standard issues such as **wages**, hours, or union recognition, but rather boiled down to a battle between the corporations' desire to return all shop-floor power to management and the USWA's determination to retain section 2(b).

Management was correct in predicting a long strike. The dispute became a battle of attrition that was settled in part because of the intervention of the federal government. The strike began to affect the national economy, and President Dwight Eisenhower declared it a threat to national security. On October 9, Eisenhower invoked the 80-day cooling-off provision of the Taft-Hartley Act to force the steelworkers back into the mills. USWA President David McDonald accused Eisenhower of strikebreaking, but once the Taft-Hartley prevision went in effect, negotiations began in earnest for the first time.

The united corporate front began to crumble when Kaiser Steel agreed to the USWA's terms in mid-October. The company had already settled when the U.S. Supreme Court ordered workers to return to work beginning on November 7. This order meant that the cooling-off period would expire in January 1960. Recognizing the rank-and-file's willingness to renew their strike at that time, the Eisenhower administration convinced the companies to settle. Eisenhower was thought to have been influenced by two factors: Vice President Richard Nixon's desire to settle in advance of his bid for the presidency and the clever legal maneuvering of USWA counsel Arthur Goldberg. An agreement was announced on January 5. The steelworkers earned a substantial wage increase and retained all their **fringe benefits**, including section 2(b) of the contract.

The USWA won because it was able to maintain **solidarity** among steelworkers, and because of the dogged efforts of Goldberg in warding off potential legal obstacles. Despite a four-month strike and two more months of intense management efforts to convince workers to drop their support of the union, the rank-and-file remained solid. This fact was especially impressive given that many younger steelworkers initially opposed the strike. Veterans of previous strikes were able to convince them that unity was necessary to defend the union and preserve wages, various benefits, and shop-floor power. Management stubbornness also focused rank-and-file anger, determination, and solidarity. When even the federal government concluded that workers stood ready to continue their battle, steel companies gave in.

The USWA hailed the contract as its best ever. Unfortunately, it may forever remain so. In 1962, USWA President McDonald agreed to relax the terms of section 2(b) and to allow more automation in the mills. That move led to his ouster as USWA leader and, in 1965, he was replaced by I. W. Abel. By the 1970s, the steel industry was in deep decline, with foreign imports undercutting domestic prices. Aging plants soon closed and steel became the poster child for **deindustrialization**. Giants such as U.S. Steel began to shift assets out of production and diversify their investments. By the late 1980s, U.S. Steel derived so many income from other sources that it rebranded itself as USX Corporation in 1991. (The company abandoned that ill-chosen name a decade later.) Specialty steel production remains in production in the United States, but steel is generally viewed as a **sunset industry** that is likely to disappear in its entirety. The USWA likewise had to reinvent itself; like U.S. Steel, the USWA expanded its organizational efforts into other fields.

Suggested Reading

Anthony F. Libertella, *Steel and Steelworkers: Race and Class Struggle in 20th-Century Pittsburgh*, 2002; Jack Metzgar, *Striking Steel: Solidarity Remembered*, 2000; David L. Stebenne, *Arthur J. Goldberg: New Deal Liberal*, 1996; Paul A. Tiffany, *The Decline of American Steel: How Management, Labor, and Government Went Wrong*, 1988.

STEEL WORKERS ORGANIZING COMMITTEE. *See* United Steelworkers of America.

STEWARD, IRA

Ira Steward (March 10, 1831–March 13, 1883) was a machinist by trade, but was considered by many of his contemporaries to be the father of the **eight-hour movement**. Although he was not the first to conceive of an eight-hour workday, few figures inspired early advocates of this policy as did Steward.

Steward was born in New London, Connecticut. His father was a humble laborer, and Steward was largely self-educated. By 1850, Steward was an **apprentice** machinist whose grueling 12-hour workdays kindled his interest in reducing the hours of toil that sapped workers' strength. He joined the International Machinists' and Blacksmiths' Union (IMBU)—a forerunner of the **International Association of Machinists**—which, in 1863, passed resolutions demanding an eight-hour workday. Steward took up the cause and the IMBU provided him with seed money to build a workers' movement in support of the eight-hour goal. Steward established several organizations in the greater Boston area, including the Labor Reform Association and the Grand Eight-Hour League (which later became known as the Boston Eight-Hour League). Boston was, at that time, a well-known **working-class** city and Steward's efforts there soon caught the attention of workers outside of Massachusetts. In 1868, federal employees won an eight-hour day.

Steward was not progressive on all issues. He held rabid anti-Chinese views, which angered fellow Massachusetts labor advocate Wendell Phillips. Nor would he live to see the eight-hour workday become standard practice. Steward did, however, pressure the Massachusetts legislature to grant a 10-hour day for women and children in 1874. In 1878, he and J. P. McDonnell founded the International Labor Union (ILU), an abortive attempt to form a **labor federation**. Although the ILU was short-lived, it did much to publicize the eight-hour day and its views on **cooperation** and redistributing wealth inspired future labor leaders, especially **George McNeill,** who idolized Steward. Some ILU ideas eventually made their way into the platform of the **Knights of Labor**.

Steward was among the first to make cogent arguments about how shorter hours would improve workers' lives and society. Others seeking to defend shorter hours often cited his numerous articles and pamphlets. One of Steward's claims that resonated with the **middle-class ideology** that dominated mid-19th-century America was his assertion that shorter hours would lead workers to improve themselves morally by giving them more time for church, community, and self-improvement. He even argued that the overall economy would benefit because reduced hours would give workers more time to become consumers. Those appeals to Gilded Age elites notwithstanding, there is little doubt that Steward saw the eight-hour day as part of a larger program to undermine **capitalism** through redistributing wealth.

Steward married twice. His first wife, Mary, died in 1878, and, in 1880, he wed Jane Henning. He died in Plano, Illinois, in 1883 and was destined to become an important symbol for the eight-hour movement throughout 19th century. Even so, he was largely forgotten by the time the 1938 **Fair Labor Standards Act** put the force of federal law behind the eight-hour day.

Suggested Reading

Philip S. Foner, *History of the Labor Movement in the United States, Vol. 1*, 1947; Timothy Messer-Kruse, "Eight Hours, Greenbacks, and Chinamen: Wendell Phillips, Ira Steward, and the Fate of Labor Reform in Massachusetts," *Labor History* 42, no. 2 (2001); David Montgomery, *Beyond Equality: Labor and the Radical Republicans, 1962–1872*, 1967.

STINT

Stint refers to an informal agreement among workers as to what constitutes a fair day's work and reasonable pace at which to accomplish it. The stint was an important part of 19th-century worker mentality that persists to the present.

The stint evolved from a built-in tension inherent in **capitalism**. Because capitalism is rooted in individualism rather than collectivism, it is in an employer's best financial interest to extract as much work as possible from employees at the lowest possible cost. Ideally, workers and management come to agreement on what constitutes reasonable profit levels and the amount of work necessary to achieve it. The stint, in essence, is a worker-defined version of standard time. In a well-run workplace in which workers and management respect one another, it is generally acceptable for employers to ask employees to work harder in extraordinary circumstances. Resistance occurs when management seeks to impose a new stint that workers deem unfair, exhausting, or arbitrary.

Taylorism and other aggressive management styles seek to circumvent the stint. Employers might attempt such seemingly positive incentives as paying **piecework** rates, or impose negative regimens such as **speedups**, **stretch-outs**, or forced **overtime**. In each case, resistance can occur. Unlike organized protests, a stint requires little more than tacit agreement among workers to maintain it. It is considered an important aspect of workplace culture that illustrates how laborers exert some degree of control over their jobs, even if a union does not represent them. All workers perform tasks and possess knowledge that evolves from the routines of work. They also learn how to pace themselves throughout the workday. Employees who feel as if their stint is being violated can **sabotage** such efforts in various ways. One of the simplest is a slowdown, a protest that might be no more complicated than working diligently only when the boss is looking. Because management is incapable of watching all employees all the time, it is hard to break a well-run slowdown. In retail work, employees can do things such as making unnecessary trips to the stockroom, taking longer than necessary when assisting customers, or imposing an informal **work-to-rule** stint in which they simply do not perform the myriad tasks they do each day that are not part of their formal job description.

Stints are usually one of the first things fellow workers communicate to new employees. New hires are often overzealous and desirous of proving themselves to be "good" employees. Older workers often advise them to "take it easy" and educate them as to what is considered a fair pace of work. Their peers often ostracize those employees who do not heed the advice. Because all workplaces function best when workers cooperate, employees who disrespect the stint can find that cooperation denied—a withdrawal of mutual help that can make their own jobs much harder.

Suggested Reading

David Montgomery, *Workers' Control in America*, 1984.

STRASSER, ADOLPH

Adolph Strasser (1844–January 1, 1939) is best known for being a cofounder of the **American Federation of Labor** (AFL) and for articulating the philosophy known as **pure and simple unionism**. He was also associated with the early Socialist Labor Party, the Cigar-Makers International Union (CMIU), and the **Knights of Labor** (KOL). Strasser's reputation is often overshadowed by that of his friend and colleague **Samuel Gompers**, but he was probably more influential than Gompers in articulating the AFL's guiding principles.

Strasser was born in a German-speaking region of Hungary. Not much is known of his early life, though his deep understanding of British trade unionism suggests he spent time in the United Kingdom prior to immigrating to the United States sometime around 1872. Gompers suggested that Strasser had upper-class roots. Like many German-speaking **immigrants** after 1848, Strasser also had radical inclinations. He settled in New York City, where he was active in the American Section of the **Marxist** International Workingmen's Association (IWA). Strasser was not long for the IWA ranks: He saw the organization as faction ridden and felt it was too German in character to appeal to American workers. He took an active part in the **Tompkins Square riot** (an unemployment demonstration on January 13, 1874), which violated IWA rules. He, **Peter J. McGuire**, and several others were expelled from the American Section.

After their departure from the IWA, Strasser and McGuire organized the Social Democratic Workingmen's Party (SDWP). Strasser became the group's executive secretary and contributed extensively to its paper, *The Socialist*, later renamed *The Labor Standard*. As in the IWA, Strasser clashed with German Americans inside the SDWP, this time over the tactical merits of trade union organization versus political action. This issue deeply divided the SDWP and various other **socialist** groups. Strasser, who had already moved toward a more pragmatic agenda, argued that workers needed to focus on immediate gains such as higher **wages**, short working hours, unemployment insurance, and sick benefits rather than investing time and energy in quixotic political campaigns. When the Workingmen's Party of the United States—soon to be rechristened the Socialist Labor Party (SLP)—was formed with an emphasis on politics, Strasser was removed from his leadership position with the SDWP.

Strasser would make a much bigger impact inside the CMIU. He also took up cigarmaking in New York City and his quick rise within the CMIU suggests he had plied the trade before arriving in America. In 1877, Strasser was promoted from organizer to president of the CMIU, a position he occupied for the next 15 years. He also met and worked with Samuel Gompers. When Strasser took over the CMIU, it was a small organization with approximately 1,000 members; he helped quadruple its size within three years.

Both Strasser and Gompers shed their socialism and developed pure and simple unionism, with Strasser insisting that the CMIU should focus on winning **collective bargaining** rights and short-range political action. The CMIU's pure and simple unionism model would prevail by the end of the 19th century, but it was considered unorthodox when it was first articulated.

The first major campaign of the Strasser/Gompers-led CMIU was to curtail the practice of tenement cigarmaking. The CMIU emphasized the unsanitary conditions of tenement labor and introduced a union label on cigars to distinguish them from the tenement-made brands. In 1878, the union appealed to the federal and state legislatures to ban **homework** in the commercial production of cigars. The several bills introduced all failed, which seemed to vindicate the arguments of socialists that political action was needed. In consequence, numerous socialists bolted the CMIU to form the SLP-affiliated Progressive Cigar-Makers Union (PCMU). In New York City, the PCMU was chartered as a Knights of Labor local assembly, a move that infuriated Strasser and Gompers, who were nominal members of the KOL; both men repudiated both the KOL and its socialist ideals. The fight between the CMIU and the PCMU touched off bitter **jurisdiction** battles between the CMIU and the KOL. Strasser became such a harsh critic of the KOL that, in 1886, he demanded that the Knights stop organizing all skilled workers.

Strasser played a key role in forming the AFL in December 1886, but he advanced Gompers to lead the federation and focused his own energies on the CMIU. In 1892, Strasser resigned as CMIU president and served the union in various lesser capacities. He served on the AFL's legislative committee and on its executive council. In the latter position, Strasser is credited with pushing through the expulsion of the **brewery workers'** union in 1907, when it embraced an **industrial unionism** philosophy.

Strasser's personal life and motives were enigmatic. A CMIU newspaper article published at the end of his presidency said, "Personally, or rather socially, he makes few friends. . . ." In the early 20th century, he moved numerous times, first from New York City to Buffalo, then to Chicago, where he resided from 1905 to 1911. He then moved back to Buffalo and, in 1914, retired from the labor movement and spent four years as a real estate agent. In 1930, Strasser moved to Florida, where he kept a deliberately low profile. He had no further contact with the CMIU, and spent his last years living in the home of a dressmaker, dying there on January 1, 1939. Strasser's considerable stock portfolio and savings were depleted during the Great Depression. He died a pauper, his burial expenses being paid by the state of Florida.

Strasser's role in cofounding the AFL was forgotten by the time of his death and he is often little more than a footnote in labor history, a mysterious omission. There is suggestive evidence that Strasser retreated from the CMIU in anger after an 1897 allegation he had misused union postage funds. He is often noted as being a close personal friend of Gompers, but the two do not seem to have had much contact after 1910. Strasser is not enshrined in the Labor Hall of Fame. Several years after his death, the CMIU paid to have Strasser's remains exhumed and shipped to Chicago for reburial. Only three people attended his interment in the Forest Home Cemetery.

Suggested Reading

Patricia Cooper, *Once a Cigarmaker: Men, Women, and Work Culture in American Cigar Factories, 1900–1919*, 1987; H. M. Gitelman, "Adolph Strasser and the Origins of Pure and Simple Unionism," *Labor History* 6, no. 1 (Winter 1965): 71–83; Julie Greene, *Pure and Simple Politics: The American Federation of Labor and Political Activism, 1881–1917*, 1988.

STRETCH-OUT

A stretch-out is an employer tactic of cutting staff, but not production, by demanding increased output from remaining employees. Stretch-outs are closely related to **speedups**. These were once routine in the textile industry. For example, weavers tending two machines might discover they were required to tend four. These practices were very common in the textile industry during the 1920s and 1930s. In fact, the term "stretch-out" appears to have originated in the textile industry during the early 1930s; newspapers routinely used it to refer to the practice of making textile workers do additional work. Stretch-outs declined when labor unions finally succeeded in organizing much of the textile industry, but they remained a feature in non-union sections of the South. They occur less frequently in the industry now because most textile manufacturing has been **outsourced** to factories outside the United States.

Stretch-outs always quicken the pace of work. Not surprisingly, workers usually resent stretch-outs, except in extraordinary circumstances such as the need to produce a greater number of goods during wartime. In other circumstances, attempts to implement them can precipitate **strikes**, especially when workload increases do not come with corresponding rises in **wages**. For that reason, in classic **Taylorism**, stretch-outs were usually accompanied by incentive pay measures such as bonuses. Taylorism was also resented, but not as much as noncompensated stretch-outs.

The term is most associated with the textile industry, but is by no means peculiar to it. Automotive workers have also complained about stretch-outs, as have workers in most other occupations. Although the term itself is seldom used any more, variants of the stretch-out are routine in the modern workforce and have accelerated since **downsizing** trends began in the 1980s. Many **white-collar** workers have expressed discontent with heavier workloads occasioned by reductions in staff, and phrases such as "doing the work of two people" are part of everyday office discourse. The declining power of labor unions is likely to result in increased use of stretch-outs in the future.

Suggested Reading

Jay T. Baldwin, *Revolt against the Plutocracy*, 2004; William J. Goode and Irving Fowler, "Incentive Factors in a Low Morale Plant," *American Sociological Review* 14, no. 5 (October 1949): 618–624; Samuel Patterson, *Social Aspects of Industry: A Survey of Labor Problems*, 1929; "Work and Protest," http://www.ibiblio.org/sohp/laf/protest.html, accessed June 18, 2011.

STRIKE

A strike occurs when workers walk off their jobs in protest against perceived injustices on the part of an employer. Common reasons for strikes include complaints over low pay, overly long workdays, or poor working conditions. Strikes are also held in an effort to force employers to grant **collective bargaining** rights, improve employee **fringe benefits**, protest management violations of union **contracts**, demonstrate employee resolve in advance of contract negotiations, or as a spontaneous reaction to arbitrary actions on the part of management. Strikes can take a variety of forms, including slowdowns, **sick-outs**, **sympathy strikes**, and memorial strikes. Workers once also used **sit-down strikes**, though most of these are now banned. They also engage in unauthorized **wildcat strikes**, wherein the rank-and-file acts on its own accord. The most common form of strike involves a vote among workers to withhold their labor by walking off their jobs and staying away until their demands are negotiated. A dominant feature of this type of strike is the use of a **picket** line in which workers voice their demands, educate the public about their plight, and attempt to prevent **scabs** from entering the business being struck.

The strike has come to be seen as the primary weapon through which organized labor expresses its discontent. It sometimes surprises students of labor history to learn that strikes have been controversial within organized labor's ranks. The first recorded use of the term in the context of a refusal to work dates comes from a British sailors' dispute in 1768. The term probably derives from the practice of striking, or lowering, a ship's sails to symbolize refusal to go to sea.

The first documented strike in the post-Revolutionary War United States occurred in Philadelphia in 1786, when printers sought a minimum wage of $6 per week. Strikes became more frequent as labor unions developed in the 19th century, but labor organizations frequently debated their wisdom, with most arguing that they should be labor's last resort, not a preemptive action. The **Knights of Labor** (KOL), for instance, officially repudiated strikes, though it engaged in many. As KOL leader **Terence Powderly** noted, strikes seldom recouped the wages lost during a work stoppage and they engendered ill will that took a long time to heal. He also noted that social conditions were such that it was often easy for employers to secure **scabs** or use legal maneuvers such as **injunctions** to break strikes and the unions that directed them. Many organizations, the KOL included, preferred to use other types of pressure against employers, including **boycotts**, public pressure, and political lobbying. The KOL and other groups called upon the government to enact mandatory **arbitration** laws that would eliminate the need for strikes. Strikes were viewed as acts of desperation. Within the United States, they were also too often acts of war. The labor history in the United States is the bloodiest of all Western democracies, with an estimated 2,500 workers losing their lives in U.S. strikes between 1870 and 1935.

It was the **American Federation of Labor** (AFL) that established the idea that the strike was labor's primary weapon in forcing employers to grant concessions to workers in a **capitalist** economy. The AFL and, later, the **Congress of Industrial Organizations** (CIO) conducted numerous strikes, many of which ended in victory for workers, but many of which did not. Left-wing groups such as **socialists**, **communists**, and the **Industrial Workers of the World** also supported the use of strikes; in their cases, the strike was viewed as a method of subverting capitalism in the pursuit of justice for the **working class** and the building of a new society. The passage of the **National Labor Relations Act** in 1935 finalized the legitimacy of labor unions and gave them some legal protections during strikes.

By the middle of the 20th century, labor strikes were such a common form of social protest that many Americans had come to assume that they were how capital/labor disputes were resolved. Historians, however, remain divided over the wisdom of the AFL's model of pursuing worker gains through strikes. Many defend the practice and doubt that significant gains could have been achieved any other way. Still others accuse their colleagues of romanticizing strikes and argue that the decision to emphasize action at the point of production rather than building independent social democratic organizations akin to European **labor parties** retarded the advance of progressive legislation in the United States and assured that American social programs and labor laws would be weak compared with those of other democracies. Historians associated with what was dubbed "the new social history" movement that emerged in the 1960s—which placed emphasis on grass-roots movements and social groups—are particularly vulnerable to the charge of having romanticized strikes. New social history advocates retort that even unsuccessful strikes served to empower groups that would have otherwise have been marginalized.

The debate over strikes is kept afloat because there is ample evidence to support each side. On the one hand, it appears doubtful that workers such as steelworkers, public employees, teachers, or professional athletes would have gained collective bargaining rights without strikes. On the other hand, the efficacy of strikes presupposes a social saturation of union strength that is no longer present in American society and helps explain why **retail** workers, **white-collar** workers, and many **service industry** employees have proved difficult to organize and why strikes among them often end in failure. Ultimately, weak labor laws make strikes of any sort hard to sustain. The prevailing sentiment since the 1980s is that most strikes that are not settled very quickly will end in failure; it is simply too easy for employers to hire scabs, use the legal system to their advantage, or leverage their superior resources to wage wars of attrition against financially strapped labor groups. During the 1980s, employers often used those very methods to precipitate **downsizing, decertification, and concessions strikes** to cripple organized labor. From the **Professional Air Traffic Controllers Organization strike** of 1981 onward, labor has fared so poorly in strikes that most unions are reluctant to call or authorize them. In 1952, the United States saw 470 major strikes in which more than 1,000 employees walked off their jobs; in 2009, there were just 5 such strikes, the lowest recorded number in U.S. history.

Prior to the 1980s, labor history studies routinely glorified strikes and touted worker victories. Since then, however, historians have paid renewed attention to the critique of strikes from individuals such as Powderly. Debates rage over whether strikes were ever the best method of obtaining rights for working people, but few would dispute the notion that they are seldom a good idea in the current economic and political climate.

Suggested Reading

Jeremy Brecher, *Strike!*, 1997; Mike Elik, "Sad, Startling Stats: Number of Union Elections, Strikes Continue Steady Decline," *In These Times*, July 7, 2010; Sidney Lens, *The Labor Wars: From the Molly Maguires to the Sit Downs*, 2009.

SUBCONTRACTING

Subcontracting is the practice in which production and/or services purchased from one firm are assigned to another by the firm under contract. It is especially commonplace in the building trades. A consumer—which could be an individual, a municipality, or even the federal government—signs an agreement with a contractor. The contract usually specifies the amount the consumer will pay for the project and the time in which the contractor will complete it, or reasonable estimates in the case of larger undertakings. Contracts are often quite detailed regarding the nature and quality of the work to be completed. In addition, building codes and consumer laws may apply. It is the contractor's responsibility to complete the project, but that individual or firm may have great flexibility in how to do so. Few general contractors complete all the work themselves. They may choose, for example, to subcontract the plumbing to one firm, landscaping to another firm, and electrical work to still a different company. It is usually the original contractor's responsibility to make certain all work is completed properly.

Subcontracting has long been a feature of American industry, and not just in the building trades. Auto manufacturers, for example, often subcontract parts fashioned in one place, but assembled at another. The same is true in the apparel industry, where cloth or even basic garments might be woven or cut in one location and tailored somewhere else.

Organized labor concerns itself with subcontracting when it undermines the jobs and **wages** of union workers. In recent years, subcontracting has emerged as another way for less scrupulous firms to subvert wages under the guise of frugality. Hospitals, for example, have replaced staff nurses with subcontracted care from firms that generally pay lower wages. Many airlines now subcontract plane maintenance, a practice that has cost jobs among union workers in the **International Association of Machinists and Aerospace Workers**. Abuses are also widespread in the building trades. In some cases large construction firms set up non-union subsidiaries into which they channel projects. The construction industry, at least, is constrained by **prevailing wage** laws; most other enterprises are not. Apparel-industry workers complain of the use of subcontracted **homework** that is little more than **sweatshop** production under a new guise. Malls and office complexes routinely subcontract services such as security, maintenance, rubbish removal, and cleaning to outside firms. In larger cities, poorly paid subcontracted work often goes to **immigrants** and the poor, though campaigns by groups such as the **Service Employees International Union**'s Jobs with Justice and Justice for Janitors campaign have helped in some cities. The hospitality and recreation industries are often cited for their widespread use of low-wage subcontracted workers such as maids, valets, and groundskeepers. Subcontracting has even made its way onto college campuses, many of which no longer employ their own dining staff, maintenance crews, sports facilities managers, or bookstore personnel. For the foreseeable future, subcontracting is likely to remain a point of contention between unions and management.

Suggested Reading

Barbara Ehrenreich, *Nickel and Dimed*, 2001; William H. Hollings, Jr., Kenneth Jennings, and Roger Wolters, *The Labor Relations Process*, 9th edition, 2009.

SUNSET INDUSTRY

"Sunset industry" is the name given to a business or manufacturing pursuit that is on the verge of obsolescence. The term applies to the entire branch of economic activity, rather than individual factories or businesses. These are generally mature industries whose future prospects are bleak.

In 1983, the *London Times* used the term "sunset industries" to refer to dying manufacturing processes that were unlikely to enjoy revitalization. These were contrasted with "sunrise" industries—particularly in high-tech fields—that were on the rise. Although the term is probably of recent vintage, the phenomenon it describes is old. Innovation and new technology have long supplanted one form of economic activity with another. In the United States, the expansion of the automobile industry during the first decade of the 20th century obliterated the carriage and buggy trade. As late as 1904, there were more than 5,000 carriage manufacturers in the United States; by 1929—the last year the Carriage Builders National Association met—there were just 88 such companies. The automobile transformed entire sectors of the economy. Towns where local businesses once supplied goods such as horse harnesses, buggy whips, and wagon wheels experienced economic stress when jobs disappeared because there was little demand for their products. Studebaker was among the very few carriage makers to make the transition. In 1900, it made nearly 100,000 horse-drawn carriages; four years later, it was nearly out of the carriage trade.

In recent years, concern over sunset industries has shifted. It is one thing for new technology to supplant old, as in the case of automobiles and carriages; it is quite another when manufacturing disappears altogether. The United States was a relative newcomer to the **Industrial Revolution** but by the early 20th century it was the world's largest industrial power, a dominance it maintained through the 1960s. Manufacturing was dealt a severe blow by the energy crises of the 1970s and by **deregulation** from the 1980s onward. By the year 2000, once-dominant economic activities such as the production of electronics, steel, aeronautics, rubber, and textiles were sunset industries producing goods for small niche markets. It is now fashionable to link sunset industries to postindustrialism, and many analysts worry that the American economy lacks a large enough productive capacity to maintain a favorable balance of trade. For workers, the loss of sunset industry jobs often means a severe cut in **wages** as the economy has (thus far) produced more lower-paying **service industry** jobs than sunrise manufacturing opportunities; indeed, jobs in such potential sunrise industries as high-tech manufacturing and medical technology have already been outsourced or moved out of the United States. The very future of work in America is uncertain, and some observers suggest that even activities such as publishing and automobile manufacturing are rapidly becoming sunset industries.

Suggested Reading

Thomas Kinney, *The Carriage Trade: Making Horse-Drawn Vehicles in America*, 2004; Jeremy Rifkin, *The End of Work: Technology, Jobs and Your Future*, 2004.

SUPPLEMENTAL UNEMPLOYMENT BENEFITS. *See* Guaranteed Annual Wage.

SWEATSHOP

Sweatshops are usually defined as small manufacturing concerns, often within a residential setting, in which men and especially women and children labor long hours under substandard conditions and receive low **wages**. The sweatshop has long been a symbol of exploitation and injustice.

In the United States, attention to sweatshop abuses was most focused during the last quarter of the 19th century and the early decades of the 20th. **Immigrants** in need of sustaining themselves were particularly vulnerable to exploitation in sweatshops, as were women in the needle trades. Sweatshops emerged in urban tenements, where workers made goods such as clothing, shoes, and cigars; laborers were usually paid **piecework** rates, which meant they needed to toil long hours to obtain basic sustenance. During the 1880s, the Cigar-Makers International Union was among the first trade unions to demand regulation of sweatshops, although there was a worldwide outrage against sweatshops by then. The battle to contain sweatshops spilled into the **Progressive Era**, and social reformers added the public appeal that sweatshop conditions increased the possibility that disease could be spread to unwary consumers through goods produced in unhealthy settings. That fear resonated, as the garment industry had long depended on "sweated" labor, a work system that served the secondary purpose of suppressing wages for all garment makers. The **International Ladies' Garment Workers' Union** led the 20th-century crusade against sweatshops, and the tragic **Triangle Factory fire of 1911** so shocked the public that legislation was passed to curtail some sweatshop abuses. In the 1930s, New Deal legislation placed further federal restrictions on sweatshops. In theory, the **Fair Labor Standards Act** outlaws most of the practices that allowed sweatshops to thrive in the United States.

Sweatshops remain a target for social reformers for the simple reason that they persist. Although many Americans believe sweatshops to have migrated overseas, thousands of sweatshops continue to exist in the United States. Many are located in depressed parts of inner cities, where employers continue to be cited for safety violations, violation of **child labor** laws, and failure to pay **overtime** rates; in some cases, Americans sweatshops have even been guilty of failing to pay **minimum wage**. Former Secretary of Labor Robert Reich claimed that in 2001, more than 60 percent of the sewing and cutting shops in Los Angeles failed to pay minimum wage or overtime; in New York City, more than 65 percent were in noncompliance with U.S. law. The U.S. computer industry has also been accused of maintaining sweatshops, as have restaurants, landscapers, hotels, and cleaning service contractors. As in the past, sweatshop employers often target recent immigrants.

Unions such as the **Union of Needletrades, Industrial, and Textile Employees** (UNITE) have led the charge to crack down on domestic sweatshop production, and have also taken part in international efforts to stop sweatshops. UNITE also charges that **homework** and **subcontracting** systems are rife with sweatshop conditions. In fact, anti-sweatshop crusaders argue that two factors have combined to make contemporary sweatshops as big a problem today as they were in the Progressive Era. First, **globalization** has made populations more mobile. **Latino** immigrants are disproportionately involved in sweatshop labor, as are recent arrivals in the United States from Asia, especially China. Second, regulation is more lax today than in the past. Government agencies such as the National Labor Relations Board have become deeply politicized and there are fewer factory inspectors today than there were decades earlier.

Globalization has also had the effect of spreading sweatshops worldwide. Many "American" firms do very little actual production in the United States, and many of the goods that end up on American shelves are produced by sweatshop labor in places such as Vietnam, China, Singapore, Bangladesh, Honduras, Nicaragua, and numerous other developing nations. Firms that have been accused of using sweatshop labor or selling sweatshop goods include Nike, Donna Karan, Levi-Strauss, Wal-Mart, Hanes, L.L. Bean, Ikea, and Abercrombie & Fitch. Shoes, clothing, rugs, toys, chocolate, bananas, and coffee are among the products most affected by sweatshop labor. UNITE and groups such as the International Labor Rights Fund, Green America, the Not for Sale Campaign, and the International Labour Organization continue to spearhead battles to end sweatshops. Consumer **boycotts** have had some effect as well. United Students Against Sweatshops, who have maintained steady pressure on colleges and universities to make certain that their branded logo-ware is produced under humane conditions, led a particularly effective boycott effort.

A small number of economists, corporate spokespersons, and social policy analysts defend sweatshops in developing nations by arguing that their presence increases the gross domestic product in host nations, thereby increasing the local living standards, providing more educational opportunities, and leading to greater development. They also assert that what Westerners see as sweatshop labor is better than existing alternatives. Such arguments are hard to sustain on a moral level and have had little effect on anti-sweatshop and anti-globalization protestors.

Suggested Reading

Eileen Boris, *Home to Work: Motherhood and the Politics of Industrial Homework in the United States*, 1994; Jennifer Gordon, "American Sweatshops: Organizing Workers in the Global Economy," *Boston Review*, Summer 2005; "Sweatshop Hall of Shame," http://www.laborrights.org/sites/default/files/publications-and-resources/sweatshop_hall_shame_2010.pdf, accessed June 17, 2011; Louie Yoon and Miriam Ching, *Sweatshop Warriors: Immigrant Women Workers Take on the Global Factory*, 2001.

SWEENEY, JOHN JOSEPH

John J. Sweeney (May 5, 1934–) served as president of the **American Federation of Labor-Congress of Industrial Organizations** (AFL-CIO) from 1995 to 2009. Sweeney took office amidst a wave of great optimism and pledged to restore organized labor's emphasis on grassroots organizing and, when necessary, defiant militancy. This promise largely failed to pan out, and labor unions continued to lose members, strength, and influence under Sweeney's watch.

John Sweeney is the son of working-class Irish **immigrants** and was raised in the Bronx section of New York City. His father, Joseph, was a bus driver and an active member of the Transport Workers Union, and his mother, Agnes, was a domestic worker.

Sweeney attended Roman Catholic schools and obtained a B.A. in economics from Iona College in 1956, after working his way through college as a gravedigger and a porter. He married Maureen Power and the couple had two adult children, including a daughter, Patricia, who works for the AFL-CIO.

Upon leaving Iona, Sweeney worked briefly for IBM, before leaving to take a lower-paying job as a researcher for the **International Ladies' Garment Workers' Union** (ILGWU). In 1960, Sweeney left the ILGWU to become contract director for the Building Service Employees International Union (BSEIU). Sweeney rose in the ranks, and the BSIU expanded and changed its name to the **Service Employees International Union** (SIEU) in 1968. That same year Sweeney joined the union's executive board. Soon thereafter, he became a SEIU vice president; in 1976, he assumed the presidency of SEIU Local 32B in New York City. Sweeney was faced with two problems that hampered Local 32B organizing efforts: corporations' disregard for their employees and the union's own passivity. Sweeney addressed both concerns. He authorized and helped mobilize two swift and hotly contested **strikes** that won important wage and job security concessions for 70,000 workers. He also labored to instill a sense of **solidarity** among local members and to encourage a combative spirit.

Sweeney became the SEIU's international president in 1980 and was also elected as a vice president of the AFL-CIO. The SEIU was one of the few American labor unions to grow stronger during the antiunion administrations of Presidents **Ronald Reagan** and George H. W. Bush during the 1980s. During this period, Sweeney spent one-third of SEIU's budget on organizing campaigns, an unheard of percentage in the era of **business unionism**. Sweeney led a number of successful SEIU campaigns including the Justice for Janitors and the Work and Family campaigns. He also agitated for legislative changes, including those that eventually made their way into the federal **Family and Medical Leave Act**. Under his watch, SEIU also launched an internal **affirmative action** program aimed at bringing gender and racial diversity to the union. Gays and lesbians also secured a foothold through the union's Lavender Caucus.

Sweeney was an outspoken critic of what he saw as the AFL-CIO's timidity in challenging conservative politicians and their anti-union policies. He was especially disappointed when **Democratic** President Bill Clinton signed the **North American Free Trade Agreement** and accused AFL-CIO President **Lane Kirkland** of not pressuring Clinton to derail the bill. Sweeney joined a coalition that worked behind the scenes to pressure Kirkland to retire. When Thomas Donahue, Kirkland's hand-picked candidate, announced his intention to succeed Kirkland, Sweeney mounted a challenge. He headed a group called "New Voices" and won election with 57 per cent of the vote, despite opposition from influential figures such as **Albert Shanker**.

Sweeney pledged to expand SEIU policies, militancy, and grassroots organizing efforts throughout the federation. He immediately launched an aggressive organizing drive backed by $20 million of newly allocated funds. As had been done in the SEIU, Sweeney sought to diversify AFL-CIO membership and leadership through active recruitment of women and **minorities**. He also vowed to promote union democracy—a call that ruffled the feathers of several notoriously autocratic affiliate leaders. Sweeney bumped heads with AFL-CIO conservatives from the start and was unable to take more aggressive action during the **Staley lockout**, which ended badly at precisely the time some observers felt it was on the verge of succeeding. He did, however, make significant changes in the AFL-CIO during his tenure as president. Although union strength declined, the horrific spate of **downsizing, deregulation, and concessions strikes** of the 1980s and early 1990s subsided. The **Teamsters'** 1997 victory in the United Parcel Service strike heartened many union supporters, and AFL-CIO unions reversed a 1980s trend by winning more strikes than they lost. Sweeney also launched initiatives to form labor/management partnerships, work on ways to preserve worker **pensions**, and explore ways to use **corporate campaigns** more effectively. In addition, he greatly expanded union training programs and sought ways to streamline union bureaucracies. He also generated controversy by revamping an older AFL-CIO nonprofit center as the Working for America Institute and shifting its focus from assisting displaced workers to economic development and political lobbying.

Sweeney made the requisite verbal commitment to cherished AFL-CIO objectives such as curtailing **runaway shops**, reining in CEO **salaries**, protecting worker security, enforcing **Occupational Safety and Health Act** (OSHA) standards, preserving **Social Security**, supporting health care reform, and passing laws that make it harder to hire **scabs** and easier to recruit union members. He was not successful in stopping the AFL-CIO's membership slide; in fact, union membership decreased during his time in office at a faster rate than it did under Kirkland. Very few unions honored Sweeney's call to devote 30 percent of their budgets to organizing. Attempts to assist the **United Farm Workers of America** (UFWA) in organizing strawberry pickers flopped, as did an expensive campaign to unionize Las Vegas construction workers.

Nor could Sweeney reconcile the various factions within the AFL-CIO. It was been plagued by defections. In 2000, the United Transportation Union quit the federation over conflicts with the **Brotherhood of Locomotive Engineers**. Even more damaging was the defection of the 500,000-member **United Brotherhood of Carpenters and Joiners**, which quit the AFL-CIO in 2001 after complaining that the federation was paying no attention to its stated goal of organizing workers or protecting **jurisdiction** rights. It also argued that the federation needed to reevaluate its relationship with the Democratic Party.

Sweeney soon faced opposition from an unlikely source: SEIU. His successor as SEIU head, Andrew Stern, tore a page from Sweeney's book. When Sweeney announced in 2003 his intention to run for reelection in 2005, Stern and other dissidents organized the New Unity Partnership (NUP), which contested existing AFL-CIO policy on issues such as union mergers and jurisdiction rights. It also charged that too many of the new programs and institutes set up by Sweeney were a waste of money and that some should be combined or eliminated so that their resources could be devoted to organizing. His NUP opponents also felt that Sweeney and the AFL-CIO should reduce political spending and concentrate on winning at the point of production rather than in Congress, where the Democratic Party had proved to be a poor ally. The NUP dissolved in 2005 and Sweeney was reelected, but shortly thereafter the SEIU, Teamsters, UFWA, and two other unions dropped out of the AFL-CIO and formed the rival **Change to Win Federation**.

Sweeney retired in 2009. It may be too early to evaluate his legacy, but the early judgment is one of promise derailed. Some critics charge that he misjudged the appropriateness of transplanting SEIU tactics to the AFL-CIO, though more believe that the problems are inherent within the AFL-CIO rather than any personal failing on Sweeney's behalf. There is little evidence to suggest that John Sweeney was disingenuous in his commitment to changing the AFL-CIO. Sweeney's inability to transform AFL-CIO culture and the continuing decline of labor unions call into question whether that **labor federation**, as currently constituted, can be an effective vehicle in advancing worker rights in a changing economic world.

Suggested Reading

Gary Chaison, "The AFL-CIO Split: Does It Really Matter?" *Journal of Labor Research* 28, no. 2 (Spring 2007): 301–311; John Sweeney and David Kusnet, *America Needs a Raise: Fighting for Economic Security and Social Justice*, 2000; Lowell Turner, Harry C. Katz, and Richard Hurd, eds., *Rekindling the Movement: Labor's Quest for Relevance in the 21st Century*, 2001; *Who's Who 2002*, 2002.

SYLVIS, WILLIAM H.

William H. Sylvis (November 26, 1828–July 27, 1869) was a Philadelphia iron molder and the visionary behind the **National Labor Union** (NLU), the first important post-**Civil War** attempt at forming a **labor federation**.

He was born in Armagh, Pennsylvania, the son of Nicholas and Maria (Mott) Sylvis. After his father's wagon-making business failed, the family moved frequently as Nicholas searched for work. When William was 11, he boarded with a Susquehanna, Pennsylvania, Whig politician who befriended the Sylvis family and provided William with his only formal education. At age 18, Sylvis became an **apprentice iron** molder. Six years later, he married 15-year-old Amelia Thomas and the couple settled in Philadelphia two years later. The couple had four sons before Amelia died in 1865. The next year he married Florrie Hunter, who bore Sylvis a fifth son.

Iron molders, who made stoves and specialty iron products, were highly skilled **artisans** whose **wages** exceeded those of workers in most other trades. Until the 1850s, molders retained great control over their craft and often operated their own foundries. Sylvis himself was briefly part-owner of a small foundry, though he usually worked as a **journeyman** molder. By the mid-1850s, however, a separate owner class had emerged in the molding trade, and it sought to wrest workplace control from independent molders. Sylvis participated in a **strike** in 1857, and was soon chosen as secretary for his local union. In 1859, he helped convene a Philadelphia convention from which the National Union of Iron Molders (NUIM) was born in 1860, with Sylvis serving as treasurer. He also authored its fiery constitution that accused organized wealth of degrading workers.

The demise of the Whig Party and the coming of the **Civil War** forced Sylvis to reevaluate his priorities. He became a Democrat when the Whigs' organization disintegrated and originally opposed both Abraham Lincoln's election and the Civil War itself. Although he opposed **slavery**, Sylvis saw the war as a disruption that would sidetrack unionization efforts. Once the war began in earnest, however, he supported the Union cause and served in a workers' militia. He left active duty in 1863 and returned to union activism, reorganizing the NUIM as the Iron Moulders' International Union (IMIU) and serving as its president.

Sylvis organized ceaselessly for the IMIU and by 1865, two-thirds of all molders were union members. Employers attempted to quash the movement by hiring more unskilled hands and by forming associations dedicated to combating the IMIU. Sylvis, however, had built a strong strike fund and an 1866 strike forced owners to capitulate. Sylvis took away from the struggle the need for even greater coordination between unions. Like many others of his generation—a time in which the permanence of **capitalism** was not a foregone conclusion— he also hoped for a future society in which economic activity would be organized around worker-controlled **cooperatives**. Sylvis felt that labor needed a national umbrella organization to represent all trades, and was the guiding spirit behind the 1866 Baltimore labor congress that created the NLU, even though he was not physically present at the meeting. The NLU came to life in 1866 and Sylvis became the co-editor of its journal, *Working Man's Advocate*. At the 1868 convention, Sylvis was elected NLU president.

The NLU was a full-fledged labor federation in name only; it held yearly congresses to which constituent unions sent representatives based on how many members they had. Estimates of NLU membership vary from 350,000 to 700,000; in practice, most NLU members were unaware that they belonged to the organization because they conducted their affairs through parent unions that had acceded to the NLU's broad reform agenda. Sylvis did what he could to give substance to the organization's demands. He was among the voices pressing President Ulysses S. Grant to enforce a recently enacted **eight-hour** workday law for federal employees. He also supported the **greenback** movement seeking to reform the nation's monetary policy. Sylvis was also convinced that a **working-class/middle-class** alliance was needed to reform society; thus he urged the seating of non-wage workers as NLU convention delegates. He also advocated limited suffrage for women and welcomed Susan B. Anthony, **Kate Mullaney**, and two other women to the 1868 convention, despite resistance from numerous male NLU members, When Sylvis ascended to the NLU presidency, he promptly appointed Mullaney as an assistant secretary in charge of organizing female workers. In a comparable spirit of inclusiveness, Sylvis urged the NLU to work with the International Workingmen's Association (IWA), a European-based **socialist** organization, and attended an 1869 IWA congress in Switzerland. He also urged African Americans to join the NLU, and several attended its 1870 congress, just two years after the NLU had rejected a proposal to admit black members. For a time, the NLU worked closely with the **Colored National Labor Union**.

Much of the NLU's promise evaporated after Sylvis's death. He died in July 1869, shortly after returning to Philadelphia from an organizing tour of the South. He was

40 when he passed away and had never enjoyed robust health, although early death was a hallmark of working-class life at the time. Without his guidance, NLU's ties to women, African Americans, and the IWA weakened. The NLU disappeared shortly after the 1872 election.

Sylvis is considered by many scholars to have been the prototype of a more modern labor leader. Many of his ideas and tactics were well in advance of the time. In later years, quite a few of his ideals were adopted by the **Knights of Labor**.

Suggested Reading

John R. Commons, *History of Labour in the United States, Vol. 2*, 1918; Jonathan Grossman, *William Sylvis: Pioneer of Labor*, 1973 (reprint of 1945 original); David Montgomery, "William Sylvis and the Search for Working-Class Citizenship," in *Labor Leaders in America*, Melvin Dubofsky and Warren Van Tine, eds., 1987.

SYMPATHY STRIKE

A sympathy strike is a self-defining term that refers to a work stoppage held in **solidarity** with another group of workers who have walked out or been **locked out**. Although sympathy strikers may face problems of their own, their walkout is usually not related to a **grievance** with their own employer. Sympathy strikes were held as demonstrations of **working-class** solidarity with the goal of forcing **capitalists** to pressure one another to resolve labor disputes. During the 1934 San Francisco dock **strike**, for example, Atlantic Coast **longshoremen** used the tactic to express their solidarity with striking West Coat comrades.

The 1947 **Taft-Hartley Act** outlawed use of sympathy strikes, though many workers ignore the law. For example, in 1996, members of the **United Auto Workers of America** walked off their jobs in Michigan in support of striking Dayton, Ohio, brake workers. Pilots and flight attendants have ignored the ban, as have teachers striking on behalf of support workers.

There are also ways around the ban on sympathy strikes. If workers in one union are on strike at a particular location, workers from other unions might plead that they felt it was too dangerous to cross **picket lines**. Most unions honor picket lines and refuse to cross them. The **National Labor Relations Act** also provides two malleable exceptions to sympathy strike bans. Workers can engage in them if the act being protected was deemed an **unfair labor practice**, or if they can argue that they are protesting an inherently dangerous situation. The sympathy strike remains a potent, if risky, tactic.

Suggested Reading

Ellis Boal, "Sympathy Strikes and the Law: Is Solidarity Legal?" *Labor Notes*, October 23, 2008; Helen Marot, *American Labor Unions*, 2006 (reprint of 1909 original).

TAFT-HARTLEY ACT

From the vantage point of labor unions, the Taft-Hartley Act is the single most unpopular piece of labor legislation ever enacted. The bill is officially an amendment to the **National Labor Relations Act** (NLRA) known as the Labor-Management Relations Act, but its common name acknowledges its two **Republican** cosponsors, Senator Robert Taft of Ohio and Representative Fred Hartley of New Jersey. The Taft-Hartley Act placed numerous restrictions on labor unions that do not apply to businesses and has been denounced as a "slave labor" bill. It was enacted in June 1947 when the Republican-controlled Congress overrode the veto of **Democratic** President Harry Truman. This action cemented the alliance between Democrats and organized labor and served further to label the Republican Party as "anti-union."

The Taft-Hartley Act is the product of a singular moment in American political history. Labor unions made unprecedented gains during the New Deal, including the passage of the NLRA. Rising levels of worker activism, including the dramatic **sit-down strikes** of the 1930s, drove those gains. Labor's willingness to cooperate with the **National War Labor Board** during World War led to additional protections for unions. Industrial, banking, and commercial leaders were appalled by what they saw as the anti-business slant of President Franklin Roosevelt and sought to undermine the New Deal, portraying it as a dangerous form of **socialism**. By 1945, however, more than 36 percent of all workers were enrolled in labor unions and preferential shops abounded. The U.S. Supreme Court's ruling that the NLRA was constitutional, Roosevelt's political finesse, and the president's popularity among **working-class** voters all combined to derail attempts to reverse the New Deal.

Roosevelt's death in 1945, the end of the war, and the changing fortunes of the Republican Party (nicknamed the Grand Old Party [GOP]) provided an opportunity for New Deal opponents to roll back pro-labor legislation during the postwar years. During the 1946 Congressional elections, GOP candidates seized upon the radicalism of the sit-down strikers, the unpopularity of the **coal miners strike of 1943** in which the **United Mine Workers of America** (UMWA) refused to honor a **no-strike pledge**, and the 1946 strike wave to portray labor unions as too powerful. The GOP was able to win control of both the House of Representatives and the Senate, thereby handcuffing President Harry Truman when he sought to expand the New Deal. The Republicans' margin of victory—246-188 in the House of Representatives and 51-45 in the Senate—allowed these legislators to advance the Taft-Hartley Act during 1947. Truman dutifully vetoed the bill, but the GOP was able to draw upon the support of conservative southern Democrats, especially those known as "Dixiecrats," to override the veto.

The Taft-Hartley Act has nine major clauses, most of which have a decided bias toward employers. The legislation curtailed preferential shops by stipulating that union-controlled shops could exist only when a union represents the majority of eligible voters and new employees have an equal say with union members. It gives new hires 30 days to decide whether they wish to join a union, a provision that unions find unfair given that the very **wages** at which new employees are hired are the result of union **collective bargaining**. In effect, new hires are "free riders" who have not paid **dues**, but who can make decisions about the union's role in the workplace. Even more damaging, the bill provides language that allows individual states to outlaw "closed shops" altogether and declare themselves **right-to-work** states.

Taft-Hartley also requires unions to give a 60-day advance notice of their intent to call a **strike** vote, a clause that unions charge allows employers to prepare for work stoppages in unfair ways such as stockpiling inventory, recruiting **scabs**, and launching anti-union publicity campaigns. The law also gives the federal government authority to issue an 80-day anti-strike **injunction** in enterprises it deems as "essential" to national interests. Work stoppages during this "cooling-off" period are illegal under the Taft-Hartley Act.

Unions particularly despise Taft-Hartley's expansion of **unfair labor practices** to outlaw sit-down strikes, secondary **boycotts, jurisdictional** strikes, and **wildcat strikes**. In some cases, employers are even allowed to discontinue the automatic **checkoff** system, thereby making it harder for unions to collect **dues**. Taft-Hartley also gives employers the right to express their opinions about unions seeking to organize their workplaces, which unions interpret as a form of intimidation that the NLRA sought to ban. They also charge that, under the guise of free speech, employers are given free reign to engage in anti-union propaganda and veiled threats against employees. Moreover, employers are allowed to sue unions for breach of contract and to spearhead **decertification** drives. These have the net effect of legitimizing anti-union tactics such as the **Mohawk Valley Formula**.

The Taft-Hartley Act also responded to the emerging **Cold War** and **Red Scare** by requiring union officers to file affidavits stating that they were not members of the Communist Party. This mandate stifled grassroots activism and eventually led labor federations to purge themselves of radical unions and unions to jettison rank-and-file ideologues. Unions are also required to file their constitutions and yearly financial statements with the **Department of Labor**. On the surface, these provisions may appear to be logical or appropriate, but neither was required of private corporations.

The rise of political action committees was an unintended effect of the Taft-Hartley Act. Republicans sought to undermine the alliance between labor unions and the Democratic Party by forbidding unions from making direct or indirect contributions to political candidates. This dictum was easily sidestepped when unions set up "independent" political action committees (PACs). PACs of all sort are now standard in American politics, a reality that leads many reformers to worry that money now unduly influences American politics.

The Taft-Hartley Act reconfigured capital/labor relations and helped tip the power balance toward capital. That was its intent. Congressman Hartley hated unions and hoped his bill would destroy them. That outcome did not occur, but the right to strike was severely curtailed and postwar militancy evaporated. Anticommunist provisos and the spectacular failure of the **Congress of Industrial Organizations'** (CIO) efforts to unionize the South during **Operation Dixie** led both it and the **American Federation of Labor** (AFL) to fall in line with the assumptions of Cold War unionism. Rank-and-file activism and grassroots organizing declined, **business unionism** became standard practice, and capital/labor disputes often shifted from the workplace to the courtroom and the ballot box. Organized labor has often not fared well in either the courts or elections. The desire to overturn the Taft-Hartley legislation prompted the AFL and the CIO to set aside their disagreements and paved the way for the 1955 merger of the two labor federations, but labor made little headway in getting Congress to repeal the act. Political stasis meant that the votes were simply not there to overturn the bill. In 1948, for instance, the Democrats regained control of the House of Representatives, but the GOP retained a majority in the Senate. The best opportunity to repeal Taft-Hartley occurred in 1950, when Democrats controlled both houses of Congress and the presidency, but Dixiecrats blocked their repeal efforts. The moment was lost in 1952, when Republican Dwight Eisenhower won the presidency and GOP candidates rode his coattails to recapture Congress.

Grassroots efforts to defy the Taft-Hartley Act have not fared much better. The CIO threatened to conduct **general strikes** to bring down the law, but those threats proved more rhetorical than actual. The UMWA openly ignored the law, but made only modest gains by doing so and, in some cases, invited the wrath of vigilantes given free reign by local law enforcement officials. By the end of the 1950s, Taft-Hartley had become institutionalized, which weakened efforts to revise or scrap it. Most unions—including the AFL-CIO—instead pinned their hopes on political solutions by backing liberal candidates and lobbying for pro-labor appointments to the National Labor Relations Board. Disdain for the act also pushed unions even deeper into alliance with the Democratic Party, which has consistently supported—though never implemented—changes to the law. Its failure to muster enough support to alter Taft-Hartley had led some unions to question the usefulness of supporting Democrats.

Nearly every union in the nation has called for repeal of the Taft-Hartley Act and continues to do so, though it is now such a defining part of capital/labor relations that repeal is unlikely and calls for such an action sound increasingly archaic. Taft-Hartley is not solely responsible for organized labor's diminished strength in recent decades, but it definitely hampers unions' ability to battle employers on legal grounds. A new generation of labor activists calls for workers simply to ignore the law and fight for justice in the workplace in defiance of it. At present, such a tactic would be very risky and few unions have the human or capital resources to wage such a battle.

Suggested Reading

Millie Beik, *Labor Relations*, 2005; Mike Davis, *Prisoners of the American Dream: Politics and Economy in the History of the US Working Class*, 2000; Taft-Hartley Act, http://

www.historycentral.com/documents/Tafthatley.html, accessed July 6, 2011; Christopher Tomlins, *The State and the Unions*, 1986.

TARIFFS AND LABOR

Tariff is another word for tax. The type that most concerns American workers are those taxes placed on goods and services that either imported into the United States or exported. Tariffs have been and remain economically complex, socially controversial, and politically divisive. Working people, like the politicians who design and enact tariffs, have split into various camps over tariffs. Generally speaking, one's point of view on tariffs largely depends upon whether one sees production and markets in national or international terms and whether one is a consumer or a producer. Nations whose import tariffs are too high face retaliatory tariffs from trading partners; moreover, manufacturers that produce goods dependent upon imported raw materials are saddled with higher production costs. Conversely, nations have historically depended upon tariffs to fund government services. This was certainly true of the United States; tariffs were its single largest revenue source until after World War I.

In contemporary **capitalism**, prevailing business sentiment generally concedes that **globalization** has created worldwide markets. Most American businesses and investors favor low tariffs so that goods and services can move freely. This was not always the case. Alexander Hamilton and other Federalists favored high tariffs as a way of encouraging the development of American enterprise. Although Federalist support for manufacturing met with fierce opposition from Thomas Jefferson and supporters of **agrarianism**, the American **Industrial Revolution** that began in the early 19th century took place within a political context in which **protectionism**, not free trade, was dominant.

Early debates over the tariff encapsulate some of the ways in which working people have split over tariffs. Workers producing finished goods favored high tariffs, whereas those engaged in agriculture and extraction of raw materials favored lower ones. A textile worker, for example, was more likely to support high tariffs as a way to protect his job and **wages** from cheaper British textiles that would flood the market if import duties were lowered. Those producing cotton, however, desired low tariffs so that the market for cotton could expand overseas. It was precisely this debate that precipitated the Nullification Crisis of 1832–1833, which many historians see as a factor in fomenting the sectional tension that led to the **Civil War**. A high tariff enacted in 1828 led South Carolina, a cotton exporter, to assert states' rights by threatening to nullify the tax.

After the Civil War, tariffs also proved a factor that retarded the **solidarity** of the **working class**. Wage-earners (then and now) have been inconsistent in their views on tariffs. As producers, they favored high ones to protect their jobs; as consumers, they wanted low tariffs on agricultural goods so that food prices remained low. This proved an obstacle for groups seeking to forge collective **class consciousness** between urban workers and farmers, such as proponents of **greenbackism**, the **National Labor Movement**, and **Populism**. Their struggles anticipated today's situation in which many of the same workers who call for protective tariffs and the reindustrialization of America also desire cheap consumer goods and food products, many of which come from abroad. During the 1980s, the **American Federation of Labor-Congress of Industrial Organizations** (AFL-CIO) launched a "Buy American" campaign to encourage consumers to **boycott** foreign-made goods. It was a failure for numerous reasons, not the least of which is that favorable tax laws allowed firms to move their assets offshore and blur the distinction, for example, between a Ford made in Europe and one made in Michigan. Mostly the AFL-CIO campaign failed for the same reason that contemporary Wal-Mart boycotts falter: Consumer behavior is generally shaped by price more than values. (Among the notable exceptions has been an anti-sweatshop boycott of college-logo goods.)

Political views on tariffs have evolved and shifted. As noted, in developing industrial economies such as that of the United States in the 19th century, high tariffs were deemed necessary to protect nascent industries from cheaper foreign imports. Today's **Republican Party** generally supports low tariffs and **fast-track legislation** to expand free trade networks; in the 19th century, the party usually took exactly the opposite position. In each case, however, Republicans' position was the one favored by the business community, the difference being that the United States was more focused on developing domestic production and markets for much of the 19th century. The 1890 McKinley Tariff, for instance, raised import duties by 50 percent to protect American manufacturers. By contrast, both before and after the Civil War, the **Democratic Party**, which drew its strength from farm voters, favored lower tariffs. Although higher protective tariffs remained the norm until after World War I, tariffs were hotly debated from the late 18th century onward, and the level at which they stood generally depended upon which party was in power. Both parties, however, sought to develop nuanced positions depending on the circumstances. Thus tariffs might be low on some items but high on others. The 1913 Underwood Tariff, for instance, is generally viewed as a low tariff; it did drastically reduce the tariff on more than 100 items, but left the rate untouched on hundreds of others.

In broad terms, most American labor unions and leaders have favored higher tariffs. This stance makes sense given that protecting jobs and securing higher wages is among the very reasons why they exist in the first place. The **Knights of Labor**, the AFL, and the CIO are among the **labor federations** that have supported protectionism. They also did so because, for the most part, there are far more restrictions on the movement of labor than of goods. Trade agreements are relatively easily negotiated, but workers seeking to cross borders must contend with national **immigration** policies. **Henry George** was among the few 19th-century labor leaders to advocate free trade, a position that may have contributed to his losing 1886 bid to become New York City mayor. In the 20th century, the **Industrial Workers of the World** called for free movement of workers around the globe, but this was and remains an unrealized ideal. Consider, for instance, the fact that under the 1993 **North American Free Trade Agreement** goods move freely between the United States and Mexico, but that undocumented Mexican workers crossing into the United States are subject to arrest, fines, imprisonment, and deportation.

Insofar as politics is concerned, free trade and low tariffs are the established order of contemporary economic life. Contemporary globalization structures began to take shape after World War II, with U.S. involvement in the **General Agreement on Tariffs and Trade**. Globalization trends accelerated from the 1970s onward and contributed to the **deindustrialization** of the United States. Currently the movement is toward even lower trade barriers, though advocates for rebuilding American industry continue to call for protective tariffs. The AFL-CIO called for high tariffs on Japanese-produced goods in the 1970s and currently supports higher tariffs on Japanese-, Vietnamese-, and Thai-made goods. Although a higher tariff policy is unlikely to emerge in the immediate future, the uncertainty of the future job market suggests that it is premature to say that the tariff debate is settled.

Suggested Reading

George B. Mangold, *The Labor Argument in the American Protective Tariff Discussion*, 2009 (reprint of 1908 original); John H. Narton, Judith L. Goldstein, Timothy E. Josling, and Richard H. Steinberg, *The Evolution of the Trade Regime: Politics, Law, and Economics of the GATT and the WTO*, 2008; Elaine C. Prange Turney and Cynthia Clark Northrup, *Tariffs and Trade in U.S. History: An Encyclopedia*, 2003.

TAYLORISM

Taylorism, also known as scientific management, is a production system based on principles outlined by Frederick Winslow Taylor in 1911. The key to Taylorism is efficiency, defined as maximizing worker output. It is the polar opposite of the **utopian** vision of **Edward Bellamy**, which envisioned a future production system in which all citizens worked in an industrial army in accordance with quotas set by a state planning board and all workers were remunerated equally. In many respects, Bellamy's vision of the future was one of collective **socialism** and Taylor's that of hyper-capitalism. Under Bellamy's approach, all labor, goods, and services benefited society; in contrast, Taylor designed a system in which greater individual profit was generated.

Taylor sought to break down all production into a series of easy-to-learn tasks. He then used time-and-motion studies pioneered by Frank and Lillian Gilbreth to reorganize tasks efficiently by eliminating needless motion. All work was designed by a planning department, which delegated the oversight of worker efficiency to line supervisors. Taylor recommended separate supervisors for setup, line speed, quality, and repairs. The goal was to increase output at a rate greater than remuneration. Taylor counseled the use of motivational tools such as incentive pay, bonuses, and **piecework** rates to get workers to increase their output. He hoped that workers would buy into the idea of increasing their wages. If, for example, a workman loading steel could be convinced to increase his workload by 20 percent as a reward for increasing his pay by 10 percent, this would result in a 10 percent savings for the firm. Taylor did not, however, base his entire system on incentives; a major component of Taylorism was the constant surveillance of the workforce.

Taylor's methods were so harsh, dehumanizing, and resented that most business leaders deemed them impractical as designed and adopted modified versions. In 1933, sociologist Elton Mayo challenged Taylor's assumptions and redefined efficiency as a worker's social capacity. He developed methods today known as human relations, which focuses on **fringe benefit** packages, group work, respect, and development of a distinct workplace culture. In some form or other, though, Taylor ideals such as central planning, time-and-motion studies, incentive pay, piecework, and worker surveillance became common features in American business firms. Most workers deeply despised Taylorism, especially when combined with the **assembly-line** discipline known as **Fordism**. As Mayo predicted, workers found informal and formal ways to resist Taylorism, ranging from **stints** or **sabotage** to union organizing and **strikes**. By the early 1970s, worker alienation was so high on assembly lines that many manufacturers sought to reconfigure production methods. Nonetheless, Taylorism persists in the American workplace, especially those in which workers are closely monitored. It also remains resented and resisted.

Suggested Reading

Frank Gilbreth and Lillian Gilbreth, *Cheaper by the Dozen*, 1949; Frank Gilbreth and Lillian Gilbreth, *Motion Stud: A Method for Increasing the Efficiency of the Workman*, 1911; Elton Mayo, *The Human Problems of Industrial Civilization*, 2003 (reprint of 1933 original); Frederick Winslow Taylor, *The Principles of Scientific Management*, 1911.

TEAM ACT. *See* Company Union.

TEAMSTERS

Teamsters are workers who load and haul goods. Although teamsters are generally associated with the trucking industry, the name predates the automotive age and reflects the fact that horse-, oxen-, or mule-drawn carts once moved freight. Skill was required at controlling the "team" of draft animals reined together.

In organizational parlance, Teamsters are members of the International Brotherhood of Teamsters (IBT), the labor union formed in Niagara Falls, New York, in 1903 when the Midwest-based Team Drivers International Union (TDIU) merged with the rival Teamsters National Union and several smaller groups. The IBT today also represents workers who are not directly involved in moving freight. The IBT is probably the most controversial labor union in American history, as its history of racketeering has resulted in several of its presidents being sent to jail. Although most of these unsavory incidents occurred decades ago, many Americans continue to view the Teamsters negatively. Those who use the term "Big Labor" in a pejorative sense often invoke the Teamsters during the presidency of **James R. Hoffa**.

Samuel Gompers, head of the **American Federation of Labor** (AFL), was influential in bringing about the merger that created the IBT, in part because the TDIU

Police confront striking Teamsters armed with pipes in the streets of Minneapolis, Minnesota, in June 1934. (National Archives)

was already affiliated with the AFL. The new organization chose Cornelius Shea as its president. The IBT won respect from other unions as it engaged in numerous **sympathy strikes** in support of the larger labor movement. An IBT sympathy strike was a powerful weapon given that American cities were dependent upon Teamsters to deliver foodstuffs and other necessities. Sympathy strikes also severely damaged the young union when, in 1905, the IBT called one in support of striking tailors employed by Montgomery Ward. In this violent 100-day strike, 21 workers lost their lives and 25,000 Teamsters suffered lost wages. Shea held onto his presidency despite the strike's loss, but it played a major role in the IBT's 1907 decision to replace him with Daniel Tobin, who would head the IBT until 1952.

Tobin oversaw the craft's transformation from one dependent upon draft animals to one in which gasoline-powered trucks took over the job of hauling freight and goods. In addition, he moved the IBT away from spontaneous sympathy strikes and sought to centralize and streamline IBT operations. One feature of his plan involved setting up "joint councils" that operated like mandatory **central labor unions**. These had the effect of breaking the power of **union locals**, which Tobin believed too often called ill-advised **strikes**. Tobin was reluctant to call strikes and preferred negotiating standardized **contracts** with employers. He did not, however, shy from battling other unions. During the **Progressive Era** the IBT was embroiled in numerous **raiding** incidents and **jurisdictional** battles with other unions, especially the International Longshoremen's and Warehousemen's Union (ILWU) and organizations representing **brewery workers**.

The IBT enjoyed growth under Tobin, especially during World War I, and Teamsters were among the first workers to win enforceable **overtime** pay. By 1925, the IBT had more than $1 million in resources, which enabled Tobin to increase strike benefits, seek alliances with the Canadian Trades and Labor Congress, and financially support other struggling unions.

During the Great Depression, the IBT sought to organize long-haul truckers. Key to this effort was gaining control of the truck terminals and using such control to organize the truckers. The IBT also engaged in interracial organizing and, by the mid-1930s, was among the AFL's more progressive unions on issues of race. Tobin welcomed President Franklin Roosevelt's New Deal and sought a political alliance with the Democratic coalition, but controversy and internal conflict dogged the IBT. Tobin and the IBT engaged in several bruising jurisdictional battles with the ILWU for the right to organize warehouse workers, and sometimes came out second best, as ILWU President **Harry Bridges** was a far more capable leader. In 1933–1934, the IBT also saw **Trotskyites** organize teamsters in Minneapolis and engage in a traumatic **general strike**. Tobin, an ardent opponent of **communism**, expelled the victorious strikers from the IBT, an act that so outraged the rank-and-file that he was forced to reverse course and recharter the Minneapolis local.

During World War II, the IBT's 530,000 members made it one of the most powerful unions in the United States. Tobin led the IBT to take a **no-strike pledge** during the war and spearheaded such popular actions as war bond sales, scrap metal and rubber drives, and seniority rights for union members returning from the armed services. Despite these steps, the IBT did sanction several strikes during the war and was plagued by accusations of corruption. It is a measure of the IBT's strength that despite these allegations, Tobin served on several presidential committees and twice turned down offers to serve as secretary of labor. When he sought to isolate the IBT from the post–World War II strike wave, however, he fell out of favor with IBT members and was effectively isolated. Most scholars studying the IBT assert that by 1948, de facto leadership of the IBT had passed to Dave Beck and James Hoffa. The two led a raid on employees who belonged to the **International Association of Machinists and Aerospace Workers** at Boeing that outraged Tobin.

In 1952, Tobin officially stepped down and was replaced by Beck, who expanded Tobin's strategy of creating multistate bargaining units, conducting area-wide negotiations, and establishing airtight control of trucking terminals—the last task allegedly accomplished with the aid of organized crime. This strategy assured almost certain victory in the event of a strike. Beck was also able to negotiate a nationwide master agreement for Teamsters as well as nationwide **grievance** procedures. The IBT grew stronger, thanks in part of the Federal-Aid Highway Act of 1956, which established the interstate highway system and assured the dominance of long-haul trucking in the nation's freight delivery system. Beck could not, however, withstand repeated Congressional investigations into the IBT's ties with organized crime, many of which allegedly dated to the days of Prohibition. In 1957, Beck invoked the Fifth Amendment 117 times during U.S. Senate hearings into Teamsters corruption. He would not be convicted until 1959 or go to jail until 1962, but Jimmy Hoffa took advantage of his weakness and replaced Beck as IBT president in 1957.

Hoffa was one of the most controversial labor leaders in American history. He was viewed as so corrupt that the **American Federation of Labor-Congress of Industrial Organizations** (AFL-CIO) demanded that the IBT replace him. When that did not happen, the AFL-CIO expelled the IBT in December 1957. Despite the racketeering allegations made about Hoffa, the IBT's political influence grew under Hoffa, in part because the union established DRIVE (Democratic, Republican, and Independent Voter Education) as a political action committee in 1959. Hoffa's clashes with Robert Kennedy, first as a Senate counsel in the late 1950s and then as U.S. attorney general in his brother John Kennedy's administration, made sensational headlines, but Hoffa was often beloved by the IBT rank-and-file. Under his leadership, Teamsters enjoyed steady advances in wages and benefits. In 1964, the Teamsters signed the National Master Freight Agreement (NMFA), a contract for 400,000 members employed by 16,000 trucking companies. The NMFA strengthened benefits, **pensions**, and working conditions for members. That same year Hoffa was finally convicted of racketeering and, in 1967, entered federal prison. Hoffa would be pardoned by Richard Nixon, but would disappear in 1975.

Frank Fitzsimmons, who would serve until 1981, succeeded Hoffa. Fitzsimmons sought to clean up some of the abuses of the IBT, and even brought the IBT into the short-lived **Alliance for Labor Action** (ALA), a progressive **labor federation**, in 1968. He did, however, share his predecessors' penchant for engaging in jurisdictional disputes, most famously a battle with the **United Farm Workers of America** that lasted from 1970 until 1977. Fitzsimmons never established himself as the strong leader that Hoffa had been, and the union continued to face allegations of underworld domination. Despite attempts at reform, it was estimated that one-third of IBT locals were dominated by organized crime, one-third were partly tainted, and just one-third were free from corruption. Before retiring in 1981, Fitzsimmons led an unsuccessful battle against **deregulation** of the trucking industry.

Both Roy Williams and Jackie Presser, the two presidents who followed Fitzsimmons, were indicted for racketeering—Williams in 1982, and Presser in 1985 and again in 1987. Presser's legal woes were ironic given that he had served as an FBI informant for the Williams investigation. Under Williams and Presser, the IBT moved sharply to the right politically. The IBT was one of just two major unions to endorse **Ronald Reagan** for president in 1980 and it routinely endorsed Republican candidates until the 1990s. Deregulation, consolidation, and ongoing struggles against internal corruption led to a decline in IBT strength, however. By the mid-1990s, the union's rolls had dwindled to approximately 200,000 members, a dip of more than 60 percent in just two decades. This decrease took place despite the IBT's decision to reaffiliate with the AFL-CIO in 1985.

Internal pressures, including the reform group Teamsters for a Democratic Union (TDU), managed to clean up some of the corruption inside the IBT. A milestone was reached in 1991, when reformer Ron Carey—who helped negotiate the union's readmittance to the AFL-CIO—fought off two establishment candidates and was elected IBT president. Carey shifted the IBT back toward a closer relationship with the **Democratic Party** and enjoyed easy access to AFL-CIO officials. He did not, however, manage to consolidate his power throughout the IBT. In 1996, Carey won apparent reelection as IBT president, only to have the election results challenged by James P. Hoffa, the son of the former IBT head. Despite the IBT's well-publicized victory in the 1997 United Parcel Services strike, Hoffa defeated Carey in a new election held in 1998; he continues to hold the presidency today.

Hoffa has expanded the IBT base into industrial manufacturing, the public service sector, food processing, and the newspaper, airline, and pipeline industries. Employers often fight IBT organizing drives by resurrecting charges of IBT corruption, but the younger Hoffa has avoided such taint. The IBT has also shifted to political positions more in keeping with its ALA period. It embraces a host of environmental initiatives and has special caucuses devoted to issues germane to women, African Americans, Latinos, and non-heterosexuals. In 2005, the IBT left the AFL-CIO and joined the **Change to Win Federation**. As of 2010, the union claimed to represent 1.4 million workers.

Suggested Reading

Steven Brill, *The Teamsters*, 1978; Teamsters, http://www.teamster.org/content, accessed December 30, 2010; Walter Sheridan, *The Rise and Fall of Jimmy Hoffa*, 1972; David Witwer, *Corruption and Reform in the Teamsters Union*, 2003.

TERRORISM AND LABOR

Labor unions responded to the terrorist attacks of September 11, 2001, with the same sense of horror, loss, and patriotism as other Americans. More than 600 union members lost their lives in the plane crash in Pennsylvania and the attacks on Washington, D.C., and New York City.

Terrorist attacks on the United States—including the foiled attempt to blow up New York's World Trade Center in 1993—have led to ongoing political and social changes, some positive and some controversial. Among the 2,819 people who died when the World Trade Center towers collapsed in 2001 were 343 firefighters, 23 New York City police officers, and another 37 law enforcement officials employed by the Port Authority of New York and New Jersey. Their deaths drew renewed attention to working people. Police and fire fighters were valorized as **blue-collar** heroes and became the focus of adoration at sporting events, parades, and public forums. In like fashion, films, TV shows, and popular music championed "ordinary" Americans.

The terrorist attacks also magnified ways in which the adoration of working people sometimes rings hollow. In November 2002, President George W. Bush signed the Homeland Security Act (HSA), which was designed to combat terrorism on U.S. soil. The HSA expanded the powers of agencies such as the Federal Bureau of Investigation (FBI), but also consolidated functions of numerous other agencies under the aegis of the Office of Homeland Security (OHS). Particularly troubling to federal workers was Section 730 of the HSA, which would have given the OHS broad leeway in defining jobs, assigning tasks, and making personnel decisions. Under Section 730, **collective bargaining** rights would have been greatly curtailed, a policy that would have affected 40,000 unionized federal employees working in agencies such as Immigration and Naturalization Services, the Custom Service Treasury Department, and Animal and Plant Health Services—all agencies absorbed by the OHS. President Bush also announced that airport security hires for the newly created Transportation Security Administration (TSA) would be non-unionized. Labor unions charged, in an argument with considerable merit, that Bush was politicizing terrorism to pursue a personal anti-union bias. In the case of the TSA, this was quite clear, as airport screeners had long been represented by the **American Federation of Government Employees** (AFGE).

The Bush administration attempted to forge ahead with plans to give OHS senior administrators broad powers in all matters related to employment and working conditions. In June 2006, however, the District of Columbia branch of the U.S. Court of Appeals ruled that the OHS's efforts to curtail collective bargaining rights were illegal. In 2008, the Bush administration and the OHS quietly dropped their plans to revise labor relations within the OHS. That same year, reports surfaced that the FBI had misused HSA powers to spy on peace activists, Chicago campaign workers associated with Barack Obama, and unions such as the AFGE, the **Service Employees International Union** (SEIU), and the **American Federation of State, County, and Municipal Employees**.

Some of the tension between unions and OHS dissipated when Barack Obama was elected U.S. president in 2008. In 2011, TSA employees voted for the AFGE to become their sole collective bargaining unit. In other moves, the National Labor College added a bachelor of science degree in emergency readiness and response management and cooperates with the OHS in student training. The **American Federation of Labor-Congress of Industrial Organizations** supports the broad parameters of the HAS, and a recent revision of its constitution bans from membership any individual or group that supports terrorism.

Conflicts continue to arise, however; the SEIU, for example, is opposed to aggressive round-ups of illegal immigrants under the HSA. Many union members and civil libertarians continue to argue that the HSA endangers free speech, privacy, and other freedoms. They also charge that the HSA is often driven by a conservative ideological agenda.

Suggested Reading

William H. Holley, Kenneth Jennings, and Roger Wolters, *The Labor Relations Process*, 2008; "Union Members Lost to Terrorism," http://www.aflcio.org/aboutus/thisistheaflcio/convention/2001/911_lostunionmembers.cfm, accessed July 7, 2011; Peter Wallsten, "Peace Activists, Labor Decry FBI Terrorism Probe," *Washington Post*, June 14, 2011.

TEXTILE STRIKES (1934). *See* Depression-Era Strikes.

TEXTILE WORKERS UNION OF AMERICA. *See* Amalgamated Clothing Workers of America.

TIME-AND-MOTION STUDIES. *See* Taylorism.

TOMPKINS SQUARE RIOT

The Tompkins Square riot took place in New York City in 1874. Although it was not bloody by the standards of the late 19th century, historians often invoke it as the symbolic opening of the brutal battles between **capitalists** and labor in post-**Civil War** America. Some view it as a harbinger of the 1886 **Haymarket Square bombing** in Chicago.

The Panic of 1873 led to high unemployment in the United States and calls for government relief in the form of public works projects to put individuals to work. As the recession deepened, various **working-class** factions began to coalesce. On January 1, 1874, several thousand New York City workers, including **socialists**, trade unionists, and antimonopoly activists, created the Committee of Safety to pressure the city to provide jobs. Their efforts were rejected by government officials and ridiculed in the press—actions that emboldened the committee to distribute a circular demanding that $100,000 be allotted to a Labor Relief Bureau. Committee members also called for a January 13 rally in Tompkins Square to demonstrate the strength of the movement. **Solidarity** flagged, however, when a rival organization headed by bricklayer Patrick Dunn denounced Committee of Safety leaders as **communists** and organized his own march on City Hall on January 5. Many workers rejected Dunn's efforts and the march was sparsely attended, though two committee leaders, **Peter J. McGuire** and Theodore Banks, appeared and marched. Mayor William Havemeyer was absent and the committee had an fruitless meeting with the board of aldermen.

Growing impatience on the part of desperate workers caused Banks to call a new meeting for January 8, where approximately 1,000 workers met in Union Square. Instead of marching on City Hall, participants proceeded to Tompkins Square, where McGuire and several hundred others were waiting. McGuire counseled solidarity and called for a mass demonstration on January 13. He also demanded that the city halt evictions of unemployed tenants and that it deliver public aid. The swelling anger frightened city officials, as did alarmist and erroneous press reports that workers were stockpiling ammunition. Nonetheless, the Committee of Safety secured a permit to meet in Tompkins Square, though they were denied a parade permit to march to City Hall. Police were ordered to arrest anyone who encouraged workers to leave their jobs to take part in the demonstration. McGuire protested the restrictions and told of the desperation of impoverished **immigrant** workers, but was chided by Police Commissioner Oliver Gardner to confine his concerns to American citizens. He was also told that police would arrest anyone approaching City Hall, though there was no statute authorizing such actions. Appeals to Mayor Havemeyer were ignored.

Once again factionalism weakened worker solidarity. Committee President George Blair resigned; New York City's Iron Molders International Union denounced the committee as communists, internationalists, and **anarchists**; and Patrick Dunn reappeared to warn the police board that committee members were communists, a charge reinforced by the involvement of the American Section of the International Workingmen's Association (IWA).

Confusion reigned when January 13 finally arrived. Mayor Havemeyer had agreed to speak at the gathering, but abruptly reneged on his commitment and permits for the march were revoked. Despite the lack of permits and subfreezing temperatures, between 4,000 and 6,000 people gathered in Tompkins Square that morning. Most were immigrants, and many were women and children. Among the crowd were future **American Federation of Labor** founders **Samuel Gompers** and **Adolph Strasser**, and Lucian Sanial, who later played a prominent role in the Socialist Labor Party. To contain the crowd, some 1,600 police were present, including mounted squads. The IWA's involvement and the intent of radicals to speak led the police board to issue orders to suppress all meetings. Several dozen officers were stationed at public buildings throughout the city; others were posted on the perimeter of Tompkins Square, prepared to arrest anyone who defied police orders. Their presence served only to enlarge the crowd.

Around 11 A.M., the First Mounted Squad was ordered to fall in behind a group of the Committee of Safety members approaching Tompkins Square, where roughly 7,000 people were now gathered. Police Commissioner Abram Duryee and officers with truncheons walked into the crowd, ordered participants to disperse, and began to club bystanders. In the corner of the square, however, the German Tenth Ward Workingmen's Organization refused to move. One German immigrant, Joseph Hoefflicher, hit an officer with a cane. When that officer attacked Hoefflicher, he was dropped by a hammer blow from another German, Christian Mayer. Mounted police entered the square and routed the protesters. Tompkins Square was sealed off, and mounted policemen chased the fleeing crowds down the city streets, clubbing them in what Gompers later called "an orgy of brutality." According to Gompers, for the next several hours policemen attacked any group of poorly dressed persons standing or moving together. Forty-six arrests were made, and those who gathered outside of the Fifth Street Police Station to protest the arrests were also beaten.

Most of those arrested that day were foreign-born, including future anarchist leader Justus Schwab. None could afford bail, and all remained in jail pending arraignment. Hoefflicher and Mayer spent several months in prison on charges of assaulting police. On January 30, 1874, a large coalition, especially of Germans, assembled at the Cooper Union to protest police brutality and to demand that the police board be dismissed, that public aid be distributed, and that free speech rights be respected. Little came of this rally, but another in Tompkins Square on August 31 secured a pardon for Christian Mayer.

City officials and most local newspapers defended the actions of the police. *Harper's Weekly* evoked the specter of the Paris Commune, which had been suppressed less than two years earlier. Most newspapers joined in whipping up fears of immigrant radicals and of plots to overthrow American institutions. Only a handful of newspapers—including the *New York Sun*, the *New York Graphic*, and the *Cincinnati Enquirer*—expressed the view that police and the city had overreacted. Post-Tomkins Square hysteria established a pattern of anti-immigrant and anti-radical rhetoric that would be used against labor movements in the years to come; some historians believe, for example, that the alleged **Molly Maguires** conspiracy several years later was an invention of Pennsylvania coal barons that played off of fears resulting from the Tomkins Square riot.

Workers were left to contemplate the need for stronger organizations. The Committee of Public Safety reorganized as the Industrial Political Party, and several other **labor parties** formed, though most were short-lived. Some labor activists lost faith in democratic political institutions altogether; the riot probably did more to encourage anarchism than to stifle it. In the short term, in fact, many individuals were radicalized by Tomkins Square, including *New York Sun* editor John Swinton. P. J. McGuire and Adolph Strasser organized the Social Democratic Workingmen's Party later in 1874—an organization that Gompers briefly joined, though he (as well as Strasser) would later repudiate socialism.

Historians have noted parallels between the Tomkins Square riot and the Haymarket Square bombing 12 years later. Chicago newspapers gave extensive coverage to the events of 1874, most of them supporting New York police. The *Chicago Tribune* encouraged city elites to build and fund a local militia to deal with agitators there. In October 1874, Cyrus McCormick became an honorary member of the First Regiment of the Illinois National Guard. In 1886, a strike at McCormick's factory was the spark that led to violence.

Suggested Reading

Samuel Gompers, *Seventy Years of Life and Labor: An Autobiography*, 1925; Herbert Gutman, "The Tompkins Square Riot in New York City on January 13, 1874: A Re-examination of Its Causes and Its Aftermath," *Labor History* 1 (Winter 1965): 44–70; Michael Wallace and Edwin G. Burrows, *Gotham: A History of New York City to 1898*, 1998.

TRADE UNION EDUCATIONAL LEAGUE. *See* Trade Union Unity League.

TRADE UNION UNITY LEAGUE

The Trade Union Unity League (TUUL) was a Communist Party of the United States (CPUSA) attempt at forming an independent **labor federation**. It was created in 1929 and disbanded in 1935, when the **Popular Front** emerged. The TUUL was the successor to the Trade Union Educational League (TUEL), which was formed by **William Z. Foster** in 1920 and won the sanction of the CPUSA in 1922.

American **communists** faced a dilemma following World War I. On the one hand, classic **Marxist** theory held that **trade unions** would be the building blocks for a post-revolutionary society; on the other hand, the **American Federation of Labor** (AFL) was a cautious organization and many of its affiliates were more interested in preserving the privileges of **craft unionists** than in building **class consciousness**. The TUEL sought to "bore within" the AFL and convert its **rank-and-file** to revolutionary ideology and the virtues of **industrial unionism**. The TUEL was largely unsuccessful in its efforts; in fact, by 1928, the AFL expelled most of its communists. The TUEL's failure to make major inroads in the AFL (or even to win **strikes**) coincided with a change in the philosophy of the Moscow-directed Communist International (Comintern). The Comintern believed that **capitalism** was entering a new era in which social stability was weakened and that revolution was imminent.

The TUUL reversed the TUEL's tactics. Instead of seeking to bore within existing trade unions, the TUUL set up new bodies committed to principles of revolutionary unionism. The AFL had denounced TUEL membership as **dual unionism**. After 1929, the CPUSA sought to compete with AFL unions and engaged in **raiding** radical members from AFL bodies. The TUEL, for example, had set up the National Miners Union (NMU) and the National Textile Workers Union (NTWU). The AFL expelled these groups in 1928, but they continued as competitors to AFL groups such as the United Textile Workers and the **United Mine Workers of America**. The TUUL also organized industries largely untouched by the AFL, including steel and metal, automobiles, shoe and leather trades, lumber, canning, foundries, food, and marine transport. Its presence in heavy industries was a major reason why the **Congress of Industrial Organizations** (CIO) forged a working relationship with communists in the 1930s.

TUUL unions were characterized by their devotion to concepts such as industrial unionism, **direct action**, rank-and-file independence, and interracial organizing. Its slogan, "Class against Class," reflected its unapologetic adherence to CPUSA principles. However, although the TUUL was part of the Communist Party, its pro-Soviet and pro-communist rhetoric was often of secondary importance. TUUL organizers and members generally worked on pragmatic concerns such as winning union recognition and securing higher wages and better conditions for workers. TUUL organizers were noted for their commitment, hard work, and perseverance as well as their ideology, though the latter often led them to take on battles they could not win. Although the TUUL called several strikes, the more usual pattern was for its leaders to offer tactical organizing support during spontaneous workplace actions. Most TUUL actions followed identical trajectories: Direct action and committed political and organizational work aroused local authorities, who used violence to defeat strikers. That was certainly the path of the NTWU and the NMU, the first TUUL unions to gain widespread recognition. Violence marred the 1929 **Gastonia strike**. The NMU was similarly crushed in failed strikes in Pennsylvania, Ohio, West Virginia, and, most famously, in Harlan County, Kentucky, where the struggles were immortalized in the Florence Reece song, "Which Side Are You On?"

Nonetheless, the TUUL also made inroads in capital/labor conflicts. From 1930 through 1934, the group's activities among farm workers in the South and West resulted in multiracial unions such as the Share Croppers Union and the Cannery and Agricultural Workers Industrial Union. During the **Depression era**, the TUUL also aided rent strikers, fought tenant evictions, and led the call for government relief. A few TUUL strikes were successful, especially those involving its strongest body, the Marine Workers Industrial Union, whose activities built upon previous work done among dockworkers by the **Industrial Workers of the World** and which also anticipated future successes among **longshoremen**.

The CPUSA and TUUL gained their greatest notoriety from their work in organizing idle workers. By early 1930, communists had created a network of unemployed councils, which sought public works jobs, government relief, unemployment insurance, mortgage moratoriums, and anti-evictions legislation. The TUUL's March 6, 1930, Hunger March led to simultaneous nationwide demonstrations in which nearly 1 million jobless workers poured into the streets of major cities. It provided the blueprint for a 1932 TUUL-led Ford Hunger March, which wended its way from Detroit to the Ford River Rouge plant in Dearborn, Michigan. That march would soon be dubbed the "Ford Massacre." Autoworkers and their families sought to present Ford with a series of demands. When they approached the River Rouge gates, however, Ford **goons** and local police clashed with marchers. Police fired into the crowd, killing 4 persons and wounding 23.

Despite its extraordinary levels of activity and its members' great personal courage, by 1933 the TUUL had little to show for its efforts. Its membership consisted mostly of unemployed and **blacklisted** workers. The TUUL faced staggering challenges, including the despair felt by unemployed workers, anticommunist propaganda, opposition from the AFL, and employer resistance. In addition, the TUUL's interracial policies proved divisive, especially in the South. The group persisted mostly because it was willing to continue to battle for workers and because AFL organizing attempts in textiles, mining, and other heavy industries proved largely unsuccessful. The events of 1933–1934 tested the TUUL even further. With Franklin Roosevelt in office, a partial economic recovery under way, and the passage of the **National Industrial Recovery Act**, thousands of workers streamed into unions, with the AFL and other traditional trade unions gaining most of the new recruits. TUUL membership soared to approximately 100,000, but this number was dwarfed by the AFL's 2.1 million members. In response, the TUUL began disbanding its unions, allowing them to rejoin the AFL or independent unions.

The TUUL came to an official end in 1935, when the CPUSA followed the Comintern's lead and political considerations superseded workplace issues for communists. In response to the rise of fascism in Europe and its perceived threat to the Soviet Union, the Comintern shifted its position and adopted policies embodied by the Popular Front, which replaced the TUUL. Nonetheless, the TUUL left a legacy of militant, industrial, antiracist organizing whose efforts came to fruition during the mid-1930s. Numerous former TUUL organizers played crucial roles in building the CIO, and some of its former affiliates became the nuclei of CIO bodies such as the **United Auto Workers of America**, New York City's Transport Workers Union, the **United Electrical, Radio, and Machine Workers of America**, and the International Longshoremen's and Warehousemen's Union. Although communism generally has negative connotations in contemporary America, the work of communist labor organizations in groups such as the TUUL profoundly shaped the U.S. labor movement.

Suggested Reading

Irving Howe and Lewis Coser, *The American Communist Party: A Critical History*, 1962; Edward P. Johanningsmeier, "The Trade Union Unity League: American Communists and the Transition to Industrial Unionism: 1928–1934," *Labor History* 42, no. 2 (May 2001): 159–177; Fraser M. Ottanelli, *The Communist Party of the United States: From the Depression to World War II*, 1991; Judith Stepan-Morris and Maurice Zeitlin, *Left Out: Reds and America's Industrial Unions*, 2002.

TRESCA, CARLO

Carlo Tresca (March 9, 1879–January 11, 1943) was a radical, an organizer for the **Industrial Workers of the World** (IWW), an independent agitator, and a crusader against fascism.

He was born in Sulmona, Italy, the sixth child of Filippo and Filomena Tresca. Carlo finished secondary school and harbored ambitions of becoming a lawyer, though his mother wanted him to become a priest. When his family fell into debt in the 1890s and lost their land, Tresca took a very different path and embraced free thought and **socialism**. He joined the Italian Railroad Workers Federation, and in 1900, became a branch secretary and editor of the group's newspaper. Tresca organized peasant workers, was arrested several times, and faced a libel charge that spurred him to immigrate to the United States in 1904, where he settled in Philadelphia. He married Helga Guerra shortly before fleeing Italy. She joined Tresca in 1905 and the couple had a daughter, but their marriage quickly failed. In 1908, Carlo was indicted for assault, rape, and adultery for a liaison with a 15-year-old girl; he served nine months in jail for adultery.

Tresca embodied a strong radical tradition among Italian **immigrant** workers, many of whom joined socialist and anarchist movements. From 1904 to 1906, he edited *Il Proletario*, the official journal of the Italian Socialist Federation of North America; he later started his own papers and edited three short-lived Italian-language radical papers between 1906 and 1917. Tresca immersed himself in the struggles of Italian immigrant workers, especially miners and mill workers in Pennsylvania. His editorials in *La Plebe* engendered opposition from the Catholic Church, as well as from capitalists, government officials, and the Italian consulate. He also gained enemies for his exposés of "Black Hand" Mafiosi figures whom he alleged had ties to the church and right-wing political movements.

Over time, Tresca converted to **anarchism**, though socialism was such a strong (and varied) force among Italian workers that he easily deflected charges of anarchism by claiming to be a socialist. Tresca was not an ideologue, though opposition to **capitalism** and authoritarianism of any sort remained constants in his speeches and writing. His popularity was such that the IWW invited him to speak during the 1912 **Lawrence textile strike**, and his powerful oratory helped maintain **solidarity** among Italian workers that was threatened when officials arrested Joseph Ettor and Arturo Giovanniti. Tresca met **Elizabeth Gurley Flynn** at Lawrence, and the two became lovers shortly thereafter.

Tresca took part in several IWW job actions, including the Paterson silk strike in 1913, and a miners' strike in the Mesabi Range in Minnesota in 1916. During the latter strike, Tresca was charged with murder and was almost lynched. He was freed from the trumped-up charge in a complicated plea bargain in which some IWW members agreed to plead guilty to other charges. IWW secretary **William D. Haywood** lashed out against the agreement, and Tresca soon quit the IWW. He, like many present and past IWW members, was arrested for antiwar agitation in 1917. Tresca moved to have his case tried separately, however, and the charges against him were eventually dropped, although he remained under surveillance for much of the rest of his life.

Tresca did not follow other radicals into the Communist Party of the United States (CPUSA) in the 1920s and 1930s; instead, he became an independent voice in defense of freedom and workers' rights. He raised money and public support on behalf of Sacco and Vanzetti, Italian anarchists accused of bank robbery and murder in 1920. He also worked hard on their appeal efforts, but the two were executed in 1927. Tresca became embroiled in numerous free-speech fights, several of which elicited support from the American Civil Liberties Union.

In 1922, fascists under Benito Mussolini took control in Italy. Tresca became such an outspoken opponent of Italian fascism that Mussolini's government pressured the United States to silence Tresca and his latest publishing venture, *Il Martello*. In 1925, Tresca was arrested and jailed for obscenity, because *Il Martello* ran an advertisement for birth control. He was sentenced to a year in jail, but served only four months before President Calvin Coolidge yielded to public outrage and commuted his sentence. Tresca redoubled his editorial attacks on fascism and many observers claim his efforts helped to sour Italian Americans on Mussolini. He was also active in the antifascist Mazzini Society.

Tresca originally supported the Bolshevik Revolution in Russia, but he reluctantly attacked the Soviet Union when he concluded that Stalin was as authoritarian as Mussolini. The expulsion of Leon Trotsky from the Communist Party in 1927 and the Spanish Civil War in the 1930s deepened Tresca's anarchism and his hatred for all forms of authoritarianism. He caused a stir in 1938, when he accused the Soviet Union of kidnapping and murdering CPUSA cofounder Judith Poyntz, who disappeared in 1937. Tresca also took part in the Italian American Victory Council in the early 1940s and zealously weeded out those whom he felt were fascists, Mafiosi, or **communists**.

Tresca was gunned down in New York City on January 11, 1943, and his murder has never been solved. Assassination theories range from the possible to the fanciful, with the motives of everyone from the Soviet secret police to the Catholic Church being suspect. Most historians point the finger at either future Mafia boss Vito Genovese who, in 1943, was a lieutenant in the Luciano crime syndicate, or to Carmine Galante of the Bonnano syndicate. Both had ties to pro-Mussolini forces and either could have been acting on their behalf. It is difficult to say with certainty, though, as the controversial Tresca seldom lacked enemies.

Tresca's activity holds significance for the labor movement on several levels. He was an important radical voice in the immigrant community, a group often spurned by more conservative union leaders as unorganizable. Tresca's efforts at Lawrence and elsewhere proved the unsoundness of that assertion. He was also an important example of the independent drive for workers' rights that took place outside the formal structure of unions. Finally, he illustrated the way in which labor rights are linked to broader questions of freedom and social justice.

Suggested Reading

Dorothy Gallagher, *All the Right Enemies*, 1988; Nunzio Pernicone, *Carlo Tresca: Portrait of a Rebel*, 2005.

TRIANGLE FACTORY FIRE OF 1911

The Triangle Factory fire occurred on Saturday, March 25, 1911. This infamous industrial accident highlighted the potential for disaster in **sweatshop** production. For many Americans, it symbolized rapacious unbridled **capitalism** at its worst, and the tragedy became a rallying cry for labor reformers and labor activists.

The official cause of the fire remains unknown, though sweatshops were filled with combustible threads, fabrics, and oily rags that would not have taken a large spark to ignite. The blaze began on the eighth floor of New York City's 10-story Asch Building. It started near the close of the business day, though the exact time is uncertain because factory owners routinely manipulated clocks to extract longer workdays from employees. The building was ill equipped with alarms or telephones, so most of the victims were unaware a fire had started until they encountered the flames. A blaze broke out just as workers were collecting their paychecks and belongings to go home for the weekend. The initial fire was small, but it quickly raged out of control as flames engulfed the shirtwaist fabric. As the predominately young female workforce attempted to flee, panic ensued when they found doors locked, an elevator out of order, and the windows blocked. (Employers routinely locked workers into rooms to discourage unauthorized breaks and, they claimed, to prevent employees from stealing cloth.)

When the fire department arrived, its ladders reached to only the seventh floor. By then, floors 8 through 10 were ablaze and smoke was thickening. As the fire gathered force and the workforce grew desperate, some women chose to jump from the windows. Firefighters tried to catch them in safety nets, but the speed of their plummeting bodies tore through the fabric. The street beneath the Asch Building

New York firemen search for bodies at the Triangle Shirtwaist Company fire in 1911. At least 146 workers died in the fire largely due to unsafe working conditions and the fact that employers had locked escape doors. (Library of Congress)

became a macabre scene of corpses piled upon corpses, as women jumped to their deaths. In the end, 146 workers died as a result of the blaze, the bulk of them recent Jewish **immigrant** women between the ages of 16 and 23. Many of those who remained inside were burned beyond recognition and remained in the city morgue for days before family members could identify them.

Recrimination began immediately after the fire. *The New York Times* reported that the Asch Building itself was fireproof, but that the building did not meet safety codes. Doors opened inward instead of outward, and were bolted shut during working hours. Moreover, there were just narrow staircases in the building, inadequate for a structure of that height. There was only one fire escape, which was broken and unusable at the time of the conflagration.

Manslaughter charges were brought against Triangle Factory owners Max Blanck and Issac Harris, both of whom escaped the building unharmed. The fire marshal ruled that either a cigarette or a match started the fire, effectively blaming the victims for the blaze, as smoking was strictly forbidden in the factory. Both Blanck and Harris were acquitted on December 27, 1911. On March 11, 1913, they settled a lawsuit by paying $75 for each life lost.

The Triangle Factory fire came in the midst of disputes in the garment trades. In fact, the Triangle Factory had been struck several times, and both the **Women's Trade Union League** (WTUL) and the **International Ladies' Garment Workers' Union** (ILGWU) had made several unsuccessful attempts to organize workers there. The company saw some of its workers spontaneously walk out during the 1909

Uprising of the 20,000 in which New York City's immigrant female shirtwaist workers successfully struck for better working conditions, shorter hours, and **wage** increases, but the Triangle Factory was mostly unaffected by that walkout and another in 1910.

After the blaze, ILGWU Local 25 organized relief services and proposed a day of mourning. Thousands of people poured into the streets for the memorial and for public funerals. Those events are best remembered for a scathing speech in which ILGWU leader **Rose Schneiderman** indicted the **middle class** for its callous disregard for immigrants, women, and workers' rights. The fire's graphic images were circulated nationwide, and the horror and senseless deaths generated great outrage. The tragedy became a cause célèbre for labor unions and social reformers, and the very mention of the Triangle Factory came to symbolize the horrendous working conditions under which factory workers toiled. The WTUL fought for major code regulations and building inspections. Although reforms were not as sweeping as advocates desired, the fire did lead to a spate of state and local factory safety laws. To many, the relatively moderate measures adopted in the immediate aftermath of the Triangle Factory fire exemplify the limited scope of **Progressive Era** reforms. Schneiderman certainly thought so, though she later moderated some of her views, befriended Eleanor Roosevelt, and advised the Franklin Roosevelt administration on the New Deal.

Suggested Reading

New York Times, March 26, 1911; Leon Stein, *The Triangle Fire*, 1962; "The Triangle Factory Fire," http://www.ilr.cornell.edu/trianglefire/, accessed July 11, 2011; David von Drehle, *Triangle: The Fire That Changed America*, 2003.

TRUMAN, HARRY, AND THE LABOR MOVEMENT

The presidency of Harry S Truman (1945–1953) was a challenging and often acrimonious time for organized labor. Truman (1884–1972) became president on April 12, 1945, when President Franklin Roosevelt died. Truman had been vice president for only 82 days, having emerged as a compromise candidate in the 1944 election to replace the controversial Henry Wallace, who had feuded with key political figures and was viewed as too sympathetic toward the Soviet Union. Truman had been a supporter of the New Deal, though he was not an insider. He would not enjoy the same admiration among working Americans as Roosevelt did.

Truman took over the presidency in the waning days of World War II. Labor unions were well aware of past history and feared that the coming end of the war would lead employers to seek termination of the **National War Labor Board** (NWLB) and the labor rights it guaranteed, just as they had done after World War I. Moreover, unions that had just weathered the Great Depression worried about the future economy and insisted that the government take an active role in regulating it, a proposal that was anathema to the business world. Worker fears were exacerbated by layoffs that occurred toward the end of 1945. (These moves proved to be temporary cutbacks related to industrial reconversion, but that was not clear in 1945.) Rising prices constituted a further concern.

Truman was no fan of the labor conflict that marred the 1930s and hoped to avoid it by creating the National Wage Stabilization Board (WSB), a new labor/capital/public consortium that would take on many of the economic and labor relations functions of the NWLB. The WSB was bitterly attacked by business leaders and by **Republicans**; Senator Robert Taft went so far as to accuse Truman of having surrendered the economy to the **Congress of Industrial Organizations** (CIO). Truman, however, insisted that **wages** could be raised without raising prices. As the debate raged, organized labor took the initiative and filed numerous **strike** votes with the NWLB. (Strike votes had to be sent to the NWLB in accordance with the 1942 **War Labor Disputes Act [Smith-Connally Act]**.) When attempts to mediate disputes failed, a series of walkouts took place that would soon make the years 1945 and 1946 the most strike-prone era in American history. Before 1945 closed, the CIO had called out autoworkers, meatpackers, electrical workers, steelworkers, and others—more than 2 million workers in all. Although the strikes were remarkably free of violence and some unions—most notably the **United Auto Workers of America** led by **Walter Reuther**—won lucrative new contracts, pressure was placed upon Truman to curtail strikes. Truman's own plan for a mandatory 30-day cooling-off period before a strike could begin met with a frosty reception from organized labor.

In March 1946, the strike wave subsided. Truman enjoyed only a short respite, however, as on April 1, 1946, **John L. Lewis** called out more than 400,000 **United Mine Workers of America** (UMWA) unionists in Pennsylvania, West Virginia, Kentucky, Alabama, Iowa, and Illinois in a strike that lasted throughout 1946. Truman assumed federal control of the mines, in accordance with the provisions of the Smith-Connally Act. The UMWA quickly negotiated a favorable settlement, which was rejected by Truman's secretary of the interior and rekindled the strike. The Truman administration secured an **injunction** against UMWA strikers and socked both Lewis and the UMWA with large fines, which were promptly appealed (and reduced). Lewis made no effort to disguise his contempt for Truman; as soon as the mines returned to private hands in 1947 and were beyond the purview of the Smith-Connally Act, the UMWA renewed its job actions and won a settlement better than that reached in 1945.

A nationwide railway strike of more than 300,000 employees also broke out in the spring of 1945, and again Truman demanded cessation of the labor action and placed the industry under federal control. He did promise a favorable settlement in May 1945, but it demanded Congressional action; Taft killed the deal in the Senate. Strikes continued apace; before 1946 closed, more than 4,600 strikes had taken place involving some 5 million workers and totaling 120 million lost workdays. In addition, **Democrats** got very little boost from their association with the unpopular president, and the Republicans gained control of Congress during the 1946 fall elections. Republican lawmakers cleared the way for states to enact antiunion legislation, including prototypical **right-to-work** laws. Only the rapidly expanding U.S. economy offered a beacon of hope for American workers.

Truman salvaged his presidency in 1947. Despite reduced labor conflict, the Republican Congress, at the behest of the **National Association of Manufacturers**, pushed through the **Taft-Hartley Act**, the most hated antilabor bill in American history and one that, among other things, gave official sanction to right-to-work laws. Taft-Hartley went into effect in June 1947, but only because Congress overrode Truman's veto. The CIO and the **American Federation of Labor** (AFL) launched vigorous campaigns calling for repeal of the Taft-Hartley Act and, by 1948, public opinion was against the act. Organized labor was unsuccessful in convincing Congress to repeal the legislation, but it exacted revenge at the polls. In the election of 1948, labor unions and their newly created political action committees funneled money into Democratic campaigns. Control of Congress returned to the Democrats. Even more surprisingly, Truman retained the presidency by defeating his heavily favored Republican challenger, Thomas Dewey.

Once again, however, Truman proved a mercurial figure whose support for organized labor was uncertain. In late 1949, Lewis again called out UMWA members, charging that coal operators were not honoring 1947 agreements. In February 1950, the Truman administration sought a temporary injunction to end the strike, with Truman asserting his authority to do so under the very Taft-Hartley Act he had vetoed. When the UMWA ignored return-to-work orders, Truman threatened to draft miners into the military. (This threat was of dubious constitutionality.) The UMWA sought and secured a settlement independent of the government in March 1950, thereby negating Truman's actions and threats.

An even bigger conflict occurred in 1952, when 560,000 members of the **United Steelworkers of America** (USWA) went on strike. In 1950, the United States had entered the Korean conflict; hence the strike threatened the supply of war materiel. The battle between steel producers and the USWA was complicated by the fact that the union had already agreed to a WSB agreement in late 1951, but manufacturers killed the agreement because it contained a **union shop** agreement and because they wished to raise steel prices, which the board had frozen. This time Truman refused to invoke the Taft-Hartley Act provisions, but he wanted to ensure that war production was unimpeded. Thus he ordered the secretary of commerce to assert federal control over key steel mills. Workers applauded Truman's action and stayed on the job; manufacturers promptly sued and the U.S. Supreme Court ruled in their favor on June 2, 1952. USWA workers walked out when private control returned to the mills, however, and the strike was not settled until the end of July, on terms favorable to the USWA and identical to those established by the WSB at the end of 1951, before strikes ravaged production.

Harry Truman chose not to run for reelection in 1952, though he would have been eligible to do so under a special clause exempting the existing officeholder when the Twenty-Second Amendment was ratified in 1951. It is doubtful he would have won; by November 1952, Truman's approval rating stood slightly more than 30 percent and he left office as the most unpopular president since Herbert Hoover. Historians generally rank Truman much higher and his reputation recovered once he left office. His relationship with organized labor, however, was at best mixed.

Suggested Reading

Robert Dallek, *Harry S. Truman*, 2008; Foster Rhea Dulles and Melvyn Dubofsky, *Labor in America: A History, Fourth Edition*, 1984; David McCullough, *Truman*, 1992.

TRUMKA, RICHARD LOUIS

Richard Louis Trumka (July 24, 1949–) is the current president of the **American Federation of Labor-Congress of Industrial Organizations** (AFL-CIO), a position he assumed in 2009. Prior to that, he was the AFL-CIO secretary-treasurer from 1995 to 2009, and president of the **United Mine Workers of America** (UMWA) from 1982 to 1995.

Trumka was born to Italian American and Polish American parents in the coal-mining town of Nemacolin, Pennsylvania. Both his grandfather and his father, Richard Ford Trumka, were coal miners, and his mother, Eola Elizabeth (Bertugli) Trumka, was a homemaker. Unlike many past labor leaders, Trumka has quite a bit of formal education, though he worked in the mines for seven years, including when he was in college. He obtained his bachelor of science degree from Pennsylvania State University in 1971, and received a law degree from Villanova University in 1974.

Trumka immediately put his law degree to work in the service of organized labor and joined the UMWA's legal staff at a critical juncture in mineworker history. In 1969, UMWA reform candidate **Joseph Yablonski** was murdered by agents acting on behalf of sitting president Tony Boyle. Although reform candidate Arnold Miller took over the UMWA presidency in 1972, the union remained riddled with corruption and populated with Boyle loyalists. Trumka quit the UMWA staff in 1979, and returned to the mines for several years.

Both Miller and his successor, Sam Church, proved weak leaders prone to authoritarianism. Trumka, by contrast, supported reform and overhaul of the UMWA, positions that helped him rise quickly in union ranks. He headed the safety committee of his **union local** and, in 1981, was elected as the southwest Pennsylvania representative on the international executive board of the UMWA. A year later, the 32-year-old Trumka rode a tide of rank-and-file insurgency and became the youngest president in UMWA history. Once again, he assumed a position at a critical time. The election of **Ronald Reagan** in 1980 emboldened anti-union forces in the United States and a series of **downsizing, decertification, and concessions strikes** decimated organized labor's strength, as did job losses associated with **deindustrialization**. Trumka sought to rekindle the rank-and-file militancy that had characterized the union under the leadership of **John L. Lewis**. His leadership of the successful 1989 **Pittston Coal strike**—which involved a **corporate campaign**—was hailed at the time as a signal event in which organized labor was beginning to reverse misfortunes suffered earlier in the decade. Trumka also won praise for his leadership during a 1993 strike against Peabody Coal. He is widely credited with helping revive the UWWA; by 1998, it represented more than 42 percent of all miners, one of the highest concentrations of union membership in any American industry, though its 240,000 members represented an overall decline since the union's high-water mark in the early 1950s.

Trumka left the UMWA presidency in 1995, when he became the youngest secretary-treasurer in the history of the AFL-CIO. He was part of an AFL-CIO reform slate that included Linda Chavez-Thompson and newly elected president

John Sweeney. Trumka pledged to bring UMWA militancy to the AFL-CIO, just as Sweeney pledged to reinvigorate the **labor federation** by infusing it with tactics used by his own **Service Employees International Union**. All of the reformers were committed to reemphasizing grassroots organizing, pursuing an independent political agenda, coalition building, increasing diversity within the AFL-CIO, and decreasing the **business unionism** of the post–World War II labor movement.

Business unionism within the AFL-CIO proved resilient, however, and many of the reformers' calls to action remained unheeded, though great progress was made in increasing AFL-CIO diversity, in leadership training, and in building alliances with other liberal groups. Trumka served on President Bill Clinton's Bipartisan Commission on the Deficit, where he argued vociferously against changes to the **Social Security** system. He was also an outspoken opponent of the **North American Free Trade Agreement** and of the World Trade Organization, but had less influence on those issues.

Trumka became embroiled in controversy during a 1996 election in which James Hoffa, son of **James Hoffa** the elder, was the clear favorite to become president of the **Teamsters** union. Trumka and the AFL-CIO favored incumbent Ron Carey. Trumka was accused of manipulating funds that led to a Carey victory, which was subsequently overturned in the courts. Hoffa easily won the court-ordered new election. Trumka vigorously denied wrongdoing and was exonerated by the AFL-CIO in 1998 and by the courts in 2001, but suspicions about his role in the election dogged him for many years.

Trumka is an unapologetic liberal who supports major health care reform, trade **protectionism** (including sanctions against China), labor law reform, international workers' rights, business regulations, and the reindustrialization of the United States. He is outspoken, advocates the use of civil disobedience, and invites the ire of conservatives and intransigents within Wall Street and the business community whom he accuses of looting the commonweal and of being driven by greed rather than loyalty to the nation. He is anathema to ultraconservatives, some of whom have advanced the ludicrous claim that he is a **communist**. Trumka was an ardent supporter of Barack Obama's campaign in 2008, but has expressed disappointment with some of the president's policies.

Trumka married the former Barbara Vidovich in 1982, with whom he has a son. He also writes a regular blog for the *Huffington Post*. It is too early to know what Trumka's presidency will portend, though some labor analysts question whether the AFL-CIO as presently constituted is a viable organization.

Suggested Reading

"AFL-CIO Top National Officers: Richard L. Trumka, President," http://www.aflcio.org/aboutus/thisistheaflcio/leaders/officers_trumka.cfm, accessed July 11, 2011; *The Huffington Post*, http://www.huffingtonpost.com/richard-trumka, accessed July 11, 2011; *Who's Who in America*, 62nd edition, 2007.

TWO-TIER WAGE STRUCTURE. *See* Concessions.

UNDEREMPLOYMENT

Underemployment refers to situations in which individuals are dissatisfied in the labor market because they lack sufficient access to jobs or are mismatched in terms of their skills or desire and their current position. They may be involuntarily working in jobs below their skill levels, or desire full-time employment but cannot attain it. The term is also used by economists to indicate a situation in which unemployment rates have risen beyond those deemed optimal for an economy to function well. It can also refer to periods in which the workforce is too large during a time of reduced productivity. A business might, for example, maintain its entire workforce during a slack period so that it can respond immediately when demand for its product or services increases. Until that occurs, however, employees simply do not have enough work to occupy their time.

Contrary to popular belief, most **capitalist** economies desire manageable levels of unemployment rather than full employment rates; otherwise, labor would be a sellers' market and employers would be forced to compete for workers. Underemployment, however, presents a different set of problems as it both undermines faith in the national economy and threatens its long-term viability. A growing type of underemployment in which individuals work below their training and educational levels has been recently dubbed "malemployment." For example, a 2010 study conducted at Northeastern University indicates that 25 percent of recent college graduates work in fields such as retail, food services, and customer services for which no college degree is needed and for which there is a negative correlation between the **wages** received and the cost of obtaining a college degree. The implications for the American educational system are profound, should such trends persist.

Changes in the U.S. economy since the stagflation of the 1970s have produced an ever-growing number of individuals who desire full-time work but cannot obtain it. This trend has touched even the ranks of highly trained professionals. Academia, for example, once offered secure and prestigious jobs for those obtaining doctorates. Now, in many fields, only one-third of new faculty hires involve full-time, tenure-track professors. Many would-be professors involuntarily find themselves working as low-wage adjuncts, usually without fringe benefits or job security.

It is not only educators who suffer from this phenomenon. Companies often cite the competitive pressures of **globalization** as a cause for streamlining their operations and cutting labor costs. Many of the underemployed are former high-salaried professionals who lost their jobs during restructuring and now find themselves malemployed. After the 1990s "dot-com" slump, for example, many former computer programmers, information-technology experts, designers, and Internet entrepreneurs found themselves unemployed and unlikely to find new jobs within their fields of expertise. To survive, they became underemployed.

Underemployment also followed in the wake of the September 11, 2001, terrorist attacks on New York City and Washington, D.C. Normal business routines, especially in the transportation and travel industries, were so disrupted that some firms went bankrupt and many others **downsized**. Once again a ripple effect took place, with professional, mid-level managers, office staff, and skilled workers in many businesses being laid off. With too many skilled people chasing too few jobs, some individuals took jobs beneath their levels of training.

Underemployment and malemployment struck again during a recession that began during the administration of President George W. Bush that some economists assert is the worst downturn since the Great Depression. During this recession, a general contraction of jobs combined with aggressive **outsourcing** of work. Even the once-stable medical field hemorrhaged jobs as new technologies allowed medical tests, x-rays, and diagnostics to be electronically transmitted and read elsewhere, often outside the United States. Moreover, a shrinking job base caused a ripple effect that led to massive cutbacks in overall spending. Hospitals furloughed staff, or dramatically changed the status of employees. Full-time nurses became part-time nurses, for instance, and speech and physical therapists who were once on staff became contract laborers.

The impact of underemployment reaches far beyond the individual level. Those forced to watch their pennies consume less, which affects the entire economy. An increase in psychological maladies has been noted as well, especially among younger workers who tend to cope less well with loss of prestige, carry more long-term debt, and have less experience making adaptations to their lifestyles. Underemployment also introduces inefficiencies into the economy in the forms of reduced capacity, disinterested workers, and structural strains on the social system. Although health care reform may alter this equation, historically frustrated workers have been less likely to carry medical insurance, and throughout the 21st century doctors and hospitals have reported a surge in the number of indigent patients treated. Underemployed workers also have fewer savings or pension plans, thereby heightening the likelihood they will burden social services in the future.

The extent of underemployment is hard to gauge, but a 2011 Gallup survey indicated that as much as 19 percent of the American workforce is underemployed. Such figures are troubling in an economy that is routinely dubbed postindustrial. Much of the health of the American economy rests with consumer spending and will be difficult to sustain if would-be buyers suffer reduced purchasing power. Some pessimists even speak of a post-work society in which underemployment, casual work, and occasional labor will become the new norm. This may be an overly bleak scenario, but the short-term forecast is that underemployment will become an even bigger problem in the future as new technology, corporate mergers, deeper immersion into the global economy, and pressure to reduce labor costs force more workers from their chosen careers. Those social critics who argue that the **middle class** is shrinking often use underemployment to bolster their claims.

Suggested Reading

D. W. Livingstone, *The Education-Jobs Gap: Underemployment or Economic Democracy?*, 1999; Joann Prause, *The Social Cost of Underemployment*, 2004; Megan Woolhouse, "Underemployed and Overeducated—and Maybe the Nation's Best Hope," *Boston Globe*, January 23, 2011.

UNEMPLOYMENT

Unemployment is the state of being jobless. This simple definition obscures the complexity and social impact of unemployment; unemployment and low **wages** are among the major factors defining the social class system.

Numerous types of unemployment exist. *Cyclical unemployment* occurs when the demand for labor drops. It is related the gross national product (GNP): In the simplest terms, when the GNP drops, unemployment rises. *Structural unemployment* occurs when changes in the economy produce a decline in certain types of work. These decreases could be the result of technological change that makes existing goods obsolete, the displacement of labor by mechanization that displaces labor, declining demand for a particular product, or factors such as **runaway shops**, **deindustrialization**, **globalization**, or free trade policies. The demand for various types of labor has declined since the 1970s, especially in the manufacturing sector in which large numbers of **blue-collar** workers are concentrated. For example, robotic welding machines have replaced human welders on automobile **assembly lines**, textile factories have relocated outside the United States, and so much production in steel, rubber, and electronics has been taken over by foreign competitors that these are now considered **sunset industries**. According to the U.S. Department of Labor, more than 9.4 million workers were displaced in the period between 1979 and 1990 due to a decline in manufacturing.

Other forms of joblessness include *frictional unemployment*, a temporary state that occurs when an individual has left one job and is looking for another, and *seasonal unemployment*, which occurs in jobs whose demand ebbs and flows at certain points in the calendar. Agricultural work, for example, peaks during planting and harvest seasons, but has low demand during the winter; likewise, according to the National Retail Federation, 27 percent of all retail sales take place in the four-week period between Thanksgiving and Christmas. There is also *voluntary unemployment*, in which an individual chooses not to work, and *hidden unemployment*, which affects those who have grown discouraged about obtaining employment or who have not reported to any official agency to be counted. Many of those persons who have stopped looking for work become chronically unemployed and are unable to maintain steady employment even when the GNP is healthy and the demand for labor is high.

The existence of voluntary and hidden unemployment—especially the latter—underscores the basic unreliability of "official" unemployment figures. Actual unemployment is always higher than stated rates. In 1933, for instance, official unemployment was 24.9 percent during the cruelest year of the Great Depression. Historians and economists looking inside the numbers argue that closer to 35 percent of workers suffered some sort of economic dislocation during that year. In more recent years, many analysts have argued that the true unemployment rate is approximately double the official rate. For example, in June 2011 the **Bureau of Labor Statistics** reported an official unemployment rate of 9.2 percent, but CNBC researchers estimate that the rate was far higher and some analysts placed it as high as 18 percent.

Marxists argue that unemployment is a built-in structural flaw of **capitalism**, whose competitive nature ensures there will be economic boom periods and corresponding downswings. Given that capitalism's goal is to maximize profits for owners and investors, it is in the best interest of employers to increase profits by manipulating variables within their control, one of which is labor. Unemployment also serves the interests of capital by creating both a reserve labor pool and a secondary labor force whose presence constrains wages.

Few contemporary capitalists would agree with Marx, but many would admit that "full employment" is undesirable. Full employment makes for seductive political rhetoric but unsound business practice within a capitalist economy. Many investors and economists speak of "natural" unemployment rate of approximately 5 percent, though some now argue that it is as high as 6.7 percent. In simple terms, if every eligible individual worked, the only way an employer could expand would be to raid workers from other firms or find new supplies through mechanisms beyond their control, such as **immigration**. Employers also fear overly low unemployment because, in a supply-and-demand-based economy, labor becomes a seller's market, wages rise, and inflationary pressure mounts. By the same token, overly high unemployment often results in a shrinking GNP, making it harder for capitalists to find a market for goods and services. Okun's law—a formula developed by economist Arthur Okun in 1962—postulates that for every 1 percent rise in unemployment above its "natural" level, there is a "GNP gap" of approximately 2.5 percent in lost productivity that produces a ripple effect in earnings.

What is indisputable is that prolonged unemployment has devastating personal and social costs. Work is strongly correlated with personal identity in the United States. Numerous studies sustain work done by social psychologists D. D. and B. M. Braginsky in 1975 that correlated a 1 percent rise in unemployment sustained for one year with a 4.3 percent rise in mental hospital admissions for men (2.3 percent for women), a 4.1 percent increase in suicide attempts, and a 5.7 percent jump in the murder rate. Other studies link unemployment to feelings of shame, lost self-esteem, rising divorce rates, upswings in the overall crime rate, and an increase in domestic violence. Public health also declines, often because displaced workers lose health insurance and cannot afford to seek preventative care. Research also suggests that men as a group deal with unemployment less successfully than women. The historical lens magnifies these assertions. Official unemployment rose to 8.5 percent in 1975, its highest level since the 1930s, peaked at 10.4 percent in late 1982, and stayed above 6 percent until 1987. Levels of violence and social stress during the 1980s exceeded the corresponding levels in the late 1960s, when unemployment was generally less than 5 percent, though the 1960s is (incorrectly) stereotyped as being more chaotic than the 1980s. The Braginsky study is also verified by rising suicide rates in the 21st century. In 2005, a non-recession year, the U.S. suicide rate was 10 deaths per 100,000 population; by 2010, as a recession eased, it had risen to 11.1 per 100,000.

What to do about high unemployment has sparked debates between (broadly speaking) demand-side and supply-side economists. Demand-side advocates take their cues from economists such as John Maynard Keynes and John Kenneth Galbraith, and point to New Deal and Great Society programs as their models. They argue that the government should take the lead in creating jobs and in putting money into the hands of workers, even if it must engage in deficit spending to accomplish such goals. In theory, social spending creates consumers who will, in turn, stimulate long-term demand. Supply-siders, who have become increasingly popular within the **Republican Party** since the presidency of **Ronald Reagan**, take the opposite position and argue for a strong monetary policy. Many suggest that tax cuts and **deregulation** would relieve the pressure on businesses and free capital for investment in the economy, thereby creating new jobs. The intensity of their disagreement was made manifest in debates during the recession that began in 2007. Republicans and **Democrats** cooperated in launching the Troubled Assets Relief Program (TARP), which bailed out banks and ailing financial institutions. It was signed into law by President George W. Bush in late 2008 and supported by incoming President Barack Obama. By contrast, nearly every Republican in Congress voted against President Obama's American Recovery and Reinvestment Act of 2009 (ARRA), which pumped more than $780 billion into infrastructure building, public jobs, tax incentives, and spending on education and health care. They also opposed extensions of unemployment benefits built into the bill.

The United States is parsimonious with unemployment benefits compared to other democracies. Until the New Deal, the country lacked a federal unemployment compensation program; instead, nearly all relief efforts were in the hands of private charities and philanthropic groups that were quickly overwhelmed during the Great Depression. The 1935 **Social Security Act** set up the mechanisms by which current unemployment compensation is given. Benefits are paid from an insurance fund financed by payroll deductions, the current rate of which is 6.2 percent of taxable income. Benefits vary slightly from state to state, but unless Congress votes to extend benefits, federal unemployment compensation is limited to 26 weeks and only workers who have been employed for a mandated "base period"—usually four of the five previous calendar quarters—are eligible to collect it. Moreover, those workers who are exempt from paying into the system are also ineligible to receive compensation. The average benefit is approximately 36 percent of what workers made before being laid off. The unemployment compensation system is also based on the assumption that recessions will be brief and shallow and that the insurance fund will be quickly replenished. During the 2007–2010 recession, some states had to borrow money to pay their unemployment claims, which led many to abrogate provisions of the ARRA that extended some benefits for 99 weeks.

Social policy disputes related to unemployment do little to gloss over the very real damage done to workers, families, and communities during periods of high unemployment. High rates jeopardize the health of the overall economy by limiting consumption, eroding the American standard of living, and undermining confidence in American institutions. Those hardest hit are often those already the most socially and economically vulnerable: **minority labor**, single-parent households, and the working poor.

Suggested Reading

Annalyn Casey, "The 'New Normal' Unemployment Rate: 6.7 Percent," *CNN Money*, February 14, 2011, http://money.cnn.com/2011/02/14/news/economy/fed_unemployment/index.htm, accessed July 18, 2011; Louis Uchitelle, *The Disposable American: Layoffs and Their Consequences*, 2006; U.S. Department of Labor, Bureau of Labor Statistics, "Labor Force Statistics from the Current Population Survey," http://www.bls.gov/cps/cps_faq.htm, accessed July 18, 2011.

UNFAIR LABOR PRACTICES

Unfair labor practices are actions on the part of employers or unions that violate Section 8 of the **National Labor Relations Act** (NLRA). On the federal level, unfair labor practices have been existed in a legal sense only since 1935. The NLRA was designed to safeguard fair play in capital/labor relations. It created both rights and obligations for unions, management, and employees within a workplace. It also laid out procedures through which **collective bargaining** rights could be pursued and the conditions that unions and management had to follow.

Although various states passed laws seeking reduce capital/labor tension, labor unions did not gain an unambiguous federal right to exist until the passage of the 1914 **Clayton Antitrust Act** during the **Progressive Era**. Although **Samuel Gompers** initially hailed the Clayton Act as "labor's Magna Charta," it was soon apparent that his was an overly optimistic assessment. The Clayton Act exempted unions from antitrust prosecution and legitimized their legal status, but it did little to curtail employer anti-union harassment practices such as employing **goons** to break up union rallies, infiltrating union ranks with company spies, spreading false propaganda to discredit unions, and hiring private armies to intimidate workers. American labor relations remained contentious and bloody, with some business moguls behaving like tyrants and some unions responding as if a literal state of war existed between employers and workers. The NLRA sought to change that situation.

The NLRA makes it illegal for management to threaten employees seeking union representation or to retaliate against those who do. Employers are also required to bargain in good faith with a union certified by the National Labor Relations Board (NLRB) and to provide information necessary for a union to fulfill its representational responsibilities. Similarly, unions must also bargain in good faith. They cannot intimidate management, retaliate against employees who do not join the union, refuse to represent non-union workers during contract talks, or sanction such things as secondary **boycotts** or **wildcat strikes**. Once a contract is in place, each side must adhere to it and can change its conditions only upon mutual agreement. If either side violates the certification process or contract terms, the NLRB has the legal authority to take legal action against parties accused of unfair labor practices.

It should be noted that the NLRB's authority was not originally accepted by all businesses. The constitutionality of the NLRA was challenged and, as the **La Follette Committee** shockingly revealed, brutality and bloodshed remained a staple in American labor relations through 1937, when the U.S. Supreme Court upheld the NLRA. The courts, the coming of World War II, and the establishment of the **National War Labor Board** helped institutionalize the NLRA and the idea of resolving unfair labor practices through bureaucratic and legal procedures rather than through unilateral action on the part of management or unions.

The NLRA did not, however, establish mandatory **arbitration** to solve disputes, so capital/labor relations remained tense after World War II. They became even more contentious with the passage of the 1947 **Taft-Hartley Act**, which was viewed by unions as a "slave labor" bill. Although this assessment seems overly histrionic, there is little question that Taft-Hartley tipped the balance of procedural dispute resolution in management's favor. That bill's provision allowing employers to express their opinions on labor unions has proved especially troublesome. Under the NLRA, complaints of unfair labor practices are filed with the NLRB. Historically, unions have filed unfair labor practice suits more often than management. From 1935 and into the 1970s, the bulk of the putative offenses occurred during organizing drives and when contract negotiations stalled. Many suits claimed that management overstepped legal boundaries in seeking to dissuade workers from joining a union, though the Taft-Hartley Act's guidelines are so ambiguous that NLRB rulings have been subject to court challenges.

The NLRA did curtail much of the violence associated with strikes before its passage and it worked reasonably well during America's late industrial age. The coming of **deindustrialization** has, however, has led some observers to question whether the current methods of determining unfair labor practices are antiquated. Organized labor could serve as a countervailing force to organized capital within an economic system that relied upon the production of capital goods. In such a system, both sides had a vested interest in resolving disagreements in a timely fashion so as to restore the flow of goods and the issuance of paychecks. **Runaway shops**, **globalization**, and the emergence of a postindustrial economy have reduced the compulsion for employers to rely upon American workers, to negotiate with labor unions, or to resolve disputes quickly.

By the 1980s, it had become commonplace for employers to use the NLRB to their advantage. The NLRB is supposed to be an impartial body, but President **Ronald Reagan** politicized the board by appointing overly pro-business members to it. Critics now complain that the NLRB fails to fulfill its statutory mandate and often unfairly favors business. That charge is open to interpretation, but what has certainly happened since the 1980s is that employers have filed numerous unfair labor practice charges against unions, hoping to precipitate **decertification** votes. In many cases, those charges were unfounded or frivolous, but because NLRB rulings could be tied up in legal challenges for years, management has been able to use its superior financial resources to exhaust unions' abilities to challenge employers. Labor unions have lost much of their former strength, and it is an open question as to whether they can be the countervailing force in capital/labor relations that acts as a check upon unfair labor practices. The 21st century has thus far witnessed an upsurge in employee complaints about management abuses, but unorganized workers are only partially covered by the NLRA's imperfect protections.

Suggested Reading

William B. Gould IV, *Labored Relations: Law, Politics, and the NLRB, a Memoir*, 2001; Kenneth Lopatika, *NLRA Rights in the Nonunion Workplace*, 2010; National Labor Relations Board, "Employer/Union Rights and Obligations," http://www.nlrb.gov/rights -we-protect/employerunion-rights-obligations, accessed July 15, 2011.

UNION LOCAL

A union local—sometimes referred to as a lodge, assembly, or similar term—is the smallest bargaining unit within a labor organization's structure. It refers to the rank-and-file members of a union at a single workplace who have won **collective bargaining** rights to represent all workers at that locale. (There are some cases in which a union local consists of workers from different workplaces, but these are rare in the contemporary movement.) The union local takes care of the day-to-day operations, negotiates **contracts**, initiates the **grievance** procedure, galvanizes members for political activity, collects and distributes **dues**, supervises **business agents**, and leads **strikes** and **boycotts**, should they become necessary.

The amount of autonomy enjoyed by union locals varies according to the organization. The term "union local" came into widespread use only after the founding of the **American Federation of Labor** (AFL) in 1886. Earlier organizations such as the **Knights of Labor** (KOL) and the **Brotherhood of Locomotive Engineers** were modeled, in part, on fraternal orders, and generally operated differently from AFL locals. The AFL's **voluntarism** principle, for example, allowed union locals to call their own strikes, whereas KOL assemblies hoping to secure support from the national office needed prior approval from an executive council loath to call strikes. These examples point to the fact that a parent international union (if one exists) generally determines procedures for defining and empowering a union local. Union locals usually have their own bylaws, officers, and procedures. Locals cooperate with one another in larger alliances, such as district councils, state federations, international unions, and **labor federations**. Many locals send representatives to larger federations with which they are affiliated, with that representation usually being defined by the larger bodies that operate under separate bylaws and constitutions.

The **American Federation of State, County, and Municipal Employees** (AFSCME) typifies modern union structures. It has approximately 1.7 million members dispersed among 1,400 union locals. Those members are also represented in 58 labor councils; Council 5 in Minnesota, for instance, represents 39 separate local unions. AFSCME members may also be represented in one of four national bodies (of nurses, **correctional officers**, retirees, and child care providers). All union members are affiliated with the international union based in Washington, D.C., which makes them virtually represented in the **American Federation of Labor-Congress of Industrial Organizations**, with which AFSCME is aligned.

Suggested Reading

"AFSCME Minnesota Council 5," http://afscmemn.org/, accessed July 17, 2011; James T. Bennett and Bruce E. Kaufman, eds., *What Do Unions Do?*, 2007.

UNION OF NEEDLETRADES, INDUSTRIAL, AND TEXTILE EMPLOYEES

The Union of Needletrades, Industrial, and Textile Employees (UNITE) existed between 1995 and 2004. It formed when two declining unions, the **International Ladies' Garment Workers' Union** and the **Amalgamated Clothing and Textile Workers Union** consolidated. In 2004, UNITE dissolved as an independent entity and merged with the **Hotel Employees and Restaurant Employees International Union** to form UNITE HERE, with a combined strength of approximately 440,000 members. UNITE HERE left the **American Federation of Labor-Congress of Industrial Organizations** (AFL-CIO) in 2005 and joined the **Change to Win Federation**, but the union split in 2009, with UNITE HERE reaffiliating with the AFL-CIO and a splinter group remaining in Change to Win.

UNITE was originally an attempt to organize workers in the various textile, garment, and needletrades industries—firms that have historically been union resistant and whose fortunes have declined precipitously due to **deindustrialization** and competition from overseas production in the age of **globalization**. At the time it formed in 1995, UNITE had just 265,000 members, about as many members as the combined UNITE HERE has today.

UNITE enjoyed its greatest success in drives against **sweatshop** labor, especially in bringing awareness of poor overseas labor conditions to college campuses. Numerous student groups were galvanized to launch anti-sweatshop campaigns and to force their universities to discontinue carrying branded logo goods created by sweated labor. In 1996, UNITE built upon reports of sweated conditions in the United States, Central America, and Asia, and led a Stop Sweatshops campaign that united trade unions, students, consumers, civil rights activists, and women's groups. UNITE also offered summer internships that tapped into student activism. A nationwide organization, the United Students Against Sweatshops, was an outgrowth of this activity; it was founded in 1998 and is now active on 180 campuses in the United States and Canada. UNITE also joined forces with students participating in anti-globalization protests. In 1999, the union took part in demonstrations against the World Trade Organization in Seattle.

On the industrial front, UNITE helped implement the **Fieldcrest settlement** in 1990. When the 5,000 workers at the Fieldcrest Cannon textile mills in North Carolina ratified a contract in 2000, a nine-year dispute was finally resolved. That victory aside, UNITE began to expand its membership beyond the needletrades, as that industry continued to decline and is now widely viewed as a **sunset industry** insofar as mass production is concerned. (Niche and specialty markers appear stronger.) In 1998, UNITE organized nearly 3,000 linen workers in 29 plants in the South. Two years later, the 40,000 members of the Laundry and Dry Cleaning International Union joined forces with UNITE. The union also brought in workers from industries as diverse as auto parts and Xerox production workers.

In the early 21st century, UNITE continued to have success in making Americans aware of sweated labor. In 2001, New York City enacted an anti-sweatshop law that outlawed the use of tax dollars to purchase city employee uniforms made under sweatshop conditions. UNITE also created the Global Justice for Garment Workers campaign to improve labor conditions around the world. Despite its successes, the continuing decline of the needletrades left UNITE with a healthy union treasury but an eroding membership base. In 2003, UNITE President Bruce Raynor approached HERE president John Wilhelm about the possibility of a merger, which was effected in 2004. The combined UNITE HERE had roughly 440,000 members at the time of the unions' merger. Few could have predicted that the merger would do great damage to both organizations.

Flush with cash and new members, UNITE HERE was drawn to the rhetorical militancy and emphasis on grassroots organizing promised by the Change to Win Federation. In 2005, UNITE HERE left the AFL-CIO and joined forces with Change to Win. Unfortunately, the UNITE HERE merger degenerated into personal acrimony, **jurisdictional** disputes, and allegations of corruption, with Raynor and Wilhelm battling over funds, organization strategies, resolution of member **grievances**, and control over a bank formerly owned by UNITE. In 2009, Raynor angrily withdrew many former UNITE affiliates and approximately 100,000 union members from UNITE HERE and formed a new body called Workers United (WU). The WU affiliated with the **Service Employees International Union** (SEIU), a key Change to Win ally. This had the net effect of drawing the SEIU into the dispute, which further degenerated into lawsuits, jurisdictional squabbles, and mutual **raiding**, especially of casino workers, which both the WU and the truncated UNITE HERE claimed. The mediation efforts of numerous individuals, including Senator Harry Reid, failed to resolve the fractiousness. A Wilhelm-engineered coup dislodged Raynor in 2009 and allegations of financial malfeasance were lodged against Raynor. Wilhelm, who assumed the UNITE HERE presidency in 2009, also charged the SEIU with meddling in UNITE HERE internal matters and promptly withdrew UNITE HERE from the Change to Win Federation in favor of rejoining the AFL-CIO. The members of Workers United remained in Change to Win.

The warring sides reached a tentative truce in 2010 in which the bank remained in WU hands, but more than $75 million of other assets went to UNITE HERE. Several other issues in dispute await future **arbitration** decisions. Although it appears that the two sides will ultimately settle their disagreements, the long dispute has taken its toll on once-promising UNITE campaigns against sweatshops and globalization. Some observers interpret the fight as a classic example of how **business unionism** badly serves union members. Whether UNITE HERE can regain its momentum remains to be seen, but the nasty internal fight at a time of eroding labor union strength did little to help the rank-and-file of any of the unions involved.

Suggested Reading

Julius Getman, *Restoring the Power of Unions: It Takes a Movement*, 2010; Stephen Greenhouse, "Service Unions Agree to End a Long Dispute," *New York Times*, July 26, 2010; "UNITE HERE!," http://www.unitehere.org, accessed July 17, 2011.

UNION SHOP

A union shop, also called a closed shop, is the opposite of an **open shop**. It refers to a workplace in which workers are compelled to join a labor union as a condition of employment. Technically, a union shop compels employers to hire only present or future union members, and a closed shop requires that employees be union members at the time of hire, but the two terms have become synonymous, perhaps because both are increasingly rare in contemporary America.

Unions have sought such provisions since the 19th century, and the **Knights of Labor** successfully set up numerous union shops, as did various craft unions. The open-shop movement supported by the **National Association of Manufacturers** and other anti-union organizations gathered strength during the 1920s and sought to derail the formation of union shops. Some unions nonetheless managed to create union and closed shops. By the end of World War II, for instance, the **United Mine Workers of America** (UMWA) had organized nearly all coal mines in the country and only an employer seeking conflict would employ a laborer without a UMWA card. Union shops are permitted under the **National Labor Relations Act** (NLRA), though the NLRA sets limits on closed shops, and the **Taft-Hartley Act** laid the groundwork for states to pass **right-to-work** laws that make closed shops illegal and union shops very hard to establish.

Laws vary slightly in states permitting union shops, but under the NLRA employees subject to union-shop clauses have at least 30 days to join a union, though a noncompliant worker can be discharged only if he or she refuses to pay **dues** or the union's initiation fee, and only if all closed-shop requirements are enforced uniformly and in a nondiscriminatory fashion. The NLRA also allows union-shop agreements to be terminated if a majority of employees vote to do so. That provision has proved controversial, as, in numerous cases, employers have sought to fire workers during a **strike** or **lockout**, hire **scabs** to take their places, and then pursue termination of union-shop agreements under Section 9(e) of the NLRA.

The very concept of a union shop magnifies ideological differences in the United States. Critics see union shops as violations of an individual's First Amendment right to free association, though courts have largely disagreed. Unions counter that attacks on closed shops are backdoor assaults on the very ideal of **collective bargaining**. It is patently unfair, they argue, for some free-loading individuals to reap identical benefits as dues-paying union members. Courts have also disagreed with parts of that logic and have ruled that an individual collective bargaining unit must negotiate on behalf of all workers within the occupation organized, whether or not they join the union. In many cases, though, such workers must pay an **agency fee** to the union. There is also opposition to closed shops from some unions. Union opponents argue that coerced membership undermines **solidarity**, breeds resentment, and is counterproductive.

Arguments on all sides are largely moot at present, as few closed shops exist. One sees vestiges of union shops in a few entertainment industries. It is difficult, for example, for actors to secure paid employment if they are not members of Actors' Equity. In like fashion, the **Major League Baseball Players Association** maintains a closed shop and most professional sports owners tolerate such arrangements. The National Hockey League's 2004–2005 lockout, which canceled the entire season, led to major changes in the financial structure of the league, but did not result in the demise of the National Hockey League Players Association, even though some disgruntled players would have supported **decertification**.

Suggested Reading

American Bar Association, *Developing Labor Law, the Board, the Courts, and the National Labor Relations Act*, 2003; Richard Freeman, *What Do Unions Do?*, 1995.

UNION STEWARD. *See* Shop Steward.

UNITED AUTO WORKERS OF AMERICA

The United Auto Workers of America (UAW) union is now officially known as the United Automobile, Aerospace, and Agricultural Implement Workers of America. It remains the largest union representing autoworkers in the United States and claims a membership of more than 1 million, though this figure includes more than 600,000 retired workers; its active membership is approximately 400,000. The UAW is generally perceived as a union in transition or decline. In its heyday from 1946 to 1970, however, it was often viewed as the template for liberal unionism.

The automobile industry embodied America's industrial might during the mature phase of its **Industrial Revolution**. By the early 1920s, automobiles were practically synonymous with the United States. Americans were fascinated by automobiles, bought them in far greater quantities than citizens of any other nation, and even today retain an unmatched reliance upon and preference for gasoline-powered private vehicles. Automobiles were not, however, invented in the United States. The idea of a motorized vehicle is ancient and a steam-powered prototype was in use in China in the 17th century. Debate rages over who should be credited with creating the first "automobile" as the vehicles came to be understood, but the German Karl Benz is generally cited as having created the first practical gasoline-powered model in 1886. The first American-made parallel is credited to Charles and Frank Duryea, a pair of Springfield, Massachusetts brothers who made their first car in 1893. The manufacturer Ransom Olds is said to have introduced **assembly-line** production in 1902, but it was Henry Ford's use of interchangeable parts beginning in 1914 that revolutionized auto production. His Model-T Fords—first available only in black because it was the only paint that dried fast enough—were produced faster and cheaper, allowing Ford to slice the price of cars by two-thirds and making them available to the masses. General Motors (GM), destined to become Ford's major rival, consolidated in Flint, Michigan, in 1908, when Buick purchased Oldsmobile. (It acquired Chevrolet, Cadillac, and Pontiac shortly thereafter and was the first company to offer multiple product lines.)

Henry Ford was the first business owner to face labor problems in the industry. In 1914, Ford offered the unheard-of **wages** of $5 per day, the equivalent of more than $110 today. Ford was hailed as a pioneering **welfare capitalist** by many and denounced as crazy by his competitors (who soon copied him). In truth, Ford was motivated less by philanthropy than by a desire to stabilize his workforce; turnover on Ford assembly lines was 380 percent in the year before he raised wages. Ford's new scheme introduced even more monotonous work, but the high pay kept workers on the job. Ford was, in fact, virulently opposed to labor unions and his firm was the last to unionize.

The automotive industry took off in the 1920s. Enormous profits were made, but pay rises failed to keep pace and averaged just 8 percent during the bull market of the 1920s. The 1929 stock market crash and ensuing depression served to magnify rising discontent on the part of autoworkers. In 1932, a Ford Hunger March saw thousands of workers organized by the Communist Party descend upon Ford's River Rouge plant in Dearborn, Michigan, where they confronted company **goons** under the supervision of Ford's security chief, Harry Bennett. Although the march ended in a rout in which four workers died, it proved a turning point in labor relations within the industry. In January 1933, more than 20,000 Detroit workers went on strike against the Briggs Corporation. In March of that year, Democrat Franklin Roosevelt took office as president and quickly thereafter signed into law the **National Industrial Recovery Act** (NIRA). NIRA Section 7(a) offered significant guarantees to protect labor unions and inspired Chrysler workers to set up the Automobile Industrial Workers Association. In the same year, left-wing tool makers and specialty auto parts workers created the **Mechanics Educational Society of America**. Although the NIRA was struck down as unconstitutional, Congress approved the even stronger **National Labor Relations Act** in 1935, the year the UAW came into being.

The **American Federation of Labor** (AFL) faced increasing pressure to organize autoworkers and, in May 1935 the UAW took shape, with the new union being headed by Francis Dillon. From the start, however, the UAW was a poor fit within the AFL, as assembly-line workers were not easily accommodated the AFL's **craft unionism** structure. UAW workers gravitated toward the **industrial unionism** model espoused by UAW dissidents organized as the Committee for Industrial Organization. The UAW and several other industrial unions were suspended in 1936, but largely ignored the AFL, replaced Dillon with Homer Martin, and continued organizing workers. Although the **Congress of Industrial Organizations** (CIO) did not officially form until 1938 with the UAW as one of its charter affiliates, both had achieved de facto existence by early 1936.

By most accounts, it was the dramatic **General Motors sit-down strike** of 1937 that legitimized both the UAW and the CIO. Victory against the world's largest corporation electrified American workers both within the auto industry and beyond. Hundreds of thousands of workers flocked to the CIO, and the UAW quickly gained collective bargaining rights for Chrysler workers. Ford, however, proved a different matter. In a repeat of the 1932 hunger march, Bennett's goons bloodied UAW activists, including future UAW president **Walter Reuther**, in a 1937 clash outside the River Rouge plant known as the Battle of the Overpass. Ford would not be organized until 1941, by which time negative publicity from Ford's tactics had negatively affected the company's sales.

The UAW took a **no-strike pledge** during World War II, and autoworkers enjoyed full employment when plants began to produce war materiel. The war also saw women join the assembly line in large numbers, as well as UAW efforts to organize workers outside of the industry. The attempt of manufacturers to break with labor guarantees made by the **National War Labor Board** precipitated a mass wave of strikes in late postwar period, with one of the most dramatic being the **United Auto Workers of America strike of 1945–1946** against General Motors. In that labor action, the UAW held out for 113 days and won a rich contract, though strike leader Walter Reuther was later criticized for abandoning a demand for the UAW to co-manage the plant, slice the work week to 30 hours, and force GM to reveal details of its finances.

Reuther parlayed the 1946 contract into union power; in 1946, he supplanted R. J. Thomas, who had been UAW president since 1938. Reuther, a moderate socialist, purged the UAW of **communist** influences and led the UAW to embrace **Cold War** unionism. Some scholars have castigated Reuther for these actions as well, but few labor unions in the history of the nation prospered to the degree of the UAW from 1946 through Reuther's death in 1970. Reuther proved adroit at **pattern bargaining** and UAW workers won large wage settlements, path-breaking **cost-of-living-adjustments**, generous **pensions**, and rich **fringe benefits** packages.

Reuther also transformed the UAW into a more progressive organization rooted in the precepts of liberal thought. The UAW was an early supporter of **civil rights**, and Reuther developed a friendship with important African American leaders such as **A. Philip Randolph** and Martin Luther King, Jr. He pushed the UAW to improve its record on racial equity, sometimes over the opposition of union locals. Reuther also hoped that the UAW and other progressive unions might become the liberal wing of the Democratic Party, and he cultivated relations between the UAW and key Democratic leaders, including Presidents John Kennedy and Lyndon Johnson. The UAW also began to address sexism within union ranks in the late 1960s, though this move was due more to agitation from women in the rank-and-file than from the actions of union officers. UAW member Dorothy Haener was a cofounder of the National Organization for Women in 1966, and Genora Johnson Dollinger, a heroine of the 1937 sit-down strike, also agitated for enlarged roles for women inside the UAW. The UAW adjusted to the changing environment; it endorsed the call for an Equal Rights Amendment, the first U.S. union to do so.

Walter Reuther became president of the CIO in 1952 and helped negotiate the 1955 American Federation of Labor-Congress of Industrial Organizations (AFL-CIO) merger. Neither Reuther nor the UAW proved a comfortable fit inside the AFL-CIO, whose president, **George Meany**, distrusted the emerging liberal politics of the UAW. The **labor federation** maintained a more cautious stance on civil rights, and many of its leaders had unbridled contempt for the **counterculture** that emerged in the mid-1960s. The UAW, by contrast, supplied seed money and tactical support for the budding radicals who created Students for a Democratic Society. It also embraced social change rather than deliberating it endlessly; Reuther advised Kennedy and Johnson on civil rights legislation, as well as other New Frontier and Great Society programs, though he later split with Johnson over the **Vietnam War**. Meany, in contrast, viewed Reuther's opposition to the war as close to treason. On July 1, 1968, the UAW disaffiliated with the AFL-CIO and, several weeks later, joined the Reuther-created **Alliance for Labor Action** (ALA), a new labor federation. The ALA was still in its infancy when Reuther died in a plane crash in 1970, and it dissolved shortly thereafter.

The dynamic Reuther was succeeded by Leonard Woodcock. Woodcock came to power at a difficult time. Younger workers were prone to launching **wildcat strikes** and militancy among black workers had given rise to groups such as the **Dodge Revolutionary Union Movement**. A 1971 UAW strike against GM went badly and nearly bankrupted the UAW. Woodcock also found it difficult to relate to younger workers alienated by assembly-line work, such as those who precipitated strikes at Lordstown, Ohio, GM plants between 1970 and 1972. His biggest crisis occurred in 1973, when the first Organization of Petroleum Exporting Countries' (OPEC) oil boycott sent petroleum costs spiraling upward. As the United States plunged into recession and stagflation in the mid-1970s, U.S. auto manufacturers found themselves saddled with a fuel-inefficient fleet that was vulnerable to foreign imports built by non-UAW workers. UAW membership was more than 1 million when Reuther died and had increased to 1.5 million by 1979, but this situation would soon change.

The UAW's immediate response to the OPEC crisis was to preserve jobs. Woodcock retired in 1977 and was replaced by **Douglas Fraser**. Fraser helped engineer a government bailout of the Chrysler Corporation in 1979, a scheme that preserved thousands of UAW jobs but at the price of sustaining a gas-guzzling fleet and with the UAW swallowing $203 million in **concessions** and givebacks. The UAW began to concentrate on jobs more than the environment, and frequently opposed plans to modernize production and replace antiquated product lines if such retooling displaced workers. Fraser became even more job conscious during the anti-union climate fostered by Presidents **Ronald Reagan** and George H. W. Bush during the 1980s. The UAW rejoined the AFL-CIO in 1981, but this did not shelter it from the **downsizing, decertification, and concessions** movements in the 1980s. By the end of the decade, it had shed more than a third of its membership from its 1979 peak, including Canadian autoworkers upset by the UAW's ignorance of Canadian affairs and its lack of militancy.

More losses were to come. German and Japanese manufacturers opened American plants in the 1980s and 1990s, but most were located in the non-union South. When Fraser retired in 1983, Owen Bieber became UAW president.

Bieber proved a lackluster leader: By the time he retired in 1995, UAW membership had slipped to less than 800,000 and the union had endured a humiliating loss in the 1992–1994 Caterpillar strike. Membership rebounded during the 1990s as the UAW began organizing groups such as freelance writers, graduate students, health care workers, and others outside the automotive industry. Under new president Stephen Yokich, union membership increased to nearly 900,000 workers by 1997, but it quickly contracted and within a decade was less than 500,000. A proposed merger with the **International Association of Machinists** failed to materialize in the late 1990s.

The UAW has lobbied hard for social changes such as a national health care plan, **protectionist** trade policies, and international labor rights. Nevertheless, it has won very few friends in the environmental community, which claims the union has paid only token attention to the need to rethink American reliance upon the internal combustion engine. The UAW has been criticized for opposing production of electric cars, though current UAW President Bob King insists the union has taken this stance only because manufacturers have been using non-union suppliers. The union has also had to fend off charges that its exorbitant pension and fringe benefits packages are partly to blame for a 2008–2009 crisis that drove GM into bankruptcy and reorganization. In 2007, the UAW was forced to accept contracts that allow new workers to be compensated at $15 per hour rather than the $28 base earned by existing workers. A 2011 study revealed that Chrysler workers averaged $76 per hour in wages and fringe benefits in 2007, but just $49 in 2011. The same day this was revealed, the UAW announced its intention to press automakers to share a greater percentage of the profits they have made.

Despite some recent setbacks, the U.S. auto industry continues to be an important industrial concern in the United States. Nonetheless, both manufacturers and the UAW face enormous challenges in the immediate future. Fossil fuel prices have proved volatile, most analysts believe that the age of cheap oil is over, and some predict that most existing petroleum supplies will be depleted by the middle of the 21st century. If they are correct, internal combustion engines will become obsolete. The UAW has been one of the most significant labor organizations in U.S. history, but its future is an open question, as is that of the auto industry itself.

Suggested Reading

John Bayard, *American Vanguard: The United Auto Workers during the Reuther Years, 1935–1970*, 2004; Kevin Boyle, *The UAW and the Heyday of American Liberalism 1946–1968*, 1995; Nelson Lichtenstein and Stephen Meyer, eds., *On of the Line: Essays in the History of Auto Work*, 1991; United Autoworkers, http://www.uaw.org/, accessed July 20, 2011.

UNITED AUTO WORKERS STRIKE OF 1945–1946 (GENERAL MOTORS)

The **United Auto Workers of America** (UAW) strike against General Motors (GM) that took place in 1945–1946 is one of the most hotly debated **strikes** in

American history. Although the UAW won one of the richest **contracts** in history, the cost of accepting the deal involved conceding the right of GM to manage its plants as it saw fit. When the strike began, the UAW had put forth a plan in which the UAW and GM would co-manage production. Numerous critics see the UAW's **concession** on this point as a turning point for the future of American labor relations.

World War II officially ended in August 1945, with the surrender of Japan. At that point, American industries geared toward the production of war materiel began the slow process of reconversion to peacetime production. By the fall of 1945, more than 300,000 Michigan workers were unemployed and some workers feared a return to the prewar **depression**. The uncertain economy corresponded with rising labor strife brought about mainly by the desire of employers to end the authority of the **National War Labor Board** and to abrogate gains made by labor unions during the war. For its part, organized labor remembered how employers after World War I had broken patterns of capital/labor cooperation and had launched vicious anti-union campaigns. With both sides primed for a fight, the summer of 1945 through the end of 1946 saw the largest wave of strikes in U.S. history. Among those walking off their jobs were workers in the steel, electrical equipment, meatpacking, **long-shore**, and trucking industries. One of the most bitterly contested of all battles was that between GM and the UAW, which began in November 1945 and raged for 113 days.

The UAW's fight with GM took place against a backdrop of internal conflict within the UAW. The UAW was headed by R. J. Thomas, an affable man whom rising star **Walter Reuther** felt was simultaneously too conciliatory and too closely aligned with the Communist Party. Although Thomas was probably never a **communist** and the **socialist** Reuther may have briefly joined the Communist Party in the 1930s, by 1945 Reuther represented a UAW faction that sought to dislodge communist sympathizers such as Martin, UAW secretary-treasurer George Addes, and key leaders such as Richard Frankensteen and Richard Leonard. Ironically, though Reuther has sometimes been identified with a rightward turn in the UAW, it was he who warned UAW leaders and their communist allies that employers were seeking to reenact the post–World War I **open-shop** drive. Reuther, a veteran of the **sit-down strikes**, was easily the most popular leader within the UAW by 1945 and his handling of the coming GM strike brought him even more acclaim from workers.

When the strike began in November 1945, Reuther put GM on the defensive by demanding a 30 percent **wage** increase for UAW workers while simultaneously insisting that GM could so without raising the price of automobiles. He challenged GM to prove him wrong. Reuther accused the company of squandering resources through inefficiency and proposed allowing the UAW to co-manage the company and **assembly lines**. Reuther argued that, in the past, carmakers had simply passed on to customers whatever gains they were forced to concede to workers. Reuther boldly asserted that unions could use their clout to prevent consumer price increases. When GM complained that UAW demands would prevent the corporation from making a fair profit, Reuther once again put management on the defensive by offering to accept less if GM would open its books to the union and reveal its costs and earnings records. GM countered that Reuther was seeking to make the United States a socialist nation, but it was staggered by gathering public demands to lay bare its internal finances.

President Harry Truman briefly interjected himself into the dispute by appointing a fact-finding board that did little to end the conflict or to bolster GM's public profile. The board recommended a 17.5 percent pay increase for UAW workers, which it opined GM could easily afford. When GM ignored that recommendation, Truman declined to pursue the matter further. But Reuther also miscalculated, perhaps because GM's financial health was even more robust than he imagined. General Motors was still subject to wartime excess-profits taxes and had, by November 1945, already earned all that it was allowed for the year. This made it to GM's advantage to endure a strike as it collected a tax refund on lost earnings that in effect, saw the federal government subsidize strike payments to the corporation.

Reuther shifted his focus to **pattern bargaining** strategies that had worked in the past. The UAW reached settlements with both Ford and Chrysler, with UAW members receiving increases of approximately 18 cents per hour. By the end of January 1946, GM and the UAW were close to agreement, but workers' savings were near exhaustion. On March 13, 1946, GM agreed to an 18.5-cent hourly increase and generous **fringe benefit** concessions on plant-pay differentials, **overtime**, vacation pay, and **pensions**. It also laid the groundwork for **cost-of-living adjustments**.

At the time, Reuther was lionized for winning the richest contract in UAW history. At the UAW's 1946 convention, Reuther defeated Thomas, assumed the union's presidency, and began a purge of communists from UAW ranks. Not many questioned Reuther's toughness or strategy at the time, but subsequent critics view the 1946 agreement as a lost opportunity for organized labor. As they see it, the UAW had within its grasp a chance to establish a principle of industrial democracy in which production decisions and labor relations would be co-managed by private corporations and public labor unions. The following year the **Taft-Hartley Act** required labor unions to make their finances public, but no such law compels corporations to do so. Although it is highly speculative to do so, many labor observers wonder if **deindustrialization**, **globalization**, **protectionism**, and **concessions** might have been played out quite differently within a co-managed economy. Reuther's decision to endorse the 1946 GM contract was, in retrospect, controversial. Those seeking to defend Reuther point out that GM was in far better shape and ready to endure a much longer strike than the UAW, and that the contract the union signed was as unprecedented as the action it did not take.

Suggested Reading

Kevin Boyle, *The UAW and the Heyday of American Liberalism 1945–1968*, 1995; Martin Halpern, *UAW Politics in the Cold War Era*, 1988; Nelson Lichtenstein, *The Most Dangerous Man in Detroit: Walter Reuther and the Fate of American Labor*, 1995.

UNITED BROTHERHOOD OF CARPENTERS AND JOINERS

The United Brotherhood of Carpenters and Joiners (UBC) represents roughly 520,000 carpenters, millwrights, cabinetmakers, and assorted woodworkers in the United States and Canada. Like many modern unions, the UBC has also absorbed some professions not directly involved in woodcrafts, including **granite workers**.

Carpenters are the craftsmen who make cabinets and moldings, frame buildings, fit and join wood, install drywall and siding, and fashion other objects from wood. They are also skilled millwrights, pile drivers, shipwrights, construction workers, and (in the case of granite laborers) stone workers. The profession has been integral to the nation since the early days of European settlement. Moreover, an organization called the Carpenters Company of Philadelphia, formed in 1724, is generally regarded as the forerunner of American labor unions, though its practices of setting prices, **wages**, and quality standards actually represented a bridge between guilds and **journeymen**'s associations, as did its mutual aid and fraternal practices and its hierarchy of **masters**, journeymen, and **apprentices**. In fact, the First Continental Congress met in Carpenters' Hall in 1774. By the end of the American Revolution, the carpenters had evolved into a prototypical journeymen's association and the **Philadelphia carpenters' strike** is considered the first labor **strike** to take place in the new nation. That strike was lost, but by 1835 carpenters had won a 10-hour workday in Philadelphia and elsewhere.

Carpenters formed various **craft unions** during the first part of the 19th century, but did not have a strong national organization until the UBC was founded in 1881 in response to changes in the post-Civil War building trades industry. In Colonial and antebellum America, skilled carpenters and joiners enjoyed tremendous bargaining power. Most projects were small and the functions of contractor, master, and capitalist were often identical. Face-to-face negotiations made it easier for skilled **artisans** to resolve disputes. After the **Civil War**, however, technological changes, changes in building techniques, and the expansion of the American economy unraveled the already frayed customary arrangements between contractors and carpenters. Masters reappeared as independent contractors, whose incentive was to hold down labor costs, which was also the goal of the venture capitalists, stockholders, developers, and the government officials that authorized and funded large scale projects.

The UBC was the brainchild of **Peter J. McGuire**, a New York City carpenter who had witnessed such Gilded Age capital/labor clashes as the 1874 **Tomkins Square riot** and the **railroad strikes of 1877**. McGuire joined the **Knights of Labor** (KOL) during the late 1870s, but did not always agree with the KOL's emphasis on forming assemblies of workers that did not share a common trade. The UBC was founded in August 1881, with slightly more than 2,000 members; McGuire served as union secretary, and Gabriel Edmonston as the group's first president. McGuire, though a **socialist**, became increasingly committed to **pure and simple unionism**. The KOL and the UBC had several **jurisdictional** disputes and McGuire was instrumental in creating the **American Federation of Labor** (AFL) in late 1886.

The UBC supported the **eight-hour movement**, and also split with the KOL in its support for the May 1, 1886, **general strike** to advance the eight-hour workday. Although some UBC members won reduced hours, the 1886 strike was not a success, and in Chicago it was marred by the **Haymarket bombing**. In 1890, the UBC led another general strike for the eight-hour day, which bore more fruit and carried the AFL's endorsement. As a result of this labor action, more than 23,000 carpenters won an eight-hour workday and another 32,000 found their workday reduced to nine hours. By the early 20th century, an eight-hour workday was the norm for nearly all carpenters.

By then, the UBC and the AFL were well established, but the UBC did not solidify its identity until the late 1890s. Prior to that time, it engaged in new jurisdictional fights with the KOL that confused many workers who were not in cities where the clashes occurred. Many UBC rank-and-file members, in fact, held dual membership in the KOL, and the UBC's assembly-room ritual was based on KOL practices. By 1903, however, the UBC contained 167,200 members, more than the entire, now-moribund KOL. The UBC's departure from the KOL also had negative fallout; the KOL was far more inclusive than most AFL affiliates, the UBC included. Many UBC **union locals** refused membership to African Americans, unskilled woodworkers, and others.

The first two decades of the 20th century saw the UBC battle against the **open-shop** movement. Employers in several major cities engaged in **lockouts** against the UBC in attempts to reduce wages and hire non-union carpenters. The effort largely backfired. In 1910, the union contained more than 200,000 members. Five years later, William Hutcheson took over as UBC president, and was successful in thwarting the Woodrow Wilson administration's back-door attempts at instituting open shops during World War I. The UBC also secured protections within the trade that anticipated those of the 1931 **Davis-Bacon Act**. The 1920s were much more difficult, however. Employers advocating the open shop under the guise of the **American Plan** engaged in concerted lockouts against the UBC. The UBC defeated open-shop plans in Chicago and San Francisco, which crippled the American Plan, but overall UBC membership fell during the 1920s. The union also faced internal challenges from **communists** attempting to assert control over UBC locals.

The Great Depression brought more challenges. With the overall decline of the American economy, only 30 percent of the UBC's members were gainfully employed at any given moment. Hutcheson grew increasingly conservative and launched bitter attacks against radicals and advocates of **industrial unionism**. At the 1935 AFL convention, Hutcheson called **John L. Lewis** a "bastard" for supporting industrial unionism, and Lewis bloodied him with a haymaker. Many historians credit the intransigence of conservative craft unionists such Hutcheson as hastening the formation of the **Congress of Industrial Organizations** (CIO). Some workers quit the UBC to join the CIO's International Woodworkers of America, a breach not entirely healed until the 1955 **American Federation of Labor-Congress** of **Industrial Organizations** (AFL-CIO) merger. Even UBC loyalists complained that leaders were out of touch with rank-and-file concerns. UBC leaders had historically embraced the AFL's **voluntarism** principle with its built-in distrust of government intervention in capital/labor relations. This made the UBC hesitant in its support for the New Deal, though union leaders ultimately lobbied for **unemployment** compensation and **minimum wage** laws. Hutcheson, however, hated President Franklin Roosevelt, and the feeling was mutual; Hutcheson and several other UBC leaders were charged with violations of the **Sherman Antitrust Act** in 1940, though the U.S. Supreme Court dismissed the charges in 1941.

The UBC enjoyed a resurgence during World War II, a time in which Hutcheson's son, Maurice, served on the Wage Stabilization Board. Membership jumped from 320,000 in 1940 to more than 700,000 by 1945. The UBC lost a key battle in 1947, however, when the **Taft-Hartley Act** was passed over President Harry Truman's veto. Section 14(b) of that bill gave legal status to the hated **right-to-work** provisos against which the UBC had long battled. Nonetheless, the UBC benefited from the building boom associated with consumerism and the Baby Boom during the 1950s, and grew to 850,000 members by 1958. Critics continued to complain that the UBC was mired in **business unionism**, and cited the purchase of properties in New Jersey and Florida, and the 1961 opening of a new headquarters in Washington, D.C., as examples of its inattention to the rank-and-file. They also charged that Maurice Hutcheson, who became UBC president in 1952, was even more autocratic than his father. For the most part, though, UBC was doing well and managed to negotiate numerous **union shops**.

The UBC was badly affected by the recession that began in 1973 and that crippled the construction industry. In 1969, nearly 80 percent of all carpenters were unionized, and the UBC had as many as 800,000 members by 1973. The 1970s recession and the anti-union climate of the 1980s led developers—spearheaded by groups like the Chamber of Commerce and the Business Roundtable—to renew their efforts to hire non-union carpenters. Their efforts were supported by conservative politicians such as **Ronald Reagan** (1981–1989) and George H. W. Bush (1989–1993). By 2000, the UBC controlled just 30 percent of the nation's carpenters. In 2001, Douglas McCarran—elected UBC president in 1995 and still serving in that role in 2012—changed the way the UBC organized by consolidating **union locals** into regional councils that corresponded more to contractor spheres of influence than to traditional geographic boundaries. He also withdrew the UBC from the AFL-CIO and affiliated it with the **Change to Win Federation**. McCarran charged that AFL-CIO business unionists wasted money on bureaucracy instead of grassroots organizing. He diverted many of the UBC's resources into organizing and in revamping the union's apprenticeship program.

In 2009, the UBC quit the Change to Win Federation; it is currently unaffiliated with any **labor federation**. In recent years the union has fought campaigns to preserve the Davis-Bacon Act, secure green building jobs for members, establish best practices codes for contractors and members alike, derail free trade agreements, and deliver continued skills training for UBC carpenters.

Suggested Reading

Thomas R. Brooks, *Road to Dignity*, 1981; Walter Galenson, *The United Brotherhood of Carpenters*, 1983; Richard Schneirov and Thomas Suhrbur, *United Brotherhood, Union Town: The History of the Carpenters' Union of Chicago, 1863–1987*, 1988; "UBC Union History," United Brotherhood of Carpenters, www.carpenters.org/WhoWeAre.aspx, accessed July 18, 2011.

UNITED ELECTRICAL, RADIO, AND MACHINE WORKERS OF AMERICA

The United Electrical, Radio, and Machine Workers of America (UE) is a case study in how social change influences the fate of an organization. The UE was founded in 1936, when a wave of **Depression-era strikes** was in the process of redefining capital/labor relations. It soon became the third largest affiliate of the **Congress of Industrial Organizations** (CIO), yet in less than a decade and a half it was reduced to a shell of its former self, the victim of the second **Red Scare** and the emergence of **Cold War** unionism. The UE-CIO once had more than 750,000 members; it is now an independent body headquartered in Pittsburgh with just 35,000 members.

The genesis of the UE lies in a successful 1933 **strike** by Philco radio workers in Philadelphia. Several **union locals** combined and won a charter from the **American Federation of Labor** (AFL). Almost immediately, however, disputes arose over the Philco charter, as its workers were organized into a federal labor union affiliated directly with the AFL. Philco workers belonged to an **industrial union**, a reality that clashed with the AFL's **craft unionism** and that invited battles over **jurisdiction**. AFL leaders tried to circumvent the dispute by transferring the Philco locals to the International Brotherhood of Electrical Workers (IBEW), an action that prompted Philco workers to quit the AFL and join forces with the newly created United Electrical and Radio Workers of America (UERW), a group emerging from electrical manufacturing locals in Lynn, Massachusetts, and Schenectady, New York.

In 1937, the UERW received a boost when James Matles, the head of the **International Association of Machinists** (IAM), led his 15,000 members out of the AFL and into an alliance with the UERW. Matles complained bitterly of discriminatory AFL racial practices and was part of a new generation of leaders who saw great potential for labor gains in emerging New Deal programs and agencies. The New Deal also proved to be a boon for industrial unionism. New industrial union locals formed in industry giants such as Westinghouse, General Electric, RCA, and Philco, and leaders such as **James Carey**, Julius Emspak, Al Coulthard, and William Turnbull emerged to lead the fight tor union recognition. By 1936, approximately 30,000 workers from various union locals had placed themselves under the aegis of the UE, a new **international union**, with Carey serving as the group's president. The UE quickly established a reputation for militant shop-floor activism and democratic unionism. It absorbed the UERW and the IAM and joined the CIO in 1938. By 1944, the UE had 720,000 members.

The UE's militancy drew heavily upon the talents of left-wing organizers, including **communists**. Although the union faced constant attacks from anticommunist crusaders in federal and state government, business, and other labor unions, the social climate of the late 1930s—including the emergence of the **Popular Front**—was such that alarmist voices could be deflected. UE leadership did, however, split over the issue of communist influence. At its 1941 convention, UE President Carey proposed banning fascists and communists from holding union offices. Matles, Emspak, and Albert Fitzgerald, a popular member from Lynn, Massachusetts, led the fight to defeat Carey's motion, and to elect Fitzgerald to succeed Cary as UE president.

The U.S. alliance with the Soviet Union during World War II (1941–1945) temporarily quelled discussions of left-wing influence inside the UE. The war years also saw the UE attain its largest membership—more than 750,000. The war's end, however, was followed by the Cold War and renewed fears of communism. The 1947 **Taft-Hartley Act** required labor leaders to sign anticommunist affidavits, which many UE leaders resolutely refused to do. The UE's defiance made it vulnerable to **raiding** from other unions, as well as attacks from internal critics such as Carey and CIO President **Philip Murray**. According to some CIO lore, the UE was expelled from the labor federation because it harbored communists. In actuality, the UE was expelled for nonpayment of **dues**, which occurred because the CIO's 1949 convention refused to endorse a UE resolution forbidding further raiding. The same convention also chartered a rival union, the **International Union of Electrical, Radio, and Machine Workers of America**.

The UE maintained its defiant stance, but its locals continued to be raided throughout the 1950s and into the 1960s, a task facilitated by the fact that the UE and the IUE often organized workers in the same shops. By the mid-1960s, the UE was greatly diminished in strength. This factor proved disastrous for electrical workers, as the 1955 AFL-CIO merger paid more rhetorical attention to industrial unionism than to its reality, at least in electrical manufacturing. Whereas the UE had once been the main organization representing electrical workers, as many as 16 different unions now represented their interests. This greatly complicated **collective bargaining** efforts with conglomerates such as General Electric and Westinghouse. Battered by the internecine union battles, the UE began to rebuild in the late 1960s, only to suffer greater losses during the 1970s and 1980s due to **downsizing** and **deindustrialization**.

The UE is a smaller union at present, but one that proudly juxtaposes its rank-and-file democracy, diversity, and militancy against what it sees as the bureaucratic **business unionism** of the AFL-CIO. It has expanded its organizing focus to include workers as diverse as plastic injection molders, tool and die makers, warehouse workers, truck drivers, day care workers, aircraft engine repairers, custodians, and graduate teaching assistants.

Suggested Reading

Ronald Filippelli and M. D. McColloch, *Cold War in the Working Class: The Rise and Decline of the United Electrical Workers*, 1995; James Matles and James Higgins, *Them and Us: Struggles of a Rank-and-File Union*, 1974; Judith Stepan-Norris and Maurice Zeitlin, *Left Out: Reds and America's Industrial Unions*, 2003; United Electrical Workers,

"The U.S.A.'s Rank-and-File Union," http://www.ranknfile-ue.org/uewho.html, accessed July 19, 2011.

UNITED FARM WORKERS OF AMERICA

The United Farm Workers of America (UFWA) is a dwindling labor union that represents approximately 5,300 agricultural workers in the United States and Canada, though the bulk of its membership is located in California and the Southwest. Although it is currently declining and contains a fraction of its peak membership, the UFWA has historically been an important voice for Filipino and **Latino** workers, especially Chicanos. The UFWA was affiliated with the **American Federation of Labor-Congress of Industrial Organizations** (AFL-CIO) until 2006, when it withdrew from that labor federation and joined the **Change to Win Federation**.

Despite the political rhetoric of modern-day xenophobes, the border between the United States and Mexico has long been a fluid boundary, and Chicanos a fixture of American society. In the 1820s, Americans moved into what was then Mexican territory in search of new farmlands to replace those worn out by cotton cultivation. Many settlers came despite prohibitions against the further **immigration** of Americans by the newly independent nation of Mexico. The desire of southern agriculturalists to introduce **slavery** into sections of Mexico was among the issues that led to the Texan war for independence in 1836. The United States annexed Texas in 1845, and border disputes between it and Mexico precipitated the Mexican War in 1848. Under terms of the Treaty of Guadalupe Hidalgo, the United States seized about one-third of Mexico, including parts of the present-day states of Arizona, California, Colorado, Nevada, New Mexico, and Utah. Thousands of Mexicans found themselves American citizens overnight.

Chicanos, Central Americans, Caribs, and South Americans often sought employment opportunities in the United States. Cubans, for example, played an important role in the south Florida cigar trade during the early 20th century. Filipino and Puerto Rican farm laborers entered the United States after the 1898 Spanish-American War, with the latter settling on the mainland in larger

A United Farm Workers of America poster urges consumers to boycott lettuce and grapes as part of an effort to pressure growers into improving wages and working conditions for farm workers. (Library of Congress)

numbers beginning in the 1920s. The U.S./Mexico border proved porous during the 1870s and 1880s, with Mexican *vaqueros* providing much of the manpower for cattle drives. In addition, large numbers of Mexicans sought employment in mining, railroading, and the auto industry between 1910 and 1930. The **Industrial Workers of the World** had success in organizing agricultural workers of various ethnic backgrounds in the 1910s.

Fewer Latinos came to the United States during the Great Depression (1929–1941), and many who were not U.S. citizens were forcibly repatriated. During and after World War II, however, the U.S. government encouraged new waves of Latino laborers to come into the country. Growers complained of manpower shortages, and the government set up the *Braceros* program to recruit Mexican agricultural workers, many of whom stayed in the United States irrespective of their temporary guest-worker status. In 1951, the tacit agreement between the United States and Mexico was formalized as Public Law 78, with a stipulation that guest workers could not replace domestic workers, a proviso seldom enforced. Contrary to popular belief, though, the majority of Latino farm workers are American citizens, with many UFWA members having deeper American roots than some of their nativist critics.

Both *braceros* laborers and American farm workers faced appalling conditions. The 1935 **National Labor Relations Act** (NLRA) exempted agricultural labor from its provisions, leaving farm workers to negotiate whatever deals they could. Only those in the *braceros* program were subject to any sort of regulation, and even they worked for low **wages**—though their $1.40 per hour pay dwarfed the wages of those outside the program, who averaged just $0.90 per hour in 1964, the year the *Braceros* program officially ended. The sanitary conditions, health standards, educational opportunities, and housing conditions of farm workers were inferior to those of America's worst ghettos, and farm workers' life expectancy was just 49 years.

The UFWA came into being as a result of small steps taken by other organizations. In 1958, **Dolores Huerta** sought AFL-CIO support for a group called the Agricultural Workers Association (AWA); one year later, the AFL-CIO absorbed the AWA as part of the Agricultural Workers Organizing Committee (AWOC). The AWOC contained some Anglo and African American workers, but the bulk of its membership was Filipino and Chicano, with Huerta and Larry Itliong, a Filipino organizer, providing much of AWOC's leadership. In 1962, **César Chávez**, a community activist, joined with Huerta to form the National Farm Workers Association (NFWA), which concentrated on organizing Chicano farm laborers in and around Delano, California. In 1965, the NWFA struck a California rose farm, an action coinciding with an AWOC **strike** against California grape growers who were not complying with the end of the *Braceros* program. Both strikes made headway, but neither resulted in a union **contract**.

The UFWA came into being during a joint NWFA/AWOC strike against grape growers in the Delano/Bakersfield area of California's southern San Joaquin Valley. The AWOC called the strike on September 8, 1965, and growers responded by importing Chicano **scabs**. On September 16, Chávez convinced the NWFA to join what was then mostly a strike involving Filipinos. Within weeks, more than 30 farms found themselves unable to field a workforce. The event that focused international attention on the farm workers and led to the founding of the UFWA was Chávez's decision to launch a nationwide **grape boycott** of California table grapes. Chávez drew inspiration from the nonviolent tactics of Mahatma Gandhi in India and civil rights leaders such as the Reverend Martin Luther King, Jr., in the United States, and proved himself an equally charismatic leader.

Grassroots mobilization spread awareness of the **boycott** across the nation, roving **pickets** tied up a 400-square-mile region, and organizers convinced numerous scabs to leave the fields. Chávez also led a 340-mile protest march from Delano to Sacramento in March 1966, which focused intense media attention on the farm workers' cause, as it coincided with the one-year anniversary of a bloody civil rights march from Selma to Montgomery, Alabama. The tactics paid off when the Schenley conglomerate buckled under public pressure and signed a contract with the NFWA, the nation's first **collective bargaining** agreement between farm workers and growers. Several weeks later, the DiGrigorio Corporation also agreed to hold union elections. That move temporarily damaged the farm workers' cause when the International Brotherhood of Teamsters (IBT) also tried to organize farm workers. Its action touched off bouts of **raiding** and an IBT campaign for workers to boycott the NWFA's first election. A second election ordered by California governor Pat Brown resulted in NWFA victory. On August 22, 1966, the NWFA and the AWOC merged to form the Farm Workers Organizing Committee (FWOC), with the support of the AFL-CIO. The name was subsequently changed to the United Farm Workers of America.

By 1970, most growers had settled with the UFWA. Chávez proved masterful at manipulating public opinion, and he undertook numerous public fasts to publicize the farm workers' plight. The UFWA gained contracts that covered issues ranging from improved housing and access to clean drinking water to the handling of pesticides. The UFWA also set up its own credit union, a health clinic, Radio Campesina, and a union hiring hall. The UFWA's stylized eagle became an instantly recognizable icon, and posters emblazoned with *Huelga! (Strike!)* and *Viva La Causa (Long Live Our Cause)* proved so popular that they became UFWA slogans. The UFW grew rapidly in the late 1960s, with its membership peaking at approximately 80,000 by 1970. Each campaign it undertook proved a bruising battle, however. Three picketers were killed in 1972, and the UFWA was forced to renew its grape boycott. The **Teamsters** also remained meddlesome; in 1973, the IBT signed side agreements with growers that undermined UFWA efforts. Particularly nasty was a prolonged battle to eliminate the use of short hoes. These took a toll on farm workers' backs and posture, but growers insisted that long hoes damaged plant roots. It took several years to replace short hoes. One of the UFW's biggest victories occurred in 1975, when California passed the **Agricultural Labor Relations Act** (ALRA), which extended legal collective bargaining rights to farm workers and set up structures that parallel those under the NLRA. Although the ALRA applied solely to California and there is currently no federal legislation regulating farm work, the bill became the template from which various states fashioned their own agricultural labor codes.

Despite its many successes and the manner in which the UFWA captured the public imagination, some labor scholars now view it as a labor offshoot of the 1960s **counterculture** and as a social phenomenon that did not age well. UFWA fortunes waned in the latter half of the 1970s and into the 1980s. Its 1979 lettuce boycott failed to capture the same support as its grape boycott, and the UFWA was forced to lodge myriad complaints against California growers it claimed acted in defiance of the ALRA. Several more farm workers died during strikes between 1979 and 1983. The UFWA also sought to call attention to studies linking farm worker handling of toxic pesticides to higher cancer and miscarriage rates, but the union achieved very little in negotiations with growers over pesticide use. In 1984, Chávez and the UFWA called for a fourth worldwide boycott, this one targeting sprayed grapes. The action lingered into 2001, when the UFW called it off.

By the late 1980s, the UFW was in serious trouble. It lost more union elections than it won, and its official membership plunged to approximately 10,000, though many observers felt that actual membership was about half that figure. Chávez underwent a 36-day "Wrath of Grapes" fast in 1988 to call attention to pesticide poisoning and the ongoing grape boycott. His action generated great publicity, but much of the media focus centered on rallies attended by celebrities such as Whoopi Goldberg, Martin Sheen, and Emilio Estevez; it is uncertain how much public sympathy this protest generated. As the UFWA's fortunes flagged, some supporters began to complain that too much of the union's focus and strategy revolved around Chávez. Even so, critics were stunned by Chávez's premature death on April 23, 1993. He was succeeded by Arturo Rodriquez, his son-in-law through marriage to Linda Chávez.

Rodriquez sought to balance dramatic public events with grassroots organizing. To mark the one-year anniversary of Chávez's death, Rodriquez and the UFW re-created the 1965 Delano to Sacramento march, an event in which 20,000 participated. The UFWA slowly rebuilt its membership base and won most union representation votes after 1994. It also signed contracts with Gallo Vineyards, Global Berry strawberry workers, and several mushroom growers. Nevertheless, it suffered setbacks as well. Its decision to lift the grape boycott in 2001 was prompted more by public indifference than by tangible gains; several of the pesticides that sparked the 1984 grape boycott remain in use, and overall pesticide use has increased. The UFWA's attempt to pressure Pizza Hut to discontinue use of Pictsweet mushrooms met with limited success, and that same year the AgJobs bill supported by the UFWA, which would have allowed some undocumented workers to stay in the country, failed to make it out of the U.S. Senate. Most observers indicate that farm workers' conditions remain poor and that many growers still flunk field sanitation standards.

The UFWA has accomplished much for an organization built on large numbers of **part-time** and **contingency** workers, and its attention to the rank-and-file has been impressive; UFWA members enjoy a union **pension** plan, health benefits, **profit sharing**, and parental leave policies. In 2005, the union won a new contract with Gallo and several other grape growers. Wages remain very low, however; in 2010, American farm workers averaged just $11.13 per hour. Given that many farm workers are employed seasonally, a substantial number continue to live in poverty. Recent studies reveal that fewer than half of farm worker children graduate from high school and that **child labor** laws are routinely violated. At present the UFWA is in a weak position to lead the charge for social change. Although it has been an important voice for farm workers, especially Filipinos and Chicanos, its future is uncertain.

Suggested Reading

Susan Ferriss, Ricardo Sandoval, and Diana Hembree, *The Fight in the Fields: César Chávez and the Farmworkers Movement*, 1998; Marshall Ganz, *Why David Sometimes Wins: Leadership, Organization, and Strategy in the California Farm Worker Movement*, 2009; United Farm Workers, http://www.ufw.org/, accessed July 19, 2011.

UNITED FOOD AND COMMERCIAL WORKERS UNION

The United Food and Commercial Workers Union (UFCW) is an **international union** that represents more than 1.3 million workers, mostly in the United States and Canada. Its members historically have concentrated in the food retailing, processing, and meatpacking industries, but like many modern unions the UFCW now represents workers in a variety of other professions, including textile manufacturing, chemical production, agriculture, and health care. The UCFW was once the second largest union affiliated with the **American Federation of Labor-Congress of Industrial Organizations** (AFL-CIO), but it quit that body in 2005 and joined the **Change to Win Federation**. The UFCW offers hope to some union watchers; although it has lost some membership in the past decade, it had made inroads into the **service industry** sector and many of the workplaces it seeks to organize are not vulnerable to becoming **runaway shops**.

The UFCW is a relatively new union. It formed in 1979, when the Retail Clerks International Association and **butchers** and other food workers associated with the Amalgamated Meat Cutters and Butcher Workmen of North America (AMCBW) merged. The latter union traced its roots to 19th-century struggles. The invention of refrigerated railcars led to a national meat industry that was dominated by corporate giants such as Armour, Cudahy, Morrell, Swift, and Wilson. Stockyards and meatpacking plants proved difficult to organize, however, though the **Knights of Labor** made some progress until a traumatic strike 1886 loss in the Chicago stockyards retarded union efforts. The AMCBW coalesced in 1897 and obtained a charter from the **American Federation of Labor** (AFL). This union made modest gains on behalf of workers, but more significant progress was made in the 1930s by the **United Packinghouse Workers of America**, which was affiliated with the **Congress of Industrial Organizations** (CIO). The two unions ceased **raiding** each other's membership prior to the AFL-CIO merger in 1955, but maintained separate identities until 1968, when the UPWA joined the AMCBW. Many supermarket meat cutters and butchers are union members, though the packinghouses remain a challenge for unions. Packinghouse organization has also proved difficult because increasing numbers of recent **immigrants** work in them—populations who are often less certain about their place in American society and who, in some cases, include undocumented workers.

Retail clerks have been affiliated with the AFL since 1890, though retailing has long been a union-resistant industry due to its historically high employee turnover rate, intransigent employers, seasonal employment cycles, and sexism. Women often dominate the ranks of retail clerks, and many unions have, in the past, not given their concerns attention equal to the concerns of male industrial workers. From the outset, however, the UFCW has had a good record in matters of gender equality. More than half of its members are women. In 1987, then UFCW President Lenore Miller became the first female union president to be elected to the AFL-CIO's executive council. The UFCW aggressively organized during the 1980s, a period in which many other unions hemorrhaged members during the **downsizing, decertification, and concessions** drives of the time. It did, however, suffer a serious blow to its prestige for its handling of the 1985–1985 **Hormel strike and lockout**. Many observers believe that Austin, Minnesota, workers would have won their battle against Hormel if the UFCW had not meddled in the conflict.

Much of the UFCW's recent success has come among **brewery**, grocery, and supermarket employees. It has targeted Wal-Mart—the world's largest corporation—for organization; Wal-Mart entered the supermarket business in 1998. Thus far the UFCW have not made much headway against the company, but its campaign is an important one. Wal-Mart's very entry into retail groceries has hastened consolidation of supermarkets. Moreover, Wal-Mart's pressure to cut costs has put the UFCW in conflict with companies previously organized, as they seek **concessions** to compete with Wal-Mart and other non-unionized chains. In 1999, the UFCW launched a campaign to organize Wal-Mart and, in 2000, it made history by becoming the first union to win a contract from the company when it won representation for grocery workers at a Jacksonville, Texas, store. It has also organized two Wal-Marts in Quebec.

In 2002, the UFCW added 80,000 new members, a rarity in the age of union contraction. The UFCW also has ongoing campaigns against other "big-box stores," such as Home Depot, and hopes to make inroads into fast-food chains such as McDonald's. It recently succeeded in organizing New York City retailers in the H & M chain and is well represented in grocery conglomerates such as A & P, Albertson's, Kroger, and Safeway. In 2008, it won a 15-year struggle to organize Smithfield Foods. Joseph Hansen was chosen to head the UFCW in 2004; the next year he led the union out of the AFL-CIO and into Change to Win.

Suggested Reading

James Lardner and David Smith, eds., *Inequality Matters: The Growing Economic Divide in America and Its Poisonous Consequences*, 2006; Eric Sclosser, *Fast Food Nation*, 2001; "UFCW: A Voice for Working America," http://www.ufcw.org/, accessed July 19, 2011.

UNITED MINE WORKERS OF AMERICA

The United Mine Workers of America (UMWA) has long been the dominant organization among coal miners. It represents miners of various kinds, though its historic strength has been in anthracite and bituminous coal fields. At one time the UMWA represented nearly every miner in the nation and had more than 500,000 **dues**-paying members. Today it has fewer than 78,000 members and its influence has declined dramatically. The UMWA had more than 200,000 members in the mid-1990s, but lost nearly half of them by 2004. Some of this erosion has been due to a shift in energy priorities; many states and municipalities now prefer to generate electricity from more environmentally friendly sources than coal. Company mergers, the closing of unproductive mines, and aggressive anti-union measures have also sapped UMWA strength at a time in which the union had begun to recover from the ravages of internal corruption in the 1970s.

The UMWA's current struggles should not obscure the historic gains made by the organization. Miners' struggle for dignity has been bloody and bitter. Mines were often located in remote areas, and mine owners ran their operations as if they were personal fiefdoms. Workers frequently toiled in **company towns** and were subject to rigid rules that regulated both work and life off the job. Some workers were paid in scrip, and many mining camps were marked by squalor, backbreaking labor, and crushing poverty. Few American industries were as deadly as mining; cave-ins, explosions, poisonous gas, and flooding frequently killed many miners in a single fell swoop. Between 1876 and 1900, there were 101 mine accidents in which more than five miners died—an incident rate that tripled from 1901 to 1925. A 1907 explosion in Monongah, West Virginia, killed 362 miners; two years later a fire in Cherry, Illinois, killed 259. Debilitating injury rates were appalling, **child labor** was standard, and the dust breathed by miners induced **black lung** disease and early death. Even today the life expectancy of underground coal miners is significantly lower than the national average, and the emphysema, lung, and cancer rates among such workers are higher than average.

The first effort to organize coal miners came in 1860, but it yielded only modest success. The Workingman's Benevolent Association (WBA) made big inroads in Pennsylvania, before it fell prey to hysteria over alleged **Molly Maguire** terrorists. Some historians believe that the Mollies were actually a fiction invented by coal operators to smash the WBA, though the presence of such an organization would not be far-fetched given the exploitation of immigrant labor in coal regions. The first miner unions to have more than a regional presence were those affiliated with **Knights of Labor** (KOL) National Trade District 135 and the 1885 National Federation of Miners and Mine Workers, the latter of which affiliated with the newly formed **American Federation of Labor** (AFL) in 1886. The UMWA was created when the KOL began to decline in power. In 1890, a union called the National Progressive Union of Miners and Mine Laborers merged with KOL District 135 to form the UMWA, spearheaded by former Knight William T. Lewis. It affiliated with the AFL.

The UMWA constitution forbade discrimination based on race, religion, or ethnicity. This was rare for the time and reflected the UMWA's KOL roots, as the KOL was one of the few **labor federations** to organize **minority labor** and unskilled workers on an equal basis with skilled, white, male **artisans**. In 1898, the UMWA won an **eight-hour** workday for most of its members, also relatively rare

Breaker Boys sorting coal in a coal mine in South Pittston, Pennsylvania. The United Mine Workers of America sought to regulate mine safety and eliminate other abuses in the industry, including crippling child labor. Breaker Boys such as these endured horrible conditions. Many lost fingers, inhaled coal dust, and were absent from American classrooms. (Library of Congress)

at the time. Most UMWA gains at the time came only after prolonged and bloody conflict such as an 1894 bituminous coal strike in which numerous miners were killed and which almost destroyed the nascent union. In 1897 **Lattimer Massacre**, company **goons** and local law enforcement officials killed 19 peacefully demonstrating **immigrant** coal miners in a Pennsylvania town. Militancy became the order of the day; the West erupted in mine disputes during the 1890s that produced such infamous incidents as the troubles at **Coeur d'Alene**, the **Colorado labor wars**, and the **Ludlow Massacre**, **Mary "Mother" Jones** was often in the midst of these and many other UMWA struggles, as well as those of the rival Western Federation of Miners.

Its militancy notwithstanding, the UMWA also benefited from prudent leadership. **John Mitchell** served as UMWA president from 1898 to 1908. He was a cautious man, but a good tactician. Mitchell was a member of the **National Civic Federation** and parlayed his contacts into bargaining advantage. In 1902, more than 150,000 miners struck in protest of low pay and appalling safety records in the mines. Mitchell met with President Theodore Roosevelt and offered to submit miner **grievances** to government **arbitration**, vowing that miners would respect the decision made. Mitchell's respectful demeanor contrasted so sharply with the intransigence and rudeness of mine operators that Roosevelt brokered a deal that prevented operators from smashing the UMWA. Although miner gains were quite modest, Roosevelt's actions heralded a coming shift in government attitudes toward organized labor. In 1910, the government set up the Bureau of Mines (BoM), one of whose tasks to regulate mine safety. This was an important step, but one that the UMWA would subsequently complain was generally more concerned with rationalizing business practices than with protecting miners. (The BoM closed in 1995 and its functions were transferred to other agencies, especially the Department of Energy.)

The UMWA continued to rely upon point-of-production action and was involved in numerous strikes and protests prior to World War I, including a 16-month strike in Westmoreland County, Pennsylvania, during 1910 and 1911 in which 15 people died. The aforementioned Ludlow Massacre involved a loss of 16 lives, 12 of them children. The UMWA agreed to a **no-strike pledge** during World War I and grew to more than 500,000 members during this period of industrial peace. Operators did not respect wartime agreements, however, and strikes broke out anew after 1920, the year **John L. Lewis** became UMWA president. The government created the Bituminous Coal Commission in 1920, which gave miners large raises and recognized the UMWA as the miners' bargaining unit, but this did little to prevent horrendous violence in Kentucky and West Virginia, including the infamous 1920 shootout between miners and Baldwin-Felts agents in **Matewan**, West Virginia. Its aftermath led to the **Battle of Blair Mountain** in which more than two dozen lives were lost. In all, some 10,000 miners battled police, company forces, and the government for more than a year, until miners were forced to capitulate. This outcome caused such palpable anger in coal fields that, in 1922, union workers responded with an atrocity of their own—the killing of 19 **scabs** during a strike in Herrin, Illinois, known as the **Herrin Massacre**. Violence was so common in Kentucky that one county was dubbed "bloody Harlan" in 1932.

Lewis won a reputation for being a hard-nosed bargainer who was not afraid to authorize strikes. UMWA militancy was aided by the fact that miners were already accustomed to hardship and many had little to lose in protracted struggles. Under Lewis, UMWA members secured retirement **pensions** and higher pay, but he grew restless with the AFL's slowness to recognize the need for **industrial unions**, and its parsimony in funding grassroots organizing. Lewis became the leading spirit behind the establishment the **Congress of Industrial Organizations** (CIO). Although a formal break did not come until 1937, the UMWA was effectively out of the AFL by 1935. Lewis became the first CIO president and rode a tide of worker militancy to win wage and benefit concessions for UMWA members. He supported the New Deal and worked to elect Franklin Roosevelt in 1932 and 1936, but supported Wendell Willkie in 1940 and resigned as CIO president when Roosevelt was reelected.

In 1941, Lewis demanded and won a **union-shop** agreement in captive mines owned by steel firms, a task accomplished by calling a risky strike against firms that the UMWA had already organized to near totality. In 1942, Lewis abruptly pulled the UMWA out of the CIO. Unlike most other unions, the UMWA refused to take a no-strike pledge during World War II. Lewis was twice cited for contempt of court during the **coal miners' strike of 1943**. Some historians believe that the UMWA's actions during the war fueled postwar antilabor legislation such as the Smith-Connally Act and the **Taft-Hartley Act**, though is likely that anti-union forces would have pushed for these bills without prompting.

The UMWA rejoined the AFL in 1946, then quit again in 1947, when Lewis refused to commit the UMWA to noncommunist affidavits required under the Taft-Hartley Act. Lewis, in fact, disliked communism and was a Republican, but he saw Taft-Hartley as an abomination and was disgusted by the AFL's strategy of seeking a political reversal of the bill. The UMWA defied the act through a series of short work stoppages, memorial strikes, and other tactics designed to test the law's limitations. From 1947 through 1950, the UMWA interrupted national coal supplies on numerous occasions. President Harry Truman issued an injunction against new strikes in 1950, while Congress debated seizing coal mines and drafting miners, actions that Lewis recognized as bluffs. Lewis continued as UMWA president into 1959. By the time he retired, his youthful activism had given way to autocratic behavior. He was one of the most important labor leaders in all of U.S. history, but his final days left a bureaucratic and nondemocratic legacy over which the UMWA would soon stumble.

Automation began to displace workers by the 1960s, and UMWA progress stalled on key campaigns such as those related to worker safety and occupational diseases. In 1963, William Boyle acceded to the UMWA presidency and almost immediately charges of corruption swirled. Rank-and-file insurgency movements formed inside the UMWA that, in 1969, supported **Joseph A. Yablonski**'s bid to unseat Boyle. Boyle used arcane UMWA bureaucratic maneuvers to win reelection, but Yablonski was murdered several weeks later. A federal judge invalidated Boyle's reelection as fraudulent, and Boyle was subsequently convicted of Yablonski's murder.

A group calling itself Miners for Democracy formed in 1970, dedicated to cleaning up the UMWA. It succeeded in electing Arnold Miller to the UMWA presidency. Miller, however, was not the strong leader reformers for whom which had hoped, and his handling of the a brutal Harlan County strike against Duke Power Company in 1973–1974 was criticized by many. During the strike, a scab murdered a UMWA member. As criticism mounted against Miller, he, too, was accused of autocracy. The UMWA remained in great turmoil until 1982, when **Richard Trumka** became UMWA president.

Trumka is credited with completing the restoration of rank-and-file democracy and of making headway on black lung disease. He also won kudos for leading the 1989 **Pittston Coal strike**, a rare victory for organized labor in an era of **downsizing, decertification, and concessions** battles. Trumka left his post to become AFL-CIO secretary-treasurer in 1995, by which time the UMWA had approximately 240,000 members. Cecil Roberts, Jr., became the UMWA president, but proved unable to sustain the growth that occurred under Trumka, who now heads the **American Federation of Labor-Congress of Industrial Organizations** (AFL-CIO). The UMWA has called attention to degrading conditions in nonunion coal mines, many of which are now operated by conglomerates. Those charges received a public airing after a 2010 explosion of a Massey Energy Company mine in Montcoal, West Virginia, that killed 10 miners, but to date the UMWA has seen few post-explosion gains.

As of 2012, Roberts still headed the UMWA, but the UMWA, like the coal industry itself, no longer commands the strength it once had. Despite political rhetoric about the future of "clean coal," under existing technology coal is not environmentally friendly, nor is it a renewable source. Unless dramatic new extraction and burning methods emerge, coal production may become a **sunset industry**. This leaves in doubt the future both of coal companies and the UMWA.

Suggested Reading

Thomas Dublin and Walter Licht, *The Face of Decline: The Pennsylvania Anthracite Region in the 20th Century*, 2005; Melvyn Dubofsky, *John L. Lewis*, 1986; John M. H. Laslett, *The United Mine Workers of America: A Model of Industrial Solidarity?*, 1996; Paul Taylor, *Bloody Harlan*, 1990; "Historical Data on Mine Disasters in the United States," United States Mine Rescue Association, http://www.usmra.com/saxsewell/historical.htm, accessed July 20, 2011.

UNITED MINE WORKERS STRIKE OF 1943. *See* Coal Miners Strike of 1943.

UNITED PACKINGHOUSE WORKERS OF AMERICA

The United Packinghouse Workers of America (UPWA) existed from 1937 to 1968 and is often studied as a model of union racial and gender cooperation. The UPWA technically came into existence in 1943, but this was simply the name change given to the Packinghouse Workers' Organizing Committee (PWOC), which was organized by **Congress of Industrial Organizations** (CIO) in 1937. Like most CIO bodies, the PWOC/UPWA was an **industrial union**.

The UPWA emerged from many decades of struggle to secure **collective bargaining** rights for **butchers** and other workers in the meat industry. Meatpacking conditions were immortalized in Upton Sinclair's 1906 novel *The Jungle*. Sinclair was accused of sensationalizing the situation, but his novel stimulated reforms during the **Progressive Era** and beyond for the simple reason that conditions had long been every bit as appalling as he described them. As a result, unionization efforts emerged in the in post-**Civil War** period side by side with expansion of meatpacking firms occasioned by advances such as refrigerated rail cars and the development of huge stockyards in locales such as Chicago, Omaha, Kansas City, and Abilene, Kansas. By the 1880s, the **Knights of Labor** (KOL) had organized packinghouse workers in small firms and was making headway with industry giants such as Swift and Armour until a disastrous 1887 **strike** in the Chicago stockyards curtailed the KOL's efforts. The Amalgamated Meat Cutters and Butcher Workmen of North America formed in 1897 and affiliated with the **American Federation of Labor** (AFL). It concentrated on organizing skilled butchers and enjoyed its greatest success during World War I, but after the war, most firms broke agreements signed with the Amalgamated and other AFL workers **scabbed** on it during struggles against Armour.

The AFL largely ignored the **immigrant** workforce that accounted for the bulk of slaughterhouse workers. The harsh conditions and long hours under which these employees toiled only worsened once the Great Depression began. As result of deteriorating conditions and the AFL's indifference, the PWOC attracted numerous militant leaders, including **communists**. The Autoworkers Organizing Committee also supplied logistical support for the PWOC. Left-wing ideology was put into practice; the PWOC maintained strict codes of racial and gender **solidarity**. It also broke down barriers that separated pork butchers from those working in beef, the latter of whom historically viewed themselves as more skilled. The UPWA probably never had more than 125,000 members, but its activism allowed it to succeed where prior efforts had faltered. A favored tactic was the use of "night riders," referring to the quick transportation of leaders and **pickets** from one town to another in support to facilitate quick organizing drives. Such actions also helped build solidarity between cities, thereby lessening the likelihood of scabbing during labor disputes. When Armour workers in Kansas City won a strike in 1937, Armour quickly settled with the PWOC in several other cities. Two years later, the PWOC forced firms to pay men and women equal wages for equal work.

The progressive PWOC took advantage of the recently passed **National Labor Relations Act** to obtain collective bargaining rights for other meatpacking workers, and it soon swamped the AFL's Amalgamated Meat Cutters in popularity. By 1943, it was the largest union in the stockyards, a status confirmed by the name change to the United Packinghouse Workers of America. In 1946, Ralph Helstein became UPWA president. Helstein was dedicated to maintaining the union's activism in the face of employer counterassaults against organized labor after World War II. The UPWA attacked the segregation policies of southern plants and the glaring wage differentials vis-à-vis northern workers. The UPWA managed to raise wage rates in the South, but was less successful in overturning the "Jim Crow" practices that relegated African American workers to the worst jobs available.

The UPWA maintained its commitment to racial equality even when it cost the union white members. In the 1950s, the union moved its headquarters to the heavily African American "Black Belt" in Chicago's South Side, and when whites dropped out, promoted African Americans to positions of union leadership. The UPWA also conducted a militant 14-month strike and **boycott** against Boston's Colonial Provision Company between 1954 and 1956, which saw remarkable levels of racial cooperation despite red-baiting and other brutal company tactics.

The UPWA declined in size and influence in the 1960s, as **mechanization** replaced line workers and firms relocated to non-union cities. Industry consolidation also eliminated many union jobs and new corporate ownership groups proved more resistant to organization. In 1968, the UPWA merged with the Amalgamated Meat Cutters and Butcher Workmen of North America. Further union streamlining resulted in the creation of the **United Food and Commercial Workers Union** in 1979. Its 1.3 million members now include the stockyard workers and butchers once represented by the UPWA.

Suggested Reading

Rick Halpern, *Down on the Killing Floor*, 1997; Roger Horowitz, *Negro and White, Unite and Fight*, 1997; Shelton Stromquist and Marvin Bergman, eds., *Unionizing the Jungle*, 1997.

UNITED RUBBER WORKERS OF AMERICA

The United Rubber Workers of America (URWA) existed from 1936 to 1995, though it traced its roots to the late-19th-century Eastern boot and shoe business, especially in New England. Rubber work is generally viewed as a **sunset industry** in contemporary American society, though a certain amount of specialty work continues and tire makers such as Bridgestone/Firestone, Cooper, Dunlop. B.F. Goodrich, Goodyear, and Kelly-Springfield still make some of their product line in the United States, as do several foreign-based manufacturers.

Rubber work was originally associated more with shoe and boot manufacturing than with automobiles. The **Knights of Labor** (KOL) was the first **labor federation** to try to unite the industry on a national basis, though this effort was thwarted when manufacturing companies formed a trust in 1892. The decline of the KOL allowed a powerful cartel, the United States Rubber Company, to operate an **open-shop** environment and set the pattern for labor/management relations throughout the industry. In the 1890s, production also expanded beyond footwear. The bicycle craze of the late 19th century led to demand for tires, as did the rise of automobile manufacturing in the early 20th century. Many tire plants located in the Midwest, with Akron, Ohio, emerging as the "Rubber Capital of the World" by the first decade of the 20th century. As rubber production accelerated, it moved from being an **artisanal** craft to an industrial occupation marked by **automation** and a deskilling of the workforce. Rubber workers toiled long hours in dirty plants. Informal protests were common as manufacturers often imposed **speedups** during high-demand seasons.

During the 1890s, the **American Federation of Labor** (AFL) sought to fill the organizational void left when the KOL declined, but the AFL's **craft union** structure led AFL President **Samuel Gompers** to charter federal labor unions that lacked organizational coherence. Numerous federal locals banded together to create the Amalgamated Rubber Workers Union in 1903, but it collapsed shortly after a 1906 **strike** centered in Trenton, New Jersey. Both the **Industrial Workers of the World** (IWW) and the machinists' union attempted to organize the field workers in Akron, but were not successful. The AFL openly competed with the IWW, which led a 1913 strike against Firestone, Goodyear, and Goodrich. The AFL's meddling had the net effect of driving both it and the IWW from the field.

Rubber was not effectively organized until New Deal labor legislation during the 1930s led to a revival of unionization. The AFL created the Rubber Workers Council in 1934, but once again its practice of dispersing industrial workers among craft union affiliates weakened its appeal for rubber workers. The AFL created the United Rubber Workers of America in 1935, but almost immediately the URWA pushed for **industrial unionism**. The infant URWA surprised industry analysts and many AFL leaders by conducting a massive **sit-down strike** at the Goodyear Rubber Company in Akron in 1936. This action was followed by a series of **wildcat strikes** in Akron and elsewhere. By then, the URWA had cast its lot with the **Congress of Industrial Organizations** (CIO). Although the CIO did not officially exist as an independent entity until 1938, most labor historians assert that it was by all meaningful measures a reality by the end of 1935. The URWA's February 1936 job action against Goodyear is sometimes considered the CIO's first strike. Although Goodyear workers did not succeed in forcing Goodyear to rescind either its **wage** cut or its layoffs, the union achieved favorable work rule changes. Subsequent strike victories over Palmer Asbestos in Chicago, Goodyear in Gadsden, Alabama, and Firestone in Akron established the URWA as a major force in the rubber industry. The URWA quickly won union recognition votes and **collective bargaining** rights with other major tire enterprises, including the United States Rubber Company, the industry pacesetter.

The URWA continued its forward momentum during World War II and changed its name to the United Rubber, Cork, Linoleum and Plastic Workers of America (URCLPWA) to reflect expansion into new **jurisdictions**. By 1945, the union had nearly 190,000 members. Like other CIO unions in the postwar era, the rubber workers union split into left-wing and conservative factions that destabilized the organization for several years, but rubber workers obtained their first **pension** plan in 1949 and health and hospitalization coverage in 1943. The URWA had been stabilized by the time of the 1955 **American Federation of Labor-Congress of Industrial Organizations** (AFL-CIO) merger and soon negotiated master contracts for rubber and plastics workers. By 1970s, the rubber workers union had more than 190,500 members.

Like many industries connected to automobiles, rubber suffered a setback in the mid-1970s from which it has never recovered. The Organization of Petroleum Exporting Countries (OPEC) instituted a series of oil **boycotts** during and after 1973, each designed to drive up the cost of petroleum by restricting supply into consumption-driven economies such as that of the United States. The OPEC boycotts posed a double threat to rubber manufacturers. First, a dip in demand for automobiles meant a lessened need for tires. Second, the boycotts caused a big jump in manufacturing costs. Tires and other rubber products are seldom made entirely from rubber latex; instead, the "vulcanization" process mixes rubber with chemicals such as sulfur that are heated to high temperatures. The need to produce such heat meant that manufacturers faced higher energy costs to produce tires. Moreover, tires—whether rubber or synthetic—depend upon polymers, many of which are petroleum based.

The rubber industry was in flux when the 1980s opened and Presidents **Ronald Reagan** and George H. W. Bush encouraged the aggressive anti-union tactics emerging in the business community. **Globalization** led to a surge in foreign imports, to which manufacturers responded by instituting layoffs, closing aging plants, and shifting production offshore to **runaway shops**. They also forced **concessions** on workers and their unions, as did foreign firms such as Japan's Bridgestone, which took over Firestone in 1976. The URWA called a strike against Bridgestone/Firestone in 1994, which stretched into 1995; during the **Bridgestone/Firestone strike of 1994–1995**, the manufacturer operated its plants with **scab** labor who produced tires for the Ford Explorer that subsequently turned out to be flawed and linked to auto fatalities. By then, the URWA/ URCLPWA had ceased to exist as an independent union. In 1995, rubber and plastics workers merged with the **United Steelworkers of America** (USWA). The USWA continues to represent rubber and plastics workers, but the future of those working in tires is unclear given that increasing numbers of the tires sold in the United States are manufactured in China, Thailand, Japan, Taiwan, and other offshore locations.

Suggested Reading

Tom Juravich and Kate Bronfenbrenner, "Out of the Ashes: The Steelworkers' Global Campaign at Bridgestone/Firestone," Articles and Chapters, Paper 38, January 2003, http://digitalcommons.ilr.cornell.edu/articles/38, accessed July 25, 2011; David Nelson, *American Rubber Workers and Organized Labor*, 1988; Bryan D. Palmer, *Goodyear Invades the Backcountry: The Corporate Takeover of a Rural Town*, 1994.

UNITED STEELWORKERS OF AMERICA

In the 1930s, the United Steelworkers of America (USWA) was the union that finally organized the American steel industry. As such, it is often studied as one of the most important **industrial unions** in U.S. labor history. The USWA is still one of the largest industrial unions in the nation and has more than 705,000 members at present. Many USWA members, however, are no longer in steel, which is now viewed as a **sunset industry**. Instead, the USWA represents rubber workers, paper producers, chemical industry employees, and health care workers, among others. Its official name is currently the United Steel, Paper and Forestry, Rubber, Manufacturing, Energy, Allied Industrial and Service Workers International Union.

The USWA emerged from the Steel Workers Organizing Committee (SWOC) in the 1930s and was the culmination of a long struggle to organize steel, the quintessential "heavy" industry associated with the maturation of America's **Industrial Revolution**. Steel—a key component in other signature industries such as weapons manufacturing, railroads, and automobiles—emerged as an industrial juggernaut after 1858, when the Bessemer process facilitated the removal of impurities from pig iron and made steel a more reliable and more cheaply produced commodity. It was also an industry that quickly fell under the control of powerful magnates such as Andrew Carnegie and J. P. Morgan, viewed by many as robber barons. The enormous wealth and political influence of such men made steel very difficult to organize. Although groups such as the **Knights of Labor** and the **Industrial Workers of the World** (IWW) made attempts to win **collective bargaining** rights for steelworkers, their efforts were more valiant than successful. Steel was the focal point of several chaotic and bloody union/management clashes, such as the 1892

Homestead Steel lockout and strike that destroyed the Amalgamated Association of Iron, Steel, and Tin Workers, a **craft union** affiliated with the **American Federation of Labor** (AFL); and the **steel strike of 1919**, a traumatic loss that made most steel mills **open shops** into the 1930s. A few firms operated **company unions**, which were controlled by manufacturers, but the only independent union of any consequence was the **International Mine, Mill, and Smelter Workers** (IMMSW), an IWW offshoot

The SWOC represented an attempt by industrial unionists to organize workers who were generally ignored by the AFL. During the mid-1930s, it was affiliated with the **Congress of Industrial Organizations** (CIO), which set up the body in 1936. SWOC/CIO efforts were assisted by the **United Mine Workers of America** (UMWA), which was keen to organize steel mills because many were owned by firms that also controlled coal mines. The UMWA lent the SWOC experienced organizers, including union executive **Philip Murray**, who served as the SWOC's chairman. The SWOC's campaign was a combination of point-of-production action and behind-the-scenes negotiation. In March 1937, secret negotiations between CIO President **John L. Lewis** and U.S. Steel chairman Myron Taylor resulted in a SWOC contract that stipulated a $5 per day, 40-hour work week that union organizers hoped would become the industry standard. The SWOC soon ran up against the intransigence and wrath of firms such as Republic Steel, Inland Steel, and Youngstown Sheet and Tube Company, however. These "Little Steel" firms—so called simply because they were smaller than U.S. Steel—were notoriously resistant to unions and were not immune to using violence to deter organizers. The SWOC launched a strike against Little Steel in the spring of 1937. In an event known as the Memorial Day Massacre, Chicago police attacked picnicking union members and killed 10 workers. The **La Follette Committee** revealed a pattern of intimidation and violence among Little Steel manufacturers, revelations that shocked the nation, though Little Steel was not finally organized until 1941.

The coming of World War II solidified gains made by the SWOC, whose members agreed to a **no-strike pledge**. In June 1942, the SWOC changed its name to the United Steelworkers of America. The name change signified both the union's permanence and its willingness to advance gains made since 1937. In 1944, the USWA absorbed an aluminum workers union and began to represent that industry as well. By January 1946, the USWA had more than 700,000 steelworkers enrolled. It called a **strike** against the steel industry when manufacturers sought to exploit the end of the war and repudiate previous agreements; it also sought **wage** increases at a time in which wage and price controls were still set by the government. The strike lasted less than a month before President Harry Truman partially lifted wartime price controls and steel producers gave workers an 18.5-cent hourly wage increase.

The USWA continued to consolidate its gains. Bethlehem Steelworkers secured a company-sponsored **pension** plan in 1949 that quickly became a standard in other USWA-organized firms. Philip Murray died in 1952 and was succeeded by Dave McDonald, who oversaw major strikes in 1956 and 1959. The **steel strike of 1959–1960** was particularly traumatic. It lasted 116 days and idled more than 500,000 workers. The USWA faced down President Dwight Eisenhower's imposed cooling-off period authorized under the **Taft-Hartley Act** and manufacturer efforts to force **concessions** and won the richest contract in steelworker history. The contract included important agreements on job classifications as well as supplemental **unemployment** benefits.

The 1960 agreement appears, in retrospect, to have been the USWA's high-water mark in the steel industry. Steel had emerged in the 1870s as a symbol of America's industrial might, but by the late 1960s manufacturers were saddled with aging equipment, had high labor costs, and faced threats from cheaper imported steel. In 1967, the IMMSW merged with the USWA, a harbinger of challenges facing both the industry and unions representing industrial workers. After 1960, the USWA avoided strikes when it could. I. W. Abel, who became USWA president in 1965, had risen through the union ranks and had overseen union political action committees. Abel preferred political pressure to McDonald's confrontational approach and was a key lobbyist in the battle to secure the passage of the 1970 **Occupational Safety and Health Act**. Abel also oversaw mergers between the USWA and the United Stone and Allied Products Worker in 1971, and between the USWA and the Allied and Technical Workers in 1972. He also brokered a deal between the USWA and steel companies known as the Experimental Negotiating Agreement (ENA); under this agreement, which lasted from 1973 through 1983, steelmakers and the USWA agreed to submit their differences to **arbitration**. Steelworker wages increased under the ENA, even as the industry contracted.

The era of peace came to an end during the 1980s, when remaining steel firms demanded concessions and givebacks from the USWA. The 1980s also saw a contraction of the USWA among steelworkers, though mergers with other bodies such as the Upholsterers International Union (1985) softened the impact of these losses somewhat. The transformation of the steel industry is symbolically represented by U.S. Steel's 1991 decision to rename itself USX Corporation, which occurred when the company began to derive more income from its merger with Marathon Oil, real estate holdings, and other pursuits than from steel manufacturing. (The much-ridiculed name was abandoned in 2001.) Layoffs and plant closures were commonplace throughout the 1980s and 1990s, with once-thriving steel towns as Birmingham, Alabama; Johnstown, Pennsylvania; Wheeling, West Virginia; and Youngstown, Ohio being portrayed in the media as the rusting faces of American **deindustrialization**.

The USWA had little alternative to diversifying its focus much as U.S. Steel had done. Its 1995 merger with the United Rubber, Cork, Linoleum, and Plastic Workers is an example of the way in which the union's focus broadened. In some cases, though, the USWA returned to pre-1963 patterns of rank-and-file militancy. It led several long and bitter strikes during the 1990s, including campaigns such as the **Ravenswood lockout** of 1990–1992, and the **Bridgestone-Firestone strike of 1994–1995**. It settled the latter dispute after absorbing the **United Rubber Workers of America** in 1995. The union also won high-profile battles against WCI Steel, Phelps-Dodge, Alcoa, Reynolds, and Newport News Shipbuilding. Long an opponent of **fast-track legislation** and a supporter of **protectionist** trade policies, the USWA also took part in the anti-**globalization** protests at the World Trade Organization meetings in Seattle during 1999.

The USWA's new direction has helped it cast off its old image of being a conservative body dominated by white male **business unionists**. The USWA is now ethnically diverse and has promoted women into positions of leadership. In the 21st century, the union has pursued a policy of militancy in steel and rubber and continued expansion of its organizational efforts outside those fields, such as among glass and wood workers. In 2005, it merged with the Paper, Allied-Industrial, Chemical and Energy Workers International Union (PACE). The following year, the USWA became one of the few unions to organize abroad, when it won representation for refinery workers in Aruba. It is too soon to know whether its strategic mix of forging alliances with other bodies, applying political pressure, and engaging in workplace militancy will yield long-term results, but it offers intriguing possibilities. The USWA is currently holding its own at a time in which other **American Federation of Labor-Congress of Industrial Organizations** (AFL-CIO) affiliates have been in steep decline.

Suggested Reading

Peter Clark, Peter Gottleib, and Donald Kennedy, eds., *Forging a Union of Steel: Philip Murray, SWOC, and the United Steelworkers*, 987; John Hoerr, *And the Wolf Finally Came*, 1988; Jack Metzgar, *Striking Steel: Solidarity Remembered*, 2011; "United Steelworkers of America," http://www.usw.org/, accessed July 25, 2011.

UPRISING OF THE 20,000

The Uprising of the 20,000 refers to a 1909 **strike** involving the United Hebrew Trades and the **International Ladies' Garment Workers' Union** (IGLWU). Despite the label associated with the walkout, at its height it actually involved more than 32,000 workers. The strike was an important expression of the militancy of Jewish **immigrant** workers in New York City's garment industry. It is also viewed as an example of the limitations of **Progressive Era** reform. Among the issues precipitating the 1909 strike were **sweatshop**-like working conditions. Just one year after the strike ended, the tragic **Triangle Factory fire of 1911** underscored the dangers of unregulated work environments.

The Triangle Factory was also a focal point in 1909. Women constituted the majority of workers in New York City's garment trades, especially recent Jewish and Italian immigrants between the ages of 16 and 24. They worked incredibly long hours—often as many as 75 hours per week—and quite a few received only **piece-work** rates for their endeavors. They also faced capricious employer deductions for garments deemed substandard, and they had to buy their own needles and thread from their meager earnings. A particularly pernicious custom was one in which employers required women to own their own sewing machines. Those who did not own these machines could "buy" one on time from their employer, with the fees being deducted from their pay. Workers were routinely fired before they completed their purchase, their machines appropriated and leased to the next unsuspecting victim.

At this point in time, only company-sponsored "associations" represented women—groups that were even less effective than **company unions**. In November 1909, Jewish women at Triangle sought to leave their employer association and be represented by the United Hebrew Trades. When Triangle fired them and hired **scabs**, other workers at Triangle walked off the job and set up **pickets** in front of the plant. Triangle hired male **goons** to harass and beat picketers. In some cases, New York City police also brutalized the individuals manning the pickets.

Five weeks into the strike, a protest rally was held at New York's Cooper Union. At the event a recent Russian Jewish immigrant worker, Clara Lemlich, upstaged the male leadership of the strike and guest speakers such as **Samuel Gompers**. Lemlich mounted the stage and urged workers, in Yiddish, to launch a **general strike** in the garment trades. Although Pauline Newman and **Rose Schneiderman** organized the ILGWU to support the strikers and the **Women's Trade Union League** also aided them, employers responded with the same sort of brutality that had greeted protestors at Triangle. Employers also engaged in tactics such as hiring prostitutes to harass the young women on the picket lines and suggest, lasciviously, that the young women could turn to prostitution if they were dissatisfied with garment-industry **wages**. Police once again sided with the corporations, and more than 700 women were arrested, 19 of whom served time in public workhouses.

The strike ended on February 10, 1910, with strikers winning union **contracts** in most garment shops; Triangle remained a holdout. The strike called attention to the ease with which employers could fire union activists, as well as the deplorable conditions, low wages, and long hours that workingwomen endured. Numerous women were **blacklisted**, including Lemlich. She was embittered by the strike and later joined the Communist Party. On the positive side, the strike proved that sweatshop workers and semiskilled workers could be organized into unions. The Uprising of the 20,000 forced the **American Federation of Labor** to reconsider its assumptions about organizing women; and not just skilled male tailors and garment cutters. It strengthened the ILGWU and placed it in a position in which it would be able to rally public support after the Triangle fire.

Suggested Reading

Charlotte Baum, Paula Hyman, and Sonya Michel, *The Jewish Woman in America*, 1976; Elizabeth Ewan, *Immigrant Women in the Land of Dollars*, 1985; Annalise Orleck, *Common Sense and a Little Fire: Women and Working-Class Politics in the United States, 1900–1965*, 1995.

UTOPIANISM AND AMERICAN LABOR

Utopianism is an imprecise term that refers to a belief in a society rooted in shared ideals. In the popular imagination, a utopia is often associated with a "perfect" society free from social and economic imperfections; in practice, the utopian impulse is merely at odds with existing social norms and followers seek alternative ways of living, working, and interacting. Utopianism is also often viewed as impractical, yet many utopian experiments and visions, especially those involving working people, sought to offer what were perceived to be pragmatic solutions to social problems. The United States has fostered thousands of utopian experiments and thinkers—so many that it is hard to find coherence and patterns that unify them. For the most part, utopias took on the character and values of those who imagined and/or created them. Their one commonality is that each was a critique of existing society.

Utopias are not unique to the United States. The term gained currency from the work of Sir Thomas More in the early 16th century, but the ancient world was also replete with utopian visions; Plato's *Republic*, for example, was the philosopher's take on how an ideal society should be run. In similar fashion, the commonwealth vision of John Winthrop outlined in his "Model of Christian Charity" essay can be viewed as utopian. Utopian experiments involving American wage-earners emerged with industrialization and appeared in great numbers during the 19th century. American manufacturers were keenly aware of social problems associated with the **Industrial Revolution** in Britain, and some hoped to create industrial models that would avoid such miseries. Samuel Slater, for instance, built a series of small textile villages in the Blackstone River Valley of Massachusetts and Rhode Island, which he hoped would absorb the best features of New England village life. By contrast, the designers of Lowell, Massachusetts, built a glittering industrial city that was to be the antithesis of grimy English textile towns. Other industrialists outside of the textile industry copied this "machine in the garden" mentality.

Industrial towns and cities were, however, usually the vision of investors rather than workers. **Capitalism**, with its emphasis on private profit, was by no means universally accepted or loved in the 19th century, nor was the industrial system. **Agrarianism** remained the dominant ideal into the early 20th century, and numerous utopias looked to agriculture—not manufacturing—to sustain communities. Religious orders such as the Amish and the Hutterites upheld the virtues of rural life, as did secular efforts such as Brook Farm (1841–1847) and Fruitlands (1843–1845) in Massachusetts, the heart of the American Industrial Revolution.

Those pre-**Civil War** utopians that focused on manufacturing from a worker's perspective often took their cues from Europe. The ideas of the Frenchman Charles Fourier were much discussed, especially his 1820 *Theory of Social Organization*, which called for a new social order based on "phalanxes" that organized labor on a rational basis, allowed greater choice, and provided for communal living. Numerous Fourier-inspired phalanxes appeared in the antebellum United States. His ideas gained currency during the **Workingmen's movement** of the 1820s and 1830s, especially as modified by **Robert Owen** at his model village of New Lanark, Scotland. Owen and his son, **Robert Dale Owen**, immigrated to the United States in 1824, where they set up a New Lanark spin-off at New Harmony, Indiana (1825–1828). New Harmony failed, but the Owens family touched off a century-long discussion of the virtues of setting up **cooperatives** as an alternative to capitalist enterprises. Until the emergence of the **American Federation of**

Labor in late 1886, the majority of working-class movements called for an end to the **wage** system and the establishment of cooperative productive and distributive networks. Belief in cooperation became a cornerstone ideological belief among American workers.

Ideology was the basis of other secular experiments as well. Many members of the Northampton (Massachusetts) Associates (1842–1846) blended cooperative labor ideals with an anti-**slavery** agenda. On Long Island, the Modern Times community (1851–1860) embraced **anarchism**. The Oneida (New York) community (1848–1881) combined radical versions of economic, religious, and sexual life and stressed Biblical-based **communism**, Christian perfectionism, and gender equality.

Marxism had a major impact on post-Civil War **working-class** utopians, though it was not the only form of **socialism** to attract attention. As capitalism matured and social problems increased during the Gilded Age, many Americans sought to reevaluate their relationships to the new social and economic order. Capitalism itself was revolutionary in its implications; hence some workers were attracted to ideals that posited a counter-revolution. Karl Marx and Friedrich Engels viewed utopianism as an incomplete expression of **class consciousness** and fancied their views to be "scientific" socialism, but there was little disguising their idealized view of future society as described in *The Communist Manifesto*. The revolutionary struggles necessary to bring about the workers' utopia bothered many Americans, however, and many opted for evolutionary socialism and communitarianism instead. In Iowa, the Icarian community (1860–1878) preferred the more romantic socialist ideals of Étienne Cabet to Marx. In like fashion, groups such as the Grange, Farmers' Alliances, and the **Knights of Labor** (KOL) embraced cooperative experiments.

Perhaps the single-most popular utopian vision in American history appeared in the late 19th century when **Edward Bellamy** published the novel *Looking Backward*. His book inspired a movement known as Nationalism in which thousands of Americans sought to make Bellamy's fictive utopia a social reality. Before the century closed, however, other utopian visions had emerged. In Roycroft, New York, an arts and crafts colony (1896–1915) appeared in which residents rejected the soullessness of industrial-made products in favor of **artisan**-made goods. (Gustav Stickley at Craftsman Farms in New Jersey revived some of those ideals in the 20th century). Californians joined the Kaweah Co-operative Commonwealth (1885–1892) in the hope of creating the interlinking cooperative networks described by evolutionary Marxist Laurence Gronlund.

Worker-based utopian movements weakened in the 20th century, but did not disappear. Job Harriman spearheaded two socialist collective communities called Llano del Rio, one in California (1914–1918) and another in Louisiana (1917–1938). Utopians in Arden, Delaware, created a community based on the single-tax precepts of **Henry George** in 1900, which is extant, as is Fairhope, Alabama, created in 1894. New York City's Greenwich Village fostered communal movements prior to World War I, and then again during the height of the **counterculture** during the 1960s and 1970s. During the Great Depression, the New Deal Community Program oversaw government-sponsored collective farms and village settlements.

As always, employers made numerous attempts to create utopian communities for their workers. Most were failures, as the capitalist profit ethos generally proved a poor fit with collective ideals. The 1892 **Pullman strike/lockout** put an end to George Pullman's utopian vision, and the Panic of 1893 led to a sharp decline in the nearby town of Harvey, Illinois, which had also demonstrated utopian ambitions. In like fashion, life in Homestead, Pennsylvania, was supposed to improve workers' conditions, until the 1894 **Homestead Steel lockout and strike** ended all pretense. Industrial utopianism nonetheless continued into the 20th century. Earle Draper designed houses for southern textile **company towns** that were supposed to elevate workers—plans that foundered on reefs of low wages and company control that tended more toward autocracy than benevolent **paternalism**. A rare exception to failed industrial utopianism was the chocolate town of Hershey, Pennsylvania, founded in 1903. Although far from a "perfect" industrial setting, most employees of Hershey considered themselves better off than other industrial workers during the lifetime of founder Milton Hershey (d. 1945).

The horrors of World War II and the Holocaust dampened enthusiasm for industrial or worker-based utopias. Many of the post-1945 utopias were associated instead with countercultural ideals, though it is also true that many of the commune dwellers in back-to-the-land experiments sought to live beyond the reaches of industrial (and emerging postindustrial) society in ways that echoed utopians of the early 19th century. Several rural communes founded in the 1960s continue to the present, including the Hog Farm in California and The Farm in Tennessee. Within the labor movement, however, the utopian impulse largely gave way to **pure and simple unionism** ideals such as wages, hours, and working conditions.

Suggested Reading

James Gilbert, *Perfect Cities: Chicago's Utopias of 1893*, 1991; Donald Pitzer, ed., *America's Communal Utopias*, 1997; Foster Stockwell, *Encyclopedia of American Communes, 1663–1963*, 1998.

VERIZON STRIKE OF 2000

On August 6, 2000, more than 87,000 Verizon workers walked off their jobs. They returned to work after an 18-day **strike** that was hailed by unions as a total victory and a harbinger of organized labor's renewal, though both assessments proved exaggerated and premature. More than a decade later, the strike's legacy is less clear and its impact on the telephone industry increasingly moot as consumers have rapidly abandoned landlines in favor of wireless cell phones.

Verizon is an offshoot of the breakup of the Bell System. The American Bell Telephone Company was founded in 1877, and named for Alexander Graham Bell, who is often credited with perfecting the telephone. After absorbing several smaller companies, Bell itself was taken over American Telephone & Telegraph (AT&T) in 1880, which retained the trademark and was generally referred to as the "Bell System." The Bell System was, technically speaking, merely the service part of AT&T, which also controlled separate long-distance services, an equipment manufacturing division, and research laboratories. Although it faced smaller telephone service competitors, the Bell System was registered as a regulated monopoly in 1934 and was so dominant that it was popularly nicknamed "Ma Bell."

In 1984, the U.S. Department of Justice ordered the breakup of the Bell System after it was determined that AT&T was in violation of antitrust laws. Instead of one giant firm, the Bell System was broken into numerous smaller companies. This decision was not universally hailed, and some customers and industry analysts argued that the Bell System had been a beneficial monopoly that delivered superior services at lower costs than its successors would be able to manage. The immediate aftermath of the breakup brought increased competition, but also consumer confusion, especially in areas in which local and long-distance services were in the hands of different firms. In some cases, competing firms failed or merged with others Verizon Communications was created early in 2000 when GTE and Bell Atlantic merged.

The initial issues precipitating the 2000 labor action were only secondarily financial; the major issues involved job security and forced **overtime** work. Under existing **contracts**, Verizon workers—including operators, customer service agents, and technicians—could be compelled to work mandatory overtime without any advance notification. The amount of overtime varied, by region, from 10 to 20 hours per week. The company also had the right to transfer workers from one center to another at its discretion. The Communications Workers of America (CWA) represented 72,000 Verizon workers, and the International Brotherhood of Electrical Workers (IBEW) approximately 15,000 employees. Between them, they controlled nearly 80 percent of all Verizon workers. Despite the unions' clout, Verizon remained adamant regarding its right to impose overtime and transfers. It insisted that the latter right was necessary to implement planned **downsizing** plans that would make the firm more competitive.

The walkout greatly disrupted telephone service on the East Coast. Managers and salaried personnel were able to prevent the company from shutting down entirely, but customers soon complained of long waits and interrupted service. Neither the CWA nor the IBEW desired a long strike, lest Verizon seek to hire **scabs** and break the unions. This led to a controversial decision that was made by union officials and resented by many rank-and-file unionists. Rather than continue to strike and impose a unified contract for all Verizon workers, the unions negotiated regional contracts in the hope that Verizon would quickly move to restore labor peace to all regions. That is precisely what happened, but the regional contracts differed from one another. Moreover, some local activists felt that their **international union** betrayed them and accepted less than they could have won by holding out. The 50,000 Verizon workers in New England and New York settled first, and won a reduction of mandatory overtime from 15 hours to 10. Several days later, Verizon workers in Delaware, Maryland, New Jersey, Pennsylvania, Virginia, and West Virginia settled, with a reduction in overtime from 10 hours to 8 (and eventually 7.5). Verizon retained the right to transfer workers, but gave vague promises of job security. Unions also won a 12 percent wage increase over three years, stock options, and a 3.5 percent wage differential for Verizon workers working in bilingual jobs. They also secured promises that Verizon would address quality-of-work issues that induced high stress in certain jobs; operators, for example, had to maintain quotas and could be dismissed for spending too long with customers. Verizon also agreed to allow the unions leeway in seeking to organize workers in its largely unorganized wireless division. Some human relations experts even began to counsel companies to stop forcing employees to work overtime and seek to hire cheaper **part-time** and **contingency** workers.

Although the pay increases were small and within the usual parameters for existing **merit pay** standards, the Verizon strike was hailed by optimists as an example of how unions were beginning to address quality-of-work issues and were moving beyond limited **pure and simple unionism** perspectives. Some also predicted that the robust economy was shifting power to the side of workers, as labor had become a sellers' market. In November 2000, however, the disputed presidential election led to financial uncertainty and the incoming administration of George W. Bush heralded a return to anti-union policies. More seriously, the terrorist attacks of September 11, 2001, led to disruption of the economy, the decision to invade Afghanistan and Iraq, and a return to deficit spending. Officially the U.S. economy went into recession in 2006, though it was already under stress by the end of 2004. High unemployment put an end to short-term plans for workers to flex their labor bargaining power.

In retrospect, technological change also doomed some of the rosier assessments made in the wake of the Verizon strike. Automated services and the rerouting of queries to offshore call centers have led to replacement of increasing numbers of local operators. The growing penetration of cell phones threatens to make landline service a **sunset industry**. In 2001, 97 percent of all households had landlines; in 2010, that share had dropped to 74 percent, and it is expected to decline much more by 2015. As of 2010, Verizon had 197,000 employees—up from 120,000 in 2000—but this figure includes 82,000 workers in its Verizon Wireless division. Neither the CWA nor the IBEW has made much headway in organizing Verizon Wireless workers.

Suggested Reading

Simon Romero, "Verizon Strike Settled in Full after Accord on Overtime," *New York Times*, August 24, 2000; Eilene Zimmerman, "HR Lessons from a Strike," *Workforce Magazine* 79, no. 11 (November 2000): 36.

VIETNAM WAR AND LABOR

The Vietnam War was both America's longest war and its most socially divisive. The labor movement was not immune to the tensions that arose from the conflict. **Cold War** unionism ideals prevailed when the first American combat troops were deployed in 1965, and nearly all affiliates of the **American Federation of Labor-Congress of Industrial Organizations** (AFL-CIO) initially supported the U.S. objectives in Southeast Asia. By the time the last Americans troops left South Vietnam in 1973, however, organized labor had split over the war, several large unions had quit the AFL-CIO, and the labor movement faced a generation gap that mirrored that in society as a whole.

The American labor movement has long prided itself on the patriotism of its rank-and-file. American flags have been a staple at union rallies since the 19th century, and groups such as the **Knights of Labor** juxtaposed the national loyalty of their members against the self-interest of monopolists and plutocrats. Even so, union members did occasionally oppose wars. Working people in both the North and the South rioted over conscription laws passed during the **Civil War**, many joined anti-imperialist leagues during the late 19th and early 20th centuries, and quite a few opposed U.S. entry into World War I, especially **socialists**, members of the **Industrial Workers of the World**, and other radicals. World War II, however, was altogether different. Nearly all unions signed no-strike pledges during the war and **working-class** men made up the bulk of enlisted men and draftees.

The passage of the **Taft-Hartley Act**, the postwar **Red Scare**, and the subsequent Cold War had a profound effect on internal labor union policies, the gist of which was that all but a handful of left-wing unionists embraced U.S. foreign policy objectives. Both the AFL and the CIO purged politically left members and embraced the broad parameters of Cold War unionism. With this stance came deep support for the U.S. **military**. A military draft for men remained in place after World War II, and military service became a rite of passage for working-class males. Labor unions and members supported the Korean War (1950–1953) with little objection, and officials within the merged AFL-CIO (1955) viewed support for the military and U.S. foreign policy initiatives as part of the bargain struck in exchange for political access. Vietnam would change this perspective so emphatically that Cold War unionism perished in its wake.

U.S. involvement in Vietnam was a product of the Cold War. Vietnam had been a French colony since the 19th century, but was taken over by imperial Japan in 1941. After World War II, the United States rejected the independence demands of Vietnamese patriot Ho Chi Minh—who had helped drive Japan from Indochina—and supported France's recolonization of Southeast Asia. France proved unable to resist Vietnamese liberation movements, however, and suffered a devastating defeat at Dienbienphu in northwestern Vietnam during 1953. The next year the United States helped broker the Geneva Accords, which divided Vietnam into North Vietnam, which was under the control of Ho Chi Minh, and the newly created Republic of South Vietnam, which was supported by the United States and other Western democracies. The division was meant to last for only two years, at which time a United Nations-monitored election would reunify independent Vietnam. The United States eventually scuttled that plan when it became clear that Ho—by then a **communist** allied with the Soviet Union—would easily win such an election. Cold War logic would not countenance the existence of another communist nation bordering China, which had undergone a communist revolution of its own in 1949. "Domino theory" adherents, who argued that a unified nation under Ho would render all of Southeast Asia and the Indian Ocean vulnerable to communist takeover, viewed a noncommunist Vietnam as crucial. North and South Vietnam began engaging in direct hostilities in 1956. Although U.S. combat troops did not directly enter the fray until 1965, South Vietnam soon became a virtual American client state awash in U.S. dollars and military advisors.

Very little of this background was known or understood by the American public until the late 1960s, nor would it have mattered to most labor leaders during the early 1960s. Few Americans were as hawkish on the U.S. role in Vietnam was AFL-CIO President **George Meany**, a vehement opponent of communism. Unfortunately for the AFL-CIO, the Vietnam conflict occurred at a time in which the **labor federation** was under stress. The merger, which had looked so promising in 1955, was already strained by unresolved internal tensions just one decade later. The failure to repeal the hated Taft-Hartley Act was a sore spot for many union leaders, as was the AFL-CIO's failure to forestall passage of the 1959 Labor Management and Reporting Act. Numerous former CIO unions complained that the AFL-CIO paid only lip service to organizing **industrial unions**, and that the federation was becoming dominated by **business unionists**. Politics and social change proved even more divisive. Former CIO unions such as the **United Mine Workers of America** (UMWA) and the **United Packinghouse Workers of America** had long practiced interracial unionism and were comfortable supporting the **civil rights** movement, as was the **United Auto Workers of America** (UAW), headed by former CIO president **Walter Reuther**. (The UMWA was not an AFL-CIO affiliate.) Meany and many key AFL-CIO members were more cautious on civil rights and were suspicious of unions that embraced social protest movements.

Little union opposition to the Vietnam War was noted in 1965, a year that Meany proclaimed that the AFL-CIO was fully behind U.S. objectives in Southeast Asia.

By 1967, however, key union leaders, including Reuther, had come to have serious doubts about the war. When 50 union leaders had the temerity to hold a Labor Leadership Assembly for Peace (LLAP) in 1967, Meany denounced those attending as "kooks." But the divisions in labor's ranks could not be glossed over by insults. Labor faced pressure from demographic and ideological changes. By the 1960s, the "Baby Boom" generation—individuals born after 1946—was the largest single age cohort in the nation; it was also the one called upon to supply ground troops for the Vietnam War and to replace retiring union members. An emerging **counterculture** called into question many prevailing social norms, including blind allegiance to U.S. foreign policy. LLAP leaders also raised such questions, with Reuther accusing Meany of allowing the U.S. State Department to dictate AFL-CIO policy.

Nonetheless, Meany spoke for a large faction of the labor movement. Public opinion polls on the Vietnam War were notoriously unreliable—they often shifted dramatically depending upon how questions were phrased—but it appears that a majority of **blue-collar** Americans supported the war until 1969 and, even then, opponents were more adamant about not expanding the U.S. role in Vietnam rather than ending it altogether. Labor's position on the war was complicated by the fact the very military-industrial complex denounced as dangerous by President Dwight Eisenhower in 1961 had been good for a lot of union workers. The U.S. economy was booming during the 1960s, and many union members enjoyed high **wages** in factories producing materiel for the Department of Defense. Some pro-war unionists became as vociferous about their position as antiwar activists. In 1970, **hard hat riots** rocked New York City and several other cities and saw union members assault antiwar demonstrators. A few commentators spoke of a gathering political conservatism within the American working class.

Pro-war labor advocates once again underestimated the generational factor. Older workers may have supported the war, but it was younger men who fought it, especially those who came from African American, Latino, and white working-class backgrounds. Working-class men and minorities were far more likely to be drafted and to serve in direct combat; **middle-class** white males often won deferments, or served out of harm's way if they did enter the military. (In the name of fairness, a lottery draft system was instituted in 1969, but it ended up being even more inequitable than the universal draft it replaced and was scrapped in 1973 in favor of an all-volunteer military.) One study revealed that every Vietnam draftee within a New Mexico Congressional district came from families with a net worth of less than $5,000. Numerous Vietnam veterans added to the perception that the war was a lost cause and that it was being perpetuated on the backs of poor and non-white soldiers; Vietnam Veterans Against the War, a group that formed in 1967, belied claims that antiwar protests addressed only the interests of "kooks" and the counterculture. Changing values and support for the war made their way to the **assembly line**, where younger workers proved more prone to engage in **wildcat strikes**, ignore the directives of local union leaders, and assume the trappings of countercultural lifestyles, such as wearing peace regalia, listening to rock music, or using drugs.

Events such as the hard hat riots, the 1970 shootings of students at Jackson State and Kent State, and President Richard Nixon's decision to escalate the Vietnam War added more fuel to already raging fires within organized labor. Reuther had pulled the UAW out of the AFL-CIO in 1968. The **Teamsters** followed the UAW, and the two formed the **Alliance for Labor Action** (ALA), an AFL-CIO rival. When chemical workers and retail workers unions were expelled from the AFL-CIO, they, too, joined the ALA, which had taken a public stand against the Vietnam War. Although the ALA did not prove to be a viable alternative to the AFL-CIO and did not survive long after Reuther's death in 1970, it did cast doubt upon the leadership of the AFL-CIO. Meany continued to head the federation until 1979, but by the early 1970s many observers viewed him and existing AFL-CIO policies as out of touch with the times. A 1972 Labor for Peace conference in St. Louis drew 1,200 union delegates, many times the number who attended the 1967 gathering.

Meany retained faith in the Vietnam War to the bitter end. The United States ended direct combat missions in 1973. Two years later, South Vietnam fell to Ho Chi Minh's troops and unification took place under communist rule. The only dominos that fell were Laos and Cambodia, whose governments were destabilized as much by U.S. expansion of the Vietnam War across their borders as by active communist aggression.

The inglorious end to the Vietnam War and the inability of the United States to win it cast severe doubt on the logic of Cold War unionism. Contentious relations with the Nixon administration also called into question blind allegiance to government policies. By 1975, Cold War unionism was on the wane. Many unions maintained their anticommunist stances until the Cold War itself ended in the late 1980s, but the post-1975 labor movement was more critical before offering support for U.S. foreign policy. Labor unions took part in the massive 1983 antinuclear protests in New York City, and the AFL-CIO endorsed a freeze on nuclear weapons production. President **Ronald Reagan** often found labor unions among the most vociferous critics of military adventurism in Central America.

Labor unions remain proud of their patriotism, but their support now tends to be more measured. Although they supported the war on terror in the wake of the September 11, 2001 attacks, in January 2003 unions also formed U.S. Labor Against the War, which has been critical of the invasion and occupation of Iraq.

Suggested Reading

Christian Appy, *Patriots: The Vietnam War Remembered by All Sides*, 2004; Philip S. Foner, *US Labor and the Vietnam War*, 1989; Frank Koscielski, *Divided Loyalties: American Unions and the Vietnam War*, 1999; Peter Levy, *The New Left and Labor in the 1960s*, 1994.

VOLUNTARISM

Voluntarism refers to one of the founding principles of the **American Federation of Labor** (AFL). Like the popular meaning—an action freely chosen without coercion—voluntarism referred to the AFL's policy of allowing unions to act according to their own choices. It specifically applied to two major areas: the decision to affiliate (or not) with the AFL, and the relationship between labor unions and government.

AFL cofounder and President **Samuel Gompers** insisted upon the liberty of workers to determine their own forms of union organization and tactics without outside interference. He had been troubled by the fact that some workers automatically became members of the **Knights of Labor** (KOL) when the KOL signed an agreement with employers compelling their employees to be represented by the KOL. He also disapproved of the KOL procedure requiring affiliated assemblies to seek the federation's approval before undertaking a **strike**, **boycott**, or other form of work disruption. Gompers was a devoted **craft unionist** who believed that individual trades were sovereign. It was, therefore, up to the rank-and-file members to decide with which **labor federation**, if any, their **international union** should affiliate. In like fashion, Gompers believed that the needs of each craft were usually separate; thus, he decided, each should have the right to call job actions that served the interests of the craft, whether or not AFL officials approved.

Gompers also believed the relationship between workers and the state should be voluntary, He, like many other early AFL leaders, distrusted governmental authority. Workers, he argued, needed to secure rights at the point of production, not rely upon government to grant them. Government, in Gompers's view, was an unreliable ally; moreover, workers looking to government for protection placed themselves in a dangerous state of dependency upon it. This, too, reflected the differences between his vision for the AFL and the practices of the KOL. The KOL called for comprehensive social reforms, many of which relied upon legislative action. By contrast, the AFL devoted itself to **pure and simple unionism** principles and regarded much of the KOL's agenda as **utopianism** in a romantic and unrealistic sense.

According to Gompers and AFL cofounder **Adolph Strasser**, voluntarism promoted the growth of unionism in several ways. First, it made workers look to their unions to deliver health, **unemployment**, and **pension** benefits. Second, voluntarism limited government interference in the labor movement and curtailed that of antilabor courts. Finally, voluntarism gave craft unions more power to pressure employers to recognize their right of self-organization. In essence, voluntarism was a union self-help principle that encouraged workers to rely upon their own judgment and strength rather than trusting government or depending upon the AFL to make decisions they should make for themselves.

Voluntarism was probably clearer to Gompers than to most rank-and-file AFL members. In addition, it did not work in practice as Gompers outlined it. For instance, the AFL built up strong strike funds by charging far higher **dues** than the KOL. In theory, affiliates could conduct their own strikes; in practice, they could draw upon the AFL strike fund only if the federation approved of their actions. As some **union locals** would discover the hard way, the AFL was sometimes as unreliable as government; if AFL leaders determined that a strike was lost or should be settled, it sometimes withdrew strike funds or unilaterally signed **contracts**. Moreover, its political nonpartisanship and suspicion of all governmental action led to decisions that members questioned. The AFL's refusal to endorse political candidates or support the creation of a **labor party** engendered tension. Some acts of nonpartisanship struck many AFL members as capricious and foolish, such as Gompers's

1919 remark that he opposed unemployment compensation laws because workers and their unions, not the state, needed to solve the problem of joblessness.

Voluntarism was dealt a mortal blow in the 1930s, when the Great Depression revealed that some social problems were so large that they begged government action. The AFL's distrust of politics also placed it in a subordinate position when New Deal policies altered the relationship of workers to the state. The newly formed **Congress of Industrial Organizations** (CIO) fully endorsed labor/political alliances and, though the AFL also gave grudging endorsement to the New Deal, the CIO was able to exert far more political influence within the Franklin Roosevelt administration than the AFL.

Voluntarism in regard to government was never officially repudiated, though it was almost a dead issue by World War II, when the AFL joined the CIO is taking **no-strike pledges** and in cooperating with the **National War Labor Board**. In like fashion, the AFL's dogged opposition to **open-shop** laws and its willingness to sign **union-shop** agreements was inconsistent with other meanings of voluntarism. It should be said, however, that the AFL (or AFL-CIO) never compelled unions to join the federation, nor prevented them from dropping out. In recent years, there has also been discussion of reviving the AFL's past distrust of government. Some activists have gone so far as to recommend that workers ignore federal labor laws.

Suggested Reading

Bruce Laurie, *Artisans into Workers*, 1989; Nick Salvatore, ed., *Seventy Years of Life and Labor: An Autobiography of Samuel Gompers*, 1984; Philip Taft, *The A.F. of L. in the Time of Gompers*, 1957.

WAGES

Wages refer to the compensation for labor received by workers who are paid by the hour. Many Americans use the term "wages" as a synonym for whatever pay they receive, but such usage is incorrect. A worker who signs a contract stipulating his or her annual compensation is receiving a **salary**, not a wage. Working for wages, in fact, has historically been among the clearest delineations of **working class** status; salaries are generally viewed as a marker of entry into the **middle class**. This has been the case even when wage-earners make more money than salaried employees. Salaried employees often have far more job flexibility than wage-earners, as the latter must actually be on site and working each hour for which he or she is paid. If wage-earners get laid off or miss work, they might receive no pay whatsoever. Wages and salaries have also served as the boundary differentiating **blue-collar** labor from **white-collar** professional work.

Although working for wages is now viewed as the norm in the United States, that was not always the case. In the **agrarian** economy of Colonial America and the early Republican period, working for wages was viewed as a dangerous form of dependency that should be of brief duration. Girls and young women, for example, often took on paid domestic work, but they hoped to leave such jobs as soon as they got married. In like fashion, **journeymen** laborers received wages, but they expected to rise to **master** status and open their own shops, complete with **apprentices** and wage-earning journeymen. Farmers prided themselves on being independent **yeomen** who worked for themselves. The **Industrial Revolution** disrupted those older systems and created a working class consisting of individuals whose entire working lives centered on receiving wages, but this was not accomplished without great resistance. Industrial workers steeped in traditions of **republicanism** resented the new social and economic regimens associated with **capitalism**. Labor organizations throughout the 19th century routinely called for an end to the wage system. The **Knights of Labor**, for instance, called upon workers to set up worker-owned **cooperatives** that would overthrow systems of private profit, and rural **Populists** called upon farmers to do the same. In the early 20th century, the **Industrial Workers of the World** called for **general strikes** to hasten the collapse of the wage system and usher in an **anarcho-syndicalist** system based on the needs of collectivized society rather than the agendas of individual investors.

The **American Federation of Labor** (AFL) was the first important labor organization to endorse the wage system unequivocally. AFL leaders such as **Samuel Gompers** believed that the wage system had become a permanent part of American society; hence it was the AFL's mission to secure the highest possible compensation for its members rather than seeking to supplant capitalism. Gompers proved prescient on that point, and now wage labor is considered the norm. In unionized environments, unions usually negotiate hourly wage scales. In non-union businesses, employers unilaterally set wages, though they often take into account the compensation in the industry or a local region.

In contemporary America, the biggest concern is no longer how to eliminate the wage system, but rather how to raise wages to keep pace with rising costs. Families working for the federal **minimum wage** simply cannot maintain a high standard of living with that level of compensation. In economic terms, one must also differentiate unadjusted wages from "real wages." The latter term refers to the actual buying power of one's wages adjusted for inflation. If, for example, a worker receives a 5 percent wage increase, but inflation rises by 10 percent, that worker has suffered a 5 percent decrease in real wages. Although some analysts disagree, most economists argue that wage-earners (and many salaried ones as well) have experienced declining real wages in the 21st century. That trend was under way even before a deep recession officially began in 2007. According to Bureau of Labor Statistics data, between April 2009 and April 2011, real wages declined an average of $0.50 per hour for most hourly wage employees. Gloomier assessments suggest that most wage-earners have less buying power now than their counterparts in 1964, and that the overall increase in family wages has been due solely to the introduction of more family members into the wage system. The uncertainty of work is also of utmost concern for American wageworkers in the postindustrial economy. Those persons forced into **part-time** and **contingency labor** do not work enough hours to earn a decent yearly wage, nor do those plagued by layoffs and **unemployment**.

Suggested Reading

Bureau of Labor Statistics, "Overview of BLS Wage Data by Area and Occupation," http://www.bls.gov/bls/blswage.htm, accessed August 8, 2011; Steven Greenhouse, *The Big Squeeze: Tough Times for the American Worker*, 2009; Geoff Mann, *Our Daily Bread: Wages, Workers, and the Political Economy of the American West*, 2007.

WAL-MART CAMPAIGN

Wal-Mart, based in Bentonville, Arkansas, is the world's largest retailer. It is popular among consumers because it undersells most of its competitors, but its low prices have come at the price of also paying low **wages**, offering few or noncompetitive **fringe benefits**, and engaging in employment practices that many critics decry as unfair and, in some cases, illegal. The company, which was incorporated in 1969, has more than 3,800 stores in the United States with approximately 1.4 million employees, whom it calls "associates." Wal-Mart's official policy is that it is "pro-associate" rather than anti-union and that its employees simply do not want labor unions. These linguistic turns of phrase do little to disguise the reality that Wal-Mart has been virulently union resistant and has a long history of contentious relations with some of its associates. When Wal-Mart associates in Jonquiere, Québec, voted to unionize in 2005, Wal-Mart closed the store rather than acquiesce to signing a union **contract**. Wal-Mart's profitability, its low wage structure, and the complaints of former and present employees have made it the target of union organizing, especially by the **United Food and Commercial Workers** (UFCW).

The UFCW sees its ongoing Wal-Mart campaign in terms akin to older **pattern bargaining** campaigns. As the world's largest retailer, a contract with Wal-Mart would certainly place pressure on the entire **retail** trade to raises wages and bargain with unions. The UFCW also worries that Wal-Mart's entry into the grocery trade will jeopardize its contracts with other grocery chains. In California, for instance, Wal-Mart grocery clerks make more than $10 per hour less than workers organized by the UFCW.

The UFCW and other unions also have other reasons for wishing to organize Wal-Mart. As numerous studies reveal, the company maintains its low prices by placing pressure on suppliers to keep their costs low. In many cases, Wal-Mart has switched from American manufacturers to foreign-made goods produced in low-wage nations. Because of Wal-Mart's dominance within American retailing, such switches have resulted in the bankruptcy of American firms such as lingerie-maker Lovable and bicycle manufacturer Huffy. Critics also charge that many of the goods that Wal-Mart imports are produced in **sweatshops** and under conditions that would be illegal in the United States. In 2010, for example, the retailer had to remove its Chinese-made Miley Cyrus jewelry line from sale because the items contained high traces of cadmium, a known carcinogenic.

The concern over lost jobs is coupled with deteriorating work conditions in those American firms that continue to supply goods for Wal-Mart. The company has, in some cases, encouraged U.S. manufacturers to shift production to low-wage nations to keep its prices low and has pressured others to cut costs however they can, which has resulted in **speedups**, **concessions** wrung from workers, and wage cuts. Numerous charges of predatory pricing have been leveled against Wal-Mart, though most have been resolved.

Wal-Mart has a troubled employment record, with roughly 70 percent of all its associates quitting within one year. The average full-time worker at Wal-Mart receives wages that would place a family of four below the federal poverty line. The company pays an average of 20 percent less to its employees than others in the notoriously low-wage retail sector. In addition, many employees receive no health care benefits; those who do have such benefits often find the plans inadequate because of high deductibles and/or restricted coverage. Connecticut found that Wal-Mart actually costs the state more than it contributes in wages due to the strain Wal-Mart workers places on Medicaid and other social welfare agencies. The firm has also faced allegations of forced **overtime**, of coercing employees to work during their breaks and "off the clock," and of violations of **child labor** laws. A 2003 raid of 61 Wal-Mart stores in 21 states yielded 250 illegal **immigrants** employed by the company. In 2011, however, Wal-Mart won a major court victory when the U.S. Supreme Court reversed a lower court's ruling in favor of a class action suit filed on behalf of 1.5 million women who charged that Wal-Mart engaged in systematic gender discrimination by denying women promotions and by paying gender-based wage differentials. Advocates for the case plan to bring new lawsuits that will circumvent Supreme Court objections to the way the original suit was configured.

It remains to be seen whether Wal-Mart's court savvy will confirm its current labor practices or fuel campaigns to unionize the giant retailer. Wal-Mart appears to be nervous about unions. In 2008, it reportedly spent several million dollars in campaigns urging associates to vote against Barack Obama because of his stated support for the Employee Free Choice Act (EFCA), which would allow workers to unionize if a majority signed cards designating a bargaining unit. Obama was elected, but the EFCA fell prey to a Senate filibuster led by conservative **Republicans**. The UFCW has sought to organize Wal-Mart for several decades. In 1999, Wal-Mart sought a trespass **injunction** against the UFCW and secured one from an Arkansas judge in 2002, which was promptly overturned by the Arkansas Supreme Court.

Wal-Mart's aggressive anti-union tactics show some signs of emboldening union activists. Recently a group formed calling itself OUR Walmart (Organization United for Respect at Walmart). It has begun to attract interest across the United States and notes that Chinese Wal-Mart workers are unionized, a right denied to American associates. (Wal-Mart claims that there are no real unions in China.) At present the UFCW and others unions face an uphill battle to organize Wal-Mart, but unions are no doubt correct in seeing its status as pivotal. If Wal-Mart can be organized, the entire **service industry** sector suddenly becomes more susceptible to unionization, a move that could dramatically alter labor relations.

Suggested Reading

Charles Fishman, *The Wal-Mart Effect*, 2006; Nelson Lichtenstein, ed., *Wal Mart: The Face of 21st Century Capitalism*, 2011; Kris Maher and Ann Zimmerman, "Union Intensifies Efforts to Organize Workers at Wal-Mart," *Wall Street Journal*, April 17, 2009; Public Broadcasting Service, "Is Wal*Mart Good for America?", http://www.pbs.org/wgbh/pages/frontline/shows/walmart/transform/employment.html, accessed August 9, 2011.

WAR OF 1812 AND THE TRANSFORMATION OF LABOR. *See* Jacksonian Era and Labor.

WAR LABOR DISPUTES ACT (SMITH-CONNALLY ACT)

The War Labor Disputes Act, better known as the Smith-Connally Act, was an early backlash against New Deal labor legislation and is widely viewed as a prelude to the **Taft-Hartley Act**. It was passed in June 1943 by a coalition of conservative **Democrats** and **Republicans**. Democratic Congressman Howard W. Smith of Virginia and Senator Thomas Connally of Texas sponsored the bill, which President Franklin Roosevelt vetoed. Congress then overrode the president's veto in the wake of the strikes led the **United Mine Workers of America** (UMWA).

The bill's intent was to curtail **strikes** and rising labor union might during World War II. The UMWA became a symbol for those arguing that labor unions had grown too powerful. Unlike most American unions, the UMWA refused to sign a **no-strike pledge**. Part of the UMWA's stance was personal—UMWA President **John L. Lewis** opposed Roosevelt's reelection bid in 1940—but part of it was situational and strategic. The UMWA was troubled by wartime inflation and viewed raises calculated according to the **Little Steel Formula** as inadequate. The UMWA also saw the time as propitious for pressing its demands, as wartime manpower shortages made labor a sellers' market. Lewis called a series of strikes that, while strategic, were exceedingly unpopular. Public opinion polls revealed widespread support for shackling the UMWA, which buoyed the efforts of Congress to override Roosevelt's veto of the War Labor Disputes Act.

The bill gave the government the right to seize any production facility in which a strike interfered with the war effort, and allowed for the prosecution of strike instigators. It also required unions to notify management of their intention to walk out, mandated a 30-day cooling-off period before a strike could take place, and required the National Labor Relations Board (NLRB) to undertake a second strike vote after 30 days to determine if workers still wished to strike. In a move that inadvertently altered the shape of political campaigns, the bill also prohibited unions from making direct contributions to candidates. Lee Pressman, the general counsel for the **Congress of Industrial Organizations** (CIO), noted that Smith-Connally Act did not prohibit contributions to primary election candidates, nor did it prevent unions from spending money on candidates through intermediary groups. In July 1943, the CIO established a political action committee (PAC) to funnel money to pro-union candidates. The PAC ultimately increased interest in politics and led the CIO to push for voter education and registration. Quasi-independent PACs have subsequently become a major force in American electoral politics.

Both the **American Federation of Labor** and the CIO opposed the bill, which Lewis predictably denounced it as a "slave act." When President Roosevelt vetoed the bill, he argued that government-imposed cooling-off periods would simply encourage walkouts, a reservation that proved prophetic. In the first three months during which the bill was in effect, the NLRB conducted 53 strike votes, 47 of which resulted in work stoppages. In all, workers engaged in more than 1,900 walkouts in the last half of 1943, heedless of the War Labor Disputes Act. The act's loopholes rendered it largely ineffective, but it also signaled congressional intent to limit union power. Key parts of War Labor Disputes Act resurfaced in anti-union bills such as the **Taft-Hartley Act** and the Labor-Management Reporting and Disclosure Act.

Suggested Reading

James B. Atleson, *Labor and the Wartime State: Labor Relations and Law During World War II*, 1998; James Foster, *The Union Politic*, 1975; Joel Siedman, *American Labor from Defense to Reconversion*, 1953; Robert Zieger, *The CIO, 1935–1955*, 1997.

WELFARE CAPITALISM

Welfare capitalism is a practice in which employers provide a variety of **fringe benefits** for their workers. Those benefits are generally in excess of institutional norms.

The reasons for offering such packages vary from employer to employer. Some are motivated by ideological reasons such as religious principles, humanitarianism, or political beliefs. Employers with deep ties to their communities may be moved by civic pride, or feel a sense of **paternalism** toward the workforce. On the opposite end of the spectrum are those employers that set up **company towns** in which they assert total control over civic affairs and, in some cases, workers' lives in the belief that they know what is best for their workforce. Still other employers use welfare capitalism strategically in the hope of deterring unionization efforts. Recent adherents of what has been labeled "ethical capitalism" offer generous benefits as an extension of their personal worldviews.

The expectation of maintaining a loyal workforce ties together all forms of welfare capitalism. The challenge facing welfare capitalism is also shared. **Capitalism** is, by nature, based on ideals of individual profit rather than shared profit, with profit itself being a primary goal. Most modern corporations are beholden to stockholders, not the vision of company founders, individual entrepreneurs, or managers. When profits decline or losses incur, pressure mounts to cut costs, and welfare capitalism programs are often targeted for trimming or elimination.

Welfare capitalism has nonetheless been a popular business practice. In the early 19th century, factory owners often cast themselves in a paternal role, taking care of the workers in exchange for their loyalty and hard work. During the early days of the textile industry, when **agrarianism** was the dominant production system, some employers operated their mills seasonally and closed them during busy planting and harvesting cycles. Even after the **Industrial Revolution** introduced economies of scale and factories operated on a continuous basis, many textile firms recruited workers less involved in agricultural production: **immigrants**, women, and children. Especially in the case of women and children, factory owners offered a host of welfare capitalist benefits that were not strictly necessary for production, including company-sponsored churches, lyceums, boarding houses, libraries, and educational opportunities. Many also tried to safeguard the morals of their workers. Lowell mill girls, for instance, were expected to comply with rigid moral codes.

Paternalism, whether the design of individuals or corporate policy, also highlights another inherent characteristic of welfare capitalism that can lead to conflict—that is, the unequal power dynamic involved. Many **utopian** experiments began life as collective visions whose fruits would be shared by participants. By contrast, welfare capitalist benefits are, in essence, "gifts" passed from masters to subordinates and, like any other gift, may or may not be what is actually desired. The problematic aspects of this practice were manifest in company towns, most of which operated according to corporate agendas and were resistant to **collective bargaining** processes that would have given workers a say in how their benefits were configured. Both Homestead, Pennsylvania, and Pullman, Illinois, were viewed by their founders as model cities, yet they were the sites of two of the 19th century's most traumatic **strikes**. In each case, the desire for higher **wages** was more important to workers than local amenities. The contradictions of top-down determination of **working-class** desires were especially obvious in company-owned towns operated by mine owners and southern textile firms. In most cases, such settlements came to be viewed as undesirable and many endured intense capital/labor battles.

During the **Progressive Era**, welfare capitalism shifted in focus and less emphasis was placed on direct control of workers' lives. As part of the period's emphasis on efficiency and social harmony, numerous business leaders sought ways to placate their workforces and to make them feel invested in the economic health of their employers. Henry Ford accomplished this feat by paying higher wages than his competitors, but others sought more creative ways to cultivate employee loyalty. Department store magnate Edward Filene (1860–1937) is often cited as a pioneer of revamped welfare capitalism. He established a credit union for his employees and took an active role in social reform, directing much of his philanthropy toward Boston-area civic improvements such as slum clearance and public health improvements rather than focusing on elite institutions such as museums and symphonies. Filene is credited with marshaling a 1911 Massachusetts **workman's compensation** law that was among the nation's first.

Filene's brand of welfare capitalism became the standard, though even it was deemed utopian and foolish by many of his contemporaries. Members of the **National Civic Federation** often implemented welfare capitalism experiments, but those in the larger and more powerful **National Association of Manufacturers** argued that employers owed workers a wage and nothing else. It must be acknowledged that welfare capitalism principles endured either because labor unions bargained for fringe benefits or because their very existence often compelled employers to implement them to avoid conflict with employees. Some employers consciously sought to counteract the appeal of unions by providing services and benefits as good as, if not better than, those found in union **contracts**. Typical welfare capitalist benefits emerging in the 20th century include **pensions**, paid vacations, sick leave, and **profit sharing**. The last of these was particularly effective, as it tied employee benefits and bonuses directly to company profitability. Companies also began to pay attention to small amenities that made workers feel more connected to employers. Rhetorical devices such as referring to all company employees as "family" appealed to some, but more effective were perquisites such as cafeterias, well-appointed restrooms, worker lounges, and company-sponsored sports teams and recreation areas. Annual picnics, employee recognition days, and outings also proved popular. A few companies even established worker-advisory councils that gave employees limited say in management decisions.

Welfare capitalism thrived during the boom economy of the 1920s, but many experiments were scuttled during the Great Depression of the 1930s. The New Deal confirmed the collective bargaining rights of workers and placed the power of federal law behind those rights. As a consequence, much of post-1933 welfare capitalism was negotiated rather than distributed as company largesse. In fact, contract negotiations were often protracted as unions sought to wrangle from employers more generous vacation, pension, and health care benefits. The term (though not the reality of) "welfare capitalism" passed from common usage by the 1950s simply because its particulars had become expectations rather than being viewed as free-will offerings.

The last decades of the 20th century saw a mild resurgence in welfare capitalism in non-union firms, especially in computer and technological industries. These industries were highly competitive and sought to obtain and retain quality workers through benefits such as stock options, research and development grants, and patent-sharing royalty agreements. Many firms also hired team-building experts and/or revived earlier practices such as athletic teams and company picnics. Companies such as Microsoft built "campuses" modeled after universities, complete with cafeterias and state-of-the-art recreational facilities.

A new breed of ethical capitalists also emerged, with firms such as Ben & Jerry's Ice Cream, The Body Shop, Patagonia, Google, and Dean's Beans directly linking corporate practices and philanthropy to social values such as environmental sensitivity, social justice concerns, and ethical treatment of employees. In like fashion, ethical capitalist investment services emerged, such as Pax World and the Aquinas Fund. Some ethical capitalist firms seek to accommodate the existing realities of two-income families or single parenthood through practices such as flex time, job sharing, and/or providing on-site child-care centers. Many also offer company-provided exercise facilities, counseling services, and generous leave policies. Nevertheless, ethical capitalism remains an imprecise and hotly debated term. Some companies that are listed as practitioners of ethical capitalism have endured labor strife, including Caterpillar, which has had acrimonious relations with the **United Auto Workers of America**. Still others, such as Nike, have been accused of **sweatshop** production and appear on lists of the "worst" firms for which to work.

Welfare capitalism, whether granted or negotiated, remains a desirable goal. Historically it has worked best during flush economic times, but has proved difficult to sustain during downturns. At its best it can be noble, even when problematic. To cite an example from the late 20th century, on December 11, 1995, Malden Mills in Lawrence, Massachusetts, burned to the ground. Malden Mills was a major manufacturer of Polartec, a synthetic fleece. Rather than furlough his employees, CEO Aaron Feuerstein used insurance money both to rebuild the factory and to continue paying employees. Employees and the general public alike hailed him as a humanist. In 2001, however, a recession sent Malden Mills into bankruptcy and Feuerstein was replaced as CEO during reorganization. The firm became insolvent again in 2007 and was closed. At present it appears that 1,500 past employees will lose their pensions.

Suggested Reading

Stuart D. Brandes, *American Welfare Capitalism, 1880–1940*, 1976; Sanford D. Jacoby, *Modern Manors: Welfare Capitalism since the New Deal*, 1997; Andrea Tone, *The Business of Benevolence: Industrial Paternalism in Progressive America*, 1997.

WESTERN FEDERATION OF MINERS. *See* International Union of Mine, Mill, and Smelter Workers.

WEST VIRGINIA MINE WARS, 1919–1923

The West Virginia mine wars were a series of violent struggles that included the infamous 1920 shootout between union sympathizers and private detectives in

Matewan, West Virginia. It culminated in the even bloodier **Battle of Blair Mountain**. Although the struggles are named for the Mountaineer State, they also spilled into neighboring Kentucky.

Although the conflict is generally said to have begun in 1919, many labor historians see the West Virginia mine wars as an extension of the 1912–1913 Cabin Creek/Coal Creek conflict in which the **United Mine Workers of America** (UMWA) and activist **Mother Jones** attempted to reorganize West Virginia miners after numerous operators cancelled UMWA contracts. That conflict resulted in an estimated 50 deaths and the imposition of martial law, but only partial recognition of the UMWA. In late 1919, the UMWA again began organizing in the largely non-union coalfields of southern West Virginia and eastern Kentucky. Mine operators had kept the region union free through tactics such as the maintenance of **company towns**, the implementation of **yellow-dog contracts**, and intimidation. The Baldwin-Felts Detective Agency was employed to ferret out union activists, enforce contracts, and evict suspected union sympathizers from company-owned homes. Baldwin-Felts agents were known for their heavy-handed methods and cavalier disregard for legal procedures; some of their agents were reputed to be thugs and former criminals. By the 20th century, many American workers hated Baldwin agents even more than the **Pinkertons**. The very presence of Baldwin agents in the coalfields was provocative.

Tensions were already high when Baldwin-Felts agents, including Albert and Lee Felts, arrived in Matewan in May 1920. Evictions deemed illegal by local sheriff Sid Hatfield led to a shootout that left the town mayor, two miners, and seven Baldwin agents dead, including the Felts brothers. It also precipitated mine shutdowns and armed conflict in the region, which intensified when Baldwin agents murdered Hatfield in cold blood as he stood outside a Kentucky courthouse in August 1921.

The region was already aflame even before Hatfield's murder, however. Mine operators imported so many **scabs** and detective that shootouts between pro-union miners and **goons** and scabs became commonplace. So, too, was destruction of company property such as shaft houses and railroad coal cars. Martial law was declared in the immediate aftermath of the Matewan shootout; and federal troops were called upon to maintain order. When the troops were withdrawn in September 1920, the violence began anew. In May 1921, a three-day gun battle erupted near Merrimac, West Virginia, a hamlet near Matewan located on the Tug River separating West Virginia and Kentucky. Miners engaged in a shootout with mine guards, state police, and deputy sheriffs that spread across the state line. When it ended, some 20 people had been killed. Because President Warren Harding was hesitant to send federal troops into the area again, West Virginia Governor Ephraim Morgan took matters into his own hands by enlarging the state police force and reconstituting the National Guard. Both institutions increased enlistments, sometimes paying little attention to the worthiness of enrollees. In like fashion, some communities deputized local businessmen. These new forces quickly moved to suppress the miners. Under martial law, all meetings were prohibited, as was conversation between two or more miners. Miners were also arrested for carrying any pro-union literature and were not released from custody unless they promised to leave the state. National Guard troops, state police, and local sheriffs invaded and destroyed the tent colonies where the evicted miners lived. The constitutionality of such actions was doubtful, even under martial law, but the remoteness of the region and the UMWA's willingness to do battle rather than litigate made the region one in which conflict superseded laws.

The August 1921 murder of Sid Hatfield, who had become a local hero after the Matewan incident, further enraged miners. Miners assembled at Lens Creek, south of Charleston, West Virginia, with the intention of marching through Logan County, Kentucky, and Mingo County, West Virginia, in defiance of martial law and with vague notions of liberating union miners from county jails. This was the spark that led to the Battle of Blair Mountain, a week-log conflict involving at least 7,000 miners and in which a least 25 (perhaps as many as 130) individuals lost their lives. President Harding reluctantly placed all of West Virginia under martial law on August 30, 1921, and 985 individuals were charged with crimes ranging from treason to murder. Because the miners' army had no significant leader, treason proved impossible to establish and nearly all miners were acquitted, though some served jail terms for other crimes.

Federal troops reestablished rudimentary order, but not total control. Sniping remained a problem and at one point in the conflict planes dropped gas bombs on miners. The rudimentary nature of air flight was such that the bombings played little role in settling matters, though they did indicate the government's resolve to end the insurrection. Most miners surrendered once federal troops arrived, but the hills of Mingo and Logan Counties remained volatile through 1923, when the UMWA officially raised the strike. Most of the coalfields involved remained no-union enterprises through 1935.

Suggested Reading

David Corbin, *Life, Work, and Rebellion in the Coal Fields: The Southern West Virginia Miners 1880–1922*, 1981; Howard B. Lee, *Bloodletting in Appalachia: The Story of West Virginia's Four Major Mine Wars and Other Thrilling Incidents of Its Coal Fields*, 1969; Lon Savage, *Thunder in the Mountains: The West Virginia Mine War, 1920–21*, 1990.

WHIPSAW STRIKE. *See* Pattern Bargaining.

WHITE-COLLAR WORKERS

The term "white-collar worker" is generally applied to those in professional, technical, office, sales, and clerical jobs. Historically, white-collar work has been a marker of **middle-class** status and stands in contrast to the **blue-collar** labor associated with the **working class**. Both terms are holdovers from the time in which most shirts had detachable collars secured to the garment by studs. Detachable collars dominated until after World War I and were washed separately from garments. Colored collars less readily showed dirt and perspiration; hence those who did manual labor favored them. White collars became associated with those engaged in nonmanual labor that would not soil collars. Their usage also implied that white-collar workers possessed more education or had acquired specialized skills that liberated them from manual toil. The author Upton Sinclair is often cited as the first to use the term specifically in reference to professional work, though he probably merely picked up what was already in popular parlance by 1911, when he first used it.

The most common distinction made is that blue-collar workers engage in physical labor and white-collar workers in mental activities. In many cases, blue-collar workers receive **wages**, whereas white-collar workers are paid a **salary**. These are now more distinctions of convenience than an accurate indicator of how hard an individual works, how much money is earned, or how compensation is paid. **Retail** workers, for example, are generally viewed as white-collar workers though many work longer hours, get paid wages, and are generally more poorly compensated than blue-collar factory workers. In like fashion, a blue-collar union autoworker frequently makes more than a white-collar public school teacher or a trained nurse. Women have long complained that female-dominated professions such as library science, clerical work, nursing, and **service industry** jobs such as hairdressing and domestic work are "pink-collar" jobs that carry neither prestige nor adequate compensation.

In the postindustrial economy of contemporary America, none of these terms carries the associations it once did, though all three remain in use. One indicator that remains in place is that children raised in blue-collar families often find the adjustment to middle-class life to be difficult, even when they obtain the education and occupational status need to sustain it. Another holdover is that white-collar professionals are harder to unionize than blue- or pink-collar workers. Scholars debate why this has been the case, though some factors appear self-evident. White-collar workers already receiving higher pay and good **fringe benefits** have less incentive to unionize, especially if they possess skills that are in demand. **Middle-class ideology** also holds self-reliance in high regard. In some cases, white-collar workers are considered management and are excluded from **collective bargaining** rights as outlined by the **National Labor Relations Act**. Unions seeking to mobilize white-collar workers in the wake of the decline of blue-collar work have met with limited success. Notable exceptions have involved unions such as the **American Federation of Government Employees**, the **American Federation of Teachers**, and the **National Education Association**

Labor unions are likely to continue their efforts to make inroads among white-collar workers, a campaign already under way by the **Service Workers International Union**. White-collar work has historically derived much of its prestige from its juxtaposition with blue-collar labor. The latter is now in decline, which has had the corresponding effect of removing some of the prestige associated with white-collar work. Moreover, white-collar workers have not been immune to the trends of cost-cutting measures and **concessions** demands facing manual laborers. Many professionals complain of abusive bosses, understaffed offices, poor fringe benefits packages, and long work hours. Lately a phrase has entered the American lexicon that would have been unthinkable decades ago: "White collar is the new blue collar."

Suggested Reading

James Kelleher, "White-Collar Blues Play Well with U.S. Labor Unions," *Reuters*, January 29, 2009; Alfred Lubrano, *Limbo: Blue-Collar Roots, White-Collar Dreams*, 2005; C. Wright Mills, *White Collar: The American Middle Classes*, 2002 (reprint of 1951 original); Daniel J. Opler, *For All White-Collar Workers: The Possibilities of Radicalism in New York City's Department Store Unions, 1934–1953*, 2007.

WILDCAT STRIKE

A wildcat strike is an unauthorized, spontaneous, and short-lived work stoppage that takes place without the sanction of either a **union local** or an **international union**. Most such labor actions occur as an immediate response to a perceived outrage and are outpourings of workers' anger. They are also sometimes called **quickies**, though that term has other meanings.

The term appears to have evolved from a shady form of banking in the early 19th century; as legend holds, one Western bank that formed and became insolvent quickly had a panther on its premises. Other sources say the phrase comes from a failed Michigan institution that had a panther logo on its banknotes. By 1838, a wildcat bank was a synonym for a risky venture. In the days before the New Deal, investors lost their assets when a bank failed. Since the 1880s, oil drillers speculating in areas of uncertain deposits have also been known as wildcatters. The first known application of "wildcat" to describe an unauthorized **strike** appeared in 1943 and replaced the 1920s term "outlaw strike."

On occasion, wildcat strikes are held to demonstrate rank-and-file displeasure with the policies and actions of union leaders. In 2001, for example, **Teamsters** working for shipbuilder Jeffboat in Jefferson, Indiana, walked out in disgust over a deal struck between the union and the company. Most wildcat strikes occur in response to local issues, however, and are unplanned, uncoordinated, and brief. Wildcat strikes occur for a variety of reasons, but relatively few of them involve **wages**. Workers may walk off the job in support of a colleague whom they feel was unfairly discharged, or because a worker was injured or killed in an incident for which the company was culpable. (The mining industry has been and remains subject to wildcat strikes when workers are injured.) They may also occur because workers perceive that they have been harassed because of their race or gender. During the early 1970s, the **Dodge Revolutionary Union** conducted numerous wildcat strikes to call attention to racism on automobile **assembly lines**. In like fashion, younger autoworkers in Lordstown, Ohio conducted wildcat strikes in response to the pace of the line, the mindless repetitiveness of their work, and disrespect from plant supervisors. In many cases, wildcat strikes have precipitated official strikes. Numerous walkouts held in 1945–1946 began as wildcat actions, as did a series of strikes in the auto industry in 1955. Some wildcat strikes are modified **sympathy strikes** in **solidarity** with other workers; during a 2011 strike by Verizon workers affiliated with the **International Brotherhood of Electrical Workers** (IBEW), some IBEW workers who did not work for Verizon refused to cross **picket** lines or do any work that involved Verizon.

Radical unions such as the **Industrial Workers of the World** advocate wildcat strikes as a tactic to disrupt **capitalism**, but wildcat strikes are anathema to most unions. The 1947 **Taft-Hartley Act** prohibits the use of wildcat strikes, and unions can be subject to heavy fines if members engage in them and the union does not do its utmost to end them quickly. Wildcat strikes have been relatively rare since the 1940s because workers engaging in them abrogate most legal protections. A 1970 Supreme Court decision, *Boys Market Inc. v. Retail Clerks Union Local 770*, dealt a further blow to wildcat strikes when the court ruled that **no-strike pledges** are implied when a union contract is in effect, even if they are not specifically stated.

Despite the danger involved in conducting wildcat strikes, some activists suggest that the tactic should be more widely used. As they see it, **business unionism** is ineffective in dealing with immediate problems and employers too easily tie up legitimate **grievances** in bureaucratic red tape.

Suggested Reading

Leigh Benin, *The New Labor Radicalism and New York City's Garment Industry: Progressive Labor during the 1960s*, 1999; Jeremy Brecher, *Strike!*, 1997; Dennis Byrne and Randall H. King, "Wildcat Strikes in U.S. Manufacturing, 1960–1977," *Journal of Labor Research* VII, no. 6 (Fall 1996): 387–401; Martin Glaberman, "Wildcat Strikes" in *Encyclopedia of the American Left*, Mari Jo Buhle, Paul Buhle, and Dan Georgakas, eds., 1992; Robert Hendrickson, ed., *Encyclopedia of Word and Phrase Origins*, 1997.

WINPISINGER, WILLIAM WAYNE

William Wayne ("Wimp/Wimpy") Winpisinger (December 10, 1924–December 11, 1997) was president of the **International Association of Machinists and Aerospace Workers** (IAM) from 1977 through 1989, and a vice president of the **American Federation of Labor-Congress of Industrial Organizations** (AFL-CIO). Winpisinger, known for his gruff personal style, was one of the last leaders of a mainstream **international union** to embrace **socialism**. Although he rose within AFL-CIO ranks, he was also a frequent critic of the **labor federation**'s timorous commitment to social justice issues, of its willingness to grant **concessions** to employers, and of its descent into **business unionism**.

Winpisinger was born in Cleveland, Ohio, the son of Edith (Knodel) and Joseph Winpisinger, the latter a **journeyman** printer for the Cleveland *Plain Dealer*. He dropped out of high school to join the U.S. Navy during World War II and served on ships in the Mediterranean Sea and the English Channel from 1942 to 1945. While in the navy, Winpisinger learned the diesel mechanic's trade. Upon his discharge from the military, he returned to Cleveland and continued working as a mechanic. In 1946, he married the former Pearl Foster, with whom he had five children.

Winpisinger became an active member of IAM Lodge 1363 and, in 1949, was elected president of the 1,300-member **union local**. His skills at contract negotiation, organizing, and handling **grievance** and **arbitration** cases led to an appointment with the IAM's midwestern field staff in 1951, and a transfer to the IAM's headquarters in Washington, D.C., in 1955. From his Washington base, Winpisinger organized truck and auto mechanics in conjunction with the **Teamsters**, but that project ended when the Teamsters were expelled from the AFL-CIO in 1957. He then served in numerous other capacities, including in the IAM's aerospace unit. Winpisinger performed masterfully as a special troubleshooter for the union president Al Hayes, and became national automobile coordinator with responsibility for 120,000 members. Eventually his responsibilities also included railroad and airline workers. In 1961, he guided negotiations with Continental Airlines that led to the IAM's first contract with the carrier. Winpisinger joined the IAM's executive council in 1967 and, 10 years later, assumed the presidency of the IAM.

As head of the IAM, Winpisinger automatically joined the AFL-CIO executive board. Despite heading a **craft union** of highly skilled workers, he was an advocate for **industrial unionism** and favored mass organizing based on the model of his heroes: **John L. Lewis** and **Walter Reuther**. Winpisinger was critical of AFL-CIO president **George Meany** even before he joined the executive board, and he stepped up his critique once he was part of the management group. Winpisinger minced no words in asserting that Meany was too old to lead the AFL-CIO, and that he did not understand a workforce conditioned by the **counterculture** and social upheavals of the 1960s and 1970s. His candor and his penchant for bluntness increased his public profile and, in 1979, he was featured on the popular CBS show *60 Minutes*. Not surprisingly, Winpisinger also gained powerful enemies, though his skill at negotiations and the IAM's large membership and treasury insulated him from reprisals.

Winpisinger took over the IAM at a crucial time. By 1977, it was the third largest affiliate of the AFL-CIO and the fifth largest union in North America. Nevertheless, membership had declined from a high of 1 million to approximately 750,000. Winpisinger understood the challenges facing organized labor in the wake of the energy crisis and stagflation of the 1970s. He insisted that both the IAM and the AFL-CIO needed a return to the activist spirit of the 1930s, a sentiment seemingly vindicated when the IAM topped 900,000 members within two years of his helmsmanship. Winpisinger also forged a group known as the "progressive bloc," consisting of AFL-CIO leaders critical of Meany's lethargic and conservative leadership. Winpisinger embarked upon a national tour to present the case both for the IAM and for unionism in general, with his goal being to restore the tarnished image of unions and defend the need to improve the economic position of American workers. His was a classic carrot-and-stick approach: Winpisinger openly embraced youth culture and engaged in populist stunts such as sponsoring prizes for auto-race mechanics, but he also insisted that broadcasters present an unbiased view of labor unions or face opposition when seeking license renewals from the Federal Communications Commission.

Nor did Winpisinger shrink from taking on politicians. Although he was nominally a **Democrat** and mindful or organized labor's historic ties with the party, he was critical of President Jimmy Carter, whom he lambasted as "the best Republican president since Herbert Hoover." Similarly, he referred to Energy Secretary James R. Schlesinger as "a Nazi," and insisted that organized labor should support only politicians whose labor record was solid. Winpisinger opposed Carter for several reasons—he was troubled by Carter's dealings with the **Business Roundtable**, felt he was too cozy with organized capital, and opposed the president's huge increases in military spending, even though the IAM had a large presence in the defense industry. In 1979, Winpisinger became a co-founder and president of the Citizen/Labor Energy Coalition, a group formed to draw attention to oil industry windfall profits in the face of workers' declining buying power. Two years later he led the IAM to file a (largely symbolic) lawsuit against the Organization of Petroleum Exporting Countries (OPEC) for artificially manipulating energy prices. As a member of the Democratic Socialist Organizing Committee (DSOC), Winpisinger led a 1979 conference on the problem of corporate power in the United States. The group adopted a series of resolutions calling upon the Democratic Party to rein in the business community. Winpisinger's anger with President Carter climaxed in 1980, when he led 300 delegates to walk out of the Democratic convention in protest of Carter's nomination for reelection.

Winpisinger was even more critical of Carter's successor, **Ronald Reagan**. At a time in which Reagan advanced a conservative political and social agenda, Winpisinger increased his involvement with the DSOC, renamed the Democratic Socialists of America in 1982. He was active in both the peace and the nuclear weapons' freeze movements and opposed Reagan's bellicose stance toward the Soviet Union (USSR); indeed, Winpisinger visited the USSR three times, even though he opposed **communism**. Winpisinger was also an advocate of gay and **Latino** rights. In 1980, he won the **Eugene V. Debs** award for his socialist activism, and was honored a second time in 1989. In open defiance of the climate of the 1980s, he helped the IAM draft a 1983 document known as the "Rebuilding America Act," an alternative to Reagan's economic agenda. He also counseled the IAM to battle against the **concessions** movement of the 1980s and co-authored (with Jane Slaughter) a 1983 book outlining battle strategy, *Concessions and How to Beat Them*.

Winpisinger, though a radical, was enormously popular within the IAM. He was viewed as a man who rose through the ranks, fought for the interests of his members, and never lost touch with his **working-class** roots. His ideology did not blind him to the need to bargain pragmatically and creatively with employers, and he won the begrudging admiration of foes such as Eastern Airlines President Frank Borman for his willingness to consider innovative **salary** agreements. Thus members of a conservative union embraced Winpisinger in spite of what labor historian Sidney Lens called "the sharpest [recent] indictment of American **capitalism** uttered by a prominent union official."

Winpisinger retired as IAM president in 1989 and died of cancer in Howard County, Maryland, on December 11, 1997. The following year the IAM renamed its facility in Hollywood, Maryland, the William W. Winpisinger Education & Technology Center.

Suggested Reading

Patrick S. Halley, *Wimpy*, 2008; "William W. Winpisinger Education & Technology Center," http://winpisinger.iamaw.org/, accessed August 11, 2011; William Winpisinger, *Reclaiming Our Future: An Agenda for American Labor*, 1989.

WOBBLY

Wobbly is a term that refers to members of the **Industrial Workers of the World** (IWW) and sometimes shortened to "Wob." The exact origins of the term are unknown, and it did not appear in print until 1913. Several theories have put forth to explain the source of the nicknamed, all of which have been repeated by IWW members. It may derive from the verb "wobble." Many members of the IWW toiled in unskilled positions on docks and railroads, and one explanation holds that the term originated from **longshoremen** wobbling under their heavy loads. A related version connects it to Irish "gandy dancers"—railroad workers who pried long tamping irons under the rails to level the beds upon which they rested. The act of getting leverage often lifted workers into the air, creating midair "wobbles." Still another theory links the term to the IWW's efforts to organize Chinese workers. The consonant *w* is difficult for native Chinese speakers to pronounce. Those Chinese workers with little English proficiency might pronounce IWW as "eye-wobble-u-wobble-u." Still others postulate Australian or exotic-dance connections. There is no conclusive proof for any theory. After 1913, however, IWW members freely and proudly appropriated the term and labor songwriter T-Bone Slim penned "The Popular Wobbly," a favorite of Wobs.

Suggested Reading

Archie Green, *Wobblies, Pile Butts, and Other Heroes: Laborlore Explorations*, 1993.

WOMEN AND LABOR. *See* Minority Labor. *See also* Protective Labor Legislation; specific organizations and individuals.

WOMEN'S TRADE UNION LEAGUE

The Women's Trade Union League (WTUL) was a cross-class organization designed to oppose **sweatshops** and campaign for shorter hours, higher **wages**, and better working conditions for workingwomen. It was founded in Boston in 1903 and partially filled the void in women's labor organizing left by the decline of the **Knights of Labor**, as most unions affiliated with the **American Federation of Labor** (AFL) either excluded women altogether or showed little interest in bringing them into the organized labor fold. The American WTUL was patterned after an eponymous group founded in England in 1874. It drew inspiration from a 1902 **boycott** by housewives of kosher butchers. William English Walling, a New York City settlement-house worker, traveled to England to observe WTUL operations. Upon returning to the United States, Walling drew up plans for an American WTUL with the assistance of **Mary Kenney O'Sullivan** and **Samuel Gompers**, though future AFL support for the WTUL was minimal.

Many of the early WTUL leaders were drawn from the **Progressive Era** settlement-house movement and included figures such as Lillian Wald, Agnes

Nestor, Vida Scudder, **Leonora O'Reilly**, and Jane Addams. The WTUL hoped to promote the cause of women trade unionists and to convince women workers to join unions. Because its leadership relied heavily on sympathetic **middle-class** women who were not wage-earners, however, some working people criticized its structure and tactics. Nonetheless, the WTUL grew under the dynamic leadership of Margaret Dreier Robins, who served as president from 1906 until 1922. The organization played an important role in the 1909 **Uprising of the 20,000** by raising money to support strikers, urging **boycotts** of firms being struck, and organizing mass protests. That labor action was said to be the largest **strike** of women in U.S. labor history to that point. The WTUL also investigated the **Triangle Factory fire of 1911** and used the tragedy to build support for factory safety reforms and other WTUL causes. It also supported the **Industrial Workers of the World** (IWW) during the 1912 **Lawrence textile strike**.

The WTUL's support for the IWW won it few friends in the AFL, which also battled the IWW in Lawrence. Robins and the WTUL often found themselves amidst controversy. Among the sources of such controversy was the WTUL's support for **protective labor legislation** that gave women both a **minimum wage** and **eight-hour** workday. It hailed these advances as true labor reforms, but because they applied only to women, feminists decried the essentialist implications of such legislation. For its part, the AFL felt that the WTUL had undermined its own **collective bargaining** efforts. The WTUL's willingness to work with radicals, moderate labor unions, and the middle class often earned it the distrust of all camps. Thus the WTUL enjoyed good relations with some unions—notably the **Amalgamated Clothing Workers of America**—but was coolly received by most AFL trades, while the ideological gap between the IWW and most middle-class reformers was simply too wide for most individuals to cross.

The WTUL was more successful in garnering interclass support for the women's suffrage movement. It was particularly effective in winning **working-class** support for the National American Woman Suffrage Association. By the 1920s, much of the WTUL's work had become more political in nature, with the WTUL continuing to lobby for protective labor legislation for women. The election of Franklin Roosevelt to the U.S. presidency in 1932 gave the WTUL a boost, as First Lady Eleanor Roosevelt was a long-time WTUL member. The WTUL's **Rose Schneiderman** gained access to the White House and was said to have influenced several pieces of New Deal legislation, including the **Social Security Act**. The WTUL was less successful in its campaign to remove laws and customs barring married women from working during the Great Depression.

The WTUL's influence waned as World War II approached, though it continued to offer classes for working women in everything from history to vocational training. It officially dissolved in 1950, but it should be considered the forerunner of groups such as the **Coalition of Labor Union Women** and various women's caucuses within both politics and the organized labor movement.

Suggested Reading

Philip Foner, *Women and the American Labor Movement*, 2 vols., 1980; Alice Kessler-Harris, *Out to Work: A History of Wage-Earning Women in the United States*, 1982; Annelise Orleck, *Common Sense and a Little Fire: Women and Working-Class Politics in the United States 1900–1965*, 1995.

WORKERS' BILL OF RIGHTS

The Bill of Rights—the first 10 amendments to the U.S. Constitution—is held in great reverence by most Americans and is widely hailed as the very foundation of personal and civil rights associated with American freedom. In recent decades, numerous erstwhile reformers have argued that the nation needs a separate workers' bill of rights to guarantee the rights of employees and ensure the dignity of all working Americans. Although such an idea is seductive, it remains elusive as there is neither agreement on what such a document would include nor the political will to bring one into being.

At present, provisions included in the 1959 Labor-Management Reporting and Disclosure Act are the closest approximation of a workers' bill of rights that exists in the United States. The act guarantees workers' electoral rights, freedom of speech, freedom of assembly, and due process safeguards when being disciplined. Workers also have the right to determine what their **dues** will be and how they are spent, and to sue when their rights are infringed. The problem is that these rights exist solely to protect rank-and-file union members from their own officers. There are no safeguards whatsoever regulating how employers must treat employees beyond those spelled out in the **National Labor Relations Act** (NLRA). The NLRA defines **unfair labor practices**, but its major thrust is to protect **collective bargaining** rights, not to regulate the day-to-day interactions between labor and management.

Many individuals would agree that the NLRA is outdated, but the content of a future workers' bill of rights is a matter of great ideological debate. Much of the political right equates the idea of a workers' bill of rights with the concept of the **right to work**—that is, with the right *not* to join labor unions. A substantial part of the political right denies the very legitimacy of labor unions and vehemently opposes a bill of rights that would make labor organizing easier or impose regulations upon the business community.

By contrast, enacting measures making it easier to organize is precisely what many labor activists mean by a workers' bill of rights. Most unions support the Employee Free Choice Act, which would have allowed a union to be recognized as a collective bargaining agent as soon as a majority of a workplace's employees signed cards authorizing the union to represent them. It would also have required unions and employers to enter into a binding **arbitration** agreement within 120 days, and would have imposed harsh penalties on intransigent employers. This bill was filibustered in the U.S. Senate and did not become law.

Many unions have developed their own versions of what a workers' bill of rights would look like; the document produced by the Labor Party, a lobby group, is typical. Its Workplace Bill of Rights notes that, at present, many workers do not enjoy even those rights allegedly guaranteed under the U.S. Bill of Rights such as freedom of speech, assembly, and due process. In many non-union workplaces, employees can be dismissed without cause, irrespective of their past employment record. The Labor Party's bill of rights would begin by making certain that the U.S. Bill of Rights applied to the private workplace, not just the public realm and inside unions. It would also include provisions such as forbidding employers from interfering with union organizing, allowing workers in all job classifications to join unions, making it easier for **part-time** and **contingency** workers to unionize, eliminating employers' right to fire workers without cause, and expanding the right to **boycott**, **picket**, and seek other redresses of **grievances**.

The idea of a workers' bill of rights is not a radical idea, as such an entity already exists in Canada, Japan, and much of Europe. Aside from proposals that make union organizing easier, most workers' bills of rights essentially ask that employers be placed under the same restraints as union members have been under since the passage of the Labor-Management Reporting and Disclosure Act. Some states have created their own workers' bill of rights laws, and New York enacted one for domestic workers in 2010. The United States generally takes more of a laissez-faire approach to business activity than other countries, however, and the overall trend of the past four decades has been toward less—rather than more—regulation of economic activity. As a consequence, calls for a workers' bill of rights currently have more moral force than political feasibility.

Suggested Reading

AFL-CIO, "Employee Free Choice Act," http://www.aflcio.org/joinaunion/voiceatwork/efca/10keyfacts.cfm/, accessed August 12, 2011; Labor Party Documents, "Workplace Bill of Rights," http://lpa.igc.org/documents/lpd_workplace.html, accessed August 12, 2011; New York State Department of Labor, "Domestic Workers' Bill of Rights," http://www.labor.state.ny.us/sites/legal/laws/domestic-workers-bill-of-rights.page, accessed August 12, 2011.

WORKING CLASS

"Working class" is a complex and malleable term whose precise meaning often depends upon who uses it. In general, it refers to those persons whose living is derived from manual or **service industry** labor, who are paid an hourly **wage**, and whose occupations do not require much formal education (though specialized skills may be involved). Normally working-class occupations carry less prestige and are not as well remunerated as jobs classified as "professional." Some scholars argue that the working class is the largest social class in America, even though most Americans believe themselves to be members of the **middle class**.

In contemporary America, the term can be used in various contexts that connote pride, shame, or snobbery. In the first sense, calling oneself a "working man" (or woman) evokes self-esteem and class **solidarity** by juxtaposing those who do hard work against an implied group of malingerers, bureaucrats, managers, and intellectuals, none of whom do "real" work. This was often the way **artisans**, **apprentices**,

journeymen, and other wage-earners viewed themselves through the 1960s. In recent years, such positive identification with the working class has waned, and many Americans now view it as an extension of the lower class—a perception fueled by the presence of large numbers of working poor. Contrary to popular belief, very few poor people are idlers; roughly one-fourth of all American workers receive sub-poverty pay. That reality, coupled with public rhetoric that falsely inflates and valorizes the middle class, has contributed to the assumption that the post-World War II economic expansion transformed the United States into a thoroughly middle-class society. So powerful were such perceptions that by the 1960s individuals such as **American Federation of Labor-Congress of Industrial Organizations** (AFL-CIO) President **George Meany** repeated the belief that the working class had become middle class, and today's AFL-CIO leaders often call for reforms to "save the middle class." This is ironic, as members of the middle and upper classes often speak of the working class contemptuously, as if it is a subordinate servant class of low ability, intellect, or social importance and is a negative referent against which to measure their own status and success.

Social scientists insist upon more rigorous criteria, but their definitions of the working class differ as well, according to ideology and research focus. Most agree that class determination is very complicated and involves factors such as objective measures of class (wealth, power, and prestige), **class consciousness**, the existence of distinct class institutions, and a host of subjective factors such as reputation and self-perception.

In an objective sense, a separate working class emerged in the United States only during the early 19th century. Before then, most working Americans were independent **yeomen**, self-employed shopkeepers and artisans, or **indentured servants** or **slave** laborers. Some individuals worked for pay, including journeymen and domestic servants, but wage-earning was viewed as a temporary status and those drawing pay did not perceive themselves as members of a separate class. An increase in manufacturing, the advent of the **Industrial Revolution**, and population growth led to the existence of those who worked for wages for their entire working lives: a distinct working class whose members came to see themselves as a class apart. Class consciousness led to the development of an active working-class culture that included theater, magazines, books, newspapers, social clubs, and **labor parties**. It also gave rise to the labor movement. In many parts of the nation, unions were still in formation by the time of the **Civil War**, but the last three decades of the 19th century witnessed the formation (or revival) of trade unions, the emergence of **labor federations**, and intense capital/labor conflict in which class lines were sharply drawn.

The meaning of class distinctions and conflicts sparked keen debate that continues to divide scholars. For **Marxists**, the working class—which Karl Marx dubbed the proletariat—was a potentially revolutionary body entrusted with the historic task of destroying **capitalism**. Marx, Friedrich Engels, and other Marxists defined social class though one's relationship to the means of production. Because industrial workers owned neither their tools nor the fruits of their labor, it was hypothesized that they would eventually develop revolutionary class consciousness and that the masses were destined to overthrow the parasitical owner classes who lived off of labor, rents, and sales of inflated goods and services. Although Marx foresaw problems in organizing the dispirited and chronically **unemployed** poor—which he called the *lumpenproletariat*—he fervently believed that a future **communist** society would eliminate all classes except the working class. Private property would be abolished and all members of society would engage in productive labor aimed at enhancing the collective good. Although Marx's predictions did not occur on American soil, his ideas have influenced numerous labor activists and continue to shape the way in which conflict theory sociologists view the working class.

Exactly why Marxism or other forms of **socialism** have had less impact among the American working class than it had in other industrial nations has perplexed scholars. Some have postulated theories collectively known as "American exceptionalism," which hold that unique American conditions such as an abundance of available land, the early development of **republican** traditions, and/or relative prosperity defused working-class radicalism. Other historians argue that American radicalism predates Marx, that the nation's ideological choices have been broader, and that socialism has had to compete with other views. Many labor historians have sided with Herbert Gutman in noting that the truly "exceptional" aspect of American society has been its heterogeneity. Rather than a single working class, the ranks of American laborers have been continually refreshed and reconstituted by **immigration**, but the work experiences of new immigrants is chronologically disconnected from those of earlier groups; instead of forging **solidarity**, this factor means that older groups see recent arrivals as economic competition and threats to prevailing cultural norms. Some scholars opt for a simpler explanation: that the American capitalist class organized more thoroughly than the working class, was more powerful, and simply crushed its opposition. Each view has both merits and weaknesses, but collectively they remind us that the term "working class" may be deceptive in that it implies unity, commonality, and singleness of purpose that perhaps never existed; indeed, some analysts use social class terms as plurals rather than singulars and speak of the working *classes* (and "middle classes," and so on).

Critics argue that Marxists oversimplify social class. Categorization is murky for those who own small service businesses such as repair shops, independent **retail** ventures, beauty parlors, and landscaping firms. In classic Marxism, such individuals belong to the petty (or *petite*) bourgeoisie and are members of the lower middle class. Yet in many cases these individuals identify more with wage-earners than with middle-class workers drawing **salaries**. German sociologist Max Weber (1864–1920) was among those who argued that the relationship to the means of production was just one of the factors that defined the working class and did not agree that unequal wealth necessarily guaranteed class conflict. Weber saw society as more complexly layered than Marx. Skilled machinists, for example, often made more money and had higher standards of living than low-level college-educated clerks, though the first would generally be categorized as working class and the latter as middle class. Weber's work cast so much doubt upon how the working class was defined that some later scholars—most notably W. Lloyd Warner (1898–1970)—did not even use the term; Warner distributed manual workers among his lower middle and upper lower class categories.

Warner's key works came in the 1950s and 1960s, at which time the term "working class" was becoming murkier. The collapse of social movements during the Gilded Age, the suppression of the **Industrial Workers of the World** and other radical groups in the early 20th century, and the intervention of the state into capital/labor relations during the **Progressive Era** and during the New Deal had the long-term effect of institutionalizing capitalism and defusing radicalism. By World War II, self-identification with the working class was still a point of pride for millions of Americans, especially those involved in labor unions, but an overall decline in labor activism occurred in the 1950s. It was occasioned by a host of factors, including the **Red Scare**, the articulation of **Cold War** unionism, restraints placed upon labor by the **Taft-Hartley Act**, and the ability of unions to secure lucrative **contracts** during the postwar economic boom. The expansion of the U.S. economy between 1946 and 1970 played a major role in democratizing consumerism and making the promises of material prosperity imaginable to the masses. This phenomenon gave fuel to those who argued that class conflict was outmoded and that the interests of capital and labor were mutual, not antagonistic. George Meany was no doubt correct in his belief that, for many workers, the boundaries between the working and middle class appeared to be collapsing.

The meaning of what it meant to be working class was in flux by the mid-1960s, a time in which the **counterculture** and New Left ideologues "rediscovered" it. Many members of the New Left romanticized the working class and admired its supposed authenticity vis-à-vis the perceived shallowness of the middle class. Some even resurrected the belief that it would be the vanguard of revolutionary upheaval. Students for a Democratic Society, for instance, set up community programs to recruit and educate workers, some radicals became blue-collar workers (and agitators), and various **anarchist**, **communist**, and socialist groups sought to enlist workers in their struggles. In truth, the American working class was less prosperous than affluence propagandists claimed, more materialistic (and less enamored of countercultural values) than the New Left held, and more polarized than most Americans realized. It contained both those enamored of upheaval, such as the **Dodge Revolutionary Union Movement**, and blue-collar conservatives, such as those who attacked **Vietnam War** protestors during the **hard hat riots** in 1970.

Some social strains within the working class were neither ameliorated by consumerism nor adequately addressed by the counterculture. The nature of work itself was often deeply resented. **Taylorism**, for instance, never fulfilled the hopes of managers hoping to instill factory discipline, as workers resisted it at the point of production, often spontaneously and without the aid of labor unions. By the late 1950s and early 1960s, leftist writers such as Harry Braverman, Irving Howe, and Harvey Swados presciently warned that many American workers had become deeply alienated from their jobs, and the outbreak of **wildcat strikes** during the late 1960s and early 1970s validated many of their concerns. When Studs Terkel's oral history collection *Working* appeared in 1974, it revealed a disturbing finding: Though workers had pride in the work they did, many of them hated their jobs and wanted their children to escape working-class life. There was also tension between older white males and younger workers, women, and people of color entering the workforce.

What few observers foresaw was the coming of **deindustrialization** and **globalization** in the wake of the stagflationary economy from 1973 through 1984. By the end of the 1970s, there was little objective evidence to validate an ideological convergence between the working and middle classes. If anything, the ruined economy and poor job prospects magnified their latent differences. As Lillian Rubin revealed, economic struggle, fear of unemployment, marital discord, fatalism, resentment, and disproportionate levels of sexism, substance abuse, family violence, and other social problems often marked working-class life. Globalization and deindustrialization led to plant closings, surging unemployment, attempts to decertify labor unions, and forced cuts in wages and **fringe benefits** for workers who kept their jobs. Rather than lash out against capitalism, however, many blue-collar voters cast ballots for **Ronald Reagan** in 1980, thereby reversing a trend that had held since the New Deal in which the working class tended to favor liberal **Democrats**. Reagan proved to be a foe of the labor movement, but progressives have struggled to rebuild working-class support to 1930s levels, and blue-collar voters also gave high tallies to conservative George W. Bush in both 2000 and 2004, and to Tea Party candidates in the 2010 Congressional elections.

Republicans have also succeeded in changing the very terms of class debate in American society. They have recognized that class is often understood in subjective terms. By the end of the 1980s, few individuals, including Democrats, continued to use the term "working class" in a prideful manner; instead, most Americans seized upon the idea that they belonged to the middle class. Although this is absurd in objective terms, it is increasingly rare to hear policy debates framed as if the working and middle classes are discrete; in the minds of most Americans, anyone who collects pay in any form is a member of the middle class. When Democrat John Edwards built his 2008 primary election campaign for president on themes of rebuilding the working class, his message gathered little traction. Ironically, ultra-conservative Republicans such as Patrick Buchanan are often at the fore of those using the term "working class," frequently in the context of calls for **protectionism** based in part upon xenophobia.

Deindustrialization has continued apace. In 1965, 53 percent of Americans worked in manufacturing jobs; by 2004, that share was just 9 percent. By 2011, a larger percentage of American workers were **unemployed** (9.1 percent) than worked in manufacturing (0.9 percent). The makeup of the 21st century working class depends upon the lens through which one views work. How, for example, does one classify the 40 percent of workers who are in nonmanagerial service-sector employment? Though such jobs are, technically, **white-collar** (or **pink-collar**) work, they are generally held in low regard and are low-paid wage labor. Writers such as Michael Zweig argue that traditional class categories should be collapsed economically and socially; one is a member of the working class if one works for wages and has a boss. By his reckoning, at least 62 percent of the labor force is working class.

Zweig's study also calls further attention to the imprecision with which social class is measured when using subjective determinations. When given a set of positive characteristics with which to associate, more than 60 percent of Americans were willing to call themselves members of the working class. So-called objective standards do not clarify matters much better, as they depend upon how data are parsed. These studies place the percentage of Americans who are working class at between 30 percent and 46 percent—a huge variance that makes the working class either the largest social class in America or marginally smaller than the middle class. Nonetheless, those who assert that working class is no longer a credible category of social analysis run afoul of the fact that the 2010 median family income was $49,777, but 90 percent of American households make less than this amount. Slightly more than 26 percent of Americans have obtained a four-year college degree, and the richest 10 percent of Americans control two-thirds of the nation's total wealth. To evoke Zweig's message, most Americans are members of the working class because they still have a boss.

Suggested Reading

Martin J. Burke, *The Conundrum of Class: Public Discourses on the Social Order in America*, 1995; Barbara Ehrenreich, *Nickel and Dimed: On (Not) Getting by in America*, 2002; The New York Times, *Class Matters*, 2006; Lillian Rubin, *Worlds of Pain: Life in the Working Class Family*, 1976; Ruy Teixeira and Joel Rogers, *America's Forgotten Majority: Why the White Working Class Still Matters*, 2001; Michael Zweig, *Working Class Majority: America's Best Kept Secret*, 2001.

WORKINGMAN'S PARTY. *See* Labor Parties.

WORKINGMEN'S MOVEMENT

"Workingmen's movement" is the term used to identify myriad efforts to form labor unions, **labor parties**, and reform groups during the **Jacksonian era**. The "Workies," as advocates of this movement were nicknamed, were strongest after 1828. Most such activity waned by 1835, and then was destroyed by the Panic of 1837. It was not a unified movement, but rather a catchall category that described **working-class** agitation that found its strongest expression in eastern seaboard cities in the North. In many cases, working-class activists allied with **middle-class** reformers, and in quite a few instances the latter directed and controlled organizations. The Workingmen's movement emerged at a time in which social reform sentiment was strong, and should be viewed within a broader context that includes religious change, **utopian** experiments, and the emergence of abolitionism, temperance, moral reform, and other attempts to improve American society.

In the 1820s, many **journeymen** began to transform traditional associations that were remnants of the guild system into prototypical trade unions. In 1827, Philadelphia carpenters struck for a 10-hour workday. That action failed, but the next year they and several other unions formed the Mechanics' Union of Trade Associations, considered by some historians to be the first American **labor federation**. From it came the Workingmen's Party of Philadelphia, which served as a model for other cities. Between 1828 and 1834, hundreds of **strikes** took place in eastern cities, scores of independent political parties formed, and at least 68 **labor journals** were published, the most influential of which was New York City's *Working Man's Advocate*.

Many of the new parties were critical of both the Whigs and the Democrats, though in some places they allied with the latter. They operated under various names including the Workingmen's Party, the Farmer and Mechanics Society, and the Workingmen's Republican Association. Coordination between groups was spotty; hence the Workingmen's movement is best seen as a series of responses to social trends, including the fact that emerging **capitalism** had created a group of wage-earners who could expect to draw paychecks for life instead of becoming independent **masters** or **yeomen** as previous generations of workers had done. Political platforms and group agendas varied, but most workingmen's associations called for land and tax reform, the passage of lien laws, free public education, the abolition of debtor prisons, shorter work hours, and strict regulations on banks, limited-liability corporations, and the use of labor-saving machinery. Many Workies adhered to the **labor theory of value**—the belief that the worth of any good or service is determined by the amount of labor put into it. All Workingmen rejected Malthusian explanations for poverty and insisted that class privilege and unfair business practices caused privation. The "Workies" advanced a mixed agenda based on progressive, preindustrial, and **agrarian** values that is sometimes called **republicanism**.

In some locales, especially the Northeast, Workingmen's parties competed for political power and initially did very well. New York City sent a carpenter to the state legislature, Philadelphia elected 20 of its 54 Workingmen's candidates, and other cities elected Workies to a variety of municipal and state posts.

Success proved fleeting, however, and by 1835 the movement was moribund in most places. Decline came for many reasons. Coordinated efforts proved difficult because Workingmen leadership varied so greatly. In New York City, for example, **Thomas Skidmore**'s call for the state to seize and redistribute land struck George Henry Evans as so radical that he conspired with others to kick Skidmore out of the party. Another Workingmen's leader, Frances "Fanny" Wright, shocked southerners and bigoted northern workers with her attempt at forming a biracial community in Nashoba, Tennessee. Her views on sexual liberation were also widely parodied. Still other leaders, such as **Robert Dale Owen**, were embroiled in utopian experiments that proved unworkable.

The Workies also generated religious controversy. Many of its leaders were free-thinkers, and though many shared the middle class's enthusiasm for the religious revivals of the Second Great Awakening, they tended to embrace unorthodox views. This left them open to attacks of being anti-Christian, which hurt their efforts to recruit workers and middle-class allies for whom religion was important.

Mostly, though, the Workingmen were undone by employer opposition and weakening economic conditions. The parties drew much of their strength from nascent trade unions whose membership rolls were unstable due to high turnover. The movement was already in deep decline by 1835, and the Panic of 1837 finished it. Many trade unions collapsed during the depression and took decades to revive.

The Workingmen's movement was nonetheless influential on many levels. First, it suggested the need to move beyond traditional forms of labor organization—considerations that led trade unions to organize around class interests rather than antiquated economic assumptions. Second, the Workies called attention to a host of unresolved issues that lived on in other forms such as the shorter-hours movement, the calling of pre-**Civil War** labor congresses, and the articulation of **cooperative** ideals. Future groups such as the New England Workingmen's Association, the **Lowell Female Labor Reform Association**, and the Boston Trades Union were offshoots of the Workingmen's movement. Third, the Workingmen's movement showed the weakness of uncoordinated agitation, a weakness that later inspired bodies such as **central labor unions** and stronger labor federations. The Workies also (inadvertently) touched off a debate that would roil labor movements for many years to come: the wisdom (or lack thereof) of forging cross-class alliances. The question, in essence, was whether the middle classes were capable of championing working-class agendas or were obstacles to enacting them.

Suggested Reading

Bruce Laurie, *Beyond Garrison: Antislavery and Social Reform*, 2005; Edward Pessen, *Most Uncommon Jacksonians: Radical Leaders of the Early Labor Movement*, 1967; Sean Wilentz, *Chants Democratic: New York City and the Rise of the American Working Class, 1788–1850*, 1984; David Zonderman, *Uneasy Allies: Working for Reform in 19th-Century Boston*, 2011.

WORKMAN'S COMPENSATION

Workman's compensation—also called worker's compensation or worker's comp—is an insurance scheme that pays benefits to individuals injured on the job and to families of employees killed while working. Worker's compensation laws are in effect in all states, but there is no single federal standard and some state laws do not cover all workers.

Workman's compensation laws are an outgrowth of the **Industrial Revolution**. The explosion of industrial output after the **Civil War** led to huge advances in personal and national wealth, but businesses went largely unregulated in an age in which laissez-faire economic values prevailed among American policymakers. Safety standards and factory inspections were spotty, if they existed at all. Workers frequently suffered appalling injuries and traumatic deaths in the workplace. Injured workers suffered a double blow in an age in which there was neither **unemployment** compensation nor a social welfare safety net. Injured workers were denied their **wages** until such time as they could (if ever) return to work and were entirely at the mercy of friends, mutual aid societies, and private charities for assistance. In some cases, businesses voluntarily made one-time payments to injured workers, but these amounts were seldom enough to sustain them and their families. It was possible to sue for damages in industrial accidents in some states, but such litigation was a long process that involved proving that the employer was at fault. In many cases, even when workers won judgments, employers refused to honor them.

As often as not, workers' lawsuits were dismissed by the courts, which frequently ruled that employee mistakes caused accidents, rather than the work conditions. In 1855, Georgia and Alabama enacted laws that made employers liable for some accidents; by 1907, 28 states had similar laws, but the first true compensation law as such came in Maryland in 1902.

The first significant push for workman's compensation from the federal government came in 1906 during the **Progressive Era**, when Congress bolstered an ineffective law passed in 1882. Laws protecting federal workers were further strengthened by the 1908 Federal Employees Compensation Act, though it also proved inadequate and has been revised several times. The federal laws empowered labor organizations such as the **American Federation of Labor** to push harder for legislation to protect non-federal workers. By 1911, various states had enacted their own workman's compensation laws; by 1949, all states had such laws. Mining was among the first industries to enact workman's compensation laws, largely because the U.S. Bureau of Mines regulated the industry after 1910.

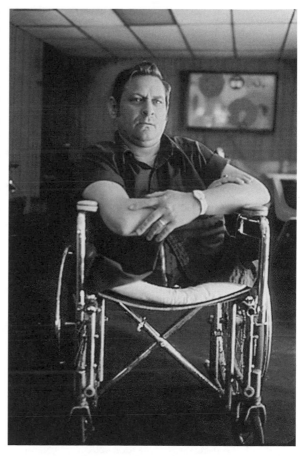

Jack Smith of Rhodell, West Virginia. He was disabled at age 21 after a year in the mines, and had to wait 18 years to collect workman's compensation. (National Archives)

At first, mine owners resisted paying into compensation funds, but they soon found the insurance fund to their advantage as it made their yearly costs more predictable and insulated them from potentially ruinous lawsuits. In some cases, mine compensation funds had the unintended effect of making mine operators less attentive to safety concerns.

Workman's compensation is of great importance, as each year one out of 10 workers in the private sector is injured while working. In addition, a host of old conditions, including **black lung disease**, have been established as legitimate work-induced conditions, and new ones have emerged, such as carpal tunnel syndrome. The goals of contemporary workman's compensation programs include alleviating the financial strain on injured workers, and making both employees and employers more attentive to the costs of injuries and the conditions that lead to them. Worker's comp funds protect both the employer and the employee. Employers are obligated to pay their employees (or their families) benefits for on-the-job injuries regardless of who was at fault. In turn, employers are protected from being sued by employees. The initial decision of whether to compensate workers is usually made by employers or insurance companies rather than by state workman's-compensation agencies. The latter generally intervene only to resolve disputes.

Approximately 90 percent of workers are covered by workman's compensation, though coverage varies by state. Texas, for instance, allows employers to choose not to participate in the state program, and roughly 40 percent of them take this route. (Companies lose anti-lawsuit immunity once they opt out.) States also vary in terms of whether the funds come from public sources, are administered by private insurers, or are a combination of the two. Workman's compensation generally pays benefits in five categories: (1) the payment of medical expenses for injured workers; (2) the payment of temporary disability monies to injured workers who cannot work, but are expected to fully recover; (3) the payment of permanent partial disability to workers suffering from injuries that affect their ability to work and support their families in the future; (4) the payment of permanent total disability benefits to workers who cannot return to work; and (5) the payment of burial and survival benefits to the families of workers killed in work-related accidents.

Disputes can arise over what level of benefits should be paid and, in relatively rare cases, employees and employers alike have abused the system. Workman's compensation is, however, an important safeguard, as each year some 66,000 Americans die from injuries or illnesses contracted on the job and millions are injured.

Suggested Reading

Price Fishback and Shawn Everett Kantor, *A Prelude to the Welfare State: The Origins of Workers' Compensation*, 2006; Margaret C. Jasper, *Workers' Compensation Law*, 2nd edition, 2008; Wiilis J. Nordlund, "The Federal Employees' Compensation Act," http://www.bls.gov/mlr/1991/09/art1full.pdf, accessed August 14, 2011; Pat Woeppel, *Depraved Indifference: The Workers' Compensation System*, 2008.

WORK SHARING

Work sharing is a self-defining term for a practice in which employers allow two or more individuals to split responsibility for a single job. It is considered by workers to be a favorable mechanism when it allows job flexibility. New parents, workers seeking **part-time** jobs, or those who would otherwise face **unemployment** generally applaud employers that offer work sharing programs. This approach is controversial, however, when it is imposed upon workers rather than chosen.

Work sharing is an old idea that received serious consideration during the Great Depression when **unemployment** soared above 20 percent; some advocates saw it as a way to allow workers to draw at least partial **wages** and remove the strain upon the private charities that delivered most of the relief to destitute families before New Deal programs created a social safety net. Work sharing has also long been in place in Europe, especially in Scandinavian nations. The idea received renewed attention in the United States during the late 1960s and early 1970s, when feminist groups seized upon it as a method of securing greater flexibility for working mothers.

Advocates for the elderly see work sharing as a way in which senior citizens can secure part-time employment. Many businesses, in turn, have been receptive to the idea because older workers tend to be more loyal, have lower turnover, have fewer discipline problems, and bring greater skill sets to the workplace. Surprising studies also reveal that, although older workers lack endurance and are susceptible to illness, their productivity per hour often outstrips that of younger workers. They also have *lower* rates of conditions such as obesity and asthma than younger workers. Longer lifespans and the strain placed on pensions and **Social Security** are likely to increase the presence of part-time elderly workers.

Government laws often encourage work sharing by requiring employers to pay an **overtime** premium for hours worked in excess of 8 hours per day or 40 hours per week. Employment laws have also fueled a major controversy over work sharing. In many states and workplaces, workers who are employed for 20 or fewer hours per week are ineligible for **fringe benefits** such as **pensions** or employer-paid health care. Some employers force workers into work sharing positions as a way to reduce payroll. In some cases, employers' practices place a strain on the social welfare agencies that underemployed workers use to compensate for inadequate wages.

Some companies used work sharing during the recession of the early 21st century. Massachusetts was among the states that promoted ideas such as reducing the work week to four days or allowing workers to share jobs instead of engaging in mass layoffs. Workers under such arrangements can still receive partial unemployment benefits, and the combination of those benefits and part-time work is greater than full unemployment compensation. Some employers are reluctant to implement work sharing in the belief that splitting jobs will reduce productivity within a given day. Studies do not sustain those fears, but they nonetheless persist.

A small but growing trend in work sharing has been an increase in companies offering work sharing as a family-friendly benefit. Another small trend is toward voluntary lifestyle downsizing. Since the 1990s, the overall trend has been for an increase in weekly hours worked. Whereas laborers in the 1960s and 1970s worked 40 hours per week, the average is now nearly 48. The lifestyle downsizing phenomenon has increased interest in work sharing, as some Americans have opted to work fewer hours and live with less money—in essence, exchanging a higher living standard for what they hope will be a better quality of life.

Suggested Reading

Anders Hayden, *Sharing the Work, Sparing the Planet: Work Time, Consumption, and Ecology*, 2008; Anthony Rienzi, "Productivity for the Ages: Maximizing the Contribution of Older Workers," *Insightout* (February 2009): 1–6.

WORK-TO-RULE

Work-to-rule is a creative and legal form of **sabotage** used by unions during contract negotiations or by workers acting on their own in an attempt to change their working conditions. It involves workers following contract provisions or company regulations exactly as they are written.

Most workplaces include many rules that are outdated or ignored by both workers and management. In addition, it is nearly impossible to write job descriptions that cover all aspects of what an employee does. Most businesses rely upon the common sense of workers to simply do the mundane tasks necessary for the smooth functioning of the workplace. They also depend upon workers to take on small tasks that increase workplace efficiency, or to accept certain jobs for little or no compensation. A public high school, for example, generally depends upon its faculty to oversee school clubs, coach sports teams, monitor cafeteria traffic, assist in the safe loading and unloading of students from buses, tutor students after hours, attend school events, meet with parents, and spend out-of-school time preparing lessons and correcting homework. In many cases, these duties are not officially part of a teacher's contract. In a work-to-rule dispute, teachers can seriously disrupt the school's functioning by doing only those tasks specified in the contract and nothing more. In like fashion, a skilled office manager performs numerous tasks not listed in job descriptions. He or she might, for instance, be required to type letters but not to proofread them. In like fashion, that individual probably makes dozens of routine decisions per day based upon his or her knowledge of organizational policy; during work-to-rule, that individual might pass on responsibility for routine decisions to management.

Labor unions often prefer the work-to-rule mechanism to strikes because members do not lose pay with this approach and cannot be replaced by **scabs**. The union can also engage in certain types of **slowdowns** without violating **collective bargaining** agreement, as contracts generally specify that workers have to perform certain jobs, but do not place a clock time limit on how long it can take.

Another form of right-to-rule involves meticulous application of rules. For example, police officers might stop and ticket all vehicles going above a usually unenforceable minimum speed limit of 25 miles per hour, thus bringing an incensed citizenry into the negotiations. Bus drivers in Providence, Rhode Island, once used a regulation requiring thorough inspection of buses to force union mechanics to examine vehicles, thereby pulling several dozen buses off the road for various alleged safety problems during the morning rush hour. In like fashion, maintenance workers have been known to use archaic state regulations during labor disputes. A state might require a licensed professional to do electrical installations. Because the word "installation" is vague, maintenance workers are within their rights to refuse to place an air conditioner in a window.

Some experts in the field of labor/management relations charge that work-to-rule is a type of strike or sabotage, but it is not legally defined as such as long as workers perform all of their assigned duties. This tactic continues to appear in different guises as the nature of work evolves.

Suggested Reading
Linda Slaughter and Judy Ancel, *Troublemaker's Handbook 2: How to Fight Back Where You Work—and Win!*, 2005.

WORLD TRADE ORGANIZATION. *See* General Agreement on Tariffs and Trade.

WRIGHT, FRANCES. *See* Owen, Robert; Owen, Robert Dale; Workingmen's Movement.

WRITERS AND ORGANIZED LABOR

The attempt to organize writers is an example of organized labor's attempt to respond to both the decline of **blue-collar** work and the **computer revolution**. To date, it has also proved an example of how volatile labor markets and the uncertain future of work have complicated the efforts of organizers.

Some writers have long been organized. Since 1933, journalists have had the option of joining the Newspaper Guild, and television, movie, and radio writers have been members of the Writers Guild of America (WGA), an organization formed in the early 1950s that belongs to the International Federation of Journalists and is an affiliate of the **American Federation of Labor-Congress of Industrial Organizations**. The WGA has led numerous strikes, including major actions in 1960, 1988, and 2007–2008. The last of these was a 14-week walkout in which a key issue was paying residuals to writers whose work appears on DVDs and other rebroadcasts. That strike cost the entertainment industry billions of dollars in lost revenue as new programming and films were delayed and advertisers were loath to spend heavily on reruns or long-run features.

The WGA is itself an offshoot of a group founded in 1912 called the Authors' League of America, now called the Authors Guild (AG). The AG now represents approximately 8,000 writers, agents, and lawyers in the book industry, though it also has representatives in magazines. Most of its members are well-established writers, and they have waged recent fights over copyright infringement for unauthorized use of their work. In 2008, for example, the AG negotiated a $125 million agreement with Google related to unauthorized scanning of copyrighted materials. It also settled a dispute with publisher Simon & Schuster over contract clauses that would have made it easier for the publisher to obtain and retain electronic publishing rights.

The Newspaper Guild, the WGA, and the AG have historically represented their members well, but the entire publishing world has been in flux in the past four decades. Newspapers have been disrupted by waves of merger activity that have accelerated since the 1980s, often resulting in **concessions**, layoffs, and firings. These shakeups in the newspaper industry have added to an already growing pool of freelance writers; the latter group is largely unrepresented and consists of individuals who are left to make the best bargain they can for their work. Most freelancers, however, have very little bargaining power, as publishers can easily find writers willing to accept whatever pay they offer. They also have had little control over what publishers did with their work in terms of editing it and reselling it. The National Writers Union (NWU) was formed in 1981 to represent freelancers, technical writers, and those journalists, fiction writers, poets, and others who were not members of the AG. It has since expanded its focus to include Web content providers. In 1992, the NWU merged with the **United Auto Workers of America** (UAW) at a time in which the UAW was rebuilding its membership base by expanding beyond the automobile industry and bringing writers, graduate students, nurses, and others into the fold.

The rise of computers and electronic publishing exacerbated the problems facing writers. Disputes arose over ownership of electronic and Web publication of materials that first appeared in print. In 2001, the NWU won a U.S. Supreme Court victory in the case of *Tasini v. Times*, which stipulated that writers were entitled to compensation when their works were republished in electronic form. The *Tasini* decision has, to date, proved more symbolic than substantive. Although the NWU won an $18 million settlement, the funds have not yet been distributed, which has led to defections from the NWU. Moreover, the ruling applied only to unauthorized republication of past work; publishers now routinely place republication language in contracts with writers, or they pay small sums to secure those rights.

The NWU's relatively high **dues** have also driven away some former union members, many of whom make too little money to justify membership. NWU leaders have faced charges that they are elitists uninterested in the struggles of authors outside the inner circle of writers dwelling in the few urban areas in which the NWU has chapters. The validity of this charge is often a matter of perception, but the NWU faces a larger challenge: It is simply difficult to organize independent workers who are spread across the nation and generally work in isolation from one another. No one knows the exact number of freelance writers in the United States. According to the **Bureau of Labor Statistics**, freelancers took on roughly 70 percent of 281,300 contracted writing jobs in 2008, but this figure surely represents a mere fraction of the actual number of freelance assignments. At present the NWU represents just 1,200 writers, making it an exceedingly small player in the overall freelance picture.

The rank of independent writers has been growing. The computer revolution has created difficulties for journals, newspapers, and magazines, many of which have drastically curtailed their operations or have gone out of business altogether. In 2009 alone, 105 newspapers ceased publishing; in 2008, 525 magazines went under. Numerous cities now have no daily paper, and even venerable publications such as *Condé Nast*, *U.S. News and World Report*, and *Gourmet* have failed. As traditional outlets for writers have dried up, many have tried their luck in such electronic fields as blogging, providing website content, and writing for online publications. Making a living at such pursuits has proved difficult for most, leaving many fields—including journalism—open to hobbyists and lesser-experienced writers. Many readers expect online content to be free, which has further suppressed the **wages** paid to writers. The current glut of writers has created a buyers' market in all industries that rely upon them. Even Hollywood now routinely hires scriptwriters on a one-time basis rather than maintaining a stable of in-studio talent.

There may be opportunities for labor unions to organize in the new electronic publishing world, but the path is unclear at present because the entire profession of writing is in flux. The UAW has certainly not been revitalized by its relationship with the NWU, and it remains to be seen whether unions will see future such ventures as worth the effort. At the same time, writers are just one example of an ever-growing sector of **part-time**, **contingency**, and contract laborers within the workforce. In many respects, freelance writers are analogous to adjunct faculty, contract health care workers, sales people reliant upon commissions, seasonal employees, and workers secured through temporary help agencies. The challenges in organizing such groups are enormous, but labor unions may find their own survival dependent upon making inroads among them.

Suggested Reading

Bureau of Labor Statistics, "Occupational Outlook Handbook, 2010–11 Edition: Authors, Writers, and Editors," http://www.bls.gov/oco/ocos320.htm, accessed August 16, 2011; Jonathan Handel, *Hollywood on Strike! An Industry at War in the Internet Age*, 2011; National Writers Union, *Freelance Writers' Guide*, 2000.

WURF, JEROME

Jerome ("Jerry") Wurf (May 18, 1919–December 10, 1981) was the former president of the **American Federation of State, County, and Municipal Employees** (AFSCME). Like **William Winpisinger**, the head of the **International Association of Machinists**, Wurf was among the last generation of labor leaders to embrace **socialism** unabashedly. He generally receives credit for building AFSME into a powerful union. When Wurf took over leadership of the AFSCME in 1964, the union had approximately 200,000 members; by his death 17 years later, it represented more than 1 million public workers.

Wurf was born in New York City, the son of Sigmund Wurf, a Jewish **immigrant** textile jobber, and Lena (Tanenbaum) Wurf. "Jerry," as he preferred to be called, survived the contraction of polio when he was just four, though he walked with a limp thereafter and was plagued by various ailments for much of his life. He moved from the Bronx to Brooklyn with his mother and her new husband following his father's death. At first he struggled in Brooklyn, but he began to excel when an English teacher at James Madison High School offered him a chance to avoid a failing grade if he improved his communication skills. Wurf took the bait, became involved in local political groups, and developed prowess at public speaking. He became active in the Young People's Socialist League (YPSL), which he credited with helping him develop a political ideology he described as "moderate radicalism." The YPSL also taught him about **Eugene V. Debs**, who was ever after Wurf's historical hero. Wurf particularly admired Debs's determination to never become "a zealot and [never to be] taken in by the **communists**." Wurf also became an admirer of perennial Socialist Party presidential candidate Norman Thomas, whom he later befriended.

Wurf enrolled in New York University and obtained his bachelor's degree in 1940, completing his studies in night school as he worked to help support his family. Following graduation, Wurf worked in a Brooklyn cafeteria. Prompted by unfavorable working conditions, he organized his fellow workers into Local 448 of the Food Checkers and Cashiers Union of the **Hotel and Restaurant Employees**. His militancy was such that the Yiddish-speaking cafeteria owners nicknamed him *Mal'ach Hamaves*, "the Angel of Death."

Wurf briefly tried his own hand at running a delicatessen, but his previous effectiveness as a labor organizer drew the attention of Arnold S. Zander, who had built AFSCME from a single-state employees' union in Madison, Wisconsin, in 1932, to a national body affiliated with the **American Federation of Labor** (AFL). In 1947, Zander hired Wurf to organize an AFL competitor to the Transport Workers' Union, which was affiliated with the **Congress of Industrial Organizations** (CIO). Wurf's efforts faltered and Zander reassigned Wurf to beef up AFSCME's New York City affiliate, a task at which he excelled. When he took over AFSME's New York District Council 37, it had fewer than 1,000 members; by 1964, it had more than 38,000. Wurf's efforts were aided by his ability to convince New York City Mayor Robert Wagner to issue a 1954 executive order giving city workers the right to unionize. Wurf was even able to pressure parks commissioner and city planner Robert Moses, a man known for exercising autocratic power, to consent to an AFSME representation election. By 1958, New York City public workers had gained equality with their organized counterparts in the private sector.

In 1962, Wurf challenged his mentor, Arnold Zander, for the AFSCME presidency when it was revealed that Zander had invested union funds in pricey housing developments at a time in which rank-and-file AFSME members were failing behind in **wage** and **fringe benefit** increases. He was unsuccessful in 1962, but defeated Zander two years later. At the time Wurf was the youngest person to dislodge a sitting **American Federation of Labor-Congress of Industrial Organizations** (AFL-CIO) **international union** president since **Walter Reuther** had done so in 1946.

Like Reuther, Wurf became a thorn in the side of cautious AFL-CIO leaders such as **George Meany**. As AFSCME president, he immediately sold the housing developments in which Zander had invested. He also sold the union's national headquarters building in Washington, D.C., and restructured the union's leadership. Moreover, Wurf did not have any patience with **Cold War unionism**. When he discovered that the Central Intelligence Agency (CIA) had been using AFSCME's international union connections to channel funds to anticommunist unionists in foreign countries, Wurf terminated the arrangements and concentrated the union's efforts on bargaining gains for AFSCME members. In New York State, the AFSCME was instrumental in persuading the legislature to repeal the Condon-Wadlin Act, which mandated the firing of striking public employees. This became the model for a similar federal executive order from President John F. Kennedy in 1962.

Wurf embraced the **civil rights** movement much earlier than most AFL-CIO leaders, and he was an early critic of the **Vietnam War**, which earned him Meany's wrath. Wurf helped establish New York's first Congress of Racial Equality chapter in the 1940s, personally recruited black AFSCME workers, encouraged AFSCME members to participate in the Freedom Rides, and was such an ardent supporter of racial justice that the Reverend Ralph Abernathy referred to him as a man "with a white skin but a black soul." He was an ally of the Reverend Martin

Luther King, Jr. On February 12, 1968, a largely black Memphis, Tennessee, AFSCME local walked off their jobs to protest racial discrimination when 22 black sewer workers were sent home without pay during a rainstorm, while white workers were allowed to remain on the job. Wurf helped coordinate mass meetings, marches, and **boycotts** of white-owned businesses and was jailed for encouraging a work stoppage in violation of an **injunction**. On April 4, King traveled to Memphis to support the strikers, was shot, and killed. Shortly after King's assassination, city leaders acceded to union demands, a victory Wurf compared to classic labor battles of the past.

During the 1970s, the AFSCME briefly became the nation's fastest-growing union and the largest union within the AFL-CIO. In part this increase in membership was a result of Wurf's recruitment of women and African Americans—two groups often ignored by more traditional labor leaders. Wurf became an AFL-CIO vice president, but his strident and confrontational style and his advocacy of positions counter to those supported by the AFL-CIO executive council blunted his effectiveness. His opposition to the Vietnam War earned him the enmity of both Meany and U.S. President Richard Nixon, who placed Wurf on the White House "enemies list." Wurf endorsed Senator George McGovern for the presidency of the United States in 1972, and simultaneously commented that the AFL-CIO's leadership was composed of elderly white men who were "products of an era and environment that is no longer." Wurf lambasted federation policies as out of touch with the moods and needs of younger workers and as insensitive to women, African Americans, and other **minority laborers**.

Wurf also feuded with AFL-CIO leadership over the formation of the Coalition of American Political Employees (CAPE), wherein he allied with the **National Education Association**, an archrival of the AFL-CIO's **American Federation of Teachers** (AFT). That position infuriated the AFT's **Albert Shanker**, and he and Wurf became implacable enemies. Despite his fieriness, however, Wurf was diplomatic enough to express public loyalty to the AFL-CIO. His personal style was such, though, that many erstwhile allies steered clear of him. During the 1970s, **United Auto Workers of America** President **Douglas Fraser** contemplated setting up a rival **labor federation** to the AFL-CIO, but abandoned the plan in part because of misgivings over the possibility of forging an alliance with Wurf.

The AFSCME experienced a temporary drop in membership during the 1970s related to fallout from plans drawn up in the 1960s to deinstitutionalize mental health treatment whenever possible, and replace mental hospitals with outpatient community health centers. Between 1955 and 1985, the number of housed mental patients dropped from 550,000 to one-fifth that number. Wurf (correctly) predicted that community treatment efforts would lag behind the pace of deinstitutionalization; by 1980, fewer than half of the facilities planned under President Kennedy's 1963 executive order had actually been opened. Although AFSCME replenished its membership by organizing other workers, Wurf considered his inability to shape mental health deinstitutionalization as among his personal failures.

Wurf devoted his later years to national labor policy. He insisted that the right of public employees to bargain collectively and to **strike** were fundamental and should not be abridged. At the same time, he agreed that strikes by police officers, fire-fighters, prison guards, and public-safety workers created social chaos and argued strongly for compulsory **arbitration** laws. Wurf, though personally militant, felt that arbitration should be extended to all public-sector employees and believed that most public-service workers were reluctant to strike. Under his leadership, the AFSCME became actively involved in public issues through its political office, Public Employees Organized to Promote Legislative Equality (PEOPLE), an organization that took outspoken positions on matters concerning public employees.

Wurf's first marriage ended in divorce. When Wurf died on December 10, 1981, he was survived by his wife of 21 years, Mildred (Kiefer), and their two children.

Suggested Reading

Joseph C. Goulden, *Jerry Wurf: Labor's Last Angry Man*, 1982; Labor and Worklife Program at Harvard Law School, "Jerry Wurf (1919–1981): A Short Biography," http://www.law.harvard.edu/programs/lwp/Wurf percent20biography3.pdf, accessed August 16, 2011; William Serrin, "A Leader for the Little Guy," *New York Times*, September 12, 1982.

YABLONSKI, JOSEPH A.

Joseph ("Jock") Yablonski (March 3, 1910–December 31, 1969) was a reform candidate who sought to head the **United Mine Workers of America** (UMWA). His 1969 murder sent the UMWA down the path of rooting out corruption and restoring rank-and-file democracy to the union when it was revealed that incumbent president W. A. ("Tony") Boyle was responsible for Yablonski's death.

Jock Yablonski was born in Pittsburgh, Pennsylvania. His father died in the mines in 1933, by which time Jock had himself been in the pits for eight years, having taken up the miner's trade at 15. The year after his father's death, Jock Yablonski was elected to a post with his **union local** that also gave him a seat on the UMWA executive board. He would serve on the board from 1932 to 1942. Although he often thought UMWA President **John L. Lewis** was dictatorial, Yablonski admired his gritty leadership and his devotion to improving the lives of miners.

In 1958, Yablonski became president of District 5, a large and important UMWA region that included the greater Pittsburgh area and parts of 11 Pennsylvania counties. In this post, Yablonski became increasingly concerned with corruption inside the UMWA's top ranks, especially after Lewis's retirement in 1960 and the death of his successor, Thomas Kennedy, in 1963. By the mid-1960s, the UMWA had shed its former militancy in favor of a **business unionism** model. There were also allegations that some union officials had ties to organized crime. Although Lewis was said to have handpicked Tony Boyle to succeed Kennedy, Yablonski sided with rank-and-file reformers determined to democratize the union and end corrupt practices. That decision prompted Boyle to force Yablonski from office in 1966.

In 1969, Yablonski announced his intention to challenge Boyle for the UMWA presidency. He had numerous powerful backers, including consumer activist Ralph Nader and Washington, D.C., attorney Joseph Rauh, the vice chair of the progressive political coalition Americans for Democratic Action. Yablonski was also popular among many UMWA miners because of his work with Labor's Non-Partisan League, a political action committee, and because of his efforts in persuading the Commonwealth of Pennsylvania to grant **workman's compensation** to **black lung** victims. Boyle, in contrast, was viewed as dictatorial and suffered from his poor public relations handling of the 1968 Farmington disaster in West Virginia, in which 78 miners died. He was also accused of embezzlement, negotiating questionable loans with UMWA monies, and illegal campaign practices. Nonetheless, arcane UMWA voting practices designed to shield leaders from the rank-and-file allowed Boyle to defeat Yablonski, who graciously conceded in public, though he filed an immediate challenge with the **Department of Labor** (DOL).

On December 31, 1969—just 22 days after the UMWA election—Yablonski, his wife, and a daughter were murdered in their Clarksville, Pennsylvania, home. The perpetrators were amateurish and left the crime scene pregnant with clues. The brutal murders also received worldwide publicity, and suspicion immediately arose that Boyle had ordered the hit on Yablonski. In 1971, the DOL ruled that Boyle's 1969 election was invalid, and a federal court ordered new elections in 1972. A rank-and-file insurgency movement, Miners for Union Democracy, spearheaded Boyle's ouster and the election of former Yablonski supporter Arnold Miller (1923–1985) to head the UMWA.

Boyle's legal woes multiplied. He was convicted of misuse of union **pension** funds in 1971, as well as making illegal political contributions during the 1968 presidential election. In 1973, Boyle was charged with first-degree murder in a plot to murder Yablonski. He was convicted in 1974 and sentenced to three life sentences. Boyle won a new trial in 1977, but was again convicted; he died in prison in 1985.

The UMWA—led by Rauh, Arnold Miller, Ed Sadlowski, Jerry Tucker, Yablonski's son (Chip), and others—began the process of reforming the UMWA, though Miller and his successors did not completely rid the union of Boyle supporters. Most observers credit **Richard Trumka**, the current head of the **American Federation of Labor-Congress of Industrial Organizations** (AFL-CIO), with finally completing Yablonski's task of reforming the UMWA after he became union president in 1982.

Suggested Reading

Paul F. Clark, *The Miners' Fight for Democracy: Arnold Miller and the Reform of the United Mine Workers*, 1981; Elizabeth Levy, *Struggle and Lose, Struggle and Win: The United Mine Workers*, 1987; Arthur H. Lewis, *Murder by Contract: The People v. "Tough Tony" Boyle*, 1975.

YELLOW-DOG CONTRACT

A yellow-dog contract is the now-illegal practice of requiring employees to sign an agreement promising not to join a labor union. Signing a yellow-dog contract was both a condition for being hired and cause for dismissal if an employee decided to join a union at some point in the future. In some cases, workers also had to sign affidavits that they had never previously belonged to a union.

The term "yellow-dog" derives from a colloquial expression that perhaps first appeared in 1902. It passed into popular use when it was used in a **United Mine Workers** journal in 1921, and quickly supplanted older expressions such as "iron-clad oath" and "infamous document." The word "dog" had long been used to refer to an unworthy, contemptuous, or unsavory individual, and "yellow" is a commonly used synonym for cowardice. Unions promoted the term "yellow-dog contract" as implying that only cowards and those of poor character would sign such an agreement, but the practice was legal until the 1930s and many destitute workers who felt they had no other choice signed such contracts.

Yellow-dog contracts were common in **company towns**, especially in coal-mining regions. Workers in such towns were threatened with firing for doing anything contrary to company policy. Because dismissal also meant eviction from company housing, workers could be left at once jobless and homeless. By the 1890s, widespread abuses led 15 states to outlaw the use of yellow-dog contracts, but the bans did little to curtail the practice. After 1903, yellow-dog contracts were a centerpiece of the **National Civic Federation**'s **open-shop** drive, and they also factored prominently in **American Plan** schemes during the 1920s, in which employers reinforced propaganda about the virtues of individual bargaining and self-reliance with yellow-dog contracts. The combination of the 1932 **Norris-La Guardia Act** and the 1935 **National Labor Relations Act** finally ended most uses of these contracts, although workers in the 1980s and onward complained that management imposes verbal forms of yellow-dog contracts. Although verbal warnings not to join labor unions are technically **unfair labor practices**, unwritten yellow-dog contracts are hard to prove or prosecute.

Suggested Reading

Foster Rhea Dulles and Melvyn Dubofsky, *Labor in America*, 1993; Daniel Ernst, "The Yellow Dog Contract and Liberal Reform," *Labor History* 30, no. 2 (1989): 251–274; Joel Seidman, *The Yellow-Dog Contract*, 1932.

YEOMAN

In American history, the term "yeoman" is an archaic term for an independent farmer who owns land. It is mostly associated with **agrarianism** as practiced in the Colonial and early Republican eras—a way of life that began to erode when industrialization appeared in the 19th century. Even then, terms such as "yeoman ideal" and "yeomanry" evoked images of independence and self-reliance. Today the term "farmer" carries much of the same symbolism that "yeoman" once implied.

"Yeoman" is of Anglo-Saxon origin. The term made its way to North America from England where, from the 17th century onward, it denoted a person holding a small landed estate, which was often granted by a social superior in appreciation of services rendered. (It was also a title associated with several high-prestige offices.) In pre-capitalist societies in which wealth was often reckoned by how much land one held, yeomanry represented a rise in social status as it meant that an individual owned property rather than renting it or toiling on someone else's land. Yeomanry was also associated with persons of high character. For the most part, yeomanry suggested a person of modest means in possession of small landholdings. As such, yeomen who were not also officeholders generally occupied a social status below that of nobles and gentry, but above that of peasants. In much of Europe the latter term could be a synonym for "yeoman and did not necessarily imply poverty or degraded status, but in English practice" most peasants worked the lands of others, not their own. Because English practices came to dominate much of the future United States and Canada, "yeoman" became a positive term and "peasant" generally carried negative associations.

Many European settlers to North America desired land, which was abundant, though claiming it often involved dispossessing **Native Americans**. English colonies were part of a mercantilist economic system designed to funnel wealth back to England, but settlers quickly engrossed themselves in farming activities that inexorably expanded westward from their original eastern seaboard settlements. Well before the American Revolution, the bulk of the Colonial population made its living from agriculture or ancillary industries such as blacksmithing, coopering, and running shops that provisioned farmers. In the minds of most, yeomanry was the highest ideal to which a male could (and should) aspire. Benjamin Franklin was among many thinkers and policymakers to equate working for **wages** with a dangerous form of subservience that was antithetical to liberty. Although it was acceptable to work for wages for a short period of one's life, the social ideal was for a man to save enough to buy land or a shop, and for a young woman to accumulate a dowry and marry a man who could support a family. In the Colonial mindset, yeomen, shop owners, and merchants were "independent" in the sense that they did not work for wages; they reaped all (or most) of the economic benefits of their own labor.

The yeoman ideal remained dominant at the time of the American Revolution, which was led by numerous individuals whose wealth derived from the lands they held. Yeomanry was also foundational in the early republic. By then, the English **Industrial Revolution** was under way. Although wealthier families often enjoyed goods made in English factories, Thomas Jefferson spoke for many Americans when he opined that America's workshops should forever remain in Europe and that Americans should remain wedded to the soil. Some of the earliest political debates within the new nation took place over matters such as Alexander Hamilton's financial schemes, Tench Coxe's recommendations for encouraging manufacturing, and Henry Clay's "American System" plans for internal improvements that would facilitate economic development. Opponents viewed each as an assault on yeomen ideals that threatened to bring to the United States horrors akin to those associated with the laboring masses of England.

Ironically, it was President Jefferson's Embargo Act of 1807 that first stimulated the development of American industry. The loss of trade during the War of 1812 further encouraged it. By the 1820s, a money-based economy was taking shape, as was a small-but-growing permanent **working class**. It is important to recognize, however, that American society remained agrarian based for many decades to come. Agriculture involved an absolute majority of the American workforce until 1880 and was the largest single occupation until 1920, when manufacturing finally overtook it. During the Great Depression, agricultural workers once again outnumbered those in manufacturing; it was not until 1940 that the number of agricultural workers slipped permanently below the manufacturing workforce. Indeed, as late as 1960, more than 12 percent of American workers were farmers.

Not all farmers were yeomen; in the South, many were renters, **sharecroppers**, and tenant farmers, especially newly freed ex-slaves and their offspring. By the 1880s, in fact, corporate farming was an accomplished reality in many parts of the nation. The yeoman ideal, however, remained in effect and, according to the U.S. Census, unclaimed lands remained available until 1890. Most 19th-century labor unions called for land reform, and as late as the 1880s, large **labor federations** such as the **Knights of Labor** (KOL) continued to see yeoman farming as a higher ideal than industrial labor. The **Populists** promoted similar notions in the 1890s. Indeed, capitalism itself remained contested and many Americans believed that alternative economic systems—including the creation of rural **cooperatives**—were preferable to the money-based private profit ideals of capitalism. In the early 20th century, the **Industrial Workers of the World** (IWW) also called for an end to the wage system.

The decline of the KOL, the disappearance of the Populists, the suppression of the IWW, and the maturation of the industrial system further eroded yeomanry as the highest ideal toward which Americans should aspire, but it persists as a powerful (though highly romanticized) concept. The possession of land is important for many Americans, and images of small farms and independent yeomen—though antiquated and based upon a mythic reading of the past—continue to evoke idealized American values analogous to those held by Franklin and Jefferson several centuries ago.

Suggested Reading

Michael J. Bowden, "The Invention of American Tradition," *Journal of Historical Geography* 18, no. 1 (January 1992): 3–26; Allan Kulikoff, "The Transition to Capitalism in Rural America," *William and Mary Quarterly* 46, no. 1 (January 1989): 120–144; Henry Nash Smith, *Virgin Land: The American West as Symbol and Myth*, 1957; Mary Weaks-Baxter, *Reclaiming the American Farmer: The Reinvention of Regional Mythology in 20th-Century Southern Writing*, 2006.

YESHIVA DECISION. *See National Labor Relations Board v. Yeshiva University.*

Chronology

1607	First indentured servants sent to North America.
1619	First African slaves arrive in Virginia colony.
1648	Boston shoemakers organize.
1676	Bacon's Rebellion.
1770	Manual workers killed during Boston Massacre.
1774	First Continental Congress convenes at Carpenters' Hall.
1786	Shays' Rebellion.
1786	Philadelphia printers' strike; possibly the first in the new nation.
1791	Philadelphia carpenters' strike—the first significant strike in the United States.
1794	Federal Society of Journeymen Cordwainers forms.
1805	Philadelphia shoemakers convicted of criminal conspiracy.
1834	Strike of mill girls in Lowell, Massachusetts.
1836	Lowell Female Labor Reform Association forms.
1837	Panic of 1837 harms labor organizing efforts.
1842	*Commonwealth v. Hunt* decision gives partial union legitimacy.
1860	Lynn, Massachusetts, shoe strike.
1865	Thirteenth Amendment abolishes slavery.
1866	National Labor Union forms.
1868	First eight-hour bill for federal workers.
1869	Knights of Labor organized.
1874	Tompkins Square riot.
1876	First trial of Molly Maguires.
1877	Nationwide railroad strike; first use of federal troops against strikers.

1881	Federation of Organized Trade and Labor Unions (FOTLU) forms.
1882	First Labor Day.
1885	Knights of Labor win first Southwest Railway strike; touches off Great Upheaval.
1886	First May Day (International Workers Day).
1886	Haymarket Square bombing.
1886	FOTLU evolves into the American Federation of Labor (AFL).
1890	Sherman Antitrust Act.
1890	Coeur d'Alene strike begins.
1890	New York Central strike.
1892	Homestead Steel strike.
1893	Cripple Creek strike begins.
1894	Pullman boycott and strike.
1897	Lattimer Massacre.
1898	Erdman Act curtails some railroad abuses.
1902	Anthracite coal strike.
1903	Women's Trade Union League formed.
1905	Industrial Workers of the World (IWW) founded.
1908	*Adair v. the United States* allows yellow-dog contracts.
1908	*Loewe v. Lawlor* curtails union organizing.
1909	Uprising of the 20,000.
1910	*Los Angeles Times* bombing.
1911	Triangle Factory fire.
1912	Lawrence textile strike.
1913	Department of Labor formed.
1914	Ludlow Massacre.
1914	Henry Ford announces $5 per day wage.
1914	Clayton Antitrust Act declares unions are not restraints of trade.
1915	Joe Hill executed in Utah.

1917	Communist revolution in Russia leads to fear in the United States.
1917	First raids of IWW halls.
1918	National War Labor Board forms; unions gain benefits.
1918	Sedition Act leads to curtailment of civil liberties; Eugene Debs jailed.
1919	Series of general strikes rock the United States.
1919	Boston police strike.
1919	Red Scare begins.
1919	Centralia Massacre.
1920	Emma Goldman deported.
1920	Matewan Massacre.
1920	Nineteenth Amendment grants women's suffrage.
1922	Herrin Massacre.
1924	AFL founder Samuel Gompers dies.
1925	Brotherhood of Sleeping Car Porters forms.
1926	Railway Labor Act.
1929	Stock market crashes; Great Depression begins.
1931	Davis-Bacon Act.
1932	Norris-LaGuardia Act.
1932	Franklin Roosevelt elected president.
1933	New Deal begins.
1934	Depression-era strike wave intensifies.
1935	National Labor Relations Act.
1935	Social Security Act.
1935	Committee/Congress of Industrial Organizations (CIO) forms.
1936	General Motors sit-down strike begins.
1936	Anti-union Mohawk Valley Formula formalized.
1937	"Sit-down fever" spreads.
1937	Brutal Harlan County strike.
1937	Memorial Day Massacre.

1938	CIO officially leaves the AFL.
1938	Fair Labor Standards Act.
1938	Little Steel strikes.
1941	Fair Employment Practices Commission established.
1941	Ford Motors is organized by CIO.
1942	New National War Labor Board set up; unions take no-strike pledge.
1943	Smith-Connally Act.
1943	CIO political action committee set up—the first PAC.
1946	Largest strike wave in U.S. history.
1946	CIO begins Operation Dixie.
1946	Hobbs Act punishes union racketeering.
1947	Taft-Hartley Act.
1948	General Motors accord with United Auto Workers of America of America.
1949	CIO purges communist unions.
1949	Final abolition of child labor.
1952	Nationwide steel strike.
1955	AFL and CIO merge to form the AFL-CIO.
1957	Select Committee on Improper Activities in the Labor Management Field holds hearings.
1959	Labor Management Report and Disclosure Act.
1959	Nationwide steel strike.
1960	New York City teachers' strike.
1962	President John Kennedy's executive order allows federal employees to unionize.
1963	Equal Pay Act.
1963	March on Washington for Jobs and Freedom.
1964	Civil Rights Act.
1965	United Farm Workers of America union coalesces; Delano strike.
1968	Rev. Martin Luther King, Jr., assassinated while leading a strike.
1968	Age Discrimination in Employment Act.

1970	Occupational Safety and Health Act.
1970	Postal workers strike.
1973	First OPEC oil embargo.
1974	Coalition of Labor Union Women forms.
1974	Suspicious death of Karen Silkwood.
1981	President Reagan fires striking air traffic controllers.
1983	Patterns of deindustrialization and union decline become apparent.
1990	Pittston Coal strike.
1992	Ravenswood lockout.
1993	Family Medical Leave Act.
1995	Reform candidate John Sweeney elected to head AFL-CIO.
1997	United Parcel Service strike.
2005	Change to Win Federation set up by dissident AFL-CIO unions.
2009	Health care reform bill signed into law.

Index

About the Author

Robert E. Weir holds a Ph.D. in American history from the University of Massachusetts Amherst, where he currently teaches. He has also taught at Smith College, Bay Path College, and Mt. Holyoke College. Weir is a former Fulbright scholar (New Zealand) and has authored (or edited) six previous books. He is also the executive secretary of the Northeast Popular/American Culture Association and a freelance journalist.